MW01596286

Dedication

To the memory of the South Carolinians of Hagood's Brigade that their service, suffering, devotion to duty, and dedication to the defense of their state be remembered by present and future generations.

J.J. Fox
Camden, South Carolina

B.G. Johnson Hagood, C.S.A.
(Circa 1863)

CWTI Collection

INTRODUCTION TO REPRINT EDITION

I am pleased to have a small role in bringing this scarce, if not rare, memoir back into the public eye. My interests in this project are several, but foremost it is to make the book available to students of the war, researchers, and ancestors who would know of the service of these South Carolinians.

This memoir is difficult to find, even at the current price of $200. Libraries no longer circulate it freely, and individuals having a copy are not prone to lending such a book.

Recent writings tend to disect and analyze major figures, their campaigns, or their performance. Many such tomes often apply contemporary criticism or solutions to arrive at conclusions which support current "progressive" concepts. A further disservice is rendered the student or historian by the faddish application of "psychohistory" presented under the guise of "new scholarship".

Lost is the real meaning of the words and lives of those who lived and fought in this epic struggle. Taken out of their time and place in history, an understanding of the motivations that drove men to follow the scarlet banner with such tenacity is lost or distorted.

Hidden is the mass of conjecture and lost in the maneuvering of corps and divisions are smaller units. These, the backbone of any army, are manned by those who began their glorious adventure with high hopes only to see their ranks dwindle to a battle-scarred band clustered around a shredded flag that had become their identity.

Johnson Hagood felt strongly that the service and courage of the Confederate Soldier should be recorded and preserved. When he wrote his memoirs, he wrote not out of political ambition, nor for financial gain. He did not even write for publication. But he did write out of pride and respect for the men of his command and the service they rendered. And, most importantly, he wrote for the survivors and future generations that a record might exist.

There is no effort to excuse or condemn. There is only the record as he knew it to be and the war as he saw it. It is the record of one who felt the fire, smelled the smoke, and counted his dead.

Here,then, are the memoirs of Johnson Hagood, Brigadier General, Confederate States Army, and of the regiments of his command, South Carolinians all.

J.J.Fox
Camden, South Carolina

"I believe it is the duty of every Confederate whose opportunities are such as to enable his to speak now, with anything like accuracy, to put on record what he knows. He owes this duty not only to himself and his associates, but to the truth."

Johnson Hagood

MEMOIRS

OF THE

WAR OF SECESSION

FROM THE ORIGINAL MANUSCRIPTS

of

JOHNSON HAGOOD

BRIGADIER-GENERAL, C.S.A

I. HAGOOD'S 1ST 12 MONTHS S.C.V.
II. HAGOOD'S BRIGADE

JIM FOX BOOKS
9 PRECIPICE ROAD
CAMDEN, SC 29020
1997

offered by

J.J. Fox
9 Precipice Road
Camden, South Carolina 29020

Produced by

John Culler & Sons, Inc.
P.O. Box 1227
Camden, SC 29020

All books produced by John Culler & Sons are printed on acid-free paper
(recycled when noted), Smythe-sewn, and exceed all requirements for
durability by libraries and discerning readers.

ISBN 1-55793-027-9

Should this book be defective, we will replace it free of charge.

Dedicated to
My Wife

CONTENTS OF VOL. I.

CONTENTS OF VOL. II.

ERRATA

The errors corrected in these Errata were made in transcribing the Author's original manuscript and were in the copy furnished the printer.—U. R. BROOKS, EDITOR.

Page 28 Read O'Cain for O'Caim.
" 32 " Steamer for stream.
" 33 " 200 pounder Parrotts for 200 Parrotts.
" 33 " Casemates for Casements.
" 33 " Ever for even.
" 42 " O'Cain for O'Caim.
" 44 " "So many" for "80 names."
" 45 Third line, second paragraph read "Further service expected from it", instead of "No further service, etc."
" 51 Second line from bottom of page read "Destination" for "Destruction".
" 53 Fourth line from top of page read J. J. Lucas for G. J. Lucas.
" 57 10th line from bottom of page read "Mere epaulments" for "Men epaulments".
" 61 9th line from top read "This" for "the".
" 62 14th line from top of page read "point" for "side".
" 63 15th line from bottom read "Going home" for "giving honor".
" 67 7th line from top of page read "O'Cain" for "O'Caim".
" 77 8th line from top of page and 14th line from top of page read "Yeadon" for "Gradon".
" 79 19th line from top of page read "exclusive" for "extensive".
" 82 Last line on page read "Warders" for "Wardens".
" 87 16th line from bottom of page read "Battery" for "Enemy".
" 88 6th line from top of page, 18th line from bottom of page, and 16th line from bottom of page read "Battalion" for "Battery".

ERRATA

Page 91 20th line from top of page read "right" for "sight."
" 93 19th line from bottom read "Boyce's" for "Boyer's".
" 94 16th and 17th lines from bottom read "Battalion" for "Battery".
" 95 15th line from bottom read "Sorely" for "slowly".
" 96 8th line from bottom of page read "beside" for "being".
" 107 Section 4. Read "drill" for "duties".
" 112 9th line from bottom and 3d line from bottom of page read "Jordan" for "Gordon."
" 113 3rd line from top and 8th line from top of page read "Jordan" for "Gordon".
" 114 9th line of note read "proudly" for "fondly".
" 114 7th line from top of page read "Jordan" for "Gordon".
" 133 18th line from top of page read "330" for "350".
" 142 16th and 17th lines from top of page read "Feu d'Enfer" for "free d'enfre".
" 142 20th line from top read "quietly" for "quickly".
" 144 16th line from top read "30 pounder Parrott" for "80 pounder Parrott".
" 145 10th line from top of page read "three" for "these".
" 150 Last line of page read "crenellated" for "cumulative".
" 155 14th line from top of page read "reverse" for "severe".
" 171 Read "Crenellated" for "crenaillare".
" 187 Second line from bottom of page read "General" for "Captain".
" 188 2nd line from top of page read "these" for "three".
" 188 6th line from bottom read "28th Georgia" for "25th Georgia".
" 190 16th line from bottom of page read "fall" for "fate".
" 192 3rd line from bottom read "traversing" for "transferring".
" 208 10th line from top of page read "bearer" for "beam".
" 210 9th line from top read "Batteries" for "Battalions".
" 234 16th line from bottom read "cowering" for "conversing".
" 235 5th line from bottom read "spun" for "strewn".
" 237 15th line from top read "inclined" for "widened".

Errata

Page 237 7th line from bottom read "plain" for "plan."
" 248 Read "Lalane" for "Lalam".
" 251 18th line from top read "straightened" for "strengthened".
" 264 19th line from bottom read "this" for "they".
" 264 14th line from bottom read "South and West" for "Southwest".
" 277 3rd line from top of page read "appear" for "approach".
" 278 12th line from bottom of page read "erect" for "east".
" 279 10th line from top of page read "omnivorously" for "ominously".
" 283 16th line from bottom read "transferring" for "transporting".
" 285 15th line from bottom read "place" for "places".
" 289 12th line from top of page read "learning" for "leaving".
" 298 7th line from bottom of page read "Major Wilds was wounded" not "captured" as printed.
" 298 2nd line from bottom read "Sligh" for "Schley".
" 308 4th line from bottom of page read "plan" for "place".
" 309 Last line on page read "feet" for "degrees".
" 310 Top line of page read "feet" for "degrees".
" 313 15th line from bottom read "fortune" for "forune".
" 339 18th line from bottom of page read "then" for "there".
" 327 14th line from top of page (*) read "Southern" for "See".
" 328 18th line from top read "prevision" for "provision".
" 330 10th line from bottom of page read "retiring" for "returning".
" 342 15th line from top of page read "20 mounted men" for "20 men".
" 345 2nd line from top of page read "Y" for "G".
" 348 18th line from bottom of page read "R. R. Depot" for "P. K. Depot".
" 354 10th line from bottom of page read "new" for "rear".
" 360 8th line from top of page read "our line" for "ours".
" 368 8th line from top of page read "Segers" for "Segus".
" 369 9th line from bottom of page read "freely" for "fully'.
" 372 12th line from top of page read "but" for "except".

Errata

Page 375   7th line from top read "64" for "65."

"   380   6th line from bottom read "O. J." for "O. G.".

"   382   11th line from bottom of page after Company K, read
            "Captain"——
            Figure 1. J. Boatwright 3rd May, 62, suspended
            on report of examining board.
            Fig. 2. Vacant.

"   384   Co. B. No. 4 read "F. J. Cannon" for "T. J. Cannon".

"   384   Read "Tarrh" for "Tant".

"   387   Company B, read "S. J. Burger" for "G. S. Burges".

"   391   Company F, read "W. W. Wise" for "M. W. Wise".

PREFACE

As has been published, I have undertaken with much pleasure the task of editing the Memoirs of the late Johnson Hagood, which gives thrilling incidents of the skill of the gallant General and of the valor of the brave men who dared to follow where he dared to lead.

Veterans of this grand old brigade, let me say that you are the remnant of many a well-fought field. You bring with you marks of honor from Secessionville, Battery Wagner, Cold Harbor, Petersburg, and other bloody battlefields. When in your youthful days you put everything at hazard in your country's cause, good as that cause was, and sanguine as youth is, still your fondest hopes were not realized. Venerable men, you have come down to us from a former generation. Heaven has bounteously lengthened out your lives. You are now where you stood fifty years ago. Behold, how changed! You hear now no roar of hostile cannon. You see no mixed volumes of smoke and flame rising from your burning homes—the ground strewed with the dead and dying—the impetuous charge, the steady and successful repulse—the loud call to repeated assault, the summoning of all that is manly to repeated resistance, thousands of bosoms freely and fearlessly bared in an instant to whatever of terror there may be in war and death. All these you have witnessed, but you witness them no more. But, alas! you are not all here—time and the sword have thinned your ranks. Comrades who fell in battle, our eyes seek for you in vain amid the broken band—you are gathered to your fathers, and live only to your country in her grateful remembrance and your own bright example.

It is hard to realize how information from good scouts has enabled our generals to win such glorious victories and how disastrous information from poor scouts has been in all armies. If General A. P. Hill had been well informed by his scouts, 21 August, 1864, General Hagood would not have made this remark: "That wielding a blade of such high temper, no wonder its brigadier hated to have to hack it against impossibilities."

I quote from the historic speech delivered before the New England Society in New York City, 12 December, 1886, by Henry W. Grady, of Atlanta, Ga.:

"You of the North have had drawn for you with a master's hand the picture of your returning armies. You have heard how they came back to you marching with proud and victorious tread, reading their glory in a nation's eyes.

"Will you bear with me while I tell you of another army that sought its home at the close of the late war—an army that marched home in defeat and not in victory, in pathos and not in splendor, but in glory that equalled yours, and to hearts as loving as ever welcomed heroes home?

"Let me picture to you the footsore Confederate soldier, as buttoning up in his faded gray jacket the parole which was to bear testimony to his children of his fidelity and faith, he turned his face southward from Appomattox in April, 1865. Think of him as ragged, half starved, heavy hearted, enfeebled by want and wounds; having fought to exhaustion, he surrenders his gun, wrings the hands of his comrades in silence, and, lifting his tear-stained and pallid face for the last time to the graves that dot the old Virginia hills, pulls his gray cap over his brow and begins the slow and painful journey. What does he find—let me ask you, who went to your homes eager to find in the welcome you had justly earned, full payment for four years' sacrifice— what does he (the Confederate soldier) find when, having followed the battle-stained cross against overwhelming odds, dreading death not half so much as surrender, he reaches the home he left so prosperous and beautiful?

"He finds his home in ruins, his slaves free, his stock killed, his barns empty, his trade destroyed, his money worthless, his comrades slain, and the burdens of others heavy on his shoulders.

"What does he do—this hero in gray with a heart of gold? Does he sit down in sullenness and despair? Not for a day. Surely God, who has stripped him of his prosperity, inspired him in his adversity. As ruin was never before so overwhelming, never was restoration swifter. The soldier stepped from the trenches into the furrow; horses that charged Federal guns marched before the plow, and fields that ran with blood in April were green with the harvest in June."

Every word contained in General Johnson Hagood's Mss. Memoirs appear in this book.

U. R. BROOKS, Editor.

From *The State*, Columbia, S. C., Wednesday, January 5th, 1898.

Out of the thinning line falls one more man in gray. The death that in his youth he so often sought in conflict has come unsummoned to Johnson Hagood in his old age and in the hallowed peace of his home. But he met it, we may be sure, with the same quiet smile of old, the serenity of a strong and fearless soul.

General and governor, planter and comptroller, banker and man of affairs, Johnson Hagood had his full share of honor and labor in the State of his birth and his devotion. The story of his career is elsewhere told, but we must set down the thoughts that come with the memories of long, and, for a time, intimate association. We first knew General Hagood during the political campaign of 1880, when he, as the Democratic candidate for governor, and the writer, as a newspaper representative, journeyed together through nearly every county in South Carolina. Six weeks of this close companionship gave an insight into his character which years of ordinary acquaintance would not have done, and the friendship there contracted and since continued prompts this contribution to a better understanding of one of the strongest and most individual of the sons of the State.

For General Hagood, although eminently honored by his people, was not known to them as he should have been. He was diffident, and was often considered haughty; he was reserved, and was thought cold; he had a wonderfully clear perception and the penalty for it was that he was sometimes set down as over-calculating.

Johnson Hagood, we have reason to believe, went into the war knowing that the South would fail, knowing that all its sacrifices of life and wealth and position would be utterly vain. But he believed in the cause of his people, and he led his men into battle as if he had the faith and confidence of a fanatic. His mind, as we have said, was intensely logical and reflective. He was a man who thought hard and reasoned icily; yet he could go against his reason when loyalty demanded.

He had perfect self-poise and was master of his emotions; for he had emotions under that calm and steady demeanor. When he was a candidate for governor and had to make his speech in each one of the thirty-odd counties his voice would choke and he would tremble as he faced his audiences, so great was his diffidence; and he was accustomed to say that he would rather charge a battery than go through such an ordeal—but go through it he did, holding himself sternly in hand. In other things his self-command was no less apparent.

He seemed often to be stern of face and thought, but for those he liked he had a smile as sweet as ever lit up a countenance and revealed an inner gentleness. Genial he was with his friends and a good raconteur, with a quiet humor that had a special charm.

General Hagood loved his State and his people, and had a sympathy with the masses in their hardships which he illustrated by his concurrence in the free silver movement of 1896. He was a banker and a man of means, and he had doubts on the silver question; but, as he said to us in that year, he was willing to take the risk in the hope that relief might come to those who needed it so sorely.

A life-long planter, he was successful in his operations, and was one of the best informed men on agricultural affairs that the State possessed. He thought much and deeply on farming and reached wise conclusions, one of which, as we remember, was that the agricultural salvation of the State was to be worked out through the development of certain little-regarded crops indigenous to the soil.

He had a remarkable capacity for organization, and was thorough, methodical and exact in all his undertakings. A man of many parts, his strongest characteristic was that he was a real and original thinker. There are far fewer such than the world assumes. Johnson Hagood did his own thinking, he made his own analyses of every question, and he reached his own clear and logical conclusions.

Much more might be said with truth, but we must be content to have drawn to the observation of those who did not know him well some of the salient points of a strong character. He had nearly reached his three-score years and ten, and the time had come for him to pass away, but the loss to South Carolina is no less real because it is late. History will give Johnson Hagood a place among the great men of his State.

From *The News and Courier*, Charleston, S. C., Wednesday, January 5th, 1898.

Crowned with nearly seventy years of honorable life, without a stain upon his shield, at peace with God and man, General Johnson Hagood has passed away from these earthly scenes forever. His life was an inspiration, his death a benediction. He lived uprightly, he died peacefully. What his hands found to do, he did with all his might. He was a great soldier, a master of men. The highest word with him was duty. His strongest ally in all the storms and conflicts through which he passed was faith—the faith of a little child. His conscience was his life, his incentive in action, his comforter in repose, his rod and staff in the final onset when he won his last great victory.

In every fibre of his soul, in every pulsation of his heart, in every aspiration of his life he was devoted to the State which he honored by his service in field and forum. He fought in South Carolina, in North Carolina and Virginia, and fought with a courage and intrepidity that challenged admiration. He was no holiday soldier. Stern in discipline, where discipline was necessary to the development of the best military qualities, he yet despised the show and sham of great parade, and measured officers and men alike by their devotion to the cause in which he was enlisted. At Battery Wagner, at Drury's Bluff, in the defence of Charleston, on the James and Chickahominy, he was ready for every command, and equal to any service. The story of Hagood's Brigade makes one of the most thrilling and glorious chapters in the military history of South Carolina. It stood of right among the bravest of the brave, and it was what it was because of the courage, the devotion, the military spirit of its indomitable commander.

General Hagood's claim to a high place among the immortals of South Carolina rests largely, but not wholly, upon his splendid services in war. But he was citizen as well as a soldier. In the Reconstruction days he remained faithful to his people and to himself; and it was due in large measure to his skill in organization, his mastery of emergencies, his fearlessness of consequences, that the rule of the alien was overthrown in South Carolina. As Comptroller-General and Governor of the State, he proved his fidelity to civic trust and, after his retirement to private life, to the end he was always the same modest man, loyal to his own conscience and unfaltering in his devotion to what was best for his people and his State.

We shall not attempt to tell the story of his life and character and achievements here—it will be written doubtless by others who are more competent for the service and who will write without the overwhelming sense of sudden bereavement upon them. We simply wish to pay tribute today to the modest gentleman, the gallant soldier, the incorruptible citizen, who has crossed the river to his waiting comrades on the other shore.

General Hagood's last public appearance in Charleston was at the reunion of the Confederate Veterans in April, 1896. The scene in the German Artillery Hall, when he responded to the call of his wartime comrades is indelibly photographed on the mind and heart of every one who heard his thrilling words. It was a soldier's greeting to soldiers, and a soldier's good-bye. There were no apologies for the past in what he said, and no regrets except for the unreturning dead. "Together we have felt," he said, "the mad excitement of the charge, the glorious enthusiasm of victory, the sullen anger of defeat. Together we have passed through the valley and the shadow of political reconstruction. . . . You believed then, and you know now, you were right. I am with you today as I have been in the past, body and heart and soul. Our service is nearly over. Most of those we knew and loved are gone. They are passing now. . . . For us there is little more left than to prepare for the final inspection and review. Let us humbly trust that we will meet the approval of the Great Commander beyond the river."

"They are passing now"; a few months ago it was McGowan; then it was Cothran; now it is Hagood.

> "The captains and the Kings depart—
> Lord God of Hosts, be with us yet,
> Lest we forget—lest we forget!"

GENERAL HAGOOD IN CHARLESTON.

General Hagood's last public appearance in Charleston was at the reunion of the Confederate Veterans, nearly two years ago.

In its report of the meeting held at the German Artillery Hall *The News and Courier* of April 23rd, 1896, said:

When it was decided to stop the reading of the report the veterans out in the hall wanted a speech, and especially one from their beloved Hagood. Some one cried out "Hagood," and that settled the matter. There could be nothing more done until the gallant Hagood had been seen and heard by the veterans. General Hagood did not want to talk, and especially not to interfere with the proceedings, but the veterans insisted and he was always too willing a man to do his duty not to respond, and so he stepped out to the front of the stage, and it must have made his heart gladden to see how he was received by his old soldiers as well as by those who fought for the same cause under different commanders. But General Hagood is always equal to an emergency, and last night he made a short talk to his old soldier friends that touched them deeply, and left even a brighter picture of the gallant soldier. General Hagood said in brief:

"I thank you for your kind greeting. It is a long time since we have met, since we have looked into each other's eyes and grasped each other's hands. In the long ago we together toiled in the weary march and looked upon 'battle's magnificently stern array.' Together we have felt the mad excitement of the charge, the glorious enthusiasm of victory, the sullen anger of defeat. And harder, sterner duties have been our lot. Together we have passed through the valley and the shadow of political reconstruction. We have seen civil rights, sacred from tradition and baptized in the blood of a patriot ancestry, trampled in the dust. We have seen the accumulations of two centuries of thrift and industry swept away, and the State plundered as a ship by a pirate crew. But 'God fulfills Himself in many ways.'

"Today our fair Southland, thanks to the indomitable energies of her blood, and the abounding resources of her gracious endowment, with her wounds cicatrized and her plumage renewed, is moving like the eagle's flight, upward and onward.

"You have met these varied fortunes as they came, and in the part you bore, you believed then, and you believe now, you were right.

"Old friends, welcome—and perhaps, good-bye. I am with you today as I have been in the past, body and heart and soul. Our service is .nearly over. Most of those we knew and loved are gone. They are passing now. Even while the drums were beating the assembly for this reunion the youngest but one of your brigadiers answered the last roll call on earth. John Kennedy, patriot, soldier, knightly gentleman, is dead. His honored place in your midst is vacant. The peace of God is on his brow.

"Younger men, as they should, are filling the ranks. They, too, are ready to live or die, 'for the ashes of their sires and the altars of their gods.' For us there is little more left than to prepare for the final inspection and review.

"Let us humbly trust that we will there meet the approval of the Great Commander beyond the river."

General Hagood was quite frequently interrupted by applause, and at the conclusion of his brief talk there was another round of applause for Hagood.

<hr>

A Sketch of His Life.

General Hagood was one of South Carolina's most distinguished sons. He was born in Barnwell County on February 21, 1829. His family was one of English extraction and settled originally in Virginia, but prior to the Revolutionary war moved to this State, located in the Ninety-Six District. Early in the present century, Johnson Hagood, the grandfather for whom he was named, removed from Charleston, where he was a prominent lawyer, to Barnwell County, and there his son, Dr. James O. Hagood, was, previous to the civil war, a successful planter. Dr. Hagood practiced his profession of medicine for more than fifty years, and greatly endeared himself to the people among whom he lived. He died in January, 1873.

General Hagood got his early education at the Richmond Academy in Augusta, Ga., and at the age of sixteen years he entered the Citadel in Charleston, graduating in November, 1847, with the highest honors of his class. After his graduation he studied law under the Hon. Edmund Bellinger, a distinguished lawyer of his day, and was admitted to the bar in 1850. The next year Governor John H. Means appointed him deputy adjutant general of militia, a portion of his duties consisting of drilling the militia at its various encampments over the State. In December,

1851, he was elected by the Legislature commissioner in equity for the Barnwell District, which important legal position he held until hostilities broke out in 1861. Then he resigned to enter the Confederate army. During the decade prior to the war he was also engaged in conducting his large plantation.

When South Carolina passed the Ordinance of Secession he was brigadier general of militia; he was at once made colonel of the First South Carolina Volunteers and took part in the bombardment of Fort Sumter under General Beauregard in April, 1861. He was then transferred from the volunteer corps to the Confederate States Army, retaining his rank as colonel. He was present at the battle of Bull Run. Returning to South Carolina he was engaged in the operations around Charleston, and at the battle of Secessionville, June 16, 1862. Immediately after that battle he was promoted by President Davis to the rank of brigadier general, and served on the coast of South Carolina until May, 1864, being engaged in the defense of Charleston during General Gilmore's siege of that city, and in the defense of Fort Wagner and the operations on James Island. In May, 1864, he was, with his command, withdrawn from Charleston and ordered to Petersburg, Va., where he arrived May 7th, and at Walthall Junction, a few miles beyond, met the advance forces of General B. F. Butler, consisting of five brigades. With 1,500 of his men, supported by 1,100 men of Johnson's Tennessee brigade, he repulsed them in the open field, many of his most gallant field and staff officers being killed and wounded. This gave time for the concentration of troops from the southward for the defense of Petersburg against Butler's advance. He served under General Beauregard at Petersburg and afterwards under the same general in Hoke's Division at Drury's Bluff against Butler and in the operations at Bermuda Hundreds. During the latter period he was instrumental in the erection of a battery at Howlett's House on the James River which, sweeping Butler's transports in the bend of the river, caused Butler to conceive the idea of cutting the famous Dutch Gap canal to escape, in his further advance up the river, the fire of this battery. The first pieces with which the battery was mounted were two 20-pound Parrots captured by Hagood's Brigade at the battle of Drury's Bluff. After General Beauregard had succeeded in bottling up Butler in the peninsular of Bermuda Hundreds, General Hagood's Brigade, with its division, was ordered to join General Lee. It reached him at Cold Harbor just prior to the battle of June 3, 1864, in which it was actively engaged. At the siege of Petersburg, which ensued, this brigade served in the trenches at one time sixty-seven days without relief, and in that period was reduced by casualties and disease from 2,300 men to 700 present for duty. At another time the next officer in rank to the brigadier present for duty was a captain, and four of the five regiments were commanded by lieutenants. At a later period during the month of August in the fighting on the Weldon road, General Hagood became the hero of as daring and gallant an exploit as is found in the history of the war. His command had been ordered to charge the enemy, and when the line of their works was reached some 200 of his men, having gotten into a re-entering angle where they were exposed to a severe cross fire, a line was pushed out surrounding them, and a mounted officer of the enemy galloping out of a sallyport, seized the colors of the Eleventh regiment and called upon them to surrender. Several officers and men prepared to do so, but had not been carried in when General Hagood, whose horse had been previously shot, proceeding towards them, called upon his men to shoot the officer. In the confusion they seemed bewildered and failed to do so. The general, having now come up to the spot, demanded the colors, telling the officer he was free to return to his troops. Instead of so doing he commenced to argue about the desperate position of the small band of Confederates. General Hagood, cutting him short, demanded a direct answer, and receiving a decisive negative, shot him from his horse. His orderly, Stoney, seized the falling colors, and the general, springing into the saddle of his adversary, succeeded in withdrawing his men with as little loss as could have been expected from the terrific fire to which they were exposed in retiring.

Some years after the war it was a pleasing incident to General Hagood that by furnishing a statement of the facts he was enabled to assist in procuring a pension from the United States Government for the gallant officer with whom the fortunes of war had placed him in conflict and who had survived the wound inflicted. General Beauregard, in forwarding the report of this affair to General Lee, remarked: "Such an act of gallantry as herein described and of devotion to his flag reflects the highest credit upon the officer who performs it and should be held up to the army as worthy of imitation under similar circumstances. Brigadier-General Hagood is a brave and meritorious officer who has distinguished himself already at Battery Wagner and Drury's Bluff and participated actively in the battle of Ware, Bottom's Church, Cold Harbor and Petersburg, June 16 and 17, 1864, and I respectfully recommend him for promotion at the earliest opportunity."

Shortly before Christmas, 1864, General Hagood was ordered to re-enforce the troops in North Carolina, and was engaged in the operations around Wilmington and afterwards in General Hoke's Division at the battles of Kinston and Bentonville. Retiring before overwhelming numbers, General Hagood's command surrendered with General Johnston at Greensboro, N. C.

His brigade entered the war 4,500 strong; at its conclusion only 499 veterans remained of that gallant band, including himself and his staff. At the termination of hostilities, General Hagood returned to active supervision of his planting interests. But he was not long permitted to devote his entire time and attention to his private affairs. In 1871 the burden of taxation under a profligate carpetbag rule in South Carolina having become well-nigh intolerable, General Hagood became a delegate to the State Taxpayers' Convention held at Columbia and composed of the most intelligent and responsible men in the State. The Convention was called to consider the enormous and increasing State debt and to ascertain if possible its actual amount and what portion of it had been legally contracted. A false statement of the State's liabilities was placed before them by Governor R. K. Scott and the State officers, and a false set of books were produced. The history of the work of this Convention looking to the final repudiation of a good proportion of the fraudulent public debt is familiar to many. General Hagood was the chairman of the committee that made the investigation, being appointed to that position on February 20, 1871.

In 1876 General Hagood was nominated on the Democratic ticket for comptroller-general, and by his patient, prudent and courageous course during the exciting campaign that followed, contributed largely to secure the great moral triumph of law and order and the downfall of the corrupt Radical rule in the old Palmetto State.

His management as county chairman of the campaign in Barnwell was perfect in its organization and such as to gain the confidence of all moderate Republicans as well as Democrats. The colored voters flocked in large numbers to the Democratic standard and joined the Democratic clubs, and although hitherto there had been a Republican majority of 1,800, almost wholly colored, the county was carried by a majority of more than 1,100 for the Democratic ticket. More than 2,000 mounted men in red shirts escorted General Hampton through Barnwell County, camping from time to time at various points where he stopped to speak, and the enthusiasm of all classes was unexampled.

During the Ellenton riots General Hagood was placed by the Republican Judge Wiggins in command of an armed posse to repress the disturbance. And during the uncertain and perilous time between the election in November, 1876, and the recognition of the Hampton government by President Hayes, when any moment might have precipitated a collision between the rival parties, Governor Hampton called only two of the State officers to his assistance—General Hagood and Attorney-General James Connor. Acting in entire accord with General Hampton they were both an advisory council and his executive officers during the existence of the dual governments. It was largely through the influence of General Hagood that over a thousand of the negroes in the county at the time united in the voluntary contribution by the citizens of the State of one-tenth of the taxes they had paid the previous year to the support of the Hampton government before it had been formally recognized by President Hayes. In May, 1877, he formally took possession of his office in the State capitol and at once entered upon the duties thereof. He applied himself to the task of thoroughly organizing and systematizing his department, which task he successfully accomplished.

At the regular election in 1878, his admirable conduct of the office was recognized and rewarded by a re-election and he continued in this office another two years, only to be still more honored by the people, who, in 1880, elected him governor of the State.

His inaugural address was an able paper; it was characteristic of the man. Brief, practical, suggestive, it discarded generalities and dealing with the matter in hand, set forth succinctly the present condition of the State, marked the improvements which had followed the restoration of honest government in 1876, and indicated in what direction, in his opinion, further progress could be made. He contrasted the then conditions with those of the period of riotous misrule that preceded. In concluding his address he said: "But the political equality of all men in South Carolina is now as fixed a feature of her policy as is the Blue Ridge in her geography. It can neither be suppressed nor evaded. The solution of the problem requires the wisest thought, the gravest counsel. It seems to me that I see it in firmness, moderation, justice. Let these characterize every act of legislation. It is my duty as governor to take care that the laws are faithfully executed in mercy. I repeat the pledge made before my election —that in the discharge of this high trust I shall know neither white man nor colored man, but only citizens of South Carolina alike amenable to her laws and entitled to their protection."

Governor Hagood's administration upon these lines was a success. Notwithstanding his expressed desire to retire at the end of his term, the disposition of the people of the State was strong for his re-election as their chief executive, and it was upon his declaration that he would not accept a renomination that they began to look elsewhere for his successor. The press of the State, upon his retirement, without exception generously voiced the universal approval he had earned.

Since Governor Hagood's retirement at the close of his term he has taken but little part in active politics. Without further aspiration for office, he took his position in the ranks and simply sought to do his duty as a citizen to his party and his country. He devoted his attention chiefly to his agricultural pursuits and to the development of the local enterprises and industries of his county. He was instrumental in the formation of a building and improvement association, an oil and fertilizer factory, a bank, a graded school and other enterprises. He always took a deep interest in agriculture and education.

In 1869 he was elected the first president since the war of the South Carolina Agricultural and Mechanical Society, holding that office for four years, when he declined re-election. He was also for two terms chairman of the State Board of Agriculture. He was the pioneer in and a strong advocate for the diversification of the State's farming industry, to which much of its present success is due; and his contributions to the agricultural press, together with his own success in the new departure, notably grass culture and stock farming, contributed much to that end.

He was always a warm supporter of the common schools and the State university.

Since 1876 he has been chairman of the board of visitors of the South Carolina Military Academy. To the welfare of this school —his alma mater—his time and his services have been given without stint.

Governor Hagood in 1854 married Eloise, daughter of Judge A. P. Butler, then United States Senator, and of whom General M. C. Butler is a nephew. He has one son, Butler Hagood.

EPITAPH WRITTEN BY GENERAL HAGOOD HIMSELF.

In Memory of
Johnson Hagood,
Planter.
Brigadier in the service
of
The Confederate States.
Comptroller-General and afterwards Governor
of
South Carolina.
For years Chairman of
The Board of Visitors in charge
of
The State Military Academy.
Born 21st February, 1829.
Died 4th January, 1898.

REST.

(*By Father Ryan.*)

———

My feet are wearied, and my hands are tired,
    My soul oppressed—
And I desire what I have long desired—
    Rest—only rest.
'Tis hard to toil, when toil is almost vain,
    In barren ways;
'Tis hard to sow and never garner grain
    In harvest days,
The burden of my days is hard to bear,
    But God knows best;
And I have prayed, but vain has been my prayer,
    For rest—sweet rest.
'Tis hard to plant in spring and never reap
    The Autumn yield;
'Tis hard to till, and 'tis tilled to weep
    O'er fruitless field.
And so I cry a weak and human cry,
    So heart-oppressed;
And so I sigh a weak and human sigh,
    For rest—for rest.
My way has wound across the desert years,
    And cares infest
My path, and through the flowing of hot tears
    I pine—for rest.
'Twas always so; when but a child I laid
    On mother's breast
My wearied little head; e'en then I prayed,
    As now—for rest.
And I am restless still; 'twill soon be o'er;
    For down the west
Life's sun is setting and I see the shore
    Where I shall rest.

INTRODUCTION

During the period to which these Memoirs relate, I kept memoranda and made notes more or less complete of events with which I was connected. I was also in most instances, at the time and at my request, kindly furnished by my superiors in command with copies of their official reports of battles and sieges in which I bore a part. The papers of Hagood's Brigade were preserved in the general wreck of Confederate military affairs. Diaries kept of portions of the war by certain of my comrades were also loaned me, and I had had preserved a complete file of the Charleston *Mercury* from the reduction of Sumter by the South Carolina forces in 1861 to the evacuation of Charleston in 1865, besides special numbers of other newspapers of that day.

From these materials, aided by my recollection, and corrected sometimes by general histories of the war and such United States congressional war documents as have been published up to this date, the Memoirs have been compiled.

It will be seen that in their character they are chiefly personal to myself and my immediate associates. My rank in the large armies in which I served was not sufficiently elevated to give me at all times a comprehensive survey of the military horizon while the war was going on, and since then I have had neither the time nor opportunity to qualify myself for a more general narrative. It will be seen also that they are purely military. My tastes and pursuits do not qualify me for entering into a discussion of the conflict of political principles having its origin in the convention which adopted the Federal Constitution itself and culminating in the secession of the Southern States, and during the war the Confederate Congress did its work on all important occasions with closed doors; but partial statements of its action reached the newspapers and it was difficult for one in the ranks of the army to learn clearly the policy that governed its course.

It only remains to state the motives that induced me to prepare these Memoirs and the object for which it is done. It is known that at the close of the war the archives of the Confederate War Department fell into the hands of the United States Government, and that Lieber, a renegade Southron, was employed to arrange them. Up to this time they have been sedulously kept a sealed book to the public. In all human probability, under the manipulation to which they have been and will be subjected, when the future historians obtain access to them

"The very mother that them bore,
If she should be in presence there,
She will not know her child."

Again, these records themselves were incomplete. The detailed reports of the campaigns of 1864 and 1865 were never made. Under these circumstances, I believe it is the duty of every Confederate whose opportunities were such as to enable him to speak now with anything like accuracy, to put on record what he knows. He owes the duty not only to himself and his associates, but to truth. It was hoped that General Lee would undertake to perpetuate the record of his men. Just after the cessation of hostilities reports of the campaigns of 1864 and 1865 were called for through the regular gradations of rank among the survivors of the Confederate army, with the avowed purpose of completing his data for the work, and they were to some extent furnished. Whatever his purpose may have been, his recent death precludes that hope.

These Memoirs are not prepared for the printer, nor will they, or any part of them, while I control them, be made public. I bequeath them to my son that he may know what part his father and his father's friends bore in the war; and with instructions at any time to show them to those whose record they give, or to their descendants. The time has not come, and may not come for fifty years, when justice can be done to the losing party in a bitter civil war. Should, then, this manuscript fall into the hands of an historian who approaches his task with the intent "to nothing extenuate, or aught set down in malice," he may use the limited material it contains for what it is worth. He will have the assurance of one, then long passed to his final account, of its accuracy as far as his knowledge and belief extends.

JOHNSON HAGOOD.

21 March, 1871.

THE FIRST REGIMENT OF SOUTH CAROLINA (12 MONTHS) VOLUNTEERS

12TH APRIL, 1861 TO 12TH APRIL, 1862 ·

FIRST SOUTH CAROLINA 12 MOS. VOLUNTEERS.
ORGANIZATION.

On the 17th December, 1860, in view of the probable passage of the Ordinance of Secession by the State Convention then in session, the Legislature of South Carolina passed "An Act to Provide an Armed Military Force." This act provided that whenever it shall appear that an armed force is about to be employed against the State or in opposition to its authority, the Governor be authorized to repel the same, and for that purpose to call into the service of the State such portion of the militia as he shall deem proper and to organize the same on the plan therein indicated. Three days afterward, the Convention passed the Ordinance of Secession, and the revolution which led to the establishment of the Southern Confederacy was inaugurated. Immediately after, the Convention provided for the raising of one or more corps of regulars, and for the acceptance of a regiment of six months' volunteers, both to be received into immediate service. Towards the last of December the Governor issued a call for volunteers under the legislative act, which resulted in the raising and organizing of ten regiments for twelve months' service. Under this call the militia regiments of Barnwell district (the 11th and 43rd of the old organization) assembled at Barnwell Village, and furnished, by volunteering, five companies. The regiment of Orangeburg District (15th old militia) assembled at its rendezvous, and furnished four companies; while the regiment of Colleton District (13th old militia) assembled at Walterboro and furnished two companies;—all on the 3rd January, 1861. The Barnwell and Orangeburg companies and one of the Colleton companies being the first ten companies which responded to the call in the State, were organized by the State War Department into a regiment under the name of "The First South Carolina Volunteers," and elections for field officers ordered. These elections were held on the 27th January, 1861, and the organization of the regiment was complete. It was officered as follows:

Colonel.. .. ..Johnson Hagood
Lieutenant-Colonel.. .. ..Thomas J. Glover
Major.. .. ..Watson A. O'Caim
Adjutant.. .. ..P. K. Moloney
Quartermaster.. .. ..G. B. Lartigue
Commissary Subsistence.. .. ..W. B. Legare
Surgeon.. .. ..Martin Bellinger
Assistant Surgeon.. .. ..E. H. Dowling
Chaplain.. .. ..Flynn Dickson
Sergeant-Major.. .. ..R. B. Wilson
Quartermaster-Sergeant.. .. ..J. H. O'Caim

COMPANY A.

Captain.. .. ..John V. Glover   Second Lieutenant...James F. Izlar
First Lieutenant.. ..John H. Felder   Third Lieutenant....S. N. Kennerly

COMPANY B.

Captain.. .. ..Daniel Livingston   Second Lieutenant.. .. ..B. F. Pou
First Lieutenant... ..S. G. Jamison   Third Lieutenant.. .. ..G. D. Jones

COMPANY C.

Captain.. .. .. ..S. M. Kemmerlin   Second Lieutenant. .. ..T. H. Cook
First Lieutenant..L. H. Zimmerman   Third Lieutenant..John J. Stroman

COMPANY D.

Captain.. .. ..Collier   Second Lieutenant. ..E. H. Holman
First Lieutenant. .. ..J. W. Sellars   Third Lieutenant..Olin M. Dantzler

COMPANY E.

Captain.. .. ..T. H. Mangum   Second Lieutenant..G. E. Steadman
First Lieutenant.. ..James M. Day   Third Lieutenant.. ..H. R. Guyton

COMPANY F.

Captain.. .. .. ..Winchester Graham   Second Lieutenant..J. J. Weissinger
First Lieutenant..George M. Grimes   Third Lieutenant.. ..G. W. Grimes

COMPANY G.

Captain.. .. ..E. J. Frederick   Second Lieutenant.. ..S. W. Trotti
First Lieutenant.. ..J. D. Rountree   Third Lieutenant.. ..G. R. Dunbar

COMPANY H.

Captain.. .. .. ..J. Vincent Martin   Second Lieutenant...W. B. Flowers
First Lieutenant.. .. ..A. T. Allen   Third Lieutenant.. .. ..W. A. All

COMPANY I.

Captain.. .. ..James White   Second Lieutenant...G. H. Breeland
First Lieutenant.. ..A. A. Hudson   Third Lieutenant.. .. ..Lewis Kinsey

COMPANY K.

Captain.. .. ..J. J. Brown   Second Lieutenant...J. A. Bellinger
First Lieutenant.. .. ..W. D. Burt   Third Lieutenant. .. ..F. M. Green

As thus organized, the regiment, together with the others raised under the act of the legislature of 1860, was directed to hold itself in readiness for service, and in the meanwhile to perfect, as far as possible, its drill and discipline. The regiment, when mustered into State service subsequently, numbered 832 rank and file.

NOTE—The regiment of six months' men provided for by the Convention assumed the name of "First South Carolina Volunteers," and were also known by this title, as well as the regiment enlisted for the war, which, in the summer of 1861, was raised by the field officers of the six months' regiment on the expiration of its service. Orr's Regiment, subsequently raised, was called First South Carolina Rifles. There was a regiment of infantry called First South Carolina Regulars. In consequence of this number of first regiments (all infantry) they were most commonly known by the names of their colonels being added to their numerical designation, thus: "1st S. C. V. (Gregg's), 1st S. C. V. (Hagood's)," etc.

FORT SUMTER.

The regulars and six months' volunteers provided for by the Convention were rapidly enlisted or accepted, respectively, and placed in service in Charleston harbor or on the adjacent islands. These, together with the volunteer militia from the city of Charleston (volunteers under the old militia organization. A. A., 1841), were employed in pressing forward the works projected for the reduction of Fort Sumter—still held by the Federal Government. In April, 1861, the batteries being well advanced and negotiations having failed to secure the delivery of the fortress, it was determined to take it by force of arms,* and vindicate the fact of secession.

---

*The immediate occasion of this conclusion was the sailing of a Federal fleet to provision and re-enforce Ft. Sumter. It arrived during the bombardment.

South Carolina's resumption of her separate sovereignty had been followed by the same act on the part of other Southern States. Each for herself had dissolved her connection with the Federal Union, and between themselves had formed a new Confederacy, with its seat of government at Montgomery. The operations against Fort Sumter had been carried on by South Carolina unaided and were continued from her own resources. Upon application of the State authorities to the Government at Montgomery, in March, General Beauregard, a distinguished officer of the army of the Confederate States, had, however, been assigned to their direction. Now it was desired to have a considerable body of troops in reserve in and near Charleston. A large fleet of Federal vessels had sailed for Charleston, and it was supposed that Sumter would be reinforced, if possible, or that at least operations in the nature of a diversion would be undertaken by the Federals. Accordingly, by an order dated 8th of April, several of the regiments raised under the legislative act of 1860 were ordered to rendezvous at Charleston. This order was received by the colonel of the First Regiment, at the hands of a special aide of Governor Pickens, on the evening of the 8th, and couriers immediately dispatched to extend it. The First Battalion arrived in the city by railroad at 10 p. m. on the 11th, and the Second Battalion just before day next morning. Upon their arrival they were marched to the race track, where they were at once mustered into the State service, and partially equipped, being supplied with arms, ammunition, and an inadequate supply of cooking utensils. At 8 a. m. on the 12th, the muster rolls were handed in to the State Adjutant-General, and the Regiment directed to report to General Beauregard. The bombardment had commenced at 4 a. m. and was then in full progress. The Regiment received orders to proceed by such transportation as should be furnished it to Morris Island, and report to the general then commanding. The Second (12 months') Regiment—Colonel Kershaw's—and a portion of the Sixth—Colonel Rion's—from the greater railroad facilities of the country in which they were raised, were enabled to reach Charleston a few hours sooner, and had been sent over to the same island directly across the harbor, just before the bombardment commenced. The Fifth Regiment (Jenkins') arrived later, and was sent to Sullivan's Island. The Third (Bacon's) and the Fourth (Sloan's) arrived still later and were held in reserve on Charleston neck. The other battalion of Rion's Regiment was placed on Stono.

In consequence of the bombardment being in progress, the First Regiment was directed to proceed across Ashley River to Dill's Landing, on James Island; thence across James Island to Legare Landing upon a creek running into Light House Inlet, and thence to Morris Island. The quartermaster, Colonel Hatch, was unable to furnish the transportation across Ashley River until 3 p. m. that day. The men had been supplied with neither haversacks nor knapsacks, and were without other camp equipage than the cooking utensils above referred to. Their rations had to be transported in bulk, and their baggage was in trunks, valises and carpetbags with which they. had left home. The movement commenced, as intended, at 3 p. m., and the Second Battalion was crossed over the Ashley without their baggage or rations (the boat being unable to carry more than the men), when the boat broke some of her machinery and the crossing stopped. A cold, driving rain came up, succeeded for the balance of the night by a bleak northeast wind. The regiment bivouacked—one battalion upon the wharf in Charleston, and the other at Dill's Landing, without food or shelter. Early next morning the remaining battalion was got across the river, and by noon the whole had moved across James Island to Legare's, where deficiency of transportation again delayed them some hours. Embarking before night, Morris Island was reached between 10 and 11 o'clock of the night of the 13th. The regiment was landed near where Battery Wagner subsequently stood, and bivouacked in the sand hills in rear of the Vinegar Hill Battery. One company of the Second Battalion (Captain Graham's) had, however, crossed James Island on the night of the 12th, and, obtaining transportation at Legare's, arrived on Morris Island about daylight on the 13th. Much suffering attended the whole movement. Ten or twelve men fainted on the wharf in Charleston from exposure and want of food. The only meal that many of the men obtained from leaving the race course to the morning of the 14th was at Legare's Landing. It was difficult to extricate the barrels, in which their rations were, from the piles of luggage on the stream, and when extricated the stomach revolted from the wet and soured mess. The proper equipment of the men with knapsacks and haversacks at the race course would have greatly mitigated their sufferings. But in the inception of a revolutionary movement, and with men and officers fresh from civil life, these troubles were unavoidable. The bombardment, which had commenced at 4 a. m. on the 12th, continued until about 1 p. m. on the 13th, when the fort surrendered. During the passage of the Ashley and the march across James Island we were in full view of the scene. The tempestuous weather of the preceding night had been succeeded by a lovely April day. Negroes were busily at work in the fields of James Island, the air was vocal with birds, and vegetation was as forward as it would have been a month later in the middle country from which the regiment had come. Contrasting strangely with this lovely rural scenery and continued pursuit of peaceful avocations, the roar and reverberation of the distant bombardment called attention to the doomed fortress in the bay. And, indeed, to eyes unused to the grand spectacles of war, it was full of sublimity. The bursting of the shells over the fort, marked by light puffs of smoke, slowly fading out into fantastic wreaths, the lurid flash from the portholes shooting out low down its level column of smoke over the water, as the besieged sent back defiance to the leaguer, the burning barracks, the consciousness that this was war, with its glories, its terrors, its uncertainties—all tended to impress vividly the imagination of the beholder. While we were at Legare's the flagstaff of the fort was shot away, and its fall was greeted with enthusiastic cheers by the regiment. These had scarcely subsided when one generous fellow called out, "Hurrah for Anderson, too," and more than one voice responded to his call. There was one person, however, a type of her class, perhaps, who did not take in fully the magnitude of the occasion. A soldier called to an aged negress, patiently delving with others in a field by the roadside, "Old woman, what's the matter over yonder?" "Eh, eh; you no see the house afire?"

The formal evacuation of the fort took place on the 14th, the garrison withdrawing with the honors of war, and being transferred to one of the Federal vessels lying in the offing. A vast concourse of people witnessed it from the shores of the harbor, and the waters of the bay were alive with boats and sightseers. Thus fell Fort Sumter. In a military point of view its defense was contemptible—to realize how contemptible one need only look to the ruins of the same work held later in the war by Rhett, Elliott and Mitchell, without a gun to reply to Gilmore's 200 Parrotts, or a casement to shelter them, save such as they themselves tunnelled in the debris, working under a merciless fire. The tenacity of purpose which could avail itself of passive resistance and fight for time had no place in their defense. A formidable fleet lay idly by and witnessed the bombardment and surrender without an effort either by force or stratagem to aid the garrison.

The means at the disposal of the Carolinians to reduce the fort, vigorously held, were totally inadequate. Their breaching guns, necessarily placed at extreme range, were old-fashioned smooth-bores of light caliber, save a rifled 12 dr., which for such a purpose was a mere toy. From their shells the casements of the fort were a perfect protection. It is true their hot shots fired the wooden barracks on the terreplein of the fort, and this, while burning, may have, as alleged, endangered the magazine, but the barracks soon burned out. Endangered magazines are an incident of every siege, and their explosion within beleaguered forts was no uncommon occurrence on both sides later in the war, and none were even surrendered in consequence. It is true that Anderson's means of damaging his assailants, sheltered behind epaulements, were as limited. He had nothing but smooth-bores, firing round shot. But neither his ammunition nor commissariat was exhausted when he surrendered. And photographs of the work taken at the time forever forbid the assertion that its tenability was seriously impaired. The walls were injured nowhere; the projectiles of the nearest batteries had given them the look of a bad case of smallpox, no more, and not a man had been killed on either side when Anderson's flag was furled. No wonder that European spectators smiled at the bombardment and defense. It had to veteran eyes, which saw only the patent facts, something of the characteristics of Chinese war. But the truth is the doctrine of State Sovereignty, with its consequent State Rights, was not then the exploded heresy which it has since become. Taught by the most venerated sages of the early

3—H.

republic, it had constituted the faith of a large majority of the people, and shaped the course of the government almost uninterruptedly from its inception. It was still a mighty, living influence, and gave to the Carolinians the benefit of that morale which is as potent in armies as is the nervous fluid in the human frame. It paralyzed the defense, and gave audacity to the assailant. The whole course of the Federal Government toward the seceded States had been that of one who admits a right but seeks to evade its consequences. The Northern press took no higher ground; and some of its most influential exponents openly admitted the Southern view of the question. Mr. Lincoln, in the face of his life-long advocacy of the principles relied upon by the secessionists, could find no higher ground upon which to put his continued tenure of Sumter than its character of property—a character in which the seceded State was more than willing to consider and account for it in an equitable distribution of assets. Major Anderson was himself a Democrat of the State's Rights school, a Kentuckian by birth and a son-in-law of Duncan L. Clinch, who had tendered his commission to the United States Government years ago, when its mandates were about to place him in antagonism to the sovereignty of Georgia.* On the other hand, he was a trained soldier of the regular army, with all of a soldier's ideas of honor. Thus situated, with his orders, such as they were, emanating from the tricky and shuffling demagogues who filled the high places at Washington; himself for some time cut off from communication with his headquarters, and the fleet (which was in direct communication with it, and which was there for nothing if not to assist him) lying idly in his view, and moving no hand to help him, no wonder that he made only such a defense as could by possibility warrant an honorable surrender. Insignificant, however, as was the defense of Sumter and facile as was its reduction, in its results it was an event of tremendous consequence. From that period what little statesmanship and reason had so far marked the controversy, fled the field, and the baleful passions of civil strife were loosed for a four years' carnival of blood and ruthless destruction.

The First Regiment remained bivouacked in the sand hills near Vinegar Hill for four days. It was then moved farther

---

*Memories of Fifty Years, Sparks, p. 134.

down the Island to Gadberry Hill, extending its left toward Vinegar Hill. Here they were again bivouacked. During this time the fleet was still lying off the bar, and the men were constantly disturbed at night by false alarms. No camp equipage was received for ten or twelve days; the weather was again tempestuous and cold; the exposure, the wretched water dug from shallow pits in the sand hills, and the inefficient policing of the camps, soon began to tell upon the health of the men. Much sickness ensued. We were a week on the island before the first drill could be had. The men were employed all the time in endeavoring to obtain such shelter as could be improvised, even in many instances constructing burrows in the sand hills, and in the difficult task of getting their rations cooked.

In ten or twelve days, however, our supply of tents, etc., began to arrive, and the men were enabled to make themselves more comfortable. Uniforms—a short grey blouse—were distributed, drilling was diligently prosecuted, and the regiment began to assume something of discipline and acquaintance with the routine of camp duty. Brigadier-General Simons (of the Charleston militia), Major-General Bonham, and afterwards Brigadier-General Nelson (the two latter of the 12 months' volunteer organization) were in command. The Charleston militia was soon after the bombardment relieved from duty. Rion's Battalion was sent to Stono, and the First and Second 12 months' Regiments, with a half troop of Charleston Volunteer Dragoons, were retained on the island until the batteries bearing on the channel were dismantled, and those bearing on Sumter were demolished. This work accomplished, they also were withdrawn.

There was one of these batteries that deserves notice, the "Stevens," or "Iron-Clad," Battery. The following diagram, drawn from recollection, will give some idea of it. The gun is "in battery" and ready for firing:

It was a structure of triangular section, presenting one of its sides at a very obtuse angle to the enemy, and open to the rear. The frame-work was of heavy timber and the side exposed to fire was plated with common railroad iron, presenting to the hostile projectiles a sloping corrugated surface thus: ⌐⌐⌐⌐. When the guns were not in battery, the portholes were closed by curtains similarly plated and worked from the inside by a lever. It was a crude affair, but sufficient for Anderson's light, smooth-bores. It was struck several times; the only injury it showed was a broken hinge to one of the curtains of a porthole, and a partial loosening of one of the iron rails. The interest attaching to this battery is that it was (the writer believes) the first instance of the actual use of iron plating for defensive purposes in war.* It was the precursor, if not the germ, of the iron-clad vessels which played so important a part later in the contest. An iron-clad floating battery had also been attempted by the Carolinians. It took some part at long range in the bombardment, but was generally considered a failure. Clement C. Stevens, then cashier in a bank in Charleston, suggested and executed this work. He subsequently raised a regiment, (24th S. C. V.), was promoted to a brigade and died in battle in the Western Army. General Stevens was a man of high character and intelligence, and earned the reputation of a most excellent officer. He was brother-in-law of Barnard E. Bee, who knighted Jackson at Manassas, dubbing him "Stonewall" a few moments before he himself was borne from that field mortally wounded. Stevens, in the same battle, was wounded on Bee's staff.

ORANGEBURG.

The First Regiment received orders on the 22nd of May to proceed to, or near to, Orangeburg and there be encamped. At 8 o'clock next morning the movement began; but the quarter-master's department was again our evil genius. It was after dark when we were landed in the city. We marched through, stopping in front of the Charleston Hotel to hear a speech from Governor Pickens, and took the cars for Orangeburg, where the regiment arrived at daylight. During our stay at Orangeburg the

---

*Mistake. See "Iron-clad Ships," Appleton's Cyclopædia.

regiment improved rapidly in drill and knowledge of military duties. The taking of Confederate service was, however, the chief topic of interest in its history while at that camp, and indeed when that question was decided the camp was broken up. Just after the fall of Sumter, the Governor of Virginia called upon the executive of South Carolina for military assistance. Virginia had not then become a member of the Southern Confederacy, though she had seceded and was threatened with Federal invasion. Governor Pickens dispatched an aide to Morris Island with a circular note to each of the colonels of regiments there, requesting them to call on their respective commands to volunteer for the service, and informing them that, in case of a favorable response, they would move at ten o'clock that night. The Second Regiment (Kershaw's) volunteered something like two hundred men, and the six months' men (Gregg's) a like number. Next day these bodies of volunteers left the island, each under command of its colonel. The balance of these regiments remained on the island. The six months' men that remained were disbanded a few days afterward, and the part of the Second Regiment that remained was subsequently recruited and known as Blanding's Regiment, while the fragments of regiments which Gregg and Kershaw carried to Virginia were rapidly filled up to full regiments by independent companies from different parts of South Carolina, who went on to join them.

The First Regiment when called upon responded by Mangum's Company volunteering nearly unanimously; the other companies volunteered from ten to thirty men each, but coupled with the condition in each case that the whole company went. No special effort was made by officers to induce the men to volunteer, for it was seen that it would disrupt the regiment, and it was thought more advisable, with a view to subsequently taking Confederate service, to keep it together. A day or so previously (16th April) Governor Pickens had sent over copies of a resolution by the Convention of the State then in session providing that "with their consent" the troops in State service should be transferred to the service of the Confederate States, and had directed the colonels commanding "to report within five days" whether their regiments would consent to be so transferred. A few days after the Virginia call, he came out in the newspapers with a proclamation (which he also directed to be read at the head of the troops) asserting his right to order the twelve months' men to march and serve wherever he deemed proper beyond the borders of the State, and declaring his intention so to do whenever in his judgment the necessary occasion arose. He called upon the Attorney-General for his legal opinion of the Governor's powers in the premises under the act of 1860, and this opinion sustained the views of the proclamation. The troops seemed to consider the proclamation as an attempt to coerce them in a matter in which the Convention, the supreme power in the land, had required their consent. They saw no practical difference, they said, in going abroad to serve the general interests of the Confederacy, though they were called State troops, and in going abroad entered into Confederate service. They imagined, too, that the proclamation was dictated by irritation at the response made to the Governor's call for Virginia volunteers. And such indignation was felt with the course of the executive that it required an exertion of authority by officers in command to prevent its public expression. No report was made under the Governor's communication of the 16th April, and the question of taking Confederate service remained in this condition at the time the regiment left Morris Island. The object of selecting Orangeburg was because the locality was deemed favorable to the consideration of the question. It was also deemed best by the field officers to obtain (which they succeeded in doing) a general furlough of ten days for the regiment before presenting the subject. The soldier suddenly called from his civil pursuits could in this interval make his arrangements for that more extended service which the necessities of the country required. The morning of the arrival at Orangeburg this furlough was announced, and, upon the reassembling of the command, the matter was fairly opened. In a communication from the Adjutant-General, dated 23rd May, and read too late to communicate to the regiment before going on furlough, was enclosed the following order:

"State of South Carolina,
"Headquarters, 19 May, 1861.

"The Secretary of War has made two requisitions for troops on the Governor, amounting to 8,000 men. If the regiments were to be retained by the State as volunteer regiments, then they are subject to orders to march whenever and wheresoever directed by the Commander-in-Chief. The resolution of the Convention seemed as intended to require that the Governor should give the honor in the first instance to the volunteer regiments to be mustered into the service of the Confederate States, and thus through the action of that body their service should be changed. The President of the Confederate States, under a recent Act of Congress, as intimated by the Secretary of War, adopted the policy of calling only for companies to be mustered in for the war, and then for the President to appoint the field officers when such companies were formed into battalions or regiments; but as eight volunteer regiments were already organized in South Carolina, it has been determined to give them the honorable opportunity of going into service as regiments with their field officers.

"Under these circumstances it is ordered that the eight regiments of volunteers be prepared by their officers to be mustered into service for their 12-months' enrollment. For this purpose the field officers and company officers with the men of each company will be required to sign a roll agreeing distinctly to the terms. It will take sixty-four privates as a minimum to make a company to be mustered in, and when a majority of the present roll of a company so agree, then that company by this decision will preserve its present organization as a basis to be filled upon, and if six or more companies in any regiment so agree, then the organization of that regiment may be preserved and a system hereafter to be adopted will be ordered to make up the companies that may thus have a majority, but not sixty-four as the case may be, in that regiment. And then, upon the same system, orders will be given to make up the remaining companies after six, always reserving the right of the company or regiment to elect officers when they (the officers) do not choose to change their service. If ten companies, with sixty-four present in each, be found to agree to the terms, then such regiment is complete.

"When the eight regiments are made up, a portion of them will be retained by order of the Governor to defend the State of South Carolina; and if the regiments decline to be mustered into Confederate service, then still a sufficient number of them, under the present organization, will be retained for seacoast defense in this State. In any case, however, this selection will be made. The mustering officer will be ready as soon as the returns are made on this.   F. W. PICKENS."

The following form of enlistment was communicated at the same time:

"We, the undersigned officers and privates of —————————— Company, —————————— Regiment of So. Ca. Volunteers, do hereby agree to be mustered unconditionally into the service of the Confederate States of America, to serve for the period of twelve months from the —————————— day of April last."

It will be observed that no plan of service is guaranteed in these papers, and the order of the 19th May distinctly sets forth that in any event a selection will be made for seacoast service in South Carolina. In his speech to the regiment while passing through Charleston, the Governor had told them that the portion of the regiment that took Confederate service would go to Virginia, and that which refused would be retained for local defense. In a speech to Blanding's Regiment, which was made a few days later and published in the newspapers (before the question was submitted to the First Regiment), he told them the same thing. And, in a conversation with the colonel and lieutenant-colonel of the First he had expressed the same purpose. It was, moreover, known that Heyward's and Manigault's Regiments (9th and 10th, under Act of 1860), raised from the seacoast district, and then being organized, preferred the local service. It may be added that the Executive's speeches and statements, it was afterwards learned, succeeded in giving to the other regiments the same interpretation of the order of the 19th May. An impression had, however, got abroad in the First Regiment that those not taking Confederate service would be disbanded, though it was never doubted that those taking it would go to Virginia.

For several days after the proposition was submitted but little progress was made. But few men could be obtained and these were distributed so equally among the companies that no company could obtain "a majority according to its present roll." The charms of home were too strong for the call of patriotism. The enemy had been expelled from South Carolina by South Carolinians unaided and at one effort; let other States do the same thing. Virginia has not yet been invaded; let her drive the Federal from Norfolk as South Carolina had done from Sumter, and the Government at Washington, seeing that the South was determined upon independence, will not be reckless enough to involve the whole continent in war. Thus many of the men and even officers reasoned; and not yet broken into the requirements of the military code, and sore from its unaccustomed restraints, they readily listened to such reasoning. The regiment was encamped in the country from which nearly half of it was raised; the friends and relatives of the men were daily in camp, and, strange to say, this outside influence was largely exerted against going into Confederate service. This, too, in the Third Congressional District, the very hotbed of secession. The people had no conception of the magnitude of the struggle in which they had embarked. Thus matters stood. The officers fearing the vacillation of Executive counsels, with the disbandment of the portion of Gregg's Regiment (nearly two-thirds) which did not take Confederate service and with the terms of the order of the 19th May before them, hesitated to take the only step by which it was evident the question could be carried. They hesitated to assure the regiment that the question was not between disbandment and Confederate service, but between Virginia and the seaboard. At length General Jamison, Secretary of War for South Carolina, happened unofficially to visit the camp, and told them that they might safely take this step, for he was apprised of the views of the Executive. The assurance was accordingly given and it was found necessary to pledge the honor of the officers that the issue was as presented.

Upon this six skeleton companies were raised, and the organization of the regiment preserved under the terms of the order. White's Company had at an earlier date unanimously declined to take Confederate service, and arrangements had, with consent of all parties, been effected to exchange it for Rice's Company of Heyward's Regiment, who desired to go to Virginia.

A report of the facts was made on the 2nd June, with a request for a mustering officer to be sent up to muster in the regiment as it stood—to dispatch it at once to Virginia—and to allow the necessary recruits to follow. The request was declined in an Executive communication dated 3rd June, and the regiment was informed that "A skeleton regiment cannot be sent to Virginia; it must be full and complete." On the 4th June Lieutenant-Colonel (afterwards General) Barnard E. Bee, having mustered in Jenkins' (Fifth) Regiment, encamped near us, informed the colonel commanding the First that he was also instructed to muster in the First, if it was completed, and at the same time handed him the following:

"Mustering Officers' Office,
"Orangeburg, S. C., 4 June, 1861.
"Under instructions from the Governor, Colonel Hagood, commanding First Regiment South Carolina Volunteers, will make the necessary arrange-

ments for transferring that portion of his regiment which has refused to enter the Confederate service to the camp at Ridgeville. This portion will be under command of Major O'Caim, and will at once be separated on the regimental records from that portion which has elected to serve the Confederacy.

"The camp equipage will be retained for the use of the regiment, consequently Major O'Caim will make requisition for camp and garrison equipage on Colonel Hatch.

"BARNARD E. BEE,
"Lt. Col. C. S. Army,
"Mustering Officer."

Previously, in a letter dated 1st June, the colonel commanding had been instructed by the Governor: "After mustering into Confederate service, the remaining companies and detachments of companies not volunteering will be placed, on the departure of the regiment, under command of the senior officer remaining, who will report for orders to the Adjutant-General's Department."

Sufficient progress had not been made for Colonel Bee, under his instructions, to muster in the regiment; but the order extended by him was communicated to the command. It was received as practical confirmation of the assurance given by the officers, and before night two more skeleton companies were made up, being eight in all and numbering near 500 men in the aggregate. Collier's Company declined, as a company, to take Confederate service, but many individuals of it had combined with a portion of Kemmerlin's Company. Rice's Company made nine, and Steadman, of Lexington, and Edward Cantey, of Camden, had each, with full companies, applied for the tenth place. Steadman being the first applicant was notified to bring his company into camp. Recruiting officers were sent out to fill up the skeleton companies, rolls dispatched to the adjutant-general with the request to send up a mustering officer on the Monday following, and the major of the regiment (who had declined Confederate service) was sent down under Bee's order to make arrangements for transferring his portion of the men to the seaboard.

On Sunday, Steadman marched his company into camp, over 80 strong, and the recruiting officers returned with recruits enough to raise the skeleton companies to the same average, but, at the same time, the major returned with the following communication from the Governor:

"State of South Carolina,
"Headquarters, 6 June, 1861.

"*Colonel Hagood.*

"Sir: I received yours of the 2nd June in which you reported your regiment ready for mustering into service. I sent the mustering officer with special instructions to muster in, and, if under the required number, to receive as a battalion, and, if under a battalion, to receive as companies. I can delay no longer, as I have already delayed longer than I ought. Colonel Glover thought if they could go to Orangeburg there would be no difficulty. Have them mustered in, and the men who decline to muster into service, I desire to have their arms, and those who muster in, I desire to receive immediately and make a permanent arrangement for the summer in the manner best suited to the public service. The five regiments recently mustered in, together with the other two already there, are all I can spare out of the State, and I must organize the rest to the best advantage for the State and the public service as soon as possible. If the companies who muster in fall below ten, then I can use them to recruit on and fill up to a regiment, if it is thought necessary hereafter. F. W. PICKENS."

Matters were thus entirely reversed. The men whose spirit had induced them to volunteer for honorable and active service abroad were condemned to an inglorious summer campaign on the coast, and those whose want of spirit had induced them to prefer the miasma and the mosquitoes of the coast, with the certainty of encountering no enemy, were to be rewarded with a return to their homes. These last were highly jubilant. The men who had signed the Confederate rolls were greatly exasperated. The officers had solemnly pledged their honor that the issue was a different one, and self-respect compelled them, as far as they were concerned, to release the men from the obligation of enlisting under the new Executive programme. The recent recruits brought in utterly scouted the idea of entering a regiment condemned to the coast. And when on Monday Captain Dunovant, the mustering officer, came, not a man would muster in.

On this report being made, orders were received to retain the whole regiment in service for State defense. A few days afterward this again was countermanded; and on the 15th June the regiment was "relieved from duty until further orders."

In the interval between the departure of the mustering officer and the order for the relief of the regiment, the colonel commanding visited Governor Pickens with a scheme to raise an independent regiment for Virginia service. His Excellency seemed utterly dismayed at the result of his communication of the 6th June, and evinced every disposition to remedy the evil by acquiescence in the scheme. The Confederate Secretary at War telegraphed his assent from Richmond; but the men failed utterly to respond. They had lost confidence in the authorities; the delights of home loomed up in magnified proportions; the last spark of volunteer enthusiasm was extinguished; and they seemed bent on disbandment at whatever discredit to themselves or consequence to the country. Desiring to disembarrass the question of every difficulty, the field officers issued a card to the regiment, pledging themselves to resign if one-half of each of eighty names as six companies would again sign the roll for Confederate service; and not a single name was given in. A few spirited company officers then proposed that the officers of the regiment band themselves into a company, and, taking the beautiful banner with which the ladies of Barnwell had presented us when the regiment was supposed to be going to Virginia, carry out the purpose of the fair donors.* This, too, failed. It was a pitch of self-devotion to which volunteer human nature could not attain.

The issue of Confederate service was presented to the other regiments who were already mustered in, in the same way that it was to the First. Similar indisposition to accept was in each of them, more or less, encountered. But the question was presented to them ten days earlier in consequence of the furlough which its field officers had perhaps unfortunately obtained for the First, and consequently they got off for Virginia before their own or any other recusants were disbanded. It may be too that they were more adroitly managed by the officers in command. When the subject of re-enlistment for the war came up, twelve months afterwards, the First regiment redeemed itself by raising and enlisting eleven companies quietly and without effort before the first enlistment of the men had expired. The writer is not accurately informed, but believes this was the only one of

---

*These gentlemen had probably never heard of "The Island of the Scots," but in this connection it will be pleasant to read "Lays of the Scottish Cavalry," p. 94.

the South Carolina regiments, and he is inclined to think the only regiment in the Confederate army, which thus by voluntary re-enlistment renewed its service at that time to that extent. The pressure of the Confederate Conscription Act* directly or indirectly gave continued existence to these original organizations. Volunteering is by far the best method of raising suddenly large armies for a popular war. The enthusiasm of the people is thus utilized before it has evanesced; but once enlisted (and that for the war) the word should be expunged from the soldier's vocabulary. It was observed, too, under similar circumstances of so large a number of offices to be filled, when an appointing power had not the time or ability to make itself acquainted with the merits of applicants, that the election of officers by the men in the first instance resulted in as good, if not a better, selection than when the government appointed. Any subsequent promotions by election after the troops are in service, and men and officers have the opportunity of exhibiting their fitness for position, is an unmitigated evil. It was in the modified form in which it existed in the regulations of the Confederate army, the lowest grade only being elective, a drawback upon discipline, which none can realize who has not experienced a similar state of affairs. Blanding's and Rion's (Sixth) Regiment struggled on manfully after the First was relieved from duty, and after a month's longer work were mustered into Confederate service. No sooner was this done than they were ordered to Virginia; and this, notwithstanding the Governor's letter of the 6th June to the First Regiment.

RELIEVED FROM DUTY.

During the time it was relieved from duty the State authorities sometimes acted as if the regiment was finally disbanded; at other times as if it was only temporarily relieved and no further service expected from it. Mangum's Company was armed and permitted to go West, where it entered Colonel Martin's First

---

*This Act was passed after the First Regiment had re-enlisted for the war.

NOTE.—*The Banner Presented by the Ladies of Barnwell.*—At Gordonsville, in the first march into Maryland, the regiment was required to assume the Confederate battle flag, and Colonel Glover left this banner in keeping of some gentleman of the town. Glover was killed shortly afterward at Second Manassas; the name of the gentleman was lost and the banner never recovered.

Mississippi Regiment, of which Mangum himself became the major. McCreery was encouraged to raise a company from individuals of the regiment to join a new regiment Colonel Gregg was raising "for the war," the time of the six months' men whom he had carried to Virginia having expired.* And though a remonstrance was made by Captain Brown, whose company was chiefly affected, and the names of his men in McCreery's Company furnished the Governor, yet his Excellency, while asserting that he had forbidden McCreery to recruit from the First Regiment, upon the filing of his roll in the Adjutant-General's office, furnished him with transportation to Virginia. Captain Lartigue, quartermaster of the regiment, and others also received Executive countenance in efforts to raise independent commands. On the other hand, individual members of the regiment were required to obtain furloughs before leaving the State, sometimes requiring the assent of the regimental commander and sometimes not. Many members of the regiment without obtaining leave straggled off to Virginia, where they permanently attached themselves to different organizations. From Orangeburg the colonel of the regiment went to Charleston and obtained a furlough for three months, not supposing the regiment would be again called into service, if at all, before the winter campaign in the South should open. Thence, after a couple of days in making the necessary preparations at home, he went to Virginia equipped as a private and prepared to do such service as might offer during his leave of absence. He was fortunate enough to be able to render some assistance as engineer in charge, under Captain Stevens, C. S. A., of the works near Fairfax Court House between the Falls Church and Flint Hill Roads, and had the honor to carry a rifle in the Palmetto Guard of Kershaw's Regiment in the retreat from Fairfax, and in the battle of Bull Run and of Manassas Plains.

At Bull Run the participation of Kershaw's Regiment was confined to sustaining a canonade behind the lines and to two sorties during the day in support of Kemper's Battery of Field Artillery. At Manassas it was more actively engaged. After

---

*McCreery, a native of Barnwell and graduate of the Citadel Military School, had been a private in the First S. C. V. He subsequently rose to the command of Gregg's Regiment and was killed in battle in 1865.

the arrival of Colonel Hagood in Virginia, the following members of the First came on with similar furloughs: Lieutenant John H. Felder, Lieutenant John A. Bellinger, Sergeant E. I. Felder, Sergeant Donald Rowe, Privates Meredith, Jaudon, Robinson, Ben Hart, and Sergeant (afterwards Lieutenant) Dibble.* They attached themselves as privates to Kershaw's Regiment and did duty as such while in Virginia.

At Manassas Lieutenant Bellinger and Sergeant Felder, together with Burwile Barnwell, of Beaufort, S. C., assisted Colonel Hagood in working one of the guns of Rickett's captured battery against the retreating enemy.

SUMMERVILLE.

The regiment assembled at Summerville on the South Carolina Railroad under the following order:

"State of South Carolina,
"Headquarters, 13 July, 1861.

"Special Orders:
  "No. 156.

"1. The Second (Blanding's) and Sixth Regiments of South Carolina Volunteers having been ordered to Virginia, and Colonel R. H. Anderson, commanding provisional forces in South Carolina, having made a requisition for troops to replace them in the defense of the State, the First Regiment of South Carolina Volunteers is ordered to rendezvous at Summerville on the 20th day of July inst.

"2. Colonel Hagood being absent from the State, Lieutenant-Colonel Glover is placed in command of the regiment and will extend this order.

---

*Member of Congress from South Carolina in 1881.

NOTE.—Lieutenant Felder contracted typhoid fever and died two months afterward. Lieutenant Bellinger, a spirited and meritorious officer, was killed in a duel, the result of an unfortunate misunderstanding with a brother officer, later in the war. Captain Stevens, Confederate States engineer, was a graduate of West Point from New York, and at the breaking out of the war was in the United States Army in Texas. He resigned his commission and cast his fortunes with the Confederacy. In 1864 he was chief engineer of Lee's Army of Northern Virginia with the rank of brigadier general, when the writer had the pleasure of agreeably renewing his acquaintance with him. After the war General Stevens, with others, accepted a voluntary exile in Mexico, where he died a few years later. The venerable and eccentric Edmund Ruffin served as a private in the Palmetto Guards, both at Bull Run and Manassas. His whole being seemed to be enlisted in the Southern Cause, and after the disastrous close of the war, declining, in his own words, "to survive the liberties of his country," he put a voluntary period to his existence.

"3. Colonel Glover will report for orders to Colonel R. H. Anderson, commanding provisional forces. . . .

"By order of the Governor.

"CHARLES H. SIMONTON,
"Acting Adjutant General."

Nine companies were represented at the rendezvous, Mangum's company having gone West. None were full and some were mere fragments. Colonel Hagood returned from Virginia during the first week in August and took command on the 10th. The recruiting of the regiment had been commenced; and the question of entering military Confederate service was again presented under the condition indicated in the following communication:

"State of South Carolina,
"Headquarters, 14 August, 1861.

"Colonel Johnson Hagood, Commanding First S. C. V.

"Sir: In order to prevent any misunderstanding, I beg leave to say that the alternative is not presented to your regiment to muster into Confederate service or to be disbanded. On the contrary, such injustice will not be done. . . . If any refuse Confederate service they will be kept on duty until their time expires.

"Very respectfully,

"CHARLES H. SIMONTON,
"Acting Adjutant General."

Under this communication all inducements to refuse Confederate service was apparently removed. Still the *bona fide* of the communication was doubted by some; and, to anticipate somewhat, the sequel showed they were well posted upon the vacillating counsels which ruled at State headquarters. After keeping the recusants in service for some time they were, on the 30th September following, disbanded. Brown's and Frederick's Companies failed to obtain a basis to recruit upon for Confederate service, as provided for in the order of 19th May, but many of their respective commands entered other companies of the regiment for that purpose. Two companies from Barnwell, commanded respectively by Captains Duncan and Brabham, and one from Williamsburg, commanded by Captain J. G. Pressly (late of Gregg's six months' regiment), were received to fill the vacant places. And thus at length the regiment was mustered into Confederate service. As soon as this was accomplished, attention was at once directed to obtaining orders for Virginia service; and, though these efforts were principally made while the regiment was stationed elsewhere, the subject will be disposed of at once. In inducing the men to take Confederate service, and especially in obtaining new companies to fill the vacant places, it was impressed upon them that they were to enlist "unconditionally," and without a pledge from the Government as to the locality of service. The seacoast from the approach of winter, when active operations might be then anticipated, had become less unpopular. Still Virginia was in general estimation the field of honor. The men composing the new Confederate regiments desired to go there, and it was clear all the way through that without the chance of the regiment being ordered to the seat of war the regiment could not be raised. Governor Pickens had made the proposition to Lieutenant-Colonel Glover, commanding, for the regiment "to muster in, upon the same terms as had been accorded to the Ninth and Tenth regiments. Those regiments are now in Confederate service upon the understanding, not expressed in writing, that they are to be used in defence of South Carolina" (see his letter), and at the same time sending him the printed "unconditional" rolls. The Governor's letter was suppressed; it was thought if he wished to limit the written contract he was encouraging a regiment, then undoutbedly under his control, to make with the Confederate Government it was his business to address his communication to that Government, and if they were unwilling to accept his modifications (as they were known to be) then to have kept the regiment on the State establishment, as he had the right to do. On applying to Anderson (now General), commanding in Charleston, for a mustering officer, the General, as a matter of form, telegraphed the Governor fir his assent and received for reply: "The Governor consents on the same terms accorded to Heyward's and Manigault's regiments." These were respectively the Ninth and Tenth. General Anderson sent the mustering officer up, and with him sent the telegram. Colonel Hagood did not communicate the telegram to the regiment, but, taking advantage of some errors in the muster rolls, sent the mustering officer back with the following communication:

4—II

"In Camp near Summerville, S. C.,
"21 Aug., 1861.

"General: Lieutenant Miles (the mustering officer sent me today and who will deliver this) desires the muster rolls made out anew in consequence of some defect of form. He showed while here a telegram from Captain Simonton, Acting Adjutant General of South Carolina, to you, saying that Governor Pickens desired the First Regiment mustered in on the terms accorded to Heyward's and Manigault's regiments. In a conversation had with you a few days ago, I understood you to say that these regiments were mustered into Confederate service *unconditionally*, and that these were the only terms upon which any regiment had been, or would be, received. The printed agreement furnished us by the State Adjutant General Department to be signed preliminary to mustering in is expressly unconditional in its terms, and I wish to state that it is upon the expressed terms of that agreement and no other that the regiment has consented to, and now takes Confederate service.

"Very respectfully,
"JOHNSON HAGOOD,
"Colonel First S. C. V."

General Anderson sent the mustering officer back next day, and we took leave of the State service with this protest on file and a part of the contract.

Desiring to remove all obstacles whatever to our Virginia scheme, General Jamison was induced to seek an interview with the Governor, which resulted in his giving his written consent to the regiment being ordered to that State. General Jamison forwarded to Colonel Hagood the paper by mail, and it had hardly arrived when Governor Pickens addressed a letter to Lieutenant Colonel Glover revoking his consent. This letter was not addressed to the "Lieutenant Colonel" with any addition indicating that his Excellency thought Glover was in command, and as Colonel Hagood was then in command, and had been since 10th August, he took no notice of the revocation but wrote to General Bonham in Virginia desiring that he would seek to have us attached to his brigade, and commenced also the following correspondence which shows the result of our aspirations in that direction:

"Headquarters First S. C. V.,
"8th Sept., 1861.

"*Hon. L. P. Walker, Secretary at War, Richmond.*

"Sir: I beg leave respectfully to enclose you a paper from Governor Pickens, giving his consent for my regiment to leave for Virginia and to apply for orders. My regiment was of the twelve months volunteers called for by the State last winter, the first organized and received into service. It has been late to take Confederate service for reasons that it is needless to speak of now; but none of which reflect either upon the spirit of the men or their readiness to serve the Confederacy. We have been in service since 13th April last, and are as well drilled as any of the Carolina troops now in Virginia. I speak from recent observation. We are receiving our winter uniforms as fast as they are made, and I feel assured that by the 20th this month our equipment for the winter will be complete. If in your judgment compatible with the interest of the service, it would be agreeable to us to be brigaded with the other South Carolina troops in Bonham's command.

"I am, sir, very respectfully,
"JOHNSON HAGOOD,
"Colonel First S. C. V."

"Adjutant and Inspector General's Office,
"Richmond, 18 Sept., 1861.

"Sir: The Secretary at War has decided, and I am instructed to inform you, that after considering the endorsement on your letter of the 8th inst. by General Ripley, it is deemed inexpedient to order your regiment to Virginia at this time. The following is the endorsement by General Ripley referred to: 'Colonel Hagood's regiment is eminently qualified to do good service in Virginia, or elsewhere, but at present and until the coast defenses are in proper condition, its services are indispensable in South Carolina. It is now at Stono—a very important post.'

"Very respectfully,
"M. Chuttal, A. A. G.
"Colonel Hagood, First S. C. V."

Thus terminated our present hopes of Virginia. But the regiment had taken no local service. It was ready to serve when the War Department thought its services were needed, and having used all the means in its power to obtain marching orders for the seat of war it felt that at length it stood straight upon the record. The tide of war soon began to roll southward. Hatteras fell; South Carolina was invaded, and the defeat of our Virginia project was no longer the subject of serious regret.

POSTS ON STONO.

On the 28th August, the sailing of the Hatteras expedition having become known, and its destruction being uncertain, General Ripley (who had succeeded General Anderson in command in South Carolina), ordered the First Regiment to Coles Island, one of the posts on Stono—the back entrance into Charleston harbor. Colonel Hagood was assigned to the command of these posts and directed to make his headquarters on Coles Island.

Here the regiment remained for the rest of its twelve months' enlistment. Its equipment was completed in every particular, and a regular course of instruction instituted. The officers were required to write on the tactics daily to the colonel, using a blackboard in demonstration; and at the same time the officers and non-commissioned officers were practically instructed in the drill. They were together drilled in the school of the "soldier squad" and "company," and then in a battalion skeleton drill. In this skeleton drill the privates of the rank were represented by two men carrying a light rod the length of a small company and the officers and non-commissioned officers occupied their proper relative positions. The colonel was throughout personally the instructor. Afterwards the course was completed by extending it to the regiment at large. Much attention was also given to the proper performance of sentry and other camp duty. The beneficial effects of these efforts were soon seen in the drill and cheerful discipline of the command, and in the creation of a high esprit du corps.

Afterwards, although the regiment was to be used only as an infantry support, it was thought proper to instruct ten men of each company in the use of heavy artillery, and subsequently two companies were assigned to batteries and thoroughly instructed in this duty. One of these companies (Captain Pressley's) was placed in charge of Fort Pickens on Battery Island, and the other (Captain Glover's) was put in charge of two batteries on Coles Island.

A large amount of fatigue duty was also done by the regiment in the construction of a wagon causeway between Fort Pickens and Coles Island, and in the erection of barracks, the building of bomb-proof batteries, etc. The island was made a strongly fortified post with barracks for 1,000 men. Commissary and quartermaster buildings, bake houses, hospital and everything else complete. A well-supplied commissariat, with a sutler's shop, added much to the comfort of the men. A daily mail, beside telegraphic communication with the city, was established. And, in short, the service for the last months of our time had more of the charaster of garrison life in time of peace than of campaigning.

In addition to the First South Carolina Volunteers there were stationed on Stono 150 Regulars under Major G. J. Lucas, and two companies of Volunteers, under A. A. 1841, from Charleston, commanded respectively by Captain J. J. Pope and Captain S. Y. Tupper. When this class of Volunteers was recalled from service, in order to reorganize the military system of the State, two companies of Volunteers "for the war" from Charleston, under Captains Simonton and Lloyd, were sent in their place. These two companies called themselves the Eutaw Battalion and carried the colors borne by Colonel William Washington's regiment in the Revolutionary battle of that name. It was a piece of red damask without device, and looked as if it had once covered a piece of furniture.

The fall of Port Royal was the only event of interest that marked the winter campaign of 1861-62 in South Carolina. It was remarkably calm on both days of the attack, and the cannonade was very distinctly heard at Coles Island. On the first day Colonel Hagood telegraphed to the general commanding the department asking for his regiment to be ordered to the scene of action, but without success. After the reduction of that post of defense, our line, which had been heretofore upon the outer beach of the island lining the coast, was withdrawn to the main. All the seacoast or island positions south of Coles Island were abandoned after being first dismantled. The new line of defense from Coles Island southwardly ran along the eastern bank of Stono to the main and thence along the main to the Savannah River. Occasional patrols visited the abandoned islands, and sometimes considerable bodies of troops in the nature of advanced guards occupied them. The enemy made an effort early in January to force his way inland from Port Royal with a view to cutting the Charleston and Savannah Railroad, but was repulsed. Subsequently his efforts were limited to marauding upon the abandoned territory, keeping well under the shelter of his gunboats. His attention seemed directed more to the City of Savannah and the coast southward and northward of South Carolina. A blockading steamer was generally lying off Stono, but sometimes it would disappear for weeks. During the last of December this steamer running in rather close, several shots were exchanged with one of our batteries. The distance, however, was too great, and had Colonel Hagood been at the post he would not have permitted the battery to reply to her fire. The blockade was run two or three times from this inlet, and once a small vessel attempting it was captured and a large one burned in our view, but unfortunately beyond our range. This last was owned and commanded by a New York Yankee, who had heard that salt was scarce in Secesscia and had hoped to make an honest penny at the expense of the "best government the world ever saw."

The posts on Stono, and their retention or abandonment in its relation to the defense of Charleston, was a subject of earnest and even angry discussion at the time, and the military critic will have to accord to the decision finally enforced a most important bearing upon subsequent operations against the city. Stono Inlet is a little southwest of, and ten miles from Charleston. A bar, as in all other Southern Atlantic bays, lies in front of it and about two miles out at sea. Directly across its mouth and a little in front of it lies Bird Key, a sand bank nearly covered at high tide. Coles Island lies at the head of the inlet towards the north. It is near two miles long and from one hundred and fifty to three hundred and fifty yards wide. Folley Island is the eastern and Kiawah Island the western boundary of the inlet. At the head of the inlet Folley River comes in from the east and Kiawah River from the west. These two rivers are mere arms of the sea, making the inland boundaries of the islands of the same name. Stono River comes into Kiawah River at the western end of Coles Island. This river is also an arm of the sea, running from the point at which it connects with Kiawah in a northerly direction till it comes within four miles of Charleston. In this part of its course it separates John's and James's Islands. At the point nearest Charleston it connects with the waters of Charleston Harbor by Wappoo Cut and creek, which last separates James Island from the main. From Wappoo Cut the Stono runs first northwesterly and then southwesterly until it communicates with the North Edisto Inlet ten miles from and south of west from Stono Inlet. From the time it leaves Wappoo Cut the Stono River separates from the main first John's Island and then Wadmalaw Island. In the latter part of its course it is known as Wadmalaw

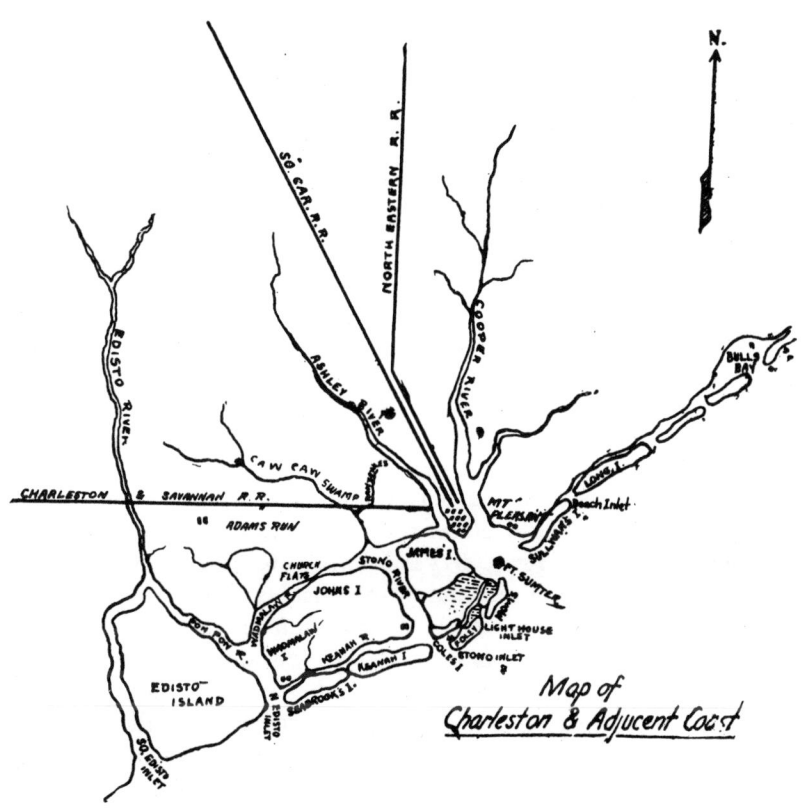

Map of Charleston & Adjucent Coast

River. Folley River communicates by a creek with the waters of the harbor at a point between James Island and Morris Island, as also with Light House Inlet. The channel across the bar in front of Stono Inlet is five feet deep at low, and thirteen feet deep at high water. It is deep but narrow after it has crossed the bar until it has come round Bird Key and entered the inlet. Here it is a mile and three-eighths from the nearest point of Coles Island. From that point the channel through the inlet up Kiawah to Stono River and up Stono River to Church Flats is wide and amply sufficient for vessels of any draft. Church Flats is the point, some ten miles beyond Wappoo, where the Stono changes its name to Wadmalaw River. Through these flats the channel is intricate and shallow, but from thence to North Edisto it is again good. Through Wappoo Cut vessels which may at low or half tide pass the Stono Bar, can pass to Charleston. Battery Island lies up Stono some two and a half miles from Coles Island and is, in fact, the southwestern point of James Island. The Stono batteries were located by General Beauregard just before the attack on Sumter. Their object then was to prevent reinforcements being thrown into the fort in small boats; no more serious efforts of the enemy were anticipated from that direction. He, therefore, located one battery on the eastern end of Coles Island to control Folley River and one on Battery Island, where the Stono is not over 600 yards wide, to control that river. Afterwards it became necessary to consider these posts in view of operations against the city. In consequence of the strength of its harbor defenses, it was supposed a land attack upon Charleston must be conducted by first obtaining some harbor above or below it on the coast as a base of operations. Bulls Bay lies northeast of the city some thirty miles, but the country between that point and the city is intricate, and Wando and Cooper rivers intervene. It would be necessary to make a detour to head the one and cross the other high up, in order to get upon the peninsular on which Charleston is built. Port Royal to the south was too far off for a good base of operations. North Edisto and Stono Inlets remained. From either of these, water communications could be had to Wappoo Cut, a point as before stated four miles from Charleston and the very place for their depot of siege material. It was the center of the semi-circumference around which only the city could be attacked. From North Edisto, however, the navigation through Church Flats was bad, and that line of communication (as well as the line from either Bulls Bay or Port Royal) was exposed to the effects of an army operating in the field to assist the besieged city. From Stono Inlet the navigation, once in, was excellent; and the line of communication was entirely in the rear of and completely covered by an advancing enemy. For these reasons it became important to strengthen the defenses of Stono Inlet.

The engineer, Major (afterwards General) Trapier, charged with the work, forgetting the different object had in view by General Beauregard in locating his battery at Coles Island, endeavored to strengthen that post by adding guns in the same locality, and running a slight infantry trench across the island near these guns to resist an enemy landed on the western part of the island and assailing in flank. While this effectually closed Folley River, it admitted of a fleet passing up the inlet at least seven-eighths of a mile from the nearest gun; and once in Stono River nothing remained but to reduce the slight barbette work at Battery Island, which could only be considered as a second line of defense, being too far to assist in the defense of Coles Island. Again, Green Creek, a navigable stream over a hundred yards wide, ran from Stono eastward and not over a half a mile in rear of Coles Island, enabling an enemy who had reached that point to take these batteries in reverse. From the length of Coles Island and its crescent-like shape, the arch being toward the inlet, Trapier's batteries could not be brought to bear upon an enemy landing upon its western end. A flank land attack and an attack in reverse were, therefore, tacitly accepted by this plan of defense; and that with sand batteries (men epaulements) not closed at the gorge, and with guns half of which could not be traversed over 150 degrees.

Colonel Hagood, on taking command, urged upon General Ripley, commanding the department, a rearrangement of the defenses, and without success at first. Subsequently the general's consent was obtained, and the following plan was adopted. A system of detached batteries with few guns in each was extended along the whole shore line of Coles Island from Folley to Stono Rivers. At each of these batteries bomb-proof shelters

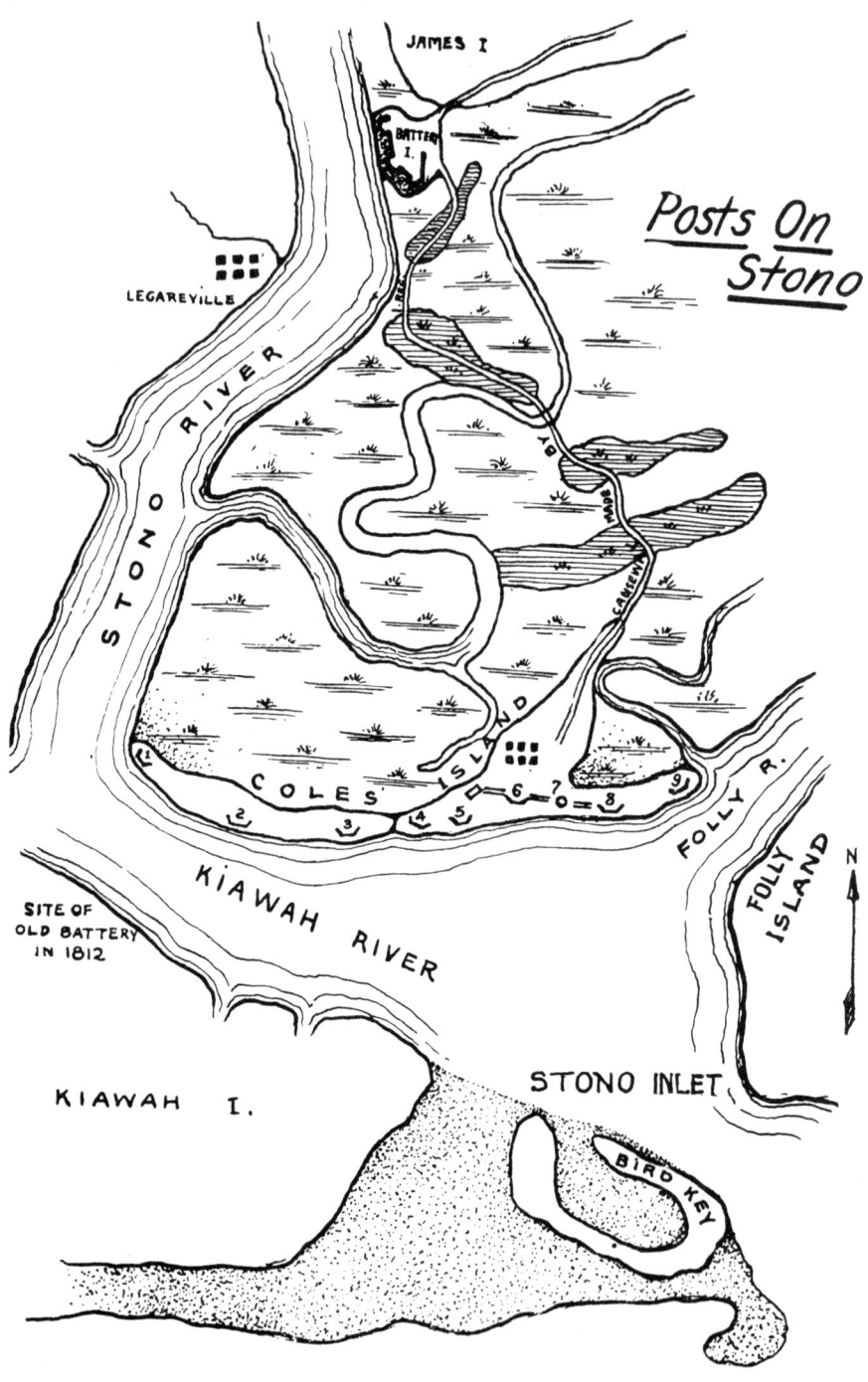

Posts On Stono

ARMAMENT.

Battery Island—2 24 drs.
Battery 1—1 32 drs. rifled.
Battery 2—2 24 drs. smooth.
Battery 3—2 24 drs. smooth.
Battery 4—2 18 drs. smooth.

Battery 5—2 32 drs. smooth.
Battery 6—1 Columb. 10'.
Battery 7—2 24 drs. smooth ; 2 24 drs. rifled.
Battery 8—3 42 drs. smooth ; 1 Columb. 10'.
Battery 9—2 32 drs. smooth ; 1 Columb. 8".

were constructed for the artillerists and infantry supports, and a large bomb-proof for the infantry reserve was located in a central position. These batteries and bomb-proof shelters were connected by covered ways where the natural features of the island did not afford sufficient protection for the passage of troops under fire. The batteries were still barbette epaulements, but the chances of being passed by a hostile fleet were diminished from the fact that along the western part of the island (along the Kiawah) the whole river was not more than 600 yards wide and in some places the channel was within 200 yards of the batteries. Colonel Hagood also recommended the piling or other obstructions of Folley and Kiawah rivers under the fire of the batteries. Trapier's infantry trench was leveled in order to give free passage in rear of the batteries; half the guns at Battery Island were brought to Coles Island; and some additional guns were obtained. General Ripley, however, directed the piling down in Stono River under the guns of Battery Island and the placing of infernal machines across the channel between Bird Key and Folley Island. By this arrangement Coles Island once passed by the enemy, even with one ship, and he had the use of Green Creek; and the great advantage of delaying him under our heaviest fire was given up. The infernal machines, or torpedoes, were a failure. A few days after they were put down, a large raft of logs intended for building bomb-proofs broke loose from Coles Island and going out with the tide floated over them. Froberg, the carpenter in charge, took some assistants in a rowboat, went after the raft and towed it back over them again without an explosion. The Confederates later brought torpedoes to a nearer approach to perfection, especially when they were not required to remain too long before use.

Such were the defenses of Stono. When the batteries were as first arranged by Trapier, General R. E. Lee, then Commander-in-Chief in South Carolina, visited them and advised General Ripley to abandon the position. Subsequently, when the changes spoken of had been made, General Pemberton, who had succeeded General Lee in the chief command, visited Coles Island and expressed the opinion that it had been made too strong to abandon now, but also expressed dissatisfaction with the selection of the island for defense at all. He seemed to think that the post could withstand a naval attack, but would fall before combined land and naval operations. The adjacent islands of Kiawah and Folley being conceded to the enemy in the plan of defense, he laid much stress upon their ability to establish mortar batteries on these. General Ripley still seemed bent on maintaining the post, and Colonel Hagood suggested that there being no adequate line of retreat for the garrison, and the comparatively large armament being invaluable to us, of which the removal in face of an enemy there was no possibility, the post should be further strengthened until it filled the requisition of an isolated self-sustaining fortress, capable of sustaining a siege as long as the City of Charleston holds out. As such it would do good service in depriving an enemy before the city of the use of Stono and compelling him to have recourse to the more exposed and difficult communication by Church Flats for bringing up his supplies and siege material. To this the reply was made that we had neither guns nor ammunition available for such a purpose.

On the 25th March, Colonel Hagood received orders, emanating from General Pemberton, to evacuate the post. Believing that an evacuation once determined upon should be rapidly executed, he, in forty-eight hours afterward, had every gun but five, with its ammunition, etc., loaded on flats ready to be towed up to Charleston, when countermanding orders were received with directions to have everything placed in statu quo, but to cease completing the works as originally designed. The best explanation he received of this vacillation of purpose was that the judgment of General Pemberton dictated the order, and that outside pressure from the State authorities induced him to defer its execution.

Hagood's Regiment remained in occupation of Coles Island until the 13th of April, 1862, when it was relieved by Stevens's Twenty-fourth South Carolina Volunteers. Stevens remained a short time on the island when the orders above referred to were renewed and the troops and material withdrawn. A picket was kept on the island with instructions to fire the buildings and withdraw before the approach of the enemy. The steamer "Planter" was used in withdrawing the material. Shortly afterward the desertion of her crew to the enemy carried information of the evacuation. This led to an immediate advance of the enemy by way of Stono against Charleston, which terminated in their repulse before Secessionville. Coles Island was never afterward occupied by the Confederates. The waters of the inlet were always held by one or more gunboats of the enemy, and Stono was the point d'appui of all subsequent operations against Charleston.

General Pemberton was severely criticized by military men for the change in the plan of defense of the city, and, in fact, so lost the confidence of the people of the State by it as to lead to his removal from the command and assignment to duty elsewhere.

There can be no doubt of the error of the movement in the light of the subsequent events of the war. There had been, however, from the beginning of the war, exaggerated ideas of the power of gunboats as compared with earthworks. Now their development into ironclads was a new element to be considered, and the success of the Virginia (or Merrimac) in silencing the enemy's batteries at Newport News, since Pemberton's visit to Coles Island, had produced the impression on the minds of many that earthworks would prove no match for these new engines of naval war. Accepting these views as correct, there was reason to eliminate this formidable agency in which the greater mechanical facilities of the enemy gave him superiority, by withdrawing our lines whenever practicable beyond its reach. General Pemberton, in a conversation with the writer in Virginia in 1864, defended his action at length as the best under the circumstances; cited General Lee's opinion when in command here, in confirmation, and referred confidently to his correspondence with the War Department on file in the office at Charleston for his vindication. An important point stated as influencing him, perhaps the chief consideration, was his supply of artillery. The majority of his guns in number and weight of metal, he said, were at Stono, and these were absolutely needed to make safe the more important harbor approach. The War Department at Richmond had positively informed him of their inability to supply more, and he had no other course left. On the other hand, the development of events showed that at this time the enemy was unprepared for, and did not contemplate, any movement, land or naval, against Charleston. The evacuation of Coles Island induced the abortive effort terminating at Secessionville; and by the time he was ready to move again in 1863, the Confederate resources in artillery were increased. The test of actual experience, too, modified the ideas entertained of ironclads. The enemy in the meanwhile, however, were wise enough to hold by their gunboats the gate we had left open, and when he came again it was ready for his use.

The writer is satisfied now that Battery Island should have been dismantled or reduced in importance to a mere cover for the communication with Coles Island, and that a strong enclosed work or moderate armament should have been erected on the south side of Folley Island, from which to Bird Key obstructions should have been placed. This, with the works on Coles Island as a second line of defense, would have effectually closed the water approach of the Stono Light House Inlet, then fortified in time, and we would never have had such a siege as Gilmore was subsequently enabled to inaugurate. A larger force than his would have been needed, operating from a more distant base, and measurably deprived of direct naval co-operation.

RE-ENLISTMENT.

The First Regiment had acquired drill and discipline and had become thoroughly organized; it had got through with all the initial diseases of the camp and become inured to the habits of the soldier; and now, just as it had become a valuable regiment, fit for efficient service, it was to be re-enlisted, and in the process was to be subjected to all the demoralizing influences of the hustings. It will be a question for the future historian how much of the disaster that attended our arms in the spring of 1862 was due to the evil of short enlistment, and to the license permitted in inducing the men to continue their service.

The attention of the Confederate Congress was directed to the subject of retaining the twelve-months men in service early in 1862, and two Acts were passed. By one of these fifty dollars bounty and a furlough not to exceed thirty full days at home were offered each twelve-months man who re-enlisted. They were also allowed to reorganize themselves into such companies, battalions and regiments as they pleased, with a general re-election of officers of every grade. By the other Act, provision was made for recruiting upon these organizations. The term of re-enlistment of the twelve-months man was to be for two years—the recruit enlisted for three years. About the same time a requisition was made on South Carolina for something over twelve thousand men—7,000 to fill the place of the twelve-months men whose term expired in April, and 5,000 in addition to her quota, then in the field.

Hitherto in South Carolina, as well as throughout the Confederacy, volunteering had been relied upon to furnish soldiers for the war. There had always been a draft or conscription held in terrorism in case volunteers failed, and, indeed, in Charleston, as well as some other cities of the South, resort had to a limited extent been had to this draft. Now, the Executive Council who had recently been constituted in South Carolina and entrusted with dictatorial powers, determined to change all this as far as that State was concerned. On the 6th March they decreed a new military system for the State, abolishing volunteering and substituting conscriptions as the only mode of raising troops during the present war. They further decreed that all conscriptions should be "for and during the war"; and that all officers from third lieutenant to colonel should be appointed by the Council.

Of course the Acts of Congress controlled in the case of the First Regiment, but the decree of the Council had the effect of destroying a project which to some extent had prevailed of giving honor to reorganize. The only way to secure a volunteer organization, with its elected officers, etc., was to re-enlist before the present term expired, and before, as citizens and no longer in Confederate service, the men came under the new military system of the State. These various enactments were, as received, published on parade, and in addition a copy furnished to each company. The men were left to discuss and digest them at their leisure, until about the 14th March, when the colonel called the regiment together and in an address of some length, after discussing and recapitulating the facts as heretofore brought to their attention, required the commandants of companies to commence the work of re-enlistment.

By the expiration of one term it resulted as follows: Martin's company failed to reorganize, but some twenty of its numbers joined other companies. Livingston's company divided and recruited up to two companies under himself and Knotts respectively. Duncan's company divided and also recruited up to two companies under himself and Sanders. The other companies each retained their organization with full numbers. The new companies were officered as follows:

First Company.
W. H. Sellars, Captain.
L. A. Harper, First Lieutenant.
J. G. Evans, Second Lieutenant.
F. Shuler, Third Lieutenant.

Second Company.
T. K. Legare, Captain.
W. W. Legare, First Lieutenant.
B. M. Shuler, Second Lieutenant.
J. B. Conner, Third Lieutenant.

Third Company.
I. S. Bamberg, Captain.
W. W. Elzry, First Lieutenant.
L. A. Wright, Second Lieutenant.
P. C. Allen, Third Lieutenant.

Fourth Company.
B. B. Kirkland, Captain.
J. F. Brabham, First Lieutenant.
R. S. Barker, Second Lieutenant.
R. B. Hogg, Third Lieutenant.

Fifth Company.
G. M. Grimes, Captain.
G. W. Grimes, First Lieutenant.
L. J. Sweat, Second Lieutenant.
L. B. Kearse, Third Lieutenant.

Sixth Company.
F. Sanders, Captain.
G. W. Stallings, First Lieutenant.
R. T. Sanders, Second Lieutenant.
S. C. L. Bush, Third Lieutenant.

Seventh Company.
W. H. Duncan, Captain.
J. H. Thompson, First Lieutenant.
P. H. Wood, Second Lieutenant.
J. R. B. Best, Third Lieutenant.

Eighth Company.
D. Livingston, Captain.
I. Inabinett, First Lieutenant.
J. C. Wannamaker, Second Lieutenant.
W. S. L. Rucker, Third Lieutenant.

Ninth Company.   J. E. Knotts, Captain.
J. Elvin Knotts, First Lieutenant.
J. H. Phillips, Second Lieutenant.
J. H. Fanning, Third Lieutenant.

Tenth Company.   J. G. Pressly, Captain.
T. I. China, First Lieutenant.
C. Logan, Second Lieutenant.
H. Montgomery, Third Lieutenant.

Eleventh Company.   John V. Glover, Captain.
J. F. Izlar, First Lieutenant.
S. M. Kennerly, Second Lieutenant.
Sam'l Dibble, Third Lieutenant.

The First, Tenth and Eleventh Companies elected to seek another regimental organization. The Eutaw Battalion, which, with the addition of these companies and some others, became the Twenty-fifth South Carolina Volunteers, of which Pressly became lieutenant-colonel and Glover major. This regiment served principally afterwards in "Hagood's Brigade." The Second and Sixth Companies attached themselves to Lamar's Battalion of Artillery, which then grew into the "Second South Carolina Artillery" and served principally afterwards in the garrison of Charleston. Sanders had been arraigned before a court-martial as first lieutenant of Duncan's company in the twelve-months regiment on charges of "conduct unbecoming an officer and a gentleman," and was in arrest awaiting sentence when the reorganization took place and when he was elected captain of the Sixth Company. The sentence of the court was promulgated shortly after he reported to Lamar, and he was dismissed the service. He went home and in a few weeks afterwards was licensed as a Baptist preacher. Stallings commanded the company, and did it well, during the remainder of the war. The other six companies elected to combine with a view of retaining their old regimental organization. They desired to retain the name, rank and banner of the First Regiment and, by filling up with four new companies, to preserve its existence. This filling up was necessarily a subsequent matter. In order, therefore, to preserve their cohesion, meanwhile, and without forfeiting their claim to be in this regiment, they went into an election "for an officer to command them, his rank and designation to be settled

5—H

by the subsequent action of the proper authority." Colonel Hagood was elected by acclamation. There never was opposition, which found expression, to Colonel Hagood in the attempt at retaining the re-organized companies in the original regiment; but for each of the other field officers there were numerous aspirants. To this cause is attributable—in part—the failure to retain them. The Eutaw Battalion and Lamar's Battalion, stationed near the regiment and in frequent intercourse with it, afforded opportunities to captains taking companies into them, for promotion. In developing into regiments they furnished field officers to be filled. One of these organizations, too, from its character of heavy artillery, promised local garrison service instead of the less comfortable life of a marching regiment. The spirit of change had also its effect. And the result of all these various sources of disorganization has been indicated.

Stevens's Regiment arrived on the 13th. On the 14th, at 2 a. m., the regiment marched for Charleston, and the following order, received on the 12th of May, was carried out:

<blockquote>
"Headquarters Military District, South Carolina,
"Charleston, 12 May, 1862.

Special Order.
    No. ——.

     *   *   *   *   *   *   *   *

"II. Colonel Stevens' Twenty-fourth South Carolina will move to Coles Island and relieve Colonel Hagood's First South Carolina as soon as possible.

"Colonel Hagood's regiment, upon being relieved, will proceed to the vicinity of Binnaker's Camp Ground on South Carolina Railroad, where such as have not re-enlisted for the war will be mustered out of service by Colonel Hagood. . . .

"IV. Such companies as have re-enlisted for the war will be granted a leave of absence until the 14th day of May; but it must be understood that the men will reassemble upon any call for service that may arise during their absence, the authorities at Richmond having consented to the leave at this time only upon this condition.

"V. Upon reassembling, six companies will report to Colonel Hagood as a portion of his regiment. Of the remaining companies, Captains Pressly, Glover and Sellars will report to Captain Simonton, commanding Eutaw Battalion, and Captains Legare and Sanders to Major Lamar, commanding battery of artillery.

     "By order of Brigadier-General Ripley.
         "F. G. RAVENEL, A. D. C."
</blockquote>

APPENDIX.

The First Regiment was at home ten or twelve days upon its re-enlistment furlough, when it was recalled into service by a special order and rendezvoused at Bamberg upon the South Carolina Railroad, whence it was transferred to the City of Charleston. Its ranks were here filled by the reception of four new companies. Glover was re-elected lieutenant-colonel. O'Caim declined to continue in service and Captain Duncan was elected to the vacant majority. Of the staff, Captain Lartigue declined reappointment and Lieutenant Flowers, of Company H of the twelve-months regiment, was appointed quartermaster. Legare having gone into the line and out of the regiment, Captain J. V. Martin was appointed commissary. Dowling had been broken by an examining board, and John S. Stoney was appointed assistant surgeon in his stead. Mortimer Glover was sergeant-major and Donald Rowe quartermaster-sergeant.

The four new companies were officered as follows:

COMPANY D.
Captain, R. L. Crawford.
First Lieutenant, J. H. Kirk.
Second Lieutenant, F. L. Welsh.
Third Lieutenant, L. J. Perry.

COMPANY H.
Captain, J. C. Winsmith.
First Lieutenant, W. A. Nesbitt.
Second Lieutenant, J. N. Moore.
Third Lieutenant, J. E. Vise.

COMPANY F.
Captain, T. D. Gwynn.
First Lieutenant, William West.
Second Lieutenant, T. W. Powell.
Third Lieutenant, F. P. Newby.

COMPANY I.
Captain, J. H. Stafford.
First Lieutenant, J. H. Harlee.
Second Lieutenant, W. L. Manning.
Third Lieutenant, R. Murchison.

The history of this regiment until July, 1862, when its first colonel was promoted to a brigade, is contained in subsequent pages of these Memoirs. In a week or ten days afterward the regiment was ordered to Virginia, where it was attached to Jenkins's (afterwards Bratton's) Brigade in the division then commanded by Hood and later by Fields. This division was a part of Longstreet's Corps. The history of the regiment, after the promotion of its first colonel, was carefully prepared by Colonel James R. Hagood, its last commander, whose manuscript is now in the possession of the writer. Suffice it to say here that its career was creditable and its services arduous and faithful among the troops which composed the distinguished corps to which it was attached.

Colonel Glover fell at the Second Manassas. He was a graduate of the South Carolina College with its first honor, and a lawyer who had already obtained distinction at an early age, when the war broke out. In the reorganization at Coles Island some temporary unpopularity was manifested toward him, the result of a faithful discharge of duty, and sickness deprived him of a share in the operations preceding Secessionville. In the active operations in Virginia his worth was conspicuous and endeared him much to his men. He fell universally lamented, and his death was marked by distinguished heroism.

Duncan succeeded Glover, but saw little service with the regiment, and resigned. Livingston succeeded Duncan and retained the command somewhat longer, when he resigned. Neither of these officers distinguished themselves and the regiment suffered in discipline and usefulness in their hands.

Colonel Kilpatrick was now appointed to the command. He was a South Carolinian and a graduate of the State Military Academy. In another regiment he had won his commission by gallant and meritorious service. He soon restored the discipline and esprit of the regiment; and after a career which added to his own and the reputation of the regiment, he, too, died upon the field of battle.

Colonel James R. Hagood joined the regiment after the battle of Secessionville and rose in two years from the ranks through the successive grades sergeant-major, adjutant and captain to its command. His colonel's commission was dated the day after he was 19 years old, and like all of his others was "for distinguished valor and skill." He got no step by seniority or election, and was at the date of his promotion the youngest regimental commander in the Confederate Army. Of him our great chieftain, General Lee, wrote from the retirement of Lexington in March, 1868: "During the whole time of his connection with the Army of Northern Virginia he was conspicuous for his gallantry, good conduct and efficiency. By his merit constantly exhibited, he rose from a private in his regiment to its command, and showed by his actions that he was worthy of the position." And Major General Fields added: "During our eventful service together, in the bivouac, on the march, or in the shock of battle, Colonel Hagood's high-toned, soldierly bearing at all times, his thorough handling of his regiment, and his distinguished gallantry in action, won my hearty admiration and regard." My brother! these immortelles are laid upon thy grave, upon which the grass is not yet green. No better soldier wore the grey. No knightlier spirit breasted the storm in twenty battles beneath the Red Cross Flag, nor struggled more bravely amid the after difficulties that befell the followers of a Lost Cause.

Colonel Hagood commanded the regiment from the death of Kilpatrick, in Longstreet's Tennessee campaign in the winter of 1863, until the surrender at Appomattox Court House, in the spring of 1865. In the terrible retreat which preceded the surrender, when the veteran Army of Northern Virginia was by hardship and hunger and fighting reduced from 27,000 to 8,000 men fit for duty, the First Regiment, which bore its full part of these trials, lost but seven unwounded men to the enemy. This fact speaks volumes for the spirit and devotion of the men and of the able manner in which they were commanded.

MARTIAL LAW IN CHARLESTON.

The reverses of the Confederate arms in the spring of 1862, commencing at Fort Donnelson and culminating at New Orleans, had anxiously excited the minds of the people of South Carolina, and daily bulletins portraying the sad fate of the Crescent City under the iron rule of Butler, "The Beast," gave warning to the people of Charleston of what might be expected should their city be, as Mr. Lincoln mildly phrased it, "occupied and possessed."

The abandonment of the Coles Island line of defense was also misunderstood, and a painful doubt had arisen in the public mind, and was shared to some extent by the State authorities, of the intention of the Confederate commander of obstinately defending the city in the event of the siege which it was felt must sooner or later come. Accordingly, the papers clamored for earnest and active preparation. Editors and correspondents alike claimed that Charleston would be disgraced unless Saragossa should be surpassed. A "Citizen," in one of our daily prints,*

---

*Courier, 5th May.

hardly exceeded the tone of other writers and talkers when he exclaimed, in contemplation of the fall of the outer forts, "What, then, shall the city be given up? We suppose not. That would be indeed a very qualified defense. . . . Let the drill of the troops be at once extended to fighting in the streets and from the houses. . . ." The governor and council warned non-combatants to depart and declared martial law in and around Charleston, empowering the Confederate Commander to enforce it. A few days later a formal resolve was promulgated from the Executive Council Chamber," "That the Governor and Council concurred in opinion with the people of South Carolina assembled in Convention, that the City of Charleston should be defended at any cost of life and property; and that in their deliberate judgment they would prefer a repulse of the enemy with the entire city in ruins to an evacuation or surrender on any terms whatever."

General Pemberton never at any moment contemplated anything but making the best defense of which he was capable, with the means at his disposal, and would no doubt, if required, have fought it while brick and mortar held together. But he was a soldier *per se*, and would have taken his inspiration from "orders" from Richmond and not from the people and civil authorities by whom he was surrounded. These he had not the tact to conciliate and use, and, for their military opinions, entertained and sometimes exhibited a most professional contempt. He, however, eagerly embraced the power placed in his hands and on the 5th of May issued his General Order No. 11, which, after reciting the Governor's proclamation of martial law over Charleston and the country within ten miles of its corporate limits, proceeded as follows:

"Now I, John C. Pemberton, . . . do sustain the said proclamation and announce the suspension of all civil jurisdiction (with the exception of that enabling the Courts to take cognizance of the probate of wills, the administration of the estates of deceased persons, the qualifications of guardians, to enter decrees and orders for the partition and sale of property, to make orders concerning roads and bridges, to assess and collect county taxes) and the suspension of the writ of habeas corpus in and over" the limits embraced in the proclamation. Another paragraph announced Colonel Johnson Hagood, First S. C. V., as provost marshal and charged him with the execution of the foregoing order and of the proclamation, under the direction of Brigadier General Ripley, commanding the military district. The provost marshal was further directed forthwith to establish a military police and to put a stop to all sales of spirituous liquors.

An express train had been sent up to the camp of the First South Carolina Volunteers at Bamberg on the 4th, with an order for Colonel Hagood to return in person upon it and report that day in Charleston; the regiment was directed to follow next day. When Colonel Hagood was made acquainted with the provision of the order about to be published making him provost marshal, he earnestly asked to be excused from the duty, the condition of his regiment requiring, in his opinion, all of his attention at that time. The General, with something of his usual curtness, peremptorily declined, but promised to relieve him as soon as he had organized the system and got it to working, or earlier in the event of active operations. To Colonel Hagood's further request for detailed instructions as to the duties required of him, the General answered that he had no further instructions than those embodied in the order. This, by the way, was copied from a recent promulgation of martial law in and around Richmond, but of how it was there construed in practice we had no information in Charleston. General Pemberton added that he expected such a system of police that a *dog* could not enter the town without the knowledge of the provost marshal and his ability to lay hands upon said dog at any moment he was required. With this chart of his duty and directions to make requisition for the means to discharge it, the new provost departed to ponder upon the work before him.

Martial Law, what was it? Very accurate ideas in relation to it have since been acquired by the Southern people—but then? General Pemberton had evidently no very definite perception of what its promulgation effected in detail,—the provost had as little. A conference with the State Attorney General, I. W. Hayne, Esq., and reference to books brought little further light; but, with such as was vouchsafed and with the order before him, Colonel Hagood proceeded to digest an organization of martial law upon the idea that it was the assumption of the execution of such existing law as it was deemed necessary to retain, with the making of such additional law as the military exigency required. Rumor soon reached him that the mayor had, in conversation, announced himself and his government as deposed; and, desiring to retain the already organized police force of the city, Colonel Hagood hastened to headquarters and obtained the publication of the following:

"Headquarters Department South Carolina and Georgia,
"Charleston, 5 May, 1862.
"His Honor Charles McBeth, Mayor of Charleston, is respectfully invited and expected to continue in the exercise of his municipal functions, as far as they shall not infringe upon any requirements of martial law. . . . It is the earnest desire of the major general commanding that the provost marshal and the mayor will act in entire unison and render such mutual aid as may be necessary to the efficient discharge of their respective duties.
"By order, etc., . . .

"J. R. Wadely, A. A. G."

The next day, the Justice of the State Court of Common Pleas and General Sessions, then sitting, adjourned his court upon the ground that the proclamation of martial law had suspended his jurisdiction. He was certainly right, under the wording of the order, but it could hardly have advanced the defense of Charleston for the provost marshal to have been hearing civil causes or even trying criminal cases already on the docket, so Order No. 13, 6th May, was obtained and published:

"It is not intended that General Order No. 11, of the 5th May, from these headquarters, shall interfere with the progress of business in the Court of General Sessions and Common Pleas now sitting in this city.
"J. C. Pemberton,
"Major-General Commanding."

In the meanwhile, however, a proclamation was received from the President of the Confederate States declaring martial law over the whole region under Pemberton's command, and using the words of Pemberton's Order No. 11, "suspending civil jurisdiction, etc." General Pemberton, therefore, rescinded his orders continuing the mayoralty and sessions of the State court, and putting his exercise of these prerogatives of martial law under the President's and not the Governor's authority. The court closed its doors; but the provost marshal never assumed cognizance of the cases on its calendar, or to decide any purely civil cases. These remained in abeyance. The organization of the Common Council was also suspended, but the police force was kept on duty under the supervision of the provost marshal. The utility of this arrangement was to some extent marred by jealousy existing between the assistant provost marshal in charge of the police department and the mayor, having inception in their past relations.

The presence of a large military force in the city was necessary to carry out General Pemberton's "dog" specification; and these troops themselves, newly raised and badly disciplined, required the enforcement of the most stringent regulations to keep *them* in order. A number were already in and near the city; their officers infested the hotels and barrooms, and an editorial in *The Mercury* of the 13th (the day on which it had been announced that martial law would at noon go into effect) called attention to outrages of a flagrant character already committed with impunity by those of lower grade. The hegira of citizens also greatly complicated the passport matter. A very stringent supervision of passports was required by the provost's instructions, and was necessary unless the whole matter was to be a farce. The city was known to be infested with spies and the enemy in daily receipt of information from it. Unfortunately the citizens had already become accustomed to a very loose passport system which had been inaugurated and put under the mayor's charge. Under this system blank passports signed by the mayor were filled up at any hour of the day or night by a policeman at the guard house of the police force, and these were sometimes examined and sometimes not by other policemen at some of the more public places of arrival and departure from the city. With a full sense of the difficulties surrounding it, Colonel Hagood entered on his labor. The following regulations, prepared and submitted for approval, on the morning of the 12th, were published in all the daily papers with the appointments and orders copied below. Headquarters were established in the court house, office hours, etc., announced, and the experiment launched.

"REGULATIONS OF THE PROVOST MARSHAL.
"UNDER MARTIAL LAW.

"Provost Marshal's Office,
"2nd Military District S. C., 12 May, 1862.

"1. During the suspension of all civil jurisdiction announced in the Proclamation of the Major-General commanding, with the exceptions therein contained, or which may hereafter be announced, a Provost Marshal's Court is established, which will take cognizance of the offenses heretofore within the jurisdiction of the Court of General Sessions, as well as of all offenses against good order or other violations of martial law.

"2. The Provost Marshal's Court will be presided over by an assistant provost marshal, his decisions to be supervised and approved by the provost marshal. The provost marshal will also, in his discretion, refer any offense to a court-martial, if circumstances make that instrumentality desirable or necessary.

"3. No person will be allowed to leave the city without a written permit from the office of the provost marshal. Every person coming into the city shall report forthwith to the provost marshal under such regulations as he may prescribe. An assistant provost marshal will be assigned to the duties of this department.

"4. The necessary guards for the execution of the above regulations and for the maintenance of good order in the city will be established. An assistant provost marshal will also be assigned to the charge of this department.

"5. Such other regulations will be made and enforced from time to time as may become necessary or expedient for the preservation of good order, and the enforcement of martial law.

"6. These regulations will be enforced after 12 m. on Tuesday, the 13th inst.

JOHNSON HAGOOD,
"Colonel First S. C. V.,
"Provost Marshal."

"Provost Marshal's Office,
"Second Military District S. C., 12 May, 1862.

"1. C. Richardson Miles, Esq., Alex. H. Brown, Esq., and Captain G. B. Lartigue are announced as assistant provost marshals.

"2. Mr. Miles is assigned to the duties of the Provost Marshal's Court.

"3. Mr. Brown is assigned to the duties of the passport office.

"4. Captain Lartigue is assigned to the supervision of the necessary guards.

"JOHNSON HAGOOD,
"Colonel First S. C. V.,
"Provost Marshal."

"Provost Marshal's Office,

"Second Military District S. C., 12 May, 1862.

"Under the Proclamation of Martial Law it is Ordered:

"1. That all distillation of spirituous liquors is positively prohibited and the distilleries will be closed.

"2. The sale of spirituous liquors of any kind is positively prohibited and establishments for the sale thereof closed subject until further orders to the following regulations and modifications:

"*Hotels* may obtain from this department licenses to allow the use of liquors to boarders at meals at the public ordinary upon terms to be specified in the license.

"*Grocers* who have obtained licenses from the city authorities may, until otherwise ordered, sell liquors in quantities of not less than three gallons to any person other than those in military service or employment: *Provided*, That the same be not consumed on the premises.

"3. All barrooms and liquor saloons and places where liquors are retailed shall be immediatley closed.

"4. No liquor shall be sold in any quantity whatever to any soldier or person in military employment without a special license from this office.

"JOHNSON HAGOOD,

"Colonel First S. C. V.,

"Provost Marshal."

Captain Molony, A. A. G., also on the same day (12th) published by order of Colonel Hagood in the daily prints for the information of parties concerned, as well as the public generally, extracts from the "Instructions to the Out Guards" and patrols "of the garrison" and of "orders" issued to the troops composing it. The following were the most important points:

A wharf was designated for the arrival and departure of small boats. One or more other wharves for the transport steamers of the department; wood, rice and provision boats were required to anchor at certain points and report by small boat to the adjacent officer of the guard where a wharf would be designated by them to land at. Persons were only permitted to enter or leave the city by land at designated points. Sentinels were ordered to fire upon boats or persons attempting to enter or leave despite their challenge.

Officers from camps without the city were required upon entering it to exhibit to the lieutenant of the guard their commissions or written leaves of absence, and immediately thereafter to report at provost marshal's office and register their names and leave of absence.* Non-commissioned officers and soldiers from the same camp were prohibited from entering the city on any pretext whatever, except upon duty, upon furlough, to pass through it, or upon furlough to visit their families, when these resided there.

As to the troops within the city it was directed that they be kept strictly within the limits of their respective camp guards. Non-commissioned officers and soldiers will not be permitted to leave the lines of their respective camps upon any pretext whatever, except upon duty or on furlough to leave the city.

Commissioned officers when not upon duty will not be permitted to leave the lines of their camps except upon special permission of the superior officer in command of the camp, who is required to exercise a sound discretion in limiting the numbers at any one time of such permits. There were other orders and instructions published, but these already given were sufficient to show how far at that time it was deemed necessary by those in command to push the stringency of martial law. To the garrison the adjutant-general said in general orders: "They were brought within the city to maintain good order. The colonel commanding trusts they will set the example. Martial law has been proclaimed. Offenses against it, however trival, become aggravated when committed by those whose duty it is to enforce it. It is earnestly hoped that the necessity for the stern punishments which must follow such offenses will not arise." *The Mercury* greeted the foregoing publications as follows: "At a juncture like the present, doubtless there are good reasons for placing the government of our ancient city in military hands. If the officers who have been invested with the control of affairs in our midst exercise their functions with wisdom, firmness and impartiality, this establishment of martial law will prove to be a welcome—as well as beneficial measure."

The Courier contented itself with the following: "Assistant Provost Marshals. By reference to an advertisement in our columns this morning, it will be seen that Colonel Johnson Hagood, Confederate Provost Marshal, has appointed C. Richardson Miles, Esq., Alex. H. Brown, Esq., and Captain Lartigue,

---

*Civilians registered all particulars with regard to themselves with the officers of the guard at point of arrival and were by him reported with their domicile in the city.

assistant provost marshals . . . The appointments are all good and acceptable as conferred upon able, worthy and patriotic men; but that of Colonel Brown especially challenges our approval. Everyone remembers what an energetic and efficient captain of the city guard or chief of police he made in bygone days, and he is now again in his proper element."

The writer, at a later day, sometimes thought with amusement of the editor's (Mr. Gradon's) commendation of Brown. He did indeed prove an invaluable assistant and Colonel Hagood was greatly indebted to him in the discharge of his duty. Brown was, however, naturally an arbitrary and overbearing man, a long resident of the city, with very decided affinities and repulsions, and when he succeeded Colonel Hagood some were disposed to think (Gradon among the number) that his little finger was heavier than other folk's hands. Mr. Miles was a lawyer of eminence and an estimable gentleman. Captain Lartigue was the ex-quartermaster of the First South Carolina Volunteers and afterwards, until the close of the war, quartermaster of Hagood's Brigade. He was a graduate of the State Military School and an old and intimate friend of Colonel Hagood's.

The enforcement of martial law came none too soon. To show how loosely and negligently matters had been managed, the following incident, added to the account given of the mayor's passport office, will suffice. The steamer "Planter" had been chartered with her officers and crew, and used as a transport and harbor guard boat. She was armed with a 32 dr. and a 24 dr. howitzer; her captain, mate and engineer were white; her pilot and four or five hands, who were negroes, completed the crew. She had taken aboard the evening previous four valuable, heavy guns for Morris Island, and laid that night at her usual wharf in front of General Ripley's headquarters on the bay. Three sentinels were stationed in sight of her, and the bivouac of Ripley's headquarter guard was near by. Between half-past three and four a. m. the "Planter" steamed up and cast loose, the sentinels supposing she was going about her business. She passed Fort Sumter blowing her whistle and plainly seen. She was reported by the corporal of the guard to the officer of the day as the guard boat. The fort was only required to recognize authorized boats passing, taking for granted that their officers are on board. This was done as usual. The run to Morris Island goes a long way past Sumter and turns. The "Planter" kept on to the blockading fleet. Her white officers were not on board. They had slept, as was their custom, on shore, notwithstanding a standing order that the officers and crews of all light draft steamers in Government employ remain on board night and day. Upon the subsequent trial of these officers it was proven that no step had been taken to enforce this order by inspection or otherwise, though it was of long standing; and they were acquitted.

The Mercury gave a lively picture of affairs in the town next day. "Martial law," said the editor, "went into force in Charleston yesterday. Squads of the provost marshal's guard were to be seen here and there, and many a luckless wight in military or semi-military costume, who had no leave of absence to show, was trotted off to the guard house, where he either did have or at some future time will have an opportunity of giving an account of himself. In more than one instance, eminently peaceful individuals, affecting the jaunty and war-like Beauregard cap, were hauled up with that true military sternness which is deaf alike to entreaties and remonstrances. The quiet precincts of the city hall were suddenly converted into a veritable camp, to the manifest delight of the urchins who thronged the railings of the enclosure gazing admiringly upon the taut canvass walls. There was a great rush to the passport office. Owing to the very limited time alloted to the issuing of passports, only a small proportion of those desiring to leave the city were accommodated with the necessary documents. Some arrangement should be made to remedy this great inconvenience to the public. . . ."

But *The Courier* blazed out indignantly at the first pinch in the working of the system, characterizing the limited time for granting passports daily "as a grievous and intolerable oppression—an unreasonable and tyrannical measure." It went on to suggest that the power to issue passports be extended to the mayor of the city again, as well as to be exercised by the military authorities.

There was much justice in the complaint, though intemperately urged by *The Courier*. In preparing the regulations, Colonel Hagood had thought the time too short; but Colonel Brown, his assistant, declared he could not spare more time from his other duties in the police department to give to this. The personal attention and attendance of the assistant provost marshal was deemed necessary in the office while passports were being issued. If the matter was to be entrusted to clerks and deputies, unsupervised, it would be a failure. These considerations had prevailed; and two hours daily, from 11 a. m. to 1 p. m., had been fixed. But the exodus of the non-combatant population which was desired, and which had been slowly going on, was not duly considered, and the panic with which the people seemed taken about getting off as soon as an impediment even of form was in the way, was never imagined. Men who crowded and pressed to get passports the first day, when they had got them, avowed that they had no intention of leaving in several days. The next day the force of men in the passport office was increased by appointing Messrs. Gourdin, Pressly, Crafts, Dingle, Gantt, and Whiting to the duty. These were all prominent gentlemen well acquainted with the inhabitants, and were permitted to grant passports only to persons personally known to them, or properly vouched for by such. Captain W. J. Gayer, A. A. G., was put in extensive charge of soldiers' passports. The civilians were continued on duty until the pressure on the office by departing citizens was relieved.

The Courier in its next issue made the amende honorable: "The Passport Matter. It affords us pleasure to state that Colonel Johnson Hagood, our provost marshal, on learning the inconvenience and distress which the original regulation in relation to passports had caused in the community, very promptly so modified it by increasing the agents and enlarging the time for issue as to completely satisfy the wants of the community. . . ."

The passport office was now at leisure and finally organized by establishing two offices in different apartments, one for citizens with separate desks of application for males and females (whites), and for negroes bond and free; another for the military with a separate desk for invalid soldiers from which all other applicants were excluded. Office hours were made from 8 to 1 and from 4 to 7 o'clock. W. E. Dingle, Esq., was placed in charge of the citizens' office, and Captain Gayer, A. A. G., continued in charge of the military office. From each of these an appeal with proper restrictions could be had to Colonel Brown, the assistant provost marshal. This gave him the time which he really needed as chief of the general police department. In this character he held also a daily court in which he investigated and summarily disposed of innumerable minor matters of petty police brought before him, but investigated and reported to the provost marshal on matters of any consequence. These the provost either disposed of or sent for trial to Mr. Miles's court. Colonel Brown had at his command a corps of detectives and, through the mayor, the regular civil police force of the city. Mr. Miles had also a daily court where he tried such cases as the regulations of the 12th May prescribed, as well as those referred to him specially by the provost. Captain Lartigue's duties were exclusively military. At night the three assistants met the provost for consultation. Colonel Hagood's duties were chiefly supervisory. The system of guards adopted was a chain of infantry sentinels completely around the city along the margin of the waters making the peninsular and across the neck at the lines in rear. These sentinels connected in their walk when the nature of the ground permitted, and at other points were within hail and musket shot. Each regiment furnished a certain number of posts, and the reliefs and guard tent were at some central point. The First South Carolina Regiment furnished the interior infantry guard, with guard tent, in City Hall Park and posts in various parts of the city. Major Frank Hampton's Battalion of Cavalry (afterwards part of the Second South Carolina Cavalry Regiment) furnished a mounted interior patrol on duty day and night. And from sunset until sunrise a boat guard patrolled the rivers (at a distance of 300 yards from shore) from a point in Ashley above the lines, around White Point Garden to a point in Cooper, again above the lines. Each boat had an infantry detachment on board and rowed backward and forward along its allotted beat. The troops in the city filled every available camping ground in the parks and malls— none occupied houses, and men and officers were rigidly kept within their camp lines under the regulations heretofore given. A large number of troops were necessary to the discharge of provost duty, as indicated. But Charleston was a very good place for the reserve troops of General Pemberton's command. Large drafts were being made upon him, too, at this time for Johnston's Army before Richmond; and when drawn from points of his department further South, they all stopped in

Charleston for a few days, reporting to Colonel Hagood as town commandant, during their stay and doing provost duty. Sometimes there were as many as six or seven thousand troops thus reporting. A brigade organization was adopted with Captain Moloney, Adjutant First South Carolina, acting as A. A. G., and Major Motte Pringle of the general staff as quartermaster. Commissary supplies were drawn by regimental commissaries direct from the post commissary. Captain R. G. Hay (afterwards Major Hay, commissary of Hagood's Brigade,) and some other unattached officers were assigned to temporary duty with Colonel Hagood. This officer had the satisfaction of receiving the approval of General Pemberton (for whom as an earnest and educated soldier he had a high respect) and believed he gave as much satisfaction to the people as could be given in the exercise of such arbitrary power for the first time in a community which had no small idea of its importance.

During this time General Ripley, in consequence of disagreement with Pemberton, and at his own request, was relieved from duty and assigned elsewhere. He was succeeded at Charleston by Brigadier-General Mercer, late commanding at Savannah.

The enemy landed on James Island 2nd June, and all the troops which could be spared from the town were hurried thither. The large drafts for Virginia had already straitened Pemberton for men; and he called on the Governor of the State for additional and temporary levies, to relieve the regular troops retained on provost duty. On the 6th June, General DeSaussure, State Adjutant General, came down from Columbia with a document from Governor Pickens, empowering him (DeSaussure) to back the Confederate commander in the defense of the city to the last extremity. General DeSaussure published a vigorous proclamation in accordance with these instructions, ordering a levy en masse of all citizens up to 50 years of age, who were not already in service, and directing them to report to the provost marshal. One man reported! Colonel Hagood called on the General for a roll of those liable to duty, under the order, that he might arrest and put them on service. He was told that it could not be furnished *under fifteen days*. Such is the value of unorganized patriotism (for certainly prior and subsequent records of Charleston in this war show no deficiency in that virtue); and the

6—H

danger of putting off organized preparation until the conflict is at hand. The regiment of Charleston Reserves were now called out and placed on provost duty, the city being left in their hands, and the regular troops, with perhaps the exception of an unattached company or two, taking the field.

This regiment had been organized some time before the proclamation of martial law and owed its purely voluntary existence*

> "Department of the Military,
> "Columbia, S. C., 12 June, 1862.
>
> "*Colonel:*
>
> ". . . Before the passage of our resolutions establishing corps of reserves throughout the State, the regiment you command had been formed upon voluntary principles.
>
> "It was accepted as formed and made subject to orders. . . .
> "Your obedient servant,
> "JAMES CHESTNUT, JR.,
> "Chief Dept. Milty.
> "To R. N. Gourdin,
> "Lieutenant Colonel commanding Charleston Reserves."

to that emulation of Saragossa alluded to as prevailing at an earlier period.

The field officers were Colonel A. H. Brown (the assistant provost marshal), Lieutenant Colonel R. N. Gourdin and Major W. A. Wardlaw—the two latter prominent merchants of the city; and in the ranks were such men as ex-Governor Aiken, Hon. W. D. Porter (president State Senate), Chancellor Lesesne, Mr. Bryan, afterwards judge of the United States Circuit Court, and many others of equal position. In fact it embodied all the exempt respectability of the city and numbered on a review before the enemy landed 1,250 men. When called on for duty, 150 responded —the balance had left the city with their families, or if present succeeded in evading the call. Those who responded did their duty with zeal and fidelity. It was at once a pitiable sight and one to elicit admiration to see these old grey-haired gentlemen, most of them wealthy, and all of them requiring and accustomed to ease and comfort, exposed to the inclemency of the weather and standing in their citizen's dress with double-barreled shotguns as wardens over the half-burned and deserted city, while the

---

*The question was for some purpose made, whether this was a volunteer regiment, and was settled in the following communication published in *The Mercury*, 14 June, 1862 :

occasional boom of a gun from James Island furnished the explanation of the spectacle.

Among these devoted men was William H. Heyward, lately colonel of the Eleventh Regiment, assigned afterwards to Hagood's Brigade. The writer of these Memoirs had not the honor of a personal acquaintance with him. Educated at West Point, and of large wealth, his life had been spent as a bachelor in the indulgence of manly and refined pleasures. He had made no effort at other than social achievement, but had certainly succeeded to an unusual extent in not only attaching to himself a circle of ardent friends, but in impressing upon them his ability for high performance had circumstances called upon him for exertion. Upon the organization of the Eleventh Regiment, he had been without opposition made its colonel—had discharged his office with ability—and had, with many other good officers, perished in the elections consequent upon the recent re-enlistment. Now, over 60 years of age, and unwell, he served as corporal in the Reserve Regiment and died a few weeks afterwards from the exposure.

When the enemy landed on James Island, Colonel Hagood claimed General Pemberton's promise to relieve him, his regiment, under Major Duncan, having been dispatched thither; but obtained leave to be absent only for the engagement then imminent. He was accompanied by his assistants, at their earnest request, as volunteers. The engagement was but partial and the experiences of the provost party were confined to sustaining a heavy gunboat shelling and a night of picket duty accompanied by heavy rain, and the dropping of an occasional shell on the line.

Now, however, the occasion for keeping him on this detached duty having passed, he on the 9th June obtained an order relieving him, with directions to resume command of his regiment.

Colonel A. H. Brown, commanding Reserves, was appointed provost marshal in his stead.

SECESSIONVILLE CAMPAIGN.

After the fall of Port Royal in 1861, in the general abandonment of the sea islands in South Carolina, possession of all of them, as far north as and including Edisto, was conceded to the enemy. When he chose, he took unopposed possession and departed with like impunity. The Confederates only visited these islands in scouting parties. Johns Island was dismantled of its defense on North Edisto Inlet and the population withdrawn, but upon it a movable Confederate force in the nature of an advanced guard had been so far stationed. The enemy had availed themselves of their success at Port Royal and were holding within their lines all of the territory conceded; and it is said that in May, 1862, the Federal chiefs, Hunter and Dupont, were considering a combined land and naval effort to wrest Johns Island also from the Confederate occupation. The escape of the steamer "Planter" and the information she gave of the abandonment of the posts on Stono, as well as of the condition of the new lines on James Island, changed their programme to a sudden blow at the city itself.*

The James Island lines, the construction of which as an interior line of defense was commenced in the winter of 1860-61, had become the main line of defense of the city upon the Stono front. At the date of Hunter's advance, they consisted of a series of redans for artillery connected by an infantry breastwork of slight profile, running from Mellichamp's house on the eastern shore of the island to Royall's house on New Town Creek. In its general course here it was parallel to the Stono and two and a half miles from the river. Advancing toward Stono along New Town Creek, redans without connecting breastworks were placed on the northern bank, and constituted the defense at a point three-quarters of a mile from the river, the line turning at right angles again became parallel to the river, and again consisted of redans with connecting breastworks, till at Lawton's house, on Wappoo, it reached the northwestern side of the island. On the right and left of this line Fort Pemberton and Secessionville (redoubts) were thrust forward. Fort Pemberton was a considerable work on the banks of Stono River below the mouth of Wappoo, and was advanced some three-quarters of a mile in front of the main line on the right; on the left, Secessionville was perhaps a mile in front and to the left of Mellichamp's. It was at the extremity of a peninsular made by the divergence of a

---

*Greely's American Conflict, 2 Vols., 460.

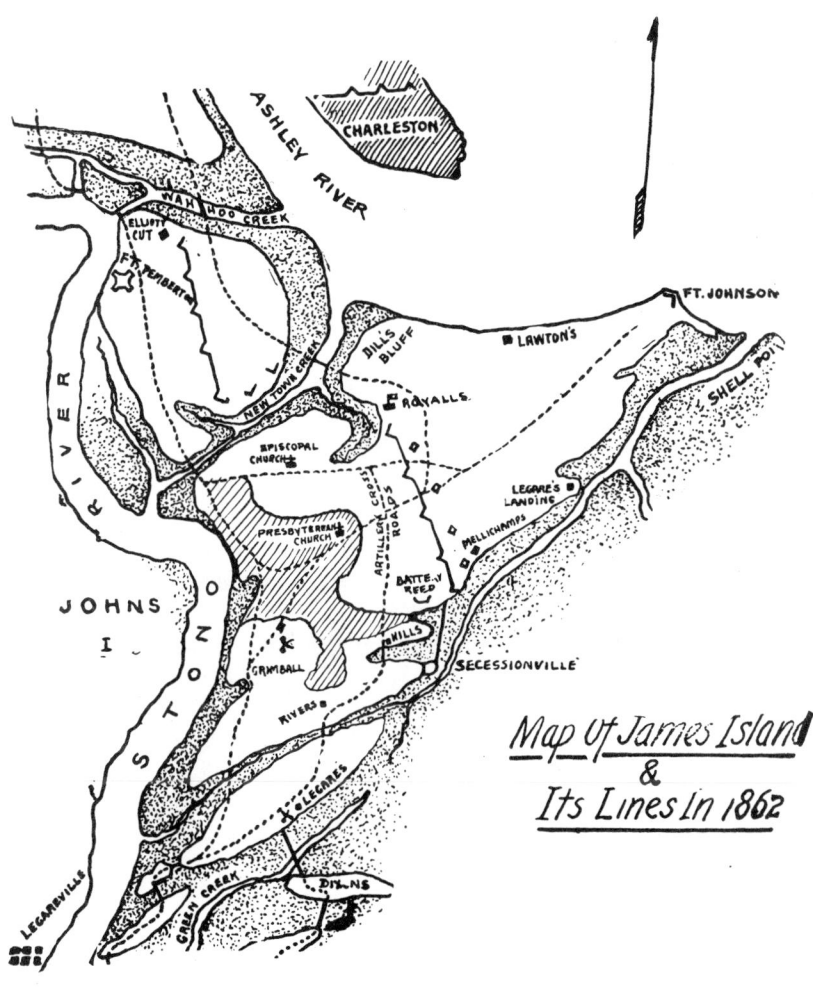

Map Of James Island & Its Lines In 1862

creek from Folley River into two branches, the land approach being from the Stono side, and communication with the rear established by a bridge. An intrenchment across the narrowest part of the peninsular made Secessionville also an enclosed work, and it was further strengthened by a small flanking battery across the northern creek or marsh, afterwards called Battery Reed, in honor of the gallant Captain Sam J. Reed, killed in this campaign. From Mellichamp's to Royall's there was a second line of defense consisting of detached redoubts, each behind an interval in redans of the first line.

Fort Pemberton was in fighting condition. But four guns were mounted at Secessionville; a bomb-proof shelter, and a powder magazine had been there constructed. The parapet was unfinished in front of the guns—indeed, its profile was so slight that after the battle of the 16th June Colonel Hagood rode his horse into the ditch and over the parapet from the exterior approach. As to the redans and redoubts of the rest of the defenses, they had no guns mounted or platforms laid.

The whole system was not only incomplete in construction, but faulty in design. The engineer, to avoid the then dreaded gunboat fire, had drawn his line so far back from Stono River as to give up full half of the island to the operations of the besiegers; and had accepted for himself full five miles of entrenchments to defend, separated into two divisions by New Town Creek, across which his communication in rear was circuitous and difficult. These evils were perceived early in the campaign, and a new line laid out along the eastern division which would have somewhat shortened it. But this line was never finished; and in the final shape which the defense of James Island took under Beauregard in 1863 to 1864, the whole system of defense heretofore indicated was abandoned, and, starting from Secessionville, a much shorter and better line was taken to Stono below the mouth of New Town Cut.

About the middle of May, the movement of the blockading vessels off Stono Inlet—sounding and buoying the channel—indicated the intention to effect an entrance. No hostile troops were then nearer than Edisto Island. The following extracts from the diary of Captain Carlos Tracy, volunteer aid-de-camp on the staff of General S. R. Gist, commanding on James Island, furnish a memorandum record of events up to 9th June:

"19 May.—Several of the enemy's gunboats attempted to enter Stono Inlet; one ran aground and the rest put back.

"20 May.—Three gunboats crossed the bar and entered Stono River about 10 a. m. One ran up and anchored below Battery Island so as to command the old (river) route, thinking probably to cut off the detachment on Cole's Island. Lieutenant-Colonel Capers withdrew his force (two companies Twenty-fourth South Carolina), by the new (back)* and scarcely completed route over Dickson's Island to James Island. Colonel Capers fired the buildings before withdrawal and acted under standing orders. Capt. L. Buist, commanding on Battery Island under similar orders, withdrew his force to James Island. On appearance of a gunboat off the mouth of Folley River, carronade on 'Marsh' Battery near the river thrown into the marsh by those in charge. Enemy shelled Coles and Battery Islands.

"21 May.—Six of our pickets (of Captain Jones' company, Twenty-fourth Regiment South Carolina,) captured. On the advance up the river of the gunboat anchored below, they concealed themselves in the old magazine, apparently expecting the enemy to pass them undiscovered. Thus, instead of withdrawing as they should have done, the enemy saw them and landed. Legare's, on John's Island side of Stono, shelled this day.

"25 May.—Gunboats to this time have been running up the river several miles each day shelling both sides of the river and returning in the evening to Battery Island. Effort today of General Ripley to draw them within effective range of Fort Pemberton failed. Gallantry of Capt. Frank Bonneau and of his men on our little floating battery stationed for the day in the creek near Dixon's Island remarked. A gunboat which engaged the enemy was driven off, the battery was moored to land. Three gunboats had been drawn up Stono by General Ripley's movements. On their return they had passed by all together when one of them returned apparently to learn what was the little dark object across the marshes and the small islands. Captain Bonneau, who was on board, had received orders not to fire unless attacked. He had his men ashore under cover. The gunboat opened on him. The captain replied, firing one of his guns himself. At the sound his men came bounding to their little *float*, and manning their two or three guns, drove the enemy away.

"31 May.—Gunboats in this time running up the Stono every morning, shelling every one who came in sight, whether on horse or foot or in vehicles. Some peaceful citizens crossing New Town Cut Bridge during this period in a buggy were startled by the near explosion of a shell sent after them and took to flight on foot across the fields. Today a few shells thrown toward Secessionville falling near the camp of the Twenty-fourth South Carolina Volunteers.

_____

*The "old" route was in use in Hagood's time and terminated at Battery Island. The "new" was constructed later and terminated near Secessionville.

"1 June.—A gunboat apparently reconnoitering in Folley River.

"3 June.—A gunboat came up Folley on the flood at 9 a. m. today, shelled Captain Chichester's Battery at Legare's house, that of Captain Warley near Secessionville and Secessionville itself, this place being occupied by the Eutaw Battalion* (Lieutenant-Colonel Simonton), the Charleston Battery (Lieutenant-Colonel Gaillard), and the cavalry companies of Disher and McKeown. Our batteries responded vigorously. No damage done except to a horse, whose leg was broken by a shell that passed first through an outhouse near General Gist's headquarters. After firing about an hour the enemy withdrew. No damage anywhere up to this time from the enemy's fire except the horses.

"Evening.—More than twenty vessels in sight. Enemy reported as being on extremity of James Island nearest Battery Island and as having driven in our pickets. Captain Tracy, of Gist's staff, and Lieutenant Winter, Wassamaw Cavalry, fired on while reconnoitering their position. General Gist and Captain Tracy repeatedly fired on same evening by enemy's advanced pickets. This firing the *first news in camp* of enemy's landing.

"3 June.—Last night the pickets lay near together at Legare's. In withdrawing Captain Chichester's guns from that point during the night they stuck in the mud. Chichester, endeavoring to extricate them, was driven off near morning. Lieutenant-Colonel Ellison Capers, Twenty-fourth South Carolina, with several companies, sent just after daylight to bring off guns and ascertain enemy's position. Sharp skirmishing with enemy at Legare's, in which Capers drove back a force far superior to his own for half a mile and took twenty-three prisoners. Retired on the advance of heavy reinforcements supported by gunboat fire. The enemy engaged was said to be the Twenty-eighth Massachusetts and One Hundredth Pennsylvania. Our loss was several wounded and one missing—taken prisoner. Lieutenant Walker, Adjutant Charleston Battery, wounded in the leg in the endeavor to bring off one of his wounded men. Gallantry and discretion of Colonel Capers was marked. Captain Ryan, of Charleston Battery, exhibited dashing courage. Capt. Ward Hopkins, same corps, wounded. Our companies first engaged were reinforced during the action. All fell back across the causeway to rivers where lay the main body of our troops. The enemy ascertained from a prisoner to be under the command of General Stevens and in strong force. Heavy bombardment all day from gunboats upon our troops in position to resist enemy's advance from Legare's. A section of Preston's Light Battery, under Captain Preston (W. C.), and Lieutenant Julius Rhett, was carried with great promptness and dash into position and worked with fierce energy under a cross fire from gunboats in the two rivers and direct fire from Legare's in front. The fire from the guns and from the more distant stationary batteries of Captain Warley and Colonel T. G. Lamar, at Secessionville, rendered the enemy's advance from Legare's across the causeway, though repeatedly threatened, too perilous to attempt. Brigadier-General Mercer in person arrived in the afternoon from the city. Colonel Johnson Hagood, First South Carolina

---

*Made Twenty-fifth Regiment a few days afterward.

Volunteers, previously detained in the city by his duties as provost marshal, joined his regiment during the day. Casualties light. Brigadier General Gist and aides covered with sand from the explosion of a shell. The screeching of the rifle shells and the heavy explosions of the 11th and 13th inch subsided a little after dark into the discharge of a single one at intervals of a half hour during the night. Our men—wet, weary and hungry—slept on their arms. The night tempestuous.

"4 June.—Main body of our troops withdrawn within the lines, advance parties only in front. Design of enemy to occupy evident.

"6 June.—Brigadier-General W. D. Smith arrived on the island and assumed command. Picket under command of Colonel Stevens, Twenty-fourth South Carolina, skirmished with enemy at Presbyterian Church. Enemy left one dead on the ground; indications of further loss. No loss on our side. A prisoner brought into camp.

"9 June.—Alarm troops to front—no fight. Enemy evidently in force at Grimball's on Stono."

On the 9th of June Colonel Hagood was definitely relieved of provost duty in Charleston, and reported in command of his regiment, which had been on the island since the 3rd under Major Duncan. The colonel had served one day with it, as noted in previous journal.

The troops on the island were sufficient for its defense, but without exception had never before seen actual service; and most of them being newly raised corps, officers and men were alike ignorant of field duty. In consequence of these facts, four of the best regiments were organized into a temporary brigade, under the name of the "Advanced Forces," and these were charged with the whole picket duty along the extended front of the southern division of the lines, except of that portion immediately in front of Secessionville, which remained in charge of the commander and was furnished by the garrison of that post until after the battle of the 16th June. General Smith did Colonel Hagood the honor to place him in command of this special brigade. It consisted of Hagood's own regiment, First South Carolina; Stevens' Twenty-fourth South Carolina, Simonton's Twenty-fifth South Carolina, and McEnnery's Seventh Louisiana Battalion. A battery of field artillery reported daily for duty·with the Advanced Forces, and ten or twelve cavalry for courier duty. Captain Moloney, Adjutant First South Carolina, acted as assistant adjutant general. Orderly Ben Martin as aid-de-camp, and Captains Hay and Lartigue were volunteer aides. The regiments drew their commissary, quartermaster and ordnance supplies through regimental channels direct from the officers of the post staff in Charleston.

Two regiments of the Advanced Forces on duty one day furnished the pickets and alternated with the other two regiments in reserve.

The arrangement of the picket system was as follows (see Map, p. 200.):

Two grand guards; one at Artillery Cross Roads and one at Frier's Cross Roads. Three outposts; one at Episcopal Church, one at Presbyterian Church, and one on Battery Island Road. The outposts furnished the chain of videttes, running from where the Battery Island Road crosses the northern Secessionville Marsh (near Hill's house), to which point the Secessionville picket came, through fields and woods to the bridge over New Town Cut near Stono River.

A section of the Light Battery on duty each day was placed with the Grand Guard at Frier's, and the other sections with the Grand Guard at Artillery Cross Roads.

The regiments of the Advanced Forces not on picket were allowed to go into bivouac at convenient points near reserve.

Skirmishing along the lines was frequent, and the firing of the videttes almost incessant—the usual custom, however, of green troops. The Yankees were as nervous as we were, sometimes in the night following up a fusillade that would break out without occasion from their videttes with volleys from their grand guards —at nothing, unless perhaps at their videttes running in. It rained almost incessantly during the whole period of active operations and there was something of ludicrous pathos in the enquiry which a half-drowned Yankee shouted out one day across the line, "I say, does it ever get dry in this country?" There was no brigade or division organization of the Confederate troops on the island except the "Advanced Forces," nor any distribution of general command by localities. There were three different generals commanding in this short campaign, and as each one arrived he took charge of everything, holding the others in reserve as

---

*It is noteworthy that Beauregard afterwards rearranged the defenses upon this idea.

second and sometimes third in command. The fact is, things were pretty generally haphazard.

On the 10th, General Pemberton directed our lines advanced, with a view to establishing a battery of heavy guns on the edge of Grimball's clearing within sufficient range to drive the gunboats from that landing and confine the enemy to the use of the Battery Island landing* as well as to break up the Yankee camp at Grimball's. General Smith took charge of the operation, and in the afternoon of the same day sent forward Colonel Hagood with the First South Carolina and the Seventh Louisiana Battalion and two pieces of Preston's Field Battery on the road through the Grimball woods, by the Presbyterian Church. Colonel Williams, with the Forty-seventh Georgia, was started more to the left from the point where these woods touched the Battery Island Road. The instructions were to drive in the enemy and seize and hold the line of the clearing. Colonel Hagood advanced along his road with a part of his forces deployed on either side of it, the rest following in supporting distance in column. The enemy were driven before him with but little resistance, and the sight of the deployed line had already reached the clearing when he was recalled in consequence of a reverse sustained by Williams. Williams had no road, but advanced in line of battle without skirmishers in front, and when he struck the clearing encountered the enemy in force behind the ditch and bank fence of the plantation and supported by artillery. The woods through which he had advanced were almost a jungle; his line had become very much disordered; and he was in action before he knew it. But his men rushed gallantly upon the enemy in squads as they came up, and, of course, were driven back badly cut up. His loss was some sixty or seventy men. Hagood lost none, and killed upon the field but two of the enemy from the feeble resistance encountered. They were not in force upon his front of attack. He was, however, subjected to a rapid fire of gunboat shells, which threatened as much damage from the falling limbs cut from the trees as from themselves.

The enemy were engaged at this period in passing troops from North Edisto to across Johns Island to Legareville on the Stono nearly opposite Battery Island. To do this they had to make a flank march of ten miles in front of an equal number of troops

---

*It is noteworthy that Beauregard afterwards rearranged the defenses upon this idea.

under General Evans, commanding the Confederate forces on Johns Island. Evans had orders to attack, information of which was communicated to Hagood with instructions upon hearing the sounds of battle in that quarter to begin to press the enemy with the Advanced Forces and at once to report the fact. It would be, he was told, the occasion of a general offensive movement for which the troops on James Island were held in readiness.

General Evans allowed the enemy to pass, and they were straggling along his front for more than two days and nights without firing a gun. He was not court-martialed, for then, as ever afterwards, it was the bane of Confederate service not to hold its commanding officers to rigid account. Evans attempted indirectly to clear himself of the slur upon his reputation by court-martialing one of his colonels for drunkenness upon this occasion, alleging in the charges that this drunkenness had balked the attack. It was the unpleasant fortune of Colonel Hagood to have been president of the court when it sat at a later period, and the facts were thus brought before him. The officer was broken* —the fact of his drunkenness was proved; but had Evans been before the court he would have found it difficult, upon the evidence elicited, to have escaped the same fate for the same offense. Nor can it be conceived how the intoxication of a single colonel of junior commission could have kept a considerable army from assuming the offensive for over two days and nights, or, indeed, for a longer period than it would have taken to arrest him and order his successor to move. Would it be believed that during the whole of the time his troops were watching for the passage of the enemy and every preparation made for momentary attack, Evans, without a subordinate general officer in his command, went back to Adams Run every night, a distance of eighteen miles, to escape the malaria of the island? Yet this fact was incidentally proven upon the trial.† The enemy having without

---

*Colonel Dunovant, South Carolina Regulars, an excellent officer, save for this unfortunate failing. A year afterwards he was restored and, guarding against his infirmity, after a useful career rose to the rank of brigadier and died gallantly in battle.

†From that relating to General Evans above, in connection with the Secession-ville fight, it seems evident that he apprehended no danger. He was a brave, able officer. At the first battle of Manassas he showed signal gallantry, saving the day to our arms.—Editor.

molestation effected the passage across Johns Island to James, General Evans, too, with a portion of his troops was transferred to the same point, and arriving on the 14th took command, Smith sinking to second and Gist to third in command. The general officers were all quartered at Royall's, and there was considerable unpleasantness among them, as much perhaps from the anomalous relations in command which they held toward each other, as from any other cause. General Evans occupied himself on the 14th and 15th in riding along the lines and examining into the condition of things, requiring Colonel Hagood to accompany him. On the afternoon of the 15th he removed his headquarters to a point near Lawton's house, on the shores of the harbor opposite Charleston and four miles to the rear. On the night of the 15th-16th June, the portion of the "Advanced Forces" on picket consisted of seven companies of Twenty-fourth South Carolina, six companies of First South Carolina, and one company of Williams' Forty-seventh Georgia, temporarily assigned to Advanced Forces. Boyer's Field Battery was on duty with the grand guards; and all were under command of Colonel C. H. Stevens. The Twenty-fifth South Carolina, the Seventh Louisiana and four companies of the First South Carolina were in reserve. Colonel Hagood was with these troops. At 4:30 a. m., on the 16th, he received a dispatch from Colonel Stevens that the Secessionville picket, which, as before mentioned, until after this date, was furnished by that garrison and did not report to Hagood, was driven in, and that the enemy were advancing in force upon that position. Colonel Hagood immediately ordered under arms the reserve; he directed Colonel McEnnery with the Fourth Louisiana Battalion to proceed by the foot bridge in rear of Secessionville to the re-enforcement of the garrison, and Colonel Simonton with the Twenty-fifth South Carolina and detachment of the First South Carolina, to proceed down the Battery Island road to operate on the flank of the enemy's advance. Having delivered these orders in person, he galloped on in advance in the same direction, ordering forward from Artillery Cross Roads one of the 6 drs. (under Lieutenant Jeter*) of the section of Boyce's

---

*President of the Senate, and by virtue of his office Governor of South Carolina in 1880 on Simpson's resignation.

Battery on duty at that point. Arriving at the scene of action, the enemy were making their second assault upon the post at Secessionville.

At 4 p. m. they had advanced upon that work, with, according to their own account, two brigades of infantry and three companies of artillery, numbering in all 3,337 men (2 Am. Conflict, 462) under command of General J. J. Stevens.† Moving swiftly and noiselessly upon the picket, they succeeded in capturing some of them and the *rest fled without firing a gun.* The gallant Lamar (as he afterwards himself told Colonel Hagood) had been superintending all night the operations of a working party, and exhausted had fallen asleep upon the parapet. Aroused by the sentinel over the guns, he discovered the enemy at the heels of his picket, not fifty yards from him. With no time to give an order, he himself pulled the lanyard of a columbiad, ready shotted with grape, and as the deadly missiles tore their way through the approaching column, the bellowing thunder aroused the garrison to the bloody work before them. It consisted of two companies of Lamar's own regiment—Second South Carolina Artillery—the Charleston Battery (afterwards Twenty-seventh South Carolina), Smith's Battery and a portion of Goodlette's South Carolina Regiment. The enemy assailed vigorously and with considerable dash; several were slain upon the parapet, and one bold fellow, jumping into the work and finding himself unsupported, effected his retreat, but carried one of Lamar's men with him a prisoner. The enemy were, however, in twenty or thirty minutes driven back with considerable loss. Stevens reformed his lines and again advanced, aided this time by another brigade under General Williams with Hamilton's Field Battery of Regulars attached, these last moving on the opposite side from Secessionville of the northern marsh forming the Secessionville peninsular. This force numbered 2,663 men and moved by Hill's house. It was on the flank of General Williams that Colonel Hagood found himself. A thicket of felled trees ran parallel with their line of advance and about 400 yards from it, on the edge of which, next to the enemy, Colonel C. H. Stevens had deployed about 100 men who had been

---

†Author of "Campaigns of the Rio Grande and Mexico."

on picket duty near that point. These men were from the Twenty-fourth Regiment and from the companies of Captains Tompkins, Pearson (Lieutenant Hamiter commanding), and Gooding (First Lieutenant Beckman commanding). The Battery Island Road, here so obstructed as to be impassable by artillery or by infantry except with difficulty as to individuals, ran between this felled thicket and the dense wood stretching towards Grimball's on the Stono. Simonton's Twenty-fifth South Carolina, about 220 strong, coming up, was placed behind this felled thicket in line of battle, its right resting near the Battery Island Road. Lieutenant Jeter's piece was placed in position on Simonton's left and directed to open on Williams's advancing column. Lieutenant Colonel Capers of the Twenty-fourth was personally dispatched to ascertain the cause of the unaccountable silence of Battery Reed and to bring its guns also to bear upon Williams. The detachment of the First South Carolina (about 120 men) was held in column as a reserve on the Battery Island Road, and directed to throw out a strong line of skirmishers on its right flank towards the Stono. The first sound of Jeter's piece brought all of Hamilton's guns upon our line from its position on the right of the Battery Island Road, beyond and in front of the felled thicket. Colonel Hagood saw the opportunity of pushing the First South Carolina through the woods against Hamilton's Battery, and advancing Simonton and Stevens against the rear of Williams's men, now enfilading and slowly galling the front despite the fire of Jeter's piece and Battery Reed, but apprehending a general advance, and charged especially with picketing the front of the southern division, he feared to take the offensive with his small force, which constituted the whole picket reserve, without re-enforcement or special orders. The disparity in men and guns between his force and General Williams's (about 5 to 1) was also perfectly apparent. While, therefore, making his dispositions to take the offensive, he despatched Captain J. V. Martin, commissary of First South Carolina, who had reported for duty as A. D. C., to report the situation and ask for orders and re-enforcements to attack. In the meantime Jeter's piece was rapidly and effectively worked, the infantry merely supporting; Battery Reed had also been opened by Capers and was doing good service. In the fort, Colonel Lamar had been wounded on the first assault and succeeded by Lieutenant Colonel Gaillard; Gaillard was now wounded and succeeded in command by Major Wagner. McEnnery arriving at a run with the Fourth Louisiana,* went into action on the right, engaging Williams's flanking line. The Third Rhode Island Heavy Artillery, acting as infantry and which had been held in reserve near Hamilton's Battery, advanced to take Jeter's piece, but were handsomely repulsed by Colonel C. H. Stevens's skirmishers, except one portion, which penetrated to Simonton's line on the left. One of his companies was engaged for a few moments in driving them back, exchanging the first volley at twenty paces, so closely had they approached without being discovered in the dense abattis of the thicket. But the Yankee bolt was shot. They fell back sullenly and unpursued, leaving their dead and wounded upon the field. Captain Martin arrived with permission for Colonel Hagood to attack, and a few minutes afterwards Slaughter's Georgia and Gadberry's South Carolina regiments reported as re-enforcements for the purpose; but the enemy had regained the shelter of his gunboats and the effort against Charleston was over for this time. For such was the result of the Battle of Secessionville—one of the decisive engagements of the war.

The Federals, by their own showing, had 6,000 men engaged and 1,500 in reserve† (part of this reserve being the Third Rhode Island). Colonel Hagood might have found Hamilton's Battery on his flank had he advanced without first sending a force against the position first occupied by it.* There were engaged on the Confederate side, in the fort and out of it, not exceeding 1,300 men, of which 450 were with Colonel Hagood. The Federals reported their loss at 574 men; the Confederates lost about 150 killed and wounded, of which 32 casualties were in Hagood's force.

---

*This was undoubtedly, from all the writer could learn, the turning point in the defense of the fort. McEnnery was a dashing and valuable officer, and the writer regrets he has not the material for giving his subsequent career. He was, after the war, a distinguished politician of Louisiana.

†Greely's American Conflict.

*General Stevens assailed the fort with 3,500 men and four field guns. General Wright commanded reserve of 3,100 men and six guns. Of the last, Williams's Brigade of 1,500 and Hamilton's Battery were in action. The remainder—1,600 men—were held in close support of Hamilton's guns on Battery Island Road.—War of Rebellion Series, Vol. XIV, p. 52.

The people of the city and State were justly elated at this stroke of good fortune. It was the first exploit upon the war path of most of those engaged in it. Newspaper reporters were anxious to obtain all the particulars and the parties interested in no wise loath to furnish them. It was amusing for weeks afterwards to see in Charleston papers the gross mistatements and, in some cases, absolutely false representations that were made, the writer or his friends always the hero of the tale. But to cap the climax of eagerness to catch "all the glory going," General Evans appeared in a card in the public papers announcing the fact that he was in command on the 16th. In General Evans's official report, which Pemberton showed Colonel Hagood before forwarding to Richmond, there were almost as many inaccuracies as in the newspaper accounts; and it really seemed as if he had not read the reports of his subordinates which he forwarded accompanying his own. For instance, he stated that he ordered McEnnery to re-enforce the garrison, yet took no notice of Hagood's or McEnnery's statements in their reports that the latter had been sent into Secessionville as heretofore stated in these Memoirs. Colonel Hagood received no order from any superior until the enemy left the field. How it was in the fort he could not say. But it always appeared to him that as far as generalship went, this battle, decisive as it was on the Confederate side, can only be characterized as an affair of outposts, in which the subordinate officers and the troops on the spot did the best they could upon the emergency; and whatever credit for generalship, if any is awarded, should be to General Smith, under whose direction the arrangement of the outposts was made. There were on the island under Evans at least as many regiments, and probably as good ones, as the enemy had, and not one was brought into action. Had his headquarters been nearer to the lines they might possibly have been used advantageously to some extent. Williams's column might have been cut off. But the affair was over very quickly, and the enemy had but a short distance to retreat before regaining the shelter of their gunboats.

No further offensive movements were undertaken by the Federals after the repulse of the 16th. They lingered upon the island, protected by their steam fleet and by defensive entrenchments, until 7th July, when the last of them embarked unmolested.

7—H

Many valuable lives were lost, and much individual heroism was displayed in this short and decisive campaign. Lamar deservedly won much reputation and commenced a career which promised much usefulness to the State, but this promise was soon cut short. He perished, a victim of malaria, the following summer. Gaillard, Wagner, Hopkins and others commenced here a series of brilliant services, traced in subsequent pages of these Memoirs. The fate of Captains Henry King, of Charleston, and Samuel J. Reed, of Barnwell, was especially deplored. The latter was an elevè of the State Military School and a most promising officer. There was an incident, too, of brave and faithful conduct in humble life, which deserves mention in any record of Secessionville. Vich Jan Vohr's henchman in the dock at Carlisle had not in his bosom a more leal and affectionate heart than the humble hero.

Lieutenant John A. Bellinger, of the artillery, was asleep in his quarters some distance from the battery when the roar of Lamar's columbiad summoned the garrison to its defense. After he had repaired to his post, his negro servant discovered that in his haste he had left his pistol, and hastened to carry it to him against the remonstrances of his companions, for the approach to the battery was now swept by bullets as with the besom of destruction. But the faithful servitor could not bear that his young master should be in such deadly conflict without his trusty weapon; and he fell, mortally wounded, in the attempt to bear it to him. Every attention that affection could suggest to Bellinger soothed poor Daniel's last moments during the week that he lingered. He said to his master just before he died, "Duncan and Normie"—Bellinger's little motherless sons—"Duncan and Normie will be sorry when they hear that I am dead."

SECOND MILITARY DISTRICT, DEPARTMENT OF SOUTH CAROLINA, GEORGIA AND FLORIDA.

On the 19th July, 1862, Colonel Hagood was, by an order from General Pemberton's headquarters, relieved from duty with his regiment, then on James Island, and assigned to the command of the "Second Military District of the Department of South Carolina, Georgia and Florida." This was in consequence of a telegraphic dispatch from Richmond that Colonel Hagood was to be

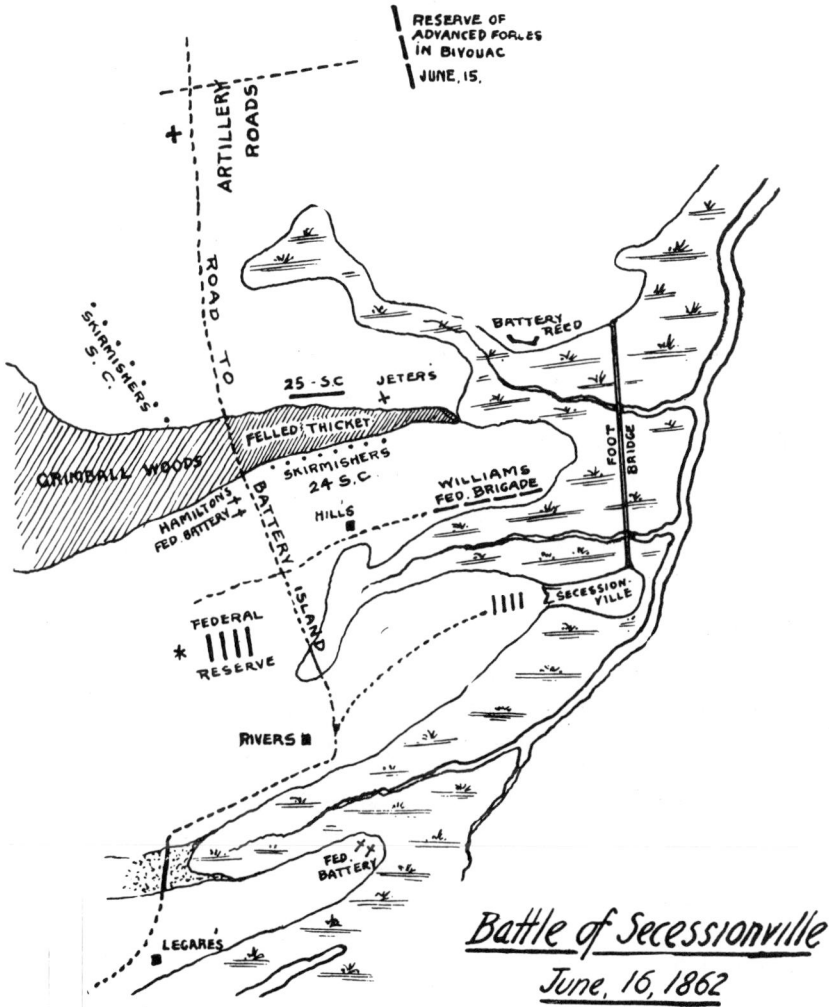

Battle of Secessionville
June, 16, 1862

*The Federal reports (War Rebellion, Series I, Vol. XIV) place the Federal reserve under Gen. Wright nearer Hamilton's Battery than in this sketch.

promoted to a brigadiership, and shortly afterwards he received his commission, bearing date 21 July. Colonel Hagood was promoted upon the recommendation of General Pemberton, and it was peculiarly gratifying to him, both because it was entirely unsolicited, and because it was a decisive mark of approval from one whom he esteemed as a thorough soldier. General Pemberton made few friends in Charleston, from his unfortunate want of tact and brusquerie of manner. He was not to the taste of a people at that time particularly disposed to be critical of military men, and matters through the Coles Island business, which was undoubtedly the cause of his removal from command in South Carolina, was much misunderstood; and his misfortune at Vicksburg, whither he was sent, completed the ruin of his reputation as a general before the country at large. His conduct afterwards, however, marked him both as a devoted patriot and a spirited soldier.

Finding that his usefulness in the high rank he then held of lieutenant general was impaired by want of public confidence, he resigned that commission and reverted to his original grade of lieutenant colonel of artillery in the Regular Army of the Confederate States; in which capacity he served until the end of the war. It was General Hagood's pleasant fortune to meet and serve with him again, both in Virginia and North Carolina.

The Second Military District embraced the country south of Charleston, from Rantowles to the Ashepoo River, with headquarters at Adams Run, about twenty-five miles from the city. Our lines of occupation chiefly followed the coast line of the main upon which the enemy had never effected a lodgement—the adjoining islands were debatable ground. The troops of the command were always mixed, combining all the different arms and varied in number from 1,000 to 1,200, or 3,000 to 4,000 from time to time. They were constantly shifting, too, regiments coming and going as the emergencies of the service required. It was not a pleasant command. While no operations of a considerable character were to be expected for some time, the country to be guarded was extensive and penetrated in every direction by water courses, giving facility for the petty marauding incursions which were to be expected. In repelling these, little reputation was to be made, and from their success much was sure to be lost.

In addition to this, the whole region was before the war considered fatally malarious during the summer months. In the winter the climate was delightful.

General Hagood's attention was given at once to a thorough personal reconnoisance of the country committed to his charge, and the perfecting of sanitary regulations for the troops consistent with their indispensable duties.

His military position was that of a local guard, having reference to the Charleston and Savannah Railroad, and the planting interest along the coast, and also an advanced guard to the City of Charleston. The result of his reconnoisance was the location of batteries armed with siege guns at certain points, with infantry entrenchments at these and other points; and the maturing of a general plan of operations in the event of an advance upon Charleston by a land force from this direction. Upon General Beauregard's succeeding General Pemberton in this quarter, which happened shortly afterwards, he called upon each of his district commanders to submit their views of operations in their respective localities. The following paper was submitted by General Hagood for the Second District and returned approved. It may be premised that the whole country was a network of swamps and water courses, and it will be seen that General Hagood, from the topography of the country, dismissed the idea of the enemy seeking the main within the limits of his district for an advance upon Charleston, except between Pon Pon and Rantowles.

"MEMOIR OF OPERATIONS CONTEMPLATED IN SECOND MILITARY DISTRICT.

"I. The first defensive line taken will be south of the Willtown and Rantowles Road—the entrenchment at Kings Creek being the right, those at Yongues Island being the center and the Church Flats batteries the left—the reserves being held in the vicinity of Adams Run. An attack by a single column upon this position will be obstinately resisted. A general attack along the whole line in strong force will compel its abandonment after holding it merely long enough to ascertain the strength and designs of the enemy. The line is too long and too near the enemy's base of operations. It is also liable to be turned by an advance from Edisto Island across to Dawhoo in the neighborhood of Pinebury.

"II. The second line taken will be behind the Caw Caw Swamp. This swamp, commencing at Rantowles, runs westward for five miles when it divides into two main branches, one continuing westward to the Edisto River, a further distance of five miles, the other running a little west of

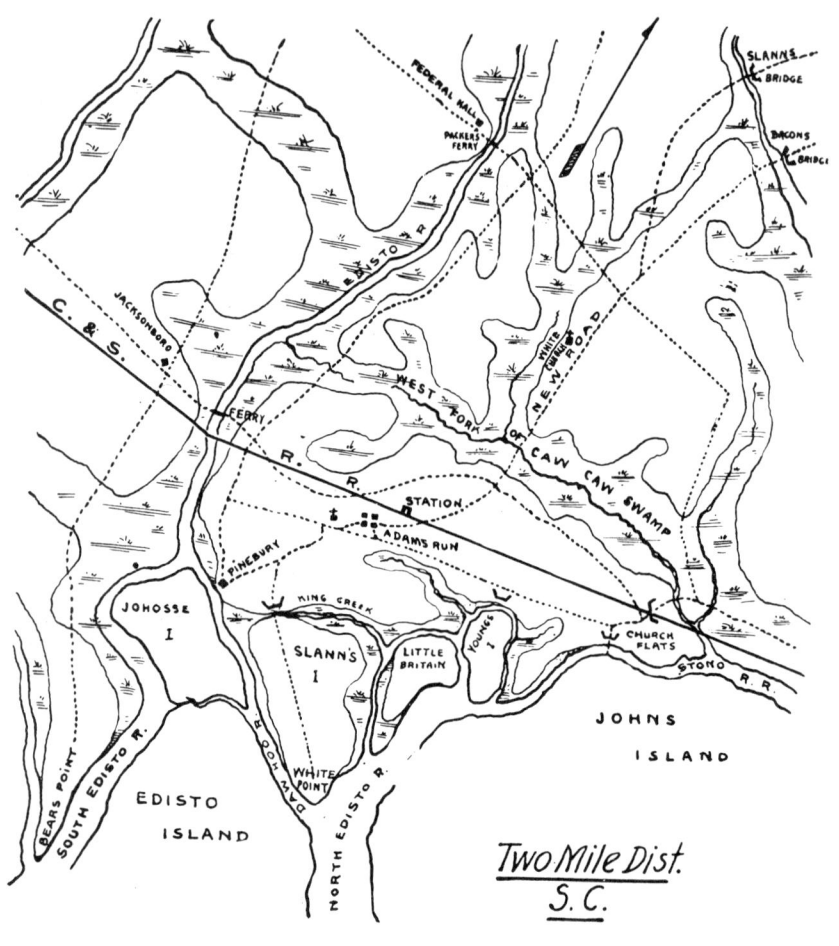

Two Mile Dist. S.C.

north toward Givhans Ferry, higher up on same river. The left of this line will be the batteries at Rantowles, the center where the new road crosses the swamp half a mile east of its bifurcation, and the right will follow the north branch. The west branch of the swamp will be held by an advanced force of mounted men. The object of taking this line is to delay the enemy and gain time for re-enforcements from the Third Military District by way of Givhans Ferry. It is objectionable from its length and from the fact that the north branch of the swamp is practicable almost anywhere to an enterprising enemy. The enemy will attack its left at Rantowles, seeking the most direct route to the city, in which case the cavalry on the right will operate offensively on his flank and rear, and the point of attack will be obstinately defended with the best means at disposal. In the event of the lines being carried at Rantowles, the troops massed there for its defense will retire within the lines proper of the city by the most direct route, and the troops on the right will retire towards Bacon's Bridge on the Ashley. Or, the enemy will attack the right of the line, where it is much weaker, and seek a more circuitous but safer route to the city. In this case this line can only be held long enough to make him concentrate and prepare for carrying it. It is hoped that time sufficient for the junction of the troops from the Third District can be thus obtained. When the line is thus carried, the troops at Rantowles will, as before, retire by the shortest route behind the city lines across the Ashley and proceed up the eastern bank of the river to unite their command at Bacon's Bridge. The troops on the right will fall back direct to Bacon's and Slann's bridges on the Ashley.

"III. The third line taken will be behind the Ashley to protect the South Carolina and North-Eastern Railroads. The troops from the Second and Third Districts united will hold the fordable portion of the river, viz.: from Shultz's Lake, a mile above Slann's Bridge, down to old Fort Dorchester. The crossings below where pontoon bridges may be thrown across will also be looked after by them, but these should be held by troops from the garrison of the city. A battle will be fought in defense of this line without orders to the contrary. The line of retreat hence will be down the peninsular into Charleston, or if this should be impracticable from the enemy's effecting a passage of the river near the city, then by way of Summerville and the Twenty-Two Mile House around the head waters of Cooper and down its eastern bank to a point near the city, where the troops can be thrown into the garrison.

"A depot of provisions for ten days for 5,000 men and 3,000 horses has been ordered to be established at White Church behind the second line of defense.

"A depot of at least twice the amount should be established at Summerville behind the third line."

General Hagood caused the country embraced in his district to be thoroughly surveyed and mapped, and made himself per-

sonally acquainted with all its intricacies. He required his staff
to do the same, as well as certain trusty and reliable mounted men
whom he kept about his headquarters as couriers and guides.

The country west of Edisto and to the Ashepoo was watched
by a cavalry company* encamped near Jacksonboro on the
Charleston and Savannah Railroad, which picketed Bear's Point,
the junction of the two rivers and a landing on the Ashepoo.
They were subsequently re-enforced by a field battery† of artillery; and were sometimes supported by infantry, when the
number of the latter arms in the district permitted. This was,
however, seldom the case. Walpole's company of fifteen or twenty
men, known as the Stono Scouts, and composed exclusively of late
planters upon the island, were kept upon Johns Island. The
Ashepoo and Johns Island pickets reported direct to headquarters.
The line of pickets from Rantowles to Edisto on the main was
placed under the charge of a permanent superintendent and
reported through him. He was furnished with the following
instructions, which were also promulgated in General Orders:

"GENERAL INSTRUCTIONS FOR PICKETS.

"1. Each picket detail from a corps will be inspected by the officer
appointed to command it, before leaving its camp, who will be held responsible that each man is properly armed and accoutred and supplied with
rations (and forage if cavalry) for the tour upon which he is ordered.

"2. They will remove to their respective stations when relieved in regular military order.

"3. On duty the horses of the cavalry will never be unbridled or
unsaddled. At feeding time, one-half will be fed or watered at a time, and
for the purpose the bits of that half will be taken out of their mouths.
The men will not be allowed to lay aside their arms; the sabres will be
continually worn and the guns be in hand or in easy reach. In the day
time one-half the men may sleep at a time, at night all will be on the alert.
A sentinel will always be with the horses when the picket is dismounted.
Fires will not be allowed under any circumstances when there is possibility
of being seen by the enemy. Concealment as far as consistent with watch-
fulness will always be aimed at.

"4. The advanced sentinels or videttes will observe the utmost watch-
fulness and keep themselves concealed as well as practicable. The horses

---

*This company was Company B, Sixth South Carolina Cavalry, and picketed
Bennett's Point on Bear's Island.—Editor.

†This battery was Walter's Horse Artillery.—Editor.

will not be unbitted under any pretense while on post, nor will either of the two videttes posted together sleep.

"5. All movements of the enemy, or clouds of dust, noises, conflagrations, etc., which may indicate movement, will be promptly reported to the officer commanding the picket, who will report the facts (in writing if possible) to headquarters.

"6. Should the enemy advance, the picket will at once report the fact to headquarters and fall back slowly, always keeping the enemy in sight and availing itself of the advantages of the ground to make such resistance as possible.

"7. The superintendent of pickets will make a daily report to headquarters."

Special instructions as to the number, station and conduct of each outpost and vidette post was also furnished the superintendent. The general scheme was a vidette post at each landing on the line, or good point of observation, with outposts at proper points to sustain them. These were all of cavalry. A strong infantry grand guard was stationed at the Church a mile from Adams Run, where the approaches from these landings chiefly concentrated. The body of the troops was held at Adams Run as a strategic center and for sanitary reasons. A permanent garrison of infantry and artillery was, however, kept at Church Flats, where siege guns were mounted; and a light battery was kept encamped sometimes with, and sometimes without, an infantry support at a landing on Wadmalaw River, known as Younges Island; and another light battery at Willtown on the Pon Pon. General Hagood was fortunate in the selection of his superintendent of pickets, Major John Jenkins, of the Third Cavalry, and the duty was in general well performed—as well as could be got out of corps newly raised and in which most commonly the officers needed instruction in every detail.

Before passing from this portion of the subject, it may not be amiss to say something of the use of cavalry, as developed in this war. Its use, as on the plains of the eastern continent and with the short range arms of former wars, seemed to have been impracticable, for it was never done. They were used generally merely as mounted riflemen, who dismounted to fight, leaving every fourth man to hold the horses. Of course there were exceptional instances. Yet throughout the war, as far as the writer's observation extended, the former mode of equipping the cavalrymen was retained. His sabre was slung to his waist, and when he dismounted to go into action, almost always as skirmisher when the greatest freedom of action was required, it was of no earthly use and a most serious hindrance. The sabre came to be regarded by most of the cavalry as an ornamental badge of their arm of service, was kept as blunt as a frow, and in many instances whole corps were without it. The rifle carbine and the revolver pistol were relied upon, whether upon horseback or afoot. Now, the use of the sabre has by no means passed away. In encounters of cavalry with cavalry, and in exceptional cases of cavalry against infantry, it still remains a more valuable weapon than any firearm discharged from a horse in motion. To hang the sabre to the pommel of the saddle on the left side, the scabbard passing under the left leg of the rider to hold it steady, and balance it on the right with a *holster* revolver, all to be for use only when mounted, and left with the horse when the soldier dismounted to fight with his carbine, apparently would relieve the difficulty. Now, the sabre, kept sharp, carried in a wooden scabbard to preserve its edge, and a repeating carbine (without a bayonet), would fit the trooper for the discharge of all the duties required of him in the most effective manner. He should be taught on horseback to rely as of yore on the sabre and pistol, and on foot upon the arms and tactics of the light infantry. Such are the reflections of one who did not serve in the cavalry arm of the service, but who had opportunities of observing cavalry fighting and sometimes commanded them in the field.

Dr. J. F. M. Geddings was the chief surgeon of the command in the Second Military District, and at his suggestion the following sanitary regulations were adopted for the sickly season, and such portions of them as had general application were continued afterward. They were enforced by the daily inspection of the doctor himself, who, for the purpose, was relieved from all other duty. He was untiring in his effort to give them effect:

"SANITARY REGULATIONS.

"1. Each camp and its vicinity will be policed thoroughly once a day, the whole command if necessary turning out for the purpose; and the offal and trash removed to a distance and thrown into tide water, burned, or buried as may be.

"2. The sinks (officer's and men's being separate) will be constructed over tide water when practicable. In other cases they will be dug to leeward—the prevailing winds being considered—be covered from view by brush or other obstructions, and dirt will be thrown once a day upon deposits. Summary and condign punishment will be inflicted upon the use of any other than the regular sink.

"3. The tents will be slit front and rear from the bottom to the ridge pole, and the flaps kept tied back night and day, when the weather permits. Blankets and bedding will be exposed daily to the air and sunlight always after the day's policing, if the weather permits. When straw is used, it will be stirred and aired daily, and removed once a week. Boards, poles and other means of raising the beds of the men a few inches off the ground will be used.

"4. Military duties during the hot months will be dispensed with except before breakfast and late in the evening. Frequent roll calls will be had during the rest of the day to prevent straggling and consequent exposure. Shelters of brush or plank will be constructed under which the necessary camp sentinels will stand.

"5. Company officers will daily inspect the company kitchens to see that the food of the men is properly prepared and especially guard against the consumption of unripe fruit or partially decomposed vegetables by the men.

"6. Every third day a strict inspection of the persons and underclothing of the men will be had, at which time the underclothing will be renewed. Daily ablutions and the wearing of the hair short will be strictly enforced."

In addition to the rigid enforcement of the foregoing regulations, quinine was at times issued to be taken as a prophylactic in daily doses of three grains, and in default of quinine a decoction of the bark of the cherry tree and dogwood with whiskey, equal parts, was used. The good effect of these precautions was soon visible in the improved health of the troops, which was alarmingly bad upon General Hagood's taking command, and we tided over the sickly season without the efficiency of the command becoming at any time seriously impaired. Most of the picket stations were upon rice swamps and some of the camps, as at Rantowles, were in localities heretofore considered deadly pestilential. The laws of malaria are subtle and but little understood. Mr. Davis, in discussing the fact of the comparative exemption of the troops on both sides from its effects during the war, for this exemption seems also to have occurred in other malarial sections, is reported to have said:* "That the excite-

---

*Craven's "Prison Life of Jeff Davis."

ment of war itself was a prophylactic." We had none of the excitement and all of the monotony of stationary camps.

To guard against the propensity of all troops to accumulate impedimenta when long in camp, and to endeavor to secure mobility to the command, the following was made a standing order:

"1. Surplus stores will not be kept on hand by the regimental quartermasters, commissaries and ordnance officers; but will be kept in the possession of the brigade officers of the several departments.

"2. Officers commanding regiments and detached corps will prevent the accumulation of baggage and keep the same within regulation limits.

"3. The following regulations are established with regard to transportation:

"(1) Whenever a general movement of the troops is contemplated, upon intimation to that effect, a *special train* will be organized before hand, containing all surplus stores, and in general terms, everything for which the troops have no immediate necessity, and the ambulances with sick in hospital. This train will always move separate from the troops and for it a special escort will be provided.

"(2) The *train* proper of wagons, etc., and containing only things needed by the troops while in camp, will follow in the offensive and precede in retreats the movements of the troops, by at least half a day's march—say six or eight miles. In it will be included ammunition and hospital wagons, baggage wagons of regiments, baggage wagons of the general staff and wagons carrying provisions and forage for immediate use.

"(3) Each regiment and independent corps will be accompanied by its ambulance and ordnance wagon following immediately in its rear.

"(4) Commanding officers will be held strictly responsible that the troops always move with three days' rations in their haversacks, and three days' forage properly packed upon the horse, if mounted, and forty rounds of ammunition in the cartridge box and sixty rounds in the ordnance wagon."

Schools of instruction by recitation were established in each regiment and independent corps, followed by reviews and drills in presence of the brigadier general commanding; and boards were organized and kept in laborious session for the examination of officers under the Act of Congress to relieve the army of incompetent incumbents.

In the discharge of these unobtrusive but important duties, General Hagood's service in the Second Military District wore away. No event of military interest beyond an occasional collision of pickets marked this time. When the enemy advanced upon

General Walker in the Third District in October, 1862, General Hagood received an urgent dispatch from him calling for assistance. Moving the Seventh South Carolina Battalion to the railroad, General Hagood stopped and emptied a passing train and dispatched the Seventh to Walker's assistance. It reached him in time to materially assist in the decisive repulse of the enemy at Pocotaligo. General Hagood, by permission of General Beauregard, followed with other re-enforcements but arrived after the battle.

In April, 1863, after the repulse of the enemy's fleet in the attack on Fort Sumter, their ironclads rendezvoused in the North Edisto Inlet, where they lay for some time with an infantry force of some 2,500 or 3,000 men, encamped close by on Seabrook's Island. General Beauregard organized a force to attempt to sink the ironclads or drive them to sea, and capture the troops on Seabrook's. He raised General Hagood's force by special re-enforcements about 3,000 good infantry, with ten or twelve field guns, and sent him a naval force of over 100 men with torpedo barges. The plan was for the torpedo barges to get amongst the fleet just before day, and as soon as they were routed, and upon condition that they were, the infantry was to attack. The barges rendezvoused safely in a creek not over a mile from the fleet on the previous night; and the land forces were brought unsuspected within short striking distance. Everything was in readiness for the next day's work, when the order was countermanded, and the troops directed to return with all speed to Charleston, to proceed, most of them, to Pemberton's assistance, then hard pressed in Vicksburg. A sailor from the naval force deserted that evening to the enemy, betraying the plan of concealment of the barges and they with difficulty escaped. Afterwards, while in North Edisto, the enemy adopted huge rafts of timber as fenders to each ironclad by way of precaution against the approach of their diminutive enemies, the torpedo boats. An instance of special gallantry occurring at this time deserves to be recorded.

When the troops above referred to landed on Seabrook Island, Captain Walpole, commanding the Scouts on Johns Island, dispatched the fact to General Hagood, and received in reply the order: "Get me a prisoner." It was between sundown and dark, and taking Sergeant Gervais and Evans Fripp with him, Walpole made his way through the enemy's chain of videttes and charging in at full speed upon a regiment which had stacked arms and was going into bivouac, discharged their six-shooting rifles right and left, shooting down two men and wounding a third, whom Walpole, a very active and strong man, jerked up, as he ran, to the croup of his horse; and the party made their escape, having obeyed the order to "get a prisoner." He was an intelligent sergeant and gave all the information wanted before he died from his wound, which proved mortal next day.

Yankee Ironclad in North Edisto April, 1863 (a monitor).

A few days after General Hagood was relieved of the command of the Second District, an effort was made by the enemy to pass up the Pon Pon River in gunboats to Jacksonboro and there destroy the Charleston and Savannah railroad bridge. They passed Willtown chiefly from the inefficiency with which the field battery at that point was worked. The guns were in barbette entrenchment upon a commanding bluff with the river obstructed by piling under their fire, and should have turned the boats back. They passed on, but Captain Walter, of the Washington Artillery, stationed, as before mentioned, on the western side of the river near Jacksonboro, came up rapidly with a section of his battery, and unlimbering in an open old field, went into action with the two gunboats just as they had reached within sight of the bridge. He turned them back and sunk one of them, which the enemy abandoned.*

Black's First Regiment of First South Carolina Cavalry served for a short time after Hagood's taking command, in the Second District. They were ordered to Virginia and Aiken's Sixth South Carolina Cavalry took their place.† These with two companies of the Third (Colcock's) under Major Jenkins composed Hagood's mounted force for the remainder of the time. The Washington Artillery (Walter's) and the Marion Artillery (Parker's) were with him all the time. Shultz's Battery was with him part of the time. The Seventh South Carolina Battalion, afterwards of Hagood's Brigade, McCullough's Sixteenth South Carolina, afterwards of Gist's Brigade, and Smith's Twenty-sixth South Carolina, afterwards of Elliott's Brigade, constituted his infantry force, details from which also acted as heavy artillery for the siege guns in position. Other regiments were with him for short periods. The Stono Scouts under Walpole were also with him from first to last. Lieutenant-Colonel Del. Kemper commanded the field batteries and the staff was:

Captain P. K. Moloney—Assistant Adjutant General.

Major G. B. Lartigue—Quartermaster.

Major R. G. Hay—Commissary Subsistence.

Lieutenant Isaac Hayne—Ordnance Officer.

Lieutenant Ben Martin—Aid-de-camp.

Captain Carlos Tracy—Volunteer Aide.

Service in the Second District had all the monotony of garrison life, with something of its advantages. The families of the officers to some extent were enabled to visit them from time to time, the ladies finding shelter in the unoccupied summer residences of the planters in the little hamlet of Adams Run. It was a fine fish and game country, and, with railroad facilities for drawing supplies from home, our tables were fairly furnished for Confederate times. The troops were supplied from the resources

---

*Captain Walter was supported by Company B, Sixth South Carolina Cavalry, which was the only support he had. The Yankee gunboat was sunk the 10th of July, 1863. Black's Cavalry Regiment was then in Virginia, and not on the Carolina coast.—Editor.

†Aiken's Sixth South Carolina Cavalry served for a short time after General Hagood assumed command; and on being ordered to Virginia Black's First South Carolina Cavalry took their place.—Editor.

of the District, and at first these were ample. Towards the last, however, these supplies became scant. Agricultural operations had been greatly interfered with by the propinquity of hostile armies, and the supply of beef cattle and sheep, at first large, became exhausted. Hogs there were none. But few of the planters continued to work the plantations south of the railroad. Among these, however, was Hawkins ·S. King. He continued to the last to carry on his several plantations, and truly his homestead appeared to be a perfect Goshen, whose abundance he dispensed with a lavish generosity. He obtained with the brigade staff the sobriquet of "*The King* of St. Pauls."

General Hagood, however, chafed at his life of inactivity— while the great game of war was being played so grandly in Virginia and in the west, his friends and former comrades being actors in the drama, and received in the spring of 1863 a promise from General Beauregard to send him into one or the other of these fields with the first brigade that left the department. Gist claimed his seniority and got the brigade sent to Pemberton in June, 1863. Two or three weeks afterward other troops were ordered in that direction and General Hagood was placed in command of the brigade organized to go. He left Adams Run and had reached Charleston on his way, when a dispatch from Richmond directed Evans's Brigade, lately arrived from North Carolina, to be substituted in his place. General Beauregard, when remonstrated with by General Hagood, under a misapprehension of the source of this order, said he knew not what induced the unusual course of the War Department in interfering in this matter. Evans did not desire to go, but was unpopular with Beauregard's chief of staff, and one of the colonels of the brigade made for Hagood, who was very intimate with General Gordon, preferred just then to remain where he was. The conclusion on General Hagood's mind, whether justly or not, was that the change had its inspiration in this ".power behind the throne," which was generally believed by those who served with General Beauregard during this period to be sometimes without the General's consciousness "stronger than the throne itself." This belief and the equally general belief of Gordon's unworthiness operated injuriously both with the officers and men. In the following summer Captain Beauregard, a brother of the General's and aid-de-camp on his staff, resigned his commission, and, calling to say good-bye to General Hagood, told him that he had himself informed his brother of the common estimate of Gordon's character, and of its injurious influence upon the General himself. But Beauregard either knew his chief of staff better, or thought he could not do without him, for he retained him until he was compelled to give him up by subsequent action of the War Department. General Gordon immediately after the war signalized himself by a very able and heartless attack in the Northern papers upon Mr. Davis, with whom he had some personal feud; and has since acquired some notoriety as the commander-in-chief, by contract for a twelvemonth, of the Cuban Insurgents.

General Hagood had to stomach his disappointment and return to Adams Run, expecting another monotonous summer within its precincts. He shortly after applied for a ten days' leave of absence to arrange his private affairs, and while at home received a dispatch from department headquarters ordering him to report at once in Charleston. Gilmore had developed his batteries against the south end of Morris Island, and the siege of Charleston had begun.

NOTE.—In the winter of 1863 the ladies of Nelson's country sent him a flag for his battalion, with a request that General Hagood should, for them, make the formal presentation. This was the last incident of the kind the writer remembers to have witnessed in the war. They were frequent at an earlier period; perhaps no one of the earlier regiments marched to the war without some such memorial of the dear ones at home to nerve them for the fray. These flags were generally beautifully embroidered State flags and were really used in but few engagements. The use of a general flag was ordered and as soon as the regiments got into the larger armies they were required to lay these aside for the regular Confederate battle flags.

General Hagood's address to the battalion in presenting the ladies' banner is appended as characteristic of the times. He said:

"I am commissioned, soldiers of the Seventh Battalion, by the ladies of the section of the State in which your corps was raised, in their name to present you with this banner.

"For two long years our fair Southern land has been drenched in blood; her plains have been torn with the rush of contending hosts; her hills have echoed and re-echoed with the dread voice of battle. The world has beheld with amazement a struggle in which a million and a half of armed men have been engaged, with almost a continent for a battlefield. Upon the one side it has seen a gigantic foe, trebling its adversary in numbers and wealth, and with all the appliances of war at its command, again and again, with a pertinacity rarely equaled, advancing to the onset. Upon the other it has seen a people cut off from all save the sympathies of the brave, standing desperately by their hearthstones and again and again repelling the insolent foe. We have met them upon our deserted fields; we have fought them by the light of our blazing homes; in rags, and with imperfect weapons, we have

THE SIEGE OF CHARLESTON.

The naval attack on Fort Sumter in April, 1863, was prefatory to Gilmore's operations, and General Ripley's report of it is given below:

"Headquarters First Military District,
"Department S. C., Georgia and Fla.,
"Charleston, 13 April, 1863.

"*Brigadier-General Thomas Gordon, Chief of Staff, etc.*

"General: Upon the first inst., the increase of the enemy's force in the Stono, and information from North Edisto, gave warning that the long-threatened combined movement upon Charleston was about to take place. Brigadier-General S. R. Gist, commanding 1st subdivision of this District

---

encountered their serried hosts. In defeat as in victory our high purpose has never quailed, and in the darkest hour of this unequal war a murmur of repining at its hardships has never passed the lips of a Southern man; it has never entered into his heart to conceive a termination to his efforts short of absolute and unqualified success. It is a spectacle, soldiers, which may well challenge comparison with the heroic struggles of classic fame, and upon this grand page of history you, too, have written your names. Upon the weary march, in the comfortless bivouac, and upon the field of battle, you have borne your part. Beneath the old oaks of Pocotaligo you have seen a comrade's glazing eye 'look fondly to heaven from a deathbed of fame,' and sadder, far sadder, in tent and hospital, afar from the gentle ministering of home, you've seen a comrade's spirit flutter its way to God, crushed out by the merciless requirements of war.

"But while the sons of the South have vindicated the blood they have inherited from patriot sires, her daughters have illustrated all that is admirable in the attributes of woman. No Joan has arisen from among them to gird on the harness of battle, no Charlotte Corday to drive the dagger home to the tyrant's heart. There has been no need for them to unsex themselves, nor will there ever be a dearth of manhood requiring such a sacrifice while woman remains the true and holy creature which God made her. But it is scarce an exaggeration to say that the voluntary efforts of our women, themselves laboring under cruel and unaccustomed privations, have clothed our armies, and organized all of comfort that exists in our hospitals. No high bred Dame of Chivalry ever belted her knight for battle with a more devoted spirit than that with which the humblest Southern woman has sent her loved ones to this war. She has checked the cry of wailing over the slaughtered corpse of her husband, to prepare her first born to take his place; and when disaster has befallen our arms and the heel of the oppressor has ground into the dust the souls of the few men who have remained to bear his yoke, the spirit of patriotism has survived in the women. Insult and injury have failed to crush it—until the indignant utterances of the civilized world have compelled the oppressor for very shame to desist.*

"It is from such women as these, soldiers of the Seventh Battalion, that I present you with this beautiful banner. Wrought by fair hands, consecrated by the pure and tender aspirations of wife, and mother, and sister, which cluster in its folds, it is committed to your keeping.

"Colonel Nelson, it is narrated in martial story that a general, desiring to hold a pass upon which much depended, posted in the defile a battalion whose metal he knew, and left them with this stern and simple charge: 'Here,' said he, 'colonel, you and your men will die.' And the order was literally obeyed. There they died! In a like spirit, and with a like confidence, I say to you: 'In defense of this flag you and your men will die.' "

---

*New Orleans.

(James Island and St. Andrew's Parish), took prompt measures for the observation and repulse of any attack in that direction. Colonel R. F. Graham, commanding 3rd subdivision, occupied the shore of Morris Island on Light House Inlet to control the passage from Folley Island, and a strict watch has been kept up to the present time on the land movements of the enemy.

"On the 5th, the ironclad fleet of the enemy, consisting of seven (7) monitors and one (1) double turreted vessel, hove in sight from Fort Sumter, and came to anchor outside in the vicinity of the Ironsides frigate, then a part of the blockading squadron. The 6th was apparently spent by the enemy in preparation, and by our artillerists in verifying the condition of their material. On the morning of the 7th, the enemy was inside the bar with all his ironclads, including the frigate, but from his proximity to the shoals and the haziness of the atmosphere his position could not be determined.

"The various works of preparation were progressed with, both upon the exterior and interior lines of defense, until about 2 p. m., when the enemy steamed directly up the channel, the Weehawken (supposed) with a false prow for removing torpedoes attached, leading, followed by three monitors; the Keokuk, double turreted, bringing up the rear.

"At each fort and battery, officers and men made preparations for immediate action, while the enemy came slowly and steadily on. At 3 o'clock Fort Moultrie opened fire. At 5 minutes past 3, the leading vessel having arrived at fourteen hundred yards, Fort Sumter opened upon it with two guns. Batteries Bee, Beauregard, Wagner and Gregg opened about this time; and the action became general, the four leading monitors closing upon the Weehawken, and taking position from the forts and batteries at an average distance of about fifteen hundred yards. In accordance with instructions the fire from the different points was concentrated upon the leading vessel; and the effort was soon apparent in the withdrawal of the leading monitor from action, her false prow having been detached and otherwise apparently injured. The remaining monitors in advance of the flag ship held their position, directing their fire principally at Fort Sumter, but giving occasional shots at Fort Moultrie, of which the flagstaff was shot away, Batteries Beauregard and Bee.

"The Ironsides meantime opened fire and drew the attention of Forts Moultrie and Sumter and Battery Gregg. A few heavy and concentrated discharges caused her to withdraw out of range, where she was followed by two other monitors.

"At 5 minutes past 4 the Keokuk left her consorts, and came to the front, approaching to within nine hundred yards of Fort Sumter, twelve hundred from Battery Bee, and one thousand from Fort Moultrie. Her advance was characterized by more boldness than had yet been exhibited by any of the enemy's fleet, but receiving full attention from the powerful batteries opposed to her, the effect was soon apparent. The ten-inch shell and seven-inch rifled bolts crashed through her armor, her hull and turrets were riddled and stove in, her boats were shot away, and in less than forty minutes she retired with such speed as her disabled condition would permit.

"The remaining monitors kept their position for a short time, but soon one by one dropped down the channel, and came to anchor out of range, after an action of two hours and twenty-five minutes at ranges varying from nine hundred to nineteen hundred yards.

"The full effect of our batteries upon the enemy could not be precisely ascertained, and, as our strength had not been fully put forth, it. was believed the action would soon be renewed. The monitor which had led in the action proceeded south outside of the bar the same evening.

"Before the commencement of the affair, I was proceeding in a boat to Battery Bee, and watched the progress of the cannonade from that point. The guns were worked with as much precision as the range would admit. There were no damages or casualties. Visiting Fort Moultrie, the damaged flagstaff was being replaced and everything prepared for a renewal of fire should the enemy again approach. One man had been mortally wounded by the falling of the staff. Crossing the channel to Fort Sumter, the effect of the impact of the heavy shot sent by the enemy against the fort they are so anxious to repossess, greater in caliber and supposed destructive force than any hitherto used in war, was found to have been much less than had been anticipated. Five men had been injured by splinters from the traverses, one 8-inch columbiad had exploded, one 10-inch carriage had its transom shot away and two rifled 42 drs. had been temporarily disabled from the effect of recoil on defective carriages.

"The garrison was immediately set to work to repair damages, and, the strength of the enemy's projectiles having been ascertained, to guard such points as might be exposed to their effect should the attack be renewed. Battery Gregg and Battery Wagner were uninjured except from the accidental explosion of an ammunition chest in Battery Wagner.

"During the night of the 7th, stores were replenished; threatened points upon land re-enforced; working parties from the Forty-sixth Georgia Regiment brought to Fort Sumter, and the renewal of the struggle in the morning awaited with confidence.

"When day dawned on the morning of the 8th, the enemy's fleet was discovered in the same position as noticed on the previous evening. About 9 o'clock the Keokuk, which had been evidently the most damaged in the action, went down about three and a half miles from Fort Sumter and three-quarters of a mile from Morris Island. The remainder of the fleet were repairing damages. Preparations for repulsing a renewed attack were progressed with in accordance with the instructions of the commanding general, who visited Fort Sumter on that day. A detachment of seamen, under Flag Officer W. F. Lynch, arrived from Wilmington, and on the 9th temporarily relieved the artillerists in charge of Battery Gregg. The operations of the enemy's fleet consisted only of supply and repair. Towards evening of the 9th, a raft, apparently for removing torpedoes or obstructions, was towed inside the bar. Nothing of importance occurred during the 10th. During the night of the 10th, Lieutenant-Colonel Dargan, of the Twenty-first South Carolina Regiment, crossed Light House Inlet, drove back the enemy's picket with loss, and returned with one prisoner.

On the 11th, there were indications that the attacking fleet were about to withdraw; and on the 12th, at highwater, the Ironsides crossed the bar and took up her position with the blockading fleet; and the monitors steamed and went toward the southward—leaving only the sunken Keokuk as a monument of their attack and discomfiture.

"In this, the first trial of the enemy's iron fleet against brick fortifications and their first attempt to enter the harbor of Charleston, in which they were beaten before their adversaries thought action had well commenced, they were opposed by seventy-six pieces in all, including mortars. Thirty-seven of these, exclusive of mortars, were above the caliber of thirty-two pounders. The guns which the enemy brought to bear were, if their own account is to be believed, thirty-six in number, including eight-inch rifled, eleven, thirteen and fifteen-inch guns, which would make their weight of metal at one discharge nearly, if not quite, equal to that thrown by the batteries.

"During the action Brigadier-General Trapier, commanding 2nd subdivision of this District, was present at Fort Moultrie. Brigadier-General Gist, commanding 1st subdivision, at Fort Johnson. Colonel R. F. Graham, commanding 3rd subdivision, at Morris Island, and Colonel L. M. Keitt, commanding Sullivan's Island, at Battery Bee, attending to their duties, and awaiting the developments of the attack.

"The action, however, was purely of artillery; forts and batteries against ironclad vessels—other means of defense, obstructions and torpedoes not having come into play. Fort Sumter was the principal object of the enemy's attack and to that garrison, under its gallant commander, Colonel Alfred Rhett, ably seconded by Lieutenant-Colonel Yates, and Major Blanding, and all the officers and men, special credit is due for sustaining the shock and with their powerful armament contributing principally to the repulse. The garrison of Fort Moultrie, under Colonel William Butler, seconded by Major Baker and the other officers and soldiers, upheld the historic reputation of that fort and contributed their full share to the result. The powerful batteries of Battery Bee was commanded by Lieutenant-Colonel John C. Simkins* and were served with great effect. Battery Wagner, under Major Cleland F. Huger; Battery Gregg, Lieutenant Lesene, and Battery Beauregard, under Captain Sitgreaves, all did their part according to their armament.

"Indeed, from the reports of commanders, it is hard to make any distinction where all did their duty with zeal and devotion. Those cases which have been ascertained will be found in the reports of the subordinate commanders. The steady preparation for receiving a renewed attack, and the discipline of the troops, especially in the garrison of Fort Sumter, the labor being necessarily great, have been quite as creditable as their conduct under fire.

*Killed at Wagner, 18 July.

"While service in immediate action is that which is most conspicuous after such a result has been accomplished, the greater credit is due to that long, patient and laborious preparation by which our works and material, never originally intended to withstand such an attack as this, have been so prepared as to enable our gallant and well-instructed officers and men to obtain their end with comparatively small loss. In that preparation the late Lieutenant-Colonel Thomas M. Wagner contributed much on both sides of the channel, and Colonel Rhett and Lieutenant-Colonel Yates, Major Blanding and other officers of Fort Sumter have been more or less engaged since the fort fell into our hands two years since. Colonel Butler, Lieutenant-Colonel Simkins, and other officers of the First South Carolina Infantry, have been for more than a year engaged in the work on Sullivan's Island. Besides various officers of engineers and other branches of the department staff known to the commanding general have been at different times principal contributors in the work, and although in the limits of this report it is impossible to mention all to whom credit is due, it is well that works like these, without which in such emergencies as the present personal gallantry avails nought, should be appreciated.

"During the seven days while the presence of the enemy's fleet threatened action, Captain William F. Nance, principal Assistant Adjutant General on the District staff, performed his difficult duties in the administration of a command of twenty thousand men in a prompt, judicious and efficient manner. He was assisted by Lieutenants H. H. Rogers and W. H. Wagner, aid-de-camps. Captain F. B. DuBarry, District Ordnance Officer, was especially active and energetic in the supply of ammunition and material for the batteries. He was assisted by Lieutenant C. C. Pinckney.

"Captain B. H. Read, Assistant Adjutant-General, Colonel Edward Manigault, and Lieutenant-Colonel St. Clair Dearing, volunteers upon the staff, were present during the action at Fort Sumter. Captain Seabrook, volunteer aid-de-camp, and Lieutenant Schirmlee, enrolling officer and acting aid-de-camp, were generally with me during the active period and all were energetic and prompt in the duties required of them. To Majors Motte A. Pringle and Norman W. Smith, post and district quartermasters, and Captain McCleneghan, assistant commissary sergeant, many thanks should be rendered. The duties of the quartermaster's department were excessively laborious on account of the limited means of transportation, and it is a matter of congratulation that with such means they were so well performed, Captain John S. Ryan, A. C. S., acted on my immediate staff.

"The reports of the engineer officers will inform the commanding general of the condition of the various works as well as of the action of the officers in that branch of the service.

"I have the honor to transmit herewith a return of the guns engaged, a return of the ammunition expended, and a numerical return of casualties, together with the reports of the different commanders.

"I have also to transmit herewith two Federal ensigns obtained from the Keokuk as she lies off Morris Island beach, by Lieutenant Glassell, C. S. Navy, one of which is evidently the ensign under which she fought and was worsted. None of the ironclad fleets flew large flags, the object having doubtless been to avoid presenting a mark to our artillerists.

"I have the honor to be

"Very respectfully,

"R. S. RIPLEY,

"Brigadier-General, Commanding."

RETURN OF CASUALTIES.

Fort Sumter .. ..Wounded 5
Fort Moultrie.. .. .. ..Wounded 1
Battery Wagner.. .. ..Wounded 5   killed 3 (by explosion ammuni-
—   tion chest)
Total Casualties.. 14

RETURN OF GUNS AND MORTARS AT BATTERIES ENGAGED.

	10-in. Columbiad	9-in. Dahlgren	7-in. Brooke	8-in. Columbiad	42 Dr. Rifled	32 Dr. Smooth	32 Dr. Rifled	10-in. Mortar	
Fort Sumter..	4	2	2	8	7	13	1	7	
Fort Moultrie..	..	..	..	9	..	5	5	2	
Battery Bee..	5	..	..	1	..	..	..	..	
Beauregard..	..	..	..	1	..	..	1	..	
Wagner..	..	..	..	..	..	..	1	..	
Gregg..	1	1	..	..	..	..	..	..	
	10	3	2	19	7	18	8	9	Total 76

CONSOLIDATED RETURN OF AMMUNITION EXPENDED.

Round Shot.. 1,539   Shot Bolts.. 233
Round Shell.. 98   Friction tubes.. 2,856
Shot, Rifle.. 359   Cannon Powder.. .. .. ..21,093 lbs.

Resuming operations against Charleston, General Gilmore, on the 10th July, assaulted and carried the south end of Morris Island. His infantry moved in a flotilla of small boats from the north end of Folley Island under cover of a heavy fire from batteries on the latter constructed without attracting serious attention from the Confederates. The movement was well planned and executed with considerable dash. Co-operative with it was the attempt to cut the Charleston and Savannah Railroad at Jacksonboro, the failure of which has already been mentioned in speaking of events in the Second Military District, and a demonstration in force from Stono on James Island.

Upon reporting on the evening of the 10th July at General Beauregard's headquarters in pursuance of the dispatch received at Barnwell, General Hagood was sent to James Island to take command of that sub-district. All day from Blackville down, whenever the cars stopped, the booming of the guns from Morris Island could be heard. Captain Moloney, Assistant Adjutant General, was with General Hagood, and Mr. William Izard Bull, acting as volunteer aide to General Beauregard, was by order of the latter directed to report to him for temporary duty. General Hagood arrived on the island about 12 o'clock at night, and learned from Colonel Simonton, in command, the condition of affairs. The enemy were in force on the Stono shore of the island, with gunboats and transports in the river. Our defensive works were the same as at the close of the Secessionville campaign; nothing had been done to them save at Secessionville, which had been much strengthened. These works looked only to an advance from the Stono front; and the enemy, now holding Folley and the south end of Morris Island with their transports in Light House Inlet, were in rear of their left flank with an uninterrupted water approach of from one and a half to two miles available for light-draft steamers, and the landings not even picketed. Had a flotilla of boats with two thousand men and a light battery landed that night at Legare's Landing, it is probable that Fort Johnson, unentrenched to the rear, would have fallen before day; and, within the limits of possibility, that before the following night the whole of James Island except the garrison of Secessionville and Fort Pemberton, which would have been cut off and isolated, would have been in their possession. A vigorous co-operative march of General Terry's force on the Stono side of the island, against the center of our line by way of Royall's house, would have made it almost a certain thing; and then the northern shore of James Island held by four thousand men would have been safe against any force at Beauregard's command for several days. Gilmore could have re-enforced afterward as fast as Beauregard, had the James instead of the

Morris Island route to Charleston been taken. This was at that time and for a day or two the promising plan.

The Confederate force on James Island consisted of the regiment of Frederick (late Lamar's), the battalions of White and Lucas, three companies of Rhett's—all heavy artillery; the siege train, consisting of four companies under Major Manigault, some cavalry as couriers, and one regiment of infantry, the Twenty-fifth South Carolina, under Colonel Simonton. This last was the only force available for movement. The heavy artillerists were barely enough to garrison the three forts in which they were stationed and to man the few guns in position on the lines. Major Manigault was with all dispatch moved that night from his camp near Wappoo to Legare's Landing, where he arrived at daylight and immediately proceeded to erect epaulements for his siege guns. This was the beginning of Battery Haskell and the series of works on the eastern shore of the island. The enemy on the Stono under General Terry remained quiet, advancing their pickets without opposition some short distance. General Beauregard rapidly pushed re-enforcements over to James Island as they arrived. Large working parties of negroes were, together with the troops, kept steadily at work, and in a few days the opportunity of doing anything by surprise or assault on James Island had passed away.

Subsequently General W. B. Taliaferro was assigned to the command of James Island, and Generals Hagood and A. H. Colquitt commanded the eastern and western divisions of the lines respectively under him. Secessionville was the dividing point in these sub-commands. These general officers served with others on the detail of commanders on Morris Island during the operations in that quarter, and when not on duty there resumed their positions on James Island.

General Hagood's tours of duty on Morris Island were: From the 18th to 22nd July, from the 6th to 10th August, from the 21st to 25th August; arriving and leaving generally on the nights of these respective dates. His next tour of duty would have commenced on the 7th September. The island was evacuated on the previous night. Of his staff, Captain Moloney, acting adjutant-general, and his aides, Ben Martin and Tracy, with his orderly, S. N. Bellinger, always accompanied him. Majors Hay and

Lartigue and Captain Hayne, commissary quartermaster and ordnance officer, were with him on the first tour; afterwards these offices on the island were made post offices and others filled them. Lieutenant-Colonel Del. Kemper served the first tour with him as chief of artillery. This officer had distinguishéd himself in Virginia at First Manassas, and subsequently an unclosed wound in his shoulder unfitted him for field duty and he was sent to this department, where he served the rest of the war. He was in person very like General Beauregard, of high mental and social culture, and an officer of much dash and merit. General Hagood was thrown much with him and formed a warm regard for him. Lieutenant-Colonel Welsman Brown served the second tour as chief of artillery, and Major F. F. Warley the third. These officers all discharged their duties with credit to themselves and to the entire satisfaction of their chief. Captain Moloney especially was invaluable, cool, intelligent and indefatigable. He relieved the command of half its burthen.

The period of active operations against Charleston, looking to its direct capture, was from 10th July to 10th September. Afterward the siege was marked only by the bombardment of Sumter and the city, with comparatively harmless cannonading of each other by the opposing batteries and some skirmishes. This continued until the spring of 1864, when Gilmore and Beauregard were both, with the bulk of their troops, transferred to the theatre of war in Virginia, where the conflict was then culminating, and Charleston was left with a skeleton garrison to hold its own against a force adequate to little more than protect from assault the long-range guns which continued day and night to hurl their crashing and exploding missiles into the ruins of the devoted city. For twelve months longer this continued, while the contest upon which depended alike the fate of Charleston and the Confederacy was elsewhere prosecuted to the bitter end. At length in the spring of '65, when all that was left of the Confederacy was concentrated for the last desperate hazard, the garrison of Charleston, her artillerists converted into infantry, silently and sadly, and bearing with them their warworn banners, marched to strengthen the hands of Johnston in North Carolina. There, upon the fields of Averysboro and Bentonville, in two field fights, they lost nearly as many men in killed and wounded as in all their service under Gilmore's guns and before his assailing columns. So much for the art of the engineer.

In arranging the material of this memoir of the siege, General Beauregard's report embracing the time from his assumption of command until the evacuation of Morris Island is taken; then General Ripley's report continues the narrative till the 10th of September; and from that time till the departure of General Hagood for Virginia in May, '64, his recollection is relied upon. In notes to these official papers, the writer has embodied such comments as appeared to him proper.

Of events in and around Charleston, subsequent to April, '64, in the absence of personal knowledge or official reports, no attempt will be made to give an account.

GENERAL BEAUREGARD'S REPORT.

Headquarters
Department Georgia, South Carolina and Florida.

General S. Cooper, Adjutant and Inspector General.

General: I arrived in Charleston on the 13th September, 1862, and assumed command on the 24th. In the interval I was engaged in ascertaining the plans and measures of Major-General Pemberton, my predecessor, for the defense, particularly of Charleston and Savannah, and in a rapid inspection of the condition and defensive resources of the department, the results of which were communicated to the War Department in two papers, dated the one relative to Charleston on the 3rd, and the other chiefly concerning Savannah on the 10th of October, 1862.

At the time the troops in this department as organized consisted:

In South Carolina—

Infantry	6,564
Artillery in position	1,787
Artillery in field	1,379
Cavalry	2,817
	12,547

NOTE.—See Publications by U. S. Government of Official Records of the War of the Rebellion, Series I, Vol. XXVIII, Parts 1 and 2.

In Georgia—
Infantry.. 3,834
Artillery in position.. 1,330
Artillery in field.. 445
Cavalry.. 1,580
                    —————   7,189

Total of all arms..   19,736

Of this force 1,787 artillery in position, 727 light artillerists, 4,139 infantry and 410 cavalry were assembled in the First Military District for the defense of Charleston; and 1,330 artillery in position, 445 light artillery, 3,834 infantry and 1,580 cavalry for the defense of Savannah. My predecessor before being relieved furnished me with his estimate of the smallest number of troops which he regarded as essential for the defense of Charleston and Savannah, to-wit:

For the defense of Charleston—
Infantry.. 15,600
Artillery in position.. 2,850
Cavalry.. 1,000
                    —————   19,450
    and 9 light batteries.
For the defense of R. R. (Charleston &
Savannah) land approaches—
Of all arms..   11,000
For defense of Savannah—
Infantry.. 10,000
Artillery in position.. 1,200
Cavalry.. 2,000
                    —————   13,200
    and 8 light batteries.
Total exclusive of light battery.. 43,650

Hence a total of 25,216 troops of all arms additional to those in the department were needed to meet this estimate.

On the 7th April, 1863, the day of the ironclad attack on Fort Sumter, the troops at my disposal in South Carolina and Georgia gave an effective total of 30,040, distributed as follows:

In the First Military District.. 11,229
In the Second Military District.. 2,849
In the Third Military District.. 5,837
Georgia.. 10,125

30,040

But the withdrawal of Cook's Brigade to North Carolina, immediately after the repulse of the ironclad fleet, of Brigadier-General S. R. Gist's and W. H. T. Walker's brigades and light batteries about the 4th May, reduced my force materially. The Department is aware of the circumstances under which this reduction took place, and in this connection I beg to refer to my letter to the Honorable Secretary of War of the 10th May and to General S. Cooper, Adjutant and Inspector General, of June 15th and July 20th, 1863.

The force in the First Military District on the 10th July was:
Infantry.. 2,462
Artillery, heavy and light.. 2,839
Cavalry.. 560
5,861
In Second Military District, of all arms.. 1,398
In Third Military District, of all arms.. 2,517
In District of Georgia of all arms.. 5,542

Grand total*.. 15,318

Meanwhile, as in duty bound by numerous telegrams and letters during the month of April, May, June and July, I kept the War Department advised both through yourself and directly of the threatening nature of the enemy's preparations upon the coast of my department and of my own fears concerning the imminence of an attack. On the 25th of April, however, in answer to my telegram of the preceding day asking for heavy guns for Morris Island and other points, the Secretary of War telegraphs:

"I regret to be unable to spare the guns even for the object mentioned. The claims of Wilmington and of the Mississippi are now regarded as paramount."

---

*Gilmore, in his "Operations against Charleston," p. 21, states his force at 17,463, exclusive of his naval strength.—J. H.

On the 1st May I was directed to send a full brigade to North Carolina to report to General Hill, and in compliance General Clingman's Brigade was dispatched. The following day the Secretary of War telegraphed, "Advices show the enemy abandoning their attack on the eastern coasts, and concentrating great forces on the Mississippi River. Send with the utmost dispatch eight or ten thousand men, including those heretofore ordered to Tullahoma, to General Pemberton's relief."

My answer was: "No orders sending troops to Tullahoma have been received. Cook's and Clingman's brigades have been returned to North Carolina. Have ordered 5,000 infantry and two batteries to report forthwith to General Pemberton, leaving only 10,000 infantry available for the whole of South Carolina and Georgia. Cannot send more without abandoning Charleston and Savannah Railroad. Shall await further orders. Enemy still occupy in force Folley and Seabrooks Islands and Port Royal. To reduce this command further might become disastrous."

On the 4th May I sent the following dispatch to Secretary of War: "Enemy's fleet reported at Hilton's Head and Port Royal yesterday is four steam frigates, five wooden gunboats, six ships, four barges, three brigs, five ocean steamers, six river steamers, five tugs, eighty-seven transports and fifty-eight schooners, being one hundred and eighty-three in all—a very remarkable increase since last report."

Hon. Mr. Sedden, Secretary of War, telegraphed on 9th May: "Foster, with his own and part of Hunter's forces, is believed to have returned to North Carolina. More re-enforcements to General Pemberton are indispensable. If General Evans's brigade has returned to you send 5,000 men; if not, with a number which with that will make 5,000 men." On the following day I telegraphed in reply: "To the Secretary of War: The order sending additional troops to Pemberton will be executed. Evans's Brigade included have but 1,000 infantry to support extensive lines and batteries at Savannah, but 750 infantry to hold line of railroad to Savannah, virtually yielding up that country and large stores of rice to the enemy, as well as opening even Charleston and Augusta and Columbia Railroads to attack at Branchville, leaving here 1,500 infantry at most, all of which will be known to the enemy in a few days. Meantime General W. S. Walker reports increased strength of enemy's outposts in his vicinity. Hagood reports 2,500 infantry on Seabrooks Island fortifying, five monitors still there. Enemy in force on Folley Island, actively erecting batteries there yesterday. Season favorable for enemy's operations for quite a month."

On the 12th, I telegraphed to the Honorable Secretary of War as follows:

"Have ordered to General Pemberton (contrary to my opinion) Evans's Brigade and one regiment amounting to 2,700 men, leaving only 6,000 infantry available in the whole of South Carolina and Georgia. The other 1,000 will await further orders of Department. General Evans reports two brigades of the enemy on Folley Island yesterday. Please answer." A letter to the same address on the 11th May exhibited certain conditions and explanations, being more fully my views on the subject of an attack, with the object of showing to the War Department the actual menacing aspect of the enemy on the coast of my department. I transcribe an extract from that letter. . . .

"A week ago, under your orders, I put in motion for Jackson, Miss., two brigades under Generals Gist and W. H. T. Walker, the former commanding South Carolina, and the latter Georgia troops,—somewhat over 5,000 infantry in all, and two light batteries of the best class in the department. Your orders have been based apparently upon the conviction that the troops of the enemy assembled in this department for operations against Charleston have been mainly withdrawn and directed to other expeditions in North Carolina and the Valley of the Mississippi. This conviction I regret I cannot share, as I am satisfied from the reports of the district commanders, and from other reasons, that there has been really but little reduction of the command of Major-General Hunter. General Walker, commanding at Pocotaligo, reports that on yesterday the outposts of the enemy in his front had been much increased in strength. General Hagood reports them to be occupying Seabrooks Island with at least 2,500 infantry. They are erecting fortifications at that point, as well as on Folley Island, which is likewise still occupied in force. Five of the monitors remain in North Edisto with some twenty gunboats and transports. With these and the transports still in the waters of Port Royal, and the forces which I am unable to doubt are still at the disposal of the enemy, he may renew the attack by land and water on Charleston at any moment. Acting on the offensive and commanding the time of attack, he could simultaneously call troops here from North Carolina, and sooner than my command could be re-enforced from any quarter out of the department. . . . A letter to you of the 20th May further calls attention to the fact that important changes are reported to be on foot in the armament of the monitors and urges strenuously that Fort Sumter be armed comfortably with the original plan, with the heaviest guns, rifled or smooth bore, which could be obtained, in anticipation of a renewal of the attack of the 7th April. I was informed, however, through your letter of 10th June, that Northern papers report the reduction of Hunter's force by sending troops to the gulf. If this be true, you will with such force as you can properly withdraw from your defensive lines proceed to Mobile to resist an attack if one be designed at that place, but if the purpose of the enemy be to send his forces to the Mississippi, you will go on and co-operate with General Johnston in that quarter."

This I answered by telegram on the 13th of same month as follows: "Enemy's ironclads and forces still as heretofore reported to department, except a gunboat expedition reported in Altamaha, and one preparing for St. John's River, Fla. I will prepare as far as practicable for contingencies referred to in Department letter of the 10th inst. Please send me any positive information relative to movements or intentions of enemy. But in order that the War Department should be thoroughly cognizant of the state of affairs in my department, I further addressed to you on the 13th June a letter in which I pointed out how utterly insufficient were the forces at my command to resist those of the enemy and that on my responsibility I could not further deplete the force in the department. I drew your attention in the same letter to the danger of an attack by way of Morris Island—indeed, to the very route which General Gilmore has since operated. I take the following extracts from that letter:

". . . Thus it will be seen that the force in this department is already at the minimum necessary to hold the works around Charleston and Savannah constantly menaced by the proximity of the enemy's ironclads. The garrison of no work in this harbor can be withdrawn or diminished, as they are all necessary links in the chain of defense. Reduce the command on James Island, and the enemy may readily penetrate by such a coup de main as was attempted last year at the weakened point. James Island would then fall, and despite our harbor defenses the City of Charleston would be thrown open to bombardment. It is not safe to have less than a regiment of infantry on Morris Island, which, if once carried by the enemy, would expose Fort Sumter to be taken in reverse and demolished. . . . Late Northern papers say Admiral Du Pont has been relieved of the command of the fleet on this coast by Admiral Foot, an officer whose operations in the west evinced much activity and enterprising spirit. And even were considerable reductions made in the enemy's forces, the valuable coast districts would be left a prey to such destructive raids as devastated the Combahee a few days ago. Thus far, however, I can see no reduction. General Hunter was at Hilton Head on the 8th July; his troops hold the same positions as heretofore and apparently in the same force—a brigade on Folley, one on Seabrooks Island and the balance on the islands about Port Royal. One of these monitors is at Hilton Head and five in the North Edisto. Nor has the number of their gunboats and transports diminished or at any time recently been increased, as must have been the case had a material removal of troops taken place."

On the 25th June his Excellency, President Davis, telegraphed the following: "From causes into which it is needless to enter, the control of the Mississippi connection between the States east and west of it will be lost unless Johnston is strongly and promptly re-enforced within the next sixty days. Can you give him further aid without the probable loss of Charleston and Savannah? I need not state to you that the issue is vital to the Confederacy." My answer was: "Telegram received. No more troops can be spared from this department without losing railroad and country between here and Savannah. Georgetown District will also have to be abandoned. See my letter to General Cooper of the 15th inst."

Thus on the 10th July, 1863, I had but 5,861 men in the First Military District guarding the fortifications around Charleston (or more than one-third the troops in my department) with an

9—H

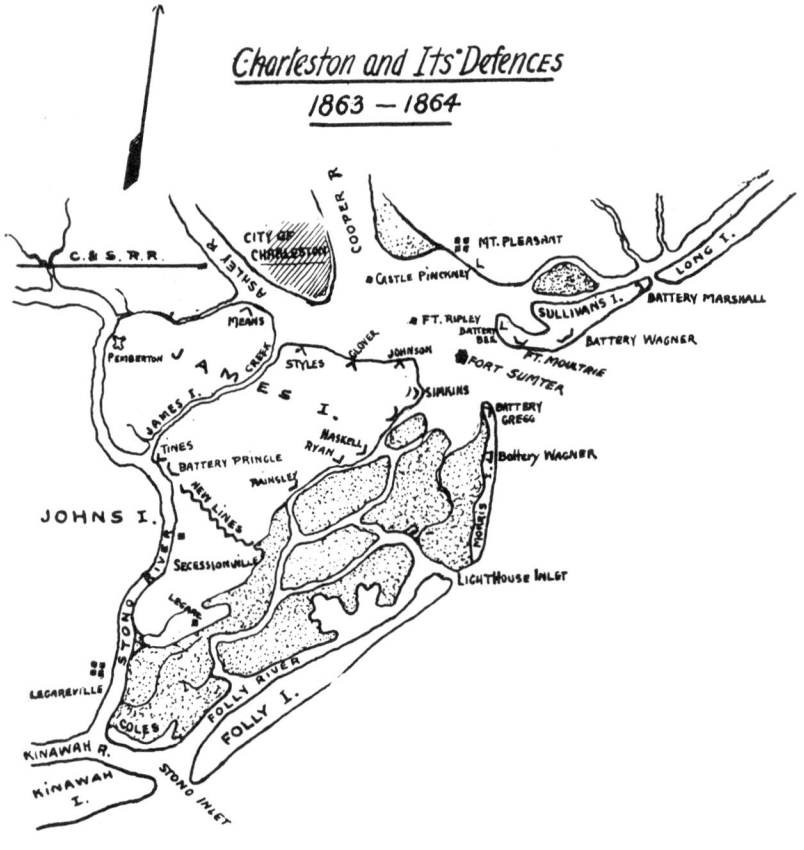

Charleston and Its Defences
1863 — 1864

enemy whose base of operations threatened Savannah, the line of coast, and the important railroad connecting the latter city with the former, with such immense transportation resources at his command as to enable him to concentrate and strike at will at any selected point before I could gather my troops to oppose.

In attacking Charleston itself five different routes of approach present themselves to an enemy. First, by landing a large force to the northward, say, at Bulls Bay, marching across the country and seizing Mt. Pleasant and the northern shores of the inner harbor. Second, by landing a large force to the southward, cutting the line of the Charleston and Savannah Railroad and taking Charleston in rear. Neither of these routes did I consider practicable or likely to be adopted by the enemy, as his numerical force would not have allowed him to cope with us, unless under the shelter of his gunboats and ironclads, a fact which General Gilmore has always carefully recognized. Before he adopts the overland approaches he will require a large addition to his land forces. The third, fourth and fifth approaches by James Island, Sullivan's Island and Morris Island, respectively, permitted the co-operation of the navy; and I always believed, as experience has demonstrated, that of the three immediate routes to Charleston, that by James Island was the most dangerous to us and the one which should be defended at all hazards; that by Sullivan's Island ranking next; and that by Morris Island last in importance for the following reasons: An enemy, who could gain a firm foothold on James Island and overpower its garrison (at that time having to defend a long, defective and irregular line of works), could have erected batteries commanding the Inner Harbor, at once taking in rear our outer line of defenses, and by a direct fire on Charleston compel its evacuation in a short period; because in such case it would have become of no value as a strategic position, and prudence and humanity would alike revolt at the sacrifice of life necessary to enable us to retain possession of its ruins. The route by Sullivan's Island was also of great importance, for the occupation of that island would not only have enabled the enemy to reduce Fort Sumter, as an artillery fortress, but would also have given entire control of the entrance to the inner harbor to his ironclad fleet. At that time, owing to the want of labor and of heavy guns, the important works which now line the shores of the inner harbor had not been erected and armed, and the enemy's fleet would have been able to shell the city comparatively unmolested, and by controlling and cutting off our communication with Fort Sumter and Morris Island would have soon necessitated their surrender or evacuation.

The remaining route by Morris Island was certainly the least injurious to us; for the occupation of that island by the enemy neither involved the evacuation of Fort Sumter, the destruction of the city by a direct fire as from James Island, nor the command by the ironclad fleet of movements in the inner harbor. The James Island route I had long thought the most likely to be attempted by the enemy, as its proximity to Folley Island (for many months back in their possession) gave them facilities for the execution of a coup de main, whilst the neighboring harbor of North Edisto gave their fleet a convenient shelter from bad weather, which they could not have had on the long island coast had their attack been by way of Sullivan's Island. Moreover the seizure of the island would have given the Federal Government opportunity of making capital with its own people and with foreign powers.*

To counteract these very apparent advantages of the enemy, I had several months previously planned and ordered to be erected on the south end of Morris Island suitable works. On Black Island, which lies between James and Morris Islands and from its position enfilades Light House Inlet, between Morris and Folley Islands, I had determined to build two batteries for two guns each. This island was further to have been connected with the mainland by a branch from the bridge, planned to connect James and Morris Islands, and nearly completed when the enemy made their attack in July.† At Vincent's Creek a battery had been commenced and had it been completed would have played effectively upon the sand hills on the south end of Morris Island. Battery Wagner was substantially strengthened and arranged for these guns on the sea face, but owing to the scarcity of labor

---

*Note A.

†The general is mistaken here. It should have been completed had his orders been carried out, but was in fact barely commenced. In sending General Hagood to command at Morris Island the first time, General B. spoke of this bridge as a means of communication; and could scarcely believe General Hagood, who had seen it but the day before, when he spoke of its unfinished state.—J. H.

and the want of the necessary ordnance to put in the works on the south end of Morris Island, they were not, on the 10th July, in that condition which would have characterized them had I had sufficient labor, transportation and ordnance at my disposal. Labor and transportation have always been serious drawbacks, not only to the defense of Charleston, but of the whole department. In reference to the labor question, I may here state that no subject relative to the defense of this department has engrossed more of my attention. Constant appeals were made to the Governors and Legislature of South Carolina and to eminent citizens since my first arrival, but few seemed to appreciate the vital necessity of securing the proper amount of slave labor for the fortifications of Charleston, and instead of the State providing 2,500 negroes monthly, as desired by me for Charleston, I received for the first six months of 1863 the following number of negroes from the State authorities, viz.: In January, 196; in February, 261; March, 864; April, 491; May, 107, and June, 60, being 1,979 in all, and an average of 350 monthly. Consequently, I had to detain these hands longer than 30 days, which was the original term of service required for each negro. This step caused considerable discontent among the owners of slaves, and in the month of July, 1863, the number of negro hands in the employ of the engineer department, provided under my call on the State, amounted to only 299 hands. In the meanwhile the troops of the command, in addition to their regular duties, were employed in erecting fortifications, nearly the whole of the works on the south end of Morris Island having been thrown up by its garrison. The engineer department used every exertion to hire labor, but their efforts were not crowned with appreciable success.

In the middle of June the batteries on the south end of Morris Island were engaged with the enemy on Folley Island, and undoubtedly retarded the progress of their operations, as the following extract from the reports of Brigadier-General Ripley will show:

". . . June 12th, 1863.—The enemy having advanced light guns to the extremity of Folley Island (Little Folley) yesterday to shell the wreck of the steamer 'Ruby' now ashore at Light House Inlet, in accordance with directions, Captain Mitchel, commanding the batteries on south end of Morris Island, opened fire, silencing them at the second shot. This morning I gave instructions to open fire in case he observed any indications of work on Little Folley on the part of the enemy; and this afternoon. about 5 o'clock, seeing parties apparently at work, he commenced shelling. About fifty men left Little Folley for the main island. The enemy replied from his batteries on Big Folley, and from his light guns." Again, on the 14th June, the same officer reports: ". . . The enemy having appeared to be at work on Little Folley, Lieutenant-Colonel Yates opened fire upon them, shelling them for about three-quarters of an hour, and putting a stop to their operations, which appeared to be erecting a shelter or battery near the inlet.*" At the time of the attack on Charleston in the beginning of April the enemy occupied Big Folley† and Seabrooks Island in force estimated at one or two brigades. This force was increased to about four brigades before July 10th, a considerable number of troops landing on Coles and James Islands. During the latter part of June and up to the first week in July, no extraordinary activity was manifested by the enemy. On Big Folley Island they were occupied as usual in fortifying the neck. strongly picketing Little Folley and interfering with wrecking parties on the steamer Ruby. On the morning of the 7th July, four monitors appeared off the bar, but no other increase of the fleet in that direction was observable. On the night of the 8th of July, a scouting party under Captain Charles Haskell visited Little Folley and discovered the enemy's barges collected in the creeks approaching Morris Island. Commencing on the 7th July, and for the three succeeding days, working parties of the enemy were seen engaged on Little Folley, supposed to be in erecting light works for guns. The wood on the island, but more especially the configuration of the ground which consists of sand hills, gave the enemy every facility for the concealment of his designs. On the

---

*"Most of the work on the batteries and all the transportation to them had to be done at night and in silence. . . . The fact that 47 pieces of artillery with 200 rounds of ammunition to each gun provided with parapets, splinter proof shelters and magazines were secretly placed in the battery within speaking distance of the enemy's pickets . . . furnishes by no means the least interesting incident." Gilmore's operations before Charleston, p. 26.

†The extreme north end of Folley Island at very high tides was separated from the rest of the island. This gave rise to the distinction of Big Folley and Little Folley. The island was densely wooded.—J. H.

night of the 8th July, considerable noise from chopping was heard, and in the morning some works were discernible, the wood and brush having been cleared away from their front. On the night of the 9th July, an immediate attack being anticipated, the whole of the infantry force on the island was kept under arms at the south end.

At 5 o'clock on the morning of the 10th July, the enemy's attack commenced by a heavy fire from a great number of light guns, apparently placed during the last forty-eight hours in the works lately thrown up on Little Folley Island. Their monitors about the same time crossed the bar and brought their formidable armament to bear upon the left flank of our position, while several howitzers on barges on Light House Inlet flanked our right. For two hours the enemy kept up their fire from these three different points, our batteries replying vigorously. The barges of the enemy having been seen in Light House Inlet in the direction of Black Island, and Oyster Point being the most accessible point for debarkation for them, it was justly considered the one most necessary to protect, and, therefore, the infantry, consisting of the Twenty-first South Carolina, about 350 men, were stationed by Colonel R. F. Graham, the immediate commander of the island, on the peninsular leading to that point. In this position the infantry were unavoidably exposed to the fire of the boat howitzers, but sheltered by the nature of the ground from that of the guns on Little Folley.

About 7 o'clock the enemy advanced on Oyster Point in a flotilla of boats, containing between two and three thousand men, a considerable portion of whom endeavored to effect a landing, in which they were opposed by the infantry until 8 o'clock, when another force of two or three regiments made good a landing in front of our batteries on the south end of Morris Island proper. These formed a line of battle on the beach and advanced directly upon our works, throwing out on east flank numerous skirmishers who very soon succeeded in flanking and taking in reverse the batteries. After an obstinate resistance, our artillerists had to abandon their pieces and fall back, leaving in possession of the enemy three 8-inch navy guns (shells), two 8-inch seacoast howitzers, one rifle 24 dr., one 30 dr. Parrott, one 12 dr. Whitworth, and three 10-inch seacoast mortars—eleven pieces in all. Two companies of the Seventh South Carolina Battalion, which arrived about this time, were ordered to the support of the batteries, but they could not make head against the overwhelming numbers of the enemy. This success of the enemy threatened to cut off our infantry engaged at Oyster Point from their line of retreat, and, consequently, about 9 o'clock, Colonel Graham gave the order to fall back on Battery Wagner, which was accomplished under a severe flanking fire from the monitor.

The enemy thus gained possession of the south end of Morris Island by rapidly throwing across the inlet a large number of troops, which it was impossible for the available infantry on the spot, about four hundred men, to resist. It was not the erection of the works on Little Folley that caused the abandonment of our position. It was clearly the want on our side of infantry supports, and the enemy's superior number and weight of guns. The woods that remained unfelled on Little Folley were of no material use to the enemy, for, even had there been labor to remove them (which I never had), the formation of the ground being a series of ridges of sand hills formed a screen which hid the enemy's movements completely from us, and afforded all the concealment he could desire. The attack was not a surprise; neither was the erection of works on Little Folley unknown to the local commander of these headquarters. The enemy, indeed, made little effort to conceal them. With a sufficient infantry support on Morris Island, the result of the attack on the 10th July, I am confident, would have been different; but, as I have already explained, the threatening position of the enemy on James Island entirely precluded the withdrawal of a single soldier from its defense until the point of attack had been fully developed, and the only re-enforcements that could be sent to Morris Island (the Seventh South Carolina Battalion, some 300 men,) arrived too late to be of any material service on the morning of the 10th July. The long protracted defense of Battery Wagner must not be compared with the evacuation of the south end of Morris Island to the discredit of the latter movement. The two defenses are not analogous. In the one a large extent of exposed ground had to be guarded by an entirely inadequate force; in the other a strong earthwork with a narrow line of approach could be held successfully by a body of men numerically quite insufficient to have opposed the landing of an enemy on the south end of Morris Island.

Whilst the enemy on the 9th July was threatening Morris Island, he also made a strong demonstration against James Island by the Stono River. At 12 m. on that day, Colonel Simonton, commanding at Secessionville, telegraphed: "The enemy are landing on Battery Island. Their advanced pickets and our's are firing. Pickets from Grimballs (on the Stono higher up) report the enemy landing at that point." Their gunboats and a monitor proceeded up the river as far as the obstructions. On the morning of the 10th July, whilst the attack was progressing on Morris Island, Colonel Simonton telegraphed that the main body of the enemy were moving in force from Battery Island to Legare's house. Later in the day, however, he telegraphed that the reported advance was premature—"They are in force on Battery Island." Though the demonstration of the enemy on Stono and on James Island was made to distract our attention from Morris Island, yet it was made in such force that at any moment it could have been converted into a real attack of the most disastrous kind to us had the garrison been weakened to support Morris Island.

On the afternoon of the 10th July, detachments of the First, Twelfth, Eighteenth and Sixty-third Georgia, under Colonel Ormstead, arrived from the District of Georgia, and with the Twenty-first South Carolina and Nelson's Seventh South Carolina Battalion became the garrison of Battery Wagner. At daylight on the 11th July the enemy assaulted Battery Wagner and were repulsed with much loss, two officers and ninety-five men being left dead in front of our works, and six officers and one hundred and thirteen rank and file taken prisoners, about forty of the latter being wounded. Our loss was one officer and five privates wounded. During the day three monitors and three wooden gunboats shelled Battery Wagner, and in the evening a fifth monitor crossed the bar. From James Island, at 7 a. m., the report was no forward movement on that front, two gunboats and several transports off Battery Island. At 9 p. m., the enemy were reported advancing in force both towards Legare's house and Grimball's, our pickets falling back before him.

On the 12th July, the Marion Artillery, four guns and thirty-nine effectives, arrived from the Second Military District and was placed on James Island, as well as the Eleventh South Carolina, from the Third Military District, four hundred effectives, but these last soon had to be returned to guard our communication with Savannah. A portion of General Clingman's Brigade, 550 men of the Fifty-first North Carolina, and 50 men of the Thirty-first North Carolina, arrived from Wilmington about the same time in consequence of my urgent call for re-enforcements.

The enemy was occupied during the day in erecting works on the middle of Morris Island, whilst five monitors and three wooden gunboats shelled Battery Wagner. The armament of Battery Wagner was increased by four 12 dr. howitzers, two 32 dr. carronades on siege carriages.

On the 13th July, the enemy was actively engaged in throwing up works on the middle of Morris Island, but was interrupted by the fire of Gregg and Sumter. During the day four monitors, three gunboats and two mortar vessels shelled Gregg and Wagner, but with light effect and slight casualty. Four monitors only were seen with the fleet, the fifth was observed going to the south without a smokestack on the evening of the 12th. Orders were issued this day for the construction of a new battery on Shell Point (Battery Simkins) in advance of Fort Johnson for one 10-inch columbiad, one 6.40 Brooke gun and three 10-inch mortars. The armament of Fort Moultrie was ordered to be increased by guns taken from Sumter. An appeal was made to his Excellency Governor Bonham for slave labor to work on the fortification.

The arrival of Clingman's Brigade and re-enforcements from other quarters having increased to some extent my available force, the consideration arose whether or not the expulsion of the enemy from Morris Island could yet be attempted. The number of men required for such an attempt would have been 4,000, the surface of Morris Island not permitting the manœuvering of a larger force. The only hope of success lay in the possibility of our troops carrying the enemy's works before daylight, otherwise the advance and attack would necessarily have been made under the fire of the enemy's fleet, in which case it must have ended disastrously for us. After a consultation with my general officers, the idea of this attack was abandoned from the consideration that our means of transportation was so limited as to make it impossible to throw sufficient re-enforcements on Morris Island in one night and in time to allow the advance of our troops to the south end before daylight.*

Two regiments under Brigadier-General Colquitt arrived on the 14th and were sent to James Island. During the day the enemy's gunboats and mortar vessels shelled Wagner at long ranges, doing but little damage. The enemy worked hard on his Morris Island works, making considerable progress, though the fire from Fort Sumter and Batteries Gregg and Wagner annoyed him much.

The impossibility of expelling the enemy from Morris Island being fully recognized, I was reluctantly compelled to adopt the defensive. Orders were issued for closing the gateway in the gorge of Fort Sumter and removing a portion of the guns also for the construction of a covered way from Fort Moultrie to Battery Bee. During the night Brigadier-General Taliaferro, commanding at Morris Island, sent out a party of 150 men under Major Rion, of the Seventh South Carolina Battalion, who drove the enemy's pickets from the rifle pits across the island some three-quarters of a mile in front of Battery Wagner. On the 15th the enemy on Morris Island appeared to be largely re-enforced, and during the night of the 14th the frigate "Ironsides" had crossed the bar.

The enemy was busy on his works, and our men employed in repairing damages in Battery Wagner, and answering the fire of the monitors and gunboats. The following instructions were given the engineer department: To have Shell Point Battery constructed for three guns instead of two; the mortar batteries at Fort Johnson to be converted into gun batteries for one heavy rifled gun, or 10-inch columbiad each; to strengthen the gorge wall of Fort Sumter by means of wet cotton bales filled in between with sand and kept moist by means of tubes or hose from upper turpline. General Ripley was also instructed to reduce the force on Morris Island to a command simply competent to hold the works against a coup de main, also to furnish the troops on that island with several hundred empty rice casks for the con-

---

*Note B.

struction of "rat holes" in the sand hills in rear of Battery Wagner.* Instructions were given to the chief of subsistence to keep rations on Morris Island for five thousand men for thirty days and on James Island for five thousand men for fifteen days, with a reserve supply in the city. On the same day the enemy's pickets along the Stono on James Island were observed to be increased by negro troops. Brigadier-General Hagood made a reconnoisance of the enemy in his front on James Island. At daybreak on the morning of the 16th July Brigadier-General Hagood, in accordance with instructions, attacked the enemy on James Island, driving them to Battery Island under shelter of their gunboats. The loss was small on both sides; three men killed, twelve wounded and three missing on our side. The enemy left forty killed on the field and fourteen prisoners (negroes) taken by us prisoners. This retreat of the enemy was followed by the advance of our troops who have occupied the ground ever since. In the engagement the gunboat Pawnee was forced to retire down the Stono under fire of our light artillery.* During the day the monitors, gunboats and mortar vessels shelled Battery Wagner. The enemy worked diligently on their batteries. In the evening large bodies of infantry were landed on the south end of Morris Island.

Colonel Harris, chief of engineers, was directed to increase the batteries on James Island bearing on Morris Island by at least twenty guns on siege carriages, so as to envelope in a circle of fire the enemy whenever he should gain possession of the north end of Morris Island; all works to be pushed on night and day.

On the morning of the 17th the enemy's fleet left the Stono River after embarking his forces at Battery Island, and appeared to concentrate them on Little Folley and Morris Islands. Both the fleet and land batteries shelled Wagner throughout the day, answered vigorously by our guns. The construction by the enemy of batteries on Morris Island proceeded rapidly. In a telegraphic dispatch today, I pointed out that the contest had passed into one of engineering skill, where, with sufficient time, labor and long-range guns, our success was very probable, owing to the

*Not used to any extent.—J. H.

*Note C.

plan of defense adopted; otherwise it was doubtful in proportion to the lack of these elements of success.

The fire of the enemy's batteries from this date prevented communication with Cummings Point during daylight, and henceforth it had to be effected at night; the very limited transportation at my command added considerably to the difficulty of relieving the garrison at Battery Wagner as often as I could have wished. The time of service was at first limited to forty-eight hours, but owing to this difficulty it was now extended to three days.

On the morning of the 18th July it became evident that the enemy were about to attempt serious operations against Wagner. The south end of Morris Island was crowded with troops, and in their batteries and advanced works great activity was apparent, large bodies of men being engaged in pushing them rapidly to completion. Troops from Folley were being continually landed on Morris Island; these advanced and took up position in line of battle behind their breastworks. At 8:10 a. m. Battery Wagner opened; five minutes afterward Battery Gregg joined. At 10 a. m. four of the enemy's vessels were in action. At 11:30 Fort Sumter opened on the enemy's rifle pits on Morris Island. The guns of Wagner about this time seemed to harass the enemy's working parties extremely. At 12:10 the frigate "Ironsides" and one monitor moved up abreast of Wagner, and at 12:30 were joined by two other monitors, when they opened fire on the work. At 1 p. m. the Ironsides, five monitors, a large wooden frigate, six mortar boats (these last could get the range without exposing themselves) and the land batteries mounting five guns, concentrated their fire on Battery Wagner and continued it till dark. The enemy's fire throughout the day was very rapid, averaging fourteen shots per minute, and unparelleled until this epoch of the siege in the weight of the projectiles thrown. Brigadier-General Taliaferro, commanding at Battery Wagner, estimated that there were nine thousand shot and shell thrown in and against the battery in the eleven and a half hours that the bombardment lasted. During that time our casualties in the work were four killed and eleven wounded. During the day the garrison replied slowly to the terrific fire to which it was exposed, whilst Fort Sumter and Battery Gregg fired rapidly. Circumstances indicating an attack at dark, Brigadier-General Hagood was relieved from the command of James Island, and, with Colonel Harrison's Thirty-second Georgia Regiment, was ordered to the re-enforcement of Morris Island. During the passage of these troops the assault was made and repulsed; but they arrived in time to dislodge a portion of the enemy who had gained a footing in the southeastern salient of Battery Wagner.

The garrison of Battery Wagner consisted of the Charleston Battalion, the Fifty-first North Carolina and the Thirty-first North Carolina, two companies of the Sixty-third Georgia Heavy Artillery and two companies of the First South Carolina Infantry, acting as heavy artillery. During the bombardment the garrison were kept under the shelter of the bomb-proofs, with the exception of the Charleston Battalion, which was stationed along the parapet of the work, a position which they gallantly maintained throughout the day, exposed to a free d'enfre. At a quarter past 8 p. m. the assaulting lines of the enemy were seen advancing from their works, and the bombardment from the fleet and land batteries subsided. The garrison were quickly called to their allotted positions and with the exception of one regiment responded manfully to the summons. The Charleston Battalion guarded the right of the work and the Fifty-first North Carolina the center. These two regiments drove back the enemy opposed to them with frightful slaughter, whilst our guns discharging grape and cannister into their shattered ranks completed their discomfiture. On the left of the work, however, the Thirty-first North Carolina disgracefully abandoned their position, and no resistance being offered at that point the enemy succeeded in crossing the ditch and gaining a footing upon the rampart. The main body of the enemy, after vainly endeavoring to gain a position on the parapet, retreated in disorder under a destructive fire from our guns, including those of Fort Sumter. The ditch and slope of the southeastern salient was then swept with a fire of grape and musketry to prevent the enemy lodged there from retiring, and after a brief resistance they surrendered.*

---

*This fire was very destructive, as the torn and mangled corpses at that point showed next morning; yet the enemy repelled an assaulting party organized by Taliaferro from the Charleston Battalion, Captain Ryan commanding. Ryan was killed; the fire was kept up, and the re-enforcements with Hagood arriving, two companies were placed in position for another assault, when, upon demand, the enemy surrendered—over a hundred.—J. H.

The assault was terribly destructive to the enemy; his loss in killed and wounded and prisoners must have been three thousand, as eight hundred bodies were buried in front of Battery Wagner next day.

The enemy's forces on this occasion consisted of troops from Connecticut, Pennsylvania, New Hampshire and the Fifty-fourth Massachusetts (negro) regiments—the whole said to have been under command of General Seymour, with Brigadier-General Strong and Colonel Putnam commanding brigades. General Seymour is said to have been wounded, and Brigadier-General Strong and Colonel Putnam killed. General Taliaferro reported that his troops, with the exception of the Thirty-first North Carolina, behaved throughout with the utmost gallantry. The heroic conduct of the Fifty-first North Carolina. counterbalanced the unworthy behavior of the Thirty-first and retrieved the honor of the State. Our loss during the bombardment and assault was 174 killed and wounded.†

At 1 a. m. on the morning of the 19th, during the engagements, I telegraphed General Ripley at Fort Sumter that Morris Island must be held at all costs for the present, and re-enforcements must be thrown there to push any advantage possible before daylight. The 19th passed in comparative quiet. The enemy sent in a flag of truce to arrange for the burial of the dead. Brigadier-General Hagood reported that 600 of the enemy's dead in and around our works were buried by our troops and at least 200 more were by the enemy.‡

The strengthening of the gorge wall of Sumter by cotton bales and sand proceeded rapidly. On the 20th the enemy opened fire from two new batteries. Throughout the day the fleet joined in the bombardment and were answered by Sumter, Gregg and Wagner. At 3 p. m. information was received that a 10-inch gun at Battery Wagner was dismounted. I impressed upon General

---

†Gilmore says he sent twelve regiments to the assault, but does not give their strength or his loss.—J. H.

‡My recollection is that there was no flag, but a practical truce was maintained for burial purposes all day, the enemy's parties being permitted to come as far as our picket at the rifle pits. From the number of dead in the confined space before the battery, in its ditch and on its rampart, the carnage impressed me more than any witnessed during the war. They absolutely lay in places crossed and piled, and horribly mangled by artillery; in many instances brains here, a leg there; sometimes a head without a body and sometimes a body without a head.—J. H.

Hagood, commanding the work, that I did not consider a 10-inch columbiad essential to the defense of the position for which siege guns, musketry, stout arms and hearts, and the strength of sand parapets must be relied on.* Orders were, however, issued for the remounting of the 10-inch gun if practicable.

The enemy's fleet this morning consisted of four monitors, the Ironsides, and seventeen vessels inside the bar; fourteen vessels outside; thirty vessels in Folley River; one gunboat and four vessels in North Edisto, and one steam frigate, one sloop of war, one gunboat and thirty-four transports at Hilton Head.

General Ripley was instructed to have the guns for Battery Haskell mounted immediately, and to open fire with them as soon as practicable. Brigadier-General Mercer was telegraphed to send on, if practicable, another 10-inch columbiad from the Savannah works. At 2 p. m. a shell struck Fort Sumter, and some eight or ten 80 dr. Parrott shot were fired at the fort from a distance of 3,500 yards. Five casualties in Wagner today and one in Sumter.

On the 21st a flag of truce was sent in with a communication from General Gilmore requesting an interview between General Vogdes and the officer commanding Battery Wagner. The proposal was agreed to and the flag of truce was met by an officer from that work. While the conference was proceeding the fleet opened a bombardment on Wagner. This gross violation of the usages of war was responded to by General Hagood by an abrupt termination of the interview. During the day the enemy's gunboats and land batteries shelled Battery Wagner. The enemy had apparently mounted eight new guns in their batteries. Colonel Rhett reported that from the want of proper appliances he had been unable to dismount the guns in Fort Sumter which I had ordered to be removed. The bombardment continued throughout the day of the 22nd, with an interval, when General Vogdes, U. S. A., requested, under a flag of truce, another interview with Brigadier-General Hagood. This was refused until an apology should be made for the breach of truce the day before. This having been given and deemed satisfactory, General Vogdes verbally proposed an exchange of prisoners, mentioning that they had but a few of ours, all except those recently cap-

---

*Note D.

tured having been sent north; that as we had the excess "of course we could select whom to exchange." He abstained from any reference to negroes, whilst intimating that a mutual parole of prisoners without regard to excess would be agreeable.*

The following instructions were given to Brigadier-General Ripley: Not to open from the new James Island batteries until their completion; then to carry on a vigorous fire on the enemy's works, sorties to be made at night whenever practicable.†

In my telegram to you of this date, I mentioned the continued re-enforcement of the enemy; that I had to guard these important lines of approach, James, Morris and Sullivan's Islands, and requested the balance of Colquitt's Brigade with more troops as soon as practicable.

No gun was fired on either side during the 23rd. Our men were engaged in repairing damages and the enemy in erecting batteries and throwing up traverses to protect them from the James Island batteries.

On the morning of the 24th a heavy bombardment was opened on Battery Wagner from five monitors, two gunboats, two mortar vessels, the Ironsides and land batteries, which continued till 9:30 a. m., when the steamer with prisoners on board proceeded to the fleet and the exchange was effected as previously agreed on. "Upon the arrival of the boat in the neighborhood of the place appointed, the fire of the enemy, which for a portion of the time had been very heavy, ceased. The 10-inch gun on the sea face was dismounted and one of the magazines so much exposed as to require the removal of the ammunition. General Taliaferro, who had previously relieved General Hagood in command, antici-pating a renewal of the bombardment upon the completion of the exchange of prisoners, as a matter of prudent precaution requested that all necessary arrangements should be made for the transfer of the troops from the island in case of necessity. The enemy, however, did not renew his attack and the time thus allowed was improved in repairing damages. . . . Instructions were sent General Taliaferro not to abandon the works without'

*Note E.

†See remarks in Note D, previously cited.

10—H

express orders to that effect."* Colonel Harris, chief engineer, having inspected Battery Wagner, reported no material damage to the work; the guns on the sea face unserviceable; those on the land face in good order; the enemy's stockade within 700 yards of the work. Brigadier-General Taliaferro came to the city to confer with me personally regarding the condition of his garrison, the officers having reported their men as much dispirited. After a conference with him, I communicated my views as follows:

The position must be held if possible until the guns en route from Richmond be received and put in position. No idea of evacuation must be entertained if there is a chance at night to repair the damages done in the day. Every night preparations will be made to remove troops from Morris Island in case of need. Battery Wagner must be held and fought to the last extremity. The garrison might rest assured that every preparation will be made for their withdrawal in case of necessity.†

My telegram to you of this date was: "The enemy shelled Battery Wagner heavily this morning. Our loss one killed and seven wounded. Am anxiously waiting for heavy guns promised from Richmond. Hope to repair damages during the night."

On the 25th the enemy's fleet remained quiet on account of the high seas, and his land battery fired but little. Fort Sumter, Battery Gregg and the James Island batteries answered. A 30 dr. Parrott was again brought to bear on Fort Sumter from the same battery as on the 20th. During the day several of my new batteries were ready for their armament. The strengthening of Fort Sumter proceeded day and night; and in anticipation of the damaging effect which the enemy's rifled guns from stationary batteries would produce on this work, a partial disarmament was carried on nightly.

On Sunday, the 26th, the bombardment of the enemy slackened. During the night shelling of the enemy's works was car-

---

*The last twenty-six lines in quotation marks have been interpolated in this report as giving a fuller account of the situation. It is an extract from Ripley's Report.—J. H.

†I am inclined to think the enemy were nearer driving the garrison from the fort today than at any time until the final evacuation. The intervention of the hour agreed upon for the exchange of prisoners and the subsequent delay in assuming offensive operations were most providential. The danger from what I learned was more from demoralization of the garrison than from damage to the works.—J. H.

ried on from Fort Sumter. Re-enforcements were seen throughout the day debarking from Morris Island. I telegraphed on this day: "Have nine positions for heavy guns ready. Not one promised from Richmond has arrived. Cannot their transportation be expedited?"

The weather on the 27th was too windy for the co-operation of the fleet, which had been increased by the addition of another monitor. During today the bombardment from the land batteries slackened. Our defenses were pushed on vigorously, whilst the strengthening of Fort Sumter and the withdrawal of guns from that work proceeded. The enemy showed great activity in advancing their works, though harassed by the fire of our batteries.

On the 28th, Battery Wagner had another very severe bombardment from the enemy's land and naval batteries, but no great damage was done. Two men were killed and five wounded. My telegraphic dispatch on the evening of the 28th was: "Many transports of the enemy are arriving with troops. At least 2,500 men are required at present for James Island. Cannot they be ordered here immediately? Enemy's land and naval batteries are now playing on Wagner, which she answers bravely, assisted by Gregg and Sumter."

On the 29th, Battery Wagner was heavily bombarded throughout the day. In a telegram to you of this date notified the arrival from Richmond of some of the promised guns: "Have received four 10-inch columbiads and four 10-inch mortars. Regret to say that by order of the Secretary of the Navy two Brooke guns have been taken from me to be shut up in a new gunboat so pierced as only to give a range of a mile and a half at most."

Throughout the 30th Batteries Wagner and Gregg were subjected to a furious fire from both land batteries and fleet. As an example of the rapidity of the enemy's fire, I may mention that between the hours of 10:30 a. m. and 1 p. m. five hundred and ninety-nine shots were fired at our different batteries—principally Gregg and Wagner. During the same time one hundred and ten shots were fired from our works. Our loss was two killed and seven wounded in Battery Wagner—no damage of any consequence to the works. Brigadier-General Ripley was instructed to transport as early as possible one of the 10-inch columbiads recently arrived from Richmond to Battery Wagner, which was accomplished on the night of the 30th.

The enemy fired heavily on Wagner throughout the 31st. Our loss was seven wounded. Our new works progressed very satisfactorily, and the strengthening of Sumter and the removal of its guns went on rapidly.

The enemy's fire on the 1st of August was slack and did but little execution, save to the front traverse of the 8-inch shell gun at Wagner, which did not, however, disable it. The casualties today were only two wounded. The enemy was industriously engaged in throwing up new batteries and advancing his trenches. Every endeavor was made by firing from Sumter, Gregg, Wagner and the James Island batteries to annoy and delay his approaches.

Throughout the morning of the 2nd August the enemy did not answer our fire, but about 2 o'clock they opened vigorously on Wagner. The damage, however, done to the work was comparatively small. In my telegram of that date I mentioned that "Transports going south from Stono, filled with troops, are reported, probably intended to operate against Savannah. Cannot some of my troops sent to General Johnston be ordered back for the defense of that city?"

Orders were given to the chief quartermaster to have trains in waiting sufficient to transport two regiments of infantry to Savannah. The difficulties attending the defense of Charleston were greatly increased by the celerity with which the enemy could remove his operations from one point to another and from the paucity of troops in my command. Savannah and the coast line were nearly denuded. All these places had to be guarded.

Instructions were given for increasing the armament of Fort Johnson by two 6-40 Brooke guns, turned over by the Navy Department, and to place floating torpedoes in certain localities. Brigadier-General Mercer was instructed to forward a detachment of artillerists to relieve that from the Sixty-third Georgia which had become reduced by casualties and sickness. The ordnance department in Richmond was applied to for Coehorn mortars.

The fire of the enemy on the 3rd was not heavy, but his sharpshooting annoyed the garrison of Wagner considerably. No casualties. Brigadier-General Mercer, at Savannah, was informed that transports were moving south from here with troops and that two regiments were held in readiness to move at a moment's notice. I was informed that Evans's Brigade was ordered to Savannah from Mississippi. In a personal visit paid to Morris Island that evening I found Battery Wagner in a very serviceable condition. The work was more solidly constructed than when the attack commenced; the garrison appeared to be in fine spirits and ready to defend the work to the last. At Fort Sumter the filling of the officers' quarters and the casemates was rapidly approaching completion. An exterior sand-bag revetment was ordered for the gorge wall, as well as a series of traverses in barbette on the east, south and northeast faces, and many changes and removals in the armament.

During the 4th August but little firing occurred upon either side. Orders were given to rearrange certain guns on the batteries of James Island. Major Trezvant, commanding Charleston Arsenal, was requested to collect all of the old iron in the burnt district to cast into projectiles. Orders were given to General Ripley to arrange with Captain Tucker of the navy an attempt to capture the enemy's picket in the marsh battery near Vincent's Creek.

On the 5th, the guns in Battery Wagner were all in fighting order. Our sharpshooters, armed with Whitworth rifles, seemed to annoy the enemy greatly, who endeavored to silence their fire with Coehorn mortars. About 9 o'clock that night a picket of the enemy, which had taken possession of our unfinished battery on Vincent's Creek and, by signalling the arrival of our steamers at Cummings Point, interfered materially with our operations, was attacked by a party from the Twenty-fifth South Carolina.* The result was satisfactory. One captain and ten enlisted men were captured. Our loss one man killed. Our defensive works at Fort Sumter and elsewhere proceeded satisfactorily. The telegram of this day was: "Enemy still being largely re-enforced from the northward. Cannot General Colquitt's other regiments be ordered here at once? Other troops are absolutely needed."

Throughout the 6th the enemy fired occasional shots from his

---

*Under Captain Sellars.—J. H.

land batteries and fleet, without material result. One casualty occurred. Our batteries fired at intervals throughout the day. Brigadier-General Cobb was ordered by telegraph to send 500 infantry and one light battery to report to Brigadier-General Mercer at Savannah. The enemy on Morris Island worked laboriously on his trenches, whilst strong **re-enforcements of** troops were daily seen arriving.

On the 7th, I received a telegram from you, informing me that the balance of Colquitt's Brigade was ordered to Charleston. There was little firing throughout the day and two casualties occurred on Morris Island.

On the 8th, Brigadier-General Evans reported his arrival at Savannah. A large increase was visible in the enemy's fleet in the Stono. During the day the firing from our batteries was carried on at intervals, but the enemy remained quiet until evening, when they opened on Battery Wagner and continued the fire throughout the night. Instructions were issued to the chief engineer to expedite the putting up in Fort Sumter of the sand-bag "chemise" to the gorge wall, the interior traverses and merlons, and to erect a covered way from Gregg to Battery Wagner.

The firing of the enemy during the morning of the 9th was heavy and rapid from his land batteries. The officer in command of the advanced pickets reported that the enemy worked industriously in his trenches till 2 a. m. The fire of our sharpshooters evidently annoyed the enemy much, as he occasionally fired with great spirit but ineffectually to dislodge them.* The effective force on Morris Island was 663 infantry, 248 artillery and 11 cavalry—total 922. During the day I received the following telegram from Brigadier-General M. Jenkins, dated Petersburg, Va.: "My scouts report shipment of troops, both infantry and cavalry, from Norfolk; supposed to be for Charleston; large quantities of forage shipped. Cavalry left 6th inst."

The chief engineer was instructed to lay out and erect a line of works on James Island, from Secessionville to Dills's house on the Stono, in lieu of the present defensive lines; to consist of lunettes with closed gorges; disposed at one-half to three-quarters of a mile apart and connected by cumulative infantry lines.

---

*Note F.

Captain Tucker, Confederate States Navy, was informed of the practice of the enemy of putting out boat pickets at night to observe the movement of our transportation to Morris Island; and it was suggested to him that steps should be taken by the navy to break up these pickets. Upon the approach of our steamers signals would be exchanged between the enemy's boats and their land batteries, and immediately a heavy fire upon Cummings' Point rendered our communication extremely dangerous and difficult. At times also the enemy illuminated the landing with a powerful light, so as to prevent the approach of steamers and forcing us to transport our supplies of men and munitions in small boats.

During the 10th the enemy remained comparatively quiet until about 8 p. m., when he opened briskly on Wagner. On our side fire was kept up from Battery Simkins (Shell Point) with columbiads from 11 a. m. to 11 p. m., when mortar firing was resumed and continued until morning. The enemy was busy during the night and his advanced works were now about 600 yards from Wagner, though no guns were yet in that position. My telegram to you of this date was: "Nothing of importance has occurred since yesterday. Evans's Brigade is arriving in Savannah and Colquitt's Regiment arriving here."

About 7 o'clock, on the morning of the 11th, the fleet and land batteries opened heavily on Wagner and were replied to by Sumter, Gregg and Simkins.* One casualty occurred during the day, the enemy as well as ourselves working persistently in spite of the heat which was excessive. Our garrison of Morris Island consisted of 1,245 of all arms.

At 5:45 a. m. on the 12th, the enemy opened on Fort Sumter with an 8-inch Parrott gun, firing from a battery to the north and west of Craig's Hill on Morris Island, the distance estimated to be at least 4,400 yards. Eleven shots in all were fired at the

---

*"About 2 o'clock on the morning of the 11th, Wagner opened a heavy fire which with the fire of James Island batteries and Sumter stopped our working parties entirely for the first time in the siege."—Enemy's Siege Journal. I had commenced this fire when Colonel Harrison arrived to relieve me.—J. H.

The Journal goes on:

"This was the most spiteful fire from Wagner since the 18th July. Indeed that work has been very quiet since that time for fear of drawing fire upon itself. Our reply to fire from whatever direction has been directed upon Wagner."—Operations against Charleston, p. 193.

fort. Four missed, three struck outside, and four struck within the fort. Again, at 5:30 p. m., the enemy opened from the same battery on Fort Sumter, firing at intervals of ten minutes till dark. Eleven 8-inch rifled shot struck the fort. Heavy firing was carried on throughout the day against Battery Wagner. Fort Sumter and Battery Gregg as well as Simkins directed their fire throughout the day against the enemy's working parties on the left of his approach and dispersed them, stopping the work they were engaged on. At dark, Battery Wagner opened with eight guns on the enemy's advanced trenches, and in conjunction with Sumter and Simkins prevented any progress on the part of the enemy.* His batteries in rear replied to the fire of Wagner and interrupted our communications with Cumming's Point.

On the 13th, the enemy endeavored several times to repair the damage done to his advanced works, but well directed shots from Wagner as often drove him back. The batteries in rear of the fleet then opened on Wagner and Gregg, and were answered by Sumter and Simkins.

At 5:30 a. m., the enemy opened with 8-inch Parrotts from the same battery as the day before, firing two or three hours only. At 11 a. m., three or four wooden gunboats approached within 4,000 and 5,000 yards of Sumter and opened slow fire. They were armed with heavy rifled guns. Some fifteen shots were fired at this great range; three only struck the fort; one shot passed over at great elevation and dropped a mile to the westward. At 5 p. m., the enemy opened again on the fort with the 8-inch Parrotts; no great damage was done, the farthest penetration into the brickwork was four feet.

On the 14th, the land batteries opened on Sumter, firing three shots; two struck. About 11 a. m. the wooden gunboats shelled the fort at long range; and at 5:15 p. m. the land batteries again opened on the fort. Throughout the day the enemy remained quiet, firing occasionally, and were replied to by our batteries. The sharpshooters on both sides kept up an incessant fire. During the night the fire of Battery Wagner put a stop to the operations on its front. The strengthening of Fort Sumter advanced rapidly

---

*"August 12 . . . Owing to a heavy fire *from Wagner*, we did not commence work until 11 (at night) and consequently did not accomplish much. . . . The infantry detail . . . broke and became so scattered it was impossible to collect them again." Operations against Charleston, p. 195.—J. H.

Battery Wagner 1863

SKETCH OF BATTERY WAGNER, 1863.—J. H.

1. Fieldpiece. 2. 10″ Mortar. 3 and 4. Carronades. 5. 32 dr. 6. 8″ Navy. 7. 32 dr. 8. 8″ Navy. 9. 32 dr. 10. 8″ Howitzer. 12. 32 dr. Rifled. 13. 10″ Columbiad. 14. 8″ Gun. 15 and 16. 12 dr. Field Howitzers.

both day and night. Brigadier-General Ripley was instructed as to the armament of a certain position of the new lines on James Island and of a new battery thrown up near Fort Johnson.

During the greater part of the 15th the enemy, both on land and sea, were unusually quiet, only occasionally firing at Battery Wagner. Later in the day they opened with some vigor on Battery Gregg. The enemy's fleet consisted this morning of the Ironsides, six monitors, eight gunboats, three mortar vessels, with thirteen other vessels inside and seven outside the bar. At Hilton Head, fifty-two vessels, including gunboats and ironclads. My telegram of this date was: "No change worth recording since yesterday. . . . Sand bag revetment of gorge wall of Sumter and traverses inside of fort progressing as rapidly as means of transportation will admit."

On the 16th, the enemy's batteries fired but little on Gregg and Wagner, but during the afternoon the two 8-inch Parrots opened on Sumter, throwing forty-eight shell. Four passed over, four fell short, two struck inside the parade and thirty-two hit in various places, exterior and interior. At this date, the armament of the fort consisted of thirty-eight guns and two mortars; at least twenty guns having been withdrawn since the landing of the enemy on Morris Island. Orders were given to Brigadier-General Ripley to remove to Battery Gregg the two mortars in Sumter as soon as it should become impossible to use them to advantage in the latter work, and to transport to other points every gun in Sumter not actually required for its defence and the new relations of that work to the defence of the harbor. The chief engineer was instructed to strengthen Castle Pinckney with sand bags; Fort Johnson to be arranged for two additional 10-inch guns; and positions to be arranged for three 10-inch guns to be placed on the James Island shore of the harbor.

Battery Wagner was bombarded heavily by the enemy about daylight on the 17th, their guns were then turned on Sumter and a heavy cannonade was directed against that work. About 9 o'clock the Ironsides and six monitors joined in the action. During the engagements Captain Rodgers, commanding the Weehawken, was killed in the pilot house of his ship. In the twenty-four hours 948 shot were fired against Fort Sumter; 448

struck outside, 233 inside, and 270 passed over. The casualties in the fort amounted to fourteen.

On the 18th, 19th, 20th, 21st, 22nd, 23rd of August the fierce bombardment of Fort Sumter by the enemy continued both from his land and naval batteries. From the 17th to the 23rd inclusive he fired against the fort a total of 5,643 shot, of which 2,643 struck inside, 1,699 outside and 1,301 missed. These projectiles were fired from 30 dr. and 300 dr. Parrotts and from 15-inch smooth bore guns. An average of 150 pounds per shot would give a weight of nearly 385 tons discharged against the walls of Fort Sumter during this period of seven days. At the end of this time nearly all the guns remaining in the fort were unserviceable and the damage to the gorge wall and the northwest face by the severe fire great; but the sand that had been placed upon the outside of the gorge wall, in conjunction with the filling up of the barracks and casemates with cotton bales, and above all the crumbling under the enemy's fire of the masonry converted this portion of Fort Sumter into a mass of debris and rubbish on which the enemy's powerful artillery could make but little impression. Throughout the siege the unremitting exertions of the engineer corps hourly increased the defensive power of the work.

The following extract from the journal of the engineer officer at Fort Sumter for August 23rd will show the condition of the work at that date: ". . . The northwest front has now five arches with ramparts fallen in; northeast barbette battery unserviceable; east front scarp much scaled by slant fire, with large craters under traverses; principal injury at level of arches and terreplein; two-thirds of southern wall east of magazine damaged; stone abutment unhurt and protected by rubbish; gorge not damaged since yesterday. Another shot has penetrated above sand filling of second-story rooms, making three since the attack began. East barbette parapets much loosened and undermined, though not displaced. One 10-inch and one 11-inch gun untouched. Brooke gun carriage shattered, but can easily be remounted on 10-inch columbiad carriage."

During the seven days that the enemy so vigorously bombarded Sumter his approaches to Wagner were slowly pushed forward under the fire of our guns and sharpshooters. On the

21st he made an unsuccessful attack on our rifle pits directly in front of that battery. The same day General Gilmore sent a demand, under flag of truce, for the surrender of Fort Sumter and Morris Island, with the threat that in the case of non-compliance he would open fire on the city; four hours were allowed for a reply. This communication was received at the headquarters of the department at 10:45 p. m.; the enemy carried his threat into execution by throwing several shells into the city on the morning of the 23rd, at about 1:30 a. m.

On the 24th, the fire against Fort Sumter lessened considerably; not more than 150 shot were thrown against it in the course of the day.

Every endeavor was made to retard the approach of the enemy to Battery Wagner. His working parties were fired upon by the guns of the battery during the night, but during the day this had to be discontinued and the embrasures closed to prevent our guns from being dismounted. Until 3 o'clock of the 25th, enemy's fire was principally directed against Sumter. After that time Wagner was fiercely bombarded, as well as the space between that work and the rifle pits. At dark the enemy endeavored to carry these pits but were repulsed. Our loss was five killed and nineteen wounded.

A very large amount of ammunition and ordnance stores were removed from Fort Sumter during the night.

On the 26th, 630 shot were fired at Sumter; Wagner and Gregg received the bulk of the fire. At 5 o'clock in the evening the enemy concentrated his fire on the rifle pits in front of Wagner. Between 7 and 8 p. m. the rifle pits were carried by an overwhelming force and seventy-six out of the eighty-nine men of the Sixty-first North Carolina, who formed the picket, were captured.*

The firing on the 27th against Sumter was limited to four shots. In front of Wagner the enemy had advanced his trenches to within 300 yards of the work, whilst the number of his guns and the accuracy of his fire prevented the opening of its embrasures except during the night. The Honorable Secretary of War informed me by telegraph, in answer to a request that I made for the services of some of the sailors stationed in Savannah,

---

*Note G.

that the Secretary of the Navy declined sending sailors from Savannah and urged a detail of men. I replied by letter setting forth the fact that the army was depleted already by details for the navy, and that no more can be spared. The importance of keeping our water transportation to Morris Island in an efficient condition was represented, and that without an additional force of boatmen it could not be preserved. Further, that our iron-clads at Savannah were safely sheltered behind obstructions, and were a portion of their crews sent to Charleston they could be returned in case of an emergency there.

On the 28th, the enemy were extremely quiet, firing only six shots at Sumter; but his approach as to Wagner advanced rapidly notwithstanding the fire from Gregg, the James Island batteries and the sharpshooters in Wagner. The enemy did not fire at Sumter during the 29th, but worked industriously upon his approaches to Wagner. His advanced works were shelled throughout the day by Wagner, Moultrie and the James Island batteries. During the night the enemy's guns were silent in front of Wagner, but they renewed the bombardment of Sumter before daylight.

During the day of the 30th they threw 634 shot against Sumter. The enemy was also busy completing his advanced works, though greatly disturbed by the fire from Wagner and the James Island batteries, which compelled them to desist from the work of advancing a sap to the left of Battery Wagner. In the evening the enemy opened a brisk fire on Wagner, both with monitors and Parrott guns. No serious damage was done the work, but several casualties occurred. During the night Wagner kept up a steady and effective fire on the enemy's advanced works.

Early on the morning of the 31st, as the steamer Sumter was returning from Morris Island with troops on board, she was unfortunately fired into from the Sullivan's Island batteries and sunk. Four men were killed or drowned, and the greater portion of the arms lost. Between 11 and 12 m. one of the monitors approached Fort Moultrie, and when within range was opened upon by that work. The enemy replied with schrapnell, all of which fell short; and after about an hour's engagement the monitor withdrew. About 2 p. m. the enemy again approached with four monitors and engaged the fort for four hours. A steady

fire was kept up on them from Fort Moultrie and other Sullivan's
fire was kept up on them from Fort Moultrie and other Sullivan
Island batteries. During the engagement the enemy fired sixty
shot, striking Moultrie fifteen times but doing no damage. The
fort fired 132 shot. The enemy's fire on Sumter was slack
throughout the day.

Captain Leroy Hammond, Twenty-fifth South Carolina Volunteers, reported today that in obedience to instructions he had
made a reconnoisance of Light House Inlet on the south side of
Black Island. On the island he saw pickets and bivouac fires, but
discovered no entrenchments. During the night the enemy succeeded in advancing their sap a short distance towards Wagner,
notwithstanding the heavy fire that was kept up on them from
that work.

At daylight, the 1st September, the enemy opened on Wagner
with mortars and continued at intervals during the entire day.
The two 32 dr. howitzers in the salient of the work were disabled.
From early morning their land batteries kept up a heavy fire on
Fort Sumter, firing throughout the day 382 shot; 166 struck
outside, 95 inside and 121 missed. This fire was very destructive,
disabling the remaining guns en barbette and damaging the fort
considerably. An extract from the report of the engineer in
charge gives the following account of its condition: ". . .
Towards noon the effect of the fire was to carry away at one fall
four rampart arches on the northeast front with terreplein platform and guns, thus leaving on this front only one arch and a
half which are adjacent to the east spiral stair. Some of the
lower casemate piers of the same front have been seriously
damaged, rendering unsafe the service of two guns hitherto
available in that quarter. On the exterior, the chief injury done
is to be noticed on the southeast pan coupiè and two next upper
casemates on east front. From these localities the scarp has
fallen away completely and left the arches exposed, as well as
the sand filling half down to the floor of second tier."

At 11:40 a. m., on the 2nd September, six monitors opened on
Sumter at distances of 800 to 1,000 yards. They were joined at
1 p. m. by the Ironsides, and together fired 185 shot, of which
116 struck outside, 35 inside and 34 passed over. The projectiles
used were 8-inch Parrott rifle shell and 11- and 15-inch smooth-

bore shot and shell. Fort Sumter was unable to answer, not having a gun in working order, but a heavy fire was kept up on the fleet by Fort Moultrie with good effect, two of the monitors being apparently injured and requiring assistance when they retired. The effect of this fire on Sumter is thus described by the engineer officer in charge: ". . . The chief external injury has been done on the east scarp, which now has lost its integrity and hangs upon the arches apparently in blocks and detached masses."

The remainder of the day was passed in comparative quiet. The fleet was occupied in placing sand bags on the decks of the monitors. The enemy's land batteries fired but 148 shot, of which 38 were directed against Sumter. In the same period our batteries fired 66 times. During the night the enemy was engaged in front of Wagner in strengthening his advanced position, which was then within 80 to 100 yards of the salient. Owing to the difficulty of transporting ammunition to Wagner the fire of that work was slack.

Early on the morning of the 3rd, the enemy opened on Wagner with mortars and continued it throughout the day. Fort Sumter was not fired at. In that work all hands were busy in repairing damages. During the past night, as usual, large quantities of ordnance stores and several guns were removed. The condition of the fort of this date was as follows: The northeast and northwest terrepleins had fallen in, and the western wall had a crack entirely through from parapet to beam. The greater portion of the southern wall was down, the upper east magazine penetrated, and lower east magazine wall cracked. The eastern wall itself nearly shot away and large portions down, ramparts gone, and nearly every casemate breached. The casemates on the eastern face were still filled with sand and gave some protection to the garrison from shell. Not a single gun remained en barbette, and but a single casemate gun that could be fired—a 32 dr. smoothbore on the west face.

During the night of the 3rd, Wagner fired steadily and the James Island batteries occasionally. Throughout the 4th the enemy confined themselves to shelling Wagner and were answered by the James Island guns. During the night of the 4th their approach was pushed close to Wagner.

At 12 m., on the 5th, the Federal flag was abreast of the south angle of the work. Throughout the day a very heavy fire was concentrated on Wagner from the Ironsides, monitors and land batteries, which severely injured the work; our casualties were also greatly increased, some forty occurring during the day. Large bodies of troops were transferred from Folley to Morris Island, and other indications pointed to an early assault. There is good reason to believe that the enemy's plan was to carry Battery Gregg by a boat attack on the night of the 5th, or early on the morning of the 6th; that the fleet should prevent the landing of re-enforcements at Cummings Point; that Wagner should be heavily shelled by ironclads, and on the morning of the 6th, on a given signal, Battery Wagner should be assailed.

This plan was frustrated, however, by the repulse of the attacking party on Battery Gregg. About 1:30 a. m., on the 6th, they were seen approaching in from fifteen to twenty barges from the passages leading from Vincent and Schooner Creeks that lie between James and Morris Islands. The garrison of Gregg* was on the alert and received them with a brisk fire of grape and musketry. The enemy was evidently disconcerted and, after discharging their boat howitzers, retired.

On the 4th September, I had convened a meeting of general officers and the chief engineer of the department to assist me in determining how much longer the Confederate forces should attempt to hold Morris Island. The rapid advance of the enemy's trenches to Battery Wagner having made it evident that before many days that work must become untenable, the following questions were propounded to the council:

"1. How long do you think Battery Wagner can be held without regard to the safety of the garrison?

"2. How long can it be held with a fair prospect of saving its garrison with the means of transportation at our command and circumstances relative thereto as heretofore indicated by actual experience?

"3. How long, after the loss or evacuation of Wagner, could Battery Gregg be held?

"4. Can the heavy guns (two in Wagner and three in Gregg)

---

*Captain Lesesne, 1st S. C. Artillery, and Major Gardner, 27th Georgia, were in command.—Ripley's Report.

in those works be removed before the evacuation without endangering the safety of the works and their garrisons?

"5. Can we take the offensive suddenly with a fair prospect of success by throwing during the night 3,000 men on the north end of Morris Island, making in all 4,000 available men, bearing in mind that no re-enforcements could be sent them until night, and probably for several nights, according to the movements of the enemy's ironclads and the fire of his land batteries?"

These questions were thoroughly discussed, as well as the probable plan of attack by the enemy, our means of defense, transportation, and reasons for prolonging our possession of the north end of Morris Island. It was agreed that the holding of Morris Island as long as possible was most important to the safety and free use of Charleston harbor; and our ability to keep up easy communication with the works on Sullivan and James Islands, in view of which I deemed it proper to renew application to the secretaries of war and of the navy, by telegraph, for some 200 sailors for oarsmen.

It was further decided that the five heavy guns at Morris Island were necessary morally and physically for the defense, to the last extremity, of the position; and such being the difficulty, if not indeed the insurmountable obstacles to their removal at this time, that no effort should be made to save them, and consequently that they should be ultimately destroyed with as much of the works as possible when further defense was abandoned.

The result was my determination to hold Morris Island as long as communication with it could be maintained at night by means of rowboats, but for which purpose sailors or men able to handle oars with efficiency were essential.

On the 5th inst., Brigadier-General Ripley prepared by my order a confidential letter to the officer commanding Battery Wagner, pointing out that it might be necessary to evacuate Morris Island, and giving full instructions for destroying the magazines and rendering the guns useless in that event.

Early on the morning of the 6th, a dispatch was received from Colonel L. M. Keitt, commanding Battery Wagner, to the following effect: ". . . The parapet of the salient is badly breached; the whole fort is much weakened. A repetition of today's fire (alluding to the 5th inst.) will make the work almost a ruin.

11—H

The mortar fire is still very heavy and fatal and no important work can be done. Is it deemed advisable to sacrifice the garrison? To continue to hold it is to do so. Captain Lee, the engineer, has read this and agrees." The casualties in Wagner on the 5th were 100 out of 900.

Another dispatch, dated 8:45 a. m., was received from Colonel Keitt: "Incessant fire from Yankee mortars and Parrott battery; can't work negroes, better look after them promptly. Had thirty or forty soldiers wounded in an attempt to work. Will do all I can, but fear the garrison will be destroyed without injuring the enemy. The fleet is opening, but I hope that we may hold till night." Again, at 10:30 a. m., Colonel Keitt signalled, "Boats must be at Cummings Point without fail." During the day a letter was received from the same officer as follows: ". . . The enemy will tonight advance their parallel to the moat of this battery. The garrison must be taken away immediately after dark, or it will be destroyed or captured. It is idle to deny that the heavy Parrott guns have breached the walls and are knocking away the bomb-proofs. Pray have boats at Cummings Point immediately after dark to take away the men. I say deliberately that this must be done or the garrison must be sacrificed. I am sending the wounded and sick to Cummings Point now, and will, if possible, continue to do so until all are gone. I have a number of them now here. I have not in the garrison 400 effective men, excluding artillery. The engineers agree with me in opinion, or rather shape my opinion. . . ."

Colonel Keitt's last dispatch was as follows: "The enemy's sap has reached the moat and his bombardment has shattered large parts of the parapet. The retention of this post after tonight involves the loss of the garrison. If the necessities of the service require their sacrifice, the men will cheerfully make it, and I will cheerfully lead them. I prefer to assail the enemy to awaiting his assault, and I will at 4 o'clock in the morning assail his works."

Things being in this condition, it became evident that an attempt to longer retain possession of Batteries Gregg and Wagner must of necessity involve the loss of the garrisons. But before giving the final order for the evacuation, I directed Colonel D. B. Harris, my chief engineer, to proceed to Morris

Island and to examine into and report upon the condition of affairs. His opinion was as follows:

". . . I visited our works on Morris Island today, and in consideration of their condition, of our inability to repair damages to Wagner as heretofore, of the dispirited state of the garrison, and of the progress of the enemy's sap, am constrained to recommend an immediate evacuation of both Batteries Gregg and Wagner. . . . In consequence of the accuracy of the fire from the enemy's land batteries which are now in close proximity (say from 500 to 800 yards) to Wagner, aided by reverse fire from his fleet, it is impossible, in the opinion of the officer commanding the fort, to keep up a fire either of artillery or small arms, and the enemy are thus left free to work in the trenches which he is rapidly pushing forward. The head of the sap is within forty yards of the salient, which is so badly damaged by a Parrott battery kept constantly playing upon it as to render it untenable. . . ."

Under these circumstances, I concluded the period had arrived when it would be judicious to evacuate Morris Island, and in the following special order detailed the manner in which I desired the movement to be accomplished:

"Battery Wagner, Morris Island, being no longer tenable, without undue loss of life and the risk of final capture of the entire garrison, that position and Battery Gregg will be evacuated as soon as practicable, to which end the following arrangements will be made by the district commander:

"I. Two of the Confederate States ironclads should take up position near Fort Sumter with their guns bearing on Cummings Point and to the eastward of it. At the same time, all our land batteries will be held prepared to sweep the water face of Battery Gregg. Transport steamers will take position within the harbor, but as near to Cummings Point as practicable, to receive the men from the row boats by which the embarkation of the men from Morris Island will be effected. As many row boats as are necessary, or which can be provided with efficient oarsmen, will be kept in readiness at once to proceed to and reach Cummings Point or that vicinity as soon after dark as may be prudent. Having reached Morris Island a courier or relay of footmen will be dispatched by the naval officer in charge with notice of the fact to the officer in command of Battery Wagner, and of the exact transport capacity of the boats. A naval officer with proper assistants will have exclusive charge of the boats and their movements.

"II. The commanding officer of Wagner having made during the day all arrangements for the evacuation and destruction of the work and armament, will, when informed of the arrival of the boats, direct first the removal and embarkation of all wounded men, and thereafter, according to the capacity of the boats at hand, will withdraw his command by companies with soldierly silence and deliberation. Two companies will remain in any event to preserve a show of occupation and repair and to defend from assault during the embarkation; and it is strictly enjoined that no more men shall quit the work and go to the landing than can be safely embarked. The embarkation will be superintended by the field officers or regimental or battalion commanders, who will halt and keep their commands about 100 yards from the boats, divide them into suitable squads for assignment to the boats in exact conformity with the directions of the naval officer in charge of the embarkation; and then superintend the disposition of the men accordingly, impressing upon all the vital necessity of silence, obedience to orders and coolness.

"III. The companies left to occupy Wagner will be under charge of a firm and intelligent field officer, who will not withdraw his command until assured that there is sufficient transportation for all the remaining garrisons of the island, including that of Battery Gregg.

"IV. The final evacuation will depend for success on the utmost coolness and quiet on the part of every man. At least two officers previously selected will be left to light the fuses already arranged and timed to about fifteen minutes to blow up the magazine and bomb-proof, and to destroy the armament in the manner already indicated in special instructions from district headquarters. But the fuses must not be lighted until it is certain there is sufficient transportation for the removal of all the garrison, or except the enemy become aware of the evacuation and are evidently about to storm and enter the work. The men must be embarked with arms loaded ready to repel an attack from the boat parties of the enemy.

"V. The garrison of Battery Gregg will stand staunchly to their posts until the last company from Wagner shall be embarked. It will then take the boats in silence and with deliberation, provision having been made as at Wagner for the destruction of the work and its ordnance. Both explosions will be as nearly simultaneous as possible; and the complete success of the evacuation will probably be in the hands of those whose high duty it will be to apply the match to the fuses at Wagner. The garrison of Gregg will be embarked with the same precautions and regulations as prescribed for that of Wagner. In case the enemy should carry Wagner immediately after the garrison shall have evacuated it, or in any way the explosion of the magazine should be prevented, a signal of three (3) rockets in rapid succession shall be made from Battery Gregg, when the naval vessels in position and our land batteries bearing on Wagner will be opened with a steady fire on the site of that work, as will be done likewise immediately after an explosion shall have taken place, and this fire shall be maintained slowly during the night.

"VI. Brigadier-General Ripley will give such additional orders as will be calculated to secure the successful evacuation of Morris Island, or to meet emergencies. He will confer with Flag Officer Tucker and procure all necessary assistance. The operation is one of the most delicate that can be attempted in war. Coolness, resolute courage, judgment and inflexibility on the part of officers—obedience to orders and a constant sense of the necessity for silence on the part of the men, are essential for complete success, and the credit which must attach to those who achieve it."

The evacuation began at 9 p. m. on the night of the 6th September. According to instructions a guard of 35 men, under Captain T. A. Hugenin, had been left to bring up the extreme rear and to fire the only magazine which contained powder. The necessary arrangements having been completed, and Colonel Keitt having been informed that the transportation was ready, the embarkation commenced and was continued with the utmost quietness and dispatch. The wounded were first embarked and were followed by the remnants of the infantry garrison. Captain Kanapaux, commanding light artillery, was then ordered to spike his guns and embark his command. Captain Lesesne, commanding Gregg,

spiked the guns of that battery and followed with his command;
and the rear guard from Wagner, coming up at that time in pursuance of orders from Colonel Keitt, the fuses communicating
with the magazines were lighted, that at Wagner by Captain
Hugenin, and that at Gregg by Major Holcombe, commissary of
subsistence, and the remainder of the command was safely and
expeditiously embarked. Owing to defects in the fuses themselves, they failed to accomplish the purpose designed, though
their lighting was superintended by careful and reliable officers.
The magazines were, therefore, not destroyed. The guns in the
batteries were spiked as far as their condition allowed, and the
implements and equipments generally destroyed or carried off.
The evacuation was concluded about 1:30 a. m., on the 7th September. The boats containing the portion of the garrison last
embarked were fired upon by the enemy's barges, but without
effect. Two of our boats containing crews of 19 sailors and 27
soldiers were captured by the enemy's armed barges between
Cummings Point and Sumter.

Thus Morris Island was abandoned to the enemy on the 7th
September with but little loss on the part of the garrison, either
in men or material. The total loss in killed and wounded on Morris Island, from July 10th to September 7th, was only 641 men;
and deducting the casualties due to the landing on the 10th July
and to the assaults of the 11th and 18th July, the killed and
wounded by the terrible bombardment, which lasted almost uninterruptedly night and day during fifty-eight days, amounted only
to 296 men, many of whom were only slightly wounded. It is
still more remarkable that during the same time when the enemy
fired 6,202 shot at Sumter, varying in weight from 30 to 300
pounds, only three men were killed and forty-nine wounded in
that work.

It is difficult to arrive at the loss of the enemy during these
operations, but judging from the slaughter made in their ranks
on the 11th and 18th July, it will be within the mark to say that
his casualties were in the ratio of ten for our one.

It may be well to remark that the capture of Morris Island
resulted in but a barren victory to the enemy, if his only object
was to gain a position from which to hurl his missiles and Greek
fire into the City of Charleston. A reference to the map will

show that the possession of Cummings Point placed him no nearer the city than he was when he held part of James Island, from whence he was driven by the Battle of Secessionville in June, 1862, and again in July, 1863, when he was driven from the same island on the 16th of the same month.*

In conclusion, I cannot express in too strong terms my admiration of the bravery, endurance and patriotism displayed by the officers and men engaged in these operations, who during so many days and nights withstood unflinchingly the extraordinary fire from the enemy's land and naval batteries, and repulsed with heroic gallantry every effort to surprise or carry the works by storm.*

I have particularly to commend the gallantry, coolness and zeal of Brigadier-General W. B. Taliaferro, Brigadier-General Johnson Hagood, Brigadier-General A. H. Colquitt, Colonel L. M. Keitt and Colonel G. P. Harrison, who at different periods had immediate command of the defenses of Morris Island. To particularize would be invidious; they one and all on every occasion did their duty nobly.

I have to express my acknowledgment of the valuable services rendered by Brigadier-General R. S. Ripley, in command of the First Military District, which included the City of Charleston and its outworks. He was invariably active, industrious and intelligent, and carried out his important duties to my entire satisfaction. Although Major-General J. T. Gilmer arrived in Charleston a few days before the evacuation of Morris Island, he was nevertheless active, zealous and of great assistance to me in holding the island to the last moment.

I also take pleasure in recording the services of Colonel Alfred Rhett, who during the siege of Wagner had command of Fort Sumter, and with his brave garrison endured a long and terrific bombardment. His conduct throughout met my entire approval and satisfaction.

To Colonel D. B. Harris, chief engineer of the department, I have to return my most sincere thanks. He was ever cool, gallant and indefatigable in the performance of his arduous duties during the whole period of the operations on Morris Island.

---

*Note C.
*Note H.

Always present in the hour of need, he exposed himself when necessary to the hottest fire and the greatest danger in the most reckless manner.* I am, General,
Respectfully, your obedient servant,
(Signed) G. T. BEAUREGUARD,
General Commanding.

EXTRACT FROM GENERAL RIPLEY'S REPORT

CONTINUING NARRATIVE OF SIEGE FROM 7TH SEPTEMBER, 1863.

". . . September 7th. The enemy occupied Battery Wagner about daylight, and was opened upon by Batteries Simkins and Cheves and Fort Moultrie with the works adjacent.

"Soon after Admiral Dalgreen, commanding enemy's fleet, sent a demand to Major Stephen Elliott, commanding Fort Sumter, for a surrender of that post. Major Elliott declined, meantime referring the matter to the headquarters of the district. Under instructions from headquarters of the department, Admiral Dalgreen was informed that he could have Fort Sumter when he could take and hold it.

"About 6 p. m., the Ironsides and five monitors came up the channel and opened fire on Fort Sumter and the batteries on Sullivan's Island, which was promptly replied to by our guns and with some effect until it was too dark to observe the results. The enemy kept up his fire until about 9 o'clock, doing but little damage to the works. Lieutenant E. A. Ervin, First South Carolina Infantry, was killed at Battery Beauregard.

"September 8th. On the morning of the 8th, a monitor, supposed to be the Weehawken, was observed aground in the channel

---

*NOTE.—High as is the tribute here paid to Colonel Harris, it is not exaggerated. He was singularly modest, and the writer has no hesitation in saying the coolest man under fire he ever met with; withal a skillful engineer and, literally, "always present in the hour of need." He was chief engineer of the department and not the local engineer of Wagner, yet always and whenever the guns of Morris Island rang out the alarm of special bombardment or assault, you might with certainty look for him at the fort whatever the difficulty or danger of getting there. Colonel H. was a Virginian, a graduate of West Point, and afterwards, and until the breaking out of this war, a large tobacco planter. His service was chiefly with General Beauregard from the First Manassas until the fall of 1864. He was then detached from Petersburg to again take charge of the engineering around Charleston, and died shortly after from yellow fever.—J. H.

leading to Cummings Point and the shore of Morris Island. A slow fire was opened upon her from a treble-banded Brooke gun and a 10-inch columbiad from Sullivan's Island and such guns as could be brought to bear from Fort Johnson. The endeavor was made to strike her below her armor, which was out of water at low tide. She was struck several times below the usual water lines, and about 9 o'clock the Ironsides and five monitors came to her assistance, engaging the forts and batteries at distances ranging from 800 to 1,500 yards, keeping up a very heavy cannonade. A shell from the Weehawken struck and disabled an 8-inch columbiad in Fort Moultrie, and glancing burst near a service magazine which was protected by a heavy traverse throwing incendiary contents into and exploding the magazine, killing sixteen and wounding twelve men of Captain R. Press Smith's company, First South Carolina Infantry. This disaster interrupted the practice but little, for Captain Bennett's company relieved Captain Smith's under a heavy cannonade, and an accurate and deliberate fire was maintained against the enemy from all the batteries on the island for about five hours, when the enemy withdrew much cut up and disabled. From personal observation, I take pleasure in commending the conduct and practice of the officers and men engaged in Colonel Butler's regiment. The effect on the ironclads I believe to have been greater than on the 7th April, and since the action but one monitor has fired a gun, and their number has been decreasing; four only are now in view. Besides the casualties from the explosion, three men and two officers were killed—Captain Wardlaw and Lieutenant DeSaussure; and fourteen men were wounded at Fort Moultrie.

"Having met with but little success in the cannonade of the Sullivan's Island batteries, the enemy's naval commander next made an attempt to take possession of Fort Sumter, and at 1 o'clock on the morning of the 9th attacked that fort with a fleet of from thirty to forty barges. Major Elliott caused his fire to be reserved until the enemy was within a few yards of the southern and eastern faces upon which the landing was attempted. He was then received with a close fire of musketry; hand grenades and fragments of epaulement were thrown over on the heads of his men, demoralizing and completely repulsing him. The crews near the fort sought refuge in the recesses and breaches of the scarp and those at a distance turned and pulled rapidly away. The gunboat 'Chicora,' the Sullivan's Island batteries and Fort Johnson opened a fire enfilading the faces of Sumter as soon as the signal was made, cutting up the retreating barges, of which several were seen floating capsized and disabled. Next morning Major Elliott succeeded in securing five boats, five stands of colors, twelve officers and one hundred and nine men, including two officers and nineteen men wounded.

"The prisoners reported the attacking force four hundred strong. It was probably larger, and the enemy's loss was undoubtedly larger than that portion which fell into our hands and under our observation. Amongst the captured colors was a worn and torn garrison flag, reported by some of the prisoners as that which Major Anderson was permitted to take from the fort on the occasion of his being compelled to surrender it in April, 1861. This had been brought to hoist and to be made the subject of boast had the assault succeeded. Whether it was really the flag in question or not, it would doubtless have been so asserted. . . . The gallant conduct of Major Steven Elliott, commanding Fort Sumter, and of his garrison, the Charleston Battalion under Major Blake, in repelling this assault, is to be especially commended. . . ."

Thus terminated the direct efforts of the enemy to take Charleston. With the capture of Morris Island, and the demolition of the offensive power of Sumter, General Gilmore, with his land forces, had done all he was able to do; and contended that he had done all he had engaged to do; and that it was enough that the gate was now open for the fleet to enter and finish the undertaking.* The fleet thought otherwise. From thenceforward, until the operations of Sherman in the interior of the State compelled the evacuation of the city, the enemy's operations before Charleston, as heretofore stated, were confined to a cannonade upon Sumter to prevent its rehabilitation as an artillery post, to the exchange of shots with our James Island batteries, from which nothing resulted, and to the regular bombardment of the city from Cummings Point. The fleet occasionally joined in the pounding of Sumter or engaged indecisively the Sullivan's Island batteries.

---

*See Gilmore's "Operations, etc."

General Beauregard's efforts were confined principally to completing the defenses of Charleston. On James Island, with which the writer was most familiar, these became very complete. Pemberton's and Ripley's lines from Secessionville, by way of Royall's house to Fort Pemberton, were abandoned. Starting at Secessionville a line much shorter was carried to Dill's, just above Grimball's on the Stono. This was a cremaillere infantry breastwork of strong profile, with heavy enclosed redoubts at distances of 700 and 800 yards, having defensive relations to each other. On the Stono were one or two heavy redoubts securing that flank. Fort Pemberton was nearly, if not quite, dismantled. From Secessionville to Fort Johnson, along the eastern shore of the island looking towards Folley and Morris Islands, heavy batteries, opened to the rear with trenches or breastworks for infantry supports, were erected, and from Johnson to opposite the city heavy batteries for the defense of the inner harbor* Bombproofs, covered ways, rifle pits and all the appliances of the engineer's art were exhausted in strengthening this system of works. Magnetic telegraphs were put up from Pemberton, Secessionville, Fort Haskell and Johnson, respectively, to headquarters at Royall's house, and a complete system of signals by rockets established. The command was divided into two divisions —Generals Hagood and Colquitt in charge, and General Taliaferro commanded the island.

In November, President Davis visited James Island. General Taliaferro was absent on leave and General Hagood in command. Mr. Davis inspected the works closely, going at a rapid gallop with his cortege from battery to battery and stopping long enough to receive a salute and ride around the regiments which were drawn up along his route, each near its post. He seemed in good spirits; the troops betrayed much enthusiasm, but he acknowledged their cheers for "Our President" by simply raising his hat. General Hagood rode with him as commander of the island, and necessarily had much conversation with him. Here and on the field of battle at Drury's Bluff when General Beauregard was pleased to present him again, with a compliment, to the President, were the only times he was ever in conversation with this dis-

---

*See map at p. 200, Ante for Old Lines. See map at p. 352, Ante for New Lines.

tinguished man. That night ex-Governor Aiken, with whom Mr. Davis was a guest, entertained the party in the city.

In February, 1864, the enemy inaugurated a campaign in Florida, covering the movement of troops from before Charleston by a demonstration upon Johns Island. Colquitt was sent with his brigade to re-enforce our troops in that quarter, and the battle of Olustee terminated the campaign. The Eleventh South Carolina was sent after Colquitt, but arrived after the battle. It was, however, creditably engaged afterwards in an affair of pickets.

Olustee, like Secessionville, was one of the decisive battles of the war, with comparatively small forces engaged. At the time, and so far since, the credit seemed to attach to General Finnigan, the district commander. From what General Hagood learned of it from those engaged he was inclined to believe the credit solely due to Colquitt. He was said to have been on a reconnoisance in force under orders from Finnigan, when he unexpectedly encountered the advance of the Yankee Army and engaged it without orders. He received no orders or re-enforcements during the fight until, just as he was preparing for his decisive charge, a message from Finnigan, five miles in rear, directed him to fall back. The charge was made, and the enemy thoroughly routed.* No fresh troops were sent in pursuit. Colquitt ordered forwarded a squadron or two of cavalry which had accompanied his reconnoisance and been unengaged in the fight. They did not get out of sight of the field of battle before they bivouacked for the night. The enemy, it was said, abandoned artillery in the road twenty miles from the field of action.

Taliaferro was now sent to Florida to take command of that district; he was in a short time superseded by Major-General Patton Anderson and returned to James Island.

The troops on James Island were generally hutted, and, from the facility of getting private supplies from home (they were chiefly Georgians and South Carolinians), lived tolerably well. The commissariat supply was irregular and bad. Major Guerrin in Charleston and Northrop in Richmond were too much for us. Under Confederate regulations, the commissary department was almost independent of even a general commanding a separate

---

*In 2 Beauregard's Military Operations.

army; and General Beauregard more than once spoke to the writer of his plans being thwarted by the interference of Northrop, the chief at Richmond. Colonel Northrop's qualifications for this high position, it was said with sarcastic bitterness, were to have been at West Point with President Davis some thirty years before and to have lived a misanthrope since without active participations in even civil life. It was a popular notion among the soldiers that he was a vegetarian and did not think meat healthy. Guerrin had been an office clerk for a physician in Charleston before the war and had married Northrop's niece. The writer knows that the movement and supply of troops is the most difficult of the problems of war; and he trusts he is not disposed to criticise harshly any man or set of men who "wore the grey." But he also knows that on James Island, had it not been for private sources of supply, the troops would have often been on siege rations, and that, too, when there was uninterrupted communication with the middle and back country of Georgia and South Carolina which teemed with provisions. A year later Sherman and his men expressed themselves amazed at the abundance they encountered here. During the winter (of 1863-64) the wives of many of the officers came down, and there was quite a pleasant society on the island. Ladies on horseback and in carriages were not an uncommon sight, and sometimes during a lull in the firing of the batteries a dancing party was had at a post liable to be opened upon at any time. Horse racing, coursing rabbits with greyhounds, and cock fighting amused the fancies of each sport; and occasionally a whole regiment would be seen on a grand battue. Deploying as skirmishers, each man armed only with a club, they would sweep over the extensive field, whooping and yelling; and it was astonishing to see what numbers of rabbits, partridges and other small game, too scared to escape, they would bring to bag. The health of the troops was good, their morale excellent, and many a tatterdemalion who followed the Red Cross flag under Lee and Johnston in '64 and '65 looked back upon this portion of his service at the siege of Charleston with fond regret.

Before leaving for Virginia, whither he had been ordered in April, 1864, General Hagood went over to Sumter to look at its condition. He had last seen it on the night of the 18th July, 1863, on his way to Wagner. Then it was an imposing artillery fortress, armed at all points, equalled for offensive power by perhaps few in the world, and triumphant in its recent decisive repulse of the ironclad fleet. The first day from Gilmore's huge rifled projectiles had demonstrated the inability of its masonry to withstand land breaching batteries, and despoiled by friends and battered by foes, it now lay in the moonlight a huge misshapen mound upon the quiet bosom of the bay. Save the battle flag floating in the night breeze, there was no sign of life or occupation, as we approached, until the quick decisive challenge of the warden obscured in the shade of the ruin arrested us. The watchword given, and landing, the visitors dived by a zigzag and obstructed entrance into the bowels of the mass of debris and came into a securely ceiled and well lighted gallery running the whole circle of the ruins, neatly whitewashed, thoroughly ventilated, widening here into a barrack room with bunks in which the reserve of the garrison were quietly sleeping; narrowing there into a covered way loopholed to give a musketry fire upon what was once the parade; and again developing itself into a hospital room, a compact headquarters office and a place of arms for defense, with ample and ingeniously defended passages for egress to summit of the ruins. Here sentinels in single rifle pits were stationed, having for giving the alarm, in addition to their guns, a wire by each, upon pulling which a bell was rung at the same time in the headquarters office and in each station of the garrison within. Boat howitzers, securely sheltered upon the interior slope of the debris, were so placed and combined with arrangements for musketry fire as to sweep every part of the parade. Wire entanglements, movable during the day or a bombardment upon the exterior slope, added to the difficulties of escalade which the action of the tides already made difficult enough. For at the edge of the water, the debris, which from the summit so far had a natural slope, was washed away, making here a nearly perpendicular wall five or six feet high. One or two heavy guns were mounted in the northwest angle of the fort which was sheltered by its position from Gilmore's land batteries. These had a field of fire upon the inner harbor, and would have been serviceable upon vessels succeeding in reaching that position in an advance of the fleet upon the city. The general appearance of the work now, as viewed from the summit ridge of the ruin and looking inward, was that of the crater of an extinct volcano.

As barrack and bomb-proof and casemate and magazine of the original fort had crumbled under the enemy's unparalleled fire, until protected alone by what had once been its defenses, no living thing could have survived even one day's ordinary bombardment; and the garrison, clinging tenaciously to the site, had burrowed into the increasing debris. Working under almost ceaseless fire, they had converted this wreck of an artillery fort, without a single gun to reply to her long range assailants, into an infantry post comparatively safe for its defenders, and with which, after one feeble effort, its assailants had never the nerve to grapple in assault.

Elliott, who had held the fort since the fall of Morris Island* without relief in the arduous and wearing duty, had just been promoted to a regiment and gone to Virginia, where in further recognition of his services he received the first vacant South Carolina brigade. Captain Mitchell was now in command and Captain Johnson remained the resident engineer. After the war, and not long before his untimely death, the writer was walking with Elliott on the streets of desolated Columbia, when they met and stopped to speak with Mrs. Pickens. After a few moments of conversation, the lady presented her little daughter to him and said in an aside to the child, "When you are old enough, my dear, to read the story of Fort Sumter, you will know why mamma wished to present you to General Elliott." Mitchell found his grave amidst its ruins, and Johnson here established a reputation for genius in his profession and for devoted gallantry unsurpassed in the war.

---

*He relieved Colonel Rhett on the 4th of September.—Ripley's Report.

NOTES TO GENERAL BEAUREGARD'S OFFICIAL REPORT.

NOTE A.

THE DIFFERENT ROUTES TO CHARLESTON.

Of the five routes of approach mentioned by General Beauregard, the two involving operations in rear appear to have been entirely beyond Gilmore's power with the land force at his disposal—by his own account some 17,000 men. It is worth noting, however, that both times when Charleston has fallen (in the Revolution and in the late war), it was from operations in this quarter after the direct attack had failed. The route by James Island is the only remaining one, the pursuit of which could have effected the fall of the city. Success upon this line of approach would undoubtedly have effected this object had Gilmore taken it. He would not have as efficient co-operation from the navy here as at Morris Island, principally from the greater facility with which the defense could have protected itself from the enfilading fire of the fleet. The lines on James Island, as already mentioned, were at that time exceedingly defective in location, incomplete in construction, and requiring a large force, not then in position, to man them. By vigorous and rapid operations against their center advancing from Grimball's and Dill's on the Stono, and a movement upon their flank and rear from Light House Inlet, as indicated in previous pages of these Memoirs, they may have been carried by assault. The slower these operations the less would have been their chance of success; and against these lines as established by General Beauregard later in the siege, from Dill's to Secessionville with heavy works from Secessionville to Fort Johnson defending that flank and rear, Gilmore with the means at his disposal would certainly have failed. He himself seemed to have had a full appreciation of the difficulties of this route. "Upon James Island," says he in his official report, "our progress would soon have been stopped by the concentration of superior force in our front. Upon Morris Island, on account of its narrowness, our force was ample. James Island was too wide to operate upon with a fair promise of success with our force."

Success on the Sullivan's Island route, from the nature of the channel, would have completely closed the channel for purposes of blockade running, would have furnished as good a point d'appui for the disabling of Sumter and given a direct fire upon almost every part of the inner harbor. But if it had taken as long to reduce Sullivan's Island as it did Morris Island (and it probably would), the same defenses would have sprung up as afterwards lined the shores of the inner harbor; and the navy would have had to exhibit more dash than it did at any time during the siege to have passed them. Charleston would not necessarily have fallen, had this route been taken. Another consideration of weight was this: To attack Sullivan's

Island, a lodgment upon Long Island, then occupied by the Confederate pickets, was necessary, when by a coup de main Sullivan's Island was to be reached across Breach Inlet. This could not have been done without attracting attention and totally depriving the coup of the attribute of surprise. Breach Inlet was also defended by works in a better state of completion than Light House Inlet was. Of Folley Island the enemy had for some time been in quiet possession as well as of the adjoining waters of Stono Bay, which gave them the opportunity of preparing measurably unobserved for a sudden descent upon Morris Island. And whatever stress they may have laid upon it, it was this element of surprise in their descent upon the south end of the island that gave them all the success they met with. What followed (the lodgment once made) was, with the conditions imposed, but a matter of time. General Beauregard in his report, it will be observed, denies the surprise, and attributes the fall of this end of the Island to the inadequate means of preparation and defense at his disposal. He undoubtedly, from his report, and, the writer may add, from very full conversations with him, appreciated the importance of strongly defending this point, and had planned and ordered a system of works adequate to the end; but they were not executed in time. Could it have been done? Could, under the circumstances of locality, the vigilance possibly have detected the massing on Little Folley for attack in time to have increased our infantry supports? Was there infantry available for this purpose? On these questions turns the whole matter. General Beauregard's report ably presents the difficulties that beset him. Gilmore says: "Wise defense would have kept us off of Morris Island entirely." And it was a general opinion of the Confederate troops, as well as the impression of the public mind, that this was the weak point in the otherwise masterly defense of Charleston. General Ripley took the opportunity of an investigation of the matter by General Beauregard's inspector-general to submit an elaborate defense of himself as district commander which he read to the writer, whose information of facts (he up to that time serving in another district) is not sufficient to warrant the expression of a decisive opinion as to where the fault was. The inclination of his mind then was and still is to attribute the laches rather to his subordinates and to circumstances, which he could not control, than to any oversight or negligence of the general commanding.

Upon the whole it appears that the route by Morris Island, though, in the language of General Beauregard, "the least injurious to us" that could have been taken, was the only one with the resources at his disposal by which Gilmore could have accomplished *anything*.

The narrow front upon which he operated and the difficult communication between Morris Island and the Confederate base of supply made difficult the concentration of a force in his front superior or even equal to that he could with easier communications at all times operate. His flanks were rendered unassailable by the ocean on one side and an impassable marsh from one and a half to two miles wide on the other. And, above all, he had the fullest possible benefit of the enfilade and reserve fire of the fleet, each vessel of which was for this purpose a movable battery. The Federal commander flatters himself, when he says in his report, "that it would have been entirely practicable to have pushed his approaches to Fort Wagner without the co-operating fire of the gunboats." The siege journal appended to his report decisively indicates the reverse. Without this fire the role would have been changed and from besieger he would probably have become besieged.

NOTE B.

TAKING THE OFFENSIVE.

When General Hagood reported, on the evening of the 11th July, to General Beauregard, the latter seemed very solicitous as to James Island front; and, in assigning General Hagood to that command, earnestly sought to impress its importance upon him. At the district headquarters immediately afterward General Hagood proposed to Ripley that instead of sending him to James Island that he be put on Morris Island that night with a sufficient force to take a vigorous offensive. General Hagood stated that he would be satisfied to do so with 2,000 fresh troops, the garrison of the island being sufficient to act as a reserve in the attack—provided, he could be landed with his men on the island by 12 o'clock that night. General Ripley thought the suggestion practicable, seemed much pleased with it, and they forthwith went together to General Beauregard with the proposition. He dismissed it summarily, with the statement that he had not the troops at hand, nor was the transportation available to put them there in time, if he had. The writer now knows General Beauregard was right. General Hagood was not at the council of general officers on the 13th. At the council, just before the evacuation of Wagner, he thought it too late to assume the offensive, and, indeed, never thought it practicable with our means to expel the enemy from Morris Island after the first night. Had the enemy's position not then been carried by assault before he had sufficiently entrenched, it would have grown under a slower approach into the dimensions of Wagner. A counter-siege, with the fire of the fleet enfilading and taking in reverse our approaches and the ground permitting no enfilade batteries for us, was simply out of the question.

NOTE C.

THE AFFAIR OF THE 16TH JULY ON JAMES ISLAND.
Headquarters First Sub-Division, First Military District.
James Island, July 18, 1863.

Captain Wm. F. Nance, A. A. G.

Captain: I have the honor to make the following report of the operations of the troops under my command on the 16th instant:

I had been instructed on the day previous to observe and report the possibility of offensive operations against the enemy in my front, and had reported two plans, the one of which limited to driving in their pickets on the left and making a reconnaisance of that part of their line with the further object of capturing or destroying the part of their force nearest Grimball's was the one approved.

The enemy occupied Battery Island and Legare's plantation principally and a part of Grimball's, and their gunboats lay in Folley and Stono Rivers, giving in front of their position a cross-fire extending as far as our picket line.

General Colquitt was ordered with about 1,400 infantry and a field battery to cross the marsh dividing Legare's plantation from Grimball's at the causeway nearest Secessionville, drive the enemy rapidly as far as the lower causeway (nearest Stono), recross the marsh at that point by a flank movement, and cut off and capture the force camped near Grimball's house. Colonel Way, Fifty-fourth Georgia, with about 800 infantry, was directed to follow en echellon on the Grimball side of the marsh, the advance of General Colquitt, and co-operate with him. A reserve of one section of artillery, supported by a company of infantry and a squadron of cavalry, under Lieutenant-Colonel Jeffords, Fifth South Carolina Cavalry, was held in hand near Rivers' house. On the extreme right a battery of four rifled twelve dr. and one of four Napoleons under Lieutenant-Colonel Del Kemper, supported by Colonel Radcliffe, North Carolina, with about 400 infantry, was ordered to engage the gunboats lying highest up the Stono.

The troops moved upon the enemy in the grey of the morning and the whole enterprise was carried out as planned. The force at Grimball's was, however, smaller than was anticipated, and, by retreating across to Battery Island, as soon as Colquitt's firing was heard, managed to save themselves before he could get into position to intercept them. Colonel Kemper engaged the Pawnee and another gunboat at 250 yards, and after some ten rounds drove them down the river beyond his range. The reserve artillery was not brought into action. The cavalry did good service in sweeping up fugitives over which the advancing infantry had run. The troops were under fire one hour and a half and behaved well. This fire was chiefly shell from gunboats and shell and cannister from a field battery. The enemy's infantry fought badly. Those encountered were chiefly colored troops, fourteen of whom were captured. These belonged to the Fifty-fourth Massachusetts. About thirty of the enemy were killed upon the field.

I beg leave to refer to the accompanying reports of subordinate commanders for full details.

The enemy were supposed to have been not above 2,000 infantry and one battery of field artillery. Upon the following night they evacuated James Island and Battery Island, leaving behind them arms and stores, of which a full return will be made. Our casualties were three killed, twelve wounded and three missing. Colonel Bull and Captain Beauregard, of the staff of General Beauregard, and Captain B. H. Reed, of General

Ripley's staff, reported to me for duty on the occasion, and, together with my own staff, rendered efficient service.

I am, Captain,

Your obedient servant,

JOHNSON HAGOOD,

Brigadier-General Commanding.

The foregoing is the official report. Colquitt drove in the pickets and the main body of the enemy with only a strong line of skirmishers until they reached the narrow neck between James and Battery Islands. Here they formed a double line of battle with field artillery on the flank and a cross-fire at close range from gunboats in Stono and Folley Rivers sweeping their front. A rapid exchange of fire of field artillery took place. The force at Grimball's had already escaped, and the instructions of department headquarters not permitting a further advance, which, too, would probably have resulted in little good, after a close reconnaissance of the position, the troops were recalled.

Federal newspaper accounts and their subsequent histories state that their force on this occasion was General Terry's *Division*, consisting of Montgomery's black brigade (two regiments) and General Stevenson's Brigade (white). This would make their force over 3,000* men. The prisoners on that day insisted that there were eight regiments. It seems they were right. The assistant surgeon of the Pawnee, who had been detailed to assist the wounded of the land forces after the assault on Wagner of the 18th July, and, wandering into our lines on the field, was picked up by our picket, told General Hagood that the Pawnee was struck forty-three times, principally in her upper works. She slipped her cables and fled after the tenth round. Kemper galloped up and unlimbered at the short range stated in an open field and fought without epaulements. The enemy's fire all passed over him, and he had neither man nor horse wounded.

Greely's History (American Conflict) states Terry's loss at 100. This is believed to have been the first time the colored troops of the Federal army were ever in action. It was certainly the first time that any were captured by the Confederates. When it was understood that such troops were being organized, by Confederate proclamation it was announced that prisoners taken from them would be turned over to the State authorities to be tried under the local laws relating to servile insurrection, and that white men commanding them would be dealt with as outlaws. It was not done in this or any subsequent case.

NOTE D.

THE STYLE OF FIGHTING WAGNER.

There was but one gun, at the time referred to by General Beauregard, on the sea face to reply to the iron-clad fire which greatly annoyed the garrison of Wagner—these vessels being enabled to take us both in reverse

---

*"About 3,800 men."—Gilmore's Report, p. 29.

and enfilade. When vigorously worked, this gun (the ten-inch columbiad spoken of) kept these vessels at a greater distance, rendered their fire less accurate, and the iron-clads seemed to have considerable respect for its missiles. On that day a monitor took up position for action within 800 yards of the fort, but, on being struck once or twice by the columbiad, withdrew two or three hundred yards, and the writer never knew them to engage the fort at closer range afterward. Besides, the demoralizing effect upon the garrison of making no reply to this very destructive fire was marked. It was in the light of this experience that General Hagood telegraphed the dismounting of the gun and asked that steps be taken to replace it that night. The gun, by the way, was an old one and was said by an artillery officer, who knew its history, to have already been fired 1,200 times. General Beauregard sent in substance the reply indicated in the report, and, with all deference, the writer would say that it foreshadowed the only defect, as it occurred to him, in the immediate defense of Wagner. *It was too passive.* Its artillery was not used enough to delay the approaches of the enemy, and the right kind of artillery was not used. Sorties, too, should have been resorted to. There was but one (Rion's, a success) during the siege. 'Tis true, no doubt, as stated in General Beauregard's report, that he ordered them made when practicable, but the writer, as a commander of the fort, does not recollect to have had this order extended to him—and it certainly should have had obedience to it enforced. Until the enemy captured the rifle pits, or ridge, as they called it, sorties were entirely practicable, notwithstanding the torpedoes in front of the work. The troops could have been moved out in column by the path which the pickets used, avoiding the torpedoes, and formed behind the pits for the attack.

With regard to the artillery—when this tour of duty was over—General Hagood brought fully to General Beauregard's attention the importance and efficiency of columbiads on the sea face, stating that he thought a battery of two or three ten-inch guns should be placed there; and further called attention to the absence of mortars for curved fire against the enemy's approaches, the only one in the fort, a ten-inch seacoast, having been disabled on the 10th July by the breaking of one of the trunnions and not having been used since. The general spoke of his inability to spare the guns and mortars, and laid less stress upon their importance to the defense of the fort. The dismounted columbiad, however, was in a few days remounted. Later in the siege another was sent down, but by this time, or shortly after, the first from continuous use had become unserviceable. So that in fact one ten-inch columbiad was the only armament opposed to the fleet during the siege. A 32 dr. rifled, on the sea face, became unserviceable after very few discharges. The landward armament consisted for offense chiefly of 32 dr. howitzers and eight-inch naval guns; a section of field guns on the left flank and one field gun on the right flank were kept for defense against assault, and this armament, in the writer's opinion, was not worked as much as it might have been by the successive commanders of the fort upon the enemy's sap.* The plan of

---

*Gilmore's operations, etc.

defense generally acted upon was a vigorous use of sharpshooters and but a moderate use of artillery from Wagner, while the fire of distant batteries was to retard the enemy's approaches, and the garrison of Wagner should be husbanded in bombproofs to repel the assault. Upon relieving his predecessor before day, on the 21st August, General Hagood found the embrasures on the land face closed with sandbags and learned that for three or four days sharpshooting alone had been used from Wagner. He directed Major Warley, accompanying him as chief of artillery, to open at once a vigorous fire from his 32 drs. This fire by the enemy's siege journal* put a stop to their work until daylight, when it ceased. At 9 o'clock we opened again, with the result, as learned from the same source, of stopping it for the day, and no further effort was made to advance their sap till the 23rd, when Wagner again opened, "completely destroying it," says the Journal. By this mode of fighting, Wagner drew a very heavy artillery fire, and we were compelled quickly after each discharge to fill the throats of the embrasures with sand bags to prevent dismounting our guns, notwithstanding which, on the evening of the 24th, the last one on the land face was temporarily disabled. General Hagood now caused Major Warley to try the experiment of wedging up into position the disabled mortar and throwing shell with small charges into the head of the sap, then some three hundred and fifty yards off. Eight ounces of powder was found sufficient, and the practice was beautiful. This was the first time curved fire was used from the fort. The enemy's progress was stopped. His siege journal says: "This mortar proved to be a great annoyance. Its fire was directed on the head of the sap, was very accurate, and our sappers had no shelter from it. Six such mortars well served would have stopped our work till subdued by superior fire." His battery of Parrotts, heretofore breaching Sumter, was now turned upon the parapet of Wagner to get at the mortar by breaching, but the mortar was not silenced.

Again, on the 25th, the mortar fire greatly retarded their sap, and Major Brooks, in their siege journal, records, "This has been the saddest day to me of the siege. Less has been done than on any other. No advance has been made." And so, throughout the siege, the enemy's record shows that whenever the artillery was actively brought to bear upon them the result was always to stop or greatly retard their progress. The value of the mortar as exhibited at this time caused another to be sent to replace it, when the old one became utterly unserviceable, and curved fire was more or less used till the end of the siege.

These comments upon the masterly defense of Wagner by General Beauregard are made with much hesitation. They are given for what they are worth.

---

*Gilmore's Operations.

NOTE E.

THE FLAG OF TRUCE AND EXCHANGE OF PRISONERS.

On the 21st July, the enemy's fire ceasing and a flag of truce appearing, Captain Tracy, A. D. C., was sent to meet it. After a short interview the flags separated, and, before either party had reached their lines, the fleet opened on the fort. Captain Tracy had to proceed a distance of two hundred yards along the exposed beach across which every projectile fired at Wagner from the fleet passed at the height of a man, they firing low to ricochet. Captain Tracy providentially reached the fort without being harmed and delivered a communication from General Gilmore requesting a personal interview between the officer commanding Wagner and General Vogdes commanding in the trenches. He also said the next afternoon had been suggested for the interview. The commander of Wagner, deeming the fire of the fleet an accident, and that it would every moment cease, did not at first permit his guns to reply. But the enemy's land batteries soon took it up; Wagner responded and the bombardment went on.

On the 22nd, at the hour suggested, the enemy's flag reappeared, and, as stated by General Beauregard, the interview was refused until the breach of truce was explained. The excuse as remembered was some misunderstanding between the naval and land commanders, and the fire could not be immediately stopped on account of General Gilmore's absence on Folley Island, and General Vogdes had no authority or perhaps means of communicating with the fleet. It was a lame excuse for the outrage, as far as the navy was concerned, for the whole interview had been on the open beach, in sight of the whole fleet, and Tracy was perfectly visible to every gunner as he returned with his flag in his hand. The explanation was, however, accepted with the profuse apologies tendered and the interview accorded.

General Vogdes stated his mission to be to ask for Colonel Putnam's body and to return to us Lieutenant Bee's with the sword of the latter. He had with him poor Bee's body for delivery. His request was complied with, and he then verbally proposed an exchange of prisoners, mentioning that they had but few of ours, all except those recently captured having been sent North, that "as we had the excess, of course, we could select whom to exchange," whilst intimating that a mutural exchange without regard to excess would be agreeable. Pending the interview, General Hagood received a dispatch from Ripley's headquarters in Charleston, where the interview and its objects were known, directing him to agree to an exchange of wounded prisoners without regard to excess on our side, except the negro prisoners; not to introduce them into the negotiations, but, if introduced by General Vogdes, to refuse, as they would not be given up; and that it was desirable on the score of humanity to get rid of the numerous white prisoners wounded in our hands, and for ·whom no adequate accommodation existed in our hospitals. The contents of the dispatch is given in substance and was not communicated to Vogdes. He carefully avoided any direct mention of negro prisoners, and his remark quoted above, that having the excess we could choose whom to exchange, etc., was in allusion to them, and all that was made. The Confederate proclamation outlawing negro troops and white officers commanding them was well known to the enemy; and, anxious to effect the exchange, it was apparent that the Federal party did not desire to complicate matters. It was observed that neither General Vogdes nor either of the three or four officers accompanying him enquired after Shaw, the colonel of the negro regiment engaged in the recent assault, although they asked after everybody else, and we subsequently learned by their newspapers that they did not then know whether he was killed or captured.

The negotiation was arranged, all in parol, by accepting the basis proposed by General Vogdes—the line to be the following Friday, at 10 a. m., and the place the point in the outer harbor from which the fleet generally conducted the attack on Wagner.

The exchange took place, and General Gilmore afterward accused Beauregard of bad faith in not sending the negro prisoners for delivery.

The foregoing narrative is believed to be perfectly correct.

NOTE F.

SHARPSHOOTING.

Whatever may be said of the artillery of Wagner not having been sufficiently active at all times, no objection on that score can be taken to her sharpshooters.

At first the infantry of the garrison served in this capacity by detail, and used their ordinary weapon—the Enfield rifle. Later, upon a suggestion which General Hagood had the honor to make, a special detail of men from the Twenty-first and Twenty-seventh South Carolina Regiments was made under Lieutenant Woodhouse, of the Twenty-first, and armed with Whitworth's telescopic rifles, a small lot of which had recently been brought through the blockade. The detail was sent to Sullivan's Island for a few days to become familiar by target practice with the weapon, and were then put on duty in the fort. At night they slept undisturbed in the hospital bomb-proof, and were excused from all fatigue duty at any time. From dawn until dark they were incessantly at work with their rifles, and of the value of their services the siege journal of the enemy gives abundant proof. They were even at times used against the monitors. In revolving their turrets, after a discharge, in order to bring the opposite gun to bear, a man on each side of the turret would for a moment expose himself, and would be complimented with the notice of a sharpshooter. The men detailed became greatly interested in the duty and were not relieved regularly as the rest of the garrison was. Later still in the siege, when the enemy got nearer to the fort, the Whitworths were returned to the city, and the Enfield resumed as better adapted to snap shooting at close quarters.

The sharpshooters perched themselves wherever they could best get a good view of the enemy from the fort, and sheltered themselves with little sandbag epaulements loopholed.

NOTE G.

THE RIFLE PITS.

About 300 yards in advance of Wagner a flattened ridge ran from the sea beach to the marsh, and here the island was narrowed. Behind this ridge in pits, two men to each, were stationed until the 26th August an infantry force, which served both as a picket and as sharpshooters. It served by ordinary detail from the garrison and used the habitual Enfield rifles. The sustained efforts of the enemy to shell them out with curved fire met with no success; and against direct artillery fire they seemed to be better sheltered than men in the fort who could be enfiladed more or less behind the breastheight. The fact of the pits being detached, one from the other, seemed to traverse them effectually against the flank fire of the fleet. The detail here served twenty-four hours; at dusk, however, it was doubled and the re-enforcement withdrawn at dawn of day.

Their sharpshooting was very annoying to the enemy, and as pickets they were invaluable, giving notice of assault in time to get the garrison out of the bomb-proofs. When the enemy's sap approached this ridge, he made an effort, on the 21st of August, to carry it by assault with the One Hundredth New York Volunteers, but failed. Again, on the 25th, a more determined effort was made. "Experience," says Major Brooks' journal, "had now proved that the sap cannot proceed unless the artillery fire of Wagner be subdued, or the enemy driven out of the ridge. . . . At 5:30 p. m., four 8-in. mortars and three Coehorn mortars opened on the ridge. At the same time the navy howitzers and *Requa Battery* fired to enfilade the reverse of the ridge. . . . The two Requa Batteries in the fourth parallel also took part."

AN INFANTRY ASSAULT AND REPULSE FOLLOWED.

Both these efforts were made during General Hagood's last tour of duty in Wagner. Upon relieving Colonel Keitt, on the 21st, he discovered after daylight that, in accordance with the practice established by the colonel on his recent tour, but 19 men were left in the pits for the day, instead of the heretofore usual number of seventy-five or eighty. They could not be re-enforced until night, and the enemy were greatly nearer them for attack than we were for support. To add to the general's anxiety, a flag of truce came in during the day, and the bearer was imprudently allowed to come near enough to observe the weakness of the force in the pits. When, therefore, in the evening a heavy and continuous bombardment of the pits and the space intervening between them and the fort commenced, it was evident what was coming, and the general drew out four companies (about 175 men) from the bomb-proofs and formed them behind the breastheight of the land force ready to go out of the right sally port by a flank when required. Having fully explained to the senior captain his anxieties and anticipations, he took his place, sheltered as best he could, to watch from the parapet the time to start this re-enforcement.

To start them too soon, before the fading light would obscure them, was to send them to butchery under the fire of artillery that could be concentrated on the intervening space; to send them too late was to lose the pits, for the enemy, once in them, would be as hard from their construction to drive out as the original occupants were. Deeming the time to have arrived, the general gave the word, "Now, captain, go." "General, I wish you would detail some other man to take this command. I don't feel *competent to it.*"

Fortunately, General Hagood saw just then Lieutenant-Colonel Dantzler, of the Twentieth South Carolina, standing in the door of the bomb-proof opening on the parade, and, beckoning to him, he came at double quick under the shelling going on. Explaining hastily the situation, the general put him in command, and, as he moved off, the assault commenced. Going at a run, Dantzler reached the pits after three on the right had been captured. The fight continued obstinately till 10 o'clock at night, when, forced out of the captured pits, the enemy gave over his efforts. After putting out his advanced videttes, who were required to crawl forward and lie on their stomachs during the night some twenty paces in front of the pits, the enemy's videttes in like position facing them some twenty paces beyond. Dantzler was going on his hands and knees down the line, inspecting them, when he discovered one post vacant. The heart of the occupant had failed him and he had slunk back into the pits. Jerking him forward into his place, with some harsh words, the attention of the opposite videttes was attracted and his fire drawn. The bullet struck the colonel, as he stood upon his hands and knees, in the breast of his coat and passed down the length of his body between his clothing and skin and out over his hip without other injury than a decided wheal. Poor Dantzler! Few braver men shed their blood in this war. At Wauboteam Church, in Virginia, in '64, he threw away his life in the effort, by a deed of "derring do," to make something of a worthless regiment to which he had been promoted. And the captain so inopportunely modest! In December, '64, on the lines before Richmond, when, in the current slang of the soldiers, chaplains were "played out," General Hagood was invited by the commanding officer of one of his regiments to attend divine service to be conducted by one of his line officers. After listening to an excellent sermon from an officer whom he had noticed during the past campaign always at his post and doing his duty well, his aide, Ben Martin, asked him if he remembered his first interview with the preacher. It was the modest Battery Wagner captain!

In the second attack (on the 25th) upon the pits, a full force was in them during the day from the Fifty-fourth Georgia, Captain Roberts commanding; and they were re-enforced at dark by Colonel Devorne's Sixty-first North Carolina. The fight was gallantly and obstinately maintained, the enemy giving over without success about 9 p. m. Captain Roberts was mortally wounded before sundown, but could not be brought into the fort before dark. When the fort had been arranged for the night, the commanding officer went into the hospital bomb-proof to enquire after him. Having expressed the hope that he was not seriously wounded, he replied that his injuries were mortal. Taking him by the hand his commander spoke of his gallant bearing in the fight, when the brave fellow half rose from his litter and said, "Thank you, general," and fell back exhausted. He asked for a chaplain, but there was none in the fort—no

> "Pious man whom duty brought
> To dubious edge of battle fought
> To shrive the dying, bless the dead."

A layman, a member of Parker's Light Battery (the Marions), a section of which was on duty in the fort, visited him at the request of the commanding officer, and spent the time, until his removal to the city, in administering to him the consolations of religion.

On the 18th of July, a Catholic clergyman was in the fort and administered the rites of his church in the bomb-proof just before the troops were drawn out to meet the assault. The chaplain of Ormstead's Georgia command and Mr. Dickson, chaplain of the Twenty-fifth South Carolina, each accompanied his regiment on its tour of duty in the fort. The writer heard of no others.

Upon being relieved before day, on the 26th, by Colonel Harrison, General Hagood called his attention specially to the critical condition of the rifle pits. They were carried by an infantry assault that night. The special circumstances the writer never learned. But the trouble was in re-enforcing them at the right time; for a sufficient force could not with safety be kept in them during the day, nor could they be re-enforced while there was light, and, as before remarked, the enemy could mass for attack closer than we were for support. Ripley's report says: "Just before dark the enemy threw forward an overwhelming force on the advanced pickets and succeeded in overpowering them before they could be supported."

NOTE H.

INCIDENTS OF SERVICE AT WAGNER.

First Sergeant Tines, of Captain John A. Gary's company, Lucas's battalion, a plain man from one of the mountain districts of South Carolina, but a true patriot and good soldier, was mortally wounded at his gun. To Gary's expression of sympathy he replied: "I am glad it is I and not you, captain; the country can better spare me." General Beauregard, on being informed of this incident, ordered one of the best of his new James Island batteries to be called "Battery Tines" in honor of the noble fellow.

Gary himself was killed a few days afterwards. He was a younger brother of Captain M. W. Gary, a generous and spirited officer, and much beloved by his comrades.*

---

*Captain John H. Gary, stationed at Battery Wagner, a shell from the enemy's gun, with a lighted fuse, fell within the fortifications, whereupon he quickly seized it and threw it outside the breastworks and it immediately exploded. Captain Gary took an active part in the capture of the Gunboat Isaac P. Smith in Stono River, a graphic account of which was given in *The Courier* of Charleston, S. C.—Editor.

On the 24th of August, Captain Robert Pringle, of the same battalion, was commanding a gun replying to the fire of a monitor. Three shells fired at a low elevation would richochet twice upon the water, the last time close to the beach and then explode just over the parapet of the fort. The practice was extremely accurate; and, although bright daylight, the huge projectiles coming straight for the spectator could be seen from the time they left the gun—presenting the appearance of a rapidly enlarging disk as they approached. One of these shells struck a school of mullet at its last rebound on the water and knocked one of the fish at least 100 yards into the gun chamber. Pringle picked it up and gaily remarked that he "had made his dinner." At the next fire from the monitor he was killed. The writer had been a good deal thrown with this young officer, and had been much pleased with his fine social traits and soldierly qualities. He was a descendant of the Mrs. Motte of Revolutionary fame.

Extracts from the diary of Lieutenant-Colonel Pressley, Twenty-fifth South Carolina:

"1st September. Ordered to Wagner. . . . Embarked from Fort Johnson all of the regiment except Company A, in a light draft steamer. Company A went in a rowboat. The steamer stopped near Sumter; harbor very rough. I got in the only boat the steamer had for debarking us, with about fifty officers and men. When we had got half way from the steamer to Cummings Point, a bombardment of Sumter by monitors commenced and the steamer returned to Fort Johnson with the balance of the regiment. At Cummings Point I found Company A, making with the men I brought, eighty or ninety men of my command, and no prospect of getting the others till next night. Reported to General Colquitt, in command, and was ordered to the sand hills in rear of Wagner. So we spent the balance of the night in what the soldiers called "private bomb-proofs"—holes in the sand. Not finding these comfortable, I myself spread my blanket between two sand hillocks. Fort Wagner and the enemy exchanged shots slowly all night.

"2nd September. Went into Wagner at daylight. Found the enemy's sap within about 120 yards of the salient; enemy working industriously. Garrison busy repairing damages and keeping up a slow fire. My command detailed as a working party for Battery Gregg. Enemy shelling Wagner, Gregg and Sumter all day. Transferred to Wagner at night, and by 11 p. m. the balance of my regiment arrived and reported to me. My companies, as they arrived, were stationed around the parapet, relieving the North Carolina regiment.

"We occupied from the extreme left along the sea face around the left salient and part of the land force; the Twenty-fifth Georgia the rest. These two regiments, with the artillerists, occupied the fort; another regiment, the Twenty-seventh Georgia, was in the sand hills in the rear. Enemy fired very little tonight. I was up most of the night posting and visiting my men; towards morning I took a nap in the left salient, resting my head against the parapet.

"3rd September. One or two of our guns and one mortar keep up a fire against the enemy's approaching sap.

"My command in high spirits,—a great many building loopholes with sand bags for sharpshooting. This has become very dangerous work; as soon as a hole is darkened on either side, a shot from the opposite sharpshooter follows, and with frequent success. Not much artillery fire by or at Wagner, but the enemy are hard at work and approaching. Our James Island batteries are firing briskly on the enemy's trenches. During the day from one-third to one-fourth the garrison are kept at the parapet, the rest in the bomb-proof—at night all are turned out. The Yankees are so near they can hear when we turn out, and quicken their fire. The garrison is heavily worked repairing damages.

"Colonel Keitt, Twentieth South Carolina, relieved General Colquitt last night in command of Morris Island. I was up nearly all night, slept a little before day in the same salient as last night.

"4th September. Quite a lively bombardment from the enemy today, number of the sand bag covers for sharpshooters knocked away. Sharpshooting still very brisk, however. . . . Batteries on James Island do good shooting, particularly Battery Simkins. Major Warley, chief of artillery, wounded; Captain Hugenin replaces him. Our parties very hard at work repairing damages. A corporal of Company A and several men wounded in my regiment. Several killed and a good many wounded in the balance of garrison. The enemy's fire slacked after dark. They display a calcium light tonight upon Vincent's creek. Towards day I tried to get a little sleep in my old place in the left salient. The shells from Fort Moultrie were passing immediately over it. A fragment from one of our own mortar shells came back into the fort and nearly struck me. This has been happening for some time, the enemy were so close. . . .

"5th September. The fleet early this morning opened upon the fort, the land batteries also cannonading with great fury—200 and 100-pound Parrotts, 8 and 10-inch mortar shells and 15-inch shell from the navy pouring into us. The shells are exploding so fast they cannot be counted. All our guns are silenced. Working them under such a fire is out of the question. The men are being wounded and killed in every direction. I have been around amongst my men a good many times and am covered with sand when I return. The three-fourths of the garrison are still kept in the bomb-proofs. The suffering of these from the heat and want of water is intolerable. The supply of water brought from the city is very inadequate; that from the shallow wells dug in the sand in and adjacent to the fort is horrible. Famishing thirst alone enables the men to drink it. . . . I have seen some horrible sights—men mangled in almost every manner. I saw a sharpshooter knocked from the parapet to the middle of the parade, some forty or fifty feet, and going fully twenty feet in the air. This was Rawlinson, of Company G, and the brave fellow clutched his rifle to the last. Of course, he lived but a short time. Lieutenant Montgomery, of Company C, was killed this morning—his head taken off by a shell.

"An attack upon Battery Gregg is expected tonight; a detachment of my regiment, under Captain Sellars, and of the Twenty-eighth Georgia, under Captain Hayne, are to be sent to re-enforce it. As they march out Captain Hayne enquires of Lieutenant Blum for Captain Sellars; a shell kills both. . . . It is apparent that our force manning the parapet tonight must be as small as possible. . . . In making our arrangements for the night there are many casualties in our detachment, commanded by Lieutenant Ramsey, Company Twenty-fifth. In a short time after it was posted every man but one was killed or wounded. The fleet has withdrawn and the land batteries slacked their fire, save the mortars, which are as active as ever. I have seen four shells start from the same battery at the same time. . . . "There was an alarm of an assault tonight. It was felt to be a relief— the prospect of changing this passive endurance of artillery into the hot blood of an infantry fight. The enemy's calcium light illuminated the whole fort, and the sharpshooters, contrary to custom, were at work all night. The enemy attacked Gregg and were repulsed. . . . Wells dug in the bomb-proofs give some relief in better water, but not enough. . . ."

Lieutenant-Colonel Pressley served until the evacuation; but the foregoing extracts from his diary are sufficient to give a picture of life in Wagner.

RESULTS AND SPECIALTIES OF THE SIEGE.

In the council before undertaking the operations on Morris Island, "the principal question," says General Gilmore's Official Report, "was to what extent the fall of Fort Sumter or the destruction of its offensive power would exert an influence on the fate of Charleston, that, of course, being the ultimate object in view. A consideration which possessed much weight was the great practical advantage of a blockade thorough and complete of Charleston harbor. The capture of Morris Island by allowing a portion of the blockading fleet to lie inside the bar, even though they should fail to finally occupy the inner harbor, would secure this end. The naval authorities at the seat of government regarded Fort Sumter as the key to the position. That stronghold once destroyed or its offensive power practically destroyed, the monitors and other ironclads, they affirmed, could remove the channel obstructions, secure the control of the entire harbor and reach the city."

Were these purposes accomplished?

1. Did Charleston fall before Gilmore's operations? Certainly not. Charleston, when it did fall, was evacuated in consequence of Sherman's march. It had withstood the direct attack

until the enemy, wearied out, had abandoned further efforts thus to capture the city.

2. Was a "blockade, in all respects thorough and complete," established? No. Moffett Channel, under Sullivan's Island, remained available to the Confederates, and though the hazards of blockade running were greatly increased it still went on.

3. Did the disabling of Sumter open the inner harbor to the fleet? Sumter was thoroughly destroyed as an artillery post, but the channel obstructions and the new batteries that sprung up on the shores of the inner harbor kept the fleet lying off Morris Island. And here it may as well be remarked that these same channel obstructions were far less formidable than imagined, the tide destroyed most of them about as fast as they were devised.

What, then, was accomplished? Narrower limits were set to blockade running, and by the bombardment much suffering and damage to property was inflicted upon the inhabitants of Charleston. Was the game "worth the candle"? It was upon the "attrition" theory, said General Grant in 1865. "The resources of the enemy and his numerical strength were greatly inferior to ours . . . I therefore determined . . . to hammer continually against him until by *attrition*, if in no other way, there should be nothing left to him but submission." And he succeeded. The "attrition" at Charleston contributed its share to the result.

In engineering the siege taught no new principles. On the contrary, its lessons enforced most emphatically the time-honored principles of the schools. The masonry of Sumter crumbled like an egg shell before the breaching batteries of the enemy; and when its debris had been pounded into earth with natural slopes, no further impression could be made upon it. On the other hand, the parapet of Wagner constructed from the first with natural slopes of sand were good to the last. For though Colonel Keitt talks of a breach, the writer is persuaded there was no breach in the engineering sense, both from Colonel Harris's report and from the diagram in Gilmore's report of the effect of his fire on the left salient, to which Colonel Keitt alludes. The truth was the superior artillery fire of the enemy could at all times, when concentrated upon the fort, make it a butcher pen, if the whole garrison were at their posts. But few men could be kept on the lines of the work during a bombardment—artillery enough to man the guns with infantry enough to act as a lookout and but little more. The practice always was during the daytime to keep a part of the garrison among the sand hillocks in rear of the fort; and during the bombardment to keep out of the bomb-proofs about 100 men.

By the 6th of September the sap of the enemy on the crest of the glacis put them in position when, deployed along its length, they could rush over the parapets of Wagner upon the cessation of the bombardment before its garrison could be drawn from the bomb-proofs to its defense. The relief of the fort was never greater than that of a strong field work, and the ditch was now half full by the drifting sand. The fort was, therefore, no longer tenable.

The great development of the merlons between the guns was claimed by General Beauregard as an improvement of his own; and it certainly is in earthworks, when casemates are impossible, a great one.

The writer became satisfied from his observation of these operations that ironclads, such as were opposed to us, could be kept out of any harbor when sand batteries could be located within 1,000 yards of the channel; *provided*, the batteries did not exceed one or two guns to each and were sufficiently detached. Where infantry supports were needed they should be bomb-proofed at convenient supporting distances and not at the guns. This, with the necessary covered ways, would be preferably his plan of defense.

The defenses of Coles Island as arranged during the latter part of our occupation were an illustration of this plan.

In this siege it is presumed more novelties were developed in artillery and larger experience gained than in any of modern times. The range and accuracy of fire obtained was never before equalled. The objections which the enemy's experience found to the larger sized Parrotts, their liability to burst, it is not thought were found by us to apply to the Brooke gun, which was the equal of the Parrott in every other respect.

An admirable invention of Lieutenant-Colonel Yates for transferring guns on columbiad carriages was used with perfect success. It was a wheel and ratchet arrangement by which the gunner alone could quickly and accurately bring the gun to bear.

The progress made in the use of torpedoes, both for offense and defense, was marked. Much, however, is yet to be attained. Where used for defense and required to be put in position for any time before hand, they were liable to get out of order and fail at the right moment. They were freely used in front of Wagner, yet the enemy sapped through them with but eight casualties from this source. About half that number occurred with us from carelessness with regard to them.

In the assault on Wagner, on the 18th July, the enemy's official report makes no mention of torpedoes; their newspaper accounts spoke of hand grenades used by the defense. This was not so, but in the night the impression might have been produced by torpedoes.

Next day the officer in charge not knowing of the torpedoes, the enemy's dead on the glacis were buried among them where they were placed and no casualty occurred. The burial party dug them up, but as they were ordinary spherical shell with the explosive arrangement in the fuse, they were deemed to have been fired the previous day without exploding. When used for offense, the writer thought more of them, and his impression is that their use at the prow of small boats, moving totally or partially submerged, was very near a success.

The fleet of "cigar boats" that sprung up in Charleston harbor and the "diving boat" were curious things to a landsman's eye; and some of the highest heroism of the war was exhibited in their use.

The writer regrets that he has not the data to speak fully of their exploits or to record the names of the gallant men who were distinguished in this service.*

The calcium light of the enemy was novel and efficient.

As a tactical movement the evacuation was an eminent success; and, though admirably executed, the chief credit is due to the comprehensive and explicit order in relation to it prepared by General Beauregard himself.

---

*IV So. Hist. paper 225 and V ditto 140, are papers on the subject by Beauregard and by Glassel.

END OF VOLUME I.

VOLUME II
HAGOOD'S BRIGADE

ORGANIZATION.

"Headquarters Dept. S. C., Ga. and Fla.
"Charleston, Sept. 20, 1863.
"(Extract)
"Special Orders.
"No. 188.

. . . .

"II. Brigadier-General Hagood's Brigade will be organized and consist of the following regiments and battalions: Eleventh, Twenty-first and Twenty-fifth Regiments, and the First (Charleston) Battalion and the Seventh Battalion South Carolina Volunteers. This organization for the present, however, will not interfere with any temporary distribution of troops by the district commander. . . .

"By command of General Beauregard.
"(Signed) JNO. M. OTEY, A. A. G."

"Headquarters Dept. S. C., Ga. and Fla.,
"Charleston, S. C., 30 Sept., 1863.
"(Extract)
"Special Orders.
"No. 198.
"I. By authority of the War Department, the First Battalion South Carolina Infantry, Lieutenant-Colonel P. C. Gaillard commanding, and the First Battalion South Carolina Sharpshooters, Major Jos. Abney commanding, will be consolidated into a regiment. . . .

"By command of General Beauregard.
"(Signed) JNO. M. OTEY, A. A. G."

A subsequent order numbered the regiment "Twenty-seventh South Carolina" and arranged the officers as follows: P. C. Gaillard, colonel; J. A. Blake (late captain, Charleston Battalion), lieutenant-colonel, and Joseph Abney, major. The regiment now had ten full companies. Subsequently, in 1864, the order of the secretary of war disbanded one of them (Clarkson's, Co. K,) on account of some illegality in its organization, and the regiment consisted of nine companies during the rest of its career. The Eleventh Regiment also consisted of nine companies, one of its companies having been permitted to organize and equip as a light battery. It was known as the Beaufort Artillery, and Steven Elliott (now Major Elliott at Fort Sumter) was its first captain. At the date of the brigade organization this company was formally detached from the regiment.

ROSTER OF BRIGADE, 30TH OF SEPTEMBER, 1863.

Johnson Hagood.. .. ..Brigadier-General, Commanding
P. K. Moloney.. .. ..Captain and Assistant Adjutant-General
G. B. Lartigue.. .. ..Major and Quartermaster
R. G. Hay.. .. ..Major and Commissary, Subsistence
E. H. Frost.. .. ..Captain and Assistant Commissary
Edmund Mazyck.. .. ..Lieutenant and Ordnance Officer
W. E. Stoney.. .. ..Captain and Assistant Inspector General
Ben Martin.. .. ..Lieutenant and Aid-de-Camp
Carlos Tracey.. .. ..Volunteer Aid-de-Camp
S. N. Bellinger ⎫
Geo. K. Ryan   ⎬ .. ..Mounted Orderlies
Dwight Stoney ⎭
G. B. Hacker ⎫ .. ..Office Clerks
F. S. Dibble   ⎭

ELEVENTH REGIMENT.

F. H. Gantt.. .. ..Colonel Commanding
A. C. Izard.. .. ..Lieutenant-Colonel
————.. .. ..Major
C. F. Davis.. .. ..Adjutant
R. P. Gantt.. .. ..Assistant Quartermaster
A. E. Williams.. .. ..Surgeon
J. B. Black.. .. ..Assistant Surgeon
A. B. Stephens.. .. ..Chaplain

COMPANY A.

(The Beaufort Artillery.)

COMPANY B.

G. J. Westcoat.. .. ..Captain
H. W. Bowman.. .. ..First Lieutenant
W. D. Ellis.. .. ..Second Lieutenant
John Black.. .. ..Second Lieutenant

COMPANY C.

T. D. Leadbetter.. ....Captain
J. J. Guerrard.. ....First Lieutenant
F. R. M. Sineath.. ....Second Lieutenant
T. W. Stales.. ....Second Lieutenant

COMPANY D.

J. J. Gooding.. ....Captain
Mac. D. Gooding.. ....First Lieutenant
O. J. Sauls.. ....Second Lieutenant
H. K. Hucks.. ....Second Lieutenant

COMPANY E.

J. H. Mickler.. ....Captain
W. Smith.. ....First Lieutenant
T. S. Tuten.. ....Second Lieutenant
Thomas Hamilton.. ....Second Lieutenant

COMPANY F.

B. F. Wyman.. ....Captain
J. S. Morrison.. ....First Lieutenant
J. M. Mixon.. ....Second Lieutenant
E. H. Wyman.. ....Second Lieutenant

COMPANY G.

W. D. McMillan.. ....Captain
W. M. Wolfe.. ....First Lieutenant
J. H. Brownlee.. ....Second Lieutenant
S. H. Brownlee.. ....Second Lieutenant

COMPANY H.

T. E. Raysor.. ....Captain
W. D. Wilson.. ....First Lieutenant
J. P. Mims.. ....Second Lieutenant
L. C. Mellard.. ....Second Lieutenant

COMPANY I.

W. S. Campbell.. ....Captain
E. B. Loyless.. ....First Lieutenant
J. C. Riley.. ....Second Lieutenant
Robert Campbell.. ....Second Lieutenant

COMPANY K.

J. Boatwright.. ....Captain (suspended)
————————.. ....First Lieutenant
L. B. Murdaugh.. ....Second Lieutenant
W. Johns.. ....Second Lieutenant

TWENTY-FIRST REGIMENT.

R. F. Graham.. .. ..Colonel Commanding
A. T. Dargan.. .. ..Lieutenant Colonel
G. W. McIver.. .. ..Major
F. Dozier.. .. ..Adjutant
A. C. McDuffie.. .. ..Assistant Quartermaster
C. Happoldt.. .. ..Surgeon
E. B. Smith.. .. ..Assistant Surgeon
J. E. Dunlap.. .. ..Chaplain

COMPANY A.

J. Harleston Read, Sr.. .. ..Captain
Thomas Ford.. .. ..First Lieutenant
J. H. Read, Jr.. .. ..Second Lieutenant
W. R. Ford.. .. ..Second Lieutenant

COMPANY B.

S. H. Wilds.. .. ..Captain
J. W. King.. .. ..First Lieutenant
J. L. Hart.. .. ..Second Lieutenant
——————.. .. ..Second Lieutenant

COMPANY D.

M. G. Tant.. .. ..Captain
J. H. Villeneuer.. .. ..First Lieutenant
S. D. Sanders.. .. ..Second Lieutenant
A. A. Vanderford.. .. ..Second Lieutenant

COMPANY E.

B. T. Davis.. .. ..Captain
A. W. Davis.. .. ..First Lieutenant
J. A. Craig.. .. ..Second Lieutenant
Alexander Craig.. .. .. .Second Lieutenant (in hands of enemy)

COMPANY F.

J. A. W. Thomas.. .. ..Captain
N. A. Easterling.. .. ..First Lieutenant
R. E. Townsend.. .. ..Second Lieutenant
W. D. Crook.. .. ..Second Lieutenant

COMPANY G.

R. W. Reddy.. .. ..Captain
J. M. Woodward.. .. ..First Lieutenant (in hands of enemy)
N. A. Bevile.. .. ..Second Lieutenant
R. H. Hudson.. .. ..Second Lieutenant

COMPANY H.

(Vacant) ....Captain
(Vacant)..................................First Lieutenant
D. G. Dubose..............................Second Lieutenant
W. H. Carlisle............................Second Lieutenant

COMPANY I.

R. G. Howard ....Captain (in hands of enemy)
H. M. Cannon..............................First Lieutenant
W. J. Altman..............................Second Lieutenant
(Vacant)..................................Second Lieutenant

COMPANY K.

J. W. Owens...............................Captain
C. L. Sansberry...........................First Lieutenant
E. B. Green...............................Second Lieutenant
H. J. Clifton.............................Second Lieutenant

COMPANY L.

H. Legett.................................Captain
W. B. Baker...............................First Lieutenant
E. L. Sweet...............................Second Lieutenant
W. D. Woodbury............................Second Lieutenant

This regiment had originally eleven companies. Company C had been transferred to another command.

TWENTY-FIFTH REGIMENT.

C. H. Simonton............................Colonel Commanding
John G. Pressley..........................Lieutenant Colonel
John V. Glover............................Major
Geo. H. Moffett...........................Adjutant
James E. Adger............................Quartermaster
W. C. Ravenel.............................Surgeon
A. J. Beale...............................Assistant Surgeon
A. F. Dickson.............................Chaplain

COMPANY A.

J. M. Carson..............................Captain
H. B. Olney...............................First Lieutenant
J. A. Ross................................Second Lieutenant
J. S. Hanahan.............................Second Lieutenant

COMPANY B.

E. W. Lloyd...............................Captain
J. S. Burgen..............................First Lieutenant
R. M. Taft................................Second Lieutenant
J. E. Bomar...............................Second Lieutenant

COMPANY C.

Thomas J. China.. .. ..Captain
E. Logan.. .. ..First Lieutenant
B. P. Brockington.. .. ..Second Lieutenant
S. J. Montgomery.. .. ..Second Lieutenant

COMPANY D.

W. J. McKerral.. .. ..Captain
D. G. McKay.. .. ..First Lieutenant
R. P. Bethea.. .. ..Second Lieutenant
M. L. Smith.. .. ..Second Lieutenant

COMPANY E.

W. B. Mazyck.. .. ..Captain
A. J. Mims.. .. ..First Lieutenant
V. Due.. .. ..Second Lieutenant
G. M. Salam.. .. ..Second Lieutenant

COMPANY F.

M. H. Sellars.. .. ..Captain
L. A. Harper.. .. ..First Lieutenant
John G. Evans.. .. ..Second Lieutenant
F. E. Shuler.. .. ..Second Lieutenant

COMPANY G.

James F. Izlar.. .. ..Captain
S. N. Kennerly.. .. ..First Lieutenant
S. Dibble.. .. ..Second Lieutenant (in hands of enemy)
G. H. Elliott.. .. ..Second Lieutenant

COMPANY H.

L. S. Hammond.. .. ..Captain
W. H. Seabrook.. .. ..First Lieutenant
F. G. Hammond.. .. ..Second Lieutenant
J. F. Ramsey.. .. ..Second Lieutenant

COMPANY I.

J. C. Burgess.. .. ..Captain
J. J. Logan.. .. ..First Lieutenant
F. B. Brown.. .. ..Second Lieutenant
R. F. Felder.. .. ..Second Lieutenant

COMPANY K.

W. B. Gordon.. .. ..Captain
F. J. Lesesne.. .. ..First Lieutenant
E. R. Lesesne .. ..Second Lieutenant
C. Lesesne.. .. ..Second Lieutenant

TWENTY-SEVENTH REGIMENT.

P. C. Gaillard..........................Colonel Commanding
J. A. Blake..............................Lieutenant Colonel
Jospeh Abney..................................Major
W. M. Smith................................Adjutant
R. Press Smith....................Assistant Quartermaster
J. L. Pressley................................Surgeon
S. P. Caine........................Assistant Surgeon
————————..............................Chaplain

COMPANY A.

F. F. Miles..................Captain (resigned shortly after)
B. W. Palmer............................First Lieutenant
J. W. Axson............................Second Lieutenant
J. M. Easterby..........................Second Lieutenant

COMPANY B.

Thos. G. Simons, Jr..............................Captain
William Sinkler........................First Lieutenant
A. H. Masterman........................Second Lieutenant
A. W. Muckenfuss......................Second Lieutenant

COMPANY C.

Samuel Lord..............Captain (resigned shortly after)
George Brown............................First Lieutenant
J. Campbell............................Second Lieutenant
H. W. Hendrix........................Second Lieutenant

COMPANY D.

J. Ward Hopkins................................Captain
J. A. Cay............................First Lieutenant
A. St. John Lance......................Second Lieutenant
J. T. Wells............................Second Lieutenant

COMPANY E.

R. Chisholm................................Captain
S. R. Proctor............................First Lieutenant
T. B. Crooker........................Second Lieutenant
S. M. Kemmerlin........................Second Lieutenant

COMPANY F.

Joseph Blythe Allston............................Captain
J. G. Hugenin..........................First Lieutenant
M. Stuart............................Second Lieutenant
(Detached in enrolling office. Never served with Brigade).
E. P. Cater............................Second Lieutenant

COMPANY G.

Henry Buist.. .. ..Captain
E. H. Holman.. .. ..First Lieutenant
C. J. McBeth.. .. ..Second Lieutenant
A. B. White.. .. ..Second Lieutenant

COMPANY H.

J. M. Mulraney.. .. ..Captain
A. A. Allemony.. .. ..First Lieutenant
J. Burke.. .. ..Second Lieutenant
R. R. Hogan.. .. ..Second Lieutenant

COMPANY I.

W. D. Walter.. .. ..Captain
T. R. Lynch.. .. ..First Lieutenant
J. C. Salters.. .. ..Second Lieutenant
W. J. Trim.. .. ..Second Lieutenant

COMPANY K.

William Clarkson.. .. ..Captain
————.. .. ..First Lieutenant
J. G. Harriss.. .. ..Second Lieutenant
A. D. Simons.. .. ..Second Lieutenant

SEVENTH BATTALION.

P. H. Nelson.. .. ..Lieutenant-Colonel Commanding
J. H. Rion.. .. ..Major
S. W. Nelson.. .. ..Adjutant
Eli Harrison.. .. ..Assistant Quartermaster
R. B. Hanahan.. .. ..Surgeon
————.. .. ..Assistant Surgeon
————.. .. ..Chaplain

COMPANY A.

B. S. Lucas.. .. ..Captain
F. McCaskell.. .. ..First Lieutenant
A. McCaskell.. .. ..Second Lieutenant
J. W. Gardiner.. .. ..Second Lieutenant

COMPANY B.

John R. Harrison.. .. ..Captain
J. L. Kennedy.. .. ..First Lieutenant
H. L. Isbell.. .. ..Second Lieutenant
S. W. Douglass.. .. ..Second Lieutenant

COMPANY C.

A. W. Pearson.......................................Captain
J. R. Manken.....................................First Lieutenant
————————.......................Second Lieutenant
————————.......................Second Lieutenant

COMPANY D.

J. L. Jones..Captain
E. A. Young....................................First Lieutenant
R. W. Young..................................Second Lieutenant
R. J. Cunningham..........................Second Lieutenant

COMPANY E.

P. P. Gaillard......................................Captain
J. M. Ross......................................First Lieutenant
————————.......................Second Lieutenant
————————.......................Second Lieutenant

COMPANY F.

Dove Segars.......................................Captain
William McSween..............................First Lieutenant
H. D. Tiller..................................Second Lieutenant
A. W. Raley..................................Second Lieutenant

COMPANY G.

William Clyburn....................................Captain
L. L. Clyburn..................................First Lieutenant
W. J. Taylor..................................Second Lieutenant
T. W. Sligh..................................Second Lieutenant

COMPANY H.

J. H. Brooks.......................................Captain
T. M. McCants..................................First Lieutenant
William Weston.................................Second Lieutenant
B. J. Randall..................................Second Lieutenant

The aggregate strength of the brigade thus formed was four thousand, two hundred and forty-six (4,246) present and absent, of whom fully five hundred were detailed in the different workshops, offices, etc., in the department. The majority of these men never got into the field. Some of them were properly detailed where they were, and from their mechanical skill or other special qualification for the detailed duty were more useful to the cause than they would have been in the ranks. But most of them were men whose native repugnance to the field endowed them with a facility in dodging, which, when backed up by more or less social influence, enabled them to skulk the war through as employees in the conscript and other military bureaus, on railroads, in printing offices, banks, blockade running and other employments supposed essential to Confederate existence.

A short notice of the history and character of the regiments now first brought together in brigade organization is necessary.

ELEVENTH REGIMENT.

Under the Act of the Legislature of South Carolina passed December, 1860, to provide "an armed military force," the original companies of this regiment were raised for twelve months and went into service on the coast, Colonel Wm. C. Heyward* commanding. It was then called the Ninth South Carolina Volunteers, and its organization was irregular, having more than ten companies, and one of these a light battery. The regiment transferred its service during '61 to the Confederate Government under arrangement made between the Convention of the State and the Confederate authorities, and was now known as the Eleventh South Carolina Volunteers. In May, 1862, it re-enlisted for "two years or the war." A more general bouleversment of officers took place upon the re-enlistment in this regiment than in any other South Carolina command at the re-elections through a most mistaken policy, permitted by the government. The regiment was seriously and permanently injured.

Its service had been uneventful to this date. Some of its companies had been engaged at the bombardment of the forts at Port Royal in 1861, and at the Battle of Pocotaligo, in '62, a portion of it had won reputation, while the remainder of the regiment had suffered some loss (its major, Harrison, included), being fired into upon a railroad train while en route to the scene of action, when it arrived after the repulse of the enemy. At the siege of Charleston, the regiment had not borne as prominent a part as some others, though here as well as in Florida, whither it had been sent in the latter part of the siege, it had done its duty well when called upon.

---

*See notice of Colonel Heyward, Vol. I, page 193.

Its present commander, Colonel Gantt, had been a lieutenant in the original regiment and was, on the reorganization, elected lieutenant-colonel. He succeeded Ellis on the latter's being compelled to resign to avoid charges of incompetency. Ellis—a cross-road politician—had been elected over Heyward without having served a day in this or any other regiment. Colonel Gantt had been at the State Military School, and his lieutenant-colonel, Izard, had held a commission in the United States navy. Colonel Izard served very little with the regiment after it was brigaded; he was most of his time on sick leave. Gooding, the senior captain, who succeeded to the majority, was an incubus upon the command, without soldierly spirit, and yet with ability enough to keep clear of such derelictions of duty as would bring him before a court. Finally, however, in the waning days of the Confederacy, he overstayed a leave under circumstances almost amounting to desertion and was dropped from the rolls.

Colonel Gantt was a good drill officer and had his regiment in fair discipline and presenting a good military appearance when it reported to the brigade. Its subsequent history will show that it had much good material in the ranks and among its officers, many of whom were worthy of their commissions.

This regiment was chiefly raised in Beaufort and Colleton Districts.

THE TWENTY-FIRST REGIMENT

Was organized 12th November, 1861, under a call upon South Carolina for additional troops and was mustered into Confederate service 1st January, 1862, for "three years or the war." It was drawn from what is known as the Pee Dee region of the State. Colonel Graham, its commander, had been an officer in Gregg's six-months regiment. Its lieutenant-colonel, Dargan, and its major, McIver, were excellent officers, and in the subordinate grades was found the usual melange—some as gallant and noble spirits as ever bore a sword or stopped a bullet—many who creditably filled their positions, and some of the earth, earthy. The regiment had been, from its organization, on the coast of South Carolina, and had borne a conspicuous part in the siege of Charleston. From its somewhat eventful service here, it was at this time more or less disorganized and required attention.

TWENTY-FIFTH REGIMENT.

Companies A and B of this regiment were raised from the Washington Light Infantry, a time-honored militia organization of Charleston, which also contributed a company to the Hampton Legion. These companies went into State service, serving at Coles Island the winter of '61-'62, and called themselves The Eutaw Battalion, Simonton, senior captain, commanding. Upon the reorganization of the First South Carolina (Hagood's) regiment in April, 1862, three of its companies (Pressley's, Glover's and Sellars') seceded, as they were permitted by the law to do, to this battalion, and it grew into a regiment by the addition of newly raised companies. On 22nd July, 1862, it was mustered into Confederate service for "three years or the war." .Captain Simonton became its colonel. He was a lawyer of prominence in Charleston, both before and after the war. His service with his regiment during its connection with the brigade was limited, he being most of the time detached on post duty. Captains Pressley and Glover became respectively lieutenant-colonel and major, and were both most excellent and meritorious officers. Among the subordinates were a number of first-class officers, and the men were of excellent material. Companies A and B were raised in Charleston; the other companies from the middle country of the State.

The discipline and esprit of the regiment was good. Its service had been principally in and around Charleston. It was creditably engaged at the Battle of Secessionville, among the troops outside of the fort. During the existing siege of the city, it had had a comparatively easy time on James Island until the last days of Wagner, when for the first time it was part of the garrison. Under its lieutenant-colonel, Pressley, it had then behaved with much steadiness, and met with considerable loss. Under the same meritorious officer it was engaged in the affair of the 16th July with General Terry's forces on James Island, and it had borne its share by detail in the other duties and events of the siege.

TWENTY-SEVENTH REGIMENT.

The Charleston Battalion, composing the first six companies of this regiment, was originally raised in Charleston and mustered into Confederate service in March, '62. In its subsequent history, it received many recruits from the country, but its officers were almost without exception Charlestonians, and the city element largely predominated in the ranks. The several companies were offshoots from the old militia organizations of the city and among themselves retained the names of their parent companies. Indeed this was common throughout the brigade, and there was scarcely a company in any of the regiments which, though known officially as Company A or Company B of such a regiment, had not some fancy name by which they were fond of calling themselves and by which they were generally known at home. P. C. Gaillard was the lieutenant-colonel commanding and David Ramsay major. Colonel Gaillard had graduated at West Point, a contemporary of General Bragg's, had served in the United States Army, and subsequently for many years was engaged in commercial pursuits in Charleston. He was a man with much of the old Roman type of character about him, had unbounded influence over his command, and was every inch a soldier. Notwithstanding his age and the loss of an arm at Wagner, he served faithfully with his regiment under every hardship of the campaign of '64 in Virginia, until, toward its close, his health succumbed and he was compelled to go upon the retired list and a post command.

Major Ramsay was a lawyer of high culture and fell at Wagner on the 18th July.

The battalion of sharpshooters composing the remaining companies of the regiment was raised in June, 1862, under orders from Richmond, partly by compulsory drafts from regiments already in service, and partly by voluntary enlistment. The officers were appointed, not elected, and the organization was rather that of Regulars than Volunteers.

In passing, it may be remarked that the scheme of the War Department of raising a special corps of sharpshooters failed, and though in this instance some excellent companies were formed, they never did duty other than infantry of the line. Indeed, as the war progressed, the whole Confederate Army rapidly became light infantry in mobility and appointments, and in a wooded country, with the Enfield rifle or its equivalent on both sides, it was seldom that anything but the ordinary skirmisher was needed. Under the circumstances, the repeating firearm was a greater advantage than any increased length of range or special accuracy of fire, the Enfield carrying its missile with deadly force and accuracy across most of the open levels encountered. There were occasions, however, such as at Wagner, at Petersburg and elsewhere in the writer's experience, when a few telescópic rifles, such as Whitworths, distributed through a regiment—say one to the company—were capable of good service. The possession of such a rifle might have been made a mark of honor as well as skill in the beam.

Major Abney, commanding the sharpshooters' battalion, had served in Mexico as lieutenant in the Palmetto Regiment; had in this war been elected to the command of one of the regiments raised in the State in the spring of '62, and, upon the inevitable reorganization upon entering Confederate service, a few weeks afterwards had been ousted by a man who was subsequently broken for cowardice. Abney was a brave man, but his habits were not good, and his virtues were rather passive than active. Blake, the lieutenant-colonel, also was a negative character. Both he and Abney had not sufficient elan and failed to command the confidence of their men. When Gaillard was absent, the regiment always did better under one of its many good subordinates. Abney's health became bad and he went on the retired list; and Blake was dropped for over-staying a leave in the spring of '65. He appealed, however, alleging great injustice done him, and was granted a court amid the rapidly culminating misfortunes of the Confederacy, the decision of which was never announced.

The Twenty-seventh was especially claimed by the Charlestonians as *their* regiment, and in consequence of its local popularity many of the best young men of the city were in its ranks. The average intelligence and social position of the rank and file were thus greater than most regiments, and its discipline and character were peculiar. It was not equal to some others in discipline, but under Gaillard, or any other of its officers who possessed its confidence, it would go anywhere and do anything. Under Blake or Abney it was far less efficient. There was too much intelligence and too little rigidity of discipline in its ranks for men without force of character to command it successfully. This regiment, like the others, had served only in South Carolina, but had been peculiarly fortunate in its service. It had won honor in the fort at Secessionville in '62; had been Talliferro's mainstay at Wagner on the 18th July; a portion of it had been Elliott's garrison at Sumter when the boat attack was repulsed; and two of its sharpshooter companies had obtained honorable mention at Pocotaligo.

THE SEVENTH BATTALION.

Lieutenant-Colonel Nelson, commanding this battalion, had commenced the war as brigadier-general of State troops at the reduction of Sumter, and General Hagood, then Colonel of the First South Carolina, had been attached to his command. When, shortly afterward, the State troops were transferred to Confederate service, the general officers lost their commissions, Nelson returned home and raised this battalion "for the war." He was a planter, a gentleman of high culture and fine presence, and an excellent officer. Major Rion had commenced the war as colonel of the Sixth South Carolina, had lost his commission in the re-election consequent upon taking Confederate service; had raised a company and joined Nelson. He was a leading lawyer of Fairfield District, both before and after the war. The subordinate officers were, with scarce an exception, good and some superior, and the men of excellent material. This battalion came nearer to Regulars in discipline and uniform efficiency at all times and under all circumstances than any volunteer troops the writer met with during the war; and this was largely due to the zeal and ability of Major Rion.

The battalion had served with distinction at Pocotaligo, arriving on a railroad train in time by a vigorous assault to decide the day. It had also borne honorable part in the existing siege of Charleston. It was drawn from the central districts of the State.

Such, briefly, was the character of the regiments now organized and known afterward as "Hagood's Brigade," as it appeared to one who knew them intimately, and who appreciated, as one appreciates a well-tried blade, that exalted heroism and unflinching devotion which marked their subsequent career as a body, but who had no respect for individuals in such a corps who fell short of its high standard—men bearing commissions in the

14—H

spirit of a conscript, while there were privates in their commands clad in rags, often infested with vermin, who went into action, or endured the hardships of the march and the trench, as if they bore a marshal's baton.

The following anecdote will show the estimate in which the regiments were held by one of the higher rank, who knew them well. On the lines before Bermuda Hundreds in May, '64, General Bragg, then holding staff position at Richmond, asked General Hagood in presence of General Beauregard what sort of a brigade he had. General Beauregard replied by narrating the incident mentioned in the Memoirs of the Second Military District (Vol. I, page 112) of Hagood's disappointment in going with the brigade sent to Vicksburg, and said: "I told him, then, that when opportunity served I would give him a good brigade with which to take the field; and I gave him the best troops I had, sir."

At the date of the order organizing the brigade, most of the regiments composing it were on James Island, constituting chiefly the infantry supports of the battalion of the east lines—a subdivision then commanded by General Hagood. The others were concentrated under his command in this position as soon as circumstances permitted. Gilmore's active operations had ceased, as before narrated, with the boat attack on Sumter, and the siege had subsided into a matter of long range fire. This state of affairs chiefly occupied the artillery, and afforded opportunity of bringing the brigade into a high state of efficiency, which was eagerly embraced.

The following circular was issued, and its directions enforced:

Headquarters Hagood's Brigade.
1 December, 1863.

Circular.

I. A course of instruction in drill will be instituted by the several commandants of regiments of the brigade as follows: The six (6) lessons in the battalion drill (Hardee's 2 Vol.) will be gone through with on successive days; and then three successive days will be devoted to the skirmish drill including the deployment of the battalion.* These duties will be had in

---

*I never saw a battalion deployed as skirmishers in actual battle. The Confederate practice was for each company to furnish men enough to cover its own front and one or more officers were detailed from the regiment. A field officer was generally detailed for the occasion to command all the skirmishers from the brigade. In some brigades these details became more or less permanent.—J. H.

the afternoon, and in the forenoon of the same day, each regimental commander will have caused his officers to recite on the lessons of the day—blackboards or some substitute being used.

II. Special attention will be given in this course to the guides, and commandants of the regiments are required to reduce to the ranks any noncommissioned officer, who, after reasonable instruction, fails to become master of his duty. The "advance in line" must be practised until the troops are perfect in its execution and its principles thoroughly understood. The troops must also be accustomed to manœuver as well by the rear rank as by the front, by inversion as by direction.

The "formation against cavalry," the "instructions for skirmishers," the "advance in line" and the "march in column" are of chief importance in the drill; and their relative importance is in the inverse order in which they are here enumerated. The points to be looked to in the march of a column, whatever the breadth of its front, are, (1) that the depth of the column never exceeds the width the troops are to occupy in line of battle. (2) That meeting an obstacle in the march, the men do not improperly break into files to pass it. (3) That no man, upon any pretense whatever, falls out of the ranks without the permission first obtained of his captain. The first two rules are to prevent fatigue to the men in closing up from time to time, and to prevent delay in the march of an army. A single battalion may lose but ten minutes on a march in thus improperly breaking into file, that will delay a brigade near an hour, and a division five hours, in which time a battle may be lost or won. The third rule is to prevent the evil of straggling, and all these rules will be enforced in this brigade on all marches, however distant from the enemy—whether going to or returning from duty, or upon any other occasion. Discipline is the result of habit, and careless habits in this particular must not be formed, or, if formed, must be broken. Officers must use such means, amounting to severity if necessary, as will enforce these rules, and they alone will be held responsible for any departure from them.

III. Commanding officers will notify these headquarters of the hours in the afternoon each may select for the drills ordered to the end that the brigadier-general may when practical be present.

By command Brigadier-General Hagood.

W. E. STONEY, A. A. A. G.

At a later day, when the brigade was in the field, a standing order, of which the following is an extract, prescribed minutely the details necessary to secure the proper conduct of marches, and regimental commandants were held directly responsible to the brigade commander for their proper observance:

"On all marches the officers second in rank present for duty with each regiment, together with the assistant surgeon, or in his absence the surgeon, will follow the regiment and be accompanied by a non-commissioned officer and a file of men. This will be the regimental rear-guard. The last regiment will, however, have instead a company as brigade rear-guard, and will be accompanied by the brigade surgeon and the surgeons who may not be immediately in rear of their regiments, filling the places of absent assistant surgeons. The ambulances will follow immediately thereafter and be succeeded by the ordnance wagons; and then the quartermaster's train, when the latter marches with the brigade. The commanding officer of the regiment will habitually march at its head, but he will frequently stop and let it march past him, to see that it marches properly. He will *always* do this upon encountering a rivulet or other obstruction which the men may be inclined to break their ranks in passing. This is most positively forbidden; all such places must be passed in proper order, and the regimental commander will immediately arrest and report any captain who fails to bring his company properly through such places. No discretion is allowed the regimental commander in such cases. An officer or man unable from any reason to keep up with the march will obtain from his immediate commander verbal permission to fall out. The regimental rear-guard will examine him, and if properly out of the ranks the assistant surgeon will give him written permission to fall to the rear, when the brigade surgeon will take such action as the case, in his opinion, requires. The brigade surgeon will be careful to allow no one to ride in the ambulances except in case of necessity. The files will be kept closed in marching and dressed, though the precision of the drill is not required. File closers will be held responsible for this by their company commanders. Cases of unauthorized straggling will be made by regimental commanders the subject of severe and summary discipline; it is the highest military offense, next to desertion.

"When in line of battle, the horses of those who do not ride in action* will be kept in the neighborhood of the field infirmary. The brigade quartermaster will see that they are supplied with forage at this point; and he will cause a light forage wagon to follow the brigade when the general quartermaster's train does not march in the column. A mounted quartermaster's man will

---

*Regimental officers.

have charge of this matter and of the ambulances, and always be with the column.

"Regimental commanders will hold their assistant quartermasters responsible for the regular supply of properly cooked food for their men. Any irregularity in this matter is *prima facie* the fault of these officers for which they must account."

The brigade inspector also habitually marched with the rearguard, which, when he was present, took its orders from him. In traveling by rail, other standing orders directed the company formation to be retained as far as practicable and *company officers were required to ride with their men*. A guard was kept in each car. In marches, which he could control, General Hagood always ten minutes after the march commenced halted for ten minutes to allow the men to adjust their packs and attend to the calls of nature. Afterwards he halted ten minutes in every hour. He always, too, after one of these halts, gave a preliminary signal to prepare to march. The writer has seen much unnecessary fatigue to the men and much discreditable lengthening of column by the absence of method in conducting a march. The practice in the Army of Northern Virginia was to have halts at no regular time, and, after a temporary halt, for the head of the column to move off without a general signal given, and each regiment arose in succession from the roadside where the men were resting and followed the march only from seeing the regiment ahead of it move. Thus the extra fatigue of hurrying up to close the column did away with the benefit of the rest. The march of the Confederate armies was habitually in "column of fours."

But to return to James Island. Subsequently to the course of regimental instruction, a school for field officers was opened at brigade headquarters with daily recitations and drills in evolutions of the line. Before this course was completed, each field officer was qualified and required to drill the brigade. The clothing, transportation and equipment of the brigade was at the same time inspected and renewed and completed, through the medium of proper requisitions. The ordnance was specially put upon an excellent footing. The long Enfield rifle, with accoutrements complete, was obtained for the whole command, except Gantt's regiment, and a small corps of artisans (selected from the ranks) was organized with traveling forges, etc., to render the command independent in matters of repair. Gantt's regiment remained armed with the smooth-bore musket until the victory of Drury's Bluff, when it armed itself upon the field with Enfields, and thenceforward the brigade was relieved from the inconvenience of having two calibres among its arms, and was in effectiveness of weapon upon a footing with the troops it encountered.

The following circular organized a Pioneer Corps and completed the preparation for the expected field service of the ensuing campaign:

Headquarters Hagood's Brigade.
James Island, 19 February, 1864.

Circular.

I. A Pioneer Corps will be organized for this brigade, and Major Gooding, Eleventh South Carolina, is assigned to its command.

II. Captains of companies under the supervision of regimental commanders will at once indicate from their respective companies each two men, having regard solely to their fitness from previous occupation for this purpose. The regimental commanders will each select a lieutenant of energetic and practical habits and report his name, rank, etc., together with the names of the men selected from their respective commands, to these headquarters.

III. The brigade quartermaster will issue, upon the requisition of Major Gooding, the necessary axes, spades and picks, together with the necessary slings for carrying them.

IV. The brigade ordnance officer will furnish to the Pioneer Corps the short Enfield rifle instead of the long Enfield, which the men now have, and see that they are supplied with proper slings for carrying them.

V. It is intended upon ordinary occasions that the officers and men of this corps shall remain and do duty, as usual, with their respective commands. In all marches, however, of the regiment, its Pioneers will be detached under its lieutenant and precede it. When the brigade moves the whole corps will precede the column under command of its field officer, the packs of the men being carried upon the baggage wagons. Upon marches, the corps will be excused from camp guard and picket duty. In action, the men and officers will return to their respective commands. Should this, under the circumstances, be impracticable, the corps will take its place in line of battle as a separate battalion.

VI. Upon all inspections and reviews, the Pioneers will appear united under their officers. The men will be held as strictly responsible for the condition of their implements as for their arms and accoutrements. Company commanders are charged with this and are held responsible that the implements are not used for ordinary camp purposes. The senior officer of the corps will inspect it once a month by regiments, and report its condition to these headquarters, commandants of regiments ordering out the Pioneers upon the request of this officer.

VII. Major Gooding will keep rolls and rosters, and take all necessary steps to make his corps efficient in the spirit of this order.

By command Brigadier-General Hagood.

P. K. MALONY, A. A. G.

Major Lartigue, the brigade quartermaster, took special interest in equipping this corps, and devised very complete slings for carrying the implements with ease to the men even at a double quick.

As thus organized, the corps was continued and did good service until the fall of '64, though, after the brigade was assigned to Hoke's Division, it was generally (under a lieutenant) a part of the Division Pioneer Corps. In October, 1864, General Lee, in an effort to increase the fighting strength of his attenuated army, ordered all such corps broken up and the men returned to the ranks. Instead, he directed one man from each company to be selected and known as "Pioneer," who, as such, was exempted from guard and picket duty, but in all other respects was considered a soldier in the ranks. In like manner commissioned and non-commissioned officers were selected who were to be put in charge when these pioneers were called together.

The fact was, that this campaign had been so much one continued siege, and the men were by this time so thoroughly indoctrinated with notions of the value of breastworks and rifle pits, that the entrenching tools with which each company had been supplied, or had supplied itself, were carried as its most valuable property. Peculations of these cherished implements were not uncommon, and on the march it was not an unusual sight to see a company officer carrying a cherished spade or pick, after it had successively passed through the hands of some half dozen wearied soldiers of his command, each of whom had borne it in addition to his arms. A special corps supplied with such implements was, therefore, no longer important.

In the general organization of the Confederate armies, at first there were brigade and regimental commissaries—all commissioned. At the date of which we are now writing, the regimental commissaries had been discontinued, and their duties assigned to the regimental assistant quartermasters, aided by regimental commissary sergeants. At a later day the regimental assistant quartermasters were discontinued, and the organization was a commissary and a quartermaster to the brigade, each ranking as major, and each with an assistant, ranking as captain. There remained throughout a commissary sergeant and a quartermaster sergeant to each regiment.

The medical corps consisted, during the whole war, of a surgeon and an assistant surgeon to each regiment, and when brigaded, the senior surgeon. assumed control and was known as the brigade surgeon.

These various staff officers in the beginning were all nominated by the line officer to whose corps they were attached. Afterwards they were transferred and assigned from corps to corps by the chief of their respective bureaus at Richmond without consulting the line officer commanding, and often to his chagrin and disgust. The same general remarks as to organization, appointment and assignment apply to the adjutants, inspectors and ordnance officers. Major-generals, lieutenant-generals and generals had each their staff officers of each department for their respective commands, and a bureau chief of each department of the staff was located at Richmond.

There were also post quartermasters, and post commissaries, whose duties never led them into the field, and who were too often corrupt speculators upon the necessities of their suffering country. It was the shortcomings of this class that brought the very name of commissary and quartermaster into odium and contempt. Of those officers of these departments who served with the armies in the field, the writer deems it but justice to say that there was as much high tone and devotion to the cause among those whom he met as among any other class of officers in the service. He desires here to record his appreciation of the gentlemen who filled these offices in his command. They yielded to no members of his staff in patriotism, high honor and personal gallantry. Their names will not as often occur in these memoirs as others, for the discharge of their necessary duties oftenest kept them in the rear, but they were always ready, when these permitted, to come to him as volunteers in action—and on these occasions did always well.

CAMPAIGN OF 1864 IN VIRGINIA.

The winter, with its comparative quiet, had closed; and the opposing parties were concentrating and marshalling their forces for a more vigorous and decisive campaign than had yet marked the history of the war. Virginia and Tennessee were respectively in the east and the west, the theaters upon which the opposing banners were unfurled, and it was evident that around these two centers would be collected in hostile array all of strength that either party possessed.

Gilmore, with the bulk of his army, had early in April been transferred to Virginia. Beauregard had been assigned to the command of the "Department of North Carolina and Southern Virginia"—a territorial command extending from Wilmington to James River in Virginia.

Wise's and Walker's (formerly Evans's) brigades had followed him, and Hagood's and Colquitt's brigades alone remained of the infantry lying at Charleston during the winter of '63-'64. These soon followed, Hagood's first and Colquitt's a week afterward.

Hagood's brigade commenced moving by rail on the night of the 28th of April for Wilmington, where it was directed to report by letter to General Beauregard, whose headquarters were at Weldon. The whole brigade, with its transportation, was not concentrated at Wilmington till the 4th May. It was encamped some two miles east of the city.

On the 5th May, the brigade received orders to proceed by rail to Petersburg, its train to move by highway. Owing to insufficient transportation, the brigade moved in fragments. Lieutenant-Colonel Dargan was dispatched with seven companies of the Twenty-first on the 5th, early in the day, and was followed by Colonel Graham with the remaining companies of that regiment and three companies of the Twenty-fifth. Next day General Hagood moved with the Twenty-seventh regiment and the remaining companies of the Twenty-fifth. Later in the day, the Eleventh regiment and Seventh battalion followed. A few cooking utensils were taken along. The horses of all the mounted officers, except the general and staff, together with the ambulances, had to go by highway with the train. No baggage was carried except upon the persons of officers and men. This with the men was excessive. They had good knapsacks, and, with the reluctance of all troops fresh from stationary quarters to throw away their little comforts, had overloaded their packs. So far it was very well, but in the active operations, into which they at once entered upon their arrival at Petersburg, in the first day's marching and fighting, off went the knapsacks, one by one, as its owner became excited or jaded; and thus was lost to him his necessaries as well as superfluities, while if he had only been burthened with the first it would have been borne and retained. Much discomfort and suffering resulted to the men from want of cleanliness, consequent upon this loss in the beginning of the campaign.

It had been foreseen by the brigade commander, when he observed the men laden like pack horses in moving from Charleston, and he had warned regimental commanders against permitting it. He should have interdicted it himself.

It is not within the scope of these Memoirs to go into the general strategy of the Virginia campaign, but some reference to it is necessary to understand the part borne by the brigade.

Grant, made lieutenant-general and commander-in-chief of all the armies of the United States a few months before, had made his headquarters with the Army of the Potomac, numbering some 140,000 men and lying behind the Rapidan, sixty miles north of the Confederate Capital. It was confronted by the Army of Northern Virginia under Lee, numbering about 52,000 of all arms.* The City of Richmond was Grant's objective, and he proposed to move upon it by the direct overland route, while Butler, moving from Fortress Monroe up the James, was to secure a point at its junction with the Appomattox from which to operate on the southern communications of Richmond. There was also to be made a co-operative move under Hunter from the Valley against the western communications of Richmond, which, when made, resulted in little but covering the Federal Army with infamy for its wanton and merciless destruction of private propery.* And in Tennessee and elsewhere in the West, Grant had ordered a heavy and continuous aggressive to be taken to keep re-enforcements from Lee. To sap the Confederate sources

---

*Swinton's Army of the Potomac, 413.

*Hunter boasted that he had reduced the theatre of his incursion to such a condition that "a crow flying over it would have to carry its rations."—J. H. Was it not Sheridan who said this?—Editor.

of material supply, razzias by light movable columns for the purpose of destroying railroads, mills, provisions, growing crops, farm stock and buildings, were to be specially organized. The regular Federal columns were to devote as much attention to these objects as was consistent with other and less congenial duties. And wherever Federal influence extended, persistent efforts were to be made in debauching the black agricultural labor of the country. These raids and these practices upon the blacks had their inception earlier in the war, but in this campaign, and as the struggle culminated, the first became more pitiless, and the last, in the decreasing area covered by Confederate arms, more effective.

The move from Fortress Monroe was, however, the most important and threatening diversion in the programme of the Virginia campaign; and with thirty to forty thousand men and a large naval armament was entrusted to General B. F. Butler, of New Orleans notoriety.

On the 4th May, Grant crossed the Rapidan and commenced his overland march. On the same day Butler commenced ascending the James. On the night of the 5th, he debarked at Bermuda Hundreds, the peninsular made by the confluence of the James and the Appomattox, and began to entrench across its narrow neck about three miles from the railroad connecting Petersburg and Richmond. On the 6th, he threw out a brigade to destroy the railroad at Walthal Junction.

Beauregard's troops were much scattered over his extensive territorial command, pending the developments of the enemy's designs. The largest portion were with General Hoke, who had recently been engaged in some successful offensive operations in Eastern North Carolina. Very few, if any, troops other than local militia of an inferior character were under General Pickett, commanding at Petersburg; and it was to meet and delay Butler's advance that Hagood's brigade had been pushed forward, while Beauregard got the balance of his troops in hand and drew re-enforcements from further South.

AFFAIR AT WALTHAL JUNCTION.

Colonel Graham, with the companies he had moved with, arrived at Petersburg and was pushed forward by General

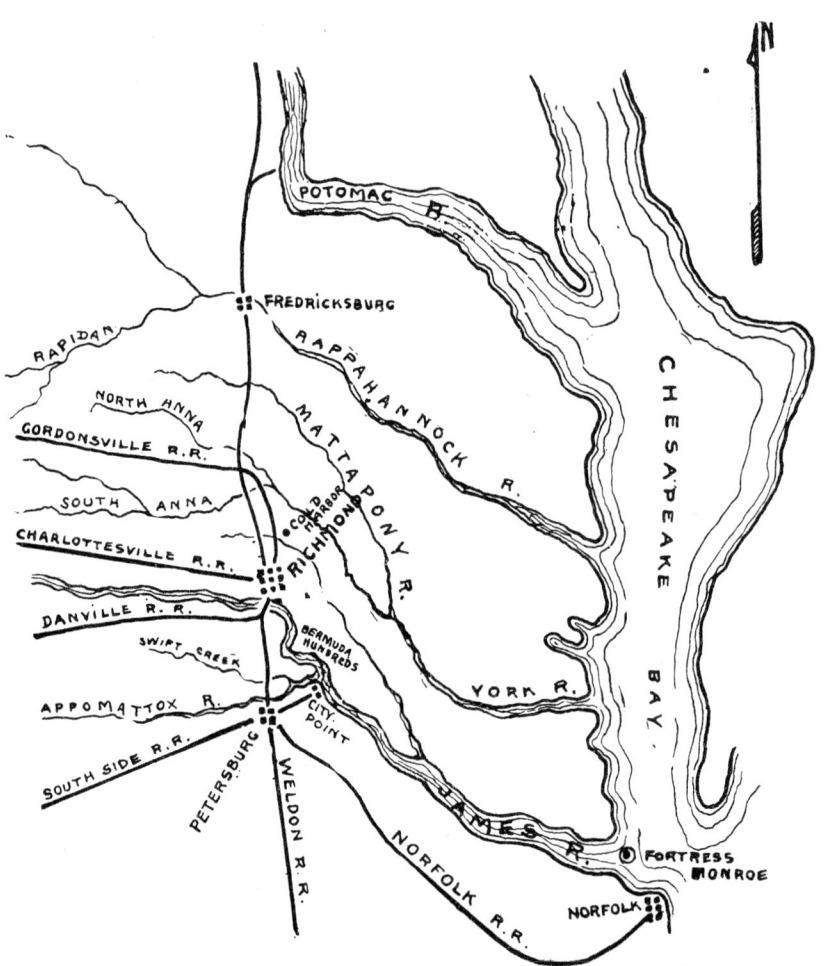

Sketch Of A Part Of Virginia

Pickett to Walthal Junction, reaching the latter place a little before 5 p. m. on the 6th May, and there found Lieutenant-Colonel Dargan's detachment which had preceded him about an hour. This raised his force to about 600 men, composed of his own regiment and three companies of the Twenty-fifth under Major Glover. As Graham's men jumped off the platform cars upon which they were borne, the brigade of the enemy,* before alluded to as thrown forward against the railroad, was in view some thousand yards off across an open field, advancing in line of battle and supported by artillery. Informed by a citizen of the topography, Graham rapidly advanced his men to a sunken road, running parallel to the railroad and some 300 yards nearer to the enemy. In this natural trench he took position across the field, his right resting upon a wood, and his left upon a ravine. A brisk action ensued. The enemy made two direct attacks, and after his second repulse, at nightfall, withdrew, leaving some of his dead and wounded upon the field. Graham's loss was two killed and thirty-one wounded.† He spoke well of the spirit and steadiness of his men.

At 8 p. m. the same evening, General Hagood arrived at Petersburg with the remaining seven companies of the Twenty-fifth, commanded by Lieutenant-Colonel Pressley. After some delay in rationing the men, he moved forward to re-enforce Graham. Roger A. Pryor, formerly a brigadier of the Confederate Army, but now a private trooper acting as guide and courier to General Pickett, piloted him to the scene of action. Arrived at the Junction, General Hagood found General Bushrod Johnson there, who informed him that hearing Graham's firing he had marched to his assistance from the direction of Drury's Bluff with a brigade of 1,168 Tennesseeans and had arrived during the night. Gaillard, with the Twenty-seventh regiment, joined Hagood at daybreak and raised his command to an aggregate of 1,500 men. General Johnson, having the senior commission, assumed the command, and shortly after daylight General D. H. Hill arrived upon the field. This officer, in consequence of some difficulty with the President and General Bragg, under whom he had recently

---

*Hickman's.

†The Federals lost 9 killed, 61 wounded.—Letter of Ed. T. Westenby of Hickman's Brigade to General Hagood, 1881.

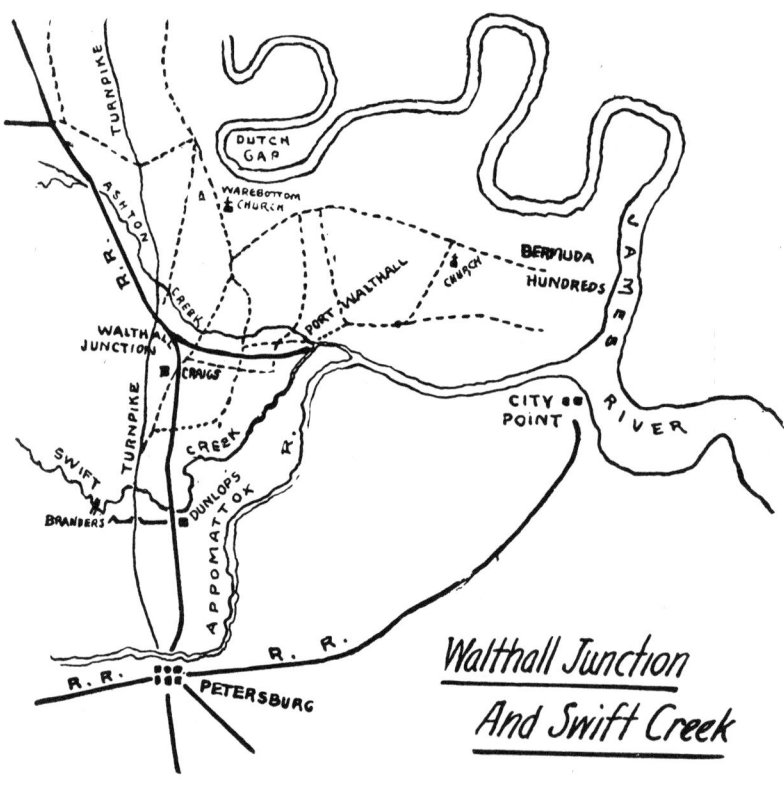

Walthall Junction And Swift Creek

served in Tennessee, was without a command at this time, but, unwilling to be idle at a time when the country had so much need of the services of her sons, had attached himself as aide to General Beauregard's staff. Although General Johnson was in command at the Junction, the ensuing operations of the day had their inspiration and direction largely from General Hill.

After daylight on the 7th, it was ascertained that the enemy had entirely withdrawn from our immediate front, and scouts reported them in the vicinity of Warbottom Church, about three miles off and somewhat to our left. About 10 a. m., General Hagood was directed to move across Ashton Creek towards the Church to feel and develop their strength and position. General Hill accompanied him, and he was told that Johnson would follow in support with his brigade. He moved in column of fours along the narrow road through the woods, the Twenty-seventh leading and skirmishers well advanced. In about a mile the skirmishers encountered the enemy's cavalry* advancing, and fired upon them, driving them back. The Twenty-seventh was at once deployed to the right of the road, and the skirmish line strengthened. A desultory skirmish ensued; and the enemy showing a disposition to develop to our left, three companies of the Twenty-fifth regiment were deployed on the line of the Twenty-seventh and to the left of the road. It soon became evident that under cover of this skirmish the enemy was moving masses of infantry to our left, with a view of flanking us and striking the railroad, and, upon General Hill's returning and reporting the fact to Johnson, Hagood was directed to withdraw and take position along the railroad at the Junction. This he did in column, usi g the skirmish line deployed and slightly engaged, first as flanke.s and afterward as a rear guard, as the direction of the road interposed them between himself and the enemy. In the meanwhile a force of the enemy had appeared south of Ashton Creek, advancing over the ground of Graham's affair of the evening before; and Johnson's brigade had not moved in support of Hagood. A few discharges from Hanker's battery of field pieces caused this force to retire. It was evident that an attack in force was now about to be made. Our line was formed along the railroad with Hagood's left resting where the turnpike crossed it

---

*Orlderdenk's N. Y. Mounted Rifles, N. Y. *Herald,* 10 May.

and Johnson's men prolonging the right toward and beyond Craig's house. Hagood had the Twenty-first regiment in reserve upon the turnpike. The artillery (six pieces) were placed by General Johnson near Craig's house. He had two other pieces sent him from Petersburg manned by uninstructed men (convalescents and men on furlough of other arms picked up in the city), who, when the action commenced, deserted their guns without firing a shot. The enemy reappeared in front of Johnson about 2 p. m. in their original force, estimated by him at four regiments and a battery of artillery, which failed to engage him except with artillery at long range, and was replied to by his batteries. This demonstration had, however, the effect of neutralizing Johnson's 1,168 men, who remained quietly watching it during the action that ensued, and lost only seven men wounded by shells.

At the same time (about 2 p. m.) the enemy appeared in two strong lines of battle with skirmishers thrown out and supported by artillery on Hagood's front. He approached from across the valley of Ashton Creek, here without swamp or woods, and his line was oblique to ours and tending to overlap it to the left. After a half hour's brisk fighting, he retired his lines somewhat, though still engaging us at longer range, and under cover of an intermediate wood moved his second line by a flank across the railroad, and it soon reappeared approaching upon Hagood's left and rear, the left of this force being upon the prolongation of our line of battle. The movement was concealed by woods until the flanking party was within easy rifle range.

The Twenty-first regiment had been ordered up into line on the left in the beginning of the action; and, upon suddenly receiving this flank fire, broke. The men went back slowly, but their organization was broken, and they were deaf to the expostulations of those officers who tried to stop them. General Hagood, perceiving the critical condition of things, proceeded at full speed with his mounted staff to lend assistance in rallying the men. The brave Lieutenant-Colonel Dargan was killed with the colors in his hands, waving them and calling to his men to rally. Graham was shot in the leg, while actively struggling against the impending rout, and had to leave the field. The command of the regiment then devolved upon Wilds, the senior captain, Major

McIver being absent. Captain Stoney, of the staff, fell from his horse with a minnie ball through his lungs, while nobly doing his duty. At length, by dint of entreaty, expostulation and threats, the retrograde movement was checked. Captain Tracy, volunteer aid-de-camp, seized the colors from the sergeant then bearing them and planted them in the ground. Lieutenant Chappell, commanding a company, rallied some dozen of his men upon it; and at once the whole current of feeling in the regiment seemed changed. The men formed right and left upon the colors, under the hot fire of the advancing enemy, with something of the precision of the dress parade. As they formed, General Hagood, to steady them, made them lie down and return the enemy's fire from that position. While this regiment was being rallied the two remaining regiments were being bent back to conform to the new position; and the result of the whole was to change our position as if he had half changed front to the rear on the right company of his right regiment. He now partially confronted at once both the force which had first engaged him and that approaching on the flank, both heavily pressing with fire, but the latter only advancing. As soon as his new line was taken, General Hagood ordered an advance. The brigade rushed forward with enthusiasm, and drove back the flanking line—they not again appearing in that direction. This advance regained us the railroad, but the right of Hagood's brigade now rested at the turnpike crossing, where his left had first been. The enemy again massed heavily in Hagood's front and essayed an advance, but his men, sheltered in the railroad cut, easily repelled this attack with little loss to themselves.

Between 4 and 5 p. m. the engagements ceased, except the firing of sharpshooters and artillery on both sides; and before dark the enemy withdrew from the field unpursued and carrying off most of his wounded. Hagood's force, as before stated, was 1,500 men and his loss during the day was 22 killed, 132 wounded, and 13 missing. The force of the enemy was five brigades of infantry, under General Brooks,* with the usual proportion of artillery and a regiment of cavalry. His loss was heavy. General Johnston estimated it at 1,000; prisoners put it larger, but it was probably not so great. During the action Hagood was assisted

---

*Army of the Potomac, p. 464.

15—H

at different times by two pieces of artillery sent to him from the right, but they were of very little service, getting twice out of ammunition after very few discharges and going half a mile to the rear to replenish it. General Johnson replied to his call for assistance, when the Twenty-first broke, that the enemy were too threatening on his front to spare it.

The Eleventh regiment and Seventh battalion arrived upon the field after the action. Pickets were thrown out and the sad duty of burying the dead and caring for the wounded was performed without distinction between friend and foe.

The brunt of this action fell upon Hagood's brigade; and in the progress of the narrative it will be seen that it saved Petersburg. By the time the enemy were again ready to advance sufficient re-enforcements had arrived to hold the place. The citizens appreciated the fact, and were enthusiastic in their gratitude. A flag was voted the brigade by the ladies; the merchants would take no pay from the men for their little purchases, and from at least one pulpit thanks were offered for the "timely arrival of the 1,500 brave South Carolinians." The brigade did acquit itself well. It was its first fight upon Virginia soil, and a creditable letter of introduction to the battle-scarred veterans of Lee among whom it was shortly merged.

Lieutenant-Colonel Pressley had his arm shattered by a rifle bullet in the charge which decided the fortunes of the day, and refused assistance, ordering back into the advancing ranks men who stopped to aid him. The arm was resected at the shoulder joint, and, though afterwards of some service to him, the colonel was never again fit for the field. The brigade from this time lost the valuable services of that meritorious officer. Glover succeeded to the command of the regiment in the absence of Simonton, who had remained upon detached duty at Charleston.

Private Vince Bellinger, a cripple from wounds received at Secessionville and on light duty with the commissary, quit the train when he heard the battle was going against us and came upon the field. Picking up the rifle of a fallen man, he joined a company and fought well during the balance of the day. Captain Sellars, of the Twenty-fifth, was wounded and returned to the fight after having the wound dressed. Lieutenants Moffett and Due, Sergeant W. V. Izler and Private I. S. Shomaker, of the

Twenty-fifth, and Sergeants Pickens Butler Watts, J. B. Abney and J. P. Gibbons, with Corporal J. Booser and Private Aemiliers Irving, of the Twenty-seventh, were mentioned for gallantry by their regimental commanders. No report of the kind was received from the Twenty-first, in consequence of the fall of its field officers and the succession of Captain Wilds to the command late in the action. There were many instances, however, of devotion in its ranks, and General Hagood often spoke with admiration of the bearing of Lieutenant Chappell in rallying the regiment. The services of the staff were invaluable in restoring order in the Twenty-first. Moloney, Mazyck and Martin did their duty with great intrepidity; and without these and Tracy and Stoney it is doubtful if the Twenty-first regiment could have been stopped. Tracy received promotion shortly after in consequence of his services in this affair, and was assigned to duty with General Earley in the Valley of Virginia. Stoney lingered a long time between life and death, and nine months afterward rejoined the brigade with one lung gone. Faithful to the last, he endured the vicissitudes and hardships of the campaign of '65; and shed bitter tears when the last hope of the Cause he loved was buried with Johnston's surrender. The extent to which the enemy had availed himself of foreign recruiting was exhibited in the fact that among the twenty or thirty prisoners taken by Hagood's brigade, there were men of six different nationalities, some of whom could not even imperfectly speak English.

SWIFT CREEK.

The arrival of the Eleventh regiment and Seventh battalion of Hagood's brigade at the Junction had raised our force to 3,500 men. The strength of Butler's force had now, however, been ascertained to be ten times that number. The line of railroad afforded no suitable position to await the advance of such an army. Without natural protection, the flanks could be turned on either side, and our line of retreat either into Richmond or Petersburg, instead of being covered by our position, was on the prolongation of our line of defense. General Pickett, at Petersburg, seemed too under the impression that an advance against the city was threatened on the south side of the Appomattox; and no re-enforcements were arriving from the South or information received as to when they could be expected. Accordingly, in a dispatch received at 10 p. m., General Pickett directed General Johnson to withdraw to the line of Swift Creek, three miles from Petersburg. At midnight the movement was commenced and by 3 a. m., of the 8th, the troops in position on the south bank of that stream and busily engaged in strengthening the entrenchments already partially constructed along that line as part of the defences of Petersburg. Hagood's brigade covered the turnpike and extended to the left as far as Brandee's Bridge and to the right as far as the railroad bridge. He also had a regiment with a section of artillery advanced by way of outpost to the top of the hill on the turnpike just beyond the creek.* The railroad bridge was held by Colonel McCauthen with the Fifty-first North Carolina regiment, of Clingman's brigade, and Johnson's brigade prolonged the right. Some eighteen pieces of artillery, consisting of Hawkins's, Owens's, Payne's and Martin's batteries, were distributed along the line, and Colonel Harris, of Beauregard's staff, arriving from Weldon, took charge of the engineering operations. A detachment of twenty-two men of Johnson's brigade was made, to work the heavy guns of Fort Clifton near the debouchment of Swift's Creek into the Appomattox, and which controlled the navigation of that river. Captain Martin commanded the fort.

The field of battle at the Junction was occupied by our advanced forces till 10 a. m., on the 9th, collecting and removing arms, accoutrements, etc. Butler unaccountably delayed his second advance upon the railroad thus long, and then our smaller force fell back before him skirmishing. The same morning, five gunboats attacked Fort Clifton, and after three hours' fighting retired with the loss of one of their number. By 12 m., Butler was in strong force on the north bank of Swift Creek and skirmishing going on between both infantry and artillery. Hagood still held the eminence on the pike upon the enemy's side of the creek.

At 11 a. m., General Pickett, from Petersburg, had instructed Johnson to maintain a defensive, advising him of re-enforcements on the way from Weldon. At 1 p. m., he enclosed a dispatch from Bragg, at Richmond, and directed him in pursuance of it

---

*See Map on page 81.

to take the offensive. Hagood was accordingly ordered to advance on his front, and the movement began. Nelson was directed with the Seventh to cross at Brandee's, and bearing to the right attack in flank the force which the rest of the brigade would encounter on the pike. Gantt, with his regiment and a detachment of the Twenty-fifth, was 150 yards across the stream holding the hill already referred to, his skirmishers thrown forward in a semi-circle of some 200 yards radius and the enemy slightly pressing. As the remaining regiments filed out of the entrenchments and moved in column down the long slope of probably 250 yards to the Turnpike Bridge, the movement was visible to the enemy on the wooded height beyond and to the right of the bridge; and a heavy fire was opened from their batteries. While the leading regiment, the Twenty-first, was crossing the bridge, Colonel Harris galloped up to General Hagood, and informing him that Pickett's plans were again changed, directed him to make a reconnoisance with the troops already over the creek and ascertain whether the present demonstration by the enemy was a feint or a real movement. Hagood told him that of course he would carry out the order, but that it was perfectly evident the enemy were in force, and that the troops he was directed to take could accomplish nothing. While they were speaking, the enemy commenced pressing heavily upon Gantt; his skirmishers were driven in, and he was warmly engaged. Gantt's line of battle was to the left of the road, beyond the crest of the hill. The Twenty-first was hurried over the bridge, and deploying to the right of the road, under cover of the hill, was directed to advance upon an alignment with Gantt. It did not behave with its accustomed spirit, was slow in deploying, advanced tardily up the broken acclivity, and was of very little assistance in the brief but sanguinary struggle that ensued.

Gantt maintained himself stoutly under the heavy pressure upon him for some minutes, until hearing firing upon his left and supposing it to be Nelson coming into action and that the whole brigade was behind him, he ordered, under his previous instructions, an advance. The roar of musketry that followed informed Hagood, who was getting the Twenty-first up the hill, of the overwhelming force in his front, and he sent Captain Moloney to order Gantt back across the creek, while the balance of the Twenty-fifth on the south bank was deployed to cover the crossing, and the regiments which had not crossed and were standing in column in the pike were ordered back to the entrenchments. The troops over the creek came back pell mell over the bridge, and were reformed on the south bank. The Twenty-fifth checked pursuit; and this most useless and disastrous reconnaisance in force was over. Colonel Nelson did not reach the scene of action, and the firing Gantt heard was from one of his own companies stationed by himself as a flanking outpost. The loss of the troops engaged was in the few minutes that the affair lasted, 31 killed, 82 wounded, and 24 missing, making an aggregate of 137 men thrown away because of too many generals, and too far away from the field of battle.

Colonel Harris, with his usual indifference to fire, remained with General Hagood during the affair, and Lieutenant-Colonel Logan, of the Hampton Legion (afterwards General Logan) acted upon his staff and was of much service. Colonel Logan had been on leave and was on his way back to his command. Captain Leroy Hammond and his brother, Lieutenant Hammond, together with Lieutenant Seabrook, being all the officers of one of the companies engaged from the Twenty-fifth regiment, were killed. The Hammonds were grandsons of Colonel Leroy Hammond of revolutionary fame in South Carolina; Seabrook was a graduate of the State Military Academy. They were brave and efficient officers. Lieutenant Wolfe, of the Eleventh, was also killed. Captain Carson, commanding the detachment of the Twenty-fifth, was severely wounded and incapacitated for service for the rest of the campaign. Tracy and Moloney, of the staff, both had their horses wounded under them. Among the missing were some valuable officers and men.

On the night of the 9th, there was some heavy skirmishing between Johnson's brigade and the enemy, with advantage to us. On the 10th, everything was quiet in our front, and General Hagood obtained permission to send a flag of truce to enquire after his wounded of the day before, and propose an exchange of prisoners he had captured at the Junction for those he had lost at the Creek. Captain Moloney was sent, and Lieutenant-Colonel Lightfoot of the artillery accompanied him. On arriving at the enemy's outpost, they found them retiring, in consequence of which our flag was forcibly detained for some hours. Butler was then an outlaw by proclamation of Confederate authorities for his conduct at New Orleans, and Captain Moloney had been directed to hold no communication with him, but to seek his ends if possible through General Turner, the officer commanding in Hagood's front.

Information was obtained, but the exchange failed; though Moloney was informed there would be no difficulty if the proposal was made in form to Butler.

BATTLE OF DRURY'S BLUFF

Butler, during the 9th May, incompletely destroyed a part of the railroad by upsetting the road structure, the crossties and rails remaining attached, and it is said* intended on the 10th to cross Swift Creek and make a determined effort at the capture of Petersburg; but deceived by tidings from Washington received the night of the 9th, that Lee was in full retreat before Grant, he determined to turn northward and assist in the capture of Richmond. Instead, however, of pressing at once upon the latter place with its meagre garrison, he withdrew aside into his entrenchments at Bermuda Hundreds, leaving the road open for the transfer by the shortest route of the troops which had been confronting him at Swift Creek, into the immediate southern defenses of the Confederate Capital at Drury's Bluff, and did not march on the latter place until two days afterward.

In the meanwhile, Major-General Hoke arrived at Petersburg with the troops (three brigades) which he had had with him in Eastern North Carolina, and, assuming command, put all our forces in march for Drury's Bluff along the turnpike left open by Butler. The movement was a flank march of ten miles along the enemy's front, he being in superior force about three miles to the right. The army moved in column of fours, with a field battery between each brigade, and the ambulances and ordnance wagons following their respective commands. The usual advance and rear guards were formed and a strong force of infantry flankers marched some three hundred yards on the right in single file at deployed intervals. Cavalry moved parallel with the

---

*Greeley's American Conflict.

march, still further towards the side of attack. The movement commenced at 1 p. m. on the 11th; Hoke bivouacked eight miles from Swift Creek, and on the morning of the 12th marched into the lines of Drury's Bluff. He was not molested. It commenced raining the night of the 11th and continued two or three days. The troops suffered much from cold and wet.

Soon after we were in position at Drury's, on the 12th, and had established our picket line, the enemy appeared. Skirmishing commenced and was maintained with more or less vigor during that day and the next. Toward evening of the 13th, some advantage was obtained over the North Carolina troops on our right, and Hoke determined to withdraw to the second or interior line of defense, which was accordingly done before day, on the 14th. At daylight on the same morning, General Beauregard joined us, having made a circuitous and forced march from Petersburg by way of Chesterfield Court House with Colquitt's brigade and a regiment of cavalry.

The lines of Drury's Bluff were in the nature of an entrenched camp. Starting at the bluff, they ran in a southwesterly direction across the pike and the Petersburg and Richmond railroad, then bending back, they returned to the river James, about a mile and a half north of the bluff. From Fort Stephens (a bastioned work on this line east of the pike) another line of slighter profile branched off in a curve still more to the southwest, forming an advanced line, with its left running into Fort Stephens and its right resting "in air" near the railroad. It was this last line that Hoke abandoned on the night of the 13th-14th May.

In the new position, Hagood's brigade occupied Fort Stephens and extended its right to the turnpike—the regiments coming from left to right in the following order: Twenty-seventh, Twenty-first, Seventh, Eleventh and Twenty-fifth. Johnson's, Clingman's and Corse's brigades came in the order named on Hagood's right. These four brigades constituted Hoke's division, as the army was temporarily organized after Beauregard's arrival. Another division was also organized with Colquitt commanding, and held in reserve. General Robert Ransom's division occupied the space from Hagood's left to the river, after it had arrived on the 15th.

Butler's skirmishing was confined to Hoke's front. Seeming inclined to operate on the Confederate right flank, he was content

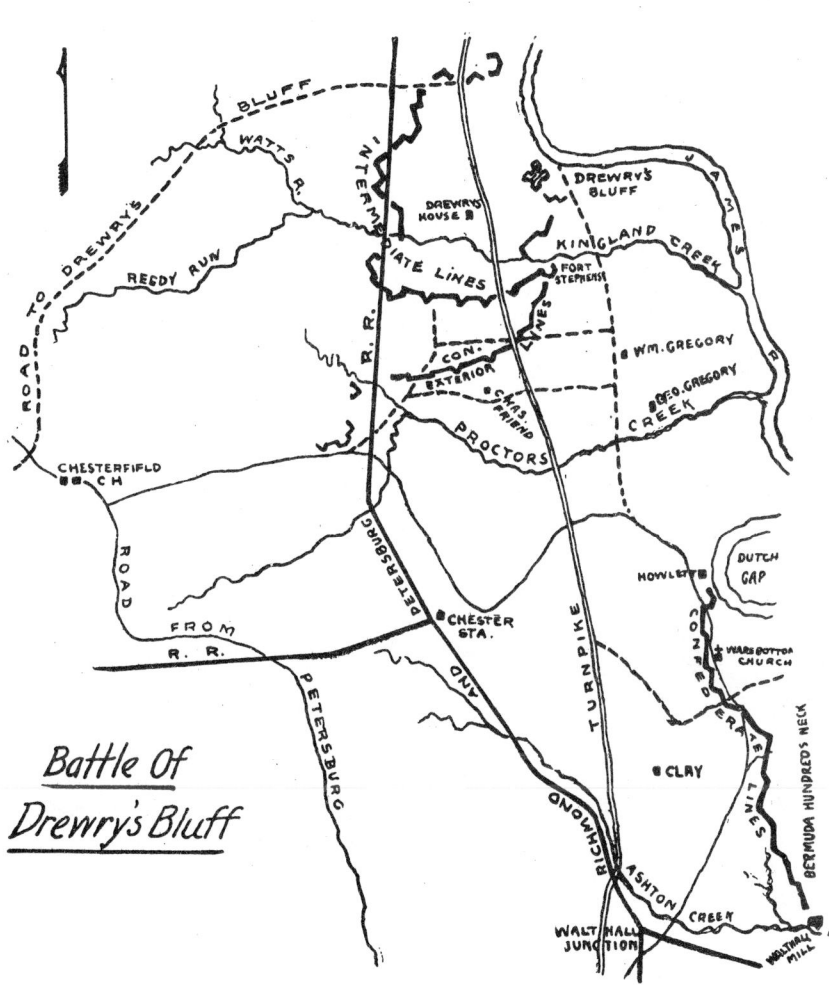

Battle Of
Drewry's Bluff

to watch Ransom's division next the river with cavalry. His gunboats had also ascended the river. The general direction of the river, the River Road,* the turnpike and the railroad was

*Or "Old Stage Road."

north and south of the two hostile lines east and west, each resting on the river. Proctor's Creek ran across these avenues and into the river, something over half a mile in front of the Confederate lines.

Hoke's evacuation of the exterior line had been made with all possible secrecy, and our pickets in front were not informed that it was contemplated. At daylight, the enemy advanced in strong force, and they quickly came running in. Hagood's picket continued on to the interior line, when they found exterior line abandoned. The enemy's skirmishers followed closely after them and obtained position close on us, within 150 yards, and sheltered by cabins which had been constructed between the two lines for barracks. Hagood immediately ordered the picket back, and to drive these skirmishers (whom he saw would do him infinite damage) to a greater distance. His picket commander, Colonel Blake, had completely lost his aplomb, and deprecatingly told General Hagood it could not be done. He was told to attempt it anyhow, and leading out his men from Fort Stephens along the prong of the abandoned line, he stopped without deploying his men, and conversing with them huddled together, remained a target for the sharpshooters from the cabins who rained their fire upon him. Major Abney was sent for to relieve Blake, and his manner while receiving instructions was not indicative that a proper selection had been made. When they were concluded, though directed to go promptly in person to take command of the picket, he went some ten steps toward the sally port and sitting down upon the banquette began vacantly to comb his hair with a pocket comb. He, too, from cause was not himself. Ordering him back to his regiment and sending Orderly Stoney to recall Blake and his men, the latter now thoroughly demoralized, Hagood directed Captain Brooks of the Seventh battalion to deploy his men behind the line of breastworks occupied by our line of battle, and at a signal to leap it and drive the skirmishers back. The company numbered about 90 men and was well officered. It gallantly performed the duty assigned to it, and succeeded in getting a good position for the brigade skirmish line.* Brooks was then relieved by the regular skirmish detail for the day composed of detachments from each regiment.

The enemy soon had artillery in position, the fire of which was chiefly directed against Fort Stephens and was very annoying, particularly that from a battery of six pieces in position where the turnpike crossed our abandoned line. The fire from these guns took the left face of Fort Stephens in reverse, and the Twenty-seventh regiment stationed there had to be put in the outer ditch for protection. The opposing lines were near enough for long range sharpshooting, and the intermediate lines of skirmishers were constantly engaged in the effort to drive each other. The casualties of the brigade on the 13th and 15th, inclusive, were 9 killed, 51 wounded, and 12 missing.

Lieutenant Archy St. John Lance, of the Twenty-seventh, was killed in the fort; Lieutenant Seay, of the same regiment, died of exhaustion; Captain Ledbetter, of the Eleventh regiment, was killed on the skirmish line, and among others who here gave their lives freely for their country was one whose history recalled that of Latour D'Avergne, "Le premier grenadier de la France." Pinckney Brown, a gentleman of means and literary culture, had taken no part in public affairs until 1860, when, an ardent Secessionist, he had been elected to the Convention and signed the Ordinance which we had all fondly hoped was to have been our second Declaration of Independence. When war followed this act, he enlisted as a private in Miles's company of the Twenty-seventh regiment and had since bravely and unflinchingly discharged every duty of the patriot soldier. Promotion was frequently offered him and invariably declined. Rifle in hand, he died "sur le champ du battaile," shot through the head upon the skirmish line.

At one time, on the 15th, the enemy appeared to be massing for assault. None followed. The Federal historians say that Butler had ordered it, but his troops were so strewn out that a sufficient number were not available for the attack, and he directed it postponed till the next day. That evening, Beauregard, passing along the lines, asked some of his soldiers if they were not tired of this sort of fighting, and said he "would change it for them."

---

*Izlar's Company, Twenty-fifth regiment, assisted Brooks in this skirmish.

At 10 o'clock at night on the 15th, Hoke's brigade commanders were summoned to his headquarters, informed that the offensive would be taken in the morning, and instructed in the plan of battle.

Beauregard's plan showed the instinct of genius. They could not under the circumstances, notwithstanding the difficulty of handling rapidly and effectively an army so recently organized, have failed substantially to have annihilated his antagonist, had not two of his division commanders failed him. The shortcomings of General Ransom and General Whiting are indicated in the official report. The first failing to carry out his instructions with vigor, and making strangely inaccurate reports of the condition of things in his part of the field, is pretty severely handled by General Beauregard. The last did not move at all, notwithstanding reiterated orders, and as far as the record goes his inaction is not explained. There is but little doubt that it was due to the unfortunate use of narcotics. Brigadier-General Wise subsequently described Whiting as stupefied from the use of these during the time Beauregard's reiterated orders to attack were being received. This was in conversation with the writer, and he also stated that he had preferred charges against Whiting on the ground of his condition, but had withdrawn them upon a personal appeal from that officer. He was relieved from this command and sent to Wilmington without an official investigation. There he resumed an important command, and his name will again occur in the Memoirs. After the war, the Federal General Ames told General Hagood that during the evening and night when Butler's routed and discouraged column was defiling within a mile of Whiting's 4,000 men of all arms, but a thin skirmish line intervened between them and destruction. The following are the official reports, or rather so much of them as without repetition continues the narrative:

"Headquarters in the Field,
"Swift Creek, Va., 10th June, 1864.
"General S. Cooper, Adjutant and Inspector-General:

. . . .

"Our army was organized into three divisions, right, left and reserve, under Major-Generals Hoke and Ransom, and Brigadier-General Colquitt. . . . Our left (Ransom) lay behind the trenches on Kingland Creek, which runs an easterly course not far in front of Drury's Bluff. Our right wing (Hoke) occupied the intermediate line of fortifications from Fort Stephens, crossing the turnpike to the railroad. Colquitt's reserve, in rear of Hoke, centered on the turnpike. The cavalry was posted on our flank and in reserve, and the artillery distributed among the divisions. A column from Petersburg, under Major-General Whiting, had been directed to proceed to Swift Creek on the turnpike, over three miles from Petersburg and nine from my lines, and was under orders to advance at daybreak to Walthal Junction, three miles nearer. The enemy's forces, under Butler, comprised the corps of Gilmore and W. F. Smith (Tenth and Eighteenth) and his line was generally parallel to ours. . . . They held our own outer lines of works, crossing the turnpike half a mile in our front. Their line of breastworks and entrenchments increased in strength with its progress westward. Its right and weakest point was in the edge of William Gregory's woods, about half a mile from James River. . . . . Going westwardly, after crossing the railroad, their line widened to the north.

"With the foregoing data, I determined upon the following plan: That our left wing, turning and hurled upon Butler's weak right, should with crushing force double it back on the center, thus interposing an exterior barrier between Butler and his base; that our right wing should simultaneously, with its skirmishers and afterwards in force, as soon as the left became fully engaged, advance and occupy the enemy to prevent his re-enforcing his right and thus form his northern barrier without, however, permanently seeking to force him far back before our left could completely outflank him and our Petersburg column close up in his rear; and, finally, that the Petersburg column, marching to the sound of heaviest firing, should interpose a southern barrier to his retreat. Thus environed by three walls of fire, Butler, with his defeated troops, could have no resource against substantial capture or destruction, except in an attempt at partial and hazardous escape westward away from his base trains and supplies. Two difficulties might impede or defeat the success of this plan; one was a possible stubborn and effective resistance of the enemy, in virtue of his superior numbers; another (probably a grave one) existed as to the efficient and rapid handling of a fragmentary army like ours, so hastily assembled and organized—half of the brigades without general officers, some of the troops unacquainted with their commanders and neighbors, staff officers unknown to each other, etc. The moral force arising from the unity, which springs from old association, was entirely wanting; and from these causes, generally so productive of confusion, great inconvenience arose. On the other hand, I reckoned on the advantage of being ready at daylight, with short distances over which to operate, a long day before me to maneuver in, plan direct routes and simplicity in the movements to be executed. Accordingly, at 10:45 a. m. on the 15th, preparatory information and orders were forwarded to Major-General Whiting, then at Petersburg twelve miles from me, with instructions to move his force to Swift Creek, three miles nearer, during the night, and at daylight next morning to proceed to Walthal Junction, about three miles still nearer. These instructions were duly received by that officer, and were as follows: 'I shall attack the enemy in my front tomorrow at daybreak by River Road, to cut him off from his Bermuda base. You will take up your position tonight at Swift Creek with Wise's, Martin's, Dearing's and two regiments of Colquitt's brigade, with about twenty field pieces under Colonel Jones. At daybreak you will march to Walthal Junction, and when you hear an engagement in your front you will advance boldly and rapidly by the shortest road in the direction of the heaviest firing to attack enemy in rear or flank. You will protect your advance and flank with Dearing's Cavalry, taking necessary precautions to distinguish friend from foe. Please communicate this to General Hill. This revokes all former orders of movement. Signed G. T. Beauregard, General Commanding. P. S.—I have just received a telegram from General Bragg informing me that he has ordered you to join me at this place; you need not do so, but follow to the letter the above instructions. G. T. B.' In the early afternoon I delivered in person to the other division commanders assembled the following circular instructions of battle, with additional oral instructions to General Ransom, that while driving the enemy he should promptly occupy with a brigade the crossing of Proctor's Creek by the River Road, which was Butler's shortest line of retreat to Bermuda Hundred's Neck.

" '(Circular.)

" 'Headquarters, Department North Carolina and South Virginia,

" 'Drury's Farm, 16th May, 1864.

" 'General: The following instructions for battle tomorrow are communicated for your instruction:

" 'The purpose of the movement is to cut off the enemy from his base at Bermuda Hundreds and capture or destroy him in his present position. To this end we shall attack and turn by the River Road his right flank, now resting on James River, while his center and left flank are kept engaged to prevent him from re-enforcing his right. Major-General Ransom's division will tonight take the best position for attack on the enemy's right flank to be made by him tomorrow at daylight. His skirmishers will drive back vigorously those of the enemy in his front and will be followed closely by his line of battle, which will, at the proper time, pivot on its right, so as to take the enemy in flank and rear. He will form in two lines of battle and will use his artillery to the best advantage. Colonel Dunovant's (South Carolina) regiment of cavalry will move with this division under the direction of General Ransom. Major-General Hoke's division, now in the trenches on the right of the position herein assigned to General Ransom, will at daylight engage the enemy with a heavy fire of skirmishers, or as soon as General Ransom's line of battle shall have become fairly engaged with the enemy. General Hoke will form in two lines of battle four hundred yards apart in front of his trenches at the proper time and in such manner as not to delay his forward movement. He will use his battalion of artillery to the best advantage. Colonel

Baker's regiment of cavalry will move in conjunction with Hoke's division, so as to protect his right flank. He will receive more definite instructions from Major-General Hoke. Colonel Shingler's regiment of cavalry will move with the same division. The division commanded by Brigadier-General Colquitt will constitute the reserve and will tonight form in column by brigades in rear of Hoke's present position, the center of each brigade resting on the turnpike. The division will be massed under cover of the hill now occupied by Hoke's troops so as to be sheltered at first from the enemy's fire in front. During the movement the head of the reserve column will be kept about 500 yards from Hoke's second line of battle. As soon as practicable, the interval between the brigades of the reserve division will be maintained at from two to three hundred yards. The reserve artillery, under Generol Colquitt, will follow along the turnpike about 300 yards in rear of the last brigade. He will use it to the best advantage. Simultaneously with these movements, Major-General Whiting will move with his division from Petersburg along the Petersburg and Richmond turnpike and attack the enemy in flank and rear. The movement above indicated will be executed, and must be made with all possible vigor and celerity. The generals commanding divisions and Colonels Shingler and Baker, commanding cavalry, will report at these headquarters at 6 p. m. today. In the meantime they will give all necessary instructions for providing their respective commands with sixty rounds of ammunition issued to each man, and at least twenty rounds for each in reserve. They will cause their commands to be supplied with two days' cooked rations.

"'(Signed) G. T. BEAUREGARD,
"'General Commanding.'

"Ransom moved at 4:45 a. m., being somewhat delayed by a dense fog, which lasted several hours after dawn and occasioned some embarrassment. This division consisted of the following brigades in the order mentioned, commencing from the left: Gracie's, Kemper's (commanded by Colonel Terry), Barton's (under Colonel Fry), and Colonel Lewis's (Hoke's old brigade). He was soon engaged, carrying the enemy's breastworks in his front at 6 a. m. with some loss. His troops moved splendidly to the assault, capturing five stands of colors and some 500 prisoners. The brigades most heavily engaged were Gracie's and Kemper's, opposed to the enemy's right, the former turning his flank. General Ransom then halted to form, reported his loss heavy and troops scattered by the fog, his ammunition short, and asked for a brigade from the reserve. Colquitt's brigade was sent him at 6:30 a. m., with orders to return when it ceased to be indispensable. Before either ammunition or the reserve brigade had arrived, he reported the enemy driving Hoke's left, and sent the right regiment of Lewis's brigade forward at double quick towards the supposed point of danger. This held the enemy long enough for the reserve brigade to arrive, charge and drive him back from the front of our left center, where the affair occurred over and along the works to the turnpike.*

*See Post.

"It will be seen from a subsequent part of this report that one of Hagood's advanced regiments had unexpectedly come into contact with the enemy and been ordered back, it not being contemplated to press at this point until Ransom should swing round his left as directed in the battle order. This possibly originated Ransom's impression as to the condition of Hoke's left, which in fact had steadily maintained its proper position. At 7:15 a. m., Colquitt's brigade of the reserve was recalled from Ransom and a slight modification of the original movement was made to relieve Hoke, in whose front the enemy had been allowed to mass his forces by the inaction of the left. Ransom was ordered to flank the enemy's right by changing the front of his right brigade, to support it by another in echellon, to advance another to Proctor's Creek, and hold a fourth in reserve. This modification was intended to be temporary, and the original plan was to be fully carried out on the seizure of the River Road and Proctor's Creek Crossing.

"In proceeding to execute this order, Ransom found the reserve brigade engaged, and his own troops moving by the right flank towards the firing at the center. He, therefore, sent Barton's brigade back instead of Colquitt's, and reported a necessity to reform and straighten his lines in the old position near the breastworks he had stormed. Here his infantry rested during the greater part of the day. Dunovant's cavalry, dismounted, were thrown forward as skirmishers towards a small force, which occupied a ridge in the edge of George Gregory's woods, north of Proctor's Creek. This force with an insignificant body of cavalry, believed to have been negroes, and a report of threatening gunboats which came some hours earlier, were the only menace to our left, as since ascertained.

"At 10 a. m., I withheld an order for Ransom to move, until further arrangements should be made, for the following reasons: The right was heavily engaged; all the reserve had been detached right and left at different times; a dispatch had been sent to Whiting at 9 a. m., which was repeated at 9:30 a. m., 'to press on and press over everything in your front and the day will be complete', and Ransom not only reported a strong force in his front, but expressed the opinion that the safety of his command would be compromised by an advance.

"On the right, Hoke early advanced his skirmishers and opened his artillery. The fog and other causes temporarily delayed the advance of his line of battle. When he finally moved forward, he soon became hotly engaged. Hagood and Johnson were thrown forward with a section of Eschellman's artillery (Washington), and found a heavy force of the enemy with six or eight pieces of artillery occupying our outer line of works on the turnpike and his own defensive lines. Our artillery engaged at very short range, disabling some of the enemy's guns and blowing up two limbers. Another section of the same battery opened from the right of the turnpike. They both held their positions, though with heavy loss, until their ammunition was spent, when they were relieved by an equal number of pieces from the reserve artillery under Major Owens.

"Hagood with great vigor and dash drove the enemy from the outer lines in his front, capturing a number of prisoners, and, in conjunction with Johnson, five pieces of artillery—three 20 dr. Parrotts and two fine Napoleons. He then took position in the works, his left regiment being thrown forward by Hoke to connect with Ransom's right. In advancing, this regiment encountered the enemy behind a second line of breastworks in the woods with abatis interlaced with wire. Attack at this point not being contemplated, it was ordered back to the line of battle, but not before its rapid advance had caused it considerable loss. This circumstance has been referred to before as the occasion of a mistake made by Ransom.

"Johnson meanwhile had been heavily engaged. The line of the enemy bent round his right flank, subjecting his brigade for a time to a fire in flank and front. With admirable firmness he repulsed frequent assaults of the enemy moving against his right and rear. Leader, officers and men alike displayed their fitness to the trial to which they were subjected. Among many instances of heroism, I can not forbear to mention that of Lieutenant Waggoner, of the Seventeenth Tennessee regiment. He went alone through a storm of fire and pulled down a white flag which a small isolated body of our men had raised, receiving a wound in the act. The brigade holding its ground nobly, lost more than a fourth of its entire number. Two regiments of the reserve were sent up to its support, but were less effective than they should have been, owing to a mistake of the officer posting them. Hoke also sent two regiments from Clingman's to protect Johnson's flank. The same mistake was made in posting these. They were placed in the woods, where the moral and material effect of their presence was lost.

"I now ordered Hoke to press forward his right for the relief of his right center. He advanced Clingman with his remaining two regiments, and Corse with his brigade. They drove the enemy with spirit, suffering some loss, but the gap between Clingman and the troops on his left induced him to retire his command to prevent being flanked, and reform it in the intermediate lines. Thus Corse became isolated, and learning from his officers that masses were forming on his right flank, he withdrew some distance, not quite as far back as his original position. These two brigades were not afterward engaged, though they went to the front, Corse about one hour after he fell back, and Clingman about 2:15 p. m. The enemy did not reoccupy the ground from which they drove them before their retreat.

"In front of Hagood and Johnson, the fighting was stubborn and prolonged. The enemy slowly retired from Johnson's right and took a strong position on the ridge in front of Proctor's Creek, massing near the turnpike and occupying advantageous ground at the house and grove of Charles Friend. At length, Johnson having brushed the enemy from his right flank in the woods with some assistance from the Washington Artillery, and cleared his front, rested his troops in the shelter of the exterior works. One of the captured pieces having opened on the enemy's masses, he finally fell back behind the wood and ridge at Proctor's Creek, though his skirmish

16—H.

line continued the engagement some hours longer. Further movement was here suspended to wait communication from Whiting, or the sound of his approach, and to reorganize the troops which had become more or less disorganized. Brief firing, at 1:45 p. m., gave some hopes of his approach. I waited in vain. The firing heard was probably between Dearing* and the enemy's rear guard. Dearing had been ordered by Whiting to communicate with me, but unsupported by infantry or artillery he was unable to do so except by sending a detachment by a circuitous route which reached me after the work of the day was closed. At 4 p. m., all hope of Whiting's approach was gone, and I reluctantly abandoned so much of my plan as contemplated more than a vigorous pursuit of Butler and driving him back to his fortified base. To effect this, I resumed my original position and ordered General Hoke to send two brigades along the Courthouse road to take the enemy in flank and establish enfilading batteries in front of the heights west of the railroad.

"The formation of our line was checked by a heavy and prolonged storm of rain. Meanwhile, the enemy opened a severe fire, which was soon silenced by our artillery. Before we were ready to advance, darkness approached and upon consultation with several of my subordinate officers, it was deemed imprudent to attack, considering the probability of serious obstacles and the proximity of Butler's entrenched camp. I, therefore, put the army in position for the night and sent instructions to Whiting to join our right at the railroad in the morning.

"During the night, the enemy retired to the fortified line of his present camp, leaving in our hands some fourteen hundred prisoners, five pieces of artillery, and five stand of colors. He now rests there, hemmed by our lines which have since from time to time been advanced with every skirmish, and now completely cover the southern communications of the capital, thus securing one of the principal objects of the attack. The more glorious results anticipated were lost by the hesitation of the left wing and the premature halt of the Petersburg column before obstacles in neither case sufficient to have deterred from the execution of the movement prescribed.

.   .   .   .

"Respectfully, your obedient servant,
"(Signed) G. T. BEAUREGARD,
"General.

"Official.
"(Signed) JOHN BLAIR HOGE, A. A. G."

On perhaps the day after the battle, General Beauregard in relieving General Ransom, that he might return to his local command at Richmond, did it in a highly complimentary order. This fact explains the following supplementary report:

---

*Cavalry.

"Headquarters Department North Carolina and
Southern Virginia.
"June 14th, 1864.

"General S. Cooper, A. & I. G.

"General: In forwarding my report of the Battle of Drury's Bluff, 16 May, 1864, it seems necessary that it should be accompanied by an explanation of the apparent inconsistency of its conclusion with my special order Number 11, May 14th, 1864, relieving the commander of the left wing, and commending in high terms the conduct of his command in the battle. A copy of the order is annexed. When it was issued, I still assumed that he had properly felt and estimated the obstacles and hostile force reported by him in his immediate front, and that his reports were to be accepted as maturely considered and substantially accurate. Subsequent investigation, necessarily requiring time, has, I regret to say, brought me to a different conclusion.

"Respectfully, your obedient servant,
"(Signed) G. T. BEAUREGARD,
"General.

"Official.
"(Signed) JNO. BLAIR HOGE, A. A. G."

Extracts from Major-General Hoke's report, comprising what related to Hagood's brigade:

"Headquarters Hoke's Division,
"25th May, 1864.

"Captain, . . . owing to the dense fog, I could see nothing of the movement of Major-General Ransom, and supposing that by this time the right of the enemy had been turned, I ordered forward the brigades of Hagood and Johnson with one section of Lieutenant-Colonel Eschelman's artillery and found the enemy still occupying our outer line of entrenchments, supported by eight pieces of artillery, with a second line of entrenchments along the line of the woods in front of our outer line of works. The attack was handsomely made and resulted in the capture by *Hagood's brigade* of five pieces of artillery, besides a number of prisoners and a great many of the enemy killed and wounded. The outer line of works was occupied, and one regiment of Hagood's brigade extended beyond it in the direction of James River. This regiment was ordered forward to connect with the right of Ransom's division, but, to my amazement, found the enemy in strong force behind entrenchments. It was not intended that this regiment should attack the enemy in that position, as the movement was to be made by the troops on the left, but it in its eagerness did so, and, I am sorry to say, suffered heavily. When it was seen that the enemy still occupied my front, this regiment was ordered back to await the further development of the flank movement. In the meanwhile, the enemy made two charges upon Hagood and Johnson, but were repulsed, and with the assistance of the artillery, *the pike was cleared of the enemy before the flanking column reached that point.* . . . The commanding general will recollect that I before stated that the strength of the enemy was in front of these two brigades, and they deserve great credit. . . .

"The loss of these commands was necessarily heavy, owing to their making a front attack. . . . I cannot refrain from calling the attention of the commanding general to the fact that his desire to relieve my command of the necessity of a front attack by the flank movement of Ransom's division was on no portion of my line accomplished. . . .

"Respectfully, your obedient servant,

"(Signed) R. F. HOKE, Major-General.

"To Captain J. M. Otey, A. A. G."

It is curious to compare the manner in which this battle was actually fought with the well-considered plan devised by Beauregard, and clearly explained beforehand to his subordinates. The plan of battle was, briefly, to seize the enemy's line of retreat, demonstrate on his front, and carry his position by a turning movement on the flank, behind which was his line of communication.

The actual fight was an almost simultaneous direct attack along his whole front, and with a hand upon the enemy's line of retreat, Whiting failed to grasp it. Thus the conceptions of genius were in the execution reduced to the least skilful of performances, and instead of a decisive defeat, Butler was merely pushed back upon his fortified base.

Some remarks are necessary upon the details of the battle as described in the foregoing official reports. The movement of the "right regiment of Lewis's brigade" and of "the reserve brigade" to the relief of "our left center" (Hagood's brigade) mentioned by General Beauregard upon information from Ransom's division, was a myth. The writer avers most positively that no part of Ransom's division ever came to Hagood's assistance, or passed in front of him till the enemy had retired from his front. General Hoke's report distinctly sustains this averment, and General Beauregard's report itself shows that the force from Ransom's division could not have performed this feat, although *it was* the duty to which the whole division was assigned. The report reads: ". . . Colquitt's brigade from the reserve was sent him (Ransom) at 6:30 a. m. Before it had arrived, he reported the enemy driving Hoke's left and sent the right regiment of

Lewis's brigade forward at a double quick towards the point of supposed danger. This held the enemy long enough for the reserve brigade* to arrive, charge, and drive him back from the front of our left center over and along the works to the turnpike." Yet, at 7:15, just three-quarters of an hour after Colquitt's brigade had moved to Ransom, and about the time it would have completed this clearing of Hagood's front, the report states, "A slight modification of the original movement was ordered to be made to relieve Hoke's front, on which the enemy had been allowed to mass his forces by the inaction of the left." This order was to Ransom, and, in substance, to resume the offensive. On receiving it, he "reported a necessity to straighten and reform his line in the old position, near the lines he had stormed. Here he rested during the greater part of the day."

General Beauregard's report also credits Johnson's brigade with a share in the capture of the five pieces of artillery on the pike. Hoke, commanding both brigades, was present in person and gives it exclusively to Hagood's brigade.

General Beauregard (adopting Hoke's report), speaks of *one regiment* of Hagood's brigade thrown forward to connect with Ransom's right. This is scarcely accurate, though there was but one regiment that actually struck the enemy's second line of breastworks. The circumstances were minutely these:

Shortly after General Ransom's division had engaged the enemy and while his advance, visible by the flash of his guns through the fog, was still on a line with Hagood's front, the brigade skirmishers under Major Rion were ordered forward. These quickly drove in the enemy's pickets and carried the enemy's first line (our abandoned trench), except that portion just on the turnpike, where the artillery was. The Twenty-fifth regiment had to be brought up to accomplish that. Hagood's brigade was now in position, without any other regiment beside the Twenty-fifth having been engaged, behind this outer line; but as it bent back on the left to run into the intermediate line at Fort Stephens, the left regiment of the brigade (the Twenty-seventh) was placed beyond the trench when this curve backward commenced, in order to have the line straight and ready for a further forward movement. There continued a desultory exchange

---

*Colquitt's two regiments.

of fire. Hagood was standing near the Twenty-seventh regiment, holding his horse by the bridle, when Hoke came up to him on foot and directed him to swing out to the right and form on the turnpike *in order to connect with Ransom*. The fog had partially lifted and a body of troops was in sight in the open, full 800 yards from Hagood, diagonally from his left front and at least three-quarters of a mile from the turnpike, on which his right was resting. This body of troops had half pivoted to the right and halted. It was Ransom's whole force (see Beauregard's report). Hagood knew that it was Ransom, for, notwithstanding the fog, he had, as before noted, been able to trace his course by the flash of his guns as well as by their sound. Now they were perfectly visible, halted, and not firing, but firing was going on ahead of them, and nearer, but still not yet in front of Hagood's left, from a line not visible which proved to have been Ransom's skirmishers. When Hagood received Hoke's order, he did not bring the position of these halted troops to the latter's attention, for he supposed they were only a part of Ransom's division, perhaps a reserve, while the line firing, and not visible, was Ransom's main line advancing through the woods to the pike with but little opposition. Confirmed in this idea by the positive direction to swing out on the pike, *and connect with Ransom*, Hagood merely spoke with Hoke of the tactical execution of the order and proceeded to obey it. He kept the Twenty-fifth and Twenty-first regiments, which were nearest the pike, in position, to give a fire down it, and, pivoting on the right company of the Seventh battalion, moved out the Seventh battalion and the Eleventh and Twenty-seventh regiments. This was done in line, and each regiment swung round by the movement technically known as "change direction," thus advancing in echellon to their new position. The distance between our outer line now reoccupied by us and the enemy's line of breastworks, on the edge of the woods, was not over two hundred yards. And it was in this space that these three regiments were maneuvering. In the change of direction their left alone would strike these works which, it seemed, Hoke thought the enemy had been driven from by Ransom's flank movement. Hagood left Hoke after receiving the order and the movement had hardly begun when a terrific fire broke out upon the advancing troops, but was hottest upon the Seventh battalion. Hagood galloped in that direction, having his horse killed under him as he reached the Seventh. This battalion, having only to wheel on its own ground, had accomplished or nearly so a change of direction at right angles to its former position and parallel to the pike, when its commander, halting it, caused his men to sit down and fire from that position while they marked the base of the movement. The Eleventh regiment, advancing firing, was steadily approaching its position on the new line, and the Twenty-seventh, coming on upon the extreme left, struck the breastworks on the edge of the woods and drove the enemy from them at the point of impact, notwithstanding the rush of its charge was impeded by wire entanglements just in front of the works. The increased fierceness of the enemy's fire brought the movement to a halt, the enemy assaying to charge, and failing. The position was obstinately held for a short time to permit relief by Ransom's approach, when General Hagood, standing behind the Seventh battalion, saw the Twenty-seventh regiment coming back, and ordered the Eleventh regiment and Seventh battalion back behind the outer entrenchments. It appeared afterward that the Twenty-seventh came back under an order sent direct from General Hoke, who had found out his mistake as to Ransom's position, and whose instructions, it will be remembered, did not permit him to press at this point at this time.

Hagood reformed his lines and remained inactive during the rest of the day with the remainder of the army. The enemy, very soon after the advance of his three regiments, withdrew from his front. Somewhat later in the day, he was hurried to Hoke's right to resist a supposed flanking movement, which not taking place, he was returned to his first position. Late in the afternoon, Ransom moved down Hoke's line to and beyond the turnpike, after the enemy had withdrawn. The Twenty-seventh regiment was thrown out to make the right of Ransom's line in this march.

During the whole battle, the brigade behaved with a steadiness and gallantry that was very gratifying. It was a spectacle to rejoice the heart of a soldier, the steadiness with which the Seventh received the enemy's onset when its new line was taken. Sitting down at the word of command, it gave and received at close range for ten minutes a murderous fire, the color bearer slowly waving his flag, and not a straggler going to the rear. When the line moved, it is no exaggeration to say that the bodies of the dead and wounded marked the position it had held. There were fifty-seven bullet marks received on its flag in the action, and in one of its companies (Brooks's) there were sixty-five casualties, of which nineteen were killed outright. The casualties of the whole brigade were 433; its field return of the previous day was 2,235.

Colonels Gaillard and Gantt, Lieutenant-Colonel Nelson, Major Glover and Captain Wilds, commanding regiments, discharged their duty with marked ability and were gallantly seconded by their men. Major Rion and Captain Brooks, of the Seventh, behaved with conspicuous gallantry, remaining in command after receiving serious wounds, Rion until nightfall, and Brooks until he was ordered to the rear by the brigade commander. The staff, Captain Moloney, Lieutenant Mazyck and Lieutenant Martin exhibited their usual courage and efficiency. Each one of them had his horse killed under him in the discharge of his duties, and Captain Moloney had a second one, which he obtained during the day, killed.

Lieutenants Taft, Lalam, Shuler, Bomar and Elliott, and Captain China (all of the Twenty-fifth regiment) were killed. Bomar was killed in an heroic exposure of himself, rendered necessary by the failure of his captain to do his duty. China, Elliott and Shuler were all originally of the First South Carolina regiment. General Hagood had served with them from the beginning of the war, and valued them highly as brave and efficient officers.

The following officers and men were mentioned for gallant conduct by regimental commanders:

Twenty-seventh Regiment—Lieutenant Gelling, Company C, acting adjutant; Color Bearer Tupper, Private H. P. Foster of the color guard, and First Sergeant Pickens Butler Watts of Company E.

In Seventh Battalion—Sergeant J. H. Outz, color bearer, killed.*

---

*In the color guard of the Seventh Battalion, Sergeants J. B. Robinson and G. W. Kennington were successively killed with the colors in their hands after Outz fell, and the colors were brought out by Sergeant Preston Cooper.

In Eleventh Regiment—Lieutenant W. G. Bowman, Company B; Color Bearer Hickman; Privates J. Jones, Company K; G. W. Hicks, Company K; A. P. Bulger, Company D, and A. Mixson, Company F.

In Twenty-fifth Regiment—Sergeant B. P. Izlar, Company G; Sergeant H. P. Greer, Company B; Privates J. T. Shumaker, Company G, W. A. Dotterer, Company A, and —— Wise, Company F.

General Hagood also reported for meritorious services, coming under his immediate observation, Private J. K. Williams, Company —, Twenty-seventh regiment. He was an Irishman and deserted to the enemy at Bermuda Hundreds a few days afterward. In the following August, after the fight on the Weldon road, one of the brigades captured on the field was carried by a battery which had been particularly destructive to us and recognized in one of the gunners, Hagood's "meritorious" Irishman. Williams greeted him cheerfully and asked after "the gineral."

President Davis was on the field during the latter part of the day. The army bivouacked among the unburied corpses of the enemy, and feasted that night upon the unwonted luxuries of coffee, sardines and canned meats, with which his abandoned camps were abundantly supplied. The brigade here obtained a good supply of shelter tents (the tent d'abies of the French); and the Eleventh regiment, as heretofore mentioned, supplied itself with Enfield rifles, throwing its old smooth-bore muskets upon the ground to be picked up by the ordnance fatigue parties.

LINES OF BERMUDA HUNDREDS.

At sunrise on the 17th, Beauregard moved forward in pursuit of Butler. The road was filled with the debris of a broken army, their dead lay unburied or hurriedly and incompletely buried upon the route, and on every side wide-spread and wanton devastation marked the spirit in which they had advanced, houses and fences burned, and stock driven off, or killed and left where they were slain. An instance of obedience to the order to destroy the

NOTE.—In the *North American Review*, Volume 144, Number 3 (March, 1887,) is an article entitled "Drewry's Bluff and Petersburg", which in all the points noted in this Memoir sustains its accuracy, and does very full justice to Hagood's brigade. It is over General Beauregard's signature.

breeding stock of the country was witnessed, which was ludicrous and at the same time had a touch of pathos in it. A hen that had evidently seen many summers, lay in front of a farm yard with her head wrung off, while her brood still lingered about her, and one little chick perched wearily upon her dead body. Poor little thing, one fancied, as it gazed unconcernedly upon the column tramping by, that it looked as if, after the turmoil and trouble of the last few days, there was for it no subject of astonishment left.

About 3 p. m., our advanced guard encountered Butler's pickets in front of his entrenched position across Bermuda Hundred Neck. Our columns were at once deployed, and skirmishers thrown out and engaged. The position at Howlett's House was seized after dark; the two 20-dr. Parrotts captured by Hagood's brigade at Drury's Bluff were here put in position and manned by Palmer's company, Twenty-seventh South Carolina, supported by infantry from another brigade. The James, running southerly from Richmond, at Dutch Gap encounters a considerable ridge, which it passes by a detour of perhaps a mile and a half to the west, and returning, after making almost a complete loop, resumes its general course. Howlett's House was on a high bluff on the western side of the river at the bend of the loop. Some 300 yards below it, the river narrowed greatly, affording a good place for obstructions under the guns of a battery at Howlett's, and immediately spreads out into a wide reach as it progressed again towards Dutch Gap. In this reach were congregated a number of gunboats and transports, upon which the two Parrotts opened in the morning, driving them beyond range. This position in the rearrangement of the defenses of Richmond that ensued during the campaign became its "Water Gate," a description applied by Beauregard to Drury's Bluff in the original plan of the fortification. It was made very strong and the desire to get up the river with their gunboats without encountering its guns and obstructions inspired Butler's famous canal across the ridge at Dutch Gap.* Like most of the enterprises of this military chieftain, it failed of success. General Beauregard named the battery in honor of Colonel Dantzler, of South Carolina, who was killed in the fighting a few days afterward near this point. Colonel Dantzler, a

---

*See 4th Battles and Leaders Civil War, p. 575.

planter of St. Matthews Parish, had commenced the war as a
lieutenant in the First South Carolina (Hagood's); had been
elected in the fall of '61 lieutenant-colonel (of Keitt's Twentieth
South Carolina), which he had commanded during the greater
part of the siege of Charleston with distinguished gallantry
and skill; and in consequence had been recently appointed to
the colonelcy of a regiment in Evans's (now Walker's) South
Carolina brigade. This regiment had been lately commanded by
Good' ., who was broken for cowardice, and trained by him was
decidedly wanting in dash. It was in an effort to inspire his
new command with something of his own spirit of daring that
Dantzler threw his life away. Beauregard's attention was now
given to establishing the shortest practicable line across the neck
and entrenching it so as to hold Butler in the cul de sac to which
he had retreated, with the fewest number of troops. His purpose
was accomplished in the next few days in a series of actions,
rising almost to the severity of battles. After each he advanced
and strengthened his lines, until, commencing at Howlett's house
on the James, they ran in a line more or less direct to Walthal's
Mill Pond on Ashton Creek near its junction with the Appomattox.* The "bottling up" process† was then complete and the
Confederate commander was at liberty to detach nearly half his
force to the assistance of Lee.

The scene of these actions was a wild, thickly wooded country
with few clearings, and in many places broken up into short but
steep hills. One day, while a sharp skirmish fight was going on.
a buck sprang up and ran for some distance between the lines;
at length one of Hagood's skirmishers brought him down and
secured the carcass.

The first position of Hagood's brigade was on Clag's Farm,
and that night it repelled a body of cavalry which was either
reconnoitering or attempting to break through our lines.

The 18th and 19th, its lines were advanced principally by
skirmish fighting.

On the 20th, a very heavy action occurred, in which the brigade
on its right was hotly engaged. Hagood's part was confined to

---

*See Map Battle Drury's Bluff, Ante 114.

†"His (Butler's) army, though in a position of great security, was as completely
shut off from further operations directly against Richmond as if it had been in a
bottle strongly corked."—Grant's Report.

severe skirmishing. In the confusion of this fight, in the woods, General Walker rode up to a regiment of the enemy before he discovered his mistake. Turning to escape, he received a volley from the whole regiment at short range, killing his horse and wounding him in several places.* He was captured and survived, but as a painful cripple for life. General Walker had gained much reputation at the battle of Pocotaligo in South Carolina, and was esteemed a valuable officer. Stephen Elliott, of Fort Sumter, now colonel of the Holcomb Legion, received the vacant brigade.

During the afternoon of the 22nd, Hagood's brigade was ordered to move further to the right, to relieve Wise's brigade. The position occupied by the latter was well entrenched, but its pickets in front were advanced in no instance exceeding fifty yards, and the enemy's in pits about 250 yards beyond made it an act of no little danger to raise one's head above our parapets. This disagreeable condition of things had to be endured until dark, when General Hagood organized a strong party of skirmishers and succeeded in getting position for his picket line beyond where the enemy's had been. By daylight each pair of men were securely entrenched in a rifle pit, and matters on the main line were more comfortable. In this affair Lieutenant Sineath, of the Eleventh regiment, was captured. After our new picket line was taken, in attempting to connect it with that of the brigade on our left, he blundered into the enemy's line.

The enemy's main line of entrenchments was here 800 yards in front of ours, and a good deal of sharpshooting took place between them, besides shelling. In the main, however, our position was comfortable enough; part of our line was in the woods, part in the open; the country was broken, giving comparatively secure passage from point to point, and a rivulet behind us gave abundant water, a blessing fully appreciated by the men covered with the dust and grime of three weeks' marching and fighting. Our train, too, here overtook us in its march by highway from Wilmington, and the officers enjoyed the luxury of clean clothing. It was sad though, as each valise was handed out and the familiar names were called, to find so many to which there was no response.

---

*See Prison Life of Jeff Davis.

"They sleep their last sleep,
They have fought their last battle,
And not until the archangel's trump
Shall sound the last reveille
Will their voices again respond to the roll call."

The casualties of the brigade on the lines of Bermuda Hundreds was one officer and one man missing, five men killed, and forty-seven wounded, making an aggregate of fifty-three.

At this time was organized Hoke's division as it continued to the end of the war, with the exception of the temporary addition to it of a brigade of reserves in North Carolina in the spring of 1865. It was made to consist of Hagood's, Colquitt's, Clingman's and Martin's (afterwards Kirkland's) brigades, the commissions of the brigadiers dating in order of seniority in the order in which the brigades are named. Colquitt's men were from Georgia; the last two brigades from North Carolina. Major-General Hoke was from North Carolina—had commenced as major, and won his way to a brigade command in Lee's Army of Northern Virginia, serving principally in Stonewall Jackson's corps. He had lately won his major-general's commission at the capture of Plymouth in North Carolina. He was not exceeding thirty years of age, of good presence and agreeable manner; a good administrative officer, of undoubted personal gallantry, and possessed of habits of vigilance. His intercourse with his subordinates was always marked with good feeling on both sides.

BATTLE OF COLD HARBOR.

While Butler's co-operative move was thus being foiled, Grant, with Meade's Army of the Potomac, was slowly urging his sanguinary way from the northward to the vicinity of Richmond.* Lee had constantly interposed his veterans across his path, and as constantly, after ineffectual and murderous assaults, Grant had essayed a turning movement by his left, to be again confronted by Lee, to again assault, and again be compelled to gain his further step towards Richmond by a further turning movement to his left. Nor did Lee oppose only a passive resistance. While standing generally upon the defensive in chosen positions, which

*See Map of Part of Virginia, p. 75.

his possession of the interior line enabled him to take, he seized every opportunity the eye of consummate genius could detect to assume a quick and sharp offensive. The spade and the mattock were brought more largely into requisition on both sides than in any war since the days of ancient Rome. "The campaign," says Swinton, "indeed resembled less an ordinary campaign than a kind of running siege. From the Rapidan to the Chickahominy, the face of the country was covered with the entrenched lines, within which the armies of the Potomac and of Northern Virginia had waged a succession of deadly conflicts."

Under cover of these entrenchments, after each unsuccessful direct attack, Grant's edgewise movements were generally effected by withdrawing the troops on his right and moving them in rear of his line to prolong his left. Lee met this with a corresponding change, and thus both armies progressed much as the wild pigeons feed and fly.

They were now approaching Richmond, and upon the banks of the Chickahominy, already rendered historical as the scene of McClellan's defeat in '62, was the safety of the Confederate capital again to be submitted to the issue of battle.

On the night of the 30th-31st May, Beauregard detached Hoke's division from the lines at Bermuda Hundreds to re-enforce Lee for the impending conflict. Its march was directed upon Cold Harbor, a strategic point beyond the Chickahominy towards which both armies were edging their way, and, upon its arrival, found itself in position upon the right of the Confederate forces.

Hagood's brigade moved last, leaving the trenches at 6 a. m., on the 31st, and marching to Chester Station on the Petersburg and Richmond Railroad, whence it was conveyed by rail to the capital, arriving at midday. Moving directly through the city and out on the Mechanicsville Turnpike, it followed the march of the division. The day was excessively hot, the pike entirely without shade, and the men suffering for water. General Hagood therefore halted at a farm house with a fine grove, where water was to be obtained, about two miles from the city, and rested his men for two hours. Here the horses of the line officers and the brigade train, which had come by highway from Chester Station, overtook us. The march was resumed, the road was now filled with wagons, artillery, and troops, and the dust and heat were intolerable. The men suffered greatly and straggling was unavoidable. Crossing the Chickahominy, we reached Mechanicsville a little before dark and took the road to the right leading to Cold Harbor. Getting beyond Gaines's Mill, we were halted at 1 a. m. by an order from General Hoke. The rest of the division was in position in front, and we were directed to rest where we were, till 3 a. m., when we also were to move forward into line. There were two taverns called respectively Old and New Cold Harbor. They were upon the same road, about a mile apart, and New Cold Harbor was nearest us. A severe cavalry combat had been in progress during the greater part of the day of the 31st for the possession of Old Cold Harbor. It had resulted in the partial possession by the enemy of the coveted position, when the arrival of Hoke's leading brigades had relieved our cavalry. In this action, the Charleston Dragoons, a company which had been old comrades of the brigade on the coast of South Carolina, had fought with desperate valor and been almost annihilated. In falling back before heavy odds, James W. O'Hear, one of its lieutenants, had stopped to aid a wounded comrade who had appealed to him not to leave him, and, refusing to surrender, was slain fighting over his friend. Hoke's advance brigades were in position between New and Old Cold Harbor, his right resting upon and covering the road between them and his left extending to the northwest towards and menacing the road from Bethesda Church to Old Cold Harbor, which comes from the northward nearly at right angles to the road upon which Hoke's right rested. At daylight on the 1st, Hagood's brigade was moved forward across a tributary of Gaines's Mill stream and posted in reserve behind Hoke's left, but facing to the northward. Grant's infantry advance was moving down from the direction of Bethesda Church upon Old Cold Harbor, and consisted of the Sixth corps. Longstreet's Corps, moving on a parallel line, led Lee's column and contemplated attacking the Sixth corps upon its march between these points. Kershaw's division was to lead the attack, and when Kershaw sent Hoke word that he had reached a certain point (Beulah Church) on the road, Hoke was to advance Hagood's brigade, posted as before described, to co-operate in the attack. Such was General Hagood's understanding of the situation as conveyed to him by his division com-

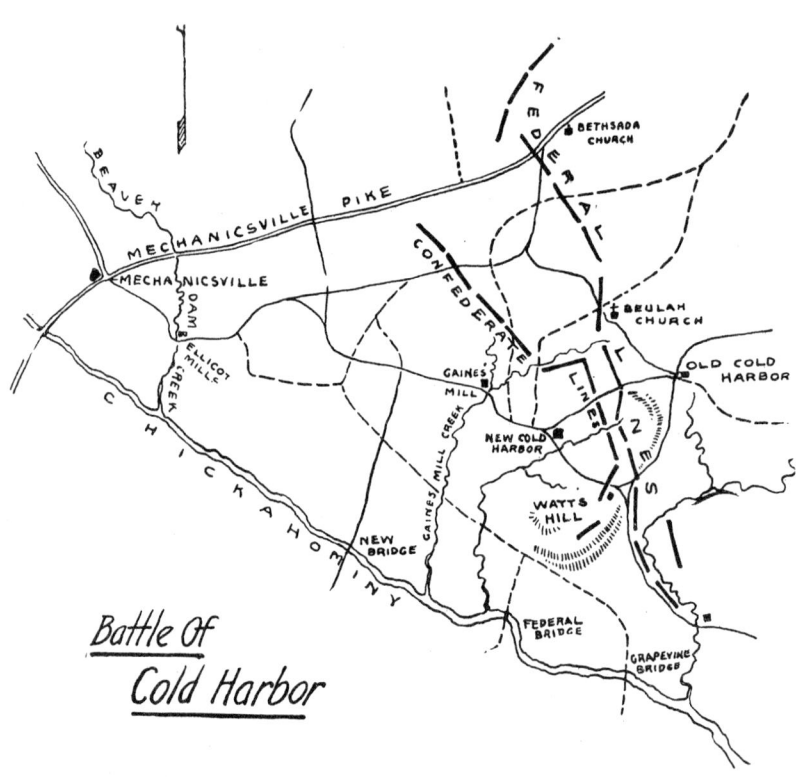

Battle Of
Cold Harbor

mander. During the morning, firing from Kershaw was heard on Hagood's left front, and afterwards a courier to General Hoke announced that the attack was foregone. In Kershaw's advance, Colonel Keitt, commanding the leading brigade, was killed, and the brigade thrown into confusion. This, with perhaps other reasons, to the writer unknown, stopped the attack.

Colonel Keitt had been a member of the United States Congress from his native State, and continued for some time to represent her in the Confederate Congress. In the second year of the war, he had been elected to the colonelcy of a newly raised South Carolina regiment, and until within the last month, his service had been around Charleston. He was a gentleman of honor and fine intellect, but his previous training and the bent of his mind qualified him for the political arena rather than a soldier's career.

Hoke now directed General Hagood to advance a company as skirmishers and feel for the enemy. He was developed to Hagood's right front, and moving down the general front of the division toward Old Cold Harbor. Shortly after, the head of Longstreet's column reached Hoke and went into position on his left. Skirmishing and artillery fire commenced and continued with more or less vigor.

The enemy now began to extend around Hoke's right beyond Old Cold Harbor, and about 4 p. m., Hagood's and Martin's brigades were hurriedly moved in that direction, the first mentioned brigade leading. Marching in column of fours in rear of our line by way of New Cold Harbor, after these brigades had passed beyond the point held by our right, they were on the field on which the battle of Gaines's Mill had been fought in McClellan's campaign. In several places, human bones were visible where they had been imperfectly buried and since uncovered by the action of the weather. The cavalry, which were guarding this flank, were driven in, as we arrived on the field. Halting and facing to the left, the column was in line of battle, but in echellon with the general line. Skirmishers were ordered forward,* and advancing handsomely drove back the enemy's pursuing skirmishers. The line of battle followed under a sharp fire of shells, and, prolonging the general line, proceeded rapidly to entrench. The point now held by these two brigades was the

---

*Under Captain J. F. Izlar of the Twenty-fifth.

17—H

tactical key of Lee's position. The field was a high plateau, with Watt's Hill behind it, and commanded most of the line now being taken up by the Confederates for the impending battle. In front, the ground fell off abruptly into a lower plateau, and on its right and right-rear were the low grounds of the Chickahominy and one of its tributaries. Had the position been seized by the enemy at this time, it is probable that Lee would have been forced across the Chickahominy and into the lines of Richmond without a general engagement. It was a race for it, won by a few minutes. The enemy's skirmishers, pursuing the small cavalry force, were already upon the field and in full view a dense mass in column was seen following in support from Old Cold Harbor. Deceived possibly by the vigor of our skirmish advance, and conceiving perhaps that this was a movement to turn the left of Grant's general line, the enemy halted and commenced to entrench along his front, and at right angles to us, keeping up meanwhile a rapid fire of artillery. Prisoners stated that this was a part of the Sixth corps, General Wright commanding, and that they were about to attack.

With the enemy in view, and under shell fire, it needed no urging to induce the men to cover themselves when the order to entrench the line we had taken was given. A windrow of rails from the adjacent fences was laid; such spades and mattocks as they had were wielded by willing hands; and bayonets, tin cups, plates, and even the unaided hands lent assistance in digging a trench inside the rails and raising a parapet upon them. The rapidity with which this was done was laughable, and would have been incredible to any one who had not seen soldiers who knew the value of earthworks, however slight, work under similar circumstances. At McGee's house, our line bent back towards the Chickahominy, and was prolonged by brigades subsequently arriving.

The enemy did not attack here this afternoon, but shortly after Hoke's two brigades had been sent to the right, the right of the Sixth corps, and Smith's corps from Butler's army, which had arrived by way of the White House, violently assailed the right of Longstreet's corps and the left of Hoke's division at the point from which Hagood had been withdrawn. Here Wofford's brigade, of Longstreet's corps, and Clingman's brigade, of Hoke's division, gave way, but the enemy were finally repulsed with a loss, by his own account, of two thousand men. He had gained, however, some advantage of position and claimed by the action to have secured the possession of Old Cold Harbor.*

In consequence of this affair, at 1 a. m., on the 2nd of June, Hagood received orders to return to his position of the day before. Martin remained where he was, and became Hoke's right; Colquitt was the center, and Hagood again became the left of the division, Clingman going into reserve to reorganize his command.

On the 2nd, Hagood, in conjunction with Hunton's brigade of Longstreet's corps, succeeded in partially re-establishing our line where the break had occurred. We were now, however, on the hither side of the tributary of Gaines's Mill Creek, beyond which our line had extended on the 1st before bending back in its continuation by Longstreet, and consequently our line was retired some 200 yards from its position of the day before. It was still, however, at this point, a salient of which the face held by Hagood was enfiladed both by artillery and infantry fire from the Sixth corps, and the fighting to secure the position was necessarily done with skirmishers, so close to the main line that the casualties were more frequent in the last than the first.

From Cold Harbor, northwestardly, the enemy's right extended to and beyond Beulah Church, and the Confederate lines confronted them somewhat confused on the extreme left. It will be perceived that this narrative confines itself chiefly to the vicinity of Cold Harbor, with the localities and movements near which the writer was most familiar. Old Cold Harbor was Grant's headquarters during these operations, and Lee's were in rear of New Cold Harbor.

On the evening of the 2nd, Lee assailed a corps of the enemy in motion on his extreme left, and inflicted considerable loss upon it. The night of the 2nd was wet and disagreeable, and the fire of the skirmishers was kept up without intermission on Hagood's front.

The next morning at half-past four (a. m.), Grant executed along the whole Confederate front of six miles a general and

---

*Swinton. The author must, however, mean the undisputed possession of the *road* from Bethesda Church to Old Cold Harbor, for the Federals had held Old Cold Harbor from the 31st May. We never held this road, but our position, as before stated, menaced it.

simultaneous assault. The historian of his army says: "It took hardly ten minutes of the figment men call time to decide this battle. There was along the whole line a rush—the spectacle of impregnable works—a bloody loss, then a sullen falling back, and the action was decided. . . . But rapidly as the result was reached, it was *decisive*. . . . Some hours after the failure of the assault, General Meade sent orders to each corps commander to renew the assault without reference to the troops on his right or left. The order was issued through these officers to their subordinate commanders, and from them descended through the wonted channels; but no man stirred, and the immobile lines pronounced a verdict silent but emphatic against further slaughter. The loss on the Union side in this sanguinary action was over 13,000, while on the part of the Confederates it is doubtful whether it reached as many hundreds."*

This was the battle of Cold Harbor, and it may sound incredible, but it is nevertheless strictly true, that the writer of these Memoirs, situated near the center of the line along which this murderous repulse was given, and awake and vigilant of the progress of events, was not aware at the time of any serious assault having been given. As before mentioned, the firing of skirmishers in front of Hunton and Hagood had not intermitted during the night; there was no line of battle assault upon their immediate front, simply an increased pressure of skirmishers, and the roar of musketry on his right and left was so quickly over, and apparently so little commensurate with such slaughter, that it is difficult even now for him to realize that it was all done in so short a time. The explanation lies in the characteristics of a direct assault upon earthworks, defended by men who have confidence in themselves, the silent rush of the assailing party, and the rapid but deliberate and deadly fire from the assailed.

There was heavy and general firing from artillery, sharpshooters and skirmishers along both army lines during the day of the 3rd of June. In Hagood's immediate front, the enemy's skirmishers had got into the swamp of the little stream along which his line was drawn, and were not fifty yards from his line of battle. They held their position pertinaciously, and the attempt to drive them out with volleys from the line or a direct advance of skirmishers

---

*Army of the Potomac.

failed. Colonel Gantt, occupying the left of the brigade, was, therefore, ordered to push a body of men across the swamp at the ford which he covered, and facing them to the right drive up the swamp, in front of the brigade, and clear it of the enemy. He sent fifty men from companies B and K of his regiment under Captain Westcoat, assisted by Lieutenants Bowman, Mims and Cassidy. After a stubborn fight, they advanced the length of the brigade, aided by sharpshooters from the lines, and cleared the swamp of skirmishers, losing thirteen of their own number, killed and wounded, among whom was Captain Westcoat, severely wounded in the leg. This enabled General Hagood to get his skirmishers beyond the swamp, and relieved him to that extent; but his position was so thoroughly enfiladed by the position of Wright's corps (the Sixth) that at 4 a. m., on the 4th, he was directed by General Hoke to pivot on his left and swing back his right until it connected with Colquitt near the road between New and Old Cold Harbor. Hunton, who had intervened between Hagood and Colquitt, was returned to his own corps, and Hagood connecting with Gregg's (Texas) brigade, of Longstreet's corps, at the stream so often mentioned, extended in a straight line some fifty yards beyond the road referred to. The salient in our line was now transferred to the point of junction of Hagood and Colquitt, but it was more obtuse and not enfiladed by any position of the enemy. The brigade was soon entrenched in its new position, indeed a trench had been partially prepared by fatigue parties before the line was moved.

The assault of the morning of the 3rd, having failed, at 4:30 that afternoon, Grant is said to have ordered each corps commander to entrench his position. On the 4th, he directed siege operations begun. Two subsequent assaults, however, were made on the point of junction of Colquitt and Hagood, and repelled principally by the fire of Colquitt's brigade with deadly effect. It is more likely that these assaults were made with a view to obtaining nearer position from which to start the approaches than with the lingering hope of breaking through our lines at this point. Here was one of the points at which siege operations were inaugurated.

Sore at his repulse, and loath to acknowledge it, Grant refrained until the 6th from asking for a flag of truce to bury his dead, and the incessant fire of his sharpshooters prevented us, as often as it was attempted, from bringing off his wounded from in front of our lines. Scattered more or less thick along their whole extent, where the assault was made vigorously, they almost paved the ground. There for three long days the dead, unburied, festered in the rays of the hot summer sun, until the stench was offensive for six hundred yards in the rear, and among them lay the wounded, suffering the tortures of wounds and heat and thirst, their moans growing fainter as the days went by.

It was over such a scene as this that the troops marched to the secondary assaults, already referred to, of the point on the road between the two Cold Harbors held by Hoke's division, and contributed their bloody quota to the mass of butchered humanity upon which they trod in their charge. When at length the flag was asked and granted, the burial parties were in most instances unable to handle the dead, corruption had extended so far, and contented themselves with covering as it lay each body with a slight mound of earth.

From the Rapidan to the close of the battle of Cold Harbor, Grant had lost sixty thousand men, seven thousand more than Lee had had during the campaign, and one thousand to every mile of his progress to Richmond. Whatever gloss success has since thrown over his style of making war, it was not, therefore, without some color of provocation that his soldiers about this time bestowed upon him the epithet of "the butcher." His severe losses and small success had a powerful effect on the Northern mind, and it is asserted by Federal historians that at this time the war was near a collapse, from which successes elsewhere alone saved it. Of Grant's tactical management of the battle of Cold Harbor, it has been said that "to criticise it as a military operation is like discussing a loaf of bread as a work of art."* It certainly can lay no claim to be classed among the efforts of genius. On this field closed the overland campaign. Each successive flank movement after his various battles had brought him nearer to Richmond; to continue them now would take him away from his goal. He had nothing left but operations against the body of the plan, either by assault, or the slower operations of siege.

---

*"Volunteer" in N. Y. *World*, September, 1868.

The casualties of Hagood's brigade during all the time at Cold Harbor were sixteen killed, one hundred and three wounded, and nine missing, making an aggregate of one hundred and twenty (120). Among these were many valuable officers and men.

Buist's company of the Twenty-seventh regiment, and Mickler's company of the Eleventh regiment, together with many individuals from other regiments, all of whom had been left behind in South Carolina, rejoined the brigade on the 4th. Among them was Colonel Simonton, of the Twenty-fifth. While he was talking with Major Glover in the trench, in the act of taking command, Glover was shot in the hand by a sharpshooter. The wound was painful and disabling but apparently not more serious. Glover was sent to the hospital, and lingering unaccountably, some days afterward the surgeon asked him if there was nothing else the matter with him, that he could see nothing in the wound in his hand to account for his prostration. Glover complained of his leg, and on examination, a wound was there discovered which had gangrened. It seemed that in receiving an order at Bermuda Hundreds, carried him by Lieutenant Martin (A. D. C.), Martin's horse, a vicious brute captured at Drury's Bluff, had kicked the major upon the leg. Receiving little attention, this wound had been fretted by his boot leg until in the general exhaustion of his system by the hard service since, it had become what it was, and the life of one of the most gallant and efficient officers of the brigade paid the penalty.

John Glover was a medium-sized, spare man, of neat figure and of reserved manner. In civil life he had made but little mark and was regarded as habitually indolent. He had a fondness, however, for military studies, and had carried a company to the bombardment of Fort Sumter in 1861. In his subsequent career, with all of which the writer was familiar, he demonstrated that he was a born soldier. Alert, vigilant and efficient in the field, he secured alike the confidence and affection of his men, and the approbation of his superiors.

BATTLE OF PETERSBURG.

Richmond and Petersburg lie about twenty miles apart, one due north of the other. In their original defences, prepared before this campaign, each city was fortified independently, its fortifications extending around each place, in a circle, more or less complete, with a radius—Richmond of about eight miles and Petersburg of about three and a half miles. In the subsequent shape which these defences assumed, they were connected by a line drawn from Drury's Bluff where the southern lines of Richmond crossed the James down the western bank of the river to Howlett's house, whence Beauregard's Bermuda Hundreds lines completed the connection with the northern lines of Petersburg. Petersburg now became the right flank of the defences of Richmond, and covering, as it did, the communications of the latter place with the rear, was the key to the position. When Grant's siege operations here languished before the vigorous defence, his efforts to turn this flank caused a gradual extension of the Confederate lines for many miles in a southwesterly prong, from Petersburg. It was at the extremity of this prong, in the spring of 1865, when Lee's army with the sources of its recruitment dried up and attenuated by the "attrition" of Grant to little more than thirty thousand rifles, with which to confront a constantly recruited foe one hundred and fifty thousand strong, that the battle of Five Forks was fought which made an immediate necessity the evacuation of the Confederate Capital. They had previously been determined upon in consequence of operations elsewhere. Lee's lines were thus eventually, from right to left, between thirty-five and forty miles long, and during the whole siege of Richmond, his army was dependent for supplies upon his still open communications with the southwest. An investment would at any time have terminated the siege.

After pushing languidly his approaches at Cold Harbor for a few days, Grant determined to transfer his operations to the south side of the Appomattox, against Petersburg, and, accordingly, commenced the movement of his army to that point. By the 13th, he was withdrawn from his entrenchments and in full march. Lee followed, still intervening between him and Richmond on the north side of the James, as it was still open to Grant to turn while north of the James and advance up the river directly against that city. When the passage of the James by Grant at Harrison's Landing had developed his designs, Lee hastened to throw himself across the James and the Appomattox higher up and again confront him. He had delayed, however, most too long and Petersburg was very nearly taken by a coup de main, as will be developed in the progress of the narrative. Hagood's brigade marched with its division from the trenches at Cold Harbor at 8 a. m., on the 13th, crossed the Chickahominy at Federal Bridge, and proceeded in the direction of Malvern Hill, passing in its march over the old field of battle at Seven Pines. It bivouacked at night on the Darby Town road three miles from Malvern Hill, Hoke's division being held in reserve by Lee. During the day an action had occurred between Grant's flanking column and our advance at Ridley's Shop. Hoke remained quiet till 5 p. m., the 14th, when he was ordered to move back some eight miles to the neighborhood of the pontoon bridge over the James near Drury's Bluff and await orders. He was then in position either to go to Lee or to Beauregard at Petersburg. On the morning of the next day he was ordered to Beauregard and marched at 11 a. m. Crossing the river, he proceeded down the turnpike, but, when opposite Chester Station, he was informed that partial transportation awaited him by rail and ordered to hurry forward his command. Hagood was at once dispatched by rail; Colquitt followed some time after, and the remaining brigades continued their march by the pike.

At noon on the 15th, Smith's (Eighteenth) corps of Grant's army, being his advance, was before the eastern defences of Petersburg, manned by Wise's brigade and the local militia composed of the boys and old men of the city. After consuming the evening in making his reconnaisance and preparations, Smith assaulted with a cloud of skirmishers and easily carried the works, capturing some artillery and prisoners. Just after this success Hancock's corps arrived, but the enemy instead of pressing on and seizing the town which lay at his mercy, determined to await the morning before making his advance.

Hagood's brigade reached Petersburg at dark, and while the men were being got off the cars and formed in the streets, the general proceeded to Beauregard's headquarters to report for orders. General Beauregard was on the lines, and Colonel Harris of his staff was instructing General Hagood to move out on the Jerusalem plank road and take position, where it issued from the fortifications, when a courier arrived announcing that the enemy had carried our works from Battery No. 3 to Battery No. 7, inclusive, and that our troops were in retreat. Hagood was instructed to move out immediately upon the City Point Road (the road uncovered by this success of the enemy) and take a position to check his advance, and upon which a new defensive line might be established. It was a critical moment. The routed troops, such as they were, were pouring into the town, spreading alarm on every hand, and there was no organized body of troops that the writer has ever heard of available at the time to resist the advance which the enemy were even then supposed to be making, except this brigade and Colonel Tabb's Virginia regiment, of Wise's brigade, which still held a portion of the lines that had not been assailed. It would be daylight before Hoke's division could all get up, and the main body of Lee's army was miles away. In this emergency, Beauregard directed the withdrawal of the troops from the Bermuda Hundreds lines and their transfer during the night to the south side of the Appomattox. Finding these abandoned, Butler next day took possession of them, and even essayed another enterprise against the Richmond and Petersburg Railroad. With the arrival, however, of the main body of the Confederate Army, he was without much trouble again "corked up" within his original limits.

It was after dark when General Hagood received his orders, and being entirely ignorant of the localities as well as unable to learn much from the confused and contradictory accounts of the volunteer guides, who accompanied him, when he reached the fork of the City Point and Prince George roads just beyond the New Market race course, he halted his column, and leaving it under Colonel Simonton, rode forward, accompanied by Captain Moloney and Lieutenant Martin of the staff, to make a personal reconnaisance. He encountered the enemy's picket on the latter road at the ford where it crosses Harrison's Creek inside of the original line of defences. The reconnoitering party had nearly ridden into it, when they were warned by a wounded Confederate by the road side. They were not fired upon. Turning across the field toward the City Point road, General Hagood was opportunely met by a courier from Colonel Harris with a map, who had also the foresight to send a bit of tallow candle and matches. With the aid of this, Hagood determined on the line of the creek he was then on (Harrison's Creek), and put his men in position.

They immediately and rapidly entrenched themselves. This creek emptied into the Appomattox in rear of Battery No. 1, which was the initial point of the defences and on the bank of the river. Its west fork crossed the line of original defences near No. 15. The line taken by Hagood was, therefore, a chord of the arc of our captured or abandoned works, and ran along the west bank of the main creek and its western fork, having very good command over the cleared and cultivated valley in its front. The old line from 1 to 2 was held by Tabb's regiment and they were relieved by the Twenty-seventh South Carolina regiment. Hagood's right did not extend to the Prince George road; his left rested on the river. By the time Hagood was fairly in position, Colquitt arrived, and took post, extending across the Prince George road, having first brushed out with skirmishers the enemy's picket at the ford. The next morning, the 16th June, was the anniversary of the battle of Secessionville, and the first shell fired by the enemy in the gloaming, and when it was yet entirely too dark to know more than the general direction in which to aim it, killed Captains Hopkins and Palmer and Lieutenant Gelling, of the Twenty-seventh regiment, who had all served with distinction in that battle, and the first of whom had been there severely wounded. The same shell also wounded several of the enlisted men of that regiment. General Hagood, wearied out, had fallen asleep some half hour before, and this shot waked him. Its successors from the same battery showed him that the position of the Twenty-seventh was completely enfiladed, and the morning light made evident to him, too, a fact that had not been appreciated in the night—the Twenty-seventh was advanced beyond his general line. This regiment was accordingly at once drawn back to the west side of the creek. Two field pieces, abandoned by our troops the day before on the City Point road beyond our present lines, were also brought in. They were found to be spiked and were, therefore, sent to the rear.

The enemy shelled Hagood furiously all day, and the skirmishers on his front were constantly engaged. They several times ostentatiously formed for battle beyond rifle range, there being no artillery on his portion of the line, and about dark assailed his center. They were repelled after keeping up the effort for an hour, never having got nearer than seventy-five yards to his entrenchments. On Hagood's right, the enemy's assault at dark was better sustained, and they suffered heavily. They met with no success. Lieutenant Allemony of the Twenty-seventh was killed today. On the 17th, the same heavy shelling and skirmishing continued on our front. About half-past six in the evening the enemy again assaulted heavily the brigade on our right. Colquitt repelled them with considerable slaughter. Their officers made a second attempt to get them on, but were unable to do so. Still further to the right several assaults were made during the day, one of which met with some success, but the Confederates rallying drove them back. The loss in the Federal ranks today was acknowledged to be four thousand. They claimed to have captured four guns, and probably got in addition some two hundred prisoners. Their long range artillery practice on Hagood's front was accurate, as it always was when there was no artillery to reply, and the brigade suffered several casualties.

In the meanwhile, General Beauregard (see Beauregard's Military Operations, II Volume, p. 253,) had determined on taking a more compact and shorter line of defence than the one now occupied, and during these two days' fighting it had been partially prepared for occupation. It was this last line which was held during the siege that ensued. It was some 800 yards nearer the city, and, like the line of the first taken, was the chord to an arc of the original defences, still more of which were now abandoned.

This line was at first a simple *trench* with the parapet on the farther side of it, and though it was afterwards amplified it retained the general character of a trench, and was always known as "The Trenches," in distinction from the portion of the original works held by us. These last were artillery redoubts, connected by infantry *breastworks*.

These "trenches" opposed Grant's front of attack, the remaining portion of the *enciente* was not assailed until perhaps the closing day of the siege of '65.

At 1:30 a. m., on the 18th, Hagood's brigade moved back on the new line to the position assigned it, which was on the left flank some 200 yards west of the house of the Younger Hare. His left was on the Appomattox, thence running off southward, nearly at right angles to the river, his line crossed the City Point road and extended to the westward end of the eminence known as

Hare's Hill, where Colquitt prolonged the general line. The New Market race course was in front of the right of the brigade, and the approach to its position was generally level. By daylight, the Confederates were quietly in position and diligently strengthening their incomplete works.

Shortly after daylight, the enemy advanced upon our old works, and finding them abandoned, came on with vociferous cheers. As soon as their skirmishers encountered ours in their new position, their line of battle halted, and heavy skirmishing commenced. This continued until about 2 p. m., the skirmishers alternately driving each other. The brigade lost several killed and wounded and a few prisoners, but inflicted an equal or greater loss upon the enemy and captured between twenty-five and thirty prisoners.

At 2 p. m., the enemy formed for assault upon the portion of the brigade between the river and the City Point road, and a little later moved forward. A regiment was pushed up along the bank of the river under cover of the grove and buildings of the Younger Hare. It came in column and, as soon as its head was uncovered, endeavored to deploy. The rest of their force attempted to come forward in line of battle. A rapid fire was opened on the column, as soon as it showed itself, and upon those in line at about 300 yards. The column never succeeded in deploying and the line broke after advancing about fifty yards under fire. They were rallied and again brought forward, but were repulsed in confusion and with heavy loss. The voices of the Federal officers in command could be plainly heard. The Twenty-first, Twenty-seventh and Eleventh regiments repulsed this attack.

South of the City Point road, the Seventh battalion and Twenty-fifth regiment were not at this time attacked. Later in the afternoon, when the enemy made a general assault upon the Confederate lines to the right, the Twenty-fifth fired a few volleys obliquely into the assaulting lines moving over Hare's Hill upon Colquitt. The skirmishing here, however, in the morning was particularly heavy and obstinate. Major Rion commanded the brigade skirmishers and distinguished himself by his usual gallantry and address. He was wounded in the arm, but continued in the field till night. Lieutenant Felder, of the

Twenty-fifth, was also wounded, and Lieutenant Harvey, of the Seventh battalion, was killed.

These three days' fighting was called the Battle of Petersburg. It resulted on the part of the Confederates in taking a line of defense which constructed, and from day to day strengthened and developed, under fire, grew into formidable siege works impregnable to all direct attack.

On the Federal side the loss of twelve thousand men in the three days was proof that even in their present incomplete state, held by such men as Lee commanded, they could not be carried by assault. Grant, accordingly, sat down regularly before the plan, and ordered siege operations begun.

Compared with the enemy's, the Confederate loss was inconsiderable. In Hagood's brigade, the casualties of the three days amounted to two hundred and twenty, of which thirty-six were killed. The loss in the character of the officers killed was, however, severely felt. Ward Hopkins was the senior captain of the Twenty-seventh regiment, and, after Colonel Gaillard, commanded the respect and confidence of the men and of his superiors more perhaps than any officer in it. His loss was a calamity to the regiment.

Captain Palmer was a graduate of the State Military Academy, and an efficient officer. Lieutenants Allemony and Harvey were also good officers and their loss was much deplored. Allemony was before the war a young lawyer, rapidly rising at the Charleston Bar, and a member of the State Legislature.

Adjutant Gelling was a young Scotch gentleman who had emigrated to Charleston a short time before the war. On the breaking out of hostilities, he had enlisted in one of the companies raised in that city, and had been promoted to his present position. General Hagood had occasion to notice and specially commend his conduct at Cold Harbor.

THE TRENCHES OF PETERSBURG.

On the 21st, Grant extended his line of investment somewhat more to his left, gaining no material advantage and losing to Lee three thousand men in the operation. His cavalry were at the same time dispatched against the railroad communications of Petersburg to the south and west, and succeeded in doing some slight damage, when they were encountered by the Confederate cavalry at Stoney Creek and completely overwhelmed. A remnant escaped into the Federal lines before Petersburg, having lost their entire artillery and train, and a thousand prisoners.

And now occurred an episode in the siege that attracted no general attention at the time, but was a bitter experience to Hagood's brigade which bore the consequences of its miscarriage. The very inception of its execution was so completely a failure that the design of the Confederate general appeared not to be suspected by either army, or by the public, and stillborn, its memory will only survive in the limbo of such memoirs as these, where individual history is the topic.

Grant's line had by this time extended a considerable distance from the river, and his communication with his base at City Point was behind his right flank and along the river. General Lee, in conjunction with General Beauregard, determined to assume the offensive, drive in Grant's right wing, seize his line of retreat, and, forcing him away from his base, inflict such a blow as would raise the siege if not put an end to the campaign. The plan was entirely feasible. The morale of the Confederate Army was at its highest, that of the enemy at probably its lowest during the campaign, and the great disparity of losses induced by Grant's sledge hammer style of fighting had brought the two armies at this time to no insurmountable inequality of numbers, other conditions being favorable. Accordingly, a powerful battery of forty-four (44) field pieces was on the night of the 23rd June secretly got into position on the north bank of the Appomattox, here quite narrow, to enfilade the enemy's line, and Fields's division of Longstreet's corps with other troops were massed behind Hagood's position next the river to follow up the attack which the latter was to lead. Anderson's brigade headed Fields's column, and Benning's brigade (under Colonel DuBose) was next. The following official papers narrate the manner in which the design was attempted to be executed:

> "Headquarters Hagood's Brigade,
> "Hoke's Division, 26th June, 1864.

"Captain Otey, A. A. G.

"Captain: I am required to make a full report of the operations of my brigade in front of Petersburg on the morning of the 24th inst. My brigade occupied the left of our line of entrenchments, resting on the south bank of the Appomattox—the Twenty-seventh, Twenty-first and Eleventh regiments filling the space from the river to the City Point Road, and the Twenty-fifth and Seventh battalion extending along the lines south of the road. The enemy's entrenchments were at this point parallel to ours at a distance of near 400 yards, an open field with a rank growth of oats upon it intervening. Each side had slight rifle pits a short distance in advance of its entrenchments. Our line of entrenchment was single, the enemy appeared to be entrenched in their lines close together, and the attack developed the fact that in their first line they had four and a half regiments, numbering some 1,600 or 1,700 men.

"My division commander, Major-General Hoke, had instructed me the night before to be ready for movement in the morning, without indicating what it would be. About dawn on the 24th he in person informed me that a general engagement was contemplated that day, and instructed me in detail as to the part my brigade was to take in bringing it on. A heavy cannonade was to be opened from the north side of the river upon the enemy's position, and five minutes after it had ceased I was to charge that portion of their line between the river and the City Point Road with the Twenty-seventh, Twenty-first and Eleventh regiments. He informed me that I was to be closely supported by Anderson's brigade. When we had succeeded in driving them from their first line, Anderson was to occupy it till *his* supports arrived, when he was to press on against their second and third lines, while pivoting my three regiments on their right and bringing up the other two regiments of the brigade, I was to form along the City Point Road perpendicular to my first position. Then, taking the enemy's first line as a directrix, I was to clear Colquitt's front as far as and including Hare's Hill, etc., etc.

"While General Hoke was still explaining the plan of battle to me, Lieutenant Andrews reported to me from General Anderson, stating that the latter was in position and had sent him to keep in communication with me. In consultation with General Hoke, my plan of attack was settled and every preparation made.

"The artillery opened precisely at 7 a. m. and ceased precisely at 7:30. At 7:20 a. m. I sent Lieutenant Andrews to General Anderson to say I would move in fifteen minutes. He left me with speed. A delay of seven minutes, however, occurred in my movement, and at precisely 7:42 I advanced. I am so far thus accurate as to time, because I did not see my support, did not know their precise distance in rear, and being governed in my instructions by time, noticed the watch closely.

"My advance was made with 400 picked men and officers as skirmishers, followed by the balance of the three regiments (about 550 men) in a second deployed line at close supporting distance. Lieutenant-Colonel Nelson, Seventh battalion, was selected to command the skirmishers. I took direction of the second line.

"The attack was made. The enemy were driven from their rifle pits without resistance of moment; their first line was gained and a portion of it captured; some thirty prisoners were taken here and sent to the rear; and the enemy's whole line was seriously shaken, his men in numbers running from the works. Discovering our small force, and the attack not being followed up, his first line rallied, re-enforcements were rapidly pushed up from his rear, and we were compelled to fall back. This was done slowly, and the enemy, endeavoring to charge us, was driven back. My men, under orders, laid down in the oats about half-way between the two hostile entrenchments to await Anderson's advance and then go with him. Numbers of them, however, got back as far as our rifle pits and were permitted to remain there with the same orders as the more advanced line. None of them came back to our entrenchment except a few skulkers, whom every attack develops, and in this case, I am happy to say, they were very few.

"How much time was occupied in these movements I am unable to say, as I did not look at my watch again. When the vigor of my attack was broken and my men had begun to fall back, the left of Benning's brigade, moving by a flank and coming from across the City Point Road, reached the right of the entrenchments I had left in advancing, and there stopped. A discussion between Major-Generals Hoke and Fields ensued, and, after some delay, this brigade moved in and was ready to advance.

"The report of Colonel DuBose, commanding Benning's brigade, will show the time of his arrival and the then condition of affairs. General Anderson's report will explain the delay in his arrival. Major-General Hoke was on the ground during the whole morning, and can speak of his personal knowledge.

"The order of attack being countermanded, I kept out all day as many of my men as my rifle pits would hold, withdrawing the rest by squads. At night all were withdrawn and the regiments re-organized. My loss was about a third of the force engaged, 25 being killed, 73 wounded and 208 missing, making an aggregate of 306.

"The gallant Lieutenant-Colonel Nelson is missing; it is hoped not killed. Captain Axson, Twenty-seventh regiment, was killed at the head of his company. Lieutenants Huguenin and Trim, of the Twenty-seventh, Lieutenants Chappell, Ford and Vandiford, of the Twenty-first, and Lieutenant Smith, of the Eleventh, were wounded.

"Captains Mulraney and Buist, of the Twenty-seventh, were captured on the enemy's works (the latter after receiving two wounds).*

"Captain Raysor and Lieutenant Riley, of the Eleventh regiment, Lieutenant White, of the Twenty-seventh, and Lieutenant Clemants, of the Twenty-first, are missing.

"I am, very respectfully, your obedient servant,

"(Signed) JOHNSON HAGOOD,
"Brigadier-General Commanding."

---

*Mistake. See post.

18—H

"Headquarters Hoke's Division, July 2, 1864.

"Captain: In obedience to orders from department headquarters (Beauregard's), I respectfully report that a plan of attack upon the enemy was settled upon on 23d June, 1864, to take place on the following morning, which plan is fully known to the commanding general. On the night of the 23d General Hagood was made familiar with the mode of attack sufficiently to make the necessary arrangements. No other officer of my command was aware of the intended advance. This precaution was taken, fearing that by some means the enemy might learn our intentions and prepare for us.

"In accordance with the plan, my arrangements were made which are fully and properly given in the enclosed report of Brigadier-General Hagood. Dividing my forces on the left of the City Point Road into two heavy skirmish lines, one to be supported by the other, and the whole to be supported by Brigadier-General Anderson's brigade of Fields's division, formed in line of battle behind the hill in rear of the entrenchments then occupied by Hagood's left. As was directed, the artillery from the batteries on the north side of the river opened fire upon the entrenchments of the enemy as soon as the morning mists had cleared away, and continued its fire with great accuracy but no execution for half an hour. After the lapse of five minutes the fire of these guns was directed upon the batteries of the enemy, drawing in a great degree their fire from the advancing infantry which, as far as I could see, was the only service rendered by our guns. Indeed, I fear we were injured more than we gained by the use of our guns, as it notified the enemy of our intended attack. My intention was to attack immediately after our guns opened upon the enemy's batteries, but as General Anderson had not reported, I delayed, and immediately one of his staff officers appeared by whom General Anderson was informed that in fifteen minutes the advance would certainly take place, which would give him time to reach the entrenchments then occupied by General Hagood. At the appointed time the advance was ordered, and immediately the second line followed. The first line gallantly entered the entrenchments of the enemy and did their duty nobly, and (as was witnessed by General Lee himself) succeeded not only in breaking the enemy, but drove them from their works.

"It was never expected that the entrenchments of the enemy could be held by these two lines of skirmishers, but that they should occupy them till the line of battle could reach them. I asked Major-General Fields, who was on the ground, to order Anderson forward, as a moment's delay would be fatal. He immediately sent the order, which had been previously sent, to General Anderson to go forward. It is proper here for me to state that this was my third effort to get General Anderson forward after my first notice to him that 'in fifteen minutes I would certainly move forward.' Some time after General Fields's second order was sent to General Anderson, he received a note from him saying that the entrenchments were still occupied by General Hagood's troops. In this he was greatly mistaken, as will be seen by General Hagood's report, and, if necessary to prove this mistake, Colonel DuBose, commanding Benning's brigade, will corroborate the fact that the entrenchments were then free of troops, except some stragglers, of whom I am sure no command is exempt. Colonel DuBose had by this time moved up in line of battle on the right of General Anderson's position, and, after reaching the trenches, moved by a left flank down them and occupied the position which Anderson was to have taken.

"After some time, I suppose an hour, General Fields put another brigade* in the trenches on the left of the City Point Road, with a view to attack, and seemed anxious to do so, but I advised against it, as the enemy had had time and had made all preparation for us, and I felt assured he would sustain a heavy loss and accomplish nothing. At this time orders were received from General Lee for me to report to him in company with General Fields, and, on hearing the position of affairs, he directed the attack abandoned.

"I was much troubled at the loss of my men, who did their duty truly and well, without results which to me appeared certain and surely ought to have been reaped.

"It is not my desire to place blame or responsibility upon others. I fear neither. In making the foregoing statements I merely give facts to the best of my knowledge, and the commanding general can draw his own conclusions. I have unofficially heard that both I and my command were censured by the commanding general. My regret is in attempting this attack without full command of all the forces which were to participate. Both the plan of battle and of attack were good, but failed in the execution. The enemy became extremely uneasy along his entire line, when the attack was made, and, had we been successful at that point, our results would have been such as have not heretofore been equalled. General Hagood did everything in his power to give us success, and desired to push forward when, in my judgment, it appeared hazardous.

"Very respectfully,
"(Signed) R. F. HOKE,
"Major-General.

"To Captain Jno. M. Otey, A. A. G."

"(Endorsement.)

"Respectfully forwarded to General R. E. Lee for his information.

"It will be seen by the reports of Generals Hoke and Hagood that they are not responsible for the failure of the attack of the 24th ulto., which would have undoubtedly been successful had the supports advanced in time. General Hoke is mistaken, if he refers to me, when he says 'I have heard unofficially that both I and my command have been censured by the commanding general.' I stated only that 'the success would have been most brilliant had the skirmishers been properly supported.' His report and that of General Hagood prove the correctness of my assertion.

---

*Anderson's. He had now got up.

"General Hoke says, on the second page of his report, 'After a lapse of five minutes the fire of the guns (*i. e.*, 44 guns on the north side of the Appomattox) was directed upon the batteries of the enemy, drawing in a great degree their fire from the advancing infantry, which, as far as I could see, was the only service rendered by our guns. Indeed, I fear we were injured more than we gained by the use of our guns, as it notified the enemy of our intended attack.'

"The object of opening the fire of the batteries referred to during the half hour preceding the infantry attack was to demoralize the enemy's troops occupying the defensive lines which were to be attacked, and which were enfiladed and taken in reverse by those batteries. It was expected also that the heavy artillery fire would throw into confusion any supports the enemy might have concealed in the woods near his line. The best proof of the entire success of the plan is the facility with which an *unsupported* line of skirmishers got possession of those lines, with a loss of only twenty-five killed and seventy-two wounded. I am decidedly of opinion that regard being had to locality and the attending circumstances, no better results could have been obtained than the plan adopted, and which failed only because not properly supported.

"Headquarters Department North Carolina and Southern Virginia, 5th July, 1864.

"(Signed)   G. T. BEAUREGARD,

"Official: John A. Cooper, A. A. A. G.   General."

———

Thus failed a brillant and entirely practical design, which might have given a different complexion to the history of this famous siege. General Hoke has noticed a fundamental error in the plan of attack, the supports not being under the same command as the attacking line. General Fields was present at the entrenchments during the whole affair, and no blame appears to have attached to him. If it was impracticable, as it probably was under the circumstances, for the attack to have been made and supported by the same division, a common superior should have been on the spot to harmonize the action of the two divisions partly engaged. Generals Lee and Beauregard were near the batteries across the river in close view of the field, but without means of direct communication, and therefore unable to take tactical direction of the affair.

So far, the plan of attack was radically wrong, but there is another and more palpable cause of failure manifest. Anderson was in line of battle (the head of a column by brigades) behind a hill about 150 yards in rear of Hagood when the attack was to commence, the "delay of seven minutes" which occurred in Hagood's movement was intentional on his part. He was waiting to see Anderson's approach advancing over the hill before he started, and he would have continued to wait, had not an aide from General Hoke, with whom General Fields was standing some forty yards off across the road, directed him to move at once. Instead of moving forward in line over the hill to the support of the attack, Anderson, when compelled by repeated orders to move, went, it was said, to the rear by file as far as the Iron Bridge nearly a quarter of a mile, thence full another quarter of a mile up the ravine of Poor Creek till he reached the shelter of the entrenchments near Hare's Hill, and then came stumbling along them already crowded with men, until he reached the part Hagood had left. He was more than one hour getting to a position to which he had little more than 150 yards to march straight forward, and with nothing in his way but the usual hazards of hostile fire. In the meantime, DuBose had got up three-quarters of an hour ahead of the brigade that was to lead him, but too late to support Hagood's attack, which was made at a charging step.

General Hagood had no personal interview with Anderson afterward and never saw his report, if any was made by him, to explain his conduct. On the record here given, there is but one comment to be made, and that the obvious one—Anderson should have been shot.* There was not even a court held, though the common sense of that portion of the army that knew anything of the affair kept afloat for two or three weeks the daily rumor that one had been ordered.

This day's experience was a peculiarly trying one to the commander of Hagood's brigade. His men were uselessly sacrificed; and from the secrecy with which the designs of the day had been kept, the delay in the arrival of the supports, and the absence of action on their part when they had come, there was a meaningless air thrown over his assault which he was not at liberty to explain. He was conscious that to some extent his command was demoralized by the result, and that it appeared to both men and officers a riddle why a skirmish line unsupported should be

---

*After twenty years this looks pretty harsh, and not having full information, ought perhaps to be omitted. 20th June, 1884. J. H.

rushed upon a triple line of breastworks garnished with artillery and manned by five fold their number of infantry. At length a Charleston editor, from which city it will be remembered two regiments of the brigade came, gave currency to the absurd idea that General Hagood had made the attack *without orders*, and with ambitious views on his part. Then, with General Beauregard's approbation, he sent for publication in the same sheet sufficient extracts from the foregoing official papers to partially explain his connection with the affair; more he could not do pending the campaign, and for some time afterward the injurious reputation of recklessness clung to him in consequence of this day's work.

A few days previous to this, in consequence of most of the regiments of the brigade being without field officers, General Hagood had divided his command into wings and given general superintendence of each to the two officers present highest in rank. Lieutenant-Colonel Nelson was put in charge of the regiments north of the City Point road, and it was thus he happened to be engaged when his regiment was not. He was standing by Hagood's side on the right of the line, when Hoke's aide brought the order to advance. The men, who had been told to follow his lead, were intently watching him, and when he was ordered to go, without speaking, he drew his handkerchief from his breast and raised it aloft. The men sprang over the parapet with a yell and rushed upon the enemy across the intervening space, he moving upon the right of the line. When they were driven back and had laid down in the oats (as they were instructed), to await the coming of the supports, he moved east along the whole length of his line under the close fire of the enemy and shortly after reaching the left, disappeared. The men of his command thought he was left by them wounded on the field. Painful rumors reached us through prisoners a few days afterward of his having been murdered by negro troops while being taken by the enemy to the rear. General Hagood brought the rumor to General Lee's attention, naming a captured lieutenant from whom he had it, and asked that a flag should enquire into the fact. The request was not granted. Thus fell a devoted patriot, a gallant soldier, a courteous gentleman.

Captain Axson was a valuable officer. He was mortally

wounded early in the charge and lingered painfully for some hours, when succor could not be rendered him. Captain Mulraney was captured literally upon the enemy's works, waving his cap and cheering on his men. Captain Buist had joined the brigade for the first time, after Cold Harbor; he was not wounded, though so stated upon misinformation, was exchanged shortly afterwards through some special influences and never again served on the field. He obtained one of the numerous exempt positions which had begun at this period of the war to be ominously sought after.

Lieutenant Trim lost his arm and was put on the retired list. Lieutenants Smith, Vandiford and Chappell died of their wounds. Chappell was the young officer whose good conduct at Walthal Junction so materially aided in rallying the Twenty-first regiment. At Drury's Bluff his coolness and efficiency attracted the attention of his brigade commander and procured him a compliment on the field. At first, he seemed likely to recover from his wound, and had procured an invalid leave. When pulling on his boot preparatory to leaving the hospital for home, he ruptured an artery near which the ball had passed, and bled to death. Some days after he had been wounded, General Hagood had sent him a handsome pistol captured from a Federal officer, with a note saying that it was intended as a testimonial of his uniform gallantry and good conduct. When the surgeon informed him that the blood could not be staunched, and that he must die, he called for his pistol and had it laid beside him on his cot. The pistol which he so treasured with its history was carefully forwarded to his widowed mother as a memorial of her noble boy. There was slain, too, upon this field among the non-commissioned officers, Pickens Butler Watts, first sergeant of Allston's company, Twenty-seventh regiment, the most distinguished soldier of his rank at that time in the brigade. He had been mentioned for conspicuous gallantry *upon every field in which his regiment had been engaged* in this campaign, and in the pursuit of the routed Federal army into its lines at Bermuda Hundreds, when, weak from sickness, he had fainted upon the march, he declined to use an ambulance, but recovering, pushed on and at nightfall was in the ranks of his company, skirmishing with the enemy.

Eldred Gantt, sergeant-major of the Eleventh regiment, and a brother of its colonel, was also wounded in this affair, and died a few days later.*

On the morning of the 18th June, when Beauregard retired from the Harrison Creek line to the one now occupied, the latter from the banks of the Appomattox to near the Jerusalem Plank road, where it ran into the line of the original defences, was in some places a trench not over two feet deep, in other places not a spade had been put in the ground—the line had been merely marked out by the engineers. The enemy following up immediately, this portion of the defences, as previously noticed, was constructed in the intervals of battle or under the constant fire of sharpshooters, and consequently remained a siege trench, the men standing in the ditch from which the earth was taken that formed the parapet, and the latter having no exterior ditch and but little elevation in place of which to impede an assaulting column abattis, chevaux du frize, palisades, breakwater, etc., were resorted to. Very little artillery was placed on the line of the infantry trench. Generally, the mortars and guns used were placed in suitable positions in rear. There were few if any guns used by the defence of heavier calibre than a Coehorn mortar or a field piece. In the progress of the siege, with incessant labor night and day, the Confederate works were strengthened in profile, drained, traversed, and covered approaches made. Bombproofs were very little, if at all, resorted to, and the men had no shelter from the weather save the few trees accidentally upon the line, or their blankets hoisted after the fashion of the tent d'abris.

Grant's lines conform to the general direction of the defence at distances varying from two to four hundred yards, and between the opposing lines each side had its rifle pits occupied by a picket line at night which was withdrawn in the day. At the Jerusalem Plank road, the lines ceased their parallelism, and the Federal line proceeded southerly towards the Weldon road, where bending back it eventually rested upon the Blackwater Swamp thus ensconcing the besieging force in a complete entrenched camp. Upon the latter portion of their line, collision was only occasional, and partook of the nature of field fighting. But from the Jerusalem Plank road back to the Appomattox, the fire of artillery

---

*This affair noticed. Alex. Stevens' History U. S., 908.

and sharpshooters was incessant, frequently continuing night and day, never ceasing from dawn till dark.

The morning of the 19th opened with heavy firing from sharpshooters which continued all day and ceased at night on Hagood's front. For this and several days the casualties were numerous from the imperfect protection as yet secured by the men. There were two Napoleons on Hagood's line, where it crossed the City Point road, and on the 21st he caused one of them to be arranged for vertical fire by depressing the train in a pit 'till the gun had an angle of 45 degrees elevation, and firing with small charges. He had seen it done at the siege of Charleston; and here as there it answered admirably as an expedient.

On the 23rd, eight Coehorns were placed in position in rear of his left; and subsequently another battery of these was established behind his right, where it joined Colquitt. The enemy had mortar batteries in our front by the 27th, but the fire from these did at no time much damage on this portion of our line. He found it difficult to drop his shell upon the thin riband of a ditch running parallel; and falling front or rear of it they did no harm. When they fell in the ditch, which was seldom, the frequent traverses limited their destructive effect. The most galling artillery fire to which the brigade was subjected was from Hare's Hill, whence its line was partially enfiladed. The enemy now also erected at some distance in rear of his right a battery of Parrotts and commenced shelling the town. The portion of it within range was soon abandoned by the inhabitants, though many of the poorer class remained, taking refuge in their cellars, when the bombardment was heavy. What number of casualties occurred among the citizens is not known to the writer, though he saw a poor woman killed by a shell in the suburb of Blanford as he was returning upon one occasion to the trenches from his baggage wagon whither he had gone to get a change of clothing.

Our picket line on the left of the City Point road was not advanced as far by many yards as it was on the right of it. The enemy's conformed somewhat to ours; and on the night of the 27th their officer inspecting his picket and coming from toward the river, crossed the road in this interval and found himself behind our picket line on the right, when he was quietly marched to the rear. The trap was kept open and for two more nights the enemy must have been mystified by the disappearance of their inspecting officers. The last night three captains walked into it, but we got no more.

An incident occurred with one of these captains that is narrated, because it seemed to be characteristic of the Puritan. When captured they were sent back to General Hagood's pit on the main line, and, as they were taken on duty, the general directed Lieutenant Moffett of his staff to ascertain if they had any official papers or orders about them. They were genteel-looking men, close shaved, neatly dressed, and one of them, near middle age, having the appearance of a substantial God-fearing and prosperous family man ere he had become "a boy in blue." The lieutenant, apologizing for the necessity, proceeded to discharge his duty, and required them to empty their pockets. Gold watches, pocket compasses and Rogers's cutlery were produced—the elder also pulling out several hundred dollars in greenbacks. These were all returned to them, and the lieutenant asked if they had nothing else about them. "Nothing," said the oldest officer with quite an air, "except *my Bible.*" "Let me see it," and from its leaves as it was handed out fell a half dozen card photographs. One was of an old lady, a good specimen of matronly respectability, and the mother of the prisoner; the others were of naked women in lewd postures!

The chronicler of a former rebellion, in which the forefathers of these people were the rebels, tells of a skirmish of Prince Rupert's in which a clergyman, a "principal governor," and a "shining light" among the then party of moral ideas, was slain after refusing quarter and provoking the soldiers by the most odious reviling of the *person* and *honor* of the king, and "in whose pockets were found several papers of memorials of his own obscene and scurrilous behavior with several women in such loose expression as modest ears cannot endure."* The stirpiculturist will note with delight how "like begets like," and might be tempted to trace the descent through Burns's "Holy Willie."

After making his own works in our front secure from assault, Grant at first appeared to have resorted to regular approaches by zigzags and parallels, but these were discontinued after little progress had been made; and the impression prevailed on the

---

*Clarendon's History of the Rebellion, I Vol., p. 409.

Confederate side that he had resorted to mining. Accordingly, counter mines were commenced at the points where the hostile lines were nearest. In the construction of these the shafts with a cross section of 6' and 4' generally began to be sunk some thirty or forty feet behind the infantry trench and descended at an easy grade until it reached the water-bearing stratum at the particular point, which was seldom over thirty feet. beneath the surface. Then pushing forward, until some sixty to one hundred feet in front of the trench had been gained, the gallery was extended laterally right and left for a greater or less distance to cover the menaced point. This was the general outline of their construction, but some were very elaborately executed, ramifying in every direction. All were ceiled with plank and scantling as the work advanced and were lighted and ventilated by perpendicular shafts. Holes were also bored with earth augurs from the galleries horizontally towards the enemy to serve as acoustic tubes in conveying the sounds of hostile mining. Sentinels were kept in the galleries night and day; and their cool, quiet aisles were delightful retreats from the heat and turmoil of the trenches. It must be confessed, however, that with the ever present death above ground there was something in the dank stillness that reigned within them suggestive of the grave.

About the 28th July, the Federal commander was discovered transporting troops to the north of the James, and Lee began to send over troops to meet this threat against Richmond.

On the 29th, Grant suddenly brought back his troops, and at daylight, on the 30th, sprung a mine under the salient on the Baxter road held by Elliott's South Carolina brigade. The breach was immediately assailed and occupied, but the enemy was unable to get beyond the crater, where he was held at bay until the arrival of re-enforcements expelled him and our original lines were re-established. This was perhaps the most prominent event of the siege, but it is not within the scope of these Memoirs to go into its details, Hagood's brigade being in no way connected with it. The fighting on the crater was desperate—the Confederates sustaining 1,200 casualties and inflicting a loss of over six thousand upon the enemy, of which 1,100 were prisoners.

The ordinary details for guard and picket and fatigue duty from the troops were very heavy. All the men were required to sit in line of battle upon the banquette, arms in hand and officers at their posts for the half hour preceding and the half hour after dark. From this time, until an hour before daylight, one-half of the men not on other duty were kept awake at a time in the same position, while the other half were allowed to get what sleep they could in the bottom of the trench, their arms and accoutrements laid aside but near at hand and disturbed by the frequent passage of inspecting officers or fatigue parties blundering along in the dark on their prostrate forms. From an hour before day until after good daylight all were roused up and stood to arms, fully equipped and prepared to repel the assault. Again during the day only one-half were allowed to lay off their equipments at a time; and none was permitted, day or night, to leave his assigned place in the trench without special permission. The company officers remained at all times with their men in the trench; the field officers and brigade staff had their respective pits, some six feet in rear of the general trench, and were permitted to use them except when the men were standing to arms. Division commanders were from six hundred yards to a half a mile in rear and generally occupied houses in the suburbs. Generals Lee and Beauregard had their headquarters near each other on the hill north of the Appomattox near Pocohontas Bridge, and with their staffs were in tents. The men in the trenches served as sharpshooters by regular detail. The constant use of the shoulder in shooting produces bruises and soreness, so that they accustomed themselves to rest the rifle on the parapet and fire it as a pistol. The accuracy of their fire was frequently spoken of by letter writers to the Northern papers; and our men, as at Wagner, became very fond of it. It was a relief to the passive endurance which made up so large a part of their duty.

Such service continued day in and day out, for so long a time, was trying to the last degree upon the men already jaded by an active campaign. For some time, during July, not a field officer was present with the brigade for duty, and four out of the five regiments were *commanded by lieutenants.* To preserve anything like organization and efficiency, General Hagood was compelled to consolidate companies temporarily, and to assign to duty, as acting commissioned officers, non-commissioned officers and even privates. In doing this he selected men who had hitherto been mentioned for good conduct in battle. This he did without authority of law, but it was acquiesced in and answered a good purpose, though it was a dangerous experiment in an army like ours. The trenches, however, were not a very congenial atmosphere for demagogy. The most rampant asserter of reserved rights would, like Esau, have sold his birthright for a mess of pottage, provided it was cooked *done*, and an hour's peaceful sleep had been added to the bargain. By the first of August (in six weeks from the commencement of this service) the strength under arms of the brigade was reduced one-half, and in three weeks more it was reduced two-thirds—numbering then but 700 men. The casualties in battle, excluding the day of the 24th of June, did not exceed one hundred, though not a day passed without more or less; and from the fact that the wounds were generally in the head or the upper part of the person, and from the enfeebled state of the general health of the men, they were mostly fatal. Diseases of a low, nervous type carried the men to the field infirmary; and at one time there were five hundred cases in Hagood's brigade alone. These field infirmaries were placed in the woods by some roadside in rear of the city, provided sometimes with a few tents, never with enough, and sometimes with none—where the men were sent whom it was thought possible to restore to duty in a short time and where the surgical operations were performed. The regimental surgeons were here. The assistant surgeons were in some places, more or less sheltered, as near as one could be found to the lines. The litter bearers brought the wounded to them, and after temporary treatment they were dispatched in two-horse ambulances to the infirmary. The various post hospitals in Petersburg, Richmond and even further off, received the severe cases. These hospitals were generally well managed; but the field infirmaries were the scene of much suffering, partly unavoidable and partly due to mismanagement. It depended entirely upon the fidelity and administrative ability of the senior brigade surgeon how each was managed. The brigade commander was expected to exercise a supervision over them which his duties in the trenches prevented from being sufficiently rigid; and the higher medical officers were not, within the writer's observation, particular enough in supervising their brigade subordinates.

From the 1st to the 20th of August nothing occurred with us to break the monotony of life in the trenches, such as it was. The foregoing narrative has given the outline of the military events and surroundings—the naked skeleton of the history; but it is difficult to convey to one who has never had a similar experience an idea of the actual reality of the labors and suffering of the men who for these long, hot summer months held without relief the trenches of Petersburg. The following extracts from the journal (MSS.) of Lieutenant Moffett, adjutant of the Twenty-fifth regiment, then acting as inspector on the brigade staff, and who gallantly and faithfully discharged his full share of the duties performed, depicts vividly but without exaggeration the life we led.

"Seldom," says he, "are men called upon to *endure* as much as was required of the troops who occupied the trenches of Petersburg during the months of June, July and August. It was endurance without relief; sleeplessness without excitement; inactivity without rest; constant apprehension requiring ceaseless watching. The nervous system was continually strained 'till the spirits became depressed almost beyond endurance. . . . . Day after day, as soon as the mists which overhung the country gave way to dawn and until night spread her welcome mantle over the earth, the sharpshooting was incessant, the constant rattle of small arms, the spiteful hissing of bullets, never ceased, and was only drowned by the irregular but daily bombardment from heavier metal. Casualties were of daily occurrence, and no place along the line could be considered safe. The most sheltered were penetrated by glancing bullets, and many severe wounds were received in this way. The trenches themselves were filthy, and though policing was rigidly enforced, yet it was almost impossible to keep down the constant accumulation. Vermin abounded, and diseases of various kinds showed themselves. The digestive organs of the men became impaired by the rations issued and the manner in which they were prepared. Diarrhea and dysentery were universal; the legs and feet of the men swelled until they could not wear their shoes; the filth of their persons from the scarcity of water was terrible; and they presented the appearance rather of inmates of a miserably conducted poor house than of soldiers of an army. But all of this was endured; and although among the meaner class desertions occurred and even self-mutilation was resorted to* to escape this horrid nightmare that brooded upon spirits not highly enough tempered to endure it, yet the great majority of the men stood all their sufferings with unflinching endurance, and never yielded 'till disease drove them to the field infirmary. Not the least of the evils encountered was the unavoidable stench from the latrines. Again, when it rained ever so little, the clay of the soil became a soapy and sticky mud; and after a heavy rain (before drainage was looked to) I have seen the water waist deep in the bottom of the trench and eighteen inches on the banquette, leaving no place for the men to sit or lie down upon. Fortunately at night the sharpshooting ceased, and the men spread their blankets on the parapet and slept. . . ."

Such was the life of the soldier in the trenches, and the following verses appearing anonymously in the Petersburg paper, during the siege, takes up the story and gives what was its frequent ending:

> "Dirty and haggard,
> Almost a blackguard,
> They bore him away
> From the terrible fray;
> From the clash and the rattle
> In the front rank of battle
> Almost dead—shot through the head—
> They reached his gory ambulance bed.
>
> "The ambulance jolts,
> But the driver bolts
> And away he flies,
> Drowning the cries
> Of the poor private:
> Glad to arrive at
> The hospital door—where, to be sure,
> The surgeon he thinks can effect a quick cure.

---

*This practice incident to all armies in hard service was effectually stopped by removing the inducement. After other means had failed, General Hagood, upon the return of the soldiers from the hospital, before signing his papers for discharge, required the facts to be examined by a regimental courtmartial, and if the mutilation was found to be self-inflicted, he retained him in the ranks at such police duty as he could perform and made him go into action under guard unarmed. The first example was enough.—J. H.

"So wan and pale,
With plaintive wail
All alone he dies:
But nobody cries.
Bear away the clay,
To the dead-house away!
Who cares, who ever sheds tears
Over ragged and dirty soldiers' biers?

"A box of pine,
Say three feet by nine,
They placed him in;
Away from the din
Of battle and strife
Then hurry for life
Under the stones to bury the bones
Of the poor soldier whom nobody mourns.

"In his home far away,
A letter some day
Perhaps may tell
How the poor soldier fell;
Then tears, ah, how deep,
The loved ones will weep,
When they hear that the bier
Of him, they so loved, awoke not a tear."

BATTLE OF WELDON ROAD.

About the middle of August, Grant threw a large part of his force across the James at Deep Bottom and advanced towards Richmond. It resulted in his repulse, but drew a large part of our force from Petersburg and thus gave him an opportunity to strike at the Weldon railroad within three miles of which his left then rested. He obtained possession of a considerable portion of it from Davis's farm near the city southward—suffering a loss of a thousand men. On the 19th, Colquitt's and Clingman's brigades, of Hoke's division, were detached to take part with other troops in an effort to dislodge him. They failed of success, though the operation resulted in inflicting heavy loss upon the enemy, including the capture of three thousand prisoners. General Clingman was wounded and never again rejoined his brigade.

The fight was to be renewed on the 20th, and on the night of the 19th, about 9 o'clock, General Hagood received an order to

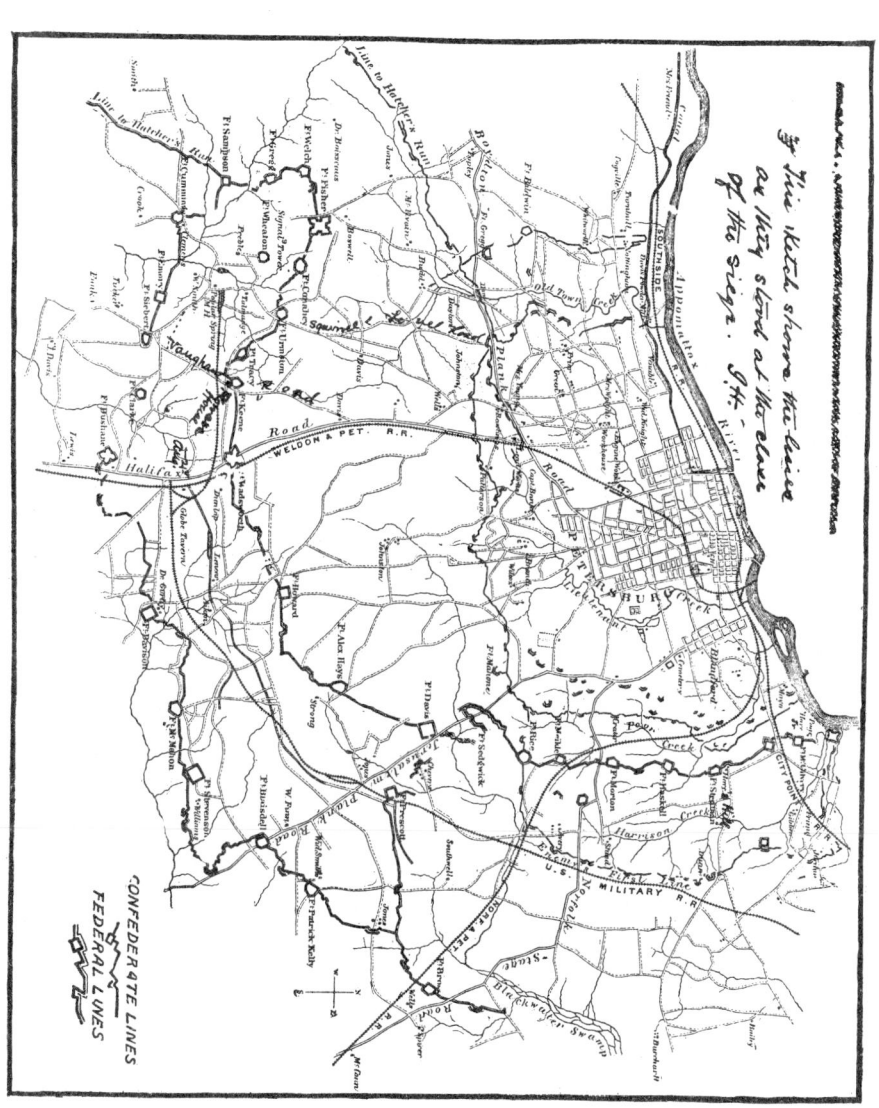

turn over his brigade in the trenches to the senior officer present, and taking with him only his personal aide report to General A. P. Hill to command a brigade from Bushrod Johnson's division in the expected fight. Bushrod Johnson was holding the lines next to Hoke, and he sent no organized brigade, but a regiment from each brigade of his division. It seemed that his habit was to keep one regiment from each of his brigades resting in rear of the lines and he sent such as happened to be there at the time. The regiments commenced arriving at the rendezvous near the lead works when Hagood was to meet them about 11:30 p. m., and by 3 a. m. Hagood had effected a brigade organization with them, appointing haphazard an acting staff and leaving their *names* and those of his regimental commanders, for it was too dark to see their faces, he reported to General Hill, who was asleep in his ambulance near by. When General Hill learned the heterogeneous character of the brigade sent him, he, much to Hagood's relief, declined to receive it, and directed the regiments returned to their division.

Nothing was done that day. The enemy were left to entrench undisturbed across the coveted road. In the afternoon, Hagood's own brigade was withdrawn from the trenches and marching through Petersburg bivouacked beyond its southern limits to the right of Battery 45.

But 59 officers and 681 men marched out of the trenches. Sixty-seven days and nights in them, without relief, had shorn the brigade of two-thirds of its numerical strength, and so debilitated were the sickly and enfeebled remainder that they tired badly in the short evening march. The brigade was itself only in the unconquerable spirit of the remnant which still clung to its banner. When General Hagood again in pursuance of his directions reported to General Hill, he felt that justice to his men required it, and he unhesitatingly asked and received the promise that he should not be used in the next day's work, if it could be avoided.

The change from the cramped and noisome trench to the freedom of the bivouac, and the call upon the men for action, instead of endurance, aroused their spirits wonderfully. And although it rained all night, the fires of the brushwood crackled merrily, and there was once more heard the light laugh, the ready joke,

19—H

and the busy hum of voices as the men prepared their suppers or smoked their pipes stretched at length before the exhilarating blaze.

At 2 a. m. (of the 21st of August) the brigade was aroused, and, moving out at half-past three, followed the column destined for the day's engagement. It still rained; and after a toilsome march through mud and water, first down the Squirrel Level road and then across toward the Poplar Spring Church, more or less skirmishing going on all the time by the flankers on our left, the brigade was directed to halt by the roadside and remain in reserve, while the column passed on. It had now ceased raining, and shortly afterwards, about a mile in front of us, the fire of skirmishers was heard, and a heavy fire of artillery opened. The men laid down and rested from the unwonted fatigue of the march. The firing became more earnest in front; and in about half an hour a courier from General Hill arrived and directed us to hasten to the front and report to Major-General Mahone.

Proceeding by a short cut into the Vaughn road, under the guidance of the courier, and up that toward Petersburg until within six hundred yards of the Flowers' house, we turned across the field to the right and proceeded towards the railroad, in the vicinity of the Globe Tavern. A number of pieces were in position in this field, shelling the railroad, and the enemy's batteries in that direction, though not visible from woods intervening, were replying vigorously. General Hagood moving in columns of fours, passed at double quick across this field, suffering some casualties from exploding shells; and as he reached its further border, a major-general rode up to him announcing himself as General Mahone. Then leading the column, he himself placed it in position in line of battle along the edge of the wood and facing the railroad. "Now," said he to Hagood, "you are upon the flank and rear of the enemy. I have five brigades fighting them in front and they are driving them. I want you to go in and press them all you can." Some fifty yards within the woods the swamp of a rivulet (or "branch") was to be seen; beyond nothing was visible, and firing both of artillery and infantry was then going on. General Mahone added, "when you have crossed the branch swamp you will come upon a clearing in which some 300 yards further is the enemy's line, and they are not entrenched." He also urged promptness in the attack.

General Hagood immediately gave the order to advance, and the men moving in line made their way across the swamp. Upon arriving on the other side, we found ourselves in the clearing, but the enemy still not visible. We were under a hill and they were upon the open plateau sufficiently far beyond to prevent the view. The advance of the brigade had, however, evidently attracted attention from the fire drawn in our direction. The line had been much broken in crossing the swamp, and Hagood immediately pushed skirmishers up the hill for protection and ordered one of his staff to accompany them and reconnoiter while he gave his personal assistance to Captain Moloney, in getting the line of battle rapidly reformed. He assisted the adjutant, instead of himself going to reconnoiter, because from the report of a courier, who had gone up the hill while the skirmishers were forming, he thought there was some danger of being himself assailed where he was and his men were so disorganized at the moment as to be in no condition to repel an attack.

In a few minutes the brigade was formed, and the report coming at the same time from the skirmishers that the enemy was but a short distance ahead of them, and *only in rifle pits*, thus confirming General Mahone's statement. Hagood, cautioning his men to move only at a quick step till he himself gave the order to charge, moved his brigade forward. He had dismounted, and, placing himself in front of the center to steady the men and repress excitement, moved backward in front of the line for a short distance as if on a drill. Himself halting before reaching the crest of the hill, the line passed and he followed with his staff behind the right of the Twenty-first regiment. The Twenty-fifth was on the left of the Twenty-first, and the other three regiments on its right. As soon as the brigade became visible, ascending the hill, a rapid fire was opened upon it, to which in reply not a shot was fired, but moving forward steadily at quick time with arms at "right shoulder shift," as we approached the line of enemy's pits, they broke from them and fled. With one accord a battle yell rang out along our line, and the men, as if by command, broke into "double quick" in pursuit. At the same moment, General Hagood discovered that the line in front of us had only been an entrenched skirmish line, though so heavy as to have deceived his skirmishers into the *notion* that it was a line of battle; and that 250 yards beyond was a strongly entrenched line, crowded with men and artillery, extending right and left as far as he could see; and the five Confederate attacking brigades nowhere visible. It also appeared to him that he was moving upon a re-entering angle of the enemy's line. In this, however, he was partially mistaken. An examination of the field after the war (see diagram at p. 321) showed that the enemy's line crossing the railroad from the east, at this time bent immediately southward, and followed its course in a comparatively straight line at some forty yards on its western side. Later in the siege their line extended farther west, as shown in the Federal sketch at p. 306. Then, recrossing the road at a point below where we struck it, their line only bit out a piece sufficient, if he could hold and permanently entrench, to prevent its further use by us. Immediately to the right of where we struck their line, a small bastioned work for field artillery was thrust forward, and our line of advance was oblique to the enemy's general line and toward its junction with the flank of this work. Thus, in fact, we were going into a reentering made more by the vicious direction of our advance than by the actual construction of the enemy's works. The flank fire from the bastioned work we could not have avoided, but from our oblique attack we had also more or less a flank fire from the straight line, which was an infantry parapet of fully five feet command with an exterior ditch eight or ten feet wide and artillery at intervals. Perceiving at a glance the hopelessness of assault under such circumstances, General Hagood stopping himself, shouted again and again the command to halt; but the crash and rattle of twelve or fifteen pieces of artillery, and probably 2,500 rifles, which had now opened upon us at close range, drowned his voice and the fury of the battle was upon his men. Moving forward with the steady tramp of the double quick, and dressing upon their colors, these devoted men, intent only on carrying the position before them, neither broke their alignment until it was broken by the irregular impact upon the enemy's works, nor stopped to fire their guns until their rush to obtain the parapet was repelled.

When General Hagood saw his men thus rushing upon certain destruction and his efforts to stop them unavailing, he felt that if they were to perish he should share their fate; and with

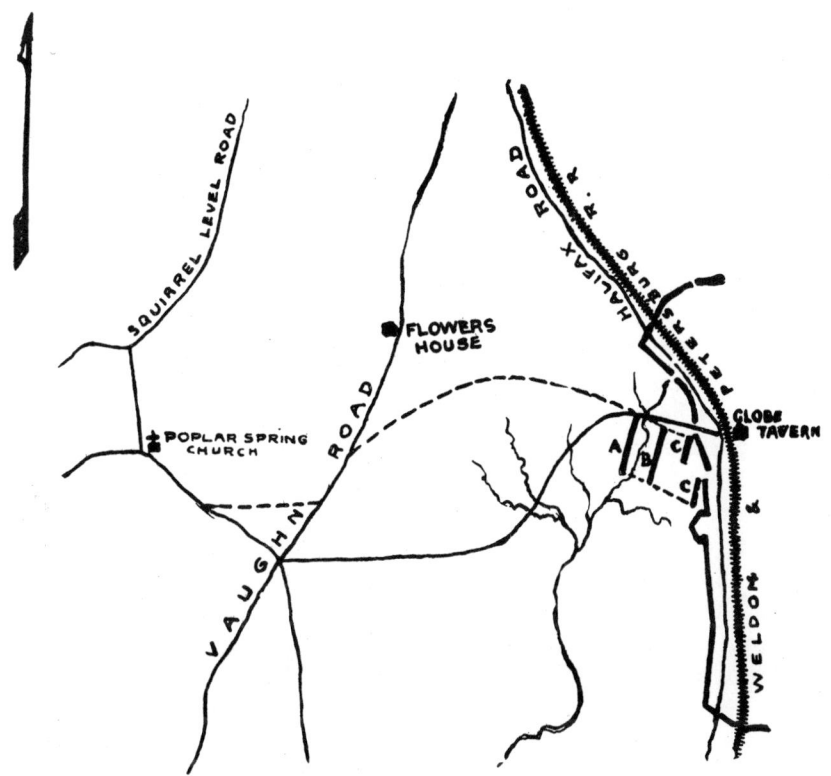

Battle Of Weldon Road

Sketch taken on the ground in 1868:

A. Hagood's Brigade as put in position by Gen. Mahone
B. Across the swamp—advancing.
C. C. An enemy's works.

Moloney and Martin and Orderly Stoney, who were all of his staff that were with him (Moffett and Mazyck were further back in discharge of their respective duties as inspector and ordnance officer), followed the advancing line. In fifty yards Lieutenant Martin fell, shot in the knee; a few steps further and Captain Moloney fell, shot through the head; and Hagood and Stoney alone reached the works—the latter shot in the shoulder but not disabled. The Twenty-fifth and Twenty-first regiments being on the left from the oblique direction of the advance, first struck the works; and while they struggled to get in, the other three regiments swept on. When they reached the ditch, there was from 75 to 100 yards interval between the two divisions into which the brigade had broken.

General Hagood was with Major Wilds, commanding the Twenty-first, who was cheering on his men to renewed assault (success being now their only hope of safety), when looking to the right he saw a mounted Federal officer among the men on the left portion of the brigade to the right, with a regimental color in his hands, and a confusion and parleying immediately around him that betokened approaching surrender. The fight was still raging to Hagood's right and left; there was no cessation on our part except in the squad just around this officer, and none whatever that was perceptible on the part of the enemy. They had pushed out from the right and left a line behind us to cut off our retreat, and this officer (Captain Daly of General Cutler's staff) had galloped out of a sally port, seized a color from the hands of its bearer, and demanded a surrender. Some officers and men surrendered, but were not carried in; others refused, but just around him ceased fighting. General Hagood called to the men to shoot him and fall back in retreat. They either did not hear him or bewildered by the surrender of part of their number, failed to obey. It was a critical moment and demanded instant and decided action. In a few minutes the disposition to surrender would have spread and the whole brigade have been lost. Making his way across the intervening space as speedily as he could, exposed to a regular fire by file from the enemy's line, scarce thirty yards off, and calling to his men to fall back—which they did not do—General Hagood approached the officer and demanded the colors, and that he should go back within his own lines, telling him he was free to do so. He commenced arguing the hopelessness of further struggle, and pointed out the lines in our rear. Hagood cut him short, and demanded a categorical reply—yes, or no. Daly was a man of fine presence and sat with loosened rein upon a noble-looking bay that stood with head and tail erect and flashing eye and distended nostrils, quivering in every limb with excitement, but not moving in his tracks. In reply to his abrupt demand, the rider raised his head proudly and decisively answered, "No!" Upon the word General Hagood shot him through the body, and, as he reeled from the saddle upon one side, sprang into it from the other, Orderly Stoney seizing the flag from Daly's falling hands.

There was no thought of surrender now. The yell from the brigade following the act and ringing out above the noise of battle told their commander that they were once more in hand and would go now wherever ordered—whether to the front or rear.

Shouting to them to face about, Hagood led them at a run against the line in his rear, Stoney holding aloft in the front the recaptured flag which he had torn from its staff. This line melted before our charge; but the fire was terrific after breaking through it, until the shelter of the valley of the branch was reached. Upon its margin a fragment from a schrapnel shell tore open the loin of the horse upon which Hagood rode; and struggling, as he fell, he kicked Lieutenant William Taylor of the Seventh battalion upon the head, rendering him for the time so confused that he had to be led from the field by one of his men. This gallant young officer had a few days before rejoined his command with an unhealed wound received at Drury's Bluff.

This ended the fighting for the possession of the Weldon Road. The Confederate losses had been very insignificant, until today, and now it was confined principally to our brigade. Grant had lost 5,000 men, *but he had the road.* A few days afterwards, Hancock with 8,000 men was dispatched southward from this point to tear up the track. A. P. Hill and Hampton met and defeated him at Ream's Station* with the loss of two field batteries and between 2,500 and 3,000 men. Grant's men might have adopted with some variation the burthen of Hood's "Song of

---

*25th August, '64.—Ed.

the Shirt"—"Ah, God! That *roads* should be so dear and flesh and blood so cheap!"

A week afterwards, in a conversation in General Lee's presence, General A. P. Hill stated to Hagood that on the morning of the 21st he was informed by his scouts as to the position and condition of the enemy's works, believing that the point upon which Hagood was sent was the left of their line, and that they had no further works down the railroad. He also added that the haziness of the morning prevented his ascertaining his error until Hagood's attack developed it. General Mahone also said to General Hagood that he shared the same misapprehension, but insisted that if the other five brigades had attacked with the same vigor that Hagood's did, we would have won. It seemed that after driving the enemy's skirmish line from the pits, out of which Hagood's men *marched* them, they stopped; and the heavy fusillade which made Mahone think they were driving the enemy was from a stationery line firing at long range.*

The frankness and freedom with which these two distinguished officers took the blame of the blunder upon themselves greatly relieved General Hagood, for he feared that this affair, in the misapprehension to which it would be subjected, would be similar to the assault of the 24th June at the City Point Road. It was, however, generally correctly understood in the army, and apparently not misunderstood by the public. Both Generals Lee and Beauregard were on the field, and the latter next day sent Hagood word through General Hoke that had it been in his power he would have promoted him before leaving it. He also, through his adjutant, called for a written report of the incident of the flag. This was briefly written and forwarded. Some months afterward, General Cooper, adjutant-general at Richmond, very kindly sent to General Hagood an official copy of the endorsements made on the report, then on file in his office. They were as follows:

---

*Captain Young, in *Philadelphia Times,* gives a different account of this part of the action. He was with one of the brigades—Scales. The statement of the text was derived from General Mahone.

"Headquarters, Dept. North Carolina and Southern Virginia.
"Near Petersburg, Aug. 23, 1864.
"Respectfully forwarded through General R. E. Lee to his Excellency, President Davis, for his information. Such an act of gallantry, as herein described, and of devotion to one's flag reflects the highest credit on the officer who performs it, and it should be held up to the army as worthy of imitation under similar circumstances. Brigadier-General Hagood is a brave and meritorious officer, who had distinguished himself already at Battery Wagner and Drury's Bluff, and participated actively in the battles of Warbottam Church and Petersburg on the 16th and 17th June last. I respectfully recommend him for promotion at the earliest opportunity. Attention is also called to General Hagood's recommendation of his orderly, Private J. D. Stoney, for a commission. I feel assured he is deserving of it.
"(Signed) G. T. BEAUREGARD,
"General."

"Headquarters A. N. V., 24 August, 1864.
"Respectfully forwarded. (Signed) R. E. LEE, General."

"Bureau A. & I. General.
Apptmt. Office, 1st Sept., 1864.
"Respectfully submitted to Secretary at War.
"By order. (Signed) E. A. PALFREY, A. A. G."

"Respectfully submitted as requested to notice of the President.
"(Signed) J. A. SEDDEN, Secty. at War."

"There are two modes of recognizing distinguished service—one by promotion, the other by announcement in orders. See recommendation for the private and note for the brigadier, whom I regard worthy of promotion when it can be consistently done.
JEFF. DAVIS, 7th Nov., 1864."
"Adj. Gen.: Note the President's endorsement and if opportunity of promotion occurs submit. 9th. Nov., 1864.
"(Signed) J. A. SEDDEN,
"Secty. at War."
"Official.
"A. & I. G. Office.
"Dec. 9, 1864,
"(Signed) H. L. CLAY,
"A. A. G."

Stoney subsequently received from the President the commission of second lieutenant in the Twenty-seventh regiment, and did his duty as faithfully and gallantly as heretofore 'till the close of the war. Captain Daly, though reported dead by the

Yankee newspaper army correspondent, was understood to have survived and to have published in the New York *Herald* many months afterward a card, among other things vindicatory of General Hagood from the charge of murder which the Yankee papers freely lavished upon him.*

General Hagood, valuing highly the approval of his superior officers in the field, sought to make no use of the foregoing handsome endorsements beyond leaving them in the war office, where they were quietly pigeon-holed. Three months later, he and many better men were overslaughed by the assignment to a division command in the army of Northern Virginia of an officer who had never previously been in battle. This it will be remembered was at the close of the fourth year of the war!

After the repulse of his brigade, on the 21st of August, General Hagood kept for some time a line of skirmishers on the field as near as possible to the enemy's works, while the litter bearers removed the wounded. Many poor fellows crawled within this line and were thus rescued from captivity; one of them, Lieutenant Harper, Twenty-fifth regiment, dragged himself from near the enemy's works with a broken leg. He was never, however, able again to resume duty with his company. Of the 59 officers and 681 men who went into the action in the brigade, only 18 officers and 274 men came out of it unhurt; being a total of 448 casualties—or about two-thirds of the force engaged. The enemy claimed to have buried 211 dead, of which most were Hagood's men. The character of the casualties was probably 120 killed, 125 wounded in our hand, and 203 captured, of which a large part were also wounded.

In the Twenty-first regiment, Major Wilds, commanding, was wounded and captured; Lieutenant Ford wounded and captured, and Lieutenants Bowles, Easterling and Atkinson were captured.

In the Seventh battalion Lieutenants McKaskell, Kennedy, Isbell and Douglass were killed; Captain Segars and Lieutenants Tiller, Raley, King, Clyburn, Taylor, and Weston wounded, and Captain Jones with Lieutenants Young, Gardner and Schley were captured. Captain Jones commanded the battalion in the action.

---

*In 1879 Captain Daly wrote from Council Bluffs, Iowa, to General Hagood for, and received an affidavit of the facts of his part in this action. He was applying for a pension.

In the Eleventh regiment, Lieutenant Minas was wounded, and Lieutenants Morrison, Bowman and Tuten were captured. Lieutenant Morrison commanded the regiment, which had scarcely the strength of a company.

In the Twenty-fifth regiment, Captains Sellars and Gordon, with Lieutenants Kennerly, Ross, Bethea and Evans were killed. Captain McKerrall and Lieutenant Duke were captured. Sellars commanded the regiment—mistake, Gordon ranked Sellars.

In the Twenty-seventh regiment, Lieutenant-Colonel Blake and Lieutenants Muckenfuss, Hendrix, McBeth and Hogan were captured. Cadet Porcher was wounded. Colonel Gaillard commanded his regiment and escaped unhurt.

Lieutenant Martin's wound in the leg proved more painful than serious. In a couple of months he was again at his post as active and efficient as ever in the discharge of his duty as aide-de-camp. Lieutenant Cassidy, of the Eleventh regiment, was noted for his gallantry; and in the ranks Sergeant Brothers, colorbearer of the same regiment, deserves especial mention. He was sick in hospital when the brigade left the trenches and hearing of the probability of its engaging the enemy, applied for his discharge, which the surgeon refused, on the ground that he was yet unfit for duty. He *deserted* from the hospital, joined his regiment on the march through Petersburg, and was shot down next day while heroically doing his duty. He lost his leg and was placed on the retired list. Many other noble men in the ranks perished or survived that day whose deeds deserve mention; but it is impossible to do justice to them all.

It was a heartrending sight to look along the line of the brigade, as it mustered in the Vaughn road after the action, and miss the familiar faces, without which it did not seem the same command. It was now shrunk to the proportions of a small battalion, yet so game and generous was the spirit of this body of men that the writer believes this poor remnant could have again been led into action that day with all the dash and gallantry that marked their morning's work. And as the news of the fiery ordeal, through which the brigade had passed, spread through the hospitals and field infirmary, the sick and wounded, who had not been present, sought their discharges, and pale and weak voluntarily hastened to rejoin their comrades and share their fate. In less than a week three hundred and thirty-nine men (339) from the sick list returned to duty, one-half of whom could not have stood a five-mile march. No wonder General Hagood was sensitive to even a suspicion of recklessly wielding a blade so highly tempered and uselessly hacking it against impossibilities.

There were two men who fell upon this bloody field who had done as much, each in his sphere, to give the character to the brigade which it had exhibited as perhaps any other two men in it—Moloney and Sellars. Captain Sellars had enlisted in the First South Carolina Volunteers (Hagood's) in December, 1860, and was made orderly sergeant of Captain Collier's company. At the reorganization of the regiment, in April, 1862, he re-enlisted in the same company, was elected its captain, and with it joined the Twenty-fifth regiment, then being organized. He was young, probably twenty-two, at the period of his untimely death —of modest bearing, strict, yet just, as a disciplinarian, and beloved by his men. In action he was cool, determined and unflinching, and exhibited a capacity for higher command, which he would assuredly have reached had a kinder fate spared his valuable life. He always did his duty well; had more than once distinguished himself; and had been recommended for promotion to the vacant majority in his regiment. The place of such a man could not well be filled.

Moloney—graduating with honor at a Northern college— engaged for a year or two in mercantile pursuits at his home in South Carolina. Then, having studied law and been admitted to its practice, was in the West perfecting his arrangements for establishing himself in Louisiana, when South Carolina seceded. Returning, he joined the First South Carolina and was made its adjutant. The foregoing Memoirs are the record of his services. In every action narrated, he was engaged, and if his name is not always mentioned, it is because the comment that must needs go with it must become monotonous—he always did his duty well and completely. His business habits, just mind, and accomplished manner, made him invaluable in the office; and on the field he had the quick intelligence and fertility of resource of the born soldier. An incident on the 24th June illustrates his coolness. He had been sent to carry an order, under very heavy fire, and on his return, when some fifteen or twenty feet from the officer who sent him, a shell from a Napoleon striking the earth between them exploded at his feet, the fragments flying on. As he emerged from the smoke which enveloped him, he quietly announced, with a military salute, "Your order has been delivered." Moloney was rather above the medium height, of slight but active frame, and of an intellectual and refined countenance. General Hagood was strongly attached to him, and in announcing his death to his family wrote, ". . . Words are idle to express the sympathy I feel for you in this great affliction. He was almost a brother to me; and to the brigade his loss is irreparable. With abilities far beyond his rank, he was assiduous and thorough in the discharge of his duty; and that with a natural urbanity which made him an universal favorite. One of the men, when he learned his fate, seized my hand and leaning on my horse's shoulder, wept uncontrollably. Wounded men, as they were borne to the rear, with their bodies torn and their limbs mangled, stopped their litter bearers to ask me after him, and express their sorrow. Generous, courteous, brave and high-toned, pure in thought and speech, ever mindful of the rights and feelings of others, jealous of his own when he thought them designedly infringed, he came up more fully to my idea of a gentleman than any man I ever knew.

"Poor fellow! As we marched that morning from our wet and comfortless bivouac, he told me that he had been dreaming all night of his mother,—may God comfort her in her sorrow."

REST FOR THE WEARY.

After the action on the Weldon Road, the brigade continued for some days to report to Major-General Mahone and was stationed on the southern lines of Petersburg, where there was no fighting. Hagood, had, however, on the 24th, in a communication to Colonel Brent (General Beauregard's A. A. G.), called attention to the worn and jaded condition of his men, and the fearful reduction in their number; and asked to be permitted to take them to some quiet camp where rest and access to water might recruit their physical condition. His application was returned approved by General Lee, and the neighborhood of the crossing of the turnpike over Swift Creek indicated for his camp. Mr. Dunlop very kindly offered his grounds to the brigade inspector sent to select the spot, and on the 2nd September we moved to this delightful camp.

Dunlop's park was near the scene of our affair at Swift Creek on the 9th May. It had been the property of an old Scotch gentleman who had accumulated a large fortune as a merchant in Petersburg and had spent years in beautifying and adorning this as his country seat. Swift Creek, a bold and handsome stream with precipitous banks, pursued its course along two sides of the park—now brawling in a rapid, now spreading into a deep, dark pool. Within the grounds artificial lakelets and mounds imitated nature. The native forest had been thinned and pruned into combinations of glade and grove and single trees; straight avenues opened upon pleasing vistas, and serpentine roads and walks meandered; the grass was the freshest of green and as perfect a carpet as any woven in the loom. Wherever a prospect opened, or the shade was densest, or the murmer of the water fell gentlest upon the ear, a summer house or a rustic seat invited repose; and from various parts of the grounds the mansion was to be seen, sometimes a glimpse, sometimes a view more or less full, but always picturesque. It was a structure in the Italian villa style, and stood upon a gentle eminence near the creek, with the grass growing up to its walls and the gravelled carriage drive approaching it in a graceful sweep.

There were perhaps not over forty acres in this beautiful park, and it appeared much larger from the artistic skill with which it was laid off; and up to this time it had escaped the ravages of war, though a cannon ball through one of the gables of the house, a straggler on the 9th May, attested the near proximity of contending armies. The old gentleman, who had delighted to adorn this retreat, had died within it while Butler's army had been on the opposite side of Swift Creek, and his son reigned in his stead. The present proprietor had been a courier for General Hagood at that time, and was now on invalid leave.

Here at last the brigade *was at rest.* It is difficult to convey an idea of the effect upon the spirits of the transfer from the heat and the glare and the filth and the turmoil and danger of the trenches, endured so long, to the shade and water, and peaceful seclusion of these grounds. An Arab entering an oasis from the burning sands of the desert might approximate its conception; a Christian arrived "where the weary are at rest and the wicked cease from troubling" would realize it. All military observances were suspended for several days. A sergeant's guard was sufficient for purposes of discipline and of restraining the men from straggling, or injuring the trees and shrubbery—especially when backed by a threat in general orders to send the first offender "back to the trenches" to serve with Colquitt's brigade, till his command returned to duty.

From dawn till dark Swift Creek was full of the men patiently scrubbing from their persons the accummulated dust of march and trench and battle, and its banks lined with others waging vigorous war upon the grime and vermin that made their garments almost uninhabitable; while the park was ornamented with groups who had undergone the cleansing process, indulging in a somnolent lethargy as profound as if inspired by hashish. Others again stretched and rolled upon the smooth and velvety surface of the grass with a kind of sensual delight.

Opportunity was now taken to refit, as far as practicable, the brigade in clothing, shoes and ordnance appointments. Its commissariat was carefully looked to; vegetable diet provided, and proper cooking enforced. The men rapidly recovered their condition and health. The field infirmary was almost emptied into the camp, and the patients got well faster here than there. In a short time the brigade began to show respectability in the number for duty. Then drills were established; at stated hours the regimental bands enlivened the air with music; sentinels and the ceremonials of camp were resumed; vacant offices filled by promotion or election, and in less than a month the brigade was itself again—sorely reduced in numbers, but ready once more "to live or die for Dixie."

About the 15th of September, the other brigades of Hoke's division were relieved from the trenches and placed in reserve on the Petersburg side of the Appomattox. And on the 26th, General Lee reviewed the division, which was concentrated for the purpose for that evening. This was the only review or other military display witnessed by the writer during the campaign of '64. It was made a gala occasion by the citizens of the beleaguered town, large numbers attending. The ladies were out in full force, and many were on horseback. General A. P. Hill rode on the staff of the commanding general upon a very graceful and beautiful silver grey; and horse and rider showed gallantly. General Lee reviewed the troops rapidly and seemed bored by the ceremonial and glad to be through with it. He was in full uniform, with a quantity of yellow sash around his waist, and did not look like himself. Even his horse looked as if he thought it was all foolishness.

After the battle of Cold Harbor and while the opposing armies still confronted each other there, the writer going to the rear in discharge of some duty was attracted by a large, powerful, well-bred horse, held by an orderly in front of the tent of a corps commander. He was a grey, perfectly groomed, and his appointments, though of the ordinary regulation character, had a neatness about them unusual during a campaign. Just then General Lee came out of the tent and slowly approaching the horse stood thoughtfully by his side for a moment. He wore blue military pants without suspenders and a short linen sack with no vest, a soft felt hat, and buff gauntlets. He had no insignia of rank about him, and carried neither sword, pistol or field glass. Recovering from his momentary reverie, he stroked the horse kindly upon the face, and with a glance at his accoutrements that bespoke the horseman, mounted, adjusted the reins in his bridle hand, settled himself in the saddle, and rode quietly away followed by the orderly. This was his usual style. He always was mounted on the same horse, and as he passed along his lines or through his army, never with more than one attendant, and sometimes with none, he looked more like some planter, with a taste for horses riding around his fields, than like the conventional military chieftain.

This absence of "fuss and feathers" in its commander gave the cue to the whole Army of Northern Virginia. The ordinary summer campaign dress of a general officer was a dark colored flannel shirt, without a coat over it, blue pants, top boots and felt hat, with a revolver buckled around his waist and a field glass swung over his shoulder. There was not a body guard in the army; and headquarter guards were small and for the protection of property, not for ceremony and display. Among the regimental officers it was difficult to get them to wear the swords which were their badges of rank. This was, however, though contrary to regulations and orders, a matter of judgment as well as taste with them. They preferred to be encumbered simply with the revolver, and in this they were right. The long range and repeating firearm had made the sword for the infantry officer as antiquated as the spontoon. It was not uncommon to see them in action directing their men without any weapon at all; and in the charge upon the enemy at the Crater, after the explosion of Grant's Petersburg mine, a South Carolina colonel—Smith, of the Twenty-sixth— was said to have led his men with a club seized for the occasion. He was also said to have been successful with his club in a hand-to-hand encounter with one of the Federal bayonets.

Our period of rest was now rapidly drawing to a close, and on the night of the 28th of September the brigade was returned to the trenches, relieving Gracie's brigade, which was stationed near the Baxter road. The enemy discovered the transfer of troops that was going on, and treated us to a most brilliant pyrotechnic display. The mortar fire was the heaviest we had yet seen at Petersburg, but the casualties were few.

THE RICHMOND LINES.

At 12 o'clock on the day after the brigade returned to the trenches it was hastily withdrawn and dispatched to the north of the James, Gracie's men resuming their old station.

On the 28th, Grant had captured Fort Harrison, a strong work on the lines of Richmond near the north bank of the river. It was feebly held by the local militia, and was easily carried by assault. Pressing on, the enemy essayed Fort Gilmer, but this was held by a company of regular artillery who had nerve enough to withstand an assault, and his career was checked. The position gained, however, seriously threatened Richmond. Fort Harrison was an important tactical point, and some mile or two of the "exterior line" to the north of it had been abandoned. The divisions of Fields and Hoke were dispatched from Petersburg to the threatened front.

Hagood followed the other brigades of his division and arrived in the vicinity of Fort Harrison at 9 o'clock the next morning. General Lee was on the ground, and it was evident an effort was

20—H

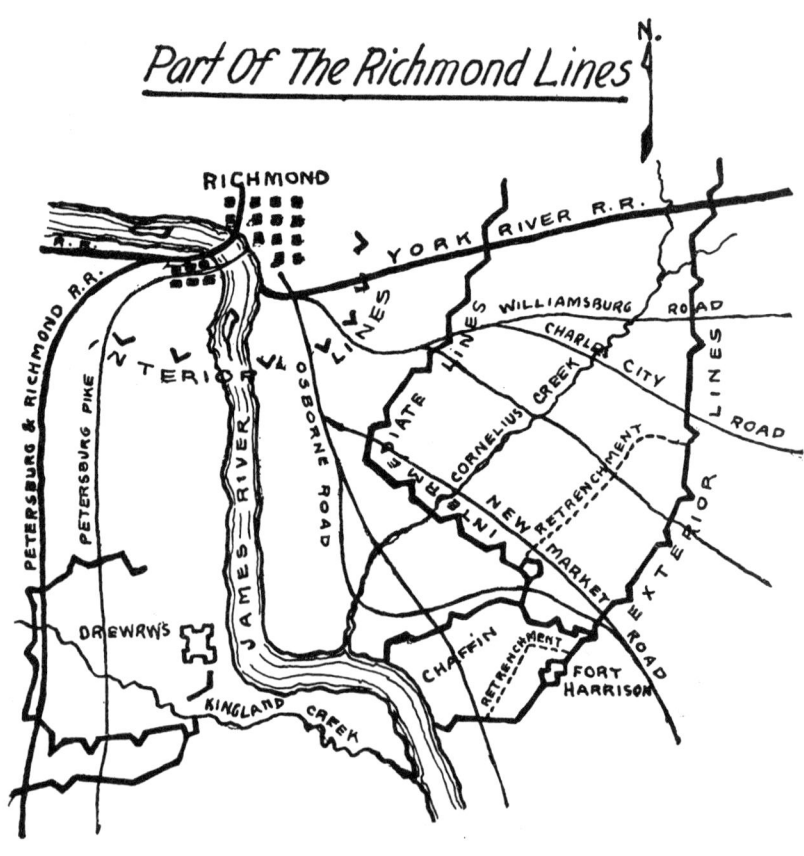

Part Of The Richmond Lines

to be made to recover the lost work. Towards midday it was made. Two separate storming columns of two brigades each (probably 6,000 men in all) were sent forward from different directions upon the fort, their assault having been preceded by a half-hour's heavy fire from artillery. Each column had a brigade front. They did not move in concert and were separately and disastrously repulsed. The column from Hoke's division was composed of the brigades of Clingman and Colquitt, and its casualties were about 800. Fields lost not so many. The First South Carolina regiment, now commanded by Colonel J. R. Hagood, composed a part of the column of Fields, and greatly distinguished itself, but lost many of its best officers and men. Our brigade was not engaged.

The Confederate commander now gave his attention to cutting off by a re-trenchment the angle of his lines held by the enemy. This was soon done, the work progressing under heavy artillery and picket fire, but the enemy not attempting to interrupt it by assault. As soon as the work was completed, the troops before Fort Harrison were relieved by militia, and General Lee again took the offensive.

The enemy had occupied the abandoned portion of the "exterior line" north of Fort Harrison, and his front was thus considerably stretched out from the river, his right resting between the Charles City and Darby Town roads. Gary's brigade of cavalry and the divisions of Fields and Hoke were available. Gary moving down the Charles City road was to turn and drive in the enemy's right flank, a small brigade of infantry and a strong force of field artillery re-enforcing him for the occasion. Fields, coming down the Darby Town road, was to take up the fight at that point, and, conjointly with Gary, press the enemy upon the river. Hoke was to follow as a reserve.

At daylight, on the 7th of October, the action commenced, Gary attacking with vigor. Fields took it up with success, and in a short time the enemy were driven across the Darby Town road for a mile towards Fort Harrison, doubling up along the line of the "exterior" works occupied by them. Fields now, in pursuance of the plan arranged, followed them up, his right resting on the line of works and taking that as a directrix, Gary on his left, all outside the line of works. At this time Hoke's division was moved from its position in the Darby Town road, where it had rested during the fight, and filing to the right followed in column behind the right of the advancing Confederate line, moving parallel to the exterior line and about 200 yards inside of them. Our advance soon encountered an entrenched line strongly manned and being rapidly re-enforced. This line ran back at right angles to the line of captured works, and had probably been constructed by the enemy to protect their flank, when it only extended thus far. It was, it will be perceived, parallel to Fields' line of advance. Two courses were now open to the Confederates. First, to make a direct assault, or second, to bring Hoke before this line, and, feeling to the left with Gary and Fields' commands, turn it. Hoke's relative position was such that he could have replaced Fields in thirty minutes. The first plan was adopted, the direct attack was made and repulsed with some loss. This terminated the day's proceedings. General Gregg, of the Texas brigade, was killed, and General Bratton, of South Carolina, was wounded in the last assault. Both were of the division of Fields. Colonel Haskell, of Gary's brigade, was severely wounded earlier in the day, after having exhibited a personal gallantry that attracted much commendation. Nine pieces of artillery, 150 horses and two or three hundred prisoners were captured. The enemy's loss in killed and wounded are unknown. Our casualties of all kinds were about 200. Though the reserve was not engaged, its advance attracted artillery fire, and there were eleven casualties from shells in Hagood's brigade. The full measure of success contemplated was not realized, and at nightfall the ground regained was once more abandoned. Why General Lee did not put in his reserve is not known. The position in which Hoke was held during the fight, it will be perceived, interposed him between the enemy and Richmond, then open to a coup de main. Possibly it was deemed important to maintain him in it. More probably the chances of success were not deemed sufficient to warrant the shattering of the whole disposable force for the defence of this front of Richmond.

For most of the foregoing details of the place and conduct of this action, the writer is indebted to a conversation with General Gary, since the war. From his own position with the reserve he saw very little of it. An impression prevailed to some extent among Fields's subordinate officers that Hoke was derelict in not joining in the final assault. In Colonel J. R. Hagood's Memoirs of the First South Carolina Regiment, these impressions are expressed. The writer never talked with Hoke on the subject, for he gave no heed to the matter though he heard rumors of it at the time. General Lee was, however, present with the reserve during most of the day, and just before and during the last assault he was with us. This settles the fact that the part borne by Hoke was under the immediate direction of the commander-in-chief.

In the evening, General Lee withdrew from the field and took up position behind Cornelius Creek, covering the New Market and Darby Town roads. Three days afterwards (10th October), he advanced his line without opposition some 400 yards and commenced another re-trenchment, cutting off the portion of the "exterior line," now finally abandoned. It ran from Fort Gilmer northeasterly in nearly a straight line till it ran into the "exterior line" near the Charles City road.

On the 13th, the enemy advanced, skirmished along the whole line, and attacked on the Darby Town road. He was repelled with a loss estimated at 1,200; ours inconsiderable.

Again, on the 27th, he advanced at daylight, skirmished along our whole line as before, but this time also making partial assaults. About noon he attacked heavily on the Charles City road, and was repulsed with a loss of 2,000 men, of whom 500 were prisoners. In both these actions, our incomplete entrenchments were defended by a single rank deployed at intervals of three to six feet, and no reserves. The troops manning the lines shifted along them as the movements of the enemy required, now closing up to repel an assault, now deploying to fill a gap, and sometimes leaving long stretches undefended except by field guns in battery.

On both days, too, the enemy attacked our extreme right below Petersburg, meeting with no success. In these affairs our brigade suffered some twenty-five or thirty casualties.

The completion of the re-trenchment was now rapidly pushed. The plan was small redans for field guns, 300 yards apart, with straight curtains for infantry. The parapet of curtains had a uniform base of 20 degrees; superior slope 12 degrees; height of interior crest 7 degrees, with a banquette; and the ditch was exterior. Where forests occurred, they were cut down for from five or six hundred yards in front, and abattis and palisades were built all along the main line some sixty yards in front. A picket line was entrenched three hundred yards in front, with small detached works V-shaped and 36 yards apart, The point of the V was toward the enemy; its splay about 6 feet, length of face 10 feet, height of interior crest 6 feet with banquette—all above ground. A chain of videttes was established 100 yards in front of picket line; they were not entrenched. As winter advanced fires were allowed on the picket line. They were built a little in rear of it* and between the detached works.

During this period, the hostile videttes were in view of each other at distances of from two to three hundred yards. There was, however, no picket or artillery fire; and the progress of our work was not interrupted except, as narrated, on the 13th and 27th of October.

An ingenious arrangement of the barbette platforms in the redans was adopted by which the advantages of this style of platform was retained and one of its disadvantages (exposure of the gunners) avoided. A little ditch two and a half feet wide, with recesses (C) for ammunition chests, was allowed around the interior slope; in it the gunners stood, and from it mostly worked the piece. The pieces were kept by a hurter from toppling into the ditch, when run "into battery," and the platform was extended back, as at D. E. to give a fire along the rear of the curtain should a lodgment be effected. Pine pole revetments were used both here and on the infantry curtains.

Winter quarters were also constructed. A continuous line of comfortable pine pole cabins, with clay chimneys, for the rank and file, ran behind the works, leaving a broad street or place of arms between it and the entrenchments.

The regimental officers had their cabins, each in the relative place of its occupant in line of battle, and the general officers had their's further in rear.

The fine bracing weather and cheerful labor and strict military observances, neglected through the more stirring parts of the

---

*See Xenophon's Anabasis Book VII (Xenophon's Works, 331), "In front of Videttes."

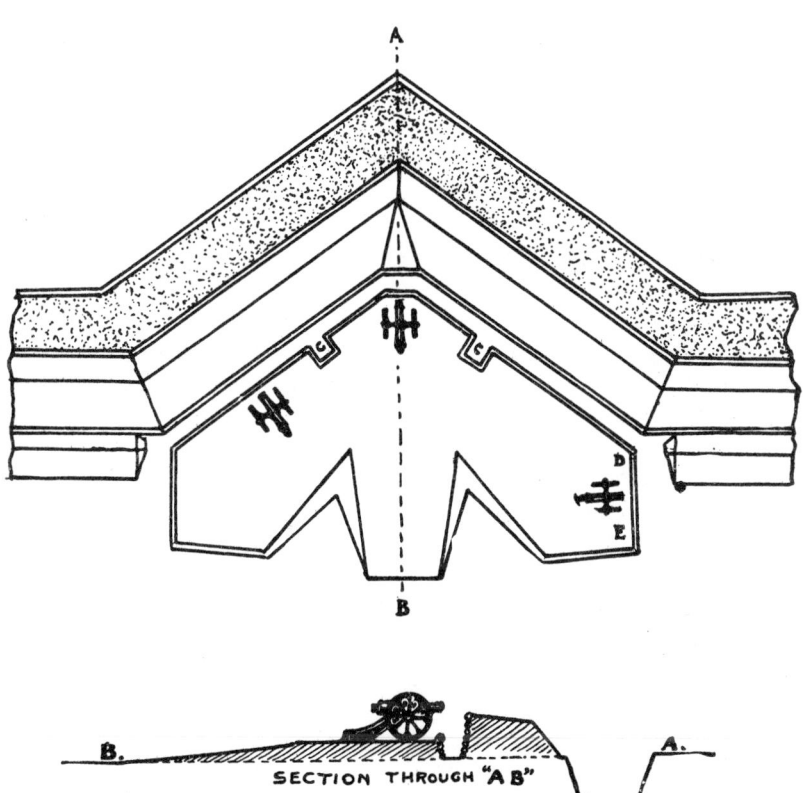

SECTION THROUGH "AB"

campaign, had a fine effect upon the health and spirits of the men. To this end, the return of the sick and wounded to duty and the easy success of the last two encounters contributed. The morale of the troops was excellent.

In Hagood's brigade, Colonel Graham (wounded at Walthal Junction) returning from invalided leave, resumed command of the Twenty-first. Gantt, absent on sick-leave during our service at Petersburg, was now in command of the Eleventh, Colonel Gaillard had been invalided. Shortly after the 21st of August, one of his field officers was in the hands of the enemy, and the other had been absent on wounded leave since Drury's Bluff; so the Twenty-seventh was in charge of one of its line officers, Captain Simons. Colonel Rion was at the head of the Seventh, and Captain Carson, wounded at Swift Creek, had returned to duty and commanded the Twenty-fifth. Colonel Simonton was taken sick shortly after joining his regiment at Cold Harbor, and, on his recovery, had obtained a detachment for post service in North Carolina. Pressly's and Glover's places had not been filled from the fact that a captain, senior to Carson, was in the hands of the enemy.

On the staff, Lieutenant Moffett had, in recognition of his valuable services, been promoted brigade aid-de-camp in place of Moloney; and Orderly Ryan, returning to duty from a wound, received in the trenches at Petersburg, was elected to a vacant lieutenancy in the Eleventh regiment. Captain Stoney was still absent with his wound, and his duties were, since Moffett's promotion, discharged by Lieutenant Mazyck in addition to his own as ordnance officer. Mazyck had throughout the campaign discharged his appropriate duties with great fidelity; and had repeatedly served in action as aide when circumstances permitted his absence from ordnance duties. He was a very gallant and meritorious officer.

The weather continued delightful up to the 1st of November, and the vicinity of Richmond and the comparative quiet in our front permitted the limited enjoyment of the society of the capital to the divisions north of the James. The officers of Hoke's division received upon two occasions a large and distinguished party of ladies. A farm house, not too near the lines, would be obtained and cleared for dancing; the walls tastefully draped with flags and garnished with arms; the Eutaw band, of Hagood's brigade (the best at that time in the army), be detailed for attendance, and ambulances dispatched for the guests. This would be the contribution on the part of the military. At an early hour, in the forenoon, the ladies would arrive, bringing not only themselves but the edibles of the feast, and immediately take charge of the festivities. A ride along the lines, when the troops were at dress parade, would complete the day. The ladies were not only of the old residents of Richmond, but were also from other States of the South—of the families of the civil and military officers of the government drawn thither by the war. It was a charming circle; refined, intelligent and accomplished, and the times had added to it the least dash in the world of the freedom of the bivouac. They were admirable specimens of high bred Southern women, as the war developed them. Devoted heart and soul to the cause, they were ready at any time to cheer their champions in battle with brave words, or tend the sick and wounded with gentle ministrations. Anything that wore the grey was ennobled in their eyes, and its welfare the subject of their prayers. They carried the refinement and delicacy of the lady into the self-imposed duties of the sick-nurse, regardless whether it was general officer or the humblest soldier who was the recipient of their kindness; and enduring their own privations bravely— banishment from home, the loss of fortune, the death of kindred —they were the first to brighten in the intervals of good forune, and the last to despair under the pressure of adversity.

During November the weather was good and bad by turns— rain, snow, and fair alternated; but the roads remained entirely practicable for military purposes. The war, however, flagged around Richmond. The armies of Lee and Grant having thoroughly tested each other's strength in the many desperate combats of the campaign, stood warily watching each other, until events transpiring elsewhere should bring new conditions into the next collision between them. The fate of Richmond was in fact being decided on other fields. This campaign had shown clearly that it was impregnable to direct attack. There was but little hope in renewed assault. Siege operations promised but little more, because of the distance of the defenses from the body of the plan. With such facility for *retrenchment*, the task would be endless. But the place had never been invested; and in its condition, with regard to supplies, an investment would certainly determine its fall.

Accordingly, after the failure of the Petersburg mine, there was no further evidence of regular approaches by the enemy; but all his efforts seemed to be given to effecting a practical investment. His success on the Weldon road was in that direction, but there he was stopped. The movements and operations, narrated north of the James, were secondary to attempts made at the same time to extend his left around our right below Petersburg. They were demonstrations to cover determined efforts against the western roads into Richmond. Lee had firmly thrust him back, and now on investment the relative proportion of Lee's and Grant's armies remaining the same, was as clearly a futile hope as assault or siege approaches.

It was at a greater distance from Richmond that its sources of supply must be cut. While Grant held Lee at bay, co-operative columns, if at all, must do the work.

The Valley Army, under General Early, after a varied experience of invasion and retreat, victory and disaster, had accomplished its main purpose of keeping the co-operative column of the enemy operating from that direction off of these same western roads. It was, however, badly shattered in discipline and efficiency, and now a part of it was drawn to the lines before Richmond, while its adversary was largely transferred to the ranks of Grant. The seasons precluded further decisive effort upon the scene of their summer operations.

In the southwestern portion of the military horizon, however, a cloud was gathering ominous of the fate of Richmond, and of the Confederacy. Hood had been dispatched into Tennessee, and by carrying the war into Africa was to recall Hannibal from Italy, but instead Hannibal had marched for Rome. While Hood was going northward to meet at a disadvantage forces equal to his own, Sherman cutting loose from his base at Atlanta had marched unopposed upon the vitals of the Confederacy. The terrible results which were to follow this ill-advised strategy of Mr. Davis had not, however, yet developed themselves, and on the lines before Richmond to Lee's army, erect and defiant, there appeared no reason why the war should not last another four years.

On the 9th December, it turned very cold and the ground remained frozen hard all day; in the afternoon it commenced sleeting, and at 9 o'clock at night, while the storm was still in progress, we received orders to be ready to move at daylight, in light marching order. Accordingly, on the 10th, the divisions of Fields and Hoke, under Longstreet, marched upon a reconnaisance around the enemy's right flank. We moved around it for nearly four miles with a strong line of flankers, between whom and the enemy there was some skirmishing. It was very cold and the roads abominable with frozen slush. The men, notwithstanding, stood it well, and at night we returned to our quarters. Longstreet was probably eleven thousand strong, including artillery and some cavalry. The object of the reconnaisance did not transpire.

The weather continued bad, and on the 20th at dark we were again ordered to prepare to move in heavy marching order and with three days' rations. At 3:30 a. m., on the 21st, the brigade started for Richmond. Kirkland's brigade had preceded it, the other brigades of the division followed. The roads were very muddy, and it was raining and freezing as it fell. We reached Richmond at 7 o'clock, crossed the river, and at 11 a. m. took the cars for Danville.

Profound secrecy as to our destination had been observed, even brigade commanders had no intimation of it, but when the order of preparation had been extended on the 20th, the impression in the command became general that we were destined for the South to meet Sherman, and every man from the sick list that could move returned to duty, many utterly unfit to march or even travel. The troops were saturated with the freezing rain on the march to Richmond, and they were loaded on freight cars without seats or fires—the men so crowded as to preclude individual motion. The rain began to be accompanied by a high wind, and lying motionless in their wet garments, the men were whistled along on the train the balance of the day and all night. At daylight we arrived at Danville. The suffering was intense. One poor fellow, of the Seventh battalion, was found dead from the exposure, and a dozen others had to be borne from the cars to the wayside hospital. General Hagood had obtained in Richmond a half-barrel of apple brandy for the brigade and caused it to be here issued to the men. It gave the poor fellows about one good drink apiece, and helped to thaw their half-frozen frames. This was the second spirit ration that had been issued to the brigade in Virginia. We had, however, during our whole connection with Lee's army, a regular ration of *genuine* coffee, a luxury that we had been strangers to for two years previous. We were detained some hours in Danville for want of transportation, and it was late in the day, the 22nd, before the brigade began to go forward over the Piedmont road. The distance to Greensboro was but forty-eight miles, and it was not until the morning of the 26th that the whole brigade was transported over it, three and a half days to go 48 miles by rail! The road and its rolling stock were evidently in bad condition, but the delays were so frivolous, and the accidents so numerous that General Hagood suspected treachery and finally got on by seizing engines and taking the trains in his own charge. It is hard to say whether there was design or only criminal mismanagement in the delay.

The Confederate Congress had adjourned a day or two before, and at Danville a party of congressmen, consisting of Senators Orr, of South Carolina, Johnson, of Georgia, a senator from Mississippi and another (Leach, of North Carolina,) presented to General Hagood an order from the Secretary at War addressed to any officer using a railroad for troops to give these gentlemen transportation homeward. They were welcomed to the "headquarters car," and for three days enjoyed its comforts. It was an ordinary freight boxcar, and in it was carried the staff horses, the baggage of the staff, the staff themselves, and their guests. From their conversation, it was evident that they were not entitled to the thanks voted by the Roman Senate to the Consul returning from Cannae, that he "had not despaired of the Republic under difficult circumstances." They were, in fact, utterly demoralized. This was the first time the writer had ever heard any one embarked in the cause, civilian or soldier, express doubts of its ultimate success; and prophetic, perhaps patent as they were, they now made but little impression upon him, for he had long looked upon the Confederate congress for the most part in the light of the *post* quartermaster and commissary officers, bomb-proofs, in which prudent men evaded the hardships and dangers of the war. He believes now, when the history of this great struggle is fairly written, that the record of our congress will be that they were utterly wanting in the discharge of the high duties of their position. They had neither the courage to control Mr. Davis in his course nor the patriotism and magnanimity when they differed with him to cordially support him in his devoted exertions.

On the evening of the 26th, the larger portion of the brigade reached Wilmington and took steamer for the neighborhood of Fort Fisher at the mouth of the river.

A day or two before we left Richmond, a fleet of war vessels, with transports, bearing a detachment of Grant's army, under Butler, had sailed from Hampton Roads in Virginia to attempt the reduction of this fort which controlled the entrance into the Port of Wilmington. It had made its effort a feeble one, and failed before our brigade arrived. Kirkland's brigade had got up in time to be of some service in the repulse. On the 31st December, we were ordered back to Wilmington to lie in reserve, and the whole division was there concentrated.

Here ended the campaign of 1864. The field return of the day showed of the brigade:

PRESENT FOR DUTY.

Officers	93	
Rifles	1,298	
	1,391	
All others present	201	
		1,592

ABSENT.

Wounded and sick, officers	31	
Wounded and sick, rifles	668	
	699	
Missing, officers	23	
Missing, rifles	554	
	577	
Without leave, officers	15	
Without leave, rifles	514	
	529	
With leave, officers	4	

```
With leave, rifles.................................    75
                                                   ------    79
Detached, officers ...............................     6
Detached, rifles .................................   122
                                                   ------   128
In arrest, rifles.................................     4
                                                   ------ 2,016
```

```
Aggregate, present and absent.....................              3,608
    Aggregate in beginning of campaign, 4,246.
    The battle casualties had been up to and including the 21st of August:
Killed, officers .................................    19
Killed, rifles ...................................   250
                                                   ------   269
Wounded, officers ................................    74
Wounded, rifles ..................................  1,067
                                                   ------ 1,141
Missing, officers ................................    28
Missing, rifles ..................................   649
                                                   ------   677
Casualties in later affairs.......................    35
                                                   ------      2,122
```

In examining these tables it must be borne in mind that among those classed as "missing" were many who filled unknown graves upon the numerous fields of the campaign just closed, and in the table of battle casualties, the "killed" are only those who died upon the field; among the "wounded" in this table are included as well as those who recovered in hospital.

Among those classed as "without leave," were many who were only technically so, sick or wounded in hospital or at home; the papers of extension had not been received at brigade headquarters when their invalid leaves had expired. Still, the number "without leave" was unduly large and was ominous of that change in popular sentiment which now began to connive at a dereliction of duty which in the earlier years of the war was deemed by that same sentiment as little less shameful than desertion. There is another class also which shows too strong—the "detached." Of course among these were individuals who may have been best serving the country where they were. Still, detachment was so convenient a cloak for skulking, that among the faithful soldiers in the ranks it was considered not much more creditable than absence without leave.

The summer work in Virginia had been to the mere soldier an interesting and desirable experience, and the brigade had much of which to be proud. It had borne its share in the most desperate campaign of the war, and had won reputation where the standard of soldierly qualities was high.

But how stood the Cause which had summoned these men from the pursuits of civil life; for these years had claimed and received their devoted effort—was it approaching success or tottering to extinction?

Events culminated so rapidly in '65, that upon looking back to this period it is difficult to realize that but little of gloomy anticipation clouded the close of '64 in the minds of those with whom the writer was associated. Conscious of discharging their duty, and with unwavering belief in the righteousness of their cause, they looked with unreasoning certainty of faith to final success. Thus, confident of ultimate triumph in the independence of their country, whatever might become of themselves, and from the position of the brigade at Wilmington certain that winter would bring no intermission in its service in the field, they regarded the situation more in its personal than in its general aspects. Looking forward to the stern duties before them, each hoped that he would continue to do "all that may become a man"; and reverting to the stirring events of the past; recalling the maddening excitement of the charge, the sullen anger of defeat— the thrilling triumph of victory, there came no feeling of gloom or sadness, save in the recollection of the gallant dead. Moloney, Dargan, Glover, Hopkins, Sellars, Nelson and others, comrades loved and true, who had marched with us on that bright spring day from the lines of Charleston, no longer filled our ranks. Whatever fate the future might have in store for us, for them the battle had been fought:

> "On Fame's eternal camping ground,
> Their silent tents are spread;
> And Glory keeps with solemn round,
> The Bivouac of the Dead."

CAMPAIGN OF 1865 IN NORTH CAROLINA

FORT FISHER.

This work, situated at the mouth of Cape Fear river, was the key to the defenses of the Port of Wilmington. There were other works auxiliary to it on both sides of the river, but they were secondary in their nature; and with the enemy in possession of Fort Fisher, backed by his large naval force, Wilmington was no longer a port of either entry or departure for the Confederates.

The Cape Fear, flowing southeasterly, enters the sea at a very acute angle, leaving between itself and the sea but a narrow strip of land for several miles before its debouchment; and this slip finally narrows to a point. The main channel turns around this point on entering the sea and leads northward for two or three miles up the ocean front of this peninsular before an outgoing vessel can depart from, or one incoming can approach the coast. The usual bar lying off the mouth of our river-made Southern harbors is the cause.

About a mile from the extremity of the peninsular, where it was quite narrow, was placed Fort Fisher, looking seaward and with its back on the river. Its trace was in general terms a redan, with one long face and one short face, meeting at a right angle. The long face conformed to the ocean front; and a detached work, Battery Buchanan, continued the defensive arrangements southward toward the point of the peninsular. The short face ran back to the river, and looked northward with a view to land attack. The line of interior crest of Fort Fisher was over a thousand yards—Pollard says 1,780 yards. The sally port on the northern or land face was upon the river bank, and was strangely weak. As remembered by the writer, it was a simple palisade and gate with no ditch in its front, and something like a causeway along the river bank leading up to it. The work elsewhere had a deep and wide ditch, except just on the seabeach. Along the land face and extending to the beach were palisades. Its parapet and traverses, which were numerous, were of extraordinary strength.

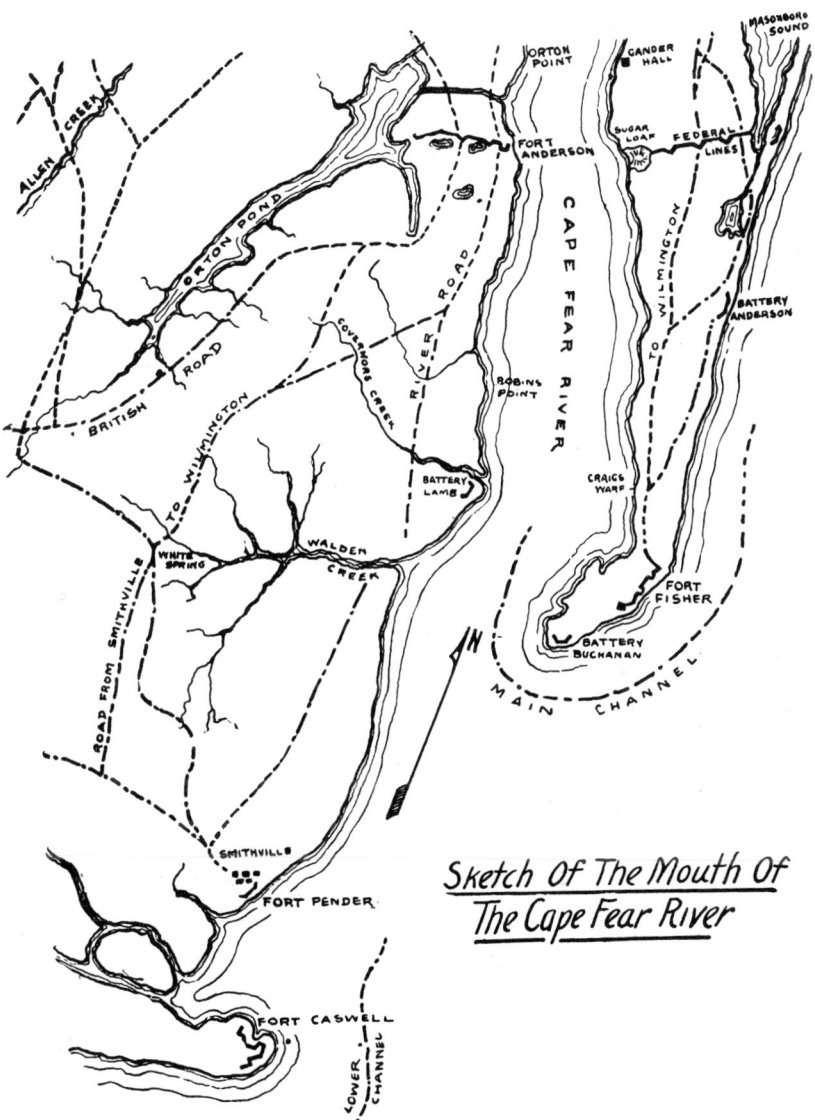

Sketch Of The Mouth Of The Cape Fear River

It had the greatest profile, and was altogether perhaps the most elaborate work built by the Confederates on the coast. On the northern front, upon which only a land attack was probable, the fort had an armament of nineteen guns. The balance of its armament was for naval encounter, and of the best the Confederate arsenals could furnish. The defects of the work were its sally port and the want of sufficient flanking arrangements for sweeping the ditch with fire.

The garrison of heavy artillerists showed well in drill and dress; had lived high and fought little during the war; and had not been benefited by the contact with blockade running speculations which their position and duties had brought about.

The Federal expedition in December against this work had been under command of General B. F. Butler and Admiral Porter. Grant had intended, it appears, another leader, General Weitzel, for the land forces, but as the troops for the expedition were drawn from Butler's "army of the James," and Wilmington was also in the limits of his department, this enterprising warrior had managed to foist himself into it when by virtue of his commission he assumed command. The effort to take the fort was embodied in a heavy bombardment of two days (intermitting at night) by the navy, when Admiral Porter pronounced the work reduced and desired the land forces previously debarked to go in and take possession. Butler declined, and for once was probably right, notwithstanding the ridicule that has since been heaped upon him in this connection. The bombardment had been heavy but diffuse, and the defensive strength of the work was substantially intact. There had been but seven guns rendered unserviceable in the whole fort, two by navy fire and five by their own imperfections. Had the garrison made but the most commonplace defense, the assault would have been a bloody failure. Butler's Federal critics, however, claimed that there would have been little or no resistance by the garrison of nine hundred men holding the work, that they were demoralized by the bombardment and cowering in the bomb-proofs. Certain it is that his skirmishers had been pushed to within 150 yards of the ditch, not only without drawing the fire of the fort, but without developing to view a defender on the walls. Indeed, one individual had even gone into the ditch and brought off a garrison flag which had fallen from the rampart, without being molested or apparently observed. Be it as it may, as to the morale of the garrison, Butler's refusal to assail terminated the expedition. The force composing it retired to Beaufort Harbor in North Carolina, where the land troops were debarked and appeared to await orders.

On the 4th January, General Hagood went upon a twenty-day leave to his home in South Carolina, leaving his brigade under command of Colonel Graham, encamped with the division upon the plank road some three miles east of Wilmington. On his return, on the 25th January, he found his brigade detached from the division and at Fort Anderson, fifteen miles below the town, on the right bank of the Cape Fear. During this time Grant had relieved Butler and sent General Terry to command the land troops of the expeditionary force at Beaufort, giving him the addition of a brigade of infantry and a siege train. This raised the force to about 8,000 men. An immediate renewal of the attempt against Fort Fisher was ordered.

On the 12th of January, a Mr. McMillan, near Topsail Sound, was said to have discovered the approach of the flotilla and sought to communicate the fact to General Bragg by telegraph. The operator was not in condition to send the dispatch. It had, therefore, to be forwarded by courier. In two hours after it was received General Hoke with his division was on the march to confront the enemy upon his landing. On the next day, the 13th, the enemy landed upon the narrow spit between the head of Masonboro Sound and the sea, near Battery Gatlin, nine miles above Fort Fisher. This he was enabled to do under cover of his fleet, which could here lie very close in shore; an assault upon his first position was difficult. Hoke deemed it very injudicious to attack and contented himself with taking up a line parallel to the beach under cover of the sand hills and scrub forest, with a view to giving battle upon any attempt of the enemy to advance. A regiment of cavalry prolonged his right flank, and watched the space thence to the beach at a point intermediate between the landing and Fort Fisher. During the night the enemy passed between or around the cavalry, without their observing it, and when day broke Hoke discovered them on his right flank securely entrenched from the ocean beach to the river and facing Wilmington. He took position in the lines previously prepared from

Sugar Loaf to the head of Masonboro Sound. Bragg now ordered Hoke to assail the enemy's newly entrenched line. Hoke reconnoitered it in person and, deeming it unadvisable, requested Bragg himself to examine the present condition of affairs on his front. This General Bragg proceeded to do, and the result was to countermand the order of assault and the determination to re-enforce the fort, accepting practically the condition that it must stand or fall upon its own resources.

Accordingly, in the afternoon of the same day (the 14th) Colonel Graham was directed to move to Gander Hall landing on the river with four regiments of Hagood's brigade and to proceed that night by steamer to Battery Buchanan, whence they were to be thrown into Fort Fisher. Graham marched with the Eleventh, Twenty-first and Twenty-fifth regiments, and the Seventh battalion. The Twenty-seventh regiment remaining, reported temporarily with Kirkland's brigade. He made a report to General Hagood upon the resumption of command by the latter, from which the following is extracted: "Shortly after arriving at Gander Hall, I received a dispatch from Colonel Anderson (Bragg's A. A. G.), directing me to embark my men on the 'Sampson' and 'Harlee' steamers, which had not as yet arrived at Gander Hall. At 7 p. m. I received another dispatch from Colonel Anderson, that the 'Sampson' would be at Gander Hall at 7:30, and that I must use her as a lighter to load and unload the 'Harlee,' as the latter drew too much water to approach either Gander Hall or Battery Buchanan. The 'Sampson' got to Gander Hall an hour later (8:30 p. m.) and was immediately loaded with troops, but got aground and did not get off till 9:30 p. m. She proceeded to the 'Harlee' with the Twenty-fifth regiment. Another steamer, the 'Pettiway,' now arrived, was loaded, got aground, and remained so. Upon the return of the 'Sampson,' I transferred part of the troops from the 'Pettiway' to her, and both boats proceeded to the 'Harlee'; found the 'Harlee' aground; tried to pull her off with the other two boats, and failed. I then had the troops on the 'Harlee' transferred to the 'Pettiway,' and ordered her and the 'Sampson' to proceed at once to Battery Buchanan. The 'Sampson' left at once with the Twenty-first regiment; but the captain of the 'Pettiway' said he had not wood enough to take her there. I directed him to take wood from the

'Harlee,' and by the time he got it aboard the 'Pettiway' was also aground, and I was informed by her captain that she would not float again before eight o'clock next morning. . . . At 2:30 a. m., the 'Sampson' returned from Battery Buchanan, having landed the Twenty-first regiment,* and I again dispatched her to the same point with the Twenty-fifth regiment under Captain Carson. . . ."

Having reported the facts by telegraph, Graham was directed to get the remainder of his men to Battery Buchanan as soon next day as the tide would float his transports, and land if the enemy's fire would permit, if not, to wait till night. He made the effort, was driven off, and crossed to Smithville as the nearest point from which to start at nightfall. Having notified General Bragg of his arrival at Smithville, he was directed to retain his command at that point.

This closed the effort to re-enforce Fort Fisher, but the garrison, with the addition of Hagood's two regiments, about 2,300 strong, was abundantly large for defense, and further transfer of troops was only necessary when those already there would need relief from arduous service. The facilities which the locality gave for this were probably about the same as those had for communication with Morris Island during the siege of Charleston.

Carson had landed at Battery Buchanan about sunrise on the 15th with the Twenty-fifth regiment and had to throw his men into Fisher under a heavy naval fire.

The bombardment which had commenced in the afternoon of the 13th, after the landing had been effected, was continuously kept up—heavily by day, and slower at night. It was somewhat heavier than the first bombardment. Admiral Porter, before the committee of the Federal Congress on the conduct of the war, seems to say, as well as his loose and bombastic statements can be reconciled (Fort Fisher Expedition, pp. 100 and 191), that in the first bombardment the navy expended 45,000 rounds of ammunition, and in the second 50,000 rounds. The naval fire (there were no batteries established on land) was directed chiefly upon the land face, and Brigadier-General Comstock of Grant's staff, who accompanied the expedition, speaking from personal inspection, said before the same committee that at the close of

---

*Commanded by Captain DuBose.

the bombardment, "so far as the earthwork was concerned, it was just as efficient as before a shot was fired." And in reference to the armament, the same officer stated that six guns and three mortars remained serviceable on the land face while "very few on the sea face were injured." These results will astonish no one who has had experience of the resisting power of earthworks and the difficulty of dismantling embrasured and traversed guns by long range shell fire. The power of artillery upon earthwork of proper slopes is little more than to deface it; and when the lines and angles of its profile are gone, and its guns disabled as they may be by concentrated fire at close range, well sustained musketry can and should hold it against assault. Whenever properly constructed and with a profile approaching permanent work, such a fort if taken, save by regular approaches, the fault is *prima facie* and almost certainly with the garrison or commander. Such has been the teaching of experience since the days of Vauban, and the lessons of this war confirm it. The bomb-proof is a protection complete for the bulk of the garrison against the preliminary bombardment; a sufficient number can find shelter on the lines behind parapet and traverse to act as sentries and guard against sudden assault; and with an entrenched picket line two hundred yards in front (each pair of men in a detached circular pit no larger than will contain them), to keep the enemy from massing for assault too close to the work and to give warning of an advance, an assault can never succeed while the garrison retain heart of grace. When by regular approaches the besieger can mass in safety for assault, in point of time nearer to the crest of the parapet than on the besieged in the bomb-proofs, then the conditions are changed.

Admiral Porter, whose dispatches are in the "furioso" vein, asserted that he had "reduced the fort to a *pulp* and *every* gun was so injured or covered with dirt that they would not work." This is on a par with his assertion that had the 400 marines whom he sent to cover a "boarding party" of sailors in the subsequent assault, by deploying in front of the sea face and opening fire, 'performed their duty,' *every one* of the rebels would have been *killed*."*

---

*Fort Fisher Exped., 189.

At 3 p. m., on the 15th, the assault was given. The garrison, cowering in their bomb-proofs from the naval fire, had permitted the enemy to approach the work very nearly. A force of sailors and marines, 2,000 strong, were massed close upon the sea face, and three brigades of infantry had obtained similar position on the land face. Upon the signal given the fleet changed its fire to other parts of the work, and the storming columns advanced. The garrison hastily and imperfectly manned the parapet. The first advance of the infantry was feeble, and apparently they recoiled. The sailors rushed on boldly and were bloodily and completely repulsed in fifteen minutes from first to last—they taking no further part in the fighting. Here the old Confederate shout of victory was being lustily given by the two regiments of Hagood's brigade* and other troops manning the sea face, when a fire in their rear called their attention to the land face. The enemy were in the fort. A detachment of the infantry column of assault rushing upon the sally port at which four uninjured field pieces remained for defense, the portion of the garrison at that point commanded by one Captain Brady, of a North Carolina regiment, cravenly surrendered without firing gun or musket.† The enemy poured in, and thenceforward on the part of the Confederates the fight was against overpowering odds with the advantage of their defensive works gone. The majority of the garrison did their duty well, and undoubtedly made as stubborn a defence as was possible under the circumstances. It was, however, more a vindication of personal pluck and character than an organized resistance. The enemy slowly won his way from gun chamber to gun chamber, the fleet firing ahead of them, and at 10 o'clock at night, after seven hours of fighting, re-enforcements brought from the lines facing Wilmington completed the work in the capture of the fort and garrison.‡

---

*See Historical Society Papers, Vol. X, page 361. Colonel Lamb seems to imply that these regiments were on land face. See Scrap Book, 1896, page 28, Captain Izlar's Refutation of Lamb.

†This is on the authority of a Wilmington newspaper of the day. See also Volume XLVI, Series I, Part 1, War of Rebellion, page 436. Lieutenant Latham, of Captain Adams' light battery, is there stated to have commanded these guns. The general statement of non-resistance is verified.

‡See Cox's March to Sea, page 137.

The enemy's loss in killed and wounded exceeded a thousand; the Confederate was some 400.

The advance of the assailing columns was witnessed from Sugar Loaf on the Confederate lines. No serious demonstration was at any time during the assault made in aid of the fort.

Such, probably, is a correct account of the fall of Fort Fisher. It is made up from such information as could be obtained after the event from the Confederates on the spot, from a study of the elaborate publications of the Federals on the subject, and from information derived since the close of the war from members of the Twenty-first and Twenty-fifth regiments engaged.

The defence is a page in the history of the war that redounds but little to our credit. Without the fort, there was inefficiency and indecision, and as a result a strong supporting force did nothing from first to last commensurate with its strength. Within the work, at the most critical point and time, there was a dastardly exhibition of cowardice, and there seemed to be but little of the careful provision of command. The absence of a picket line, in pits, upon the land front, the almost open gateway, the insufficiency in the number of men kept out of the bomb-proofs and on the lines, look like absolute military fatuity. Crimination and recrimination was rife among the Confederates after the disaster, but it is useless to perpetuate it here. Poor Whiting laid down his life in atonement of any errors he may have committed in the defence, and it is certain that in the hour of trial he personally bore himself with knightly valor. And as for Bragg, disaster had already so linked itself with his fortunes, that when a few months before Mr. Davis had assigned him to the command of this department, a Richmond paper had given expression to the feeling of both army and people in the curt paragraph,—"Bragg has been sent to Wilmington, good-bye Wilmington."

Hagood's brigade suffered a loss of thirty-one officers and four hundred and forty-four enlisted men in the fort, being all of the Twenty-first and Twenty-fifth regiments then present for duty with the brigade, and a few individuals from the Eleventh regiment. But three of its officers were wounded slightly, and none killed. It is believed that the casualties among the enlisted men were in proportion equally few.

THE SITUATION.

With the fall of Fort Fisher, a change occurred in the conditions of military affairs in this quarter that materially affected the relations and objects of all the different armies of the Confederacy, now in depleted numbers concentrating upon the small area and upon which the issue was destined to be decided.

Wilmington, in a military point of view, had had value in Confederate eyes, first as a seaport, and second as a point of railroad connection. In its first relation, it had lately become of immense consequence, being the best and almost the only point of contact left to us with the outer world. With the fall of Fisher it was hermetically sealed as a seaport, and its only value remaining was as a railroad connection on the seaboard route from Richmond to the south and west. Below Petersburg a portion of this route was already in possession of the enemy, the result of Grant's last summer operations on the Weldon road, and a detour had to be made towards the mountains to pass this point. The portion remaining to us was threatened by the troops below Wilmington and by a force at New Berne. It required a small army to guard it, and its possession by the enemy at points sufficient to deprive us of its use was a foregone conclusion, whenever he chose to move against it with a sufficient force. Richmond had another communication with the south by rail, running westward to Danville, and thence by Charlotte, Columbia and Branchville to Augusta, Georgia. Sherman's march through Georgia had cut the railroad communications westward of Augusta, and they had now to be repaired. This route from Richmond to South Carolina lay mostly close under the mountains, and it ran through the heart of the Confederacy. By transferring to it the rolling stock of the seaboard route and taking up so much of the rails as was practicable for repairs on the interior route, the communications of Richmond would not have been impaired in efficiency and would then have been established solely behind our center instead of partly on an exposed flank. Bragg's troops would have been released for action, and their number was not inconsiderable. He had probably at this time 16,000 troops of all arms in his department.

About 10,000 men (infantry and artillery), the fragments of Hood's army after his disastrous Tennessee campaign, were being directed upon Augusta, Georgia. About 10,000 men, a large portion of them unaccustomed to the field but veterans of four years' siege service, thoroughly disciplined, well equipped and of high morale were lying in and around Charleston.

Butler's and Wheeler's cavalry, under General Hampton, amounted to 8,000 men, and there were perhaps 6,000 more men in North and South Carolina (militia and reserves) available for post duty.

This gave an aggregate of 50,000 men, of whom from 40,000 to 45,000 could have been massed to meet Sherman, who was now lying at Savannah with probably 70,000 men, preparing for an advance to a junction with Grant at Petersburg.

Charleston was in the same category as Wilmington in a military point of view. Its value was solely as a seaport remaining partially open though its use was greatly restricted by the fall of Morris Island. To abandon its walls, rendered so illustrious by its heroic defence, would have been a severe blow to the morale of the Confederacy, and even the limited value of its port was now of great importance to us. It should, therefore, have been retained if possible. To arrest the march of Sherman was, however, now the pressing necessity, before which every other consideration sunk into insignificance.

Had, therefore, upon the fall of Fort Fisher, Wilmington been immediately evacuated and all the troops available in South Carolina, North Carolina and Georgia been concentrated in South Carolina upon the line of the Combahee and Salkahatchie to Barnwell Village and thence to the Savannah river, the position would have covered Charleston and the railroad connection from Branchville to Augusta. It was a strong one, and the key line to the possession of South Carolina. Had it been forced by the enemy, then abandoning Charleston and returning before him, here a resistance could have been made that would have deflected him from important points, limited his devastation in South Carolina, harassed and weakened his force, and finally the Confederates touching a depot at Fayetteville, in North Carolina, could have given decisive battle in front of the Cape Fear as Sherman emerged from the semi-desert country between Camden and that river, and before he had refitted his troops and received the munitions which he had been unable to transport on his march from the steamers that met him at Fayetteville.

Embracing in the view a larger field of strategy, the Confederates should have been re-enforced for this decisive fight from Lee's army, even at the cost of abandoning Richmond. Had the fortune of war here pronounced in our favor, Sherman's defeat so far from his natural base, the sea, could have been converted into a rout; and with his army disposed of, the failing fortunes of the Confederacy would have revived. It is true that Grant would have been on the heels of Lee, and with his command of the sea and rivers, and our wornout railroad transportation, it is doubtful which in point of time would have had the shortest line. But in such decisive strategy, as that indicated, now lay our only hope of escaping the fate which was fast encircling us. If the columns of the enemy converging to a junction could not be beaten in detail, there could be but one result in the coming campaign.

The necessity of concentration and the abandonment of all secondary points was patent, and among subordinates freely discussed at the time, but the paralysis of approaching death seemed to be upon the direction of our affairs.

Bragg, with the independent command of North Carolina, remained in Wilmington, as will be subsequently narrated, until he was pushed out, frittering away his strength in skirmishes, and letting the dry rot of desertion unchecked by vigorous action gnaw into his army until in a few weeks he had no troops left but Hoke's division and a regiment of cavalry. Hardee, commanding in South Carolina, lay supinely on the coast, not even reorganizing and refitting his troops for service (but popularly supposed to be giving his attention to ignoble cotton speculations), until Sherman moved, and then retired before him with all the haste and disorder of a flight. With such haste and want of judgment was the withdrawal from Charleston effected that the troops (men on their first march during the war) were hurried twenty-nine miles the first night and they unpursued. Leaving the coast with upward of 10,000 men, it was said that Hardee reached North Carolina with but 4,000, and not even a combat on the way. Straggling and desertion had done the work.

The cavalry of Hampton offered a skirmishing resistance to Sherman's march, and was almost all the opposition he met with in South Carolina. Consolidation of command of the troops, that should have been opposing this march, at length was made by the appointing of Joe Johnston, after Columbia had fallen and when concentration for defence must necessarily take place beyond the Cape Fear. In the meanwhile the available Confederate force had without a battle dwindled to 30,000 men, and the already overwhelming Federal strength had received another increment. The army which under Thomas in Tennessee had confronted Hood had now been largely transferred to North Carolina, and was marching to a junction with Sherman in two columns moving respectively from Wilmington and New Berne.

Beauregard was announced by General Johnston on the 16th March as second in command.

The aspect of civil affairs at this time had much of painful interest. The increasing estrangement between Mr. Davis and the Congress, the enlistment of slaves, the refusal of the Trans-Mississippi Army to cross the river for service in the east, were all occasional subjects of discussion in camp. The Hampton Roads Conference had been held and its results officially announced from Richmond to be that there was no peace for us save in unconditional submission to the will of the conqueror. These matters were all talked of, but not much dwelt upon. Our information upon them was not full and we were not sure always that it was correct. Besides, four years of service in subordinate military grade is apt to give one the habit of confining his attention to the matters before him. But one unmistakable evidence of our rapidly failing fortunes was constantly forcing itself upon commanders of troops in February and March, 1865, and that was the intercepted appeals *from friends at home* to the soldiers to desert. Absentees, both officers and men, away upon any pretext, were also with difficulty gotten back. During February the brigadier commanding had five officers dropped for absence without leave from Hagood's brigade. And later two colonels of regiments sent to South Carolina to get up absentees, failing to return in due time, the brigadier himself was dispatched by the major-general commanding the division on the same errand. The people had lost heart and their influence was reacting badly upon the soldier wearied by long and lately disastrous service.

The narrative returns to the brigade and events at Wilmington.

LINES BELOW WILMINGTON.

Battery Buchanan, on the extremity of Federal Point, was captured with its garrison of artillerists the night Fort Fisher fell. Hoke continued to hold the entrenched lines above, running from Sugar Loaf, a promontory on the Cape Fear river to the head of Masonboro Sound. On the right bank of the river, in the next few days, Fort Caswell and the other defences were abandoned aş high up as Fort Anderson near Orton Point, and the Confederates withdrew to the previously entrenched lines at this place. Fort Anderson was opposite Sugar Loaf, and the lines raa from this work to Orton Pond which stretches out in a southwesterly direction seven miles from the river in an air line, and nine or ten as the road ran. On the left bank of the river the Sugar Loaf lines were enfiladed or taken in reverse at will by the enemy's fleet outside, the concealment of the forest alone rendering them tenable, and they were liable to be turned by a landing from the sea behind them. On the right bank the line was short and strong enough against a direct attack. It could be turned by the head of Orton Pond.

The river channel ran close under Fort Anderson and was not in all over six or eight hundred yards wide, though the whole river was at this point three miles in width. The fort, however, had only nine (9) guns, all 32 drs., two of which were rifled but not banded. These with their carriages were old and worn, and bore across and down the river. No gun could be brought to bear up the river, and consequently if any portion of the fleet should have passed the fort we would have had no fire upon it, while it would have taken nearly every gun in reverse. Torpedoes in the river completed the defensive arrangements. There were obstructions in the river eight or nine miles above Fort Anderson, and there was no communication between the Sugar Loaf and Fort Anderson lines, except through Wilmington, fifteen miles above. They were thus practically thirty miles apart, while, with his abundant steam transportation in the river, to the enemy they were not wider apart than five miles march.

OPERATIONS ON THE FORT ANDERSON LINES.

Up to the 11th February, operations had been confined on the left bank to skirmishing and occasional shelling from the sea, and on the right bank there had been occasional engagements at long range between Fort Anderson and a monitor and a gunboat from the fleet. The fort used generally a 12 dr. Whitworth taken from a field battery. Against the monitor it was of little use, but against the gunboat it was effective.

The Confederate fighting strength of all arms was about 4,000 men on the left bank, and 2,300 on the right bank. Of these there was one regiment of cavalry, Colonel Lipscomb's Second South Carolina; the infantry was Hoke's division, and part of the heavy artillerists of the recently abandoned forts converted into infantry. The remaining part of these garrisons manned the heavy guns remaining in position, and there were three or four very good light batteries.

The enemy, on the 11th February, had a fleet in the river of 1 monitor, 15 gunboats, 1 flagship, 1 armed blockade runner, 16 transports and 5 tugs. The armament of these vessels appeared to be 11- and 15-inch shell guns and Parrotts. Outside, the fleet was also large. At Smithville our scouts reported 500 infantry, and at Battery Lamb some two or three hundred. On the other side their force was probably 9,500 land troops (of which a few cavalry), with ability to throw on shore two thousand sailors and marines. Of the enemy's land troops two thousand or twenty-five hundred had recently arrived.

The enemy were reported massing a large force at New Berne to strike at the road from Wilmington towards Petersburg. The telegraph reported that Sherman had the South Carolina railroad from Branchville to Williston, and, while moving on Columbia, was demonstrating at once upon Charleston and Augusta.

Bragg had gone to Richmond temporarily and left Hoke in command of the department of North Carolina.

Brigadier-General Hagood, having, on his return from South Carolina, relieved Brigadier-General Hèbart, commanded in person on the Fort Anderson lines. His force was his own brigade, about 925 enlisted for duty, and the fragments of the garrisons, before alluded to, converted into infantry, and brigaded under Colonel Hedrick, Fortieth North Carolina. These numbered 805 enlisted for duty. In addition, there was Moseley's and Bradham's light batteries, together 132 enlisted for duty, and 152 enlisted mounted men of the Second South Carolina cavalry.

The total enlisted under his command was, therefore, something over 2,000, and his force, including officers, about 2,300.

On the 15th of February, the enemy made a reconnaisance in force from Smithville as far as White Spring Branch, where the road from Smithville to Wilmington forks, one going straight on up the river by Fort Anderson, the other turning westward and leading around Orton Pond. This party was met and skirmished with by Hagood's mounted force, and retired at night-fall without pressing vigorously.

On the 16th February, the enemy passed over from Battery Buchanan to Smithville five large transports with troops, and at dark a considerable force were still visible at the wharf at Buchanan, apparently waiting transportation. Subsequent events showed that these troops were the Twenty-third Army Corps, General Scofield commanding,* recently arrived before Wilmington from Tennessee. It was accompanied by field artillery, a small force (probably two hundred) of cavalry, and a brigade (Abbott's) of Terry's command. General Hagood had on the 15th asked for, and on the 18th received, some fifty additional mounted men. Colonel Lipscomb was at the same time sent over to take command of this arm. This re-enforcement raised the Confederate force to 2,350 men, with which to confront fully 20,000.

General Hagood now massed all his mounted forces upon right flank at the head of Orton Pond, keeping but twenty to act as a patrol in his front, and endeavoring to remedy the want of mounted men here by doubling his infantry picket and pushing them further out, say a mile and a quarter.

On the 17th, the enemy advanced in force from Smithville and halted for the night in front of Hagood's infantry picket. The mounted patrol and the infantry picket skirmished with them, and the monitor with seven (7) gunboats engaged the fort at long range. The monitor engaged at 1,000 yards, and the gunboats out of range of our 32 drs. Firing commenced at 1:30 p. m. and continued till sunset; 170 shell were thrown into the fort; one man was wounded, and no damage done to the work. Forty-seven (47) shot were thrown by the fort at the monitor, of which

---

*Cox's and Ames' divisions with Moon's brigade of Crouch's division, Cox commanding. Scofield in general command. Cox's March to the Sea, page 149.

several struck, doing no apparent damage. The Whitworth 12 dr. threw a few shot at the gunboats, when its ammunition became exhausted, and it was sent back at night to the Lower Town Creek bridge to await a supply of ammunition telegraphed for to Wilmington. But thirty rounds could be obtained, and these arrived too late for any subsequent operations on the Fort Anderson lines.

Colonel Simonton, Twenty-fifth regiment, was placed in immediate command of Hagood's brigade for all purposes of military movement. This officer had a few days before been returned to the brigade, having been detached since June, 1864, and Colonel Graham, the senior colonel, was on recruiting service in South Carolina.

On the 8th of February, a communication from General Bragg had directed that "except in an extreme case, involving the safety of the command, the present position should not be abandoned." The chief danger apparently apprehended by the department commander, as exhibited in this communication, was the passage by the fort of the fleet, and he went on to say, "A point for communication across the river has been selected from the mouth of Town Creek on the west to the old State Salt Works landing on the east. By this route re-enforcements can be sent to and from both detachments of the command until the fort is passed. Thus any land attack can be met."

It is well to remark in passing that this route of communication was never established.

On Saturday morning, the 18th of February, the monitor took position within 800 yards of the fort, and the fleet of wooden gunboats anchored just beyond the ascertained range of our smooth bore 32 drs., the rifled 32 drs. could not be brought to bear upon the position of the wooden fleet. At 6:30 a. m., the bombardment commenced, and continued till 6 p. m. Twenty-seven hundred and twenty-three shell were thrown at the fort, nearly all of which struck the work or exploded within it. The fort fired fifty-three shot and shell, twenty of which were fired from the rifled guns at the monitor. Of these, seven struck without doing apparent damage. The smooth bores were fired at intervals, more in defiance than in the hope of injuring the enemy. The land forces of the Federals pressing our advanced skirmish line after daylight, the right was driven back, the left continuing to hold its position. General Hagood, about 9 a. m., directed this whole line to fall back upon a second line which he had entrenched in rifle pits some 250 yards in front of his entrenchments; and sent the Second cavalry, hitherto acting as a patrol on their front, to re-enforce the right flank at the head of Orton Pond. The enemy now advanced, taking position in the skirt of woods some 600 yards in our front, and sharpshooting commenced and continued during the day. The two light batteries of Moseley and Bradham shelled the woods in our front during the same time. The enemy developed no field pieces.

Colonel Lipscomb reported today with the re-enforcement of fifty mounted men, before alluded to, and was sent with them to the right and directed to take command. Entrenching tools (some 20) had on the previous evening been sent the officer then in command, and he had been instructed to strengthen his position by such available means as were practicable. These mounted troops were simply mounted infantry; their arms were the short range cavalry carbine intermixed with Enfields.

Shortly after Colonel Lipscomb arrived at his post, the enemy, who had previously appeared on his front, advanced. Sharp skirmishing ensued, and by nightfall he was pressed back a mile or more. Lieutenant Jones, of Bradham's battery, was sent to his assistance and with one howitzer. Lipscomb's position was now directly across from Orton Pond to Allen Creek, covering the road leading into Fort Anderson and Wilmington road, and about four (4) miles from this last, the force in his front being thus on the right rear of the Fort Anderson position, and at that distance from its sole line of communication.

The casualties in the fort, which was held by Hedrick's men, from the bombardment were slight; one officer (Lieutenant Vans, Fortieth North Carolina,) being killed and six men wounded. And in this connection it is worthy of mention that not a man of the garrison took shelter in the bomb-proof, confirming the previous observation of experience that traverses and parapets are sufficient protection, when the garrison is not too numerous, against anything but the heaviest mortar fire. The damage to the earthwork was considerable. The wooden revetment had gradually given way; the epaulement was much torn up; in fact, in

22—H

one place breached nearly to the level of the gun platform; and the traverses knocked out of shape. No gun, however, was dismounted, nor its working injured beyond repair during the night.

The casualties in the infantry today did not exceed half a dozen.

After 6 p. m. the fire of the fleet on the fort averaged one in five minutes, until 11 p. m., when it was reduced to a shot every half hour till 2 p. m. For the rest of the night it was increased to a shot every ten minutes. Working parties were kept diligently employed all night repairing damages, and an obstruction was made to the sally port of the fort on the river side in view of an infantry assault up the beach.

About 10 p. m., written dispatches from Colonel Lipscomb and the report of Captain Barnes, Fortieth North Carolina, acting as scout, together with the examination of prisoners and deserters, satisfying General Hagood that the force on his right and rear was large and of the three arms, and that Lipscomb's force was entirely too few to check it, he became satisfied that an evacuation was necessary to save his command. As he was, however, in telegraphic communication with his division commander, General Hoke, and the facts as learned had been laid before him, General Hagood awaited orders and continued diligently preparing to fight the position next day.

About 1 a. m., on the 19th, after sending over a staff officer to confer with General Hagood, General Hoke invited the expression of General Hagood's opinion upon the propriety of withdrawing from the Fort Anderson lines. It was given by telegraph as follows:

"1. The enemy are on my right and rear, in point of time less than three (3) hours' march. Their force is certainly, from data heretofore sent you, one-half to two-thirds of my whole strength.* It will take me three-quarters of an hour to hear of their advance, which reduces the time to two and a quarter hours. It is impossible for me to strengthen the small force opposed to them. You know its strength.

"2. I have a very much larger force than my own 600 yards in

---

*Two brigades were in front of Fort Anderson entrenched, and Ames' division, with two additional brigades, had turned Orton Pond.—Cox's March to the Sea, p. 149.

my front, in full view by daylight, and with the fleet to co-operate. Therefore, when the force on my right rear moves, I must abandon this position, or sacrifice my command.

"3. I have two defiles in my rear (the bridges and causeways just behind me) to move through, and two and a quarter hours in which to extend the order, execute it, and confront the enemy on my right rear. Even at night there is a possibility of having to do this pursued by the force in my front. In the daytime it is certain, and then I can use but one bridge, on account of the fire of the fleet. Could I re-enforce my right sufficiently to hold the turning force in check, the case presented would be different."

To this General Hoke replied: "Dispatch received. . . . What do you think best?" General Hagood replied: "I think this place ought to be evacuated and the movement commenced in half an hour." This last dispatch was sent at 2:05 a. m., and at 2:48 a. m. the reply was received from General Hoke ordering the evacuation and the taking up of a line behind Town Creek.

The movement was immediately commenced. The quarter-master and commissary train had in the beginning of the fight been placed behind Allen Creek. It was ordered to Lower Town Creek bridge. The field batteries, ordnance wagons and ambulances were sent across Orton causeway, and there the infantry commenced to withdraw. When the infantry began to move, a dispatch was sent Lipscomb directing him to fall back quietly towards Anderson till he reached the road leading from Anderson to Wilmington via Upper Town Creek bridge, and then taking that road act as a flanking column to the main column which would move on the road to the Lower bridge. As soon as the infantry and heavy artillerists had crossed the Orton canal, orders were sent the infantry pickets in the pits ahead of the entrenchments to withdraw. It was in the early dawn when this last move was commenced, and almost simultaneously with it the enemy advanced with a heavy skirmish line at double quick, followed closely by a line of battle. The picket retired at a run, and fifty or sixty were captured. The enemy most probably had prepared for an assault at daybreak, and their advance was in pursuance of this preparation. The sluices of Orton Pond were cut, and the bridges of the canal burned. This checked pursuit, and the fleet kept back till the torpedoes opposite the fort could be raised. Our march to Town Creek was undisturbed. The force in front of Lipscomb coming down between Orton Pond and Allen Creek struck the lower road upon which the main column had retreated an hour after the rear had passed. It proved to have been a larger force than Lipscomb thought. It was probably two divisions of the Twenty-third Corps, while the other division had been in our front. (See pencilled note 469.)

No effort was made to blow up the magazine of the fort or to destroy its armament, because of the shortness of the time till daylight after the order of evacuation was received; and because General Hoke had requested by telegraph that the magazine should not be exploded before 6:30 a. m., which was later than General Hagood designed to hold the fort.

ENGAGEMENT AT TOWN CREEK.

Town Creek enters the Cape Fear river from the west about six miles above Fort Anderson and on the same side of the river. The upper and lower bridges had each been previously slightly fortified by General Hagood, his only communication with Wilmington being over them, and were held by bridge guards, the upper by eighty infantry and the lower bridge by twenty. The Whitworth sent back from Anderson had been directed to stop at the lower bridge, and had there received a small supply of ammunition. The creek was forty or fifty yards wide, and was navigable for craft of four feet draft as far as the upper bridge; at its mouth, however, was a hard sand bar only one foot under water at low tide. The two bridges were the only regular crossings, and at both the high ground was on the southern bank. From three-quarters of a mile above the lower bridge to the river were rice fields; above that point were rice fields at intervals, but not on both sides at once. The swamp was generally half a mile wide, but there were frequent bluffs where the highland approached the stream first on one side and then on the other. Between the lower bridge and the mouth there were bluffs on the north side with open rice fields and the usual dams to the highland opposite. The channel of the Cape Fear lay between Big Island and the east bank; but there were boat landings at Cowan's and above. It was between nine and ten miles between the bridges by the road we were obliged to use—about six (6)

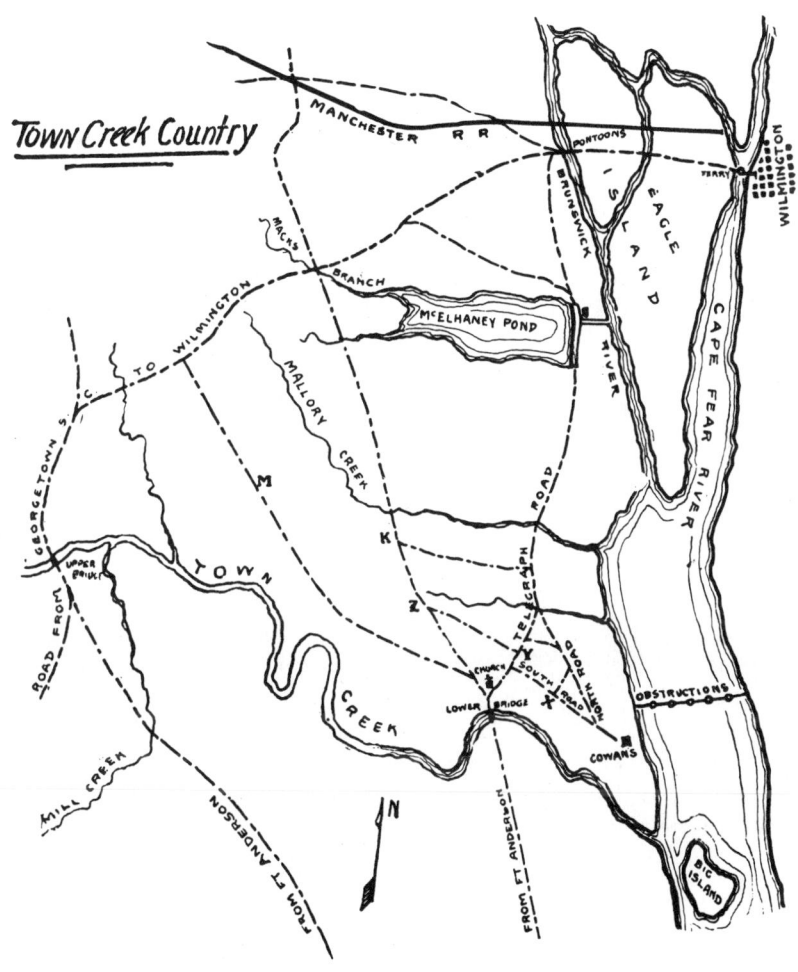

Town Creek Country

miles from the upper bridge to the cross roads at Marks' Branch, about seven (7) miles to the lower bridge to same points, and four (4) miles from these cross roads to the pontoon bridge over Brunswick river. Mallory Creek was between Marks' Cross Roads and the lower bridge, and two and a quarter miles from the last. Cowan's landing by the road was about the same distance from the lower bridge.

At 9:45 a. m., on the 19th, the main column crossed the lower bridge and went into position—Taylor's regiment, of Hedrick's brigade, in the entrenchments with three (3) pieces of artillery—Gantt's Eleventh South Carolina (under Captain Westcoat), picketing Cowan's—and the balance of Hagood's brigade, under Simonton and Hedrick's own regiment, the Fortieth North Carolina, with the balance of the artillery in reserve near the church. A patrol of twenty men were kept to the front down the Fort Anderson road. Lipscomb arrived soon after at the upper bridge and reported himself in position with the balance of the cavalry, eight infantry and one howitzer.

General Hagood reported by telegraph his arrival to General Hoke and asked for orders. He received the following reply: "Future operations will depend on circumstances. Will telegraph you in the morning."

The enemy appeared in front of lower bridge, at 3:30 p. m., and slight skirmishing ensued. At 5:35 p. m., Hagood telegraphed Hoke: "Thirteen (13) gunboats in the river above Big Island, and small boats ahead sounding. . . . Town Creek is a line can be held whenever occupied. I have examined several miles of it today. From my observation it can be crossed almost anywhere that sufficient troops are not stationed. Let me know your views and intentions." In reply the same evening General Hagood received the following: "Hold Town Creek till you hear from me." On the next day, the 20th, General Hoke telegraphed, "You must move your command as you think best; at same time recollect the importance of your communication with Wilmington. . . . I leave the matter to your judgment." And again and finally, on same day, "Dispute their advance at every available point." Shortly afterwards an officer from the staff of General Bragg, who had returned from Richmond and resumed command, was sent to General Hagood to impress upon him the necessity of delaying the enemy's advance. He stated that a large number of Federal prisoners, some ten thousand, had been sent to Wilmington, for delivery in exchange under a convention entered into between Generals Grant and Lee—that the Federal commander had been notified of it under a flag about the time he had commenced his advance; that he had declined to receive them, alleging some reason—not now remembered—that he was probably pressing forward in the hope of obtaining possession of them by recapture; and that time was essential to get these prisoners off, out of reach, as well as valuable commissary and quartermaster stores—all of which were being transported slowly with our imperfect railroad facilities.

These were the orders and instructions under which General Hagood acted.

When the enemy's skirmishers began to press on the evening of the 19th, Lieutenant Jeffords with his mounted patrol were brought in; and the lower bridge thoroughly destroyed. Jeffords' command was then used until late next day to patrol the north bank of the stream towards Lipscomb, meeting with Lipscomb's patrol on that bank. Colonel Lipscomb was also directed to scout to his front and left on the enemy's flank and rear, and for that purpose to keep his bridge intact until compelled by the enemy in large force to destroy it.

At daylight, on the 20th, the enemy were in large force in front of lower bridge; he got a battery of Parrotts into position and pushed forward skirmishers. The fire of artillery and rifles was at this point brisk throughout the day. He seemed also to be feeling right and left for a crossing. No demonstration was made on Lipscomb.

About 11:30 a. m., the Twenty-first South Carolina was sent to relieve the Eleventh South Carolina at Cowan's. Shortly after it started a dispatch was received from Captain Westcoat, commanding Eleventh, that the enemy were landing at Cowan's. Major Wilds, commanding Twenty-first, was immediately directed by courier to retain the Eleventh and engage the enemy. At 12:40 p. m., he reported the enemy in force and driving him. Colonel Simonton, commanding Hagood's brigade, was directed to take the Twenty-fifth and Twenty-seventh regiments with him and, assuming command, take position at the first fork of the road coming from Cowan's and hold it. At 2:10 p. m., he reported from a point on the south road short of this fork, "The enemy are in my front and appear to be extending on the north road. From my position I cannot guard both roads. No demonstration since Major Wilds reported." General Hagood had previously ordered two pieces of artillery to Colonel Simonton. He immediately went in person and found Colonel Simonton skirmishing sharply with the enemy, his reserves and two pieces of artillery on south road (at point marked X—see Map at p. 476), and his skirmish line not reaching the north road. The enemy were endeavoring to overlap him on both flanks. A reconnaisance satisfied General Hagood that the enemy had landed in sufficient force on this flank to render the position on Town Creek insecure,* and with the crossing on the bar at the mouth of the creek now in his possession and the point covered by the guns of his fleet, it was evident he could fling across the bulk of his forces whenever he pleased. Considering the overwhelming number opposed to him, General Hagood determined at once to withdraw from Town Creek. His small force, however, from the necessity of his position, had been scatttered over twelve (12) miles, with the line of retreat behind the left flank, the one that had been turned. It was necessary, therefore, that resistance should be obstinately made by Colonel Simonton in order to give time to concentrate.

The colonel was accordingly directed to extend his line of skirmishers to the left (so as to cover both roads), to put a reserve behind each flank (one on each road), to keep one piece of artillery with each reserve (on the south road), and to fall back making an obstinate *skirmish* fight, until his reserves reached the telegraph road: then to close his reserves together at the point marked Y, where General Hagood promised himself to place the other piece and to retire down the road (YZ)—making that his direction.

Having made these dispositions and given these directions, General Hagood returned rapidly to his headquarters at the Church, and dispatched Colonel Lipscomb immediately to withdraw with his whole force to Marks' Cross Roads; called in Lieutenant Jeffords with his mounted men and sent him to Colonel

---

*Three brigades of Cox's division.—Cox's March to the Sea, p. 151.

Simonton to keep up the connection between his two reserves; sent Lieutenant Moffett, A. A. G., to the point G to bring word when Simonton should be driven to within 200 yards of the Telegraph road; ordered the trains which had previously been stationed at Marks Cross Roads into Wilmington and sent with them his sick and wounded and two of his field pieces that had been disabled; and placed the Seventh South Carolina and the Fortieth North Carolina, under command of Lieutenant-Colonel Rion of the Seventh, in line of battle on the Wilmington road (at the points K to Z). Two men were sent to burn the bridges at McElhaney's mill and cut the sluices to prevent the enemy's use of the telegraph road to intercept the retreat to Wilmington. Mr. Young, signal operator, with George Addison, courier at brigade headquarters, was sent on this duty.

Colonel Lipscomb was absent from his command examining the creek above his position when the courier reached the upper bridge, and the officer next in command most improperly delayed to execute the order till Colonel Lipscomb could be found—thus losing two hours in his movement.

Judging from the firing that Simonton was hard pressed, General Hagood gave the order to Colonel Hedrick, commanding at the lower bridge, to commence withdrawing at 3 p. m. He was instructed to leave a strong rear guard in the work till he was fairly off. Lieutenant Moffett arrived before the order was fully executed and reported Simonton near the telegraph road. When Hedrick's column was within half a mile approaching Colonel Rion's lines (of the point Z), Captain Stoney was dispatched with a courier accompanying him at speed (down the road Z Y) to order Simonton to fall back rapidly, and to guide him. Stoney found on the left (of the road Z Y) a body of skirmishers very slightly engaged, and Simonton on the right (of this road and in the telegraph road) with one piece of artillery and in a line of battle (extending to the left and backward towards the skirmishers—thus making his line oblique to the road Z Y and thrown forward towards the enemy on his right). The enemy were advanced with a heavy line of battle, and Simonton firing rapidly upon them both with his artillery and rifles. Captain Stoney delivered his order, and Simonton ordered his piece limbered up and his line of battle to move to the left towards the skirmishers (and the road Z Y), but the enemy pressing him again, he revoked the order and sent Stoney to say he was too heavily engaged to withdraw. Captain Stoney was immediately returned to Colonel Simonton at the full speed of his horse to tell him "*he must come;* to throw away his artillery and make a run for it; that a line of battle was formed in his rear to protect him."

Stoney arrived in time to see the overwhelming lines of the enemy sweep over Simonton—the artillery firing till the enemy got within a few feet of it, and the infantry standing by the gun and resisting till overpowered hand to hand. He did not get to Simonton, and, his own horse being shot, he became involved in the mêleè. The body of skirmishers, before alluded to, coming out and straggling from the right and informing Hagood of the state of affairs, he now took position behind Mallory creek, keeping out a strong skirmish line (across the road between K and Z) and the squad of cavalry under Jeffords patrolling towards the Church direct straggling in.

This position he held till after dark, when stragglers ceasing to come in and Colonel Lipscomb reporting with his mounted men, his infantry and artillery being in march on the Georgetown road approaching Marks's Cross Roads, General Hagood ordered a retreat. One-half of Lipscomb's mounted men formed a rear guard at the distance of a mile, and the other half was sent forward to hold the position of McElhaney's mill. The infantry and artillery were passed over the pontoon bridge across Brunswick river, and by steam ferry over the Cape Fear by 12 o'clock at night; and the former marched to report to Hoke who upon the left bank had fallen back to near Wilmington. The cavalry, after burning the pontoons and the railroad bridge over Brunswick river and leaving the picket on Eagle Island, crossed into Wilmington about daylight on the 21st.

In this engagement the loss was two pieces disabled and brought off, two pieces captured by the enemy, and 461 men and officers killed, wounded, and missing—all of whom were from four regiments of Hagood's brigade. Colonel Simonton carried into action six hundred men and officers. His fault was in allowing his greatly inferior force to become engaged in a line of battle behind obstructions rapidly thrown up, when the occasion required him, and he had been directed, to make an obstinate skirmish fight.* Again, when ordered to withdraw, instead of facing the rear and withdrawing directly from the approaching enemy at a double quick, if necessary, he endeavored to make a flank march along the enemy's front, with, it is presumed, a view to getting a road down which to retire in column. The country was an open pine forest. His troops behaved with their accustomed gallantry, and to their obstinate defense of the flank, which had been turned, was due the safety of the whole command that day. The thing would have been completed had they themselves not been sacrificed in the discharge of the duty. Colonel Simonton, however, was inexperienced in the command of troops in the field and his errors certainly leaned to virtue's side.

Of the missing, mentioned above, Colonel Simonton subsequently reported 330 men and officers, including wounded captured by the enemy. Twenty killed upon the field is a very large estimate, and this would leave over a hundred men and officers, who, coming out of the rout and not finding the brigade that night, straggled off to South Carolina, and were no more, with very few exceptions, heard of in the war. Captain Stoney himself, included among the missing above reported, with fifty-two men and officers came out of the rout and did not find the brigade that night. These men, misinformed on reaching the Lumberton railroad of affairs in Wilmington, took the cars to Lumberton to rejoin the brigade via Fayetteville (this, however, they never did). Captain Stoney separated from them and rejoined his command at Rockfish creek some days later.

In all these operations Hagood's command fell back for four days before a force of ten to his one, taking this time to go a distance of eighteen miles and crossing two rivers. Everything that was movable was brought off, and the loss in battle was inconsiderable, when the circumstances of fighting to delay so superior a force is regarded, and especially the powerful aid the enemy derived from his navy. Without this he could not with such facility have turned the Town Creek position. The propriety of making the obstinate stand at Town Creek at all rests with the direction of affairs. It delayed the evacuation of Wilmington but little and was a hazardous venture. Had the junction been made at Wilmington on the night of the 19th, the

---

*For this the country was admirably suited.

enemy would have got into position on the 20th near the pontoon bridge, and would at most have shelled the town with field artillery. The nearest point of the town to the Brunswick shore being two and a quarter miles, this would have been a mere bagatelle. Did humanity forbid exposing non-combatants to this, we would have had to evacuate the town only one day sooner. As it was, a large number of prisoners could not be got off by railroad, and were marched ahead of us to a point on the railroad beyond the Northeast river where they were placed on the cars next day for further transportation.

EVACUATION OF WILMINGTON.

General Hagood, on reporting at Bragg's headquarters on the arrival of his column in Wilmington, was directed to send his infantry on to Hoke, while he should remain in the town and take the command. He was also instructed, with Lipscomb's cavalry, to watch the crossings of the Cape Fear as high up as Hilton Ferry. Two light batteries and a few infantry under Colonel Jackson, the post commander, were also left with him for provost duty.

In the afternoon the enemy's advanced parties drove our picket off of Eagle Island and appeared at P. K. depot, opposite the foot of Market street. General Hagood ordered a force of dismounted cavalry with a howitzer across the ferry, and soon drove the enemy back, re-establishing the picket.

During the day the Federal prisoners before alluded to were marched across the Northeast river; and the able-bodied male slaves, and the horses of citizens fit for military purposes were seized by direction of General Bragg and sent in the same direction. Arrangements were made for burning the naval stores and cotton stored in the town, as also shipping in the river, some half a dozen vessels. Arrangements were also made for distributing to the retiring troops as they marched through the town such portable quartermaster stores as shoes, etc., which could not be got off by rail. At night, guards were stationed with rigid orders to put down all pillage that might be attempted by the most summary measures. At daylight, on the 22nd, Hoke had marched into and through the town. The cotton, naval stores and vessels were in flames, and as the rear guard left in the early dawn a mass of black smoke had settled like a pall over the silent town; in its extent and density suggestive of the day of doom.

The army marched up the railroad toward Petersburg to its crossing of the Northeast river, some eight or nine miles from Wilmington, crossed on a pontoon bridge, and encamped. The enemy's advance guard came on thus far and slight skirmishing ensued. On the 23rd, the army moved on to Rockfish creek unpursued, where it remained till the 5th March. It rained, more or less, during all this time, and the roads got into bad condition. The exchange of Federal prisoners heretofore declined took place during this time, we delivering at Northeast river and receiving on the Richmond front.

OPERATIONS NEAR KINSTON.

A reference to the general map of North Carolina is necessary to an understanding of the subsequent movements and events of the war in this quarter.

Sherman was approaching from South Carolina, with Goldsboro for his objective; and had directed co-operative columns to move from Wilmington and New Berne to a junction with him at or near this railroad center. With Goldsboro in his possession and the roads back to the coast at Wilmington and New Berne, he could refit his army and with his united force of nearly one hundred thousand men* in hand be ready to co-operate with Grant as soon as the advancing spring released the armies in Virginia.

Fayetteville was an important Confederate arsenal and depot, from which there was steamboat navigation to Wilmington. And the Neuse river was also navigable for river steamers up and above Kinston.

On the 5th of March, Hoke's division began to move by railroad for Kinston, General Hagood bringing up the rear. He left with his last regiment on the 7th, and reached Kinston at 7 a. m., on the 8th. Lipscomb's cavalry was left to watch the enemy at Northeast river, which they had shown no disposition to cross; the light batteries and their infantry support of some

---

*Sherman's Report to Committee on Conduct of the War, p. 366.

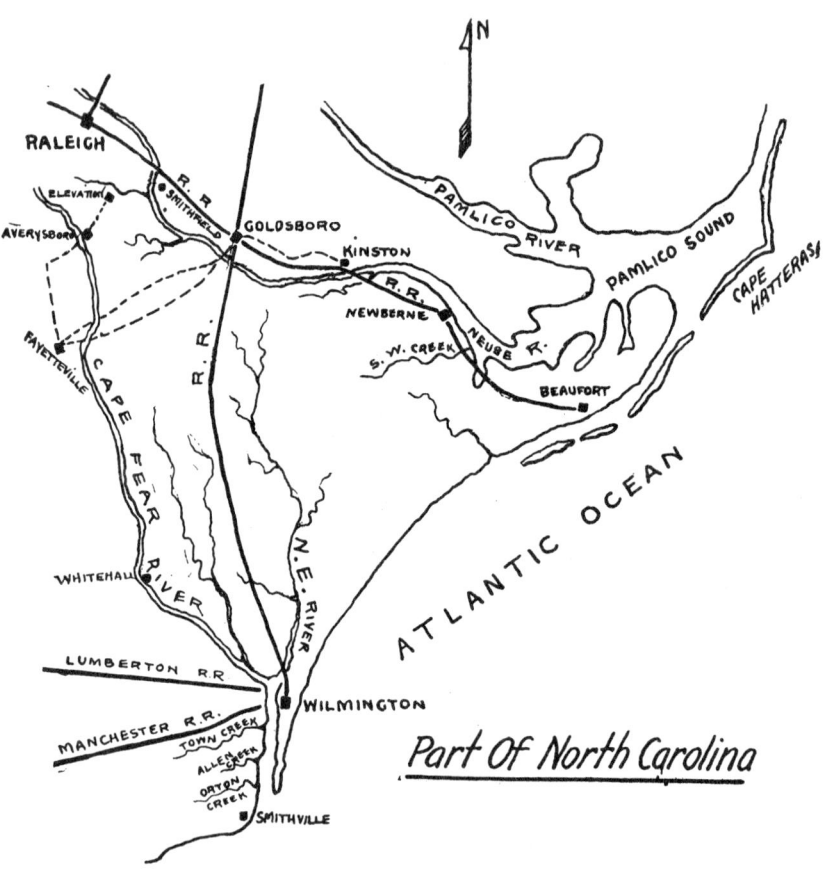

Part Of North Carolina

150 men, which were on the Cape Fear river at White Hall, while we lay at Rockfish creek, were ordered to report to General Joe Johnston at Fayetteville; and the artillery and train of the division moved by highway. On arriving at Kinston it was found that the column of the enemy which was to move from New Berne, in accordance with Sherman's plans, was before the place. Scofield had transferred from Wilmington enough men to New Berne to make, with the troops already there, some 20,000 men* and with himself in command.† He had left with Terry something over 10,000 men to move at the proper time from that point.

Major-General D. H. Hill, with some 2,500 effective arms-bearing men of Hood's Army of Tennessee and a brigade of junior reserves, had come by rail from the direction of Raleigh, and with Hoke's division constituted our force (between 7,000 and 8,000), which was confronting the enemy at Southwest creek two miles from the town. The regiment, heretofore spoken of as "Hedrick's brigade," had, by order of General Bragg issued at Rockfish, been assigned to Hagood's brigade, and this command was now organized as follows:

1. Rion's command, consisting of his own (Seventh) battalion and the remnants of the other four South Carolina regiments, making a regiment of twelve companies about 500 strong.

2. Hedrick's (Fortieth North Carolina) regiment, consisting of six companies (the other four captured at Fort Fisher), about 375 strong.

3. Taylor's command, consisting of one company, being fragments of the Thirty-sixth North Carolina, captured at Fort Fisher, and three (3) companies of the First North Carolina battalion of heavy artillery converted into infantry. This battalion was about 275 strong.

When General Hagood arrived with Rion's regiment at Kinston, he was ordered forward to report to General Hill, by whom he was placed in reserve. Taylor's battalion and Hedrick's regiment, that had preceded him, were reporting the one to Brigadier-General Baker, of Hill's command, and the other to Clingman's brigade, of Hoke's division.

---

*Report of Commander in Conduct of the War.—Sherman's Report, p. 366.
†Johnston's Narrative, p. 79, says "3 divisions under Major-General Cox." See also Cox's March, etc., p. 155.

The Neuse river runs at this point nearly due east; and South-west creek, coming from a southwesterly direction, empties into it two miles below Kinston. Kinston is on the north bank. About a mile from the mouth of the creek is a mill, with its pond backing water for some distance; and between the mill and the river the creek is not fordable though narrow and without swamp of any consequence. General Hagood was placed by the staff officer who conducted him at the fork of the Dover and Neuse road, and riding forward in person found General Hill's troops extending from the mill to the river behind slight entrenchments on the banks of the creek, skirmishing going on, and the enemy's line apparently parallel to our's and overlapping us on our right. General Hill informed him that Hoke's division had moved that morning by the upper Trent road around the head of the mill pond to strike the enemy's left flank; and that he was waiting Hoke's attack to himself advance.

About 11:30 a. m., General Hoke's guns were heard; and at 12 m., Hill ordered up his reserve to take the place of some junior reserves, who had become rather shaky under a moder-ately sharp skirmish to which they had been exposed; and advanced, driving the enemy easily in his front for a short dis-tance, when he received a dispatch from Bragg, commander-in-chief, that Hoke had met with considerable success and that Hill should move down the Neuse road to intercept the enemy at its intersection with the British road, down which he was retreating.

Hill moved immediately with Rion's regiment at the head of his column and arriving at West's house halted to await the retreating enemy. He picketed the British road and scouted a mile or so towards the enemy without meeting even a straggler. At 4:30 p. m., Hill received another dispatch from Bragg to march on the British road towards the enemy and attack him in the rear, but not to do so and return, if it was too late to accom-plish anything before dark. Hoke's fire still continuing without advancing from the position which he apparently held when Hill first moved, and then being but one hour and a half before dark, with the enemy between three and a half and four miles from him, Hill decided to withdraw, and returned behind Southwest creek.

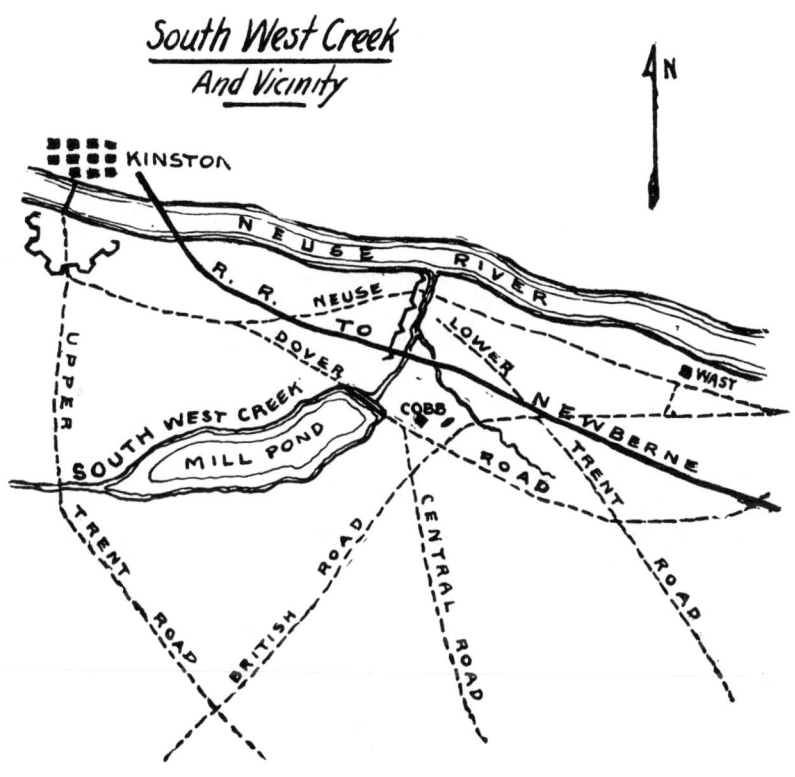

South West Creek And Vicinity

Hoke's success was a thousand prisoners captured and five hundred killed and wounded of the enemy who fell into his hands. He struck the enemy unentrenched on their flank and rolled them up with but little loss to himself, until the disarangement of his own advance caused by the tangled underbrush of the forest compelled him to halt to arrange his lines. By the time he was ready again, and had found the enemy in the new position they had taken, night arrested further action.

At the close of the day, the enemy occupied a position oblique to his first and in the general direction of the lower Trent road—his right not *reaching* the Neuse road. Hoke took position in front of the mill pond on the British road, his left short of the railroad. Our general line at nightfall was, therefore, en echellon, Hoke being in advance of the creek, and the second echellon on the banks of the creek—Hill's position of the morning. That night the second echellon was occupied by reserves, and Hill's forces were sent across the creek and went into line with Hoke. Hagood's brigade was got together again.

On the next day, the 9th, at daylight, Hoke marched with three brigades back across the mill, and moved by the Neuse road around the enemy's right with a view to attack; but, finding the enemy strongly entrenched, returned without making an attack. Hagood's brigade reported to Hill today and occupied his left. It was engaged in heavy skirmishing all day.

On the 10th, reserves held the bank of the creek as before; Hill held the position of the advanced echellon, and Hoke moved with his whole division (Hagood's brigade returning to him) at daylight down the central road, and making a wide detour marched through a low swampy country in the woods all the time, and struck the enemy's left in his rear position on the lower Trent road. The attack was made en echellon, Kirkland's and Colquitt's brigades in advance, and Clingman's and Hagood's in the second line, and in position from right to left as named. Kirkland was the only one heavily engaged; and the position of the enemy being discovered strongly entrenched, with abattis, etc., the troops were withdrawn and returned to the position of the night before. General Hill engaged the enemy with artillery and a heavy skirmish line, when Hoke attacked; but Hoke desisting did not press. Kirkland's loss was about 300, and was the chief loss sustained in all these operations, the first day's loss of the Confederates having been very inconsiderable.

On the night of the 10th, General Hagood was informed that we were to withdraw from before Kinston. The movements of the enemy in other quarters, and the necessity of concentrating in front of Sherman was the cause. There was nothing in the local situation that required it.* The Federals had been offered battle for three successive days, and had quietly accepted the defensive role of ditch digging and waiting to be attacked.

The retrograde movement commenced next morning and the enemy made no effort to molest it. Hill went by rail with his troops to Smithfield on the Neuse, some forty miles from Raleigh; and Hoke's division marched leisurely to the same point, our brigade remaining for two or three days in Kinston without being attacked. Scouts reported that the Federal army commenced a retreat upon New Berne at the same time that Bragg withdrew and only halted when they learned the fact of the Confederate retrograde.

Colonel Hedrick was wounded on the 8th himself, and lost three men. On the 9th, Rion lost two wounded and Taylor three. These men were all the losses of Hagood's brigade.

Hoke's column, after a pleasant march through a fine planting country up the valley of the Neuse, arrived at Smithfield on the 16th March. Here General Joe Johnston was in command, and Sherman's main column before him. He had marched, unopposed through South Carolina, spreading havoc and desolation, compelling the evacuation of Charleston and burning Columbia and numerous smaller towns, but attempting to hold no part of the State except Charleston. The head of his column was now near Fayetteville.

Johnston's army consisted of the troops of Bragg, Hardee and part of Hood's Tennessee army, with Hampton's cavalry, probably 30,000 of all arms. Sherman's force was 65,000 to 70,000, and the approaching co-operative columns of Scofield and Terry would raise it to a hundred thousand.

With these odds against them, the Confederates were once more to try the fortune of battle.

---

*They fell back to Goldsboro by General Bragg's order.—Johnston's Narrative, p. 380.

```
Army Tennessee ...............................   5,000
Hardee .......................................  11,000
Bragg ........................................   8,000
                                              ------- 24,000
Cavalry—Wheeler ..............................   3,000
Cavalry—Butler ...............................   1,000
                                              -------  4,000
                                                      ------- 28,000
Sherman's four corps..........................          70,000
Cavalry ......................................           5,000
                                                        ------- 75,000
```

Johnston's Narrative, 372, 377 and 378.

BATTLE OF BENTONVILLE.

From the vicinity of Raleigh to Goldsboro, the Neuse has a southeasterly course for a distance of fifty miles; and Smithfield is on the north bank half way between the two places.

To the southward, and twenty miles off, the Cape Fear runs parallel for half this distance; then at a little town called Averysboro diverges to the south. Fayetteville is west of the Cape Fear and forty-five or fifty miles southwest of Smithfield. Averysboro is half way between the two places. Two roads lead out of Fayetteville, cross the Cape Fear ten or fifteen miles below Averysboro, and, uniting on the south bank of the Neuse, go into Goldsboro.

From Smithfield is a road down the southern bank of the Neuse, and crossing Hannah and Mill creeks it passes by Bentonville and enters the upper road from Fayetteville to Goldsboro.

On the 16th March, Hoke's division arriving at Smithfield, crossed the river at Turner's bridge, two miles below the town, and encamped on Black creek. We had been having artillery fire all day, and at night learned that it was an engagement Hardee had had with the advance of one of Sherman's columns at Averysboro, and that he had, at its close, fallen back upon an elevation ten miles in our front. Hardee's loss was said to be 500 casualties of all kinds, and the enemy's supposed to be much larger. The Confederates were entrenched, the enemy made two direct attacks which were repulsed, and then turned our position, compelling its abandonment.

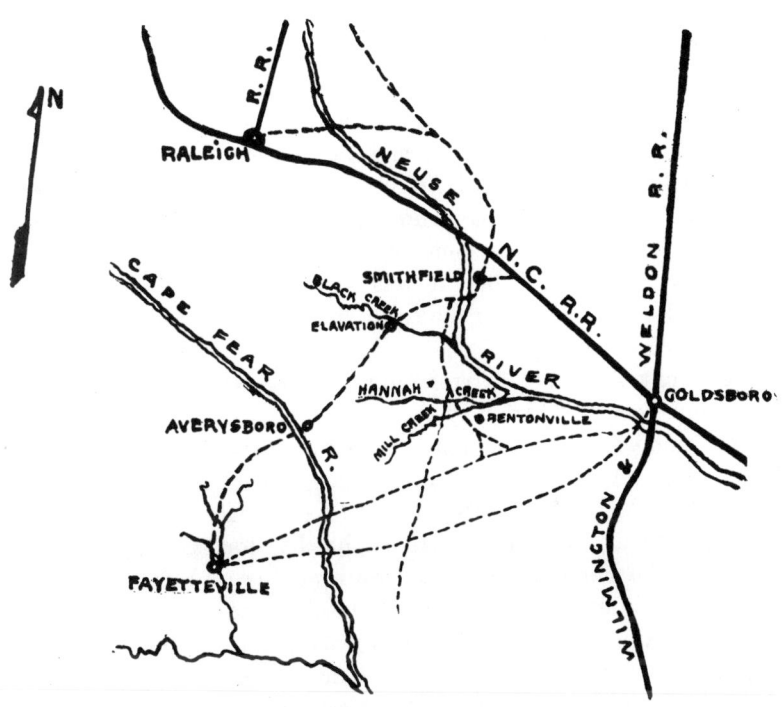

Vicinity Of Bentonville

Hardee's loss was trivial until his position was turned, when Rhett's brigade of South Carolina Regulars, commanded by Colonel William Butler, which was upon the flank, was badly cut up. The chief loss was in this brigade. Colonel Rhett had been captured a few days before. Sherman now ceased to press toward Smithfield and turned upon Goldsboro, moving by both the roads leading from Fayetteville to that point.

On the 18th Johnston moved down the south bank of the Neuse—Hoke's division marching thirteen miles to a point a little above Bentonville. On the 19th, the division went into line of battle beyond the upper road from Fayetteville to Goldsboro and on the prolongation of the western fork of the Bentonville road, and formed the left wing of Johnston's line. Hardee took the right of the Fayetteville road and was the right wing. In front of Hardee the ground was somewhat elevated, with more or less clearing. In front of Hoke it was low, wet pinewoods, interspersed with bay gulls and sluggish drains and having considerable undergrowth.

Butler's cavalry were skirmishing heavily with the enemy a mile in our front toward Fayetteville as we went into position, and were immediately afterward withdrawn. The enemy's skirmishers came on after them and striking the infantry skirmish line were checked and began feeling to our left. At this time Hagood's brigade was on the left of the division, and Colquitt's brigade next to Hagood,—making the first line of battle; Clingman's and Kirkland's brigades constituted the second line. General Hoke having been informed by Hagood of the enemy's moving to the left brought up Kirkland's from the second line and placed him on Hagood's left. Very soon after Kirkland's was in position, the enemy assailed, striking half of Hagood's front (Rion's regiment on the left) and the whole of Kirkland's. He was handsomely repulsed, leaving a good many dead and wounded men and abandoned rifles in our front. Our skirmish line was immediately re-established, the arms secured and the wounded brought in. Our loss was trivial, the men having with great rapidity covered themselves with log and earth obstructions. Lieutenant E. H. Bell, Company C, Seventh South Carolina battalion, was, however, killed. He was an excellent officer of his grade, and had served with fidelity throughout the war.

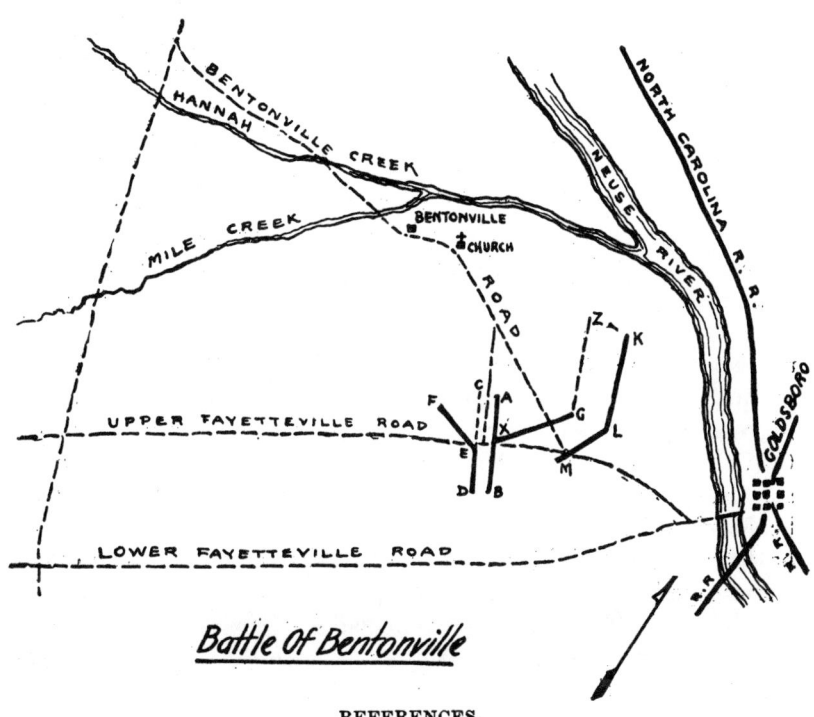

Battle Of Bentonville

REFERENCES.

A B—Johnston's line, 19th.
C E D—Sherman's first line, 19th.
F E D—Sherman's second line, 19th.
A X G Z—Johnston's line, 20th and 21st.
K L M—Sherman's 17th Corps, 20th and 21st.
F E D—Sherman's 14th and 20th Corps, 20th and 21st.

The staff standing unprotected behind the line, Lieutenant Martin had the sole of his shoe taken off by a rifle bullet striking between his foot and the earth, and Major Hay, commissary of subsistence, acting as aide-de-camp on this occasion, was painfully bruised by a ball glancing from a tree.

Heavy skirmishing continued on our front during the morning, the enemy still feeling for our left, which was now prolonged by dismounted cavalry. Our's was not engaged, but occupied in entrenching.

About 2 p. m., General Johnston advanced his right wing and forced back the enemy's left until it was at an angle of 45 degrees with its original position, the point of the angle being opposite Colquitt's center; his right wing remained parallel to our immediate front, and by this time was well entrenched. In swinging out, Hardee had lost connection with the left wing, and about 4:30 p. m., Hoke was ordered to move out two brigades and regain it. He had thrown out a regiment from the right of Colquitt's brigade, secured the angle of the enemy's entrenched position, and was sweeping down to the left to clear the front of Colquitt's left, and Hagood's before advancing, when an order arrived from Bragg, who had not been on the field and had heard of Hoke's movement through some aide or courier, to move both brigades straight out and make a direct attack. The order was obeyed and the works carried, though with considerable loss, over 500 men in the two brigades. General Hood was behind his center regiment, Hedrick's, commanded by Major Holland; Taylor was on the right of the brigade connecting with Colquitt, and Rion was on the left. Colquitt struck the works full, as did Taylor's regiment; Holland met with nothing but a line of battle; and Rion on the extreme left encountered only a skirmish line. After the first works were carried and the line was advancing steadily upon a second series of breastworks some 500 yards from our original line, General Hagood observed the troops on his right beginning to retire, first Colquitt (he could not see beyond that brigade) and then Taylor, and ordered his center and left back. There was nothing on his front nor on Colquitt's, as he subsequently learned from Colonel Zachery, commanding that brigade, to prevent a continued advance. The retrograde movement commenced with Hardee and resulted, it was said, from encountering works which could not be carried without undue sacrifice.

The loss in Hagood's brigade was chiefly in Holland's and Taylor's (North Carolina) regiments, and was from fire upon them in retiring; Colquitt's men received little or no fire in their retreat.

The Confederates at night re-occupied their first line of battle, but the enemy continued with their left wing bent back in the position into which it had been driven.

We had been fighting all day the Fourteenth and Twentieth U. S. Army Corps, as we learned from prisoners. The loss in our division at least would have been inconsiderable and our success eminent had it not been for Bragg's undertaking to give a tactical order upon a field that he had not seen. Hardee had captured a number of prisoners and several pieces of artillery, part only of which he was enabled to bring off on account of the tangled nature of the ground and the battery horses being killed. His losses were probably 800. From subsequent information it was learned that three Federal divisions were broken.

During the afternoon and night Sherman marched the Seventeenth corps by the lower Fayetteville road to its junction with the Upper road near the Neuse, succeeded in putting it in position on the Upper road in our immediate rear, and General Johnston, before it arrived in striking distance, next morning, the 20th, retaining the position of his right wing, swung back his left behind and nearly parallel with the upper Fayetteville road. His extreme left was somewhat refused, and prolonged and protected by cavalry. Hagood occupied the left of Hoke's division, Kirkland being the right. Harrison's Georgia brigade, of Hardee's command, prolonged and terminated the infantry line on the left. The rest of Hardee's command was in reserve behind this flank, and the Tennessee troops (of Hood's army) were on the right where they had been on the previous day and engaged in the operations of the right wing.

Johnston's line was now across the two branches of the Bentonville road by which after forking it enters the Upper Fayetteville road. His wings were each broken back to protect his flanks. The Fourteenth and Twentieth corps were on his right flank and front, the Seventeenth corps was on his left and front, and between the two divisions of the enemy's army was free communication along the Upper Fayetteville road. This position was scarcely taken when the enemy on the right attacked partially but heavily, Kirkland's brigade repelling the assault. On the left he deployed heavy skirmish lines, and severe skirmishing ensued but no assault. Our troops rapidly entrenched their new position. No further effort at assault was made, but the respective skirmishers were engaged all day and night along the whole line.

Next day, the 21st, the enemy having massed infantry in force on the extreme left, where Wheeler's cavalry extended and protected our flank, drove him some 2,000 yards and reached the field near the church and within 100 yards of the Bentonville road, our only line of communication. Here some 200 men of Alfred Cumming's Georgia brigade and the Eighth Texas cavalry on horseback fell furiously upon the right flank of the enemy's advancing line, and threw it into confusion. Wheeler rallied and succeeded in forcing them back, regaining his former position. At this time Hagood's brigade and Walthal's command of 950 men of the Army of Tennessee,* detached for the purpose, arriving, took the place of the cavalry, which moved further towards Hannah creek for the protection of the flank.

The enemy made no further demonstration here, but remained in line of battle with a heavy line of skirmishers engaged the rest of the day and night.

When Hagood's brigade was detached to re-enforce Wheeler, the enemy perceiving the movement immediately attacked the position he had left, but Clingman's brigade extending behind the really good entrenchments handsomely repulsed the assault. Colonel DeVorn, commanding the brigade, was, however, badly wounded, and Lieutenant-Colonel Mallett was killed. The latter General Hagood had first met at the defence of Battery Wagner in the siege of Charleston. He was a brave man and an excellent soldier.

On the morning of the 22nd, General Johnston commenced withdrawing from the field, skirmish lines covering the movement, and by 7 a. m. had taken position behind Hannah creek

---

*This was all that was left of Stewart's Army Corps.

three miles to the rear. He was unmolested in withdrawing. The enemy felt his new position with cavalry and skirmishers, but did not press. In the afternoon, the Confederates marched for their former position on Black creek, Hoke's division bringing up the rear.

Sherman moved on to Goldsboro, and the junction with the co-operative columns from New Berne and Wilmington took place.

Hagood's brigade in this battle lost 249 men killed, wounded and missing, of whom all but 17 were from the North Carolina troops of the command. Among these were some valuable officers and men. Colonel Taylor (Thirty-sixth North Carolina) was wounded and lost his arm, and Captain R. G. Rankin (First North Carolina battalion) attracted General Hagood's attention by his heroic bearing. He was wounded and died shortly after. Our general casualties were understood to be 2,500,* and the enemy's evidently heavier.†

The affair was indecisive. Johnston had evidently hoped, by falling rapidly upon one of Sherman's columns in march, to beat him in detail, and prevent his concentration at Goldsboro. While inflicting considerable injury upon the enemy, and raising the morale of that portion of his army which had been in one unvaried retreat since Atlanta, he failed to accomplish his purpose. With odds against him, it could only have been by that chance which so often determines military affairs that he could have succeeded.

Confederate forces present:

Infantry and artillery.. .. .. .14,100
Cavalry.. 4,000
——— 18,100
Federal forces:
On 19th.. .. .. .35,000
On 20th and 21st.. .. .. .70,000

*Killed, 223; missing, 653; wounded, 1,467; total, 2,343.—Johnston's Narrative, page 393.

†Johnston puts it at 4,000. Cox (page 197) at 1,604.

Johnson's Narrative, page 393.

FLARING UP OF THE CANDLE. THE END.

On the 24th of March, the army crossed the Neuse and went into camp on the north bank of the river above the railroad station. The distance of the enemy with cavalry intervening did away with the necessity of infantry outpost duty, and vigorous efforts were at once inaugurated by General Johnston to put his army in effective condition for further service. Drills, reviews, and inspections were the order of the day, and what was known as the consolidation Act was commenced to be enforced. This Act had been passed by the Congress some time before, but its provisions, for which there was a great necessity, had not been up to this time enforced. The supply of recruits to the Confederate army had for a year past failed, and indeed the Bureau of Conscription did not even efficiently return to their colors the men who upon various pretexts, legitimate and illegitimate, were at home. From the casualties of war, brigades had become regiments, regiments companies, and some organizations had almost ceased to exist. This was the condition of the armies in the field, while upon the rolls were borne men enough to constitute an army ample to hold the Federal hordes indefinitely at bay. Numbers of these were prisoners of war, and Grant's policy of obstructing exchange made their return too uncertain to be counted upon. There was but one course left to put the armies of the Confederacy upon a footing of efficiency sufficient to continue the contest, and that was to consolidate and reorganize the good men and true, who still clung to their banners, into new regiments and brigades of proper strength and rely for recruits to supply the waste of war upon returned prisoners of war, and such skulkers at home as a more vigorous execution of the powers of the conscription could return to the ranks.

This consolidation was a matter of much interest to both officers and men. In our particular case, a strong feeling was manifested to unite the volunteer South Carolina troops, which had come on with Hardee, to our old brigade. There were old acquaintances, Frederick's regiment of artillery now converted into infantry, and others, comrades of ours in the siege of Charleston.

These on the evacuation of Charleston had been brigaded under General Stephen Elliott, and their number had been considerably reduced by the hasty march from South Carolina, and casualties in the recent actions at Averysboro and Bentonville. Their addition, however, would have put the old brigade once more upon a respectable footing as to numbers in the field. General Elliott, who was now compelled to retire from active service by a recent wound and the reopening of the wound received at the explosion of the mine at Petersburg, felt impelled to return home, and his officers and men desired it, and General Hagood requested his division commander to seek to have it done. General Hoke, for some reason, was laggard in his efforts, enough to call for a remonstrance from his subordinate. Nominally there were yet men enough on the brigade rolls, present and absent, if returned to duty, to restore it to efficiency, and General Hoke seemed more inclined to give his efforts to recovering these. After conference with General Johnston, but without previous indication of his purpose to Hagood, he procured an order detailing Hagood himself to go to South Carolina on this duty. This order was handed to the brigade commander on the 30th March, and the same evening he issued a complimentary farewell order, which they had well deserved, to the North Carolinians who had been serving with us, and the following address to his own men:

"Headquarters Hagood's Brigade,
"Near Smithfield, N. C., 30th March, 1865.
"To the Officers and Men of Hagood's Brigade:

"There are now in South Carolina, absent without proper leave from the command, 828 men. There have been captured from the brigade in its long and arduous service, 1,505 men and officers, all of whom are, or soon will be, in South Carolina on the usual exchange furlough. In the present interrupted state of communication, both within South Carolina and from thence to the army, General Johnston thinks it necessary to adopt some other than the usual means to secure the prompt return of these men to their standards. With, too, this large number of men or any considerable proportion of them back in the ranks, the different regiments of the brigade will be saved from the action of the consolidation act, and the general appreciates the natural desire of his men to finish the war in the same organization in which they have heretofore served.

"Influenced by these considerations, the general commanding has ordered me to turn over the command of the brigade temporarily to the ranking officer present, and to proceed to South Carolina to secure, by my personal exertions, as far as may be, the rapid recruiting of our command. This has been done without previous intimation of his views, or without suggestion from me. When I learned his intention I applied to have the remnant of the brigade now here temporarily returned to the State, there to gather up the absentees; but I was informed that, small as their number was, they could not be spared from the army here. Our general possesses your unbounded confidence. He had been called to the command at this critical juncture by the universal voice of the army and the country, and it becomes us implicitly and cheerfully to carry out his views.

"I shall be absent forty days, perhaps a short time longer, but so soon as the purpose of my absence shall be accomplished you have the guarantee of my past history that I will be back where I have hitherto found the post of duty—amid your ranks.

"In my absence you will not be consolidated, and although the North Carolina troops will be taken from the command, the old brigade will be kept intact and redeveloped into its old proportions as the returning members arrive.

"In concluding this frank and full statement of the condition of our command, let me urge upon both officers and men to give their hearty co-operation in carrying out the views of our general—views dictated not only by the interest of the country at large, but by the welfare of our beloved brigade. When I return, greet me, comrades, with the announcement that in my absence no man has left his standard—that the word deserter has been expunged from the vocabulary of Hagood's brigade.

"Remember your glorious record. Recall the spirit that animated you at Walthal when almost single-handed you held the invader at bay until the arrival of Beaureguard's avenging army. Think of your triumph at Drury's; your services at Cold Harbor, at Bermuda Hundreds, the sixty-seven days in the trenches of Petersburg, the bloody but glorious Sunday on the Weldon road, the Richmond lines, Fisher, Anderson Town Creek, Kinston, Bentonville. What men before ever made such a record in eleven months? Will you let such a history terminate ingloriously, and the verdict of posterity be that the men who made the record perished in the making, and that the degenerate survivors were unable to sustain the weight of glory their more gallant comrades had already won?

"Officers and men of the Eleventh, Twenty-first and Twenty-fifth and Twenty-seventh, to you especially do I appeal to keep your commands together. You are the nucleus upon which your regiments must be rebuilt. Suppress any rising spirit of discontent at unavoidable unpleasantness in your present condition; lend me your zealous efforts; and again your regiments will be in the condition they were when the swords of Ledbetter and Dargan and Glover and Hopkins flashed in your van, and their gallant spirits proudly departed to heaven from a death won in your ranks.

"JOHNSTON HAGOOD, Brigadier-General."

General Hagood was directed to select a detail of officers to company and assist him; and given transportation for them and their horses by rail as far as these roads remain in running order. This was to the edge of Sherman's "swath" through South Carolina. Lieutenant-Colonel Rion, Seventh battalion, was left in charge of the brigade, aided by Stoney, Mazyck, Lartigue and Hay of the staff. Moffett and Martin of the staff and Captain Brooks (Seventh battalion) accompanied General Hagood; and next morning they started for South Carolina.

The brigade now numbered of all grades present 493 men! This was the last time General Hagood saw it; or saw the Red Cross flag floating over armed men in the field. Before his mission in South Carolina had been accomplished,—before the forty days had expired—the Confederacy had gone down in blood and gloom.

Captain Stoney kept a memorandum diary of events after General Hagood's departure; and the following extracts from it conduct the history of the brigade through the few days that remained to the bitter end. They at the same time give such glimpses of the general course of events, now familiar history, as were obtainable at the time by a subordinate and show, too, how in the shadow of approaching doom the ignoble traits of poor human nature are as perceptible as the heroic.

"March 31st.—General Hagood having left for South Carolina. Lieutenant-Colonel Rion assumed command of the brigade, being the ranking officer present. The North Carolina troops, lately brigaded with us, assigned by division orders to Kirkland's and Clingman's North Carolina brigades. The division is now attached to Hardee's corps.

"April 4th.—Hardee's corps reviewed by General Johnston. In the absence of Lieutenant-Colonel Rion on courtmartial duty, the brigade commanded by Captain Thomas, Twenty-first regiment.

"April 7th.—Corps again reviewed in honor of Governor Vance, of North Carolina. In the afternoon he made a speech to the brigade of junior reserves lately attached to Hoke's division, speaking plainly of the critical condition of affairs, but impressing upon them that with anything like a proper discharge of duty the cause was by no means hopeless.

"April 9th.—Received orders to have wagons packed by reveille tomorrow; no intimation of what movement is on foot.

"April 10th.—At 10 a. m. orders to prepare to move. At 11:30 a. m. marched in a heavy rain; passed through Smithfield and encamped five miles beyond on Raleigh road. Colonel Graham, Twenty-first, arrived at headquarters just before we marched, but did not assume command. being required by division commander, before doing so, to account for his prolonged absence in South Carolina, whither he had been sent on similar duty upon which the brigade commander is now detailed. Colonel Gantt, Eleventh, is absent under similar circumstances. Major Cleland K. Huger, of the artillery, upon today's march, intimated to me that General Lee had met with a disaster; a few hours later the army was filled with vague rumors upon the subject.

"April 11th.—Marched fifteen miles and bivouacked five miles from Raleigh. Troops out of marching condition from even the short rest at Smithfield; straggled badly.

"April 12th.—Passed through Raleigh at midday. The city was being rapidly evacuated and immense quantities of stores destroyed and abandoned. Captain Segus and his company (Seventh battalion) left behind in city as provost guard. Division encamped on Hillsboro road five miles beyond Raleigh. Rumors in regard to General Lee assuming an unpleasant air of probability.

"April 13th.—Marched at 6:30 a. m. Camped four miles from Chapel Hill.

"April 14th.—Route altered from Hillsboro to Greensboro. Marched twenty-two miles; but little straggling.

"April 15th.—Division prepared to march at 4:30 a. m., but for some unexplained reason did not move until 6 a. m. under arms in a heavy rain during the interval. Our division was the rear of the column; the enemy following, but not pressing, and not nearer than Chapel Hill. Early in the day encountered the Haw River swollen with a freshet; crossed with much difficulty but no loss; a few men were washed away by the current but not drowned. Three miles beyond the river the direction of the march was changed to Salisbury. On this road a mill stream was encountered, about twenty feet wide, but so rapid and deep that the wagons were gotten over with difficulty. The Allemance, out of its banks, next crossed our path. A few men had succeeded in crossing by *chaining their hands* or by holding on to horses' tails of the mounted men, who half waded, half swam over, but the wagons were at a hopeless standstill. General Hardee was on the further bank, evidently anxious for rapid movement and nonplussed by the obstacle. At length the leading teamster was ordered to attempt the passage. With a crack of the whip, and a shout to his mules he is in and under, rises, struggles, and is swept away. Everything was again at a standstill; the rain was falling in torrents, the river was rapidly rising, something had to be done, and our lieutenant-general determined to try to swim another wagon and team across. The order was given, and followed by the same result. Mules, wagon and teamster were swept down the stream; and it was hard to tell which was uppermost in the struggle with the flood. The general's resources seemed now exhausted and he ordered the destruction of the train. General Hoke suggested that a more practicable crossing might be found, and he was permitted to seek it. Four miles higher up we crossed without difficulty at Holt's mill, and the train was saved. Encamped half a mile beyond the river after a most fatiguing day's march. Tonight, Colonel Olmstead, of the First Georgia regiment, tells me positively that *General Lee has surrendered.* Great God! can it be true? I have never for a moment doubted the ultimate success of our cause. I cannot believe it.

"April 16th. March resumed at 6:30 a. m. Roads almost impassable. To facilitate movement, the division train was divided—each train had its own wagons in its front with details to assist them along. Marched twenty miles and encamped with instructions to move at 4:30 a. m. tomorrow without further orders.

"April 17th. At 12 last night, the order to move this morning was countermanded, and we remained stationary during the day. Early in the day it was reported *our army* was to be surrendered. This rumor was at first disregarded, but presently began to assume shape and force. The wildest excitement seized the troops. I rode to division headquarters to learn the truth. I saw Majors Cross and Adams of the staff, who informed me that beyond a doubt the army would be surrendered tomorrow. In reply to my question whether I was at liberty to make this known, Major Adams replied, 'Yes, and you may further say that any one who desires to leave can obtain a written permit from division headquarters.' I returned to camp and made the announcement. Colonel Rion immediately ordered the brigade into line and urged them not to leave. The enemy were now supposed to be not only in rear, but on both flanks, and it would be difficult to escape; that if any considerable number left it might compromise the terms given to those that remained. The men seemed at this time ready to do anything that their officers advised, to march that night in the effort to cut their way out, or to remain and abide the issue where they were. All the afternoon the cavalry were passing us saying they 'were going out.' The infantry soon become almost frantic, and in every direction were rushing to beg, borrow, buy and steal horses. Disorganization was complete. Horses and mules were everywhere taken without the least regard to ownership. Trains were openly carried off after plundering the wagons. The division supply train was thoroughly stripped. The flags of the brigade were burned by the men in the certainty of surrender. About dark an order came from army headquarters to keep the men together, but with that day the army perished—a mob remained.

"April 18th.—No further development of events. About dark Major Cross, A. A.-G., came to Colonel Rion with directions from General Hoke to say to the brigade that there was no truth in the reported surrender. Demoralization, however, is utter and complete; there is no spark of fight left in the troops. General Johnston expresses, we are told, great displeasure at the report. It came to Hoke from corps headquarters, and is now there denied to have been warranted by anything that passed. Our remaining supplies of commissary and quartermaster stores are fully issued, but forage for the animals is failing.

"April 19th.—A strange rumor in camp that Lincoln has been assassinated. In the afternoon a circular from General Johnston expressing profound regret at the report of his intended surrender, and positively denying its truth. Accompanying the circular was a general order announcing to the army 'that a suspension of arms had been agreed upon pending negotiations between the two governments. During its continuance the two armies are to occupy their present position.'

24—H

"No one who has not seen and mixed with demoralized troops will be disposed to credit my statement that this announcement appeared unwelcome to many of the men. They regretted to have to remain in camp a few days longer, although the difference was between going home as prisoners of war on parole or as freemen under an honorable peace. This was undoubtedly the prevailing sentiment with the mass. Others drew high hopes from the expression underscored in the official copy, 'the two governments.' Recognition of independence was deduced from it, whatever minor terms might be agreed upon, and when later in the evening a courier from corps headquarters reported the news that Captain Fielden, an assistant adjutant-general at army headquarters, had stated that peace was declared, and upon most favorable terms, we were in the highest spirits. The impression prevails that the United States have become embroiled with France in the matter of Mexico, and that our independence is recognized on condition of an alliance offensive and defensive between the North and South.

"April 20th.—Nothing definite as to the terms of the impending peace. Rumor now has Reconstruction as the basis. The universal sentiment of the brigade is opposed to anything like submission or reconstruction of the accursed Union. The feeling, I noticed the other day, I am sure arose from no desire of giving up the Cause, but going home as prisoners of war included in their minds the sequence of exchange and renewal of the struggle.

"April 21st.—General Hoke returned from Greensboro with various items of news. We are to return to the Union under the status of 1860, the rights of property to be respected, and property as defined in each State to be recognized. All laws passed since 1860 to be submitted to the Supreme Court, negro slavery to be untouched, the troops to be marched to their respective State capitals, and there ground their arms; at the capital, too, each soldier is to take an oath of allegiance to the United States.

"April 22d.—There being reason to think that many of the brigade were contemplating leaving for home, Colonel Rion issued a circular advising them to remain to the end. Immediately the whole command collected at headquarters to hear more fully from him. He addressed them at length. He stated the position of affairs, as far as known to him, and urged that their departure would be a violation of the truce, compromising their personal safety, compromising General Johnston, and finally compromising their personal honor.

"April 23d.—Seven men of the Seventh battalion and fifteen men of the Twenty-seventh regiment left for home yesterday and today. The division is being rapidly reduced in this way. They are going in large bodies and at all hours without an effort being made to stop them.

"April 24th.—Desertion on the increase throughout the army. Thirty men and one officer (Lieutenant Brownlee, Eleventh South Carolina), of our brigade, left yesterday.

"April 25th.—Informed that the truce would terminate at 11 o'clock tomorrow. Received orders to be ready to move at that time. Men still leaving in crowds. Our brigade lost thirty-nine, all from Seventh battalion.

"April 26th.—Marched at 11 a. m. May I ever be spared such a sight as I witnessed when the order to move was given. Whole regiments remained on the ground, refusing to obey. In the last ten days desertion had reduced Kirkland's brigade from 1,600 to 300 men; Clingman's and the brigade of junior reserves from the same cause were each no stronger; Hagood's and Colquitt's brigades had suffered, but not so much. Now not more than forty men in each brigade followed Kirkland and Clingman from the ground. Officers as high as colonels, not only countenanced, but participated in the shameful conduct. Major Holland, of the North Carolina troops, formerly attached to our brigade, went off with all his men, and officers of higher rank did the same. Hagood's brigade here left forty men; Colquitt's about two hundred. These commands being from South Carolina and Georgia, are willing to hold together while movement is towards their homes. I fear a march in another direction would equally reduce their numbers. For all this demoralization I must hold our higher officers responsible. All the sensational reports which have so loosened the bands of discipline originate at their headquarters, and many of them are playing first hands in the shameless appropriation of public property that is going on. This last remark applies principally to General Hardee's headquarters, and much feeling is elicited among the troops by the appropriation there of supplies intended for and much needed by them. Halted on the Trinity College road five and a half miles from Trinity, having marched ten miles.

"April 27th—Remained quietly in camp all day. Rumors rife as usual, at length culminating in the sad and solemn truth of surrender.

" 'Headquarters Army of Tennessee,
" 'Near Greensboro, N. C., 27th April, 1865.

" 'General Order No. 18.

" 'By the terms of a military convention, made on the 26th instant by Major-General W. T. Sherman, U. S. A., and General J. E. Johnston, C. S. A., the officers and men of this army are to bind themselves not to take up arms against the United States until properly relieved from that obligation, and shall receive guarantees from the United States officers against molestation by the United States authorities so long as they observe that obligation and the laws in force where they reside.

" 'For these objects duplicate muster rolls will be made out immediately, and after the distribution of the necessary papers, the troops will march under their officers to their respective States and there be disbanded.

" 'The object of this convention is pacification to the extent of the authority of the commanders who make it.

" 'Events in Virginia, which broke every hope of success by war, imposed on its general the duty of sparing the blood of this gallant army and of saving our country from further devastation and our people from ruin.

" 'J. E. JOHNSTON, General.

" 'Official: ARCHER ANDERSON, Lieutenant-Colonel and A. A.-G.'

"April 28th.—The brigade was paid today one dollar and a quarter in silver per man, the last, I suppose, of the Confederate treasury. I shall have mine made into a medal to keep and value as received from the dying hands of my government. It is the greatest earthly satisfaction and my only consolation now, that I entered her service on the day of the inauguration of this war; was never absent from my command except by authority or from wounds, and continued in the field until the last day.

"30th April.—Still in camp. Rumor seems to have tired of her occupation. The stern reality of accomplished defeat is upon us. Famine begins to threaten us.

"May 1st.—Still here, disorganized, dissatisfied. No right acknowledged now except might, no property safe which is not defended with pistol and rifle. Regimental and higher commanders ordered to High Point to receive paroles. Colonels sign for their regiments, brigadiers for their staff, and colonels, major-generals for their brigades, and so on. Paroles are not to be issued to individuals until we reach the end of our journeys to our respective States.

"May 2d.—Lancaster courthouse has been indicated as the point in South Carolina where our brigade is to disband, and there seems no reason now why we should not start for it. General Hardee has quietly slipped off; General Hoke is with us still, though his division consists only of the remnants of Colquitt's and Hagood's brigades. Our brigade surrendered forty officers and three hundred and ten men; Colquitt's about the same.

"In all these terrible days of desertion but one officer (Lieutenant Brownlee, already mentioned) had fallen away from this brigade. Our horses have for a week been reduced to one quart of corn per day, while the mules get no grain and but a handful of long forage.

"Expected issues from the Federal authorities have not been received. Ten days' rations of bacon are in the brigade commissariat and no meal. No orders to leave have been received, but with famine staring us in the face, General Hoke consents to our starting. As it might, however, turn out a serious step, in the event of our not being able to get food on our route, the question of waiting for the Federal issue of supplies, or of starting now was submitted to the men. Of course, they voted to go. They would go with the certainty of starving. Received General Hoke's farewell address to his division. It is full of feeling.

"May 3d.—This morning at 8 a. m. our brigade started upon its last march. The Twenty-seventh led the column with *seven* men in its ranks; the Twenty-fifth followed next with *five;* the Seventh battalion, which had not suffered so much in battle as the other regiments, had near a hundred men in ranks; the Twenty-first not quite so large, and the Eleventh regiment, numbering sixteen in all told, was the rear guard. We stopped at Hoke's headquarters to pay him our respects and say good-bye. He and his staff seemed to feel the occasion deeply, and their expressions of regard and good will were very grateful to us all. The last link that bound us to the army thus severed, we resumed our weary journey homeward. At sunset we had made eighteen miles. The Washington artillery overtook and camped near us.

"May 4th.—The men straggled off at daylight and are scattered widely on both sides of our route seeking provisions. The wagons are all that mark the march during the day, and at night the men reassemble as they come up to where headquarters are made. Crossed the Yadkin at Stokes' Ferry; marched twenty-eight miles and bivouacked at Colonel Kendall's farm. During the day the commissary obtained and had ground into meal twenty bushels of corn. This gives bread for the rest of the march to South Carolina, but our mules and horses are starving.

"May 5th.—No incident on the march. Our animals still without forage. At night they attack the wagon covers and essay to devour them. There is no grass; gnawing rails and trees is their only feed. The country through which we are marching is of the poorest description.

"May 6th.—Made a march without incident, passing through Monroe and camping eight miles south of it.

"May 7th.—Arrived at Lancaster courthouse, in South Carolina, about 11 a. m. Halted in a grove on the edge of the village and proceeded to the work of disbandment.

"We first distributed the transportation of the brigade, as directed by General Johnston, officers and men taking an equal chance in the lottery, then the paroles were given out to the men and the work was done."

Thus ended the military history of a body of men who struck for what they believed to be inalienable right, and staked their all upon the issue. *Deo Vindice.*

Individuals found their way as best they could to the ruins and desolation which were now their homes, there in patience to abide the event; the brigade, like the Cause in which it had enlisted, was dead.

APPENDIX

In the autumn of 1864, when the brigade then attached to Longstreet's corps was serving upon the Richmond lines, the following rosters of its different regiments were made out and officially forwarded under directions from corps headquarters. They are correct from the organization of each regiment up to that date; subsequent changes are not given, nor is the means of accuracy in noting them at hand. The most important, however, may be gathered from the preceding narrative.

SEVENTH SOUTH CAROLINA BATTALION.

Organized 22d February, 1862. Mustered into Confederate service 22d February, 1862.

FIELD OFFICERS.

Lieutenant-Colonel.

(1) P. H. Nelson, major 22d February, 1862. Promoted lieutenant-colonel 10th July, 1862. Killed in battle 24th June, 1864.

(2) J. H. Rion, captain 22d February, 1862. Major 5th March, 1863. Lieutenant-colonel 24th June, 1864.

Major.

(1) L. W. R. Blair, captain 22d February, 1862. Major 10th July, 1862. Resigned 3d March, 1863.

(2) J. H. Rion. (See above.)

(3) Vacancy not filled.

STAFF.

Surgeon.

R. B. Hanahan, 30th March, 1863. Assistant Surgeon.

(1) Chas. R. Taber, December, 1861. Promoted.

(2) Wm. Weston, 2d February, 1865.

Ensign.

(1) A. P. Irby, 20th June, 1864. Resigned.

(2) Vacant.

Assistant Quartermaster.

(1) Eli Harrison, 6th March, 1862. Transferred.

(2) Office abolished.

Adjutant.
(1) S. W. Nelson, 20th March, 1862. Resigned.
(2) W. M. Thomas, 12th December, 1864.

COMPANY A.

Captain.
(1) L. W. R. Blair (see field officers).
(2) B. S. Lucas, first-lieutenant 22d February, 1862. Promoted 10th July, 1862. Wounded and retired June, 1865.

First-Lieutenant.
(1) B. S. Lucas. See above.
(2) D. Segars, second-lieutenant 22d February, 1862. First-lieutenant 27th May, 1862.
(3) F. M. McCaskell, second-lieutenant 22d February, 1862. First-lieutenant June, 1864. Killed 21st August, 1864.
(4) A. M. McCaskell, second-lieutenant July, 1862. First-lieutenant 21st August, 1864.

Second-Lieutenant.
(1) D. Segars. See above.
(2) F. M. McCaskell. See above.
(3) A. M. McCaskell. See above.
(4) J. W. Gardiner, junior second-lieutenant 14th October, 1862. Promoted second-lieutenant 21st August, 1864.

Junior Second-Lieutenant.
(1) J. W. Gardiner. See above.
(2) Vacant.

COMPANY B.

Captain.
(1) J. H. Rion (see field officers).
(2) J. R. Harrison, first-lieutenant 22d February, 1862. Captain 5th March, 1863. Resigned.
(3) J. L. Kennedy, second-lieutenant 22d February, 1862. First-lieutenant 5th March, 1863. Captain 23d November, 1863. Died of wounds 8th August, 1864.
(4) S. W. Douglass, junior second-lieutenant 2d April, 1863. Second-lieutenant August, 1864. First-lieutenant August, 1864. Died of wounds September, 1864.
(5) J. L. Tidwell, second-lieutenant September, 1864. First-lieutenant 13th December, 1864. Captain 18th December, 1864.

First-Lieutenant.
(1) J. R. Harrison. See above.
(2) J. L. Kennedy. See above.

(3) H. L. Isbell, junior second-lieutenant 22d February, 1862. Second-lieutenant 1st April, 1863. First-lieutenant 23d November, 1863. Died of wounds 27th August, 1864.

(4) S. W. Douglass. See above.

(5) J. L. Tidwell. See above.

(6) S. H. Cook, 13th December, 1864.

Second-Lieutenant.

(1) J. L. Kennedy. See above.

(2) H. L. Isbell. See above.

(3) S. W. Douglass. See above.

(4) J. L. Tidwell. See above.

(5) S. H. Cook, 8th September, 1864. Promoted. See above 13th December, 1864.

(6) J. P. Cason, junior second-lieutenant 8th September, 1864. Second-lieutenant 13th December, 1864.

Junior Second-Lieutenant.

(1) H. L. Isbell. See above.

(2) S. W. Douglass. See above.

(3) R. W. Kennedy, 3d April, 1863. Killed 21st August, 1864.

(4) S. H. Cook. See above.

(5) J. P. Cason. See above.

(6) Vacant.

COMPANY C.

Captain.

(1) W. H. Sligh, 22d February, 1862. Resigned.

(2) A. W. Pearson, junior second-lieutenant 22d February, 1862. Second-lieutenant 11th November, 1862. First-lieutenant 29th June, 1863. Captain 29th June, 1863. Resigned 25th October, 1864.

(3) J. R. Mankin, junior second-lieutenant 19th November, 1862. Second-lieutenant 29th June, 1863. First-lietuenant same date. Captain 25th October, 1864.

First-Lieutenant.

(1) M. H. Howell, 22d February, 1862. Resigned 11th November, 1862.

(2) F. H. Elmore, second-lieutenant 22d February, 1862. First-lieutenant 11th November, 1862. Resigned 29th June, 1863.

(3) A. W. Pearson. See above.

(4) J. R. Mankin. See above.

(5) Vacant.

Second-Lieutenant.

(1) F. H. Elmore. See above.

(2) A. W. Pearson. See above.

(3) J. R. Mankin. See above.

(4) W. D. Hill, junior second-lieutenant 7th October, 1863. Promoted same day.

Junior Second-Lieutenant.
   (1) A. W. Pearson. See above.
   (2) J. R. Mankin. See above.
   (3) W. D. Hill. See above.
   (4) E. H. Bell, 7th October, 1863. Killed at Bentonville in 1865.

COMPANY D.

Captain.
   (1) J. L. Jones, 2d January, 1862. Captured 21st August, 1864. Prisoner until end of war.

First-Lieutenant.
   (1) W. Clyburn, promoted to Company G.
   (2) E. A. Young, second-lieutenant 22d February, 1862. First-lieutenant 27th May, 1862.

Second-Lieutenant.
   (1) E. A. Young. See above.
   (2) R. W. Young, 14th July, 1862.

Junior Second-Lieutenant.
   (1) R. Moseley, 22d February, 1862. Resigned.
   (2) R. I. Cunningham, 19th November, 1862.

COMPANY E.

Captain.
   (1) R. E. Boykin, 22d February, 1862. Resigned 25th May, 1863.
   (2) P. P. Gaillard, second lieutenant 22d February, 1862. First-lieutenant 6th November, 1862. Captain 25th May, 1863.

First-Lieutenant.
   (1) A. G. Sanders, 22d February, 1862. Resigned 6th November, 1862.
   (2) P. P. Gaillard. See above.
   (3) James Ross, junior second-lieutenant 22d February, 1862. Second-lieutenant November, 1862. First-lieutenant same date.

Second-Lieutenant.
   (1) P. P. Gaillard. See above.
   (2) James Ross. See above.
   (3) F. W. Lenoir, junior second-lieutenant 19th November, 1862. Second-lieutenant 19th November, 1862.

COMPANY F.

Captain.
   (1) Dove Segars, 27th May, 1862.

First-Lieutenant.
(1) Wm. McSween, 27th May, 1862. Died 1864.
(2) H. D. Tiller, junior second-lieutenant 27th May, 1864. Second-lieutenant 1st November, 1864. First-lieutenant 2d June, 1864.

Second-Lieutenant.
(1) J. E. Horton, 27th May, 1862. Died 1st November, 1862.
(2) H. D. Tiller. See above.
(3) A. W. Rabey, junior second-lieutenant 19th November, 1862. Promoted second-lieutenant 2d June, 1864.

Junior Second-Lieutenant.
(1) H. D. Tiller. See above.
(2) A. W. Rabey. See above.
(3) G. P. King, 13th August, 1864.

COMPANY G.

Captain.
Wm. Clyburn 27th May, 1862.

First-Lieutenant.
L. L. Clyburn 27th May, 1862.

Second-Lieutenant.
Wm. J. Taylor, 27th May, 1862.

Junior Second-Lieutenant.
Thomas Sligh, 27th May, 1862.

COMPANY H.

Captain.
(1) J. H. Brooks, 14th July, 1862.

First-Lieutenant.
(1) T. M. McCants, 14th July, 1862. Killed in battle 3d June, 1864.
(2) Wm. Weston, second-lieutenant 14th July, 1862. Promoted first-lieutenant 3d June, 1864. Resigned 20th January, 1865. Appointed assistant surgeon.
(3) Vacant.

Second-Lieutenant.
(1) Wm. Weston. See above.
(2) B. J. Randall, junior second-lieutenant 14th July, 1862. Promoted 3d June, 1864.

Junior Second-Lieutenant.
(1) B. J. Randall. See above.
(2) A. P. Irby, 27th October, 1864.

ELEVENTH SOUTH CAROLINA REGIMENT.

The officer commanding this regiment reported an absence of records which forbade an attempt to give a roster until 3d May, 1862, when the regiment was reorganized on re-entering the Confederate service. Colonel Wm. C. Heyward had commanded it during that period of its service. The following roster commences with the 3d May, 1862.

After the reorganization Company A, commanded by captain, afterwards general, Stephen Elliott, had by the Secretary at War been permanently detached for service as light artillery.

FIELD OFFICERS.

Colonel.
: (1) D. H. Ellis, 3d May, 1862. Resigned.
: (2) F. H. Gantt, lieutenant-colonel 3d May, 1862. Colonel 22d November, 1862.

Lieutenant-Colonel.
: (1) F. H. Gantt. See above.
: (2) A. C. Izard, Captain 5th July, 1862. Major 22d October, 1862. Lieutenant-Colonel 22d November, 1862.

Major.
: (1) J. J. Harrison, 3d May, 1862. Killed 22d October, 1862.
: (2) A. C. Izard. See above.
: (3) J. J. Gooding, captain 3d May, 1862. Major 27th November, 1862.

STAFF.

Surgeon.
: (1) A. E. Williams, 8th July, 1862.

Assistant Surgeon.
: (1) J. B. Black, 25th June, 1862.

Assistant Quartermaster.
: (1) R. P. Gantt, 9th June, 1862. Transferred (office abolished).

Chaplain.
: (1) A. B. Stephens. (Never served with regiment after it was brigaded.)

Adjutant.
: (1) C. F. Davis, 3d May, 1862.

COMPANY A.

Captain Elliott commanding permanently detached.

COMPANY B.

Captain.
: (1) J. J. Westcoat, 15th May, 1862.

First-Lieutenant.
(1) J. H. Dawson, 3d May, 1862. Resigned.
(2) H. W. Bowman, second-lieutenant 3d May, 1862. First-lieutenant 1st May, 1863.

Second-Lieutenant.
(1) H. W. Bowman. See above.
(2) W. D. Ellis, junior second-lieutenant 12th May, 1863. Second-lieutenant same date.

Junior Second-Lieutenant.
(1) Ed Chaplain, 3d May, 1862. Cashiered.
(2) W. D. Ellis. See above.
(3) John Black, 15th June, 1863.

COMPANY C.
Captain.
(1) T. D. Ledbetter, 3d May, 1862. Killed in battle 14th May, 1864.

First-Lieutenant.
(1) J. J. Guerrard, 3d May, 14th September, 1864. Died of wounds 14th September, 1864.
(2) Vacant.

Second-Lieutenant.
(1) F. R. M. Sineath, 3d May, 1862.

Junior Second-Lieutenant.
(1) Thomas Stall, 3d May, 1862.

COMPANY D.
Captain.
(1) J. J. Gooding. See field officers.
(2) Vacant.

First-Lieutenant.
(1) McD. Gooding, 3d May, 1862.

Second-Lieutenant.
(1) O. G. Sauls, 3d May, 1862. Resigned.
(2) H. K. Huck, junior second-lieutenant 3d May, 1862. Promoted second-lieutenant.

Junior Second-Lieutenant.
(1) Huck. See above,
(2) W. I. Gooding.

COMPANY E.

Captain.
(1) J. H. Mickler, 3d May, 1862.

First-Lieutenant.
(1) Wilson Smith, 3d May, 1862. Died 24th July, 1864.
(2) Thomas Tuten, second-lieutenant May, 1862. First-lieutenant 24th July, 1864.

Second-Lieutenant.
(1) Thomas Tuten. (See above.)
(2) Thomas Hamilton, junior second-lieutenant 3d May, 1862. Second-lieutenant 24th July, 1864.

Junior Second-Lieutenant.
(1) Thomas Hamilton. (See above.)
(2) B. M. Wells, 25th November, 1864.

COMPANY F.

Captain.
(1) B. F. Wyman, 3d May, 1862.

First-Lieutenant.
(1) J. T. Morrison, 3d May, 1862.

Second-Lieutenant.
(1) W. H. Wyman, 3d May, 1862. Resigned.
(2) J. M. Mixson, junior second-lieutenant 3d May, 1862. Second-lieutenant 18th May, 1863.

Junior Second-Lieutenant.
(1) J. M. Mixson. (See above.)
(2) E. H. Wyman, 18th April, 1863.

COMPANY G.

Captain.
(1) Capt. W. D. McMillan, 3d May, 1862.

First-Lieutenant.
(1) W. M. Wolfe, 3d May, 1862. Killed in battle 9th May, 1864.
(2) Vacant.

Second-Lieutenant.
(1) J. H. Brownlee, 3d May, 1862.

Junior Second-Lieutenant.
(1) S. H. Brownlee, 3d May, 1862.

COMPANY H.

Captain.
T. E. Raysor, 3d May, 1862.

First-Lieutenant.
W. G. Wilson, 3d May, 1862.

Second-Lieutenant.
J. P. Minus, 3d May, 1862.

Junior Second-Lieutenant.
L. C. Mellard, 3d May, 1862.

COMPANY I.

Captain.
(1) A. C. Izard. (See field officers.)
(2) W. S. Campbell, first-lieutenant 5th July, 1862. Captain 22d October, 1862.

First-Lieutenant.
(1) W. S. Campbell. (See above.)
(2) E. B. Loyless, second-lieutenant 5th July, 1862. First-lieutenant October, 1862.

Second-Lieutenant.
(1) E. B. Loyless. (See above.)
(2) J. C. Riley, 22d October, 1862. Dead.

Junior Second-Lieutenant.
(1) R. J. Dandridge, 5th July, 1862. Dead.
(2) J. C. Riley. (See above.)
(3) Robert Campbell, promoted second-lieutenant.
(4) George K. Ryan, 25th November, 1864.

COMPANY K.

Captain.
First-Lieutenant.
(1) J. H. Murdaugh, 3d May, 1862. Resigned.
(2) L. B. Murdaugh, second-lieutenant 3d May, 1862. First-lieutenant 29th September, 1863.

Second-Lieutenant.
(1) L. B. Murdaugh. (See above.)
(2) William Johns. (See below.)

Junior Second-Lieutenant.
(1) William Johns, 3d May, 1862. Promoted 29th September, 1863.
(2) F. J. Cassidy, 4th January, 1864.

TWENTY-FIRST SOUTH CAROLINA REGIMENT.

Organized 12th November, 1861. Entered Confederate Service 1st Jan., 1862.

FIELD OFFICERS.

Colonel.
Robert F. Graham, 26th January, 1862.

Lieutenant-Colonel.
(1) Alonzo T. Dargan, 26th January, 1862. Killed in battle 7th May, 1864.
(2) George W. McIvor, major 26th January, 1862. Lieutenant-colonel May, 1864.

Major.
(1) George W. McIvor. (See above.)
(2) J. Harleston Read, Sr., captain 1st January, 1862. Major 7th May, 1864. Retired October 8, 1864.
(3) S. H. Wilds, captain 1st January, 1862. Major 8th October, 1864.

STAFF.

Surgeon. See above.
(1) Theodore A. Dargan. Transferred.
(2) C. Happolt. Resigned.
(3) Samuel Muller, October, 1863.

Assistant Surgeon.
(1) W. A. Player. Resigned October, 1863.
(2) E. B. Smith.

Assistant Quartermaster.
(1) John C. McClenaghan. Died.
(2) N. C. McDuffie.

Adjutant.
(1) Thomas E. Stanley. Appointed A. C. S.
(2) L. F. Dozier. Appointed assistant surgeon.
(3) D. R. W. McIvor, 1st February, 1864.

COMPANY A.

Captain.
(1) J. Harleston Read, Sr., lieutenant. (See field officers.)
(2) Vacant.

First-Lieutenant.
(1) Paul Fitzsimons. Resigned.
(2) Thomas Ford, second-lieutenant 1st January, 1862. First-lieutenant November, 1862.

Second-Lieutenant.
(1) Thomas Ford. (See above.)
(2) J. H. Read, junior, 1st May, 1862.   Junior second-lieutenant November, 1862.

Junior Second-Lieutenant.
(1) C. E. Wiggins, 1st January, 1862.   Resigned.
(2) J. H. Read, Sr. (See above.)
(3) W. Reese Ford, December, 1862.

COMPANY B.

Captain.
(1) S. H. Wilds (see field officers).
(2) Vacant.

First-Lieutenant.
(1) D. C. Milling, 1st January, 1862.   Resigned.
(2) J. W. King, second-lieutenant 1st January, 1862.   First-lieutenant July, 1863.   Resigned December, 1863.
(3) J. S. Hart, junior second-lieutenant 1st January, 1862.   First-lieutenant December, 1863.   Killed 16th May, 1864.
(4) J. C. Clements, junior second-lieutenant December, 1863.   Second-lieutenant July, 1863.   First-lieutenant 1st June, 1864.

Second-Lieutenant.
(1) J. W. King. (See above.)
(2) J. L. Hart. (See above.)
(3) J. C. Clements. (See above.)
(4) T. J. Cannon, October, 1863.

Junior Second-Lieutenant.
(1) J. L. Hart. (See above.)
(2) J. C. Clements. (See above.)
(3) T. J. Cannon. (See above.)
(4) T. D. Zimmerman, 1st June, 1864.

COMPANY C.

Transferred to Twenty-fifth South Carolina Regiment, becoming Co. I of that regiment.

COMPANY D.

Captain.
(1) M. G. Tant, 1st January, 1862.

First-Lieutenant.
(1) H. P. Lynch, 25th January, 1862.   Resigned.
(2) J. H. Villeneure, 1st May, 1862.   Retired.
(3) J. D. Sanders, 28th April, 1864.

Second-Lieutenant.
   (1) J. H. Villeneure. Promoted.
   (2) J. D. Sanders. Promoted.
   (3) A. A. Vanderford. Died 3d July, 1864.

Junior Second-Lieutenant.
   (1) J. D. Sanders. (See above.)
   (2) A. A. Vanderford. (See above.)

COMPANY E.
Captain.
   (1) B. T. Davis, 1st January, 1862. Killed 28th May, 1864.
   (2) Vacant.

First-Lieutenant.
   (1) A. W. Davis, 1st January, 1862.

Second-Lieutenant.
   (1) John A. Craig, 1st January, 1862. Killed 15th May, 1864.
   (2) A. P. Craig, 1st May, 1862.

Junior Second-Lieutenant.
   (1) J. L. Freeman, 1st January, 1862. Resigned.
   (2) A. P. Craig. (See above.)
   (3) Thomas Wilkes, 1st January, 1864. Died 1st September, 1864.
   (4) F. Rivers, 25th November, 1864.

COMPANY F.
Captain.
   (1) J. A. W. Thomas, 1st January, 1862.

First-Lieutenant.
   (1) W. L. Legett, 1st January, 1862. Resigned 1st May, 1862.
   (2) N. A. Easterling, second-lieutenant 1st January, 1862. First-lieutenant 1st May, 1862.

Second-Lieutenant.
   (1) N. A. Easterling. (See above.)
   (2) R. E. Townsend, 1st May, 1862.

Junior Second-Lieutenant.
   (1) R. E. Townsend, 1st January, 1862. (See above.)
   (2) W. D. Cook, 1st May, 1862.

COMPANY G.
Captain.
   (1) E. C. Stockton, 1st January, 1862. Resigned.

25—H

(2) R. Dickerson, first-lieutenant 1st January, 1862. Captain 1st May 1862. Resigned December, 1862.
(3) R. W. Reddy, junior second-lieutenant 1st January, 1862. Second-lieutenant 1st May, 1862. First-lieutenant same date. Captain December, 1862. Retired August, 1864.
(4) Vacant.

First-Lieutenant.
(1) R. Dickerson. (See above.)
(2) R. W. Reddy. (See above.)
(3) J. M. Woodward, second-lieutenant 1st May, 1862. First-lieutenant December, 1862.

Second-Lieutenant.
(1) J. C. Dove, 1st January, 1862. Resigned 1st May, 1862.
(2) R. W. Reddy. (See above.)
(3) J. M. Woodward. (See above.)
(4) W. A. Bevel, December, 1862. Killed 16th May, 1864.
(5) R. A. Hudson, killed June, 1864.
(6) P. Bowles, June, 1864.

Junior Second-Lieutenant.
(1) R. W. Reddy. (See above.)
(2) J. M. Woodward. (See above.)
(3) Samuel Petty, 1st May, 1862. Resigned December, 1862.
(4) W. A. Bevel. (See above.)
(5) R. A. Hudson. (See above.)
(6) A. B. White, 25th November, 1864.

COMPANY H.
Captain.
(1) J. F. A. Elliott, 8th January, 1862. Died December, 1863.
(2) H. P. Spain. Resigned December, 1863.
(3) D. G. DuBose, December, 1863.

First-Lieutenant.
(1) C. I. Flynn, 8th January, 1862. Resigned May, 1862.
(2) H. P. Spain. (See above.)
(3) D. G. DuBose. (See above.)
(4) F. D. Dalrymple. Killed 1st July, 1863.
(5) W. H. Carlisle, 10th August, 1863.

Second-Lieutenant.
(1) H. J. Lee, 8th January, 1862. Resigned 1st May, 1862.
(2) F. D. Dalrymple. (See above.)
(3) D. G. BuBose. (See above.)
(4) W. H. Carlisle. (See above.)
(5) H. Wilson, 10th July, 1864.

Junior Second-Lieutenant.
   (1) W. W. Moore, 8th January, 1862. Resigned 1st May, 1862.
   (2) E. M. Rogers, 1st May, 1862. ·Resigned 10th January, 1863.
   (3) D. G. DuBose. (See above.)
   (4) W. H. Carlisle. (See above.)
   (5) H. Wilson. (See above.)
   (6) P. W. Atkerson, 10th February, 1864.

COMPANY I.

Captain.
   (1) A. M. Woodberry, 1st January, 1862. Resigned 1st February, 1862.
   (2) R. G. Howard, March, 1862.

First-Lieutenant.
   (1) H. A. Gasque, 8th January, 1862. Resigned 1st May, 1862.
   (2) A. B. Jordan, 1st May, 1862. Resigned August, 1862.
   (3) H. M. Cannon, 7th December, 1862. Resigned 20th April, 1864.
   (4) H. J. Chappell, 28th April, 1864. Killed 24th June, 1864.
   (5) W. J. Altman, August, 1864.

Second-Lieutenant.
   (1) H. M. Cannon. (See above.)
   (2) D. Shelly, 7th December, 1862. Resigned December, 1862.
   (3) J. H. Jarrott, died June, 1863.
   (4) H. J. Chappell. (See above.)
   (5) W. J. Altman, June, 1863. (See above.)
   (6) H. M. Cannon (former first-lieutenant re-elected.)

Junior Second-Lieutenant.
   (1) O. B. Jordan, 8th January, 1862. Resigned 1st May, 1862.
   (2) D. Shelly. (See above.)
   (3) J. H. Jarrott. (See above.)
   (4) H. J. Chappell. (See above.)
   (5) W. J. Altman. (See above.)
   (6) H. M. Cannon. (See above.)
   (7) Vacant.

COMPANY K.

Captain.
   (1) J. W. Owens, 8th June, 1862. Killed 15th May, 1864.
   (2) E. B. Green, 15th May, 1864.

First-Lieutenant.
   (1) C. L. Sandsberry, 8th January, 1862. Killed 16th May, 1864.
   (2) H. J. Clifton, 16th May, 1864.

Second-Lieutenant.
   (1) E. B. Green. (See above.)
   (2) Vacant.

Junior Second-Lieutenant.
   (1) H. J. Clifton. (See above.)
   (2) Vacant.

COMPANY L.

Captain.
   (1) N. C. McDuffie, 8th January, 1862. Resigned November, 1862.
   (2) H. Legett, 7th December, 1862. Died 2d July, 1864.
   (3) W. B. Baker, September, 1864.

First-Lieutenant.
   (1) H. Legett, 8th January, 1862. (See above.)
   (2) W. B. Baker, 7th December, 1862. (See above.)
   (3) W. D. Woodberry, 20th September, 1864.

Second-Lieutenant.
   (1) W. B. Baker, 8th January, 1862. (See above.)
   (2) E. L. Sweat, 7th December, 1862. Dropped 7th July, 1864.
   (3) W. D. Woodberry, 7th July, 1864. (See above.)
   (4) Vacant.

Junior Second-Lieutenant.
   (1) E. L. Sweat. (See above.)
   (2) W. D. Woodberry. (See above.)
   (3) Vacant.

TWENTY-FIFTH SOUTH CAROLINA REGIMENT.

Mustered Into Confederate Service 22d July, 1862.

FIELD OFFICERS.

Colonel.
   (1) C. H. Simonton, 22d July, 1862.

Lieutenant-Colonel.
   (1) John G. Pressly, 22d July, 1862. Disabled by wounds 7th May, 1864.

Major.
   (1) John V. Glover, 22d July, 1862. Died from wounds 19th June, 1864.
   (2) Vacant.

STAFF.

Surgeon.
   (1) W. C. Ravenel, 24th May, 1862.

Assistant Surgeon.
    (1) J. M. Warren. Transferred.
    (2) A. J. Beale. Transferred.
    (3) A. G. Bradley, 13th July, 1864.

Chaplain.
    (1) A. T. Porter. Resigned.
    (2) E. C. Winkler. Transferred.
    (3) A. F. Dickson. Resigned September, 1864.
    (4) Vacant.

Assistant Quartermaster.
    (1) J. E. Adger. Transferred to brigade staff July, 1864, (office abolished).

Adjutant.
    (1) George H. Moffet, 30th July, 1862. Transferred to brigade staff July, 1864.

COMPANY A.

Captain.
    (1) James N. Carson, 30th July, 1862.

First-Lieutenant.
    (1) H. B. Olney, 30th April, 1862.

Second-Lieutenant.
    (1) W. W. Finley, 30th April, 1862. Resigned July, 1863.
    (2) James A. Ross, 30th April, 1862. Killed 21st August, 1864.

Junior Second-Lieutenant.
    (1) W. W. Finley. (See above.)
    (2) James A. Ross. (See above.)
    (3) J. S. Hannahan. Transferred.

COMPANY B.

Captain.
    (1) E. W. Lloyd, 24th February, 1862. Retired 22d August, 1864.

First-Lieutenant.
    (1) Robert A. Blum, 24th February, 1862. Killed 5th September, 1863.
    (2) G. S. Burges, second-lieutenant (junior) 24th February, 1862; second-lieutenant September, 1863. First-lieutenant same date. Retired 29th November, 1864.
    (3) H. J. Greer, junior second-lieutenant 22d November, 1864. Second-lieutenant same day. First-lieutenant 29th November, 1864.

Second-Lieutenant.
(1) R. W. Greer, 24th February, 1862. Killed 16th June, 1862.
(2) J. S. Burges. (See above.)
(3) R. M. Taft, 20th June, 1862. Killed 16th May, 1864.
(4) J. S. Hannahan. Transferred 29th November, 1864.
(5) H. G. Greer. (See above.)
(6) Vacant.

Junior Second-Lieutenant.
(1) S. J. Burges. (See above.)
(2) Robert M. Taft. (See above.)
(3) J. E. Bomar, 15th September, 1863. Killed 16th May, 1864.
(4) J. S. Hannahan. (See above.)
(5) H. G. Greer. (See above.)
(6) Vacant.

COMPANY C.
Captain.
(1) John G. Pressley, 5th September, 1861. Promoted lieutenant-colonel.
(2) Thomas J. China, 30th April, 1862. Killed 18th May, 1864.
(3) Calhoun Logan, 18th May, 1864.

First-Lieutenant.
(1) T. J. China, 5th September, 1861. (See above.)
(2) Calhoun Logan, 30th April, 1862. (See above.)
(3) S. J. Montgomery, 18th May, 1864.

Second-Lieutenant.
(1) Calhoun Logan, 30th April, 1862. (See above.)
(2) H. Montgomery, Jr., 5th September, 1861. Killed 5th September, 1863.
(3) B. P. Brockington, 1st May, 1862. Resigned June 26, 1864.
(4) S. J. Montgomery, 19th September, 1863. (See above.)
(5) J. R. China, 26th June, 1864. (See above.)
(6) Vacant.

COMPANY D.
Captain.
(1) W. J. McKerrall, 15th April, 1862.

First-Lieutenant.
(1) J. G. Haselton, 15th April, 1862. Resigned 19th September, 1863.
(2) D. J. McKay, 19th September, 1863.

Second-Lieutenant.
(1) D. J. McKay, 15th April, 1862. (See above.)
(2) P. P. Bethea, 19th September, 1863. Killed 21st August, 1864.
(3) M. L. Smith, 5th October, 1863.

Junior Second-Lieutenant.
(1) P. P. Bethea, 15th April, 1862. (See above.)
(2) M. L. Smith, 5th October, 1863.* (See above.)
(3) N. D. Currie, 27th November, 1864.

COMPANY E.
Captain.
(1) R. D. White, 22d February, 1862. Resigned 3d September, 1862.
(2) N. B. Mazyck, 3d September, 1862.

First-Lieutenant.
(1) N. B. Mazyck, 22d February, 1862. (See above.)
(2) A. J. Mims, 3d September, 1862.

Second-Lieutenant.
(1) M. W. Bythwood, 22d February, 1862. Resigned 3d September, 1862.
(2) A. J. Mims, 22d February, 1862. (See above.)
(3) V. Due, 10th September, 1862.

Junior Second-Lieutenant.
(1) A. J. Mims. (See above.)
(2) V. Due. (See above.)
(3) F. E. Denbee, 13th September, 1862. Resigned 17th February, 1863.
(4) Geo. M. Lalane, 17th February, 1863. Died May, 1864.
(5) John E. Prince, 22d November, 1864.

COMPANY F.
Captain.
(1) J. D. Collier, 22d August, 1861. Died October, 1861.
(2) J. W. Sellers, October, 1861. Resigned 10th April, 1862.
(3) M. H. Sellers, 11th April, 1862. Killed 21st August, 1864.
(4) L. A. Harper, 4th August, 1864.

First-Lieutenant.
(1) J. W. Sellers. (See above.)
(2) L. A. Harper. (See above.)
(3) E. H. Holman, 21st August, 1864. Transferred.

Second-Lieutenant.
(1) E. H. Holman. (See above.)
(2) O. M. Dantzler, promoted lieutenant-colonel Keitt's regiment.
(3) M. H. Sellers. (See above.)
(4) John G. Evans, 11th April, 1862. Killed 21st August, 1864.

Junior Second-Lieutenant.
(1) O. M. Dantzler. (See above.)
(2) M. H. Sellers. (See above.)
(3) L. P. Collier, December, 1861. Resigned 10th April, 1862.
(4) F. E. Shuler, 10th April, 1862. Killed 16th May, 1864.
(5) M. W. Wise, 11th November, 1864.

COMPANY G.

Captain.
(1) John V. Glover, 7th February, 1861. Promoted major.
(2) James F. Izlar, 22d July, 1862.

First-Lieutenant.
(1) James F. Izlar, 15th August, 1861. (See above.)
(2) S. N. Kennerly, 22d July, 1862. Killed 21st August, 1864.

Second-Lieutenant.
(1) S. N. Kennerly, 15th August, 1861. (See above.)
(2) Samuel Dibble, 23d August, 1862.

Junior Second-Lieutenant.
(1) Samuel Dibble, 23d August, 1861. (See above.)
(2) Geo. H. Elliott, 26th July, 1862. Killed 16th May, 1864.
(3) Joseph Graves, 22d November, 1864.

COMPANY H.

Captain.
(1) S. Leroy Hammond, 26th May, 1862. Killed 9th May, 1864.
(2) W. H. Bartless, 21st May, 1864.

First-Lieutenant.
(1) W. H. Seabrook, 26th May, 1862. Killed 21st May, 1864.

Second-Lieutenant.
(1) F. G. Hammond, 26th May, 1862. Killed 9th May, 1864.

Junior Second-Lieutenant.
(1) F. C. Jacobs, 26th May, 1861. Resigned 30th April, 1862.
(2) J. T. Ramsey, June, 1863. Resigned 19th February, 1864.
(3) W. H. Bartless, 27th February, 1864. (See above.)
(4) E. W. Rush, 18th November, 1864.

COMPANY I.

Captain.
(1) E. N. Plowden, 1st January, 1862. Resigned 1st May, 1862.
(2) Y. N. Butler, 1st May, 1862. Resigned 1st June, 1863.
(3) James C. Burgess, 17th June, 1863. Retired 29th August, 1864.
(4) J. J. Logan, 29th August, 1864.

First-Lieutenant.
(1) Y. N. Butler, 1st January, 1862. (See above.)
(2) James C. Burgess, 1st May, 1862. (See above.)
(3) J. J. Logan, 29th August, 1864. (See above.)
(4) F. B. Brown, 29th August, 1864.

Second-Lieutenant.
(1) James C. Burgess, 1st January, 1862. (See above.)
(2) J. J. Logan, 1st May, 1862. (See above.)
(3) F. B. Brown, 29th August, 1864. (See above.)
(4) R. F. Felder.

Junior Second-Lieutenant.
(1) E. R. Plowden, 1st January, 1862. Resigned 1st May, 1862.
(2) F. B. Brown, 1st May, 1862. (See above.)
(3) R. F. Felder, 17th January, 1863. (See above.)

COMPANY K.
Captain.
(1) W. B. Gordon, December 29, 1861. Killed 4th August, 1864.
(2) E. R. Lesesne, 21st August, 1864.

First-Lieutenant.
(1) F. J. Lesesne, 29th December, 1861. Killed 9th May, 1864.
(2) Charles Lesesne, 21st August, 1864.

Second-Lieutenant.
(1) G. N. McDonald, 29th December, 1861. Killed 10th September, 1863.
(2) E. R. Lesesne, 29th December, 1861. (See above.)
(3) W. Salters, 22d November, 1864.

Junior Second-Lieutenant.
(1) E. R. Lesesne. (See above.)
(2) Charles Lesesne. (See above.)
(3) Vacant.

TWENTY-SEVENTH SOUTH CAROLINA REGIMENT.
FIELD OFFICERS.
Colonel.
(1) P. C. Gailliard, major Charleston battalion April, 1862. Colonel 27th October, 1863.

Lieutenant-Colonel.
(1) J. A. Blake, 2d October, 1863.
(2) Major Joseph Abney, 2d October, 1863 (previously major First battalion sharpshooters).

STAFF.
Surgeon.
(1) J. L. Pressly, 2d October, 1863.

Assistant Surgeon.
(1) James P. Cain, 2d October, 1863.

Assistant Quartermaster.
(1) R. P. Smith, August, 1863. Resigned, 1864.

Adjutant.
(1) W. Mason Smith, killed April, 1864.
(2) A. D. Simons, 1864, (18th April).

COMPANY A.

Captain.
(1) F. T. Miles, 17th February, 1862. Resigned 18th April, 1864.
(2) B. W. Palmer, 18th April, 1864. Killed June, 1864.
(3) J. W. Axson, 16th June, 1864. Killed 24th June, 1864.
(4) Vacant.

First-Lieutenant.
(1) B. W. Palmer, 17th February, 1862. (See above.)
(2) J. W. Axson, 18th April, 1864. (See above.)
(3) Vacant.

Second-Lieutenant.
(1) J. W. Axson, 17th February, 1862. (See above.)
(2) J. M. Easterby, 18th April, 1864. Retired July, 1864.
(3) Vacant.

Junior Second-Lieutenant.
(1) John M. Easterby, 17th February, 1862. (See above.)
(2) Vacant.

COMPANY B.

Captain.
(1) Thos. Y. Simons, Jr., 17th February, 1862.

First-Lieutenant.
(1) Wm. Clarkson, 17th February, 1862.

Second-Lieutenant.
(1) Wm. Sinkler, 17th February, 1862.

Junior Second-Lieutenant.
(1) A. H. Masterman, 17th February, 1862. Killed 16th April, 1862.
(2) A. W. Muckenfuss, 16th April, 1862.

COMPANY C.

Captain.
(1) David Ramsey, 17th February, 1862. Killed 18th August, 1863.
(2) Samuel Lord, Jr., 18th August, 1863. Resigned 26th January, 1864.
(3) George Brown, 26th January, 1864. Killed 22d June, 1864.
(4) Vacant.

First-Lieutenant.
(1) Samuel Lord, 17th February, 1862. (See above.)
(2) George Brown, 18th August, 1863. (See above.)
(3) James Campbell, 26th January, 1864.

Second-Lieutenant.
  (1) George Brown, 17th February, 1862. (See above.)
  (2) Henry Walker, April, 1862. Killed July, 1862
  (3) James Campbell, July, 1862. (See above.)
  (4) H. W. Hendricks, January, 1864.

Junior Second-Lieutenant.
  (1) Henry Walker, 17th February, 1862. (See above.)
  (2) James Campbell, 16th June, 1862. (See above.)
  (3) H. W. Hendricks, July, 1862. (See above.)
  (4) George B. Gelling, January, 1864. Killed June, 1864.
  (5) Vacant.

COMPANY D.

Captain.
  (1) Henry C. King, 17th February, 1862. Killed 16th June, 1862.
  (2) J. Ward Hopkins, 16th June, 1862. Killed 16th June, 1864.
  (3) J. A. Cay, 16th June, 1864.

First-Lieutenant.
  (1) J. Ward Hopkins, 17th February, 1862. (See above.)
  (2) B. J. Barbot, 16th June, 1862. Resigned August, 1862.
  (3) J. A. Cay, August, 1862. (See above.)
  (4) J. T. Wells, June, 1864. Retired November, 1864.
  (5) Vacant.

Second-Lieutenant.
  (1) J. J. Edwards, 17th February, 1862. Killed 16th June, 1862
  (2) J. A. Cay, 16th June, 1862. (See above.)
  (3) A. St. John Lance, August, 1862. Killed 15th June, 1864.
  (4) J. T. Wells, 15th June, 1864. (See above.)
  (5) C. M. Hopkins, September, 1864.

Junior Second-Lieutenant.
  (1) B. J. Barbot. (See above.)
  (2) A. St. John Lance. (See above.)
  (3) J. T. Wells. (See above.)
  (4) Vacant.

COMPANY E.

Captain.
  (1) R. Chisholm, October, 1862.

First-Lieutenant.
  (1) S. R. Proctor, 1st July, 1862.

Second-Lieutenant.
  (1) F. J. Dunovant, 3d July, 1862. Resigned October, 1862.
  (2) T. B. Crooker, October, 1862.

Junior Second-Lieutenant.
   (1) J. G. Guignard, 23d June, 1862. Resigned October, 1863.
   (2) S. M. Kemmerlin, October, 1863.

COMPANY F.

Captain.
   (1) Joseph Blythe Alston, 1st July, 1862.

First-Lieutenant.
   (1) J. G. Hugenin, 2d July, 1862.

Second-Lieutenant.
   (1) M. Stewart, 3d July, 1862.

Junior Second-Lieutenant.
   (1) E. P. Cater, 3d July, 1862. Dropped 1864.

COMPANY G.

Captain.
   (1) Henry Buist, 30th June, 1862.

First-Lieutenant.
   (1) E. H. Holman, 1st July, 1862.

Second-Lieutenant.
   (1) Charles J. McBeth, 2d July, 1862.

Junior Second-Lieutenant.
   (1) A. B. White, July, 1862.

COMPANY H.

Captain.
   (1) Edward Magrath, 17th February, 1862. Resigned April, 1862.
   (2) W. H. Ryan, April, 1862. Killed 18th July, 1863.
   (3) James M. Mulraney, 18th July, 1863.

First-Lieutenant.
   (1) Wm. H. Ryan, 17th February, 1862. (See above.)
   (2) James M. Mulraney, April, 1862. (See above.)
   (3) A. E. Allemony, 11th July, 1863. Killed 19th June, 1864.
   (4) Vacant.

Second-Lieutenant.
   (1) James M. Mulraney, 17th February, 1862. (See above.)
   (2) A. E. Allemony, April, 1862. (See above.)
   (3) John Burke, April, 1863. Retired.
   (4) P. R. Hogan, April, 1864.

Junior Second-Lieutenant.
(1) A. E. Allemony, 17th February, 1862. (See above.)
(2) John Burke, August, 1863. (See above.)
(3) P. R. Hogan, August, 1864. (See above.)
(4) J. F. Preston, November, 1864.

COMPANY I.

Captain.
(1) Julius A. Blake, 17th February, 1862. See field officers.
(2) W. D. Walters, August, 1863.

First-Lieutenant.
(1) W. D. Walters, 17th February, 1862. (See above.)
(2) F. C. Lynch, August, 1862. Died October, 1863.
(3) J. C. Salters, October, 1863.

Second-Lieutenant.
(1) F. C. Lynch, 17th February, 1862. (See above.)
(2) J. C. Salters, August, 1863. (See above.)
(3) W. J. Trim, 14th August, 1863.

Junior Second-Lieutenant.
(1) J. C. Salters, 17th February, 1862. (See above.)
(2) W. J. Trim, 14th August, 1863. (See above.)
(3) R. B. Seay, October, 1863. Died 15th May, 1864.
(4) A. G. Cudworth, January, 1865.

COMPANY K.

Captain.
(1) W. Clarkson, September, 1863.

First-Lieutenant.
(1) J. B. Gardiner. August, 1863. Killed 9th September, 1863.
(2) J. G. Harris, 9th September, 1863.

Second-Lieutenant.
(1) J. G. Harris, 14th August, 1863. (See above.)
(2) A. D. Simons, October, 1863.

Junior Second-Lieutenant.
(1) A. D. Simons, 14th August, 1863. (See above.)
(2) R. B. Seay, 14th August, 1863. Died 15th May, 1864.

This company was organized in 1863 by an order from General Beauregard's headquarters, and served as such until the summer of 1864. It was then, by an order of the War Department, disbanded on account of some irregularity in its organization. The men were distributed and the officers provided for. The regiment afterwards had but nine companies.

EDITOR'S APPENDIX

COMPANY A, 21ST REGIMENT, INFANTRY.

Read, J. Harleston.....................................Captain
Ford, Thomas..Captain
Fitzsimons, Paul...............................First Lieutenant
Read, J. Harleston, Jr........................First Lieutenant
Ford, William Rees.. .. ..Second Lieutenant
Wiggins, C.....................................Third Lieutenant
Ford, John...................................First Sergeant
Powers, John J...............................First Sergeant
Bath, Thomas................................Second Sergeant
Avant, Jerry R..............................Third Sergeant
Goude, Francis M............................Fourth Sergeant
Goude, Matthew..............................Fourth Sergeant
Grier, G. Benjamin........................Fifth Sergeant
Avant, Samuel...............................Fifth Sergeant
Cohen, Jacob B..............................Fifth Sergeant
Cribb, Henry...............................First Corporal
Vaux, Robert W.............................First Corporal
Owens, John................................Second Corporal
Peal, Daniel...............................Second Corporal
Owens, Daniel...............................Third Corporal
Goude, Stevens.............................Third Corporal
Etheridge, Isaac J........................Fourth Corporal
Cumbie, Daniel C.. ..   ..Fourth Corporal

PRIVATES.

Ackerman, James	Cribb, William L.	Gradeless, David
Altman, James	Cribb, Frank	Garrett, Wesley
Bone, Benjamin J.	Cartwright, Samuel	Goude, John
Bone, David	Carlisles, F. P.	Goude, Jos.
Cribb, Alex. F.	Collins, Grier B.	Grier, Samuel J.
Cribb, A. Jack	Currie, W. Thomas	Grier, T. Coke
Cribb, John	Cumbie, Elias	Grier, T. B.
Cribb, Benjamin	Cumbie, Moses S.	Grier, W. Kennedy
Cribb, Italy	Carter, George	Grouter, John
Cribb, John F.	Cribb, Emanuel	Griggs, Martin
Cribb, John	Elliott, Washington F.	Hathaway, Sam'l
Cribb, Thomas J.	Exum, Zack J.	Hamlin, Joseph
Cribb, Wesley	Fenters, Thomas J.	Harrelson, Frank

Heyward, James	Moore, Robert	Rawls, James L.
Hinson, John	Moore, Samuel	Rhames, Nathaniel
Holliday, Henry	Nealey, Robert	Rogers, James H.
Howard, Joseph A.	Nichols, Frank	Rowe, Jerry
Hunt, J. Eneas	Owens, Leonard	Rowe, Steven
Jacobs, A. Jack	Owens, Jesse	Roberts, William
Jacobs, James S.	Owens, Elisha	Sanders, Ephraim
Jacobs, N. L.	Owens, Sam	Sanders, George E.
King, Simeon	Owens, Thomas	Skipper, Allen
Kelly, William	Owens, William	Skipper, Timothy
Lewis, Daniel M.	Owens, William W.	Skipper, Sam
Mace, James C.	Palmer, Asa B.	Stokes, Ezander
Miller, E. John	Phillips, John	Smith, Jordan
Miller, Clayton	Phillips, Nelson	Springs, William
Miller, B. Taylor	Powers, Barfield	Turner, Jesse
Moore, David D.	Powers, John H.	Tavean, Augustus
Moore, Ebenezer	Powers, James	West, John M.
Moore, John J.	Powers, Gaidl	Williams, Wilson G.
Moore, John	Powers, Levi	Williams, James R.
Morgan, Isaac	Philips, E.	Webb, T. T.
Myers, Nicholas		

COMPANY B, 21ST REGIMENT, INFANTRY.

Wilds, Samuel H..............................Captain
Milling, David C...........................First Lieutenant
Hart, John L..............................First Lieutenant
Clements, John C..........................First Lieutenant
King, John W.............................Second Lieutenant
Cannon, Theo. J..........................Second Lieutenant
Dargan, Zimmerman T.....................Second Lieutenant
Dargan, Alonzo T.........................Brevet Lieutenant
Dargan, George W.........................First Sergeant
Stuckey, Edmund..........................First Sergeant
Fountain, Wm. A..........................Second Sergeant
Morse, Geo. W............................Sergeant
McCall, J. Muldrow.......................Sergeant
King, J. P. Z............................Sergeant
Williamson, J. Wilds.....................Sergeant
Du Bose, Alfred..........................Sergeant
Frierson, James M........................Sergeant
Crawford, H. L...........................Sergeant
Hepburn, Clem C..........................Sergeant
Watford, L. E............................Corporal
Fruitt, Pinckney.........................Corporal
Beck, Caleb..............................Corporal
Fountain, James C........................Corporal
King, T. Preston.........................Corporal
Kelley, James............................Corporal

PRIVATES.

Abraham, I.	Galloway, James	Parrott, George
Burch, J. Blackwell	Galloway, James E.	Parnell, Robert
Byrd, E. J. C.	Gee, John	Parnell, Thomas
Beasley, David	Garner, Alex	Register, Ira *
Barnes, Hubbard	Galloway, Emory	Register, James
Bass, Jesse	Heath, Andrew	Rhodes, J. Burt
Beasely, Ivy	Hagood, Robert	Rhodes, Joseph
Best, George	Harllee, Thomas H.	Rhodes, Ashton
Beasely, I. M.	Harrell, Joel E.	Rugg, R. P.
Beck, William	Harrell, S. Miller	Smith, Monroe
Backus, John A.	Harrell, James	Stewart, Wm. F.
Bryant, William	Isgette, Allison	Stewart, Samuel
Bryant, W.	Johnson, James T.	Stuckey, Hardy
Beasley, J. Wesley	Kelly, Harrison	Snipes, John
Bryant, Jesse	Kelly, Ladson	Stokes, W. F.
Bryant, Jefferson	Kelly, Wesley	Stokes, Joseph
Barnes, William	Kelly, Wiley	Sanders, H. E. P.
Blackman, Wade	King, Scarboro W.	Sanders, James N.
Blackman, Henry	King, John W.	Truitt, Amos
Bryant, Gray	Lewis, Zack	Williamson, Edwin P.
Collins, Joseph E.	Law, Augustus E.	White, Hugh B.
Cohen, Isaac	Lunn, Thos. E.	White, James A.
Coats, James P.	Lide, Hugh R.	Witherspoon, J. Boyd
Coggeshall, Peter C.	McDonald, Wm.	Yarborough, Thos.
Cole, Wm.	Moore, Frank	Zimmerman, Dozier P.
Du Bose, Theo.	Moore, James	Barnes, Hubbard
Du Bose, Henry K.	Mowry, Peter R.	Blackman, James
Du Bose, Edward C.	McIlveen, John	Blackwell, Jas.
Dozier, Frank	McCall, J. De Witt	Blackwell, Henry
Dargan, J. Furman	McCall, G. Walter	Galloway, Chap.
Dozier, Peter C.	Muldro, Elihu	Gregg, Thomas
Ellis, James	McCall, Geo. W.	Grantham, John J.
Ellis, Wesley	McLendon, Kinnon	Hill, Eli
Fountain, William J.	Northcutt, Travis	Kelly, Thomas
Fields, James	Northcutt, John W.	Kelly, David
Fields, Wesley	Northcutt, William	McKenzie, William
Fields, Bartholomew	Northcutt, Abraham	Nichols, Duncan
Frazier, John	Oats, Jas. P.	Rhodes, Jno. J.
Frazier, Wm. B.	Player, Wm. A.	Rhodes, Wm. E.
Frazier, Charles	Parrott, J. Perry	Teel, James
Flowers, Andrew	Parrott, John	Williamson, Frank
Flowers, Wesley	Parrott, James	Walker, Jesse
Gandy, Ephraim	Parrott, Samuel	Warr, J. J.
Goodson, Joshua	Parrott, Frank	Warr, J. R.
Galloway, George	Parrott, Jesse K.	

COMPANY D, 21ST REGIMENT, INFANTRY.

Tarr, Milford G................................Captain
McIver, George W.........................First Lientenant
Sanders, Samuel D........................First Lieutenant
Lynch, Hugh P...........................Second Lieutenant
Villeneuve, Jos. H.........................Third Lieutenant
Campbell, J. C............................First Sergeant
Wilson, Alexander J.............................Sergeant
Patrick, J. M..................................Sergeant
White, Evander F...............................Sergeant
Vanderford, Alonzo.............................Sergeant
Graffts, C. N..................................Sergeant
Wicker, Rufus W...............................Sergeant
Bryan, William D..............................Sergeant
Ousley, H. C..................................Sergeant
Grimsley, Wesley E............................Corporal
Williams, Alex H..............................Corporal
Chapman, B. F................................Corporal
Powe, J. E...................................Corporal
Eddings, James...............................Corporal
Campbell, H. B...............................Corporal
Powell, Willis A...............................Corporal
Smothers, A..................................Corporal
Graffts, Charles A.............................Corporal
White, Ellison S...............................Corporal

PRIVATES.

Atkinson, Alexander	Cross, Thomas	Edwards, A. H.
Atkinson, J.	Crawford, John T.	Edwards, Franklin
Atkinson, Jas. S. T.	Campbell, John	Edwards, John
Atkinson, William	Cross, Randall	Edwards, John H.
Atkinson, R.	Curry, John C.	Edwards, Joseph C.
Braddock, Ellerbe	Croley, Wm. H.	Ellerbe, A. W.
Braddock, Franklyn	Campion, B. Franklin	Freeman, Chapman
Braddock, John	Dixon, Archibald	Freeman, Irvine
Braddock, Joseph	Dixon, Charles	Freeman, Hamilton
Braddock, George	Dixon, James	Freeman, John
Braddock, Ralph	Dixon, Daniel	Freeman, William
Braddock, Thomas	Dixon, C. P.	Goodwin, Alexander
Benton, E.	Dozier, James W.	Goodwin, William T.
Brock, Calvin	Driggers, H. C.	Goodwin, Samuel
Brock, Thomas	Driggers, Rilah	Grant, John
Brown, J. D.	Edwards, Alexander	Grant, Rilah
Chapman, Calvin E.	Edwards, Alexander	Grant, William
Coker, Caleb	Edwards, J. V.	Grant, Thomas
Coker, Thomas L.	Edwards, Edward	Gulledge, John

26—H

Head, Robinson
Hainey, Benjamin
Hatchell, W. H .
Huggins, John L.
Huggins, S.
Johnson, John W.
Kirvin, G. W.
Lide, Robert T.
McIver, David R. W.
McLaughlin, Alex.
Ousley, J. H.
Outlaw, Edward
Patrick, James M.
Patrick, John C.
Patrick, Eli
Parker, Richard
Parker, Calvin
Pelletier, L. L.

Polk, John B.
Porter, D. J.
Polson, James H.
Powe, Ellerbe F.
Powe, James F.
Powe, Joseph E.
Pressley, William
Richardson, Asa
Robbins, Henry
Roler, William
Rushing, Elijah
Rye, W. W.
Scarboro, William
Smith, W. A.
Talbot, Andrew
Teal, W.
Terry, Champ. P.
Thomas, J. T.

Thomas, J. H.
Thompson, Samuel D.
Thompson, W.
Turnage, William A.
Turnage, William H.
Watson, David
Watson, John
Wade, W. E.
Wetherford, John
Wicker, W. R.
Wilkes, Joseph
Williams, A. H.
Winburn, William
Wise, Charles J.
Yarborough, Geo. H.
Yarborough, Moses C.
Yarborough, William C.
Yarborough, L.

COMPANY E, 21ST INFANTRY.

Davis, B. T...Captain
Davis, A. W..Captain
Craig, John A..Lieutenant
Freeman, Jesse..Lieutenant
Craig, Alex. P..Lieutenant
Wilkes, Thos. W...Lieutenant
Rivers, Fred...Lieutenant
Knight, Moses E...Sergeant
Wilkes, A. M..Sergeant
Oliver, Wm. P...Sergeant
Boan, Archie A..Sergeant
Wadsworth, Lewis H..Corporal
Douglass, Duncan D..Corporal
Johnson, Nelson...Corporal
Craig, William D..Corporal
Boan, Archie E..Corporal

PRIVATES.

Allan, Robert A.
Alexander, Benjamin F.
Boan, Charles D.
Boan, Richard J.
Boan, Matthew
Boan, James D.
Boan, John
Boan, Daniel

Burr, Alston
Burr, Jacob
Burr, Burrell
Brown, Stephen
Brown, William
Brown, Wilson
Brown, Wilson, Jr.
Brown, John B.

Brown, James
Brown, Valentine T.
Bachelor, Joel
Cato, Henry
Cato, John
Cassidy, Andrew J.
Cross, William
Cross, William F.

Cross, Henry
Crowley, Mally
Crowley, Andrew J.
Coley, E. B.
Davis, John W.
Davis, Elisha
Davis, Thomas P.
Davis, Thomas F.
Davis, William A.
Davis, Wm. B., Jr.
Davis, John F.
Davis, Wm. R.
Dickson, John W.
Dickson, Richard
Dickson, William
Dickson, Samuel
Dickson, Elias
Dixon, Henry
Edwards, B. Frank
Ellis, Archibald
Elliott, Franklin
Freeman, William
Freeman, Lewis L.
Freeman, John
Gardner, John
Gainey, Green
Gainey, George
Gainey, William
Gandy, Ephraim
Huggins, John C.
Huggins, Nathan
Huggins, Jacob

Huggins, John
Huggins, Solomon
Jordan, William
Jordan, William C. A.
Jordan, Richard
Jordan, Thomas M.
Jordan, John
Jordan, Allan
Jordan, J. Henry
Jordan, Wm. E.
Jordan, Alex, Sr.
Jordan, Alex, Jr.
Johnson, Henry
Johnson, John R.
Johnson, Wesley
Jones, John
Jones, William
Keith, Abel
Kesiah, John H. M.
Lisenby, Samuel
Langley, William
Langley, John B.
Langley, Robert
Levi, A.
McFarland, Archibald
McFarland, Duncan
McLean, John J.
McLean, John P.
Merriman, Burrell
Odom, William
Odom, J. Kelly
Odom, Morgan C. T.

Odom, Gillam
Odom, Elisha
Oliver, Steven
Parker, James
Parker, Badgegood
Perkins, James F.
Purvis, James
Purvis, William
Purvis, John
Purvis, Alex.
Polson, Amos
Polson, John
Polson, Robert
Polk, Robert
Polk, James
Perdue, Archibald
Perdue, Colleton
Roscoe, Joseph F.
Rickett, William
Rivers, Mark
Tarlton, Andrew J.
Turnage, Robert B.
Turnage, James P.
Teal, William W.
Teal, T. Benj.
Teal, David R.
Teal, William
Talbert, Archibald
White, Hosea
Wilkes, Daniel
Young, Jeremiah B.

COMPANY F, 21ST REGIMENT, INFANTY.

Thomas, J. Alexander W................................Captain
Leggett, William L.................................First Lieutenant
Easterling, Nelson A...............................First Lieutenant
Townsend, Robert E................................First Lieutenant
Cook, William D..................................Second Lieutenant
Hamer, Phillip M...................................First Sergeant
Moore, John R.....................................First Sergeant
Easterling, Andrew B.............................Second Sergeant
McCaskill, Neal C................................Second Sergeant
Adams, William F.................................Second Sergeant
Easterling, Jesse...................................Third Sergeant
Odom, William B....................................Third Sergeant

Lester, Thomas C.. .. ..Fourth Sergeant
Quick, Herbert T.. .. ..Fourth Sergeant
Feagan, Edward J.. .. ..Fourth Sergeant
McIntyre, John T.. .. ..Sergeant-Major
Moore, Alfred W.. .. ..First Corporal
Gibson, James M.. .. ..Second Corporal
Hamer, Robert H.. .. ..Third Corporal
Stubbs, D. Derrick.. .. ..Third Corporal
St. Clair, Duncan M.. .. ..Fourth Corporal
Easterling, George W.. .. ..Fourth Corporal
Newton, David D.. .. ..Fourth Corporal

PRIVATES.

Adams, Joshua D.	Dunn, William	Leggett, A. J.
Adams, John R.	Dunn, Thomas	Locklear, Alexander
Adams, William L.	Easterling, A. Jackson	Locklear, Sandy
Anderson, John G.	Easterling, Harris R.	Manship, Aaron
Anderson, William T.	Easterling, Joel A.	McCall, John N.
Barrington, Peter	Easterling, John A.	McDaniel, Ira W.
Barrington, Phillip	Easterling, William L.	McKenzie, Joseph C.
Barrentine, William	Easterling, William T.	McInague, John R.
Bennett, Frank	Easterling, John L.	Moore, Benjamin J.
Bennett, Thomas	Easterling, James J.	Nelson, Erwin
Bowen, Charles	Fields, Silas	Newton, John C.
Bowen, Frank L.	Fletcher, Thomas	Odom, D. A.
Bigman, George	Gay, P. W.	Odom, S. Durant
Bristow, David M.	Gibson, Andrew H.	Odom, Henry
Bristow, Robert N.	Guin, George	Odom, James E.
Bristow, Wiley J.	Grice, Ephraim G.	Odom, Samuel F.
Bundy, G. Washington	Hamer, Abner C.	Owens, John
Butler, Elijah	Hamer, Charles H.	Pate, Willis
Butler, William, Sr.	Hamer, Elijah C.	Pate, Alfred D.
Butler, William, Jr.	Hamer, James C.	Peel, Eli T.
Calder, John D.	Hamer, Thomas C.	Peel, Thomas
Calder, Stanford	Haywood, Anderson	Polson, William
Cottingham, Twiman	Haywood, Isham	Powers, Erwin
Covington, Abijah B.	Haywood, William	Quick, Angus
Covington, Alfred D.	Herndon, Dave	Quick, Henry
Creech, David L.	Hewstiss, George Wash-	Quick, Jno. B.
Clark, Archie	ington	Roscoe, Alexander H.
Clark, John	Howard, John	Roscoe, William M.
Cummings, Elisha	Hudson, Joshua H.	Scott, Wash.
Coward, John H.	Jacobs, Snowden	Smith, Cholson
Currie, Neal R.	Jacobs, B. L.	Spears, James A.
David, William J.	Johnson, Wm. D. Chand-	Steen, Allen
Dial, Jacob	ler	Stephens, James E.

Stephens, Reuben	Stubbs, Thomas E.	Wallace, Thomas G.
Stogner, William	Stubbs, Thorough-	Weathersford, James
Stogner, Thomas	good P.	Williams, Henry
Stubbs, David	Tait, William J.	Williams, Samuel
Stubbs, Albert A.	Terrell, William T.	Willis, Allen
Stubbs, Campbell E.	Thomas, Joseph	Wise, William W.
Stubbs, John B.	Turnage, Luke	Woodall, Ransom
Stubbs, Samuel F.	Usher, M.	Williams, John
Stubbs, Maston W.	Walters, Reuben	

COMPANY G, 21ST REGIMENT, INFANTRY.

Stockton, E. C...Captain
Dickenson, Robert......................................Captain
Reddy, R. W...Captain
Dove, J. Calhoun..............................Second Lieutenant
Woodward, James M............................Second Lieutenant
Bevil, W. A...................................Second Lieutenant
Bowles, Peter................................Second Lieutenant
Boyle, John..................................Second Lieutenant
Hudson, R. A.................................Second Lieutenant
Petty, S. D..................................Second Lieutenant
Brown, Thomas J..................................Sergeant
Doten, Thomas J..................................Sergeant
Mathews, Samuel P................................Sergeant
Wells, Ebby M...............................First Sergeant
Codey, Moses M...................................Corporal
Brown, T. B......................................Corporal
Rhodes, John B...................................Corporal
Howell, T. J.....................................Corporal

PRIVATES.

Barfield, Peter	Douglass, H.	Hunter, John
Blackman, Wade W.	Ellerby, A. Cooper	Hall, Daniel
Belk, James K.	Ellerby, Hossack	Harrell, S. K.
Booth, J. D.	Ellerby, Z.	Hawkins, John
Byrd, Mathew	Farmer, Brantley	Hearon, John Z.
Byrd, W.	Galloway, S. P.	Howell, E.
Byrd, John	Galloway, Ferdinand	Howell, J. D.
Browder, John	Gandy, David R. W.	Hutson, W. J.
Campbell, J. H.	Gandy, J.	Jenkins, James
Cannon, L. W.	Griggs, W. C.	Johns, D. R.
Coker, R. E.	Griggs, Clement	Jones, Riley
Cook, B. D.	Gainey, John	Knight, Frank
Dove, A. B. C.	Gainey, Thomas W.	Kelley, Simon
Dagan, W. H.	Gairey, Evander	Kelley, Thomas
Dyson, Archibald S.	Graves, John	Landreth, Peter

Lundy, Allison	Parnell, A. W.	Tiner, Hugh
Marshall, J. R.	Polson, R. H.	Tiner, John
McKissick, Wm. J.	Polson, W. H.	Teel, James
McClendon, J. M.	Poe, James	Toler, R. E.
McClendon, L. A.	Ruggs, E. T.	Vann, Jerry E.
Miller, J. H.	Ruggs, Andrew J.	Webb, E. P.
Morrell, E.	Sandsbury, Daniel	Winburn, Joseph
Nettles, W. W.	Spence, Moses E.	Winn, Colin
O'Nails, James	Spell, Gillam	Wells, T. G. F.
Parker, T. F.	Stanley, John T.	

COMPANY H, 21ST REGIMENT, INFANTRY.

Elliott, John F. A..Captain
Spain, Hartwell...Captain
Du Bose, D. G..Captain
Flinn, C. J...First Lieutenant
Dalrymple, Thos. H.....................................First Lieutenant
Carlisle, W. H...First Lieutenant
Lee, Henry J...Second Lieutenant
Atkinson, Peter W....................................Second Lieutenant
Rogers, Elisha M.......................................Third Lieutenant
Wilson, Harvey...Third Lieutenant
Moore, W. W...Third Lieutenant
Odom, Joel...First Sergeant
Lawson, W. R. S...First Sergeant
Elliott, Z. W..Sergeant
DuBose, Wm. H. B...Sergeant
Mixon, W. P..Sergeant
Dalrymple, Peter L..Sergeant
Beasley, Abram..Corporal
DuBose, Henry J...Corporal
Stokes, Henry Y...Corporal
Witherspoon, David W..Corporal
Best, William...Corporal

PRIVATES.

Andrews, Thomas	Best, Nicholas B.	Cody, M. M.
Abbott,	Best, Robert D.	Campbell, James H.
Andrews, Aris	Blackman, Henry	DuBose, Robert S.
Boykin, Hiram	Buffkin, Hugh	DuBose, Andrew
Boykin, Harrison	Blackwell, James	DuBose, Jeremiah
Boykin, W. Franklin	Brown, William	Davis, Thomas
Boykin, Henry	Beasley, Elijah	Dean, J. L.
Bass, Burrell	Bruce, George H.	Elliott, J. Franklin
Best, James P.	Crosswell, Wm. H.	Elmore, Wilson W.

Elmore, Simpson E.	Hill, James	Red, J. F.
Elmore, Ellis	Inkles, Richard	Rogers, Evans
Galloway, L. C.	Jones, Henry	Rhodes, John B.
Galloway, Timothy P.	Joy, Henry M.	Stuckey, Howell C.
Galloway, J. Ferdinand	Josey, J. R.	Stuckey, Wiley D.
Galloway, Thomas	King, William	Scarborough, George P.
Galloway, Pipkin	King, Wesley	Smith, Phillip D'.
Galloway, Abram M.	Kelly, Thomas	Stewart, Ira
Grantham, Robert W.	Lawson, Joseph T.	Skinner, Simpson
Gardner, John B.	Logan, Joseph	Skinner, James
Grooms, Reese	Lee, Judge L.	Skinner, Wm. W.
Herring, William	McLendon, Robert	Skinner, Thomas C.
Hearon, Joseph N.	Mixon, M. Townsend	Skinner, R. Zimmerman
Hearon, Wm. E.	Marshall, William H.	Skinner, Franklin
Huggins, Alex. G.	Moore, Wesley	Shumake, Morgan'
Huggins, John H.	McKenzie, Joseph R.	Stokes, Henry Y.
Huggins, W. Middleton	McKenzie, Israel G.	Stokes, W. Elias
Hurst, Henry W.	Nicholson, James	Thomas, Henry B.
Hurst, Samuel F.	Newsom, Bennett	Woodham, H. Middleton
Hurst, Simeon	Outlaw, Benjamin	Woodham, John E.
Harris, Wiley M.	Peebles, Edward S.	Woodham, Jared
Harris, Franklin H.	Parnell, Henry E.	Woodham, Emberry
Harrison, Madison W.	Parnell, T. Joshua	Witherspoon, David
Howell, Alex.	Plummer, E. B.	Witherspoon, Jefferson W.
Howell, J. Barry	Quick, James D.	
Harrell, Nathan	Quick, Jesse E.	Warren, Gilham
Harrell, Robert	Register, Calvin	Warren, William

COMPANY I, 21ST REGIMENT, INFANTRY.

Woodberry, Evander M..........................Captain
Howard, Richard G..........................Captain
Gasque, Henry A.....................First Lieutenant
Cannon, Henry M.....................First Lieutenant
Shelly, David.....................Second Lieutenant
Jordan, A. Bennett.............Brevet Second Lieutenant
Jarrett, J. Alston.....................Second Lieutenant
Altman, Wm. J.....................Second Lieutenant
Chappell, Henry C.....................Second Lieutenant
Noble, J. Hardy.....................First Sergeant
Gasque, C. Marion.....................Second Sergeant
McDaniel, John R.....................Third Sergeant
Jordan, John S.....................Fourth Sergeant
Cannon, George H.....................Fifth Sergeant
Hucks, John R.....................Sergeant
Dozier, J. Valentine.....................First Corporal
Cannon, Wm. H.....................Second Corporal
Wright, John W.....................Third Corporal
Altman, J. Hamilton.....................Fourth Corporal

PRIVATES.

Avant, Orlando R.	Ham, Charles W.	Richardson, David W.
Altman, Samuel S.	Herrin, Allison W.	Richardson, J. Graves
Altman, J. Benjamin	Herrin, David F.	Richardson, James H.
Altman, J. Wesley	Hewitt, Thomas	Richardson, Thomas J.
Bone, John	Hewitt, Joseph R.	Rowell, James W.
Bone, Robert G.	James, James V.	Rowell, David A.
Bailey, G.	Jarrett, James B.	Rowell, Valentine
Boatright, Robert S.	Jarrett, Charles Ed.	Rowell, William P.
Brown, George W.	Jordan, W. King	Stanley, John F.
Brown, Henry	Lowrimore, John	Sampson, Joseph
Brown, Jesse C.	Lowrimore, Moses	Sampson, Samuel
Brown, William J.	Lowrimore, Hanson L.	Shelley, John C.
Brown, Evander	Marlow, R. William	Shelley, Zachariah
Bellflowers, Jesse	Martin, Stephen H.	Shackleford, Stephen P.
Burroughs, Thomas	Martin,	Sineath Joseph P.
Cannon, Samuel W.	McClellan, Daniel B.	Tindal, Emanuel
Collins, Valentine	McClellan, Enos	Tindal, Solomon
Cook, James Ervin	McDaniel, J. Randall	Tucker, John
Davis, James H.	Miller, John P.	Turbeville, Asa
Davis, H. Foster	Pace, James A.	Williams, Henry S. B.
Dozier, John F.	Powell, Noah P.	Williams, John C.
Dozier, Tully	Parker, Thomas	Williams, Jacob H.
Foxworth, Ervin J.	Prior, William M.	Williams, Jordan
Foxworth, Joseph B.	Rogers, Thomas G.	White, James H.
Gasque, Ervin A.	Rogers, J. Benjamin	Whaley, John H.
Gregg, Thomas C.	Richardson, Pinckney G.	Whaley, William M.
Gregg, Wesley L.	Richardson, E. Franklin	Wall, Lawson J.
Gunter, William	Richardson, Thomas	Wallace, John J.

COMPANY K, 21ST REGIMENT.

J. W. Owens..Captain
Cowen, L. Sandsbury....................................First Lieutenant
Green, E. B...Second Lieutenant
Henry, J. Clifton.....................................Third Lieutenant
Bristow, James, T.......................................First Sergeant
Brand, Alvin..Second Sergeant
Brockington, E. S......................................Third Sergeant
McLeod, Geo. W..Fourth Sergeant
Lockhart, O. Francis...................................First Corporal
Hodge, William H......................................Second Corporal
Hilary, Powers..Third Corporal
Hall, Isaac...Fourth Corporal

PRIVATES.

Ard, Ben	Gregg, Eli A.	Nettles, Robert
Ard, E. H.	Gatlin, John G.	Oliver, Claton
Anderson, Stephen H.	Grantham, James	Oliver, Sidney
Anderson, Brylie H.	Gowdy, Benjamin	Oliver, Lazrus
Anderson, Joel	House, George	Purvis, Henry
Anderson, Wiley H.	Hicks, John	Purvis, Thomas
Anderson, S. Pinckney	Hall, James	Powers, Thomas J.
Anderson, Silas	Hooten, John	Pierce, John B.
Anderson, Miles R.	Hudson, Thomas	Revell, George W.
Anderson, Jesse.	Hodge, John C.	Scaff, Samuel
Amerson, Cooper	Hayley, James	Scaff, James R.
Amerson, Capers	Haley, Jesse	Scaff, Mathew
Brand, William	Harper, Ricks	Smith, Thomas
Bates, George W.	Hewitt, Thomas	Sandsbury, Burdell
Brown, Nelson	Jordan, Henry	Stuart, James
Brown, Samuel	Jeffords, S. King	Thornhill, Evander
Brown, George	Jeffords, Joseph	Thornhill, John
Byrd, George	Jeffords, John	Truitt, Pinckney
Blackwell, James H.	Jeffords, Rufus J.	Tolar, Street
Cade, John L.	Johnson, John W.	Tolar, Robert
Cooper, Joel J.	Jackson, John	Vaughro, Henry H.
Carter, Ira	Jordan, Andrew	Wilson, Geo. W.
Clifton, M. Webster	King, James	Wilson, John W.
Cotingham, William	Kilpatrick, Reese	Wilson, John
Cook, Ezecal	Kilpatrick, William	Wilson, Archibald S.
Crawford, Henry I.	Langston, John	Wilson, William C.
Chandler, Daniel S.	Lawrence, Moses	White, Jarry
Cole, Cefus F.	Lee, William	Windham, William J.
Dority, John	Loyd, Wesley	Windham, Samuel
DuBose, Zimmerman J.	McCall, John	Wadford, Lazarus
DuBose, Elias H.	Mims, Jacob	Wadford, William C.
Davis, Thomas H.	Mims, Jesse	Weatherspoon, Jefferson
Davis, George W.	Mims, James E.	Wadford, Nelson
Dewitt, Samuel	Marshall, William	Wooten, John
Daws, A. S.	Muldrow, Andrew	Young, William H.
Gray, Daniel A.	McKoy, Samuel	Young Thomas

COMPANY L, 21ST REGIMENT.

McDuffie, Neal C.. .. .. .Captain
Le Gette, Hanibal.. .. .. .Captain
Baker, Wm. C.. .. .. .Captain
Woodberry, Wm. D.. .. .. .First Lieutenant
Sweet, Ebenezer L.. .. .. .Second Lieutenant
Gibson, Albert.. .. .. .Second Lieutenant
Williamson, Robert L.. .. .. .First Sergeant

Gasque, A. M.................................First Sergeant
Collins, Wm. T.................................Sergeant
Huggins, Christopher..............................Sergeant
Reaves, Robert H...........................Orderly Sergeant
Willimson, Leonard..........................Fourth Sergeant
Coleman, Samson J................................Corporal
Baker, William W.................................Corporal
Lane, Joseph V...................................Corporal
Sawyer, James A..................................Corporal
Carmichael, Franklin.............................Corporal
White, Augustus K................................Corporal

PRIVATES.

Ammons, W. Edward	Carmichael, J. B.	Haywood, James
Ammons, H. Calhoun	Cale, E.	Herring, Pinckney L.
Ayers, William D.	Cohen, Isaac	Harrell, Ephraim
Ayers, Joseph	Carter, John	Jones, Frederick D.
Ayers, Thomas	Deas, Franklin	Jones, James A.
Avant, Jordan	Dennis, George W.	Jordan, William
Anderson, James R.	Edwards, Richard W.	James, William P.
Bailey, Nias	Evans, N. J.	Jacobs, M.
Bailey, Wesley	Flowers, Elly	Le Gette, Henry C.
Bailey, Mathew	Flowers, William	Le Gette, Levi
Baker, John E.	Fowler, James F.	Lane, Robert L.
Baker, Benjamin B.	Frierson, J. M.	Lambert, Robert
Bird, Hugh G.	Gardner, Daniel	Martin, Mac F.
Bethea, Edwin A.	Gerald, John	McCall, Barney
Brown, William	Gasque, J. Martin	Matthews, Samuel P.
Brown, John O.	Gasque, Samuel O.	Miller, Charles W.
Beaty, Thomas	Gasque, Wesley E.	Oliver, Alexander R.
Campbell, Mike C.	Gasque, Wm. B. R.	Powell, William
Clarke, Robert C.	Gasque, Henry	Potter, James
Cooper, Ralph	Gibson, Robert W.	Porter, James
Criddle, James R.	Gibson, Oscar E.	Porter, S. Goss
Collins, John W.	Gibson, John S.	Pitman, David G.
Collins, David C.	Godbold, Huger	Richardson, Stephen
Collins, Joel B.	Godbold, Thomas W.	Richardson, John
Collins, Shadrack	Hair, James	Richardson, Thomas
Collins, Richard	Huggins, S. Lewis	Rogers, Jno. W.
Carmichael, Archibald B.	Huggins, Wesley	Rogers, Owen M.
Carmichael, Evander	Huggins, Wm. D.	Rogers, Carey
Carmichael, Franklin	Huggins, William	Rogers, Fred. G.
Carmichael, Archie	Harrelson, John L.	Rogers, Bethel
Carmichael, Judson D.	Harrelson, Timothy	Rogers, T.
Carmichael, Daniel M.	Harrelson, Benjamin	Rowell, Valentine
	Haywood, John W.	Rowell, William

Robertson, L. D.	Smith, Enoch	Williamson, Bright J.
Sawyer, John	Thompson, James T.	Williamson, Joseph M.
Sawyer, Thomas	Tedder, Daniel M.	Williamson, David R.
Shelley, Joseph G.	Townsend, Francis M.	Williamson, Sol. M.
Snipes, Moses	Thomas, Samuel B.	Williamson, Samuel W.
Summerford, William	Tyler, Richard	Worrell, James
Shackleford, John B.	Webb, John	
Shaw, Benjamin A.	Wise, J. M.	

COMPANY A, 1ST REGIMENT.

Glover, Thomas Jamison.. .. ..Captain
Glover, John Vingard.. .. ..Captain
Felder, John H.. .. ..First Lieutenant
Izlar, Jas. Ferdinand.. .. ..First Lieutenant
Kennerly, Samuel N.. .. ..Second Lieutenant
Dibble, Samuel.. .. ..Second Lieutenant
Felder, Edmund J.. .. ..Sergeant
Williams, James A.. .. ..Sergeant
Elliott, Geo. H.. .. ..Sergeant
Legare, Thomas K.. .. ..Sergeant
Ray, W.. .. ..Sergeant
Frederick, J. P.. .. ..Sergeant
Fox, T. S.. .. ..Sergeant
Zimmerman, Daniel.. .. ..Sergeant
Izlar, Benj. P.. .. ..Sergeant
Hook, John H.. .. ..Sergeant
Rast, J. E.. .. ..Sergeant
Izlar, William.. .. ..Sergeant
Culler, L. Hayne.. .. ..Sergeant
Andrews, Thadeus C.. .. ..Corporal
Rowe, Daniel Jacob.. .. ..Corporal
Shuler, B. M.. .. ..Corporal
Wiles, Robert H.. .. ..Corporal
Wannamaker, Francis Marion.. .. ..Corporal
Paulling, W.. .. ..Corporal
Kohn, Theodore.. .. ..Corporal
Robinson, Jude.. .. ..Corporal
Kennerly, J. R.. .. ..Corporal

PRIVATES.

Andrews, E. W.	Ayers, D. A.	Brooker, James
Austin, M. L.	Ballentine, S.	Brunson, William
Avant, J. H.	Buzzard, J. C.	Buyck, F. G.
Antilley, F. M.	Brickle, V. V.	Baxter, J. D.
Ashe, John	Brooker, A. F.	Baxter, E. J.

Black, M. G.
Boyd, M. T.
Brickle, V. V.
Brooker, A. F.
Brooker, James
Brunson, Wm.
Buyck, F. J.
Bozard, J. S.
Bozard,
Bull, W. A.
Crawford, W. E.
Crider, G. B.
Cannon, James
Carson, B. A.
Champy, A.
Champy, T.
Church, W. A.
Collins, A.
Conner, A. A.
Conner, F.
Crider, J. H.
Culclasure, D. J.
Curtis, G. H.
Culler, J. W.
Dantzler, D. W.
Dantzler, M. J. D.
Denaux, E. C.
Dolen, M.
Doscher, Eiber
Doyle, P.
Ehney, W. L.
Ehney, E. T.
Ezekial, E.
Fanning, John A.
Felder, Samuel J.
Felder, E. L.
Gardner, D.
Glover, W. P.
Glover, C. L.
Grambling, Martin
  Luther
Glover, Mortimer
Hall, S. P.
Hook, S. P.
Hitchcock, L. W.

Houser, E. M.
Houser, F. D.
Houser, J. D.
Houser, G. M.
Inabinet, Frank S.
Inabinet, A. J.
Inabinet, C. G.
Irick, L. A.
Izlar, L. T.
Izlar, A. M.
Inabinet, J. M.
Izlar, B. W.
Jenkins, L. W.
Jaudon, P. B.
Jaudon, S. W. A.
Kelly, Thomas
Kemmerlin, T. A.
King, W.
Legare, W. W.
Law, W. P.
Lucas, A.
Meredith, W. C., Jr.
Murphy, E.
Myers, Esau
Miller, A. V.
Moody, W. A.
Murph, J. C.
Murrow, O. H.
Meredith, W. C.
Norris, T. P.
Ott, W. F.
Ott, J. V.
Pape, F. W.
Pike, Jno. C.
Pool, T. C.
Pooser, E. E.
Pooser, J. P.
Pooser, W. H., Jr.
Pooser, W. H., Sr.
Pooser, J. H.
Prickett, J. H.
Prusner, William
Pooser, William
Rawlinson, M. A.
Rawlinson, A. S.

Robinson, Murray,
Ray, John D.
Reynolds, F. S. H.
Reed, J. V.
Reed, J. N.
Riley, John W.
Rickenbacker, M.
Rowe, A. G.
Rush, H. M.
Ruple, Andrew J.
Rowe, William Sabb.
Riley, D. A.
Sanders, B. H.
Shoemaker, Ira T.
Shunight, L.
Sanders, J. D. D.
Shuler, J. M.
Shuler, J. W.
Smoak, B. Z.
Smoak, H. O.
Staley, E. S.
Stroman, D. P.
Stroman, Michael
  Gramling
Stroman, P. B.
Summers, Jacob W.
Summers, William
Stroman, J. P.
Tatum, John S. C.
Taylor, W. W.
Tucker, J. R.
Tyler, H. Alonzo
Valentine, W. W.
Van Tassel, James
Williams, W. E.
Williams, S. W.
Wolf, Z. Marion
Wolf, E. M.
Wolf, J. J.
Wright, R.
Wolf, Andrew J.
Zeigler, H. H.
Zeigler, M. C.
Zeigler, John A.

COMPANY B, 1ST REGIMENT.

Livingston, Daniel.................................Captain
Pou, B. F.....................................First Lieutenant
Jones, James D.............................Second Lieutenant
Knotts, Joseph E...........................Second Lieutenant
Ehney, W. L..................................First Sergeant
Geiger, F. J.......................................Sergeant
Menecken, J. A...................................Sergeant
Phillips, James H.................................Sergeant
O'Cain, J. A.......................................Sergeant
Fanning, J. H.....................................Corporal
Inabinet, James A................................Corporal
Martin, H. O......................................Corporal
Geiger, R. Baker..................................Corporal

PRIVATES.

Axson, J. W.	Horsey, J. H. W.	Rucker, U. S. L.
Brown, J. F.	Hughes, W. F.	Redmond, Job
Brown, E.	Huffman, Jacob	Robinson, Jos. F.
Brown, William	Huffman, J. H. S.	Richter, J. J.
Brown, L. S.	Huffman, J. W.	Riley, J. W.
Brown, S. W.	Hooker, David H.	Stevenson, Benjamin
Brown, J. P.	Hildebrand, D. L.	Stevenson, W. M.
Bailey, J.	Hooker, F. F. M.	Stevenson, J. P.
Bennett, J. F.	Inabinet, P. D. P.	Smithheart, John
Courtney, P.	Inabinet, J. V.	Smith, J. W.
Craft, J. S.	Johnson, P. P.	Smith, W. D.
Craft, T. W.	Jeffcoat, H. E.	Stricklin, H. S.
Culclusure, A. D.	Jeffcoat, S. W.	Slagle, W. F.
Crim, D. G.	Kaigler, F. G.	Sightler, T. M.
Corbett, M. F.	Knotts, T. D.	Sightler, S. B.
Crider, D. H.	Lucas, J. R.	Sightler, W. S.
Cook, W. D.	Lucas, Rufus	Stabler, G. W.
Davis, T. J.	Lorick, P. C.	Schumpert, S. A.
Dannelly, G. W.	Lorick, J. H.	Ulmer, A.
Douglass, M. P.	Martin, A. T.	Vann, T. J.
Fanning, Jos. A.	Martin, J. J.	Williams, F.
Flake, J. R.	Mack, B. A.	Williams, James
Flake, J. W.	McIver, J. J.	Williams, M. F.
Flake, J. T.	Ott, James P.	Wise, A. J.
Flake, T. B.	Peeples, Jos. E.	Whetstone, J. A.
Furtick, J. H.	Plimale, A.	Yon, W. P.
Furtick, L. D.	Quattlebaum, J. J.	Zeigler, D. W.
Hutto, R. S.	Rucker, G.	Zeigler, D. A.
Hutto, James	Rucker, A. E.	

COMPANY C, 1ST REGIMENT.

Kirkland, B. B.. .. ..Captain
Brabham, J. F.. .. ..Captain
Hayes, J. N.. .. ..First Lieutenant
Barker, R. S.. .. ..Second Lieutenant
Hogg, R. B.. .. ..Third Lieutenant
Barker, J. H.. .. ..Third Lieutenant
Brabham, C. F.. .. ..First Sergeant
Brabham, H. J.. .. ..Second Sergeant
Williams, J. A.. .. ..Third Sergeant
Breland, W. E.. .. ..Fourth Sergeant
Young, G. F.. .. ..Fifth Sergeant
Hayes, J. A.. .. ..Fifth Sergeant
Kirkland, R. C.. .. ..First Corporal
Burke, W. B.. .. ..Second Corporal
Wilson, L. J.. .. ..Third Corporal
Bowers, M. C.. .. ..Fourth Corporal

PRIVATES.

Allen, J. M.
Barker, Owen W.
Bennett, J. W.
Bennett, J. A.
Best, L. C.
Best, W. W.
Billing, E. W.
Blackwood, F. A.
Blackwood, T. W.
Bowers, E.
Bowers, M.
Brabham, W. R.
Brabham, J. Medicus
Bonnett, R. W.
Connelly, William
Cope, Mc.
Cradock, W. P.
Cone, G. P.
Creech, F. H.
Creech, J. W.
Curtain, Jack
Deer, Anderson

Frohberg, H. C.
Frohberg, P. A.
Garvin, C. H.
Gray, Joseph
Harrod, G. M.
Harrod, Wm. P.
Harley, John E.
Harrison, R. R.
Hartnett, M.
Hoover, George H.
Hoover, J. J.
Hiers, N. T.
Holly, J. Calvin
Hagood, James R.
Jenny, J. Wyman
Jenkins, J. A.
Johnston, C. E.
Jones, James
Loadholt, C. U.
Loadholt, J. M.
Lynes, B. F.
Lynes, Geo. W.

Lott, Joshua
Lucas, C. D.
Myers, P. O.
Mixon, Frank
McMillan, F. M.
McMillan, J. E.
McMillan, R. H.
Morris, Gideon
Myrick, J. W.
Myrick, Eli
Platts, Geo. W.
Platts, W. F.
Priester, J. R.
Smith, C. E.
Smith, W. E.
Smith, Moses
Thompson, W. O.
Williams, J. B.
Williams, J. D.
Williams, W. W.
Wood, Allen

COMPANY D, 1ST REGIMENT.

Crawford, Robt. L.. .. ..Captain
Kirke, James H.. .. ..Captain
Welsh, Francis M.. .. ..Captain

Perry, L. J.. ....First Lieutenant
Witherspoon, John C.. ....Lieutenant
Hilton, Joseph B.. ....First Sergeant
Gregory, Owen.. ....Second Seregant
Langely, Robert.. ....Third Sergeant
Crockett, James E.. ....Fifth Sergeant
Bennett, James K.. ....Third Sergeant
Sings, W. C.. ....Fourth Sergeant
Welsh, T. J.. ....Fifth Sergeant
Sims, Michael J.. ....Sergeant
Latham, I. T.. ....Second Corporal
Adams, J. W.. ....Corporal

PRIVATES

Caskey, Jefferson J.	Faile, J. Thomas	Patrick, William
Hilton, S. J.	Faile, C. C.	Plyler, General W.
Adams, John	Gregory, W. H.	Plyler, D. H.
Arant, James	Gregory, D. J.	Pitman, Jethro
Arant, Samuel	Gregory, N. B.	Pitman, Bennett
Bailey, E. J.	Ghent, Jackson	Perry, Robert D.
Bailey, Wm. G.	Garris, F. M.	Richardson, W. A.
Bradley, Nelson	Gettis, Franklin M.	Smith, James E.
Bailey, Jno. H.	Graham, James P.	Sweat, Edward
Blackman, John S.	Glenn, John D.	Sweat, John T.
Blackman, Simson	Harrell, T.	Sullivan, Robert M.
Bowers, Samuel J.	Hilton, William H.	Small, Annias
Bush, Beverly	Hilton, T. F.	Sistare, A. J.
Caskey, John D.	Harris, William	Sutton, Zachariah
Cauthen, William	Horton, Doniver	Secrest, John C.
Caskey, W. R.	Johnson, S. S. Burdett	Seay, John
Caskey, Thomas P.	Kirk, Robert M.	Strain, W. W.
Clyburn, Jesse	Latham, Thomas A.	Shute, Elihu
Crenshaw, James M.	Lamaster, James	Taylor, A. J.
Crenshaw, John S.	Larke, John F.	Taylor, Alexander
Cook, J. Crawford	Montgomery, Josiah A.	Taylor, J. R.
Caskey, Eli A.	McAbee, S.	Ussery, Samuel M.
Corbett, James J.	McQuirt, John	Watson, Levin A.
Deas, Sandford	McManus, Robert H.	Wilkerson, Thos O.
Doster, W. G.	McAteer, J. Porter	Wallace, Manus
Flynn, James	McAteer, Robt. H.	Wallace, J. F.
Flynn, Thomas	McInnis, D. A.	Wallace, H. J.
Faile, Emanuel	McAteer, F. M.	Welsh, James V.
Faile, Samuel	Nesbit, W. E.	

COMPANY E, 1ST REGIMENT.

(July to April, 1865.)

Duncan, W. H................................Captain
Thompson, J. H........................First Lieutenant
Wood, P. H..........................Second Lieutenant
Stansell, Jack........................Third Lieutenant
Best, J. R. B.........................Third Lieutenant
Bryan, R. A..........................Third Lieutenant
Hair, J. M...........................Third Lieutenant
Wood, W. J...........................Third Lieutenant
Hall, D. P..................................Sergeant
Mixon, G. D.................................Sergeant
Ogden, D. S.................................Sergeant
Johnson, S. W...............................Sergeant
Woodward, W. W..............................Sergeant
Mixon, F. M.................................Sergeant
Thomson, Arthur.............................Sergeant
Patterson, D. P.............................Sergeant
Manville, A. P..............................Sergeant
Colding, J. C...............................Sergeant
Ogden, Isaac................................Sergeant
Key, S. M...................................Corporal
Harley, Edward..............................Corporal
Best, W. T..................................Corporal
Cane, J. B..................................Corporal
Thomson, Arthur.............................Corporal
Sprawls, D. P...............................Corporal

PRIVATES.

Beck, Noah	Driggers, John	Hall, Nathan
Bellinger, C. W.	Drummond, Augustus	Hayne, Job
Bellinger, S. N.	Drummond, John	Jackson, Isaac
Bryant, William	Gass, R.	Joel, Julius
Brunson, St. M.	Gill, Val.	Johnson, J. F.
Burckhalter, Basil	Goodwyn, J. B.	Kapham, M.
Cameron, J. J.	Green, Jeff.	Kapham, Theodore
Cameron, Joe	Green, John	Kitchen, W. F.
Cameron, Pink	Green, W. Frank	Lambert, John
Canada, John W.	Hagood, E. Augustus	McLain, Wiley
Cane, J. Milledge	Hagood, Wm. A.	Mixon, W. J.
Damish, J. Chris.	Hagood, Thomas B.	Morgan, J. A.
Diamond, James	Hair, J. W.	Morgan, L. H.
(Deserted)	Hair, Mathias	Nelson, A. P.
Dias, W.	Hale, John	Nelson, W. P.

Owens, John	Scott, P.	Sweat, George
Parker, M. P.	Sheppard, Joseph	Weathersbee, Ben
Pender, D. Farrar	Stansell, John M.	Woodward, J. A.
Roundtree, Job	Stewart, C.	Woodward, Nick.
Scott, C.	Stivander, W. F.	

COMPANY E, 1ST REGIMENT.

(Originally Company K, from January to June, 1861.)

Mangum, T. H.............................Captain
Pressley, Jno. G..........................Captain
Day, James M..........................First Lieutenant
China, T. J.............................First Lieutenant
Steedman, G. E........................Second Lieutenant
Logan, C..............................Second Lieutenant
Guyton, H. R..........................Second Lieutenant
Montgomery, H........................Second Lieutenant
Langley, Samuel.........................Sergeant

PRIVATES.

Allen, D. A.	China, S.	Dickson, J. S.
Ard, J. J.	Christmas,	Dickson, B. E.
Ard, J.	Cook, M. D.	Dunn, M. C.
Ard, R.	Cook, T. J.	Epps, J. H.
Ard, E. J.	Coker, J. S.	Evans, J. J.
Brown, H. J.	Coker, P. J.	Ellis, E. S.
Brown, M. A.	Conner, S. S.	Feage, R. E.
Baker, M. R.	Cameron, H. G.	Floyd, G.
Baunsean, J. T.	Cameron, J. W.	Fleming, L. B.
Bradshaw, J.	Cooper, A. B.	Fleming, W. E.
Burgess, J. M.	Cullum, W. P.	Footman, J. M.
Browders, S. W.	Cannady, Wm.	Footman, H. E.
Brickles, J. M.	Cumings, J. E.	Garner, H. G.
Braxton, J.	Clark, J. M.	Guess, A.
Brockington, B. P.	Cook, J. F.	Gist, G.
Blockman, W.	Christmas, J. E.	Gamble, J. R.
Burckhalter,	Cooper, W. N.	Gamble, R. K.
Brown, James	Cooper, J. H.	Graham, S. J.
Bryant, R. A.	Cook, E. R.	Guyton, J. C.
Blalock, J. G.	Dukes, W. D.	Holly, L. A.
Blalock, R.	Dukes, J. E.	Haweston, G.
Brown, W. P.	Dukes, B. F.	Hair, H. M.
Brown, J.	Dennis, E. G.	Hatcher, J. M.
China, J. R.	Dennis, S. R.	Holly, G. W.

27—H

Hester, J. L.	McCullough, J. E.	Rush, E. W.
Harris, J. B.	McConnell, L. A.	Red, N. R.
Holly, C. C.	McKensie, S.	Ramsey, J.
Hair, N. G. W.	Markey, J.	Sanders, J. C.
Hair, J. W.	Montgomery, S.	Surney, W. J. C.
Hall, J. W.	Montgomery, S. C.	Shaw, W. D. J.
Hart, H. H.	Mitchum, J. S.	Singletery, E. J.
Hogg, J. C.	Mitchum, G. K.	Slingfield, E.
Hutto, J.	Mitchum, C. S.	Sigler, A. S.
Hair, J. J.	Matthews, J. M.	Spawls, J. F.
Harvey, J. C.	Matthews, R. C.	Smith, W. R.
Heath, A. J.	Matthews, William	Scherarty, G. W.
James, S. S.	Menet, J. A.	Schroder, H.
Jandow, J. J.	Mitchell, A. M.	Thigpen, J. E.
Johnston, E.	Moseley, W. H.	Thigpen, W. N.
June, S. N.	Moseley, W. F.	Tisdale, A. G.
Jannegan, W.	Mims, R. H.	Tisdale, W. W.
Jordan, A. F.	McCreany, C. W.	Tyler, H.
Jones, W. B.	Mims, J. A.	Teague, G. A.
Johnson, J. J.	Merritt, G. A.	Tool, J. L.
Knox, W. J.	Mitchum, S. S.	Turner, J. G.
Kelly, J. W.	Nolen, J.	Taylor, G. W.
Langley, P. G.	New, M.	Waters, R. B.
Logan, W. D.	New, J.	Wilson, P.
Lyles, W. R.	Owens, J. O.	Wilson, Jack
Lee, J. E.	Owens, E.	Weeks, W. J.
Lamb,	Owens, S.	Weathersbee, J. E.
Lane, J. W.	Parker, H. G.	Weaver, O. F.
Montgomery, E. P.	Parsons, A. J.	Wolf, W. S.
McClure, C. W.	Price, J. M.	Walker, Nat.
McClary, D. R.	Peacock, E. L.	Williams, H. L.
McClary, J. L.	Player, J. N.	Young, L. E.
McClary, S. A.	Parsons, W. H.	Young, W. H.
McCormick, P. B.	Parsons, F. R.	Young, J. H.

COMPANY F, 1ST REGIMENT.

Grimes, G. M...Captain
Gwin, T. D..Captain
Weisinger, J. J.......................................First Lieutenant
Southern, J. L..First Lieutenant
Grimes, G. W...Second Lieutenant
Newby, F. P..Second Lieutenant
Jimison, R. R..Second Lieutenant
Baker, T. P...Third Lieutenant
Kearse, J. F..First Sergeant
Feaster, N. A...First Sergeant

Shockley, W. T. . . . . Second Sergeant
Hagood, A. . . . . Second Sergeant
Sweat, L. J. . . . . Third Sergeant
Hall, S. D. . . . . Third Sergeant
Gwin, J. T. . . . . Fourth Sergeant
Gwin, R. A. . . . . Fifth Sergeant
Odom, D. G. . . . . Fourth Sergeant
Patterson, A. . . . . Fifth Sergeant
Gosnell, Geo. . . . . First Corporal
Flircnet, Henry. . . . . Second Corporal
Thompson, J. L. . . . . Third Corporal
Hawkins, Joe. . . . . Fourth Corporal
Kinard, E. F. . . . . First Corporal
Jennings, A. B. . . . . Second Corporal
Rush, C. E. . . . . Third Corporal
Copeland, J. J. . . . . Fourth Corporal

PRIVATES.

Anderson, Brown	Newby, William	Carter, D.
Brown, Morgan	Nelson, Joseph	Clayton, C. R.
Brice, T. K.	Adams, J. J.	Choen, D. A.
Brookshire, Day	Roy, Joseph	Calsen, J. W.
Burdette, J. W.	Southern, W. R.	Copeland, J. C.
Bridges, A.	Smith, William	Dyches, B. H.
Bridges, W. N.	Trammell, B. F.	Evals, S. W.
Clary, S. F.	Trammell, P. L.	Folk, C. L.
Crain, S. R.	Tor, Joseph	Ford, E.
Collens, E. O.	Vermillion, T.	Furman, H. S.
Clark, J. H.	Thomas, W. Powell	Gillam, J. J.
Cely, W. H.	(Second Lieutenant.)	Grimes, J. F.
Davis, W. R.	Runnels, Adams	Hemingway, F. K.
Emery, J. B.	Johnson, Elias	Hemingway, W. C.
Harnby, W. S.	McAuly, A. A.	Hunter, J. B.
Hartley, Grabial	Bishop, John	Jeffcoat, M. M.
Hartley, Jeremiah	West, William	Johns, J. S.
Hawkies, Hamp.	(First Lieutenant.)	Kearse, L. R.
Hall, Thomas	Barbers, B. J.	Kush, J. A.
Hunson, G. B.	Basset, J. J.	Kinard, G. J.
Johnson, John	Beard, W. T.	Kinard, M. A.
Johnson, Pleas	Businger, J. J.	Kinard, M. O.
Lafay, P. B.	Businger, J. A.	Kirkland, J. K.
Lafay, A. E.	Businger, W. C.	Lane, W. S.
Lafay, Isaac	Bennett, J. M.	Main, J. A.
Multy, J. A.	Bennett, W. A.	Main, J. W.
Moore, James	Bishop, J. M.	Millhouse, C. H.
Morris, Harry	Brealmed, T. J.	Miller, C. D.

Mitchell, B.	Road, R. L.	Hughes, A. J.
Morris, W.	Sease, J. D.	Jones, V.
Morris, T.	Smith, J.	Loper, S. D.
Morris, R.	Smith, J. M.	Morris, H. W.
Mase, Geo. W.	Steedley, A. T.	Pellom, H. R.
McFadden, J.	Steedley, D. O.	Road, W. B.
McMillan, H. C.	Steedley, J. E.	Smith, J. J.
Patrick, C. M.	Steedley, R. J.	Steedley, L. B.
Pellon, E.	Thompson, J. H.	Zoney, S. S.
Preston, A.	Thompson, J. W.	Fender, J. S.
Rentz, J. D.	Zeigler, J. J.	Still, A.
Rentz, W. A.	Zurox, J. W.	Hunter, H. R.
Riley, G. S.	Beard, C.	Main, M. M.
Risher, H. B.	Fender, J. M.	McKenzie, W.
Road, J. M.		

COMPANY G, 1ST REGIMENT.

Frederick, E. J................................Captain
Romsire, J. V..............................First Lieutenant
Trotti, S. W..............................Second Lieutenant
Dunbar, G. R..............................Third Lieutenant
Dunbar, S. S..............................First Sergeant
Asheley, R. C..............................Second Sergeant
Dunbar, T. S..............................Third Sergeant
Horey, J. I..............................Fourth Sergeant
Starling, G. W..............................Fifth Sergeant
Asheley, L. A..............................First Corporal
Wood, P. H..............................Second Corporal
Darlington, J. H..............................Third Corporal
Romsire, M. A..............................Fourth Corporal
Barker, W. E..............................Fifth Corporal
Garvin, M. H..............................Sixth Corporal

PRIVATES.

Anderson, B. I.	Black, T. S.	Dicks, Graney
Benson, Alex.	Brady, J. M.	Chatman, W. A.
Benson, Ben	Bunghman, A. T.	Frust, F.
Bailey, Alex.	Dunbar, F.	Goss, R.
Bewmot, C. F.	Dunbar, R. J.	Glover, J. W.
Bush, W. D.	Darlington, W. R.	Hawley, E. H.
Bowers, B. F.	Dicks, A.	Holman, G. W.
Baxley, W. M.	Dicks, Anne	Holland, I. I.
Rush, S. C.	Dias, W. L.	Hall, Franklin
Bates, I. B.	Dias, H.	Hallam, William
Bowers, H. C.	Dunbar, Samuel	Hawley, James

Killingsworth, I. I.	Newman, Steph.	Rawford, Shade
Killingsworth, W. L.	Newman, Geo.	Roundtree, C. L.
Killingsworth, T. H.	Nicholson, Roger	Stallings, M. C.
Key, S. M.	Owens, Jno.	Smith, W. H.
Key, Darbin	Parker, Jno.	Thomas, M.
Layton, F. M.	Pucson, William	Williams, Ed.
Lowe, Ancil	Rottenberry, Wm.	Williams, Wiley
Moody, Mat	Romasire, G. F.	Witherspoon, M.
Meyer, C. C.	Robinson, I.	Young, Tom
Nelson, But	Roundtree, M.	

COMPANY H, 1ST REGIMENT.

Martin, J. V..Captain
Allen, A. T...First Lieutenant
Flowers, W. B.......................................Second Lieutenant
All, W. A..Second Lieutenant
Erwin, E. A..Sergeant
Bryan, R. A..Sergeant
Colding, J. C..Sergeant
Hammond, W. R...Sergeant
Sanders, R. T...Sergeant
Best, W. C..Sergeant
Roberts, R. C...Sergeant
Erwin, S. M...Sergeant
Minors, C. T..Sergeant
Bellinger, J. A...Sergeant
Martin, Abraham...Corporal
Bonnet, R. W..Corporal
Billing, E. N...Corporal
Jenkins, J. A...Corporal
Harden; W. M..Corporal
Gray, J. P..Corporal
Richardson, J. M..Corporal
Garvin, J. W..Corporal
Erwin, J..Corporal

PRIVATES.

All, G.	Bennett, John	Best, Wilson
All, J.	Bennett, James	Barker, R. S.
Allen, J. M.	Best, W. W.	Barker, J. H.
Ashe, T. M.	Block, G. W.	Bassett, M. P.
Allen, W. W.	Bodiford, H.	Bates, J. W.
Allen, J. C.	Bowers, E.	Bowers, M.
Barker, J. G.	Brown, P.	Barker, W. J.
Baxley, J. M.	Brunson, W. M.	Bennett, J. N.

Billings, E. W.	Hardin, A.	Myrick, E.
Black, J. R.	Hayes, J.	Mallard, J.
Boils, O. S.	Hewlitt, A. S.	Mixson, R. H.
Bradley, D. C.	Hutto, M.	Murdaugh, J.
Bryan, H. P.	Harley, W. M.	Myrick, J.
Burke, Wm.	Harley, J. P.	Owens, L.
Canty, James	Hiers, O.	Oliver, James
Carroll, H.	Hadwin, J.	Patterson, D.
Colding, T. B.	Hays, John	Plath, Charles
Cone, G. P.	Harvey,W. J.	Priester, E.
Connelley, W. L.	Hiers, G.	Platts, J. P.
Connelley, Wm.	Hoover, D.	Richardson, J. M.
Creech, J.	Haphan, T.	Rouse, M. D.
Curtain, John	Hayne, E. S.	Shuler, W.
Canty, S. C.	Jones, James	Sightler, W. A.
Castilon, W. H.	Jenkins, J. A.	Sightler, A. M.
Cave, D. C.	Johns, E.	Sauls, B.
Daly, H.	Kirkland, C. S.	Smith, J.
Daly, Pat	Lancaster, J. C.	Sanders, J.
Edenfield, J. L.	Lawton, F. A.	Sanders, W.
Fennell, J. W.	Lipsey, W. M.	Strange, H.
Fowke, G.	Lon, A.	Taylor, P.
Garvin, C. H.	Loadholt, M.	Williams, J. D.
Garvin, W. H.	Martin, Ben	Williams, D. W.
Garvin, J. W.	Moody, J. B.	Wooley, N.
Gray, Joe	Moody, William	Williams, R. H.
Gibsinger, J.	Morris, J.	Wood, J. A.
Gooding, W. M.	Morris, R. W.	Young, C. M.
Gray, J. A.	Mims, F.	Young, J. F.
Hall, N.	Murden, J. J.	Youmans, R.

COMPANY I, 1ST REGIMENT.

Stafford, Jas. H...................................Captain
Harllee, John W.................................First Lieutenant
Manning, Wm. L................................Second Lieutenant
Murchison, Roderick............................Second Lieutenant
Murphy, Duncan................................Third Lieutenant
Butler, Gilbert.................................First Sergeant
Blue, William..................................First Sergeant
McKeller, John D...............................First Sergeant
McInnes, Daniel................................Second Sergeant
McCall, Nathan................................Third Sergeant
Carmichael, Malcolm C..........................Fourth Sergeant
Campbell, Daniel...............................Fifth Sergeant
Carmichael, Daniel A...........................Corporal
McCormack, Jno. H.............................Corporal

Loftin, Jno. H..................................Corporal
McInnis, Murdoch..............................Corporal
Brigman, Arthur P..............................Corporal

PRIVATES.

Ammons, Phillip	Garner, James	Jackson, Warren A.
Ammons, Asa	Gaddy, Ithanner J.	Jackson, Charles T.
Bailey, Christopher	Graham, Dugald	Jackson, James R.
Bethea, Holden	Gray, Franklin	Jackson, John T.
Bolton, Britton	Gray, Henry	Jackson, John C.
Butler, Eli T.	Hamilton, Tobias	McCall, John C.
Butler, Alfred W.	Hamilton, Tristram	McDaniel, Amos
Buie, William H.	Hamilton, Whitton	McDaniel, Joseph
Bendy, Jno. A.	Horton, Thomas T.	McDaniel, Randall
Burnett, John	Hairgrove, Isaac H.	McArthur, James
Carmichael, Alex. J.	Herring, Harmon	Owens, Redlin
Campbell, Jno. C.	Henry, Edward	Paul, William
Clark, Kenneth	Herring, Daniel M.	Stackhouse, William R.
Cottingham, Stewart	Herring, Samuel	Stackhouse, Tristram F.
Crawford, Jas. D.	Hyat, Solomon	Sherwood, Richard
Coward, Abner	Hyat, Jno. C. D.	Surles, Archibald
Coward, Ansel	Hyat, James K.	Taylor, Ephraim
Dillon, William	Hyat, John	Townsend, Daniel A.
Easterling, Henry	Hyat, Hugh	Turner, John C.
Evans, William T.	Hyat, David	Turner, Joel
Fitzgerald, Robt. E.	Hulon, Wylie	Walter, Phillip D.
Fore, Tracey	Hamilton, John	

COMPANY K, 1ST REGIMENT.

Brown, J. J....................................Captain
Burt, W. D....................................First Lieutenant
Bellinger, Jno. A..............................Second Lieutenant
Green, F. M....................................Third Lieutenant
Hart, B. A.....................................First Sergeant
Kitching, J. H.................................Second Sergeant
Cary, W. H....................................Third Sergeant
Tyler, M. V....................................Fourth Sergeant
Johnson, J. L..................................Fifth Sergeant
Ogden, D. S....................................First Corporal
Hair, J. M.....................................Second Corporal
Hankinson, J. N................................Third Corporal
Blankensie, D..................................Fourth Corporal
Thompson, A. W................................Sixth Corporal

PRIVATES.

Allen, B. B.	Harley, Virgil	Ray, W. T.
Askew, G. N.	Hext, G. B.	Redd, S.
Balentine, J. C.	Holman, J. F.	Riley, J. P.
Bates, E.	Holland, I.	Robinson, W. D.
Bellinger, V. W.	Howard, D. A.	Sightler, F. M. (First in
Bellinger, S. W.	Jones, J. A.	Co. B, then in K.)
Birt, W. B.	Karney, I.	Stallings, C. A.
Bowman, L.	Kelly, T.	Stiernder, W. L.
Brown, P.	Kirkland, P.	Tyler, I. M.
Cain, G. N.	Manvire, A. P.	Tyler, R. E.
Clark, J. I.	Martin, M. H.	Twiaal, Z. A.
Collins, T.	Mims, R.	Ussery, W.
Damish, J.	Mason, B. F.	Walker, J. N.
Diamond, Jas.	Wilson, I. H.	Weathersbee, C. W.
Enicks, A. C.	Nix, W. W.	Weatherston, T.
Giles, W. A.	Adam, R. W.	Walker, W. D.
Goss, J. A.	Mason, W. P.	Williamston, W.
Green, M. V.	Owens, S. S.	Wooley, A.
Halford, W.	Patterson, A. A.	Yon, P.

25TH REGIMENT.

FIELD OFFICERS.

Simonton, C. H.. .. .. .Colonel
Pressley, Jno. G.. .. .. .Lieutenant-Colonel
Glover, Jno. V.. .. .. .Major
Moffitt, G. H.. .. .. .Adjutant
Dibble, S. W.. .. .. .Adjutant
Prendergrass, J. M.. .. ..Ensign
Adger, J. E.. .. .. .Quartermaster
Barr, D. D.. .. ..Commissary
Ravenel, W. C.. .. ..Surgeon
Warren, J. M.. .. ..Assistant Surgeon
Wardin, W. H.. .. ..Assistant Surgeon
Beall, A. J.. .. ..Assistant Surgeon
Bradley, A. G.. .. ..Assistant Surgeon
Dickson, J. F.. .. ..Assistant Surgeon
McDowall, J. R.. .. .. .Quartermaster Surgeon
Smyth, J. Adjer.. .. .. .Quartermaster Surgeon
Fersner, W. F.. .. .. .Orderly Sergeant
Hirsch, M. J.. .. ..Commissary Sergeant
Dantzler, M. J. D.. .. ..Hospital Steward

COMPANY A, 25TH REGIMENT.

Simonton, Chas. H..Captain
Carson, Jas. M...Captain
Olney, Hiram B.....................................First Lieutenant
Finley, W. Washington.............................Second Lieutenant
Ross, James A.....................................Second Lieutenant
Hannahan, Jos. S..................................Second Lieutenant
Cotchett, W. Dana, Jr.............................Second Lieutenant
Owens, Wm. Capers....................................First Sergeant
Muckenfuss, W. M.....................................First Sergeant
Sheppard, Jno. L....................................Second Sergeant
Jones, D. Henry......................................Third Sergeant
Edgerton, Jas. E....................................Fourth Sergeant
Honour, Fred. H.....................................Fourth Sergeant
Ragin, Charlton H....................................Fifth Sergeant
Stevens, Jas. A......................................Fifth Sergeant
Olney, Alfred L......................................Fifth Sergeant
Miller, Frederick W...................................First Corporal
Black, C. T...Second Corporal
Ellis, Chas. S......................................Second Corporal
Newcomer, Jno. G....................................Second Corporal
Dickinson, Jas. H...................................Second Corporal
Phelps, Jno. B.......................................Third Corporal
Muckenfuss, W. G.....................................Third Corporal
Dibble, Sam'l W.....................................Fourth Corporal
Kellers, J. Fred....................................Fourth Corporal
Blackwood, G. Gibbs.................................Fourth Corporal
Rowand, C. Elliott...................................Fifth Corporal
Cowperthwait, Wm. B..................................Fifth Corporal

PRIVATES.

Adger, J. Ellison	Burrows, Sam'l L.	Cross, B. H.
Anderson, Sam'l W.	Burrows, F. Marion	Cudworth, A.
Baker, Henry G.	Burnham, Edward S.	Dixon, Geo. W.
Baker, E.	Bird, W. Cooper	Douglass, Campbell
Ballot, F. G.	Calder, William	Dooley, W.
Barbot, Julian	Calder, James	Dukes, T. Charlton H.
Barton, A. J.	Calder, Edward E.	Dotterer, William A.
Berry, Thos. T. E.	Carter, Jno. W.	Enslow, J. A., Jr.
Beesley, E. B.	Chapman, Thos. B.	Folker, O. F.
Blackwood, J. C.	Clayton, W. H.	Forbes, W. H. F.
Blanchard, T. S.	Cox, E. P.	Gibson, Walter E.
Bodow, H. R.	Conner, George D.	Gowan, Peter
Breese, S. Van Vecton	Coste, N. E.	Gallwey, William
Burn, Orville J.	Cross, E. Frank	Haas, John

Harper, F. M.	Marsh, David C.	Proctor, Henry G.
Hall, John	Marsh, Jas. G.	Proctor, Wm. E.
Honour, J. Lawrence	Martin, J. S.	Ramsey, J. T.
Honour, Theo. A.	Masters, A. W.	Reid, George
Holmes, Wm. E.	Mey, Florian C.	Robb, James
Humphries, Wm.	Mellichampe, Jas. M.	Riols, A. T.
Jones, J. Walker	Mellichampe, Wm. A.	Robinson, S. A.
Jervey, Wm. C.	Milnor, Vincent	Salvo, James F.
Jeter, W. L.	Miller, Gustavius	Seyle, Samuel H.
Klinck, Jno., Jr.	Mintzing, J. F.	Small, Joseph J.
Kingman, Jno. W.	Muckenfuss, Wm. C.	Sheppard, Benjamin F.
King, S. H.	McNamee, Jas. V.	Shelton, H. S.
Kingman, Oliver H.	McCabe, J. W.	Shokes, G. W.
Kiddell, Charles	O'Sullivan, Thos. F.	Shackleford, E. H.
Lambert, W.	Ortman, W. I.	Smyth, J. Adger
Lawton, J. Frampton	Ortman, Julius F.	Smyth, Augustine T.
Lanneau, Wm. S.	Patterson, W. N.	Steinmeyer, Wm. H.
Lee, L. S.	Pennall, A. F.	Schmidt, J. M.
Lee, B. M.	Pennall, R. E.	Warren, W. Dalton
Locke, P. P.	Prevost, Clarence	Mortimer, Jack
Locke, F. Otis	Prichard, Wm.	(col. cook)
Lovegreen, Lawrence B.	Porcher, Chas. F.	Perrineau, Isaac
Lucas, Benjamin	Petit, J. J.	(col. cook)
Mahoney, D. A.		

COMPANY B, 25TH REGIMENT.

Lloyd, Edward W.......................................Captain
Hannahan, Joseph S....................................Captain
Blum, Robert A...................................First Lieutenant
Burger, Sam'l J..................................First Lieutenant
Greer, Henry I...................................First Lieutenant
Greer, Richard W................................Second Lieutenant
Taft, Robert M..................................Second Lieutenant
Bomar, J. Edward.........................Brevet Second Lieutenant
Lanneau, Fleetwood...............................First Sergeant
Simons, T. Grange................................First Sergeant
Marion, Jno. F.................................Second Sergeant
Jamison, Wm. H.................................Second Sergeant
Gyles, Frank E.................................Second Sergeant
McLeod, Robt. A................................Third Sergeant
Oliver, Frederick K............................Third Sergeant
Force, Alexander, W...........................Fourth Sergeant
Whittaker, Wm. M...............................Fifth Sergeant
Caldwell, J. Shapter..........................Fifth Sergeant
Gaillard, Jno. P...............................First Corporal
Hayes, LeRoy W.................................First Corporal
Laurence, R. De Treville......................Fourth Corporal
Gray, Alfred..................................Fourth Corporal

PRIVATES.

Atkinson, Anthony O.
Adams, Etsell L.
Baker, Geo. S.
Beckman, Christian J.
Bomar, Geo. W.
Blakely, R.
Brown, Samuel N.
Brown, T. K.
Butler, H. W.
Boyce, J. Jeremiah
Burns, Lawrence T.
Brown, J. H.
Cochran, Wm.
Cantwell, Pat. H.
Copes, Frederick
Culler, W. V.
De Treville, Ed. W.
Devoe, James H.
Doucin, P. M.
Dorre, C. Frederick
Dibble, Marion W.
Duff, A.
Edmondson, George
Estell, Henry P.
Flynn, Wm. E.
Flynn, W. H.
Force, George H.
Flynn, Charles H.
Gadsden, Thomas N.
Gilliland, Daniel B.
Gilliland, Edward B.
Glover, Jno. B.

Glover, Leslie
Gibbs, Isaac B.
Grady, James T.
Grady, Edward
Graham, Stephen G.
Grice, George D.
Greer, W. Robert
Happoldt, J. H.
Houston, Jno. H.
Hernandez, B.
Johnston, Chas. H.
Lanneau, J. Bennett
Lebby, Thos. D.
Little, Wm.
Logan, E. W.
Mathews, Christopher
Molloy, Lawrence E.
Martin, Jno. C.
Mellard, J. Pettigrew
Mellard, Joel P.
Moffitt, Geo. H.
Moore, Wm. H.
Murray, D. D.
Myers, H.
McCutchen, R. G.
McDowell, Robt. H., Jr.
McMillan, W. F.
Muller, R.
Ortman, Louis
Ortman, Henry
O'Hara, W. P.
Oliver, Thos. P.

Prior, Barney R.
Riecke, Gerhard
Renneker, Fred. W.
Renneker, J. Henry
Robbins, E. Frank
Saltus, Samuel
Schulte, J. Herman
Shaffer, R. Randolph
Shaffer, Wm. H.
Shaffer, C. P.
Simons, W. Lucas
Silcox, James
Silcox, Daniel S.
Scherer, John
Shecut, J. Fraser
Smith, Jno. B.
Stocker, John D.
Strong, S. J.
Taft, A. Walton
Tavernor, J. H.
Tharen, Edward B.
Trumbo, Augustus S.
Warren, Benjamin W.
Westendorff, Chas. H.
Williamson, Chas. A.
Williams, Henry H., Jr.,
Wittschew, E.
Woodberry, Stratford B.
Wilkie, Octavius
West, Chas. H., Jr.
Hunter, T. (col. cook)
Lawrence, J. (col. cook)

COMPANY C, 25TH REGIMENT.

China, Thos. J.....................................Captain
Logan, Calhoun....................................Captain
Montgomery, Henry, Jr.....................Second Lieutenant
Brockington, Burrows P.....................Second Lieutenant
China, J. Randolph..........................Second Lieutenant
Montgomery, S. Isaac.......................Second Lieutenant
Scott, Junius E............................Second Lieutenant
Tootman, Jno. M................................Sergeant
China, Samuel M................................Sergeant

McClary, G. Franklin..............................Sergeant
Mitchum, Sylvester S..............................Sergeant
Montgomery, Samuel................................Corporal
Epps, J. Henry....................................Corporal
Baker, Major R. D.................................Corporal
Jayroe, John W....................................Corporal
Montgomery, Isaac.................................Corporal
McKnight, Wm. H...................................Corporal

PRIVATES.

Ard, Edward G.	Feagin, Madison S.	Montgomery, J. Alexander
Ard, S. Reuben	Feagin, Richard	
Ard, James, Jr.	Gist, George	Montgomery, J. Franklin
Ard, Joseph	Guess, William	
Allen, Drue A.	Guess, G. Adolphus	Montgomery, Wm. J.
Adams, D. Elliott	Guess, Burgess M.	Montgomery, James B.
Brown, Harvey J.	Gamble, Robert K.	McConnell, Thomas A.
Brown, Madison A.	Gamble, Isaac K.	Mathews, James M.
Barrineau, J. Thomas	Garner, Henry S.	McCrary, S. Alex.
Barrineau, R. Henry	Graham, Samuel	McClary, Lidney B.
Barrineau, Edwin M.	Grayson, Harvey L.	McClary, Wm. D.
Barrineau, Ebbin G.	Grayson, John M.	Mouzon, Wm. E.
Barrineau, Geo. W.	Johnson, J. Bird	Murphy, J. Calvin
Browder, S. Warren	Johnson, Edward	McCants, John E.
Brabham, J. Augustus	Jaudon, Dicky J.	McKnight, Daniel Baker
Brabham, John	June, Samuel N.	Owens, J. Manson
Brown, James M.	James, Wm. E.	Parsons, Wm. H.
Brockinton, William	James, Samuel S.	Parsons, A. Jack
Cook, T. James	Jones, J. Ferdinand	Parsons, George
Cook, W. Dorsey	Kelly, John W.	Pressley, Hugh M.
Cook, Elihu R.	Kelly, Elbert J.	Pendergrass, Jno. M.
Cooper, Archie B.	Kaler, James E.	Pendergrass, B. Robert
Dennis, Edward G.	Lee, Isaac E.	Rush, Emory W.
Dennis, Samuel R.	Logan, Washington D.	Shaw, H. David
Duke, W. David	Liles, Robert K.	Smith, Erwin R.
Duke, Robert E.	Lambert, A. Jack	Smith, David M.
Duke, Benjamin F.	Mitchum, J. Sessions	Tisdale, Wm. W.
Duke, Thomas J.	Martin, Ebbin R.	Wilson, Pinckney
Duke, David M.	Martin, J. James	Wilson, John
Ellis, Ellie S.	Montgomery, S. Edgar	Young, W. Henry
Footman, Henry E.	Montgomery, T. Warren	Young, James H.
Feagin, J. Alfred	Montgomery, Edward P.	Young, Levi E.

COMPANY D, 25TH INFANTRY.

McKerrall, Wm. Jasper..............................Captain
Haselton, James...........................First Lieutenant
McKay, Daniel J...........................First Lieutenant

Bethea, Pickett P.. .. ..Second Lieutenant
Smith, Marcus L.. .. ..Second Lieutenant
Alford, Artemus.. .. ..Sergeant
Richard, Meyer.. .. ..Sergeant
McIntyre, Joseph.. .. ..Sergeant
Barfield, Jesse.. .. ..Sergeant
Sweet, David.. .. ..Corporal
Cox, Lewis J.. .. ..Corporal
Greenwood, E. B.. .. ..Corporal
Herring, Jno. C.. .. ..Corporal
Herring, Marcus C.. .. ..Corporal

PRIVATES.

Turbeville, George	Godbold, James V.	Kennedy, Evander
Allen, John	Graves, W. M.	Lane, Ferdinand
Atkinson, Tulley	Goodbad, Eli	Lane, Franklyn
Barrentine, Wilson	Graham, E.	Lundy, John
Berry, Nathan	Hoyt, Hugh	Lovell, J. W.
Blackman, David	Hoyt, Washington	Lane, Robert
Barrentine, Nelson	Herring, D. M.	Lane, S. D.
Bullard, P. D. B.	Hamilton, Whitner, Jr.	Lundy, Wm.
Barnett, D.	Hunt, George	McCorkle, J. F.
Beverly, Douglass	Hunt, Charles	Mekins, Phillips B.
Coward, Ansel	Hunt, P. C.	Mekins, Oscar
Candler, William	Hays, W. M.	McKnight, J. E.
Candler, Noah	Hays, Nicholas W.	Moore, G. W.
Cook, Hiram	Hays, W. C.	Norton, Sandy
Coats, Evander	Hays, H. R.	Nees, John
Cottingham, Wesley	Hays, R. H.	Owens, Hewitt
Coals, James	Hays, A. G.	Owens, Lott
Candler, Wm., Sr.	Hays, Jesse H.	Ransom, John
Coleman, Louis	Hays, E. W.	Rushing, James
Clark, Johnson	Hays, C.	Riley, D. S.
Carter, Henry	Hairgrove, Wm.	Rucker, Ruff
Daniel, Harllee	Hairgrove, W. H.	Smith, J. K.
Drew, R.	Haselden, James	Redman, Jake
Daniel, Dargan	Hyatt, Hugh	Turner, Willis, Jr.
Drew, Turrentine	Hyatt, John	Turner, Martin
Drew, John W.	Herlong, James	Turner, Joel
Edge, John	Ikner, James	Tart, G.
Edge, Hamilton	Johnson, J. F.	Withington, W. G.
Foxworth, John	Jordan, Jacob	Watson, David
Foxworth, W. K.	Jackson, J. R.	Wilkes, James
Freeman, Robert	Johnson, George	Wilkinson, James
Freeman, Rob.	Johnson, Barney	Wood, John
Gaddy, J. J.	Jones, F. D.	Yates, Wm.
Graham, James	Keever, David A.	

COMPANY E, 25TH REGIMENT.

White, Robert D..Captain
Mazyck, Nat B...Captain
Bythwood, Mat W....................................First Lieutenant
Mims, Alfred James..................................First Lieutenant
Duc, Virgil..Second Lieutenant
Durbee, F. Eugene..................................Second Lieutenant
Lalane, Geo. M.....................................Second Lieutenant
Prince, John E.....................................Second Lieutenant
May, P...Sergeant
Norris, E. J...Sergeant
Dunn, Geo. A...Sergeant
King, John...Sergeant
Sanders, Joseph T....................................Sergeant
Mahoney, William.....................................Sergeant
Milligan, H. A.......................................Corporal
McEvoy, P..Corporal
McLeish, Jno...Corporal
Manning, John..Corporal
Vocelle, Leon..Corporal
Kettleband, S. D.....................................Corporal
Gory, P..Corporal

PRIVATES.

Adams, Geo. P.	Doughty, E. B.	Husseman, H. H.
Arnum, M. V.	Daggett, J. W.	Hirsch, Melvin J.
Arnum, W. D. P.	Dunn, James	Hutson, J. H.
Abrams, A. F. W.	Dallwick, L.	Hudson, Elias
Bilton, John J.	Duc, John E.	Hutson, Edward R.
Bilton, William	Dufort, J. L.	Halverson, J. H.
Bilton, George	Easterby, S. D.	Ittner, J.
Baker, Fred. G.	Englert, John W.	Jacobs, F.
Brooks, J. D.	Flotwell, R.	Johnson, Jno. R.
Burns, John	Farris, J. E.	Jones, J. W.
Bain, M.	Frank, Joseph	Jones, William
Brennan, John	Foster, C. H.	Kressell, Frank
Boyce, W.	Fourcher, V.	Kenny, J.
Burck, E.	Fannigan, T.	Lalane, Paul B.
Broughton, J. J.	Funk,	Laler, M.
Bergen, P. J.	Gerkin, E. H.	Long, John
Campsen, J. H.	Gordon, W. C.	Leitch, Gilbert M.
Carey, M.	Gordon, J.	Lolly, J.
Carpenter, W.	Gaymon, M.	Laverne, J.
Christophel, M.	Gerry, Wm., Jr.	Marshburn, E. H.
Crosby, James	Haselton, D. B.	Mahoney, D.
Cohen, Julius	Hall, George	Martin, John

McIntyre, Thomas	Puckharber F.	Stay, W. P.
Morris, J.	Papham, J. R.	Schroder, John
Metts, John	Preston, Jno. F.	Schroder, Claus
Meyers, John	Ruger, Wm. T.	Seele, Charlie
Nickerson, A. J.	Rosis, J.	Stewart, Richard
Nickeson, G. W.	Reeves, George	Sanran, H.
O'Mara, John	Rose, A.	Smith, John S.
O'Mara, William	Ryan, J.	Stafford, H. R.
O'Brien, D.	Speissegger, T. W.	Trainer, J.
Petit, George W.	Smith, Thomas	Vanderpool, L.
Phillips, Lemuel M.	Smith, P.	Voyleberg, L.
Pundt, A. M.	Smith, Joseph	Vayler, C.
Peck, O. M.	Sevetus, S.	Vocelle, A.

COMPANY F, 25TH REGIMENT.

Sellers, M. Henry...Captain
Harper, Leonidas A.......................................Captain
Evans, John G.....................................Second Lieutenant
Shuler, Franklin E................................Third Lieutenant
Wise, Wade W..Lieutenant
Carson, Robert J...............................First Sergeant
Hart, Capers H...Sergeant
Gramling, Mike W.......................................Sergeant
Fralic, W. J...Sergeant
Avinger, A. P..Sergeant
Dantzler, B. M...Sergeant
Dantzler, E. L...Corporal
Prickett, J. W...Corporal
Ulmer, Thomas W..Corporal
Way, D. A...Corporal
Harmon, J. W..Corporal

PRIVATES.

Avinger, D. J.	Dantzler, W. H.	Fertic, Boyd
Avinger, Lewis H.	Dantzler, Lewis W.	Fertic, Charles
Barber, G. D.	Dantzler, George M.	Fertic, George
Barsh, W. F.	Dantzler, Fred. W.	Fertic, John
Braddy, D.	Dantzler, Ervin P.	Fertic, Joseph
Braddy, E. W.	Davis, O. S.	Fersner, Wm. F.
Clayton, D. J.	Davis, Thomas	Fersner, Frank
Clayton, W. W.	Davis, Morgan A.	Fersner, Lawrence W.
Clayton, F. R.	Douglas, Brince	Fogle, W. J.
Dantzler, Arthur P.	Evans, R. M.	Golson, J. D.
Dantzler, Henry F.	Felder, Carson E.	Gramling, Martin
Dantzler, J. N.	Felder, O. J.	Luther

Griffin, A. B.	Pailer, O. J.	Smith, J. W.
Griffin, James	Parler, Leonidas	Smith, R.
Griffin, Henry	Prickett, J. H.	Shurlnight, Lon
Griffin, John	Rast, J. T.	Strock, William
Griffin, Silas D.	Rooke, E. C.	Strock, E. B.
Grainger, Henry E.	Rucker, John	Taylor, Middleton E.
Haigler, F. M.	Rucker, Henry	Taylor, Pinckney H.
Haigler, F. G.	Rickenbacker, Nicho-	Thompson, D. V.
Heckle, A. J.	las F.	Ulmer, F. F.
Heaner, Jno. C.	Shirar, Henry	Ulmer, G. L.
Holmes, Sam	Shuler, Erastus V.	Vogt, L. C.
Houck, Daniel D. S.	Shuler, F. Pinckney H.	Walling, Jos. A.
Huffman, David J.	Shuler, George L. V. S.	Walling, R.
Huffman, W. R.	Shuler, D. G. B.	Walling, Jas.
Huffman, John	Shuler, Merrick W.	Wannamaker, Irvin W.
Jones, James	Snell, W. D.	Way, Wad B.
McIver, David A.	Smoak, A. A.	Wiles, Henry
McIver, Bruner A.	Smoak, A. E.	Wiles, William
Murray, D. D.	Staley, H. J.	Wiles, G. A.
Meyers, Fred.	Stroman, Charles	Wiles, V. P.
Meyers, J. W.	Stroman, Emanuel	Zeigler, Fred.
Ott, Samuel	Spigener, Edward	Zimmerman, R. D.
Ott, J. Frank	Stone, Adam	Zimmerman, W. C.

ST. MATTHEWS CO., 1ST REGIMENT.

PRIVATES.

Barber, John	Hungerpeler, J. T.	Rush, Davie H.
Bookhart, D. B.	Hart, Tom C.	Shuler, P. C.
Evans, Lewis W.	Jones, L. C.	Way, James F.
Evans, R. F.	Mims, F.	Williams, Capers
Godfrey, Pink	Powers, George	

COMPANY G, 25TH REGIMENT.

Glover, John V...Captain
Izlar, Jas. Ferdinand.......................................Captain
Kennerly, Samuel N................................First Lieutenant
Dibble, Samuel...................................First Lieutenant
Elliott, George H..............................Second Lieutenant
Graves, Joseph................................Second Lieutenant
Izlar, Benjamin Pou............................Orderly Sergeant
Hook, J. Hilliard....................................Sergeant
Rast, Jacob E......................................Sergeant
Izlar, William Valmore.............................Sergeant
Culler, L. Hayne...................................Sergeant
Shoemaker, Ira T...................................Sergeant

Paulling, William..Corporal
Kohn, Theodore..Corporal
Robinson, Jude..Corporal
Kennerly, J. Robert.....................................Corporal

PRIVATES.

Adger, A. M.
Austin, Morgan L.
Arant, James H.
Antilley, M. Furman
Ashe, John
Ayers, D. A.
Bailey, Henry
Bailey, Charles
Benton, J. W.
Bozard, Jacob C.
Bozard, John S.
Bozard, David T.
Bozard, Steven E.
Brabham, Lawrence F.
Bronson, Marion D.
Brown, Henry
Brown, David
Bruce, James P.
Bull, W. Aiken
Collins, A.
Crawford, Wm. E.
Crider, Geo. B.
Culcleasure, D. J.
Culler, W. Wesley
Culler, J. W.
Culler, Jacob
Dantzler, J. M.
Dantzler, David W.

Dantzler, Manley J. D.
Darnold, Esau
Darnold, S. C.
Dibble, Frederick S.
Fairy, Geo. W. B.
Frieze, Franz J.
Froberg, H.
Hall, Sylvanus
Hall, Samuel R.
Holman, Jas. M. O.
Holstein, Joseph A.
Hook, Samuel P.
Hook, John
Hook, Lawrence L.
Inabinet, A. Jeff.
Inabinet, Frank S.
Inabinet, Charles G.
Inabinet, E. E.
Izlar, Lauriston Theodore
Izlar, Adolphus Madison
Irick, Laban A.
Irick, Alex. D.
Irick, Elliott H.
Jenkins, Lewis W.
Meredith, William C.
Moody, W. A.
Murphy, Emanuel

Murphy, David F.
Myers, Esau
Myers, Luther
Myers, Fred.
O'Cain, Jno. M.
Ott, Elmore
Ott, Elias
Ott, J. David
Rast, Fred. M.
Rast, Lewis
Rawlinson, Moses
Rawlinson, Abram S.
Rawlinson, Wm. J.
Rives, Wm. C.
Robinson, Murray
Rush, Lewis F.
Scott, Junius L.
Sanders, Ben H.
Shultnight, Low
Smoak, Andrew J.
Stokes, Jefferson
Syphret, Obadiah J.
Sanford, Jesse
Tatum, Jno. S. C.
Taylor, William W.
Wolfe, Edward M.
Wolfe, Peter

COMPANY H, 25TH REGIMENT.

Hammond, Sam'l LeRoy.....................................Captain
Bartless, Wm. H...Captain
Seabrook, Whitmarsh H............................First Lieutenant
Hammond, F. G..................................Second Lieutenant
Rush, E. W....................................Second Lieutenant
Jacob, F. C...................................Second Lieutenant
Ramsey, J. T..................................Second Lieutenant
Prickett, J. H................................Second Lieutenant
Toye, R. G......................................First Sergeant
Horton, R. A....................................First Sergeant

28—H

Oliver, F. K.. .. .. .Sergeant
Rochester, W. A.. .. .. .Corporal
Lamb, Robert.. .. .. .Corporal
Williams, M. R.. .. .. .Corporal
Brown, F. H.. .. .. .Corporal
Fagan, J. H.. .. .. .Corporal

PRIVATES.

Adams, A.	Gary, J. W.	McCoy, R.
Adams,	Gregorie,	O'Donnell, E.
Ardas, G.	Hodgson, P. P.	Odom, J. A.
Ashe,	Hyman, J. C.	Odom, James
Baugh, M.	Hyman, T.	Powell, C.
Baugh, L.	Hall, G.	Powell, D.
Bartley, J. L.	Hyde, J. C.	Powell, E.
Bentley, E. B.	Jones, Henry	Pearson, J. W.
Bergin, R. H.	Jones, William	Popham, G. H.
Cunningham, W. H.	James, H. V.	Pundt, A. M.
Cook, Alexander	Kelly, J. C.	Peck, C. M.
Crawford, Major	King, R. W.	Reed, J. R.
Chastine, W. B.	Keenan, P.	Ronan, P.
Dobbins, T. C.	Lynch, E.	Rivers, C. H.
Davis, James	Long, J.	Rosis, J.
Davenport, J. C.	Lee,	Sears, G. P.
Ducine, P. M.	Matthews, H. W.	Stephens, James
Doling, John	Matthews, W. J.	Smith, James
Dunn, J.	McFeely, J. G.	Steadham, G. D.
DuBose, S. C.	McAlister E.	Scott, O. H. P.
Dougherty, F.	Moore, R. A.	Seignous, J. P.
Drose, T. C.	Metts, W. D.	Smoak,
Evans, J. R.	Moise, H. C.	Thompson, A.
Esta, J.	Mezzer, James	Wescoat, St. J. D.
Farrell, H. C.	Melton, E. F.	Wallace, Barney
Farmer, E.	Murphy, L. D.	Williams, A.
Green, P.	McCalvey, A. C.	Wolfe,
Gordon,	Maul, H. C.	
Gray, James	Mullins, F.	

COMPANY I, 25TH REGIMENT.

Butler, Y. N.. .. .. .Captain
Burgess, J. C.. .. .. .Captain
Logan, John J.. .. .. .Captain
Brown, F. B.. .. .. .Second Lieutenant
Felder, R. F.. .. .. .Second Lieutenant
Cockran, Jno. W.. .. .. .Sergeant
Lowder, W. A.. .. .. .Sergeant
Bagnal, J. Moultrie.. .. .. .Sergeant

Fleming, J. W.................................Sergeant
Arledge, Thomas W.............................Sergeant
Ridgway, Reuben F.............................Sergeant
Haley, H. V...................................Corporal
Tobias, Thomas E..............................Corporal
Freeman, Wm. D................................Corporal
Plowden, Wm. B................................Corporal
Evans, J. L...................................Corporal

PRIVATES.

Anderson, A. G.	Hodge, S. N.	Richburg, Joseph E.
Barnes, James	Hodge, E. S.	Richburg, Jno. A.
Burgess, James A.	Hodge, W. J.	Ridgeway, J. N.
Brunson, Josiah C.	Haley, F. W.	Raffield, Thomas N.
Bell, Jas. M., Jr.	Haley, Isaac A.	Rodgers, William
Bell, Manning A.	Hill, N. H.	Rodgers, John
Burgess, D. J.	Hodge, J. N.	Rodgers, Ervin
Burgess, S. H.	Hodge, Jas. D.	Rodgers, J. Ladson
Burgess, Jno. A.	Hodge, Samuel.	Reardon, D. E.
Barwick, Geo. W.	Herrington, Kinder	Ridgeway, Jno. M.
Brewer, J. F.	Johnston, F. M.	Richburg, B. D.
Barnes, Francis	Johnson, Daniel	Richburg, J. N.
Burgess, Robert B.	Johnson, Jno. J.	Setzer, Alfred
Burgess, J. Calvin	Jacobs, Mitchell	Steadham, G. D.
Brogden, Joseph	Johnson, Pinckney	Smith, Wm. A.
Burgess, W. R. (M. D.)	Johnson, Neighbor	Stukes, F. M.
Burgess, Andrew	Knowlton, Jno. W.	Tobias, Isaac N.
Cockran, Allen	Kelly, Jno. M.	Tobias, Wm. M.
Cutler, James	Lowder, C. A.	Tobias, F. W.
DeLoach, Nelson	Lowder, J. J.	Tobias, J. W.
Davis, J. Elbert	Lowder, H. S.	Tobias, J. Henry
Dickson, Geo. W.	Lowder, J. O.	Tobias, Thomas N.
Evans, Peter	Loyd, Santa	Timmons, J. A.
Evans, C. W.	McCullough, Wm.	Timmons, Wm. J.
Evans, J. H.	McIntosh, John F.	Teetz, Martin
Evans, T. Rush	Mixon, A. W.	Tindal, A. J.
Evans, Joseph W.	Moyd, E. M.	White, Isaac B.
Ervin, L. Nelton	McDonald, R. D.	White, H. Y.
Fleming, B. F.	Pelt, John	White, H. T.
Fleming, H. F.	Plowden, Jno. M.	White, Wm. R., Jr.
Fleming, H. L. B.	Plowden, J. C.	Witherspoon, R. J.
Fleming, W. D.	Pendergrass, Jno. M.	Weston, Geo. W.
Fleming, S. W.	Pendergrass, B. R.	Whitehead, R. W.
Gamble, Thomas E.	Plowden, Joseph	Worsham, Joseph
Gamble, John F.	Richburg, Canty	Worsham, Peter
Gibbons, Gabriel	Richburg, Jas. H.	Windham, Flinn
Hodge, A. J.		

COMPANY K, 25TH REGIMENT.

Gordon, W. B...Captain
Lesesne, E. R..Captain
Lesesne, T. J...First Lieutenant
McDonald, S. W.......................................First Lieutenant
Lesesne, C...First Lieutenant
Saltus, William.....................................Second Lieutenant
Davis, T. B..First Sergeant
Cooper, J. J..Sergeant
Lifrage, T. M..Sergeant
Mims, J. N...Corporal
Micham, W. E...Corporal
Micham, Sam..Corporal
Matthews, C. M...Corporal

PRIVATES.

Altman, W. T.	Dennis, T. J.	Mictham, T.
Ard, John	Dennis, A. J.	Player, J. G.
Ard, E.	Dennis, W.	Player, J. D.
Ard, B.	Duke, W. D.	Player, L.
Barfield, T. E.	Evans, W. T.	Pipkin, J. R.
Blakeley, S. S.	Flowers, J. J.	Rowell, W. T.
Browder, E.	Gamble, J. W.	Smith, W. W.
Browder, McK.	Gamble, A. M.	Smith, F. N.
Browder, W.	Hicks, B.	Stukes, W. N.
Browder, G.	Hodge, J. C.	Scott, M.
Browder, B. R.	Horn, W. W.	Scott, J. F.
Browder, J.	Hodge, J. H.	Scott, L. V.
Byrdick, W. R.	Keels, T. T.	Salters, John
Byrdick, W.	Kirby, J. H.	Terry, G. W.
Brunson, J. H.	Lamb, J. H.	Thomas, J. D.
Baggott, J. A.	Lesesne, P. H.	Thomas, E.
Blakely, T. W.	Lesesne, W. C.	Tanner, J. B.
Cannon, R. J.	Lovell, B. L.	Thomas, H. B.
Cubstead, W. J.	Lamb, Samuel	Wilder, B.
Cubstead, J. E.	Martin, G.	Wilder, John
David, John	McConnell, S. L.	Wilder, L.
Davis, John	McConnell, W. H.	Wilder, S.
Davis, T. H.	Mictham, J. S.	Windham, John
Davis, W.	Mictham, B.	Walters, J. P.

FIELD AND STAFF OF 7TH S. C. BATTALION OF ENFIELD RIFLES.

Nelson, Patrick H....................................Lieutenant-Colonel
Rion, James H.......................................Lieutenant-Colonel
Nelson, Patrick H..Major

Blair, L. W. A.................................Major
Rion, Jas. H..................................Major
Hannahan, R. B...............................Surgeon
Tabor, Chas. R.................Captain and Assistant Surgeon
Weston, Wm..................Captain and Assistant Surgeon
Profest, Wm. K...............Acting Assistant Surgeon
Harrison, Levi..............Captain and Assistant Quartermaster
Mosely, R....................Captain and Assistant Commissary
Nelson, Warren R.............First Lieutenant and Adjutant
Thomas, Wm. M...............First Lieutenant and Adjutant
Irby, A. P...................First Lieutenant and Ensign
Mayrant, Wm.................Color Bearer and First Sergeant
Outz, J. H..................Color Bearer and First Sergeant
Robertson, Jno. B...........Color Bearer and First Sergeant
Cooper, Preston.............Color Bearer and First Sergeant
Remington, Geo. W...........Color Bearer and First Sergeant
Elmore, Albert R.............Sergeant-Major
Fooshee, James W.............Sergeant-Major
Gadsden, Christopher.........Orderly Sergeant
Pate, Henry..................Orderly Sergeant
Smith, Joel A................Orderly Sergeant
Baum, Mannes.................Commissary Sergeant
Harrison, Jno. D.............Commissary Sergeant
Nunnamaker, Henry............Quartermaster Sergeant

COMPANY A, 7TH BATTALION, INFANTRY.

Blair, L. W. R...............................Captain.
Lucas, Benj. S...............................Captain
McCaskell, Finley............................First Lieutenant
Segurs, Dove.................................Second Lieutenant
Gardner, J. W...............................Second Lieutenant
McCask, Allen...............................Second Lieutenant
Hough, Moses................................Second Lieutenant
McSween, Wm.................................Sergeant
Tiller, H. D................................Sergeant
Horton, J. E................................Sergeant
Hargraves, J. E.............................Sergeant
Newman, B. S................................Third Corporal

PRIVATES.

Burns, Isaac	McLaurin, Dan'l	Atkinson, W. H.
Outlaw, M. J.	Pitts, J. C.	(Color)
Outlaw, B. F.	Campbell, Jno.	Allen, Elias
Bethune, Daniel M.	Campbell, Chas.	Allen, W. A.
Clyburn, Jno. H.	Yarborough, W. A.	Allen, W. W.
Gardner, S. L.	McLauren, J. A.	Anderson, John
(Corporal)	(Corporal)	Atkinson, J. J.

Brannar, Elias
Brannon, J. E.
Bateman, W. J.
Blackwell, T. J.
Blackwell, M. T.
Blackwell, U. A.
Berry, J. W.
Bone, J. W.
Bone, J. E.
Bruce, James
Barnes, R. E.
Bethune, N. A.
Beasley, S.
Cameron, W. J.
Cato, James
Caston, J. W.
Clyburn, J. Henry
Clyburn, W. A.
Copeland, Moses
Daniels, W. N.
Douglas, Ed.
Douglas, James
Davis, T. H.
Dunn, T. P.
DeBruhl, Jesse E.
Evans, T. P.
Folsom, S. T.
Gardner, S. T.
Gardner, T. D.
Gardner, W. J.
Gardner, D. W.
Gee, W. N.
Hall, C. L.
Hall, F. M.
Hall, J. M.
Hall, Joseph
Hall, L. McC.
Hall, John J.
Hall, James
Hall, J. R.
Hall, J. E.
Hammerslaugh, S.
Harris, A. T.
Hough, Amos
Hough, Samson
Hyatt, C. W.

Hyott, J. W.
Horton, Ransom
Horton, J. S.
Horton, J. W.
Herron, J. E.
Herron, Samuel
Hopkins, James
Holland, T. R.
Johnson, Noel
Jordan, Colin
Jones, N. W.
Jones, Calvin
King, G. B.
King, G. P.
King, George
King, J. E.
Kelly, J. F.
Lucas, S. D.
Leach, John
Marshall, A. C.
Mosely, Isaac
Mosely, Milberry
Mosely, Reddick
McCaskill, J. D.
McCaskill, J. H.
McCaskill, C. W.
McLendon, Wm.
McGourgan, A.
McGourgan, Jno.
McLaurin, Angus
McPherson, L. B.
Mixon, J. S.
Mixon, L. S.
Daniel, Peter
Murchison, Columbus
Newman, Nelson
Newman, J. H.
Newman, J. T.
Newman, B. W.
Newman, Milberry W.
Nichols, Isaac
Norris, George
Norris, A. C.
Outlaw, Curtis
Parker, Michael
Phillips, S. F.

Rodgers, W. J.
Rodgers, S. C.
Rodgers, J. D.
Randolph, W. F.
Randolph, Thomas
Radcliff, W. C.
Raley, A. W.
Shaw, William
Shirley, J. E.
Sinclair, James
Sinclair, John
Stein, Henry
Scarborough, B. A.
Stokes, E. E.
Stokes, Simeon
Stokes, W. J.
Stokes, Ephraim
Stokes, E. J.
Smith, John
Shumaker, G. N.
Surles, E. M.
Tiller, John
Tiller, J. M.
Tiller, P. W. C.
Turner, R. J.
Turner, B. J.
Warr, H. L.
Waters, Thomas
Watkins, E. M.
Watkins, J. A.
Watkins, P. H.
Watkins, Jesse E.
Watkins, Jno. E.
Watkins, J. J.
Warley, B. M.
Watson, James
Webb, Samuel
West, Joseph
West, R. E.
Woodham, Jno. W.
Williams, A. N.
Yarborough, Wilson
Yarborough, J. C.
Yarborough, E. N.
Young, Samuel

COMPANY B, 7TH BATTALION.

Rion, James H.................................Captain
Harrison, Jno. R..............................Captain
Kennedy, John L...............................Captain
Douglas, S. Wade..............................Captain
Tidwell, Jno. S...............................Captain
Isbelle, H. Lawrence...................First Lieutenant
Cason, Jas. P..........................First Lieutenant
Kennedy, R. W.........................Second Lieutenant
Cook, S. Henry........................Second Lieutenant
Harvey, W. A...............................Lieutenant
Phillips, R. W.........................First Sergeant
Duke, S. H.................................Sergeant
Smith, Joel A..............................Sergeant
Gerig, Francis.............................Sergeant
Gadsden, C. E..............................Sergeant
Rabb, Jas. K...............................Corporal
Duke, H. Oscar.............................Corporal
Fraser, Daniel.............................Corporal
McDonald, Jas. M...........................Corporal

PRIVATES.

Abbott, D.	Brown, J. W.	Dunlap, P. W.
Abbott, John	Brown, W. C.	Dye, J. L.
Abbott, J.	Carter, D.	Easler, Adgena
Allen, J. A.	Castles, J. S.	Easler, E.
Anderson, T.	Cloud, D. G.	Easler, John
Bailey, J. A.	Cloud, J. F.	Eastler, H.
Bagley, W. L.	Cloud, T. E.	Eastler, James
Barber, G.	Cohen, Morris	Estes, E. W.
Barber, N. C.	Cooper, W. J.	Estes, W.
Barber, T. J.	Cork, John	Evans, W. D.
Barker, T. W.	Coleman, J. F.	Faust, J. J.
Baum, M.	Cotton, J.	Field, R. W.
Bell, E. H.	Crawford, D.	Gladden, James
Black, L. D.	Christmas, Thos. H.	Gladden, Silas
Blizzard, D. A.	Crawford, S. L.	Gibson, D. H.
Blizzard, E. J.	Crawford, T.	Goza, E. A.
Blizzard, J. T.	Crosby, C. N.	Gray, G. M.
Brazill, D. L.	Crosby, R. F.	Grunnell, Jos. S.
Bookhart, J. A.	Crumpton, Z. A.	Hammond, H.
Boyd, John	Dawkins, H.	Harrison, Eli
Broom, E. T.	David, Morris	Harrison, J. Edmunds
Broom, C. P.	Dickey, Chas. A.	Hayes, C.
Boney, Jno. T.	Dunbar, H. A.	Haynes, E. W.
Brown, J. L.	Dunbar, S. B.	Hagood, H. W.

Hagood, Joel	McCully, J.	Sharp,
Hagood, J. A.	Melton, L.	Scott, J. Y.
Hagood, G. M.	Mobley, R. L.	Sexton, J. B.
Hinnant, A. R.	Mundle, J. D.	Shepard, W. W.
Hinnant, J. S.	Murray, W. B.	Smith, W. W.
Hobbs, J. A.	Martin, G. E.	Sims, T.
Hogan, M. A.	Neely, J. B.	Simpson, J. D.
Hollis, J. L.	Neil, J. H.	Starnes, J. W.
Hood, H. E.	Ooten, Thos.	Steel, J. A.
Hood, J. J.	Perry, Allen	Sterling, J.
Hood, J. T.	Peake, D.	Stevenson, S. H.
Howell, Sam'l M.	Perry, Isaac	Stevenson, R.
Huey, A. M.	Perry, J. J.	Stevenson, S.
Jamison, A. L.	Perry, S. G.	Stewart, J. Dallas
Jamison, W. H.	Perry, S. N.	Stewart, J.
Jeffers, R. L.	Perry, W. F.	Stewart, W.
Jeffers, A. McK.	Poteat, Jacob A.	Stone, J.
Johnson, R. Thos.	Powers, James	Tidwell, C. L.
Kelly, W. D.	Powers, Lawrence	Thomas, W. L.
Kennedy, A. B.	Propst, H. E.	Trapp, Allen
Kennedy, John	Propst, W. K.	Watts, J. A.
Kennedy, J. F.	Price, C. P.	Watts, J.
Kennedy, J. T.	Price, E.	Wilson, John
King, Benjamin	Rabb, W.	Wilson, J.
Land, F.	Rains, J. M.	Wilson, J. W.
Lewis, R.	Reid, D. J.	Wilson, D.
Levister, J.	Rimer, A.	Wilson, J. M.
Lee, J. S.	Robinson, J. A.	Williamson, J. C.
McDonald, Leander	Roe, W. F.	Wooten, T.
McGrath, H. A.	Rose, J. A.	Wright, J. C.
McGrath, N. C.	Rose, W. C.	Wyrick, J. Z.
McIntyre, John	Rosbore, J. F.	Young, C. B.
McLain, W.	Rush, W.	

COMPANY C, 7TH BATTALION.

Sligh, Wm. H..Captain
Pearson, A. W..Captain
Mankin, Joel R...Captain
Howell, Malley.......................................First Lieutenant
Bell, E. H...First Lieutenant
Elmore, Franklin H.................................Second Lieutenant
Taylor, Wm. H......................................Second Lieutenant
Sligh, T. W..Third Lieutenant
Hill, W. D...Third Lieutenant
Davis, Elihu...First Sergeant
Telford, Wm..Second Sergeant

Johnston, Henry....................................Third Sergeant
Wilson, W. M.....................................Fourth Sergeant
McGill, Wm. P....................................Fifth Sergeant
Hawkins, William....................................Corporal
Braswell, James....................................Corporal
Daniels, Starke....................................Corporal
Neil, R. Y....................................Corporal
Kelly, Asa C....................................Corporal
Medlin, Wesley....................................Corporal

PRIVATES.

Abbott, Wesley	Faust, John	Marsh, Jonathan
Antonio, L. W.	Futril, Sam'l	Martin, Asa
Arledge, Moses	Garner, James	Martin, D.
Augustine, Sam	Gibson, Nicholas	Martin, Joseph
Bayley, James	Gibson, S. D.	Martin, Phillip
Boyer, Moses	Goins, Ainsley	Martin, Thomas
Broughton, Edward	Goins, Henry	Maxey, John
Broughton, Frank	Goins, Ransom	Mayrant, James
Brown, Allen	Goins, Wesley A.	Mayrant, John
Bysander, B.	Haithcock, Hopkins	McCrady, A.
Campbell, D.	Hawkins, Augustus	McCrady, James
Campbell, John	Hawkins, Jno. C.	McLain, Daniel
Campbell, Thos., Sr.	Hawkins, Peter S.	McNeill, Henry
Campbell, Thos., Jr.	Hill, John	McNeill, James, Jr.
Cloud, D. G.	Hill, Lonnie	Medlin, Daniel
Coleman, A.	Hood, John	Medlin, E.
Cook, John	Hornsby, J.	Medlin, Hilliard
Cooper, Eben	Hornsby, Wesley	Medlin, Isaac
Corder, Henry	Horton, Samuel D.	Medlin, John
Corder, James	Hughes, A. F.	Medlin, Samuel
Corley, Jas. D.	Huggins, Daniel	Miles, H.
Cotton, N.	Huson, Robert S.	Mitchell, D. D. D.
Daniels, Edward	Hussey, George	Morrill, Alexander
Daniels, Nathan	Jacobs, Chris.	Outen, Daniel
Daniels, Starke	Jones, Wesley	Powers, James
Davis, David	Justice, Hilliard	Price, Chas.
Davis, James	Justice, William	Price, Frederick
Davis, John	Kelley, F.	Price, George
Davis, R.	Kelley, James	Price, Hugh
Davis, Thomas	Kelley, Pleasanton	Price, John
Davis, W. D.	Lee, James	Price, Thomas J.
Dennis, Gabriel	Lomas, William	Price, Thos. N., Jr.
Deveaux, S. L.	Lorick, J. A.	Rials, John
Dorritty, Thomas	Lovett, Frederick	Rials, Thomas
Elders, John	Lovett, Robert	Rush, William
Evans, James	Lovett, Thomas	Senn, Jacob

Shannon, D. Davis
Sharpe, George
Sharpe, Samuel
Shirley, Rich
Shirley, William
Sidler, Jesse
Sightler, H.
Smith, George
Smith, Henry, Jr.
Smith, Henry, Sr.
Smith, John
Starke, Wm. Pinckney

Strange, Henry
Strickland, John
Thomas, W.
Thompson, Sam
Thornton, John
Thornton, Peter H.
Trapp, Levi
Turnipseed, Edward
Usher, J. C.
Watts, William
Welch, J. J.
Welch, T. R.

Wells, John
Wells, William
Windom, O. K.
Williams, Daniel
Williamson, Wade
Williamson, William
Wilson, M. F.
Wilson, McKenzie
Wilson, Thomas
Wilson, Wm. M.
Wooten, Dan

COMPANY D, 7TH BATTALION.

Jones, J. L..Captain
Clyburn, W...First Lieutenant
Young, E. A..First Lieutenant
Mosley, R...Second Lieutenant
Cunningham, R. J...................................Second Lieutenant
Young, R. W..Second Lieutenant
Malone, W. R..First Sergeant
Clyburn, L. L...Sergeant
Goodale, J. R..Sergeant
Wilson, T...Sergeant
Jones, W. J...Sergeant
Cauthen, W. C...Sergeant
Bell, L. C..Corporal
Young, M. J...Corporal
Young, G. W...Corporal
Lewis, R. T...Corporal
Twitty, L. M..Corporal
Young, W. J...Corporal
Sheorn, J. A..Corporal
Cauthen, L. M...Corporal

PRIVATES.

Adams, W.
Allen, J. W.
Atkinson, R. R.
Ballard, J. F.
Banks, J. M.
Bailey, D.
Barnes, G. W.
Bell, J. L.
Boon, S.
Boon, Z.

Boon, J. W.
Brace, J. T.
Brazil, L.
Brown, T. W.
Brown, J. T.
Billings, C. T.
Bryant, W.
Bullock, G. N.
Capell, H.
Carroll, J.

Cauthen, J. M.
Cauthen, W. C.
Cauthen, W. B.
Cauthen, L. M.
Clyburn, J. C.
Clyburn, J. N.
Copeland, D. J.
Copeland, G. B. T.
Carter, J. F. G.
Coward, J. H.

Dabney, J. H.
Dabney, J. A.
Davis, A. E.
Dixon, G. L.
Denton, W. C.
Duren, W. R.
Dunlap, R. M.
Elmore, A.
Elmore, D.
Farmer, J. A.
Farmer, E. J.
Falconburg, J. A.
Ferrell, J. R.
Fitzpatrick, T.
Gardner, R. J.
Gardner, W. R.
Gaskins, J. G.
Gaskins, J. B.
Gaskins, R.
Gillrane, M.
Green, J.
Gray, S. F.
Griggs, J.
Henderson, W. M.
Henderson, J.
Herbert, S.
Holland, J. C.

Holland, J. R.
Horton, T. C.
Kelley, H.
Kelley, J. J.
Kirby, F.
Latta, R.
Lewis, W. H.
Meggs, S.
Mickle, J.
Marshall, J. C.
McNeill, D.
McNaughton, W. D. N.
Moseley, C. L.
Moore, W.
Moseley, J. C.
Munn, D. A.
Munn, D. M.
Outlaw, R.
Payton, B. M.
Peach, D.
Pendergrass, J.
Price, D. K.
Quinlin, G. M.
Randolph, H.
Ray, N.
Reaves, D.
Reaves, D. R.

Rider, L. F.
Roe, A.
Rutledge, W. F.
Rutledge, J. E.
Ryan, G. R.
Sanders, P.
Self, S.
Self, W. F.
Spears, B. F.
Smith, D. R.
Smith, William
Smith, W.
Smyrl, Thos. I.
Stokes, W. C. J.
Stuckey, A.
Sutton, T. G.
Thomas, J. H.
Thorne, J. R.
Wall, W.
Warren, J. M.
White, R. J.
Williams, J. B.
Williams, J. N.
Wilson, J. T.
Wilson, J.
Young, A.
Vincent, J.

COMPANY E, 7TH BATTALION.

Boykin, B. E..Captain
Gaillard, Phillip P..Captain
Ross, James M...First Lieutenant
Sanders, A...Second Lieutenant
Lenoir, Thos. W...Second Lieutenant
Goodale, Jno. R...Second Lieutenant
Harvey, W. A...Second Lieutenant
Bracey, J. H..Sergeant
Ross, W. A...Sergeant
Atkinson, Chas. M...Sergeant
Gayle, J. Robert..Sergeant
Hox, Thomas..Sergeant
Richardson, Thomas..Sergeant
Cater, John J...Sergeant
Moody, W. M..Corporal
Sanders, Jas. A...Corporal
Brown, Wm. R...Corporal
Benton, J. W...Corporal

Thompson, J. S.....................................Corporal
Berry, Jas. J......................................Corporal
Frost, Charles E...................................Corporal

PRIVATES.

Anderson, W. E.	Dixon, Benjamin	Mitchell, John M.
Allen, James A.	DuBose, William C.	Morris, Henry
Allen, J. P.	Easterling, E. M.	Morris, William
Ammons, Alcien	Goza, E. A.	Moody, Charles E.
Ammons, James	Gerrald, Wm. C.	Myers, Thos. S.
Belk, S. Lawson	Goodale, Joseph	Nunnery, Anderson
Belk, Joseph A.	Gatlin, John T.	Nunnery, Peter
Bracey, Ransom M.	Gaillard, James E.	Nunnery, Peter P.
Brown, Rich C.	Haley, Jno. B.	Prescott, Thos. D.
Brown, Simon	Haley, James B.	Phillips, Henry D.
Brunson, B. D.	Haley, Ferdinand B.	Shull, Martin A.
Bradley, Herbert	Hendricks, James R.	Sanders, John
Cater, James	Hatfield, James W.	Sanders, Garner
Cater, Wm. H.	Ives, James M.	Scott, Abijah
Cater, Henry	Ives, William T.	Scott, Henry
Chambers, S. Oliver	Jolly, John J.	Scott, Geo. W.
Chewning, Jas. H.	Jenkins, Lodolphus F.	Scott, James J.
Cheatham, W. H.	Jeffers, A. McKenzie	Stuart, Dallas
Crawford, D.	Leach, Wm. T.	Thompson, Jno. A.
Cain, James	Moore, L. A.	Willson, Wm. H.
Deas, Henry	McIntosh, James	Willson, S. G.
Dunbar, Adam H.	McDowell, James T.	Willson, John
Dunbar, Robert	McKenzie, Langdon C.	Willson, Wylie

COMPANY F, 7TH BATTALION.

Segar, Dove.......................................Captain
McSwan, William...............................First Lieutenant
Horton, Jas. Ervin............................Second Lieutenant
Tiller, Henry D...................................Lieutenant
Raley, Andrew W...................................Lieutenant
King, Gillam P....................................Lieutenant
Gardner, Stephen L.................................Sergeant
Kelly, Jas. F.....................................Sergeant
Hough, Sampson....................................Sergeant
Pate, Henry.......................................Sergeant
Phillips, Steven F................................Sergeant
McCaskill, Jas. H.................................Sergeant
Gardner, Thos. D..................................Sergeant
Sowell, James E...................................Sergeant
Turner, Benjamin J................................Corporal
Folsom, Stephen T.................................Corporal

Dunn, Thomas P.. .. ..Corporal
Horton, James S.. .. ..Corporal
West, Joseph.. .. ..Corporal
Raley, Reddick.. .. ..Corporal
Newman, Jno. T.. .. ..Corporal

PRIVATES.

Bone, James E.
Bone, William W.
Bruce, James
Barnes, Reddin E.
Barnes, William
Bennen, Neill J.
Bell, Robert J.
Blacknell, Geo. P.
Cato, James
Cato, Wm. T.
Cato, William
Caston, Jno. W.
Cantey, Thos. R.
Culpeper, Jno. H.
Copeland, Thos. R.
Clanton, Lovick
Campbell, Benjamin
Campbell, James
Davis, Thomas H.
Dickson, Jesse
Elliott, William
Folsom, Wm. W.
Folsom, Jno. J.
Gardner, D. Whitfield
Gardner, Wm. J.
Gardner, Milus L.
Gee, Wm. N.
Gibson, Nathan W.
Hall, James
Hall, Wm. E.
Hall, Jacob R.
Hall, Joseph
Holland, Thomas R.
Holland, James
Holland, Thomas
Herron, James E.
Herron, S. Samuel
Horton, Ramsour
Horton, Jas. Wyatt
Horton, Thomas R.
Hopkins, James

Hopkins, Lucius
Hopkins, Malcolm
Hough, Laban C.
Hough, I. Sheppard
Hollis, Hiram F.
Hagood, Jesse M.
Holleyman, Geo. W. L.
Hogan, J. L.
Hornsby, Jesse
Ingram, Moody
Jones, Richard T.
Jones, John T.
Jones, Nathaniel W.
Jones, Samuel N.
Jamieson, C. Alex.
King, George
Kennington, George W.
McCaskill, C. Wesley
McCaskill, Wm. P
McLendon, William
McLendon, Elias
McLendon, Gillis
McGougan, Angus
McGougan, John
McGougan, Archibald
Moseley, Reddick
Miller, R. Peel
Munn, Henry J.
McCoy, Benjamin D.
Newman, John H.
Newman, B. Wylie
Newman, M. W.
Newsom, Henry
Norris, Hubert
Outlaw, Curtis
Pace, J. L.
Phillip, Robert J.
Phillip, Chas. I.
Phillip, Geo. W.
Phillip, W. Riley
Phillips, S. F.

Pate, Levi, Jr.
Pate, Chapman
Raley, Dove
Raley, William
Radcliff, Wm. C.
Robinson, James
Robinson, Hilton
Rains, Muses B.
Smith, John
Searles, Edward M.
Shumake, Geo. N.
Stroud, Lilly T.
Stroud, Jno. M.
Stokes, C. Spencer
Scott, Timothy
Sutton, J. Fred
Sowell, Wylie
Sullivan, James
Shaw, J. Duncan
Turner, Benj. D.
Turner, Robert J.
Thompson, Wm. B.
Thompson, Henry
Tiller, Joseph J.
Thorne, Thos. S.
West, Joseph
Watkins, Jesse E.
Warley, B. M.
Watkins, Jas. J.
Watkins, Jno. E.
Warr, H. L.
Ware, Henry L.
West, Richard E.
Woodham, J. Wesley
Williams, Alex. N.
Williams, Jas. E.
Warren, Wylie L.
Young, Samuel
Yarborough, Eben N.
Yarborough, Thos. G.
Young, Sam

COMPANY G, 7TH BATTALION.

Clyburn, William..Captain
Clyburn, L. L..First Lieutenant
Taylor, W. J..Second Lieutenant
Sligh, Thos. W..Second Lieutenant
Clyburn, L. C..First Sergeant
Rabb, Jas. K...Second Sergeant
Mayrant, J. G...Third Sergeant
Smyrl, Thos. J...Third Sergeant
Smith, Joel A...Fourth Sergeant
Murray, Wm. B...Fifth Sergeant
Cooper, Pres..Color Sergeant
Shears, B. F..First Corporal
Daniels, Edmund.......................................Second Corporal
Cooper, W. J..Third Corporal
Horton, Thos. C.......................................Fourth Corporal

PRIVATES.

Augustine, S. W.	Hays, James	Pendergrass, Joseph
Brown, E. T.	Hill, J.	Price, Thos. N.
Bagley, W. L.	Justice, Hilliard	Peach, William
Broughton, E. L.	Justice, William	Phillips, E. D.
Bradley, D. T.	Jones, L. C.	Perry, Jno. J.
Baskins, W. D.	Jeffers, Thomas	Quinlin, G. W.
Cooper, J. P.	Kirby, T.	Ryder, L. F.
Corder, Jas. A.	Kirby, John	Roe, J. W.
Clyburn, J. N.	King, Benjamin	Robinson, J. W.
Dickey, C. A.	King, Edmund	Rabon, John
Dean, G. A.	Latta, Robert	Smith, Henry
Drakeford, W. H.	Martin, Thomas	Smith, W. L.
Fields, R. H.	Martin, Phillip	Sutton, G.
Gaskins, J. D.	Mikell, Joseph	Sutton, T. G.
Gilliam, Martin	Motley, Samuel	Self, G. W.
Gardner, C. L.	Morris, J. J.	Smyre, J. N.
Gardner, W. R.	Marsh, James	Stuckey, Anderson
Gardner, H. N.	McMullin, A. L.	Tiller, H. A.
Gaskins, G. W.	Marshall, J. C.	Thorne, J. R.
Gay, C. B.	McKennon, L.	Villipigue, J.
Holland, J. R.	Munn, D. D.	Ward, Allen
Holland, Jno. C.	McNeill, Henry	Williams, J. B.
Horton, J. C.	Medlin, C.	Williams, J. N.
Hughes, A. F.	McDowell, A. J.	West, Joseph
Hornsby, J. D.	Nelson, Columbus	Wilkes, William
Honey, Henry	Nelson, Francis	Wilson, John
Hall, H. H.	Outlaw, Bentley	Wilson, W. M.
Henson, Henry	Outlaw, Richard	Wilson, James
Hocutt, Richard	Outlaw, Rosier	

COMPANY H, 7TH BATTALION.

Brooks, J. Hampden..Captain
McCants, Thos. M....................................First Lieutenant
Randall, B. J..First Lieutenant
Weston, William...................................Second Lieutenant
Irby, A. P..Second Lieutenant
Fooshe, J. W..First Sergeant
Drennan, W. A..First Sergeant
Walker, E. P...Second Sergeant
Neal, Wm. M...Third Sergeant
Motley, R. L..Sergeant
Outz, J. H...Color Sergeant
Rush, W. H..Sergeant
Gregory, J. J...Sergeant
Robinson, J. S..Corporal
Brooks, S. J..Corporal
Davis, W. S...Corporal
Johnston, J. W. I...Corporal
Braddy, J. G..Corporal
Hunsucker, F. C...Corporal
Robinson, Jno. B......................................Color Sergeant

PRIVATES.

Addison, H. F.	Fox, James	**Lasure, Fell**
Addison, Hiram	Franklin, J. M.	Laddingham, J. W.
Addison, J. J.	Franklin, W. M.	Livingston, S. D.
Bagley, W. R.	Furness, Mathew	Livingston, Wm.
Bailey, William	Gates, Robert	McCants, G. B.
Bailey, J. D.	Coleman, Jacob	McGill, A.
Bell, John	Gray, Joel	McLaughlin, W. B.
Bell, Henry	Guillebeau, J. C.	McManus, G.
Boykin, H.	Hammond, Asa	Milford, R. W.
Bird, Peter	Harris, J. W.	Martin, J. J.
Cheatham, Alfred	Harrison, Robert	Miles, Stephen
Cogburn, R. M.	Harvely, James	Miller, J. M.
Cothran, S. N. B.	Henderson, J. C.	Miner, J. H.
Cotton, J. L.	Hollingworth, E.	Miner, R. S.
Cotton, T. W.	Hollingworth, J. M.	Powell, J. E.
Dougherty, B.	Holloway, J. S.	Prince, Oliver
Douglas, E. C.	Holloway, W. C.	Roberts, D. S.
Dunning, Reeves	Johnstone, Randall G.	Roberts, W. C.
Durst, G. E.	Jones, D. M.	Rogers, Jasper G.
Elkins, W. F.	Jones, W. H.	Rush, H.
Ellenburg, John	Kennedy, A. D.	**Rush, Jacob**
Ellenburg, Martin	Langley, T. R.	Rush, J. H.

Rush, J. N.	Stalnaker, R.	Walton, J. F.
Rush, W. A.	Stalnaker, T.	Walton, J. S.
Rambo, Warren	Strange, Henry	Whittaker, N.
Scott, T. A.	Street, R. J.	Wyrick, L. V.
Seay, William	Smith, E. P.	Wideman, E.
Shinall, G. W.	Talbert, M. S.	Wideman, F.
Strickland, Starling	Taylor, Wm.	Wideman, S. B.
Sturgeon, Thomas	Thomas, J. S.	Wooten, W. T.
Sturgeon, R. D.	Thomas, Jesse	Wright, B. B.
Sturgeon, J. O.	Thomas, W. M.	Wright, E. C.
Shirley, Samuel	Tinkler, L. D.	Young, Alex.
Shinall, J.	Tyson, W. C.	Young, J. M.
Stalnaker, D. F.	Vandiver, J. B.	

FIELD AND STAFF OF 27TH REGIMENT.

Gaillard, Peter C.............................Colonel
Blake, Julius A.......................Lieutenant-Colonel
Ramsay, David...............................Major
Abney, Joseph...............................Major
Smith, R. Press............Captain, Quartermaster and Commissary
Smith, W. Mason..................Adjutant and Lieutenant
Williams, Winthrop.................Adjutant and Lieutenant
Simons, Alfred D.............Acting Adjutant and Lieutenant
Pressley, J. L.......................Surgeon and Major
Cain, Jos. P...............Assistant Surgeon and Captain
Oxlade, Thomas.........................Sergeant-Major
Howland, W. E...................Commissary Sergeant
Notte, J. O..........................Orderly Sergeant

COMPANY A, 27TH REGIMENT.

(Calhoun Guards.)

Miles, Francis T............................Captain
Palmer, Barnwell W..........................Captain
Axon, J. Waring.............................Captain
Easterly, John M.....................Third Lieutenant
Webb, Daniel C.....................Orderly Sergeant
Baker, Henry H............................Sergeant
Alexander, Geo. W..........................Sergeant
Black, Samuel C............................Sergeant
Gadsden, Thomas............................Sergeant
Smyser, J. William.........................Sergeant
Calvo, C. A...............................Sergeant
Brown, Edmonds T...........................Corporal
Britton, Richard A.........................Corporal

Baker, Eugene B.............................Corporal
Spady, Southey G...........................Corporal
Britton, J. Francis.........................Corporal

PRIVATES.

Axson, Wm. J.	Hall, J. Gadsden	Parker, Thomas
Addison, Capers P.	Hall, F. M.	Petigru, Dan'l
Brown, C. Pinckney	Hammett, Ripley	Radcliff, Geo. T.
Brown, Josiah S.	Horry, Edward S.	Rankin, George F.
Buist, Chas. B.	Hughes, Henry M.	Randall, Edward
Baker, Barnard E.	Hughes, Edward	Schnierlie, Vincent
Buckheister, J. Andrew	Holmes, Isaac	Smith, James, E.
Champlain, Jackson	Innis, Chas. H.	Smith, Julius.
Choate, Eben	Irving, Dr. Aemelius	Smith, Horace
Choate, Thomas	Jervey, Theodore D.	Shannon, Henry
Clayton, David B.	Jervey, Lewis	Sutton, William
Champlain, Edward	Johnston, William	Swinton, J. Ralph
Cherry, William	Johnston, Pringle	Tennent, Josiah S.
Caldwell, Wm. A.	Jackson, Thomas	Tennent, Gilbert V.
Davis, Calvin T.	Kingman, Oliver H.	Trenholm, Paul C.
Davis, G.	Kiddell, Theodore	Vincent, William
Easterly, Washington N.	Martin, T. Ogier	Waring, Dr. Jno. B.
Fengas, Hippolyte V.	Mellichampe, Wm. S.	Westendorff, Jas. S.
Gibbes, J. Perroneau	Miot, Jno. C.	Westendorff, Charles
Heriott, Wm. B.	Millikin, Adam E.	Webb, Paul H.

COMPANY B, 27TH REGIMENT.

Simons, Thomas Y....................................Captain
Clarkson, William.............................First Lieutenant
Sinkler, Wm. W..............................Second Lieutenant
Masterman, Alfred H.........................Second Lieutenant
Muckenfuss, Allen W.........................Second Lieutenant
Chamberlain, Henry A...........................First Sergeant
Wright, J. D..................................Second Sergeant
McMahon, D.....................................Third Sergeant
Bluitt, A. J..................................Fourth Sergeant
Gardner, Jas. A................................Fifth Sergeant
Summerall, Wm. H...............................First Corporal
Buckheister, Wm. C............................Second Corporal
Crosby, Jno. C.................................Third Corporal
McSweeny, M...................................Fourth Corporal
Masterman, Edwin J.............................Lance Corporal
Walsh, James..................................Lance Corporal

PRIVATES.

Arnold, John	Hellers, William	Phosphal, John
Anderson, Wm.	Harris, Jno. C.	Perry, John
Adams, Henry	Harris, William	Perry, Robert
Addison, Jno. C.	Hynes, James, Sr.	Page, William
Addison, Jos. A.	Hynes, James, Jr.	Page, Henry
Betschman, John	Horlbeck, Edward	Palmer, Lewis M.
Bates, Henry	Hughes, Thomas	Phelan, Michael
Bowers,	Johnson, John	Pool, James M.
Boyd, Chas. J.	Johnson, Capers	Pearson, John
Bee, Norman	Johnson, Paul T.	Quinn, Russell
Burns, Edward	Knight, Absolom	Seabrook, E. Smyley
Blocker, Hamilton W.	Kimmey, Francis E.	Stutts, Mathew M.
Barnett, John	Kirby, Lee	Seay, Henry M.
Belcher, William	Kirby, John M.	Sweeney, Michael
Conlon, Jno. B.	Lamb, Wm. J.	Steward, Richard
Christmas, Andrew J.	Lucas, George	Simon, Alfred D.
Carey, Thomas	Littlejohn, John	Symmers, Geo. W.
Canten, Richard	Littlejohn, George	Symmers, Jno. H.
Conroy, Thomas	Lotz, Peter	Sullivan, Andrew J.
DuPre, James C.	Lake, Edward	Sheridan, Thos., Sr.
DuPre, Joseph	Lake, John	Sheridan, Thos., Jr.
Doyle, George W.	Linstedt, Henry	Stevens, John H.
Donahoe, John	Lindsay, Chas. T.	Staley, John
De Veaux,	Maull, Bernard P.	Sauls, Benjamin
Deverin,	Murphy, Timothy	Smith, James
Edwards, John	Moss, William	Smith, John
Edwards, Jno. W.	Mabry, Jno. C.	Sutcliffe, Wm. H.
Friend, Robert	McCreery, William	Sineath, Joseph A.
Foucher, J. Victor	McAteer, John	Tavell, Edward
Floyd, John	Molloy, John	Taylor, William H.
Gruber, Charles	Murray, Thomas	Turner, C. C.
Gibbon, Michael	McDowell, Robert	Turner, Geo. W.
Graser, George	McCarthy, Lawrence	Vaughan, Wm.
Gibbes, J. Reeves	Morrisey, Patrick	Van-Wiper, Henry
Herbert, Chas. W.	McManus, Robert E.	Wood, Robert
Hollander, Matthew	McLane, Wm. T.	Webb, Walter
Hollander, John	Nunan, Cornelius	Wheeler, James G.
Hammett, Jno. C.	Neill, Daniel	Williams, Jefferson
Hanahan, Whitridge	Nesbitt, Wm. J.	Whitlock, Wm. F.
Halsall, William H.	Petch, Emanuel M.	

COMPANY C, 27TH REGIMENT.

Lord, Samuel.....................................Captain
Brown, Geo. W.....................................Captain
Campbell, James.............................First Lieutenant
Hendricks, H. W.........................Second Lieutenant

Riley, J............................First Sergeant
Connolly, P........................Second Sergeant
Ristig, W..........................Third Sergeant
Wood, W. C........................Fourth Sergeant
Cassidy, J.........................Fifth Sergeant
Dangerfield, R.....................First Corporal
Smith, E. P........................Corporal
Jackson, A. M......................Corporal
Kirby, H. N........................Corporal
Sherer, Jno. M.....................Corporal

PRIVATES.

Anderson, J. R.	Edwards, P.	Malone, P.
Ashe, J. J.	Faulbeer, A.	Maccabee, N. P.
Brown, J.	Ferris, J. B.	Maccabee, J. N.
Butt, J. F.	Falls, E. C.	Miskelly, J. W.
Berry, W. P.	Flynn, J.	Mullings, W.
Barry, W. L.	Glenn, M.	Nagle, L.
Bomar, W. B.	Gill, E. H.	Patrick, C.
Bomar, J. E.	Griffith, J. G.	Pierson, D. W.
Biggers, A. J.	Harshaw, H. J.	Pringle, J.
Biter, Alex.	Hughes, E.	Quinn, J. M.
Beardon, S. S.	Hughes, J.	Quinn, R.
Brown, S. S.	Hesch, C.	Rhode, D.
Blake, Charles	Hines, J.	Robinson, A.
Bagwell, Jos. B.	Hanna, J. C.	Rees, B. F.
Braner, H.	Heigh, T. P.	Riley, J.
Baker, F.	Heffner, M.	Stanton, A.
Boesch, J. J.	Herbert, J. C.	Sobbe, E.
Breene, P. J.	Hamby, A.	Seay, J. H.
Brice, A.	Hudson, H. C.	Sellers, R. A.
Buchanan, C.	Harrington, W.	Shillinglaw, W. A.
Cooper, W.	Jeffers, B.	Schultiess, E.
Caldwell, S. A.	Jackson, W. P.	Stack, J.
Caldwell, A. P.	Kelly, John	Schroeder, H.
Childers, J.	Lay, C.	Shoefflin, J.
Chesney, G. W.	Lindon, I.	Seibert, F.
Cassidy, D.	Leive, E.	Smith, E.
Cook, H.	Lawton, G. W.	Thomas, S. A.
Davis, P.	Lowry, S.	Taylor, H.
Daly, T.	Lipscomb, W. L.	Ussery, T. B.
Drummond, J. F.	McDonald, A. A.	Weddigan, E.
Duncan, Alexander	McDavitt, J.	Whitehead, B.
Dugan, R. E.	McNeill, J.	Watson, C.
Eggerking, F. W.	McCarley, J. M.	Wooten, J. H.
Evans, L. K.	McCaffrey, J.	Williamson, J.
Edwards, J. P.	Michaelis, J. H.	West, A. J.
Epps, B. W.		

COMPANY D, 27TH REGIMENT.

King, Henry C..Captain
Hopkins, J. Ward...Captain
Cay, John A..Captain
Wells, Joseph T..First Lieutenant
Hopkins, Chas M..First Lieutenant
Barbot, Peter J.......................................Second Lieutenant
Lance, A. St. John....................................Second Lieutenant
Stoney, Isaac D.......................................Second Lieutenant
Edwards, Jno. J................................Junior Second Lieutenant
Foster, Charles.......................................First Sergeant
Arnold, Thomas..Sergeant
Smith, W. Kirkwood....................................First Sergeant
Beckman, Wm. W..First Sergeant
Foster, Henry P..Sergeant
Gilliland, Arthur..Sergeant
Saylor, Henry E..Sergeant
Williams, Winthrop...Sergeant
Valentine, Isaac D...Corporal
Neufville, H. S..Corporal
Frouche, Augustus F..Corporal
Dingle, G. Wesley..Corporal
Poole, Frank S...Corporal
Starnes, Robert C..Corporal
Stegin, J. H...Corporal

PRIVATES.

Armstrong, D. A.	Beason, Samuel	Cleary, William
Abrams, T. H.	Blanton, L. L.	Cleary, J. E.
Alley, James A.	Bryson, Thos. J.	Clopton, G. W.
Aldrich, C. F.	Bryson, John H.	Compton, W. B.
Arlington, C. H.	Bumpers, A.	Davis, W. A.
Austin, Sam'l	Butler, John W.	Dewees, Thos. H.
Atkinson, T. W.	Bullington, D. G.	Davenport, J. C.
Barbot, A.	Burns, W. L.	Edgerton, Sam'l F.
Barbot, A. A.	Byars, N.	Ellison, A. E.
Ball, Y. J.	Brown, J. S.	Evans, R. C.
Ball, J. J.	Brown, A. J.	Foster, Chas. B.
Bailey, Wm. A.	Casey, Thomas	Fickling, J. H.
Ballentine, G. P.	Cash, M. S.	Fisher, Sam'l W., Jr.
Barksdale, J. C.	Cannon, W. H.	Fowler, Jno. F.
Barksdale, Jno. A.	Colson, Andrew C.	Fowler, W. W.
Beadle, R. T.	Cook, James C.	Fowler, James F.
Beadle, B. A.	Check, John	Fooshe, J. H.
Bee, Sandiford	Chandler, J. W.	Fooshe, John
Bee, William E.	Chandler, J. J.	Floyd, Miles

Garland, W. H., Jr.	Martin, S. B.	Saxon, J. F.
Garrett, E. B.	Martin, L. S.	Saxon, Jack
Garrett, T. B.	Miler, David A.	Shaffer, Fred J.
Gibbes, Allen S.	Miller, Daniel	Stone, M.
Graves, W. W.	Milford, J. W.	Smith, Whiteford S.
Graves, W. B.	Milam, William	Saylor, Jacob J.
Grant, A. A.	Moodie, A. G.	Strange, Perry
Griffin, W. H.	McPherson, J. M.	Strange, J. A. W.
Gyles, W. Alfred	Middleton, Thos., Jr.	Stroble, A. Stuart
Hamilton, Jno. A.	Moses, Edward L.	Suran, Henry T.
Harrison, F. M.	Moore, W. B.	Sweeney, J. R.
Harrison, J. F.	Moore, R. L.	Soxby, J. H.
Haselton, E. E.	Moore, J. H.	Switzer, L. O.
Helames, J. H.	McAbee, W. C.	Taylor, E. G.
Helames, W. H.	Martin, S. V.	Tennant, Edward S.
Helames, Y. C.	McCrady, J. P.	Tennant, Wm., Jr.
Hitch, S. G.	Motes, A. Y.	Tennant, Chas. J.
Howland, Wm. E.	Nathans, J. N.	Terry, E. L.
Hughes, Thos. S.	Nelson, Josiah	Theus, S.
Hyde, Samuel T.	Nelson, W. A.	Timms, J. M.
Johnson, Thomas N.	Nelson, Thomas	Toomer, Edward P.
Johnson, Wm. W.	Owings, M. J.	Tupper, James, Jr.
Joel, John	Owens, R.	Turner, John G.
Kennedy, M. B.	O'Sullivan, M.	Walker, G. W.
King, Wm. L.	Pinson, Jno. H.	Walker, E. T.
Knight, J. A.	Pinson, Jabez R.	Walker, John
Lamotte, Henry J.	Plane, Thomas	Ware, W. A. J.
Levin, S. M.	Poole, Andrew B.	Watts, R. S.
Lindsay, Henry A.	Pitts, James Y.	Wells, Clement
Lucius, J. R.	Porter, Joseph H.	Wells, B. M.
Lockwood, Thos. P.	Pope, M. T.	Watson, J. D.
Macbeth, Edward W.	Posnanski, Gustavus	Withers, T. R.
Macbeth, Wm. L.	Roumillat, A. J. A.	Withers, James
Mahoney, Michael	Ray, F. T.	Wilson, W. A.
Madden, Z. L.	Reeder, R. S.	Wilson, A. B.
Madden, J. A.	Ried, C. Henry	Williams, J. C.
Madden, Moses	Redden, Henry	Wheeler, G. R.
Martin, H. H.	Roberts, Jno. F.	Wharton, John
Martin, L. D.	Rutledge, Jno. E.	

COMPANY E, 27TH REGIMENT.

Chisolm, R.. .. ..Captain
Proctor, S. R.. .. ..First Lieutenant
Crooker, T. B.. .. ..Second Lieutenant
Remmerlin, S. M.. .. ..Brevet Second Lieutenant
Cady, W. N.. .. ..Second Sergeant
Jackson, J. M.. .. ..Fifth Sergeant

Davis, J. R.. .. ..Third Sergeant
Cady, T. N.. .. .. Fourth Sergeant
Wood, F.. .. ..First Corporal
Castin, W. J.. .. .. Second Corporal
Watts, W. P.. .. .. Third Corporal

PRIVATES.

Abney, J. B.	Garrick, J. R.	Owens, J. L.
Barse, D. J.	Gleaton, W. M.	Owens, W. R.
Beck, M. J.	Gregory, John T.	Owens, J. A.
Bolin, S. E.	Hammond, H.	Poole, John
Brown, Josiah	Hallman, J. W.	Rice, J. N.
Brown, Joshua	Hall, J. C.	Ready, J. P.
Brooker, B. D.	Hendrix, G. S.	Redmore, J. L.
Carson, J. C.	Humphries, M.	Rumbly, A. J.
Cartin, E.	Humphries, W. L.	Shirey, S. W.
Cartin, W. C.	Hull, J. M.	Scott, F. T.
Chapman, D. N.	Jackson, J. P.	Smith, E.
Crabtree, G.	Jones, L. M.	Smith, W. S.
Coats, D. N.	Jones, W. F.	Slaggs, R.
Craft, J.	Jones, J. A.	Thrift, John
Cromer, J. R.	Kissick, J. W.	Ulm, R. M.
Centerfield, S.	Kissick, T. R.	Varnes, W. M.
Cockerell, J.	Leach, J.	Walker, James
Coffee, J. H.	Murphy, J. M.	Wood, Jesse
Dockins, L.	Madden, L. C.	Whetten, A. M.
Duncan, G. W.	McGill, A.	Williams, D. N.
Duncan, T. J.	Nates, J. C.	Willson, J. C.
Davenport, H.	Neal, B.	Zeigler, D. F.
Fowler, R.	Neal, R. L.	

COMPANY F, 27TH REGIMENT.

Allston, Thos. Blyth.. .. ..Captain
Huguenin, Julius G.. .. ..Lieutenant
Stuart, Middleton.. .. ..Lieutenant
Cater, E. P.. .. ..Lieutenant
Porcher, Chas. Pettegru.. .. ..Cadet
Watts, Pickens B.. .. ..First Sergeant
Floyd, Thos. G.. .. ..First Sergeant
Gibbons, J. P.. .. .. Second Sergeant
Staubs, Jacob.. .. .. · .. ..Third Sergeant
Boozer, Jacob.. .. .. Fourth Sergeant
Stone, W. L.. .. ..First Corporal
Lemon, W. O.. .. .. Second Corporal
Attaway, T. G.. .. ..Third Corporal
Kirby, Evander.. .. .. Fourth Corporal

Boatwright, Eli.. .. ..Corporal
Welch, Joseph.. .. ..Corporal

PRIVATES.

Aaron, J. J.	Galloway, W. T.	Reddy, James
Arthur, J. T.	Gant, W. H.	Reddy, Wm.
Attaway, J. A.	Gibbs, Joseph	Smith, S. M.
Aultman, Thomas	Gibbs, Thos. E.	Smith, James
Barfield, M.	. Glisson, J. C.	Seay, Geo. W.
Barfield, W. H.	Graham, G.	Smith, J. R.
Bailey, Samuel	Goodman, J. H.	Singletary, Jno. J.
Bladon, T. J.	Gibbons, J. C.	Tanner, Edward D.
Bowman, J. W. D.	Griffith, H. W.	Thomas, Oliver
Brodie, M.	Hulon, Ervin	Thomas, Rowan
Brown, William	Hunt, Chas.	Thomas, Huger
Bryant, J. T.	Hunt, George	Thomas, James
Butler, C. W.	Healy, F. W.	Thomas, D. R.
Birkett, W. H.	Healy, J. B.	Thornhill, B. B.
Benenhaley, Jno.	Jones, David	Tolson, B. G.
Benenhaley, Randall	Keaton, John	Taylor, Henry
Calder, Malcolm	Keels, D. E.	Tanner, James
Calder, W.	Long, W. W.	Turner, G. W.
Calder, James	Long, Jno. M.	Traynham, A. J.
Chandler, Isaac J.	Long, Wm.	Taylor, J. W.
Cockerill, Wesley	Logan, A. J.	Vausse, J. J.
Coulter, Alexander	Logan, F. S.	Vausse, A. E.
Deas, Franklyn	Lane, Jas. D.	Walden. J.
De Loach, George	Lemmon, W. H. B.	Welch, S. W.
De Loach, Caleb	McDaniel, P. B.	Williams, J.
De Loach, Allen	Moore, J. K.	Woodward, J. M.
De Loach, Wm.	Moore, S. R.	Walker, Nathaniel
De Loach, Milledge	Moyd, E. M.	Woodward, W.
Dean, John	Murrell, B. L.	White, J. W.
Desnoyers, L.	Newberry, A. McCants	Welch, Samuel
Dorman, D.	Padgett,	Weaver, J. P.
Earle, T. T.	Plunkett, C.	Weaver, Oscar
Floyd, W. H.	Proctor, D.	Wightman, W. S.
Fulmer, W. T.	Rutland, Ezekial	Wright, James
Galloway, S. P.		

COMPANY G, 27TH REGIMENT.

(Charleston Sharpshooters or Palmetto Guards.)

Buist, Henry.. .. ..Captain
Holman, Edward H.. .. ..Lieutenant
Macbeth, Chas. J.. .. ..Lieutenant
White, Abbott B.. .. ..Lieutenant

Harr, Thos. C.. .. ..Sergeant
Mims, Fletcher.. .. ..Sergeant
Bookhart, D. B.. .. ..Sergeant
Shuler, P. C.. .. ..Sergeant
Way, J. F.. .. ..Sergeant
Johnson, R. C.. .. ..Corporal
Gordon, J.. .. ..Corporal
Huffman, J. H. S.. .. ..Corporal
Burke, I. J.. .. ..Corporal

PRIVATES.

Ables, N.	Hames, G.	Lucas, J. R.
Andrews, W.	Hart, A. R.	McMakin, W. G.
Bailey, J. D. A.	Harvey, Wm.	Meadows, J.
Barber, John	Horsey, W.	Moore, G. W.
Baum, C.	Hays, W.	Moore, E. W.
Blakely, J. K.	Hill, B. W.	Neese, G.
Brock, G.	Hollingsworth, W.	Neighbours, W.
Bryant, B.	Huffman, M.	Neighbours, J.
Bryson, W.	Huffman, F.	Nelson, T.
Bryson, J.	Hungerpeeler, Jim	Oshields, J.
Burgess, J.	Irby, S. V.	Perkins, T. C.
Burkitt, Wm.	James, F.	Poole, L.
Burroughs, T. C.	James, R.	Powers, G.
Campbell, W. J.	Jennings, J.	Pyles, M.
Campbell, J. McD.	Johnson, H.	Rainwater, J. P.
Copeland, H.	Jordan, H.	Rice, H.
Crossley, E.	Keaton, J.	Riddle, S. T.
Dodd, Dixon	Kemerling, S.	Riddle, William
Duckett, J.	King, D. A.	Rodgers, A. M.
Dunn, E.	Knight, T.	Rodgers, L. P.
Dunford, A. J.	Lamb, J.	Rourke, A. V.
Dunford, M.	Lambreth, R.	Shuler, C. E.
Emory, J.	Lartigue, E. J.	Smith, William
Evans, L. W.	Lamson, J.	Smith, F. J.
Floyd, D.	Leaird, D.	Smith, W. B.
Fuller, J.	Leaird, J. H.	Smith, J. F.
Gantt, Z.	Leaird, J. J.	Stevens, J.
Gartman, S.	Leaird, T. L.	Stone, J.
Gilliam, B. B.	Leaird, I. J.	Stone, W. A.
Godfrey, T. P.	Leaird, R. S.	Sumeral, J. H.
Gossett, W.	Lewis, J. R.	Taylor, A. S.
Grice, F.	Lewis, G. W.	Teague, L. K.
Givin, T. D.	Lewis, T. J.	Templeton, R. J.
Givin, W. P.	Livingston, L. M.	Thomas, E.
Givin, J.	Lovett, W. L.	Tribble, C. E.

Vise, J. E.	Wiles, P. E.	Michael, B.
Vogt, T. P.	Witkofsky, J.	McKenzie, A.
Waldrup, B. W.	Woofe, R.	Floyd, H.
Ward, J.	Woodward, T. J.	Floyd, W.
Whitmire, B.	Woodward, H. P.	Scott, A.
Whitten, M. B.	Wyatt, R.	John, Marco
Whitten, A.	Zeikle, A.	

COMPANY H, 27TH REGIMENT.

Ryan, W. H...Captain
Mulvaney, J. M...Captain
Allemong, A. A..First Lieutenant
Burke, John...Second Lieutenant
Hogan, P. R..First Lieutenant
Hogan, Thos. L..First Sergeant
O'Neil, F. L..First Sergeant
Carroll, Patrick....................................Second Sergeant
Ward, Daniel...Third Sergeant
Lee, Edward..Third Sergeant
Preston, Jno. F.....................................Fourth Sergeant
Madigan, Lawrence...................................Fourth Sergeant
Lanigan, Edward......................................Fifth Sergeant
Moran, Michael.......................................Fifth Sergeant
Harrington, Wm.......................................First Corporal
Jager, J. Adolphus.................................Second Corporal
Conroy, John...First Corporal
Culleton, Patrick...................................Third Corporal
Doherty, Luke......................................Fourth Corporal

PRIVATES.

Brooks, Robert	Dougherty, James	Gratton, Daniel
Bresman, Thomas	Driscoll, Timothy	Goodrich, Allan
Chandler, W. M.	Dinan, William	Goodrich, Henry
Callager, James	Dinan, Cornelius	Goodrich, Thomas
Carmady, J.	Dougherty, J. C.	Gleason, Thomas
Carroll, Thomas	Dairy, Thomas	Gaffney, R.
Cavanah, Thos.	Dunn, J.	Hartwell, Michael
Cullinane, M.	Edwards, James	Hancock, J.
Carey, Thomas	Edwards, John	Hayden, Thomas
Cummings, James	Egan, Thomas	Hurley, Jerry
Carroll, James	Fowler, James	Hanley, Patrick
Crowley, Richard	Fitzgerald, S.	Hanley, Edward
Connelly, Thos.	Flannigan, Patrick	Hill,
Cosgrove, James	Flaherty, Thos.	Hogan, Patrick
Dodds, George	Fludd, Luke	Howard, D.
Divine, John L.	Flynn, James	Hughes, Thos.

James, T. C.
Kenny, Peter
Liddy, J.
King, John
Lipscomb, W. S.
Lee, Edward
Lee, Patrick
Maher, John
Molone, Jas.
Molone, Thos.
Murphy, Joseph
Murphy, Tim
Manion, Patrick
Manion, Thomas
Martin, Peter
Millan, Charles

May, John
McManigal, Jas.
McDonald, James
McMahon, John
Moloney, John
Nunan, John
O'Neil, D.
O'Neil, Patrick
O'Neil, Henry
Phillips, James
Ramey, Thos.
Ryan, Edward
Ryan, Thomas
Reynolds, Samuel
Sullivan, Martin

Sheahan, Thos.
Shelton, William
Shannon, M.
Todd, James
Toole, Michael
Walsh, James
Walsh, J.
Whelan, Rhody
Whelan, Edward
Wise, Thomas
Wise, Richard
Warren, Christopher
Warren, John
Wiley, Rudolph
Wiley, Henry

COMPANY I, 27TH REGIMENT.

Blake, Julius A...Captain
Walter, W. Dove...Captain
Salters, J. C...First Lieutenant
Lynch, Frank..Second Lieutenant
Cudnorth, Arthur G..Lieutenant
Trim, Wm. J..Lieutenant
Patterson, E. R..First Sergeant
Hurst, James...Second Sergeant
Lumbers, Frank..Sergeant
Pooser, B. W...Sergeant
Swinton, Hugh...Sergeant
Guy, John W..Sergeant
Jeannerette, E. N...Sergeant
Roach, E. L..Sergeant
Rowand, Robert...Sergeant
Seybt, Robt. F..First Sergeant
Badger, Joseph...Corporal
Champlain..Corporal
Campbell, Geo..Corporal
Badger, David..Corporal
Gouvenir, Julius...Corporal
Manude, J. A...Corporal
Speissigger, C. A..Corporal

PRIVATES.

Adams, C. D. C.
Adams, John
Adams,
Adkins,
Addickes, Henry
Addickes, C. E.
Anderson, W. H.
Allen, Edward
Buchanan, Thos.
Bee, Norman
Bee, John P.
Brown, Edwin
Barclay, James
Badger, Joseph
Betsell, Henry
Bale, William
Binder,
Collins, Samuel
Cheney, I. S. R.
Colson, Henry
Collier, Joseph
Carstin, F. H.
Carstin, C. G.
Cheney, S.
Davy, George
Deal, William
Danner, John M.
Danner, A.

DuBois, J.
Egan, F. C.
Egan, C. E.
Gradick, Edward
Gibson, Geo. B.
Gowan, John F.
Groverman.
Grover, George
Grover, John
Horlbeck, Edward C.
Ham, William
Ham, H. U.
Ham, Henry
Hudgins, Henry
Jordan, E. W.
Johnson, T. H.
Jarcks, G. H.
Kelly,
Lynch, F. L.
Lequeux, Marion
Miller, William
McAbee
McAbee,
McIntosh, D.
Maxie, George
Maunde, J. A.
Newton, T. E.
Newton, H. D.

Note, J. O.
Oxlade, Thomas
Oliver, Joseph
Pollard, W. C.
Pierce, Henry
Powers, Thomas
Rhodes, James
Rhodes, George
Randall, Henry
Ryan, J.
Ross, Jno. H.
Riggs, J. S.
Steinmeyer, James
Seyle, William J.
Sanders, Henry
Suares, J. E.
Sires, S.
Sassard, J. A.
Speissinger, L. P.
Strain, William
Thompson, John
Thompson, J. W.
Williams, Henry
Wilder, J. F.
Wood, James
Young, Henry
Zimmerman, W. A.

COMPANY K, 27TH REGIMENT.

Clarkson, William.......................................Captain
Harris, J. G.....................................First Lieutenant
Simons, A. D...................................Second Lieutenant
Seay, R. B...............................Brevet Second Lieutenant
McSweeny, M......................................First Sergeant
Montgomery, P. S....................................Sergeant
Collins, J. A..Sergeant
Turner, T. H..Sergeant
Lotzen, H. L..Corporal
Chapman, W. D......................................Corporal
Bishop, W. P..Corporal
Perry, Wm. L..Corporal

PRIVATES.

Anderson, Wm.
Alley, R. C.
Bates, G. W.
Bishop, H.
Blackwood, C.
Bridges, G. H.
Bragg, D. W.
Brannon, J. J.
Beardon, G. L.
Cantrell, E.
Cantrell, T. B.
Cantrell, R. H.
Cannon, T. H.
Carlton, J. T.
Carlton, M. S.
Castleberry, J. H.
Crosby, J. J.
Conlin, J. B.
Cooksey, T. L.
Chapman, M. B.
Davidson, H. M.
De Young, William
Duberry, D. J.
Dupre, J.
Edwards, W. P.
Eskew, Y. D.
Ford, M. D.
Floyd, J.
Floyd, M.
Fowler, H.
Foster, J. J.

Gentry, H.
Griffin, T. B.
Griffin, N.
Goforth, J. P.
Harnes, L. B.
Harnes, F.
Harvey, J.
Hawley, A. M.
Henderson, M.
Hendricks, T. M.
Heller, William
Hullender, M.
Humphries, T.
Horton, W. R.
Kirby, L.
Kirby, J. M.
Kirby, L. C.
Kay, James
Lucas, George
Lewis, Poser
Lindsay, W. H.
Lindstedt, H.
Maul, B.
Mayfield, J. M. C.
McElrath, D. T.
McElrath, J.
McDowell, W. G.
McCarter, S.
Page, J. C. C.
Parris, W. B.

Perry, A. J., Sr.
Pearson, J. T.
Pearson, A. P.
Pearson, G. L
Poole, E. V.
Poole, L.
Powers, J. A.
Quinn, A. R.
Quinn, L. C.
Ray, W.
Rodgers, J. D.
Roberson, J. R.
Smith, A.
Smith, J. P.
Spell, J. D.
Turner, H. H.
Turner, Wm.
Turner, B. O.
Timmons, A. J.
Vaughan, W. S.
Williams, E.
Wilson, W.
March,
   (col. musician)
Williams,
     (col. cook)
Manly,
     (col. cook)
Jeffrey,
     (col. cook)

FIELD AND STAFF, 11TH REGIMENT.

Heyward, W. C.................................Colonel
Ellis, Dan'l H................................Colonel
Gantt, F. Hay................................Colonel
Shuler, Wm...............................Lieutenant-Colonel
Campbell, Robert.........................Lieutenant-Colonel
Izard, Allen C...........................Lieutenant-Colonel
Smith, Benj. B...............................Major
Harrison, Jno. J.............................Major
Gooding, J. J................................Major
Fraser, Edward R...........................Adjutant
Porter.....................................Adjutant
Bell.......................................Adjutant

Davis, Charles F...Adjutant
Gantt, Richard P......................Assistant Quartermaster
Sams, B. B..Commissary
Williams, A. English..Surgeon
Black, Benjamin.............................Assistant Surgeon
Gantt, Eldred S...Sergeant
Ervin, Samuel..........................Commissary Sergeant

COMPANY B, 11TH REGIMENT.

Westcoat, J. J...Captain
Bowman, H. W. G..............................First Lieutenant
Ellis, W. D...................................Second Lieutenant
Stutts, R. R..................................Second Lieutenant
Rumph, D. A..................................Third Sergeant
Platt, John.................................Fourth Sergeant
Stutts, Geo..................................Second Corporal
Wilkinson, W...............................Second Corporal
Black, John.................................Second Lieutenant
Farr, Thomas...............................First Sergeant
Martin, H. P...............................First Corporal

PRIVATES.

Ayer, John	Groomes, H.	Price, W
Atkinson, W.	Groomes, R.	Ritts, John
Barr, James	Hollins, J.	Ritts, Thomas
Benton, H.	Hutson, J.	Rivers, B.
Benton, S.	Howard, W.	Rose, A. W.
Branton, R.	Harris, W.	Rudd, J. L.
Blumingby, D.	Hucks, John	Rush, S.
Bishop, M.	Infinger, N.	Rush, James
Bowman, W.	Johnson, G. A. T.	Rictor, N. G.
Bowman, N.	Johnson, John	Simmons, J. L.
Corley, John	Lester, James	Simmons, J. A.
Caddin, W.	Lacey, Thomas	Thompson, James
Caddin, R.	Martin, Ed.	Thompson, Thomas
Cordes, G.	Manning, James	Varner, M. T.
Dilk, W. L.	Mizzles, Joe	Weatherly, J. D.
Doyle, A.	Newton, A.	Willis, J.
Doyle, M.	Newton, George	Wood, W.
Driggers, John	Pendavis, R.	Waldorf, A.
Floyd, M.	Platt, J. H.	

COMPANY B, 11TH REGIMENT.
(Added as Supplementary Roll.)

Smith, Benj. B..Captain
Meggett, Wm. C..Captain
Westcoat, Julius J..Captain

Corbett, D. H................................First Lieutenant
Dawson, J. H................................First Lieutenant
Bowman, W. H...............................First Lieutenant
LaRoche, Richard...........................Second Lieutenant
Chaplin, E. D..............................Second Lieutenant
Ellis, W. D................................Second Lieutenant
Simmons, W. C..............................Second Lieutenant
Black, Jno.................................Second Lieutenant
Wilkinson, D. J....................................Sergeant
Freshwater, J. H...................................Sergeant
Farr, Thos...Sergeant
Stutts, R. R.......................................Sergeant
Wilkinson, J. M....................................Sergeant
King, A. Sidney....................................Sergeant
LaRoche, Ed. D.....................................Sergeant
Bunch, Jno...Sergeant
Rumph, D...Sergeant
Simmons, J. S......................................Sergeant
Simmons, J. T......................................Sergeant
Platt, Jno...Corporal
Wilkinson, J. O....................................Corporal
Platt, Jno., Jr....................................Corporal
McMillan, J..Corporal
Martin, H. P.......................................Corporal
Malloy, Lewis......................................Corporal

PRIVATES.

Atkinson, W.	Driggers, John	Jenkins, Jos. E.
Allen, J. T.	Doyle, A.	Johnson, Geo.
Albers, James	Doyle, Marion	Johnson, James
Barr, James	Daniels, A. W.	Johnson, John
Benton, H.	Floyd, M.	Lacey, James
Bishop, Hill	Gibson, O.	Lester, Thomas
Blumingburg, D.	Grimes, James	Manning, Jas.
Bowman, W.	Grooms, R.	Measels, John
Brantley, A. P.	Grooms, H.	Martin, E. D.
Benton, S.	Harris, W.	McGuire, J. J.
Bowman, W. J.	Hollis, James	Meagles, J.
Cadden, Wm.	Howard, W.	Newton, A.
Cadden, Richard	Haynes, Alfred	Newton, Geo.
Cahill, P.	Hucks, John	Pendavis, R.
Cordes, George	Hughes, O.	Prine, Wm.
Cordrey, J.	Hutson, J.	Ritts, John
Cammer, Lewis	Hurdman, N.	Ritts, Thomas
Davis, J.	Infinger, Nat	Rector, N. G.
Dilk, W. L.	Jenkins, Geo. M.	Rivers, B.

Rose, A. W.	Smith, W., Jr.	Willis, A. J.
Rush, James	Thompson, John	Wilkinson, T. W.
Rush, J.	Thompson, James	Wilkinson, W.
Rush, C.	Terry, S.	Wilder, Jno. B.
Rush, S.	Varner, M. T.	Washer, A. E.
Rudd, J. J.	Verrell, L.	Williams, Benj.
Seaborn, Wm.	Veree, Wm.	Whatley, Aleck
Shaw, William	Waldorf, A.	Wood, N.
Simmons, J. A.	Weatherly, J. D.	Winnougham, N.
Smith, W.	Willis, James	Yeadon, Richard

COMPANY C, 11TH REGIMENT.

Ledbetter, Thos. E............................Captain
Guerard, Jacob..........................First Lieutenant
Sineath, Tecfrick......................Second Lieutenant
Stull, Thos. W.........................Third Lieutenant
Smidd.................................Orderly Sergeant
Ledbetter, Daniel.......................Second Sergeant
Limehouse, Thos. R......................Third Sergeant
Weatherford, Watson.....................Fourth Sergeant
Jamison, H. A........................Commissary Sergeant
Smith, Broglin..........................First Corporal
Redmore, Chas..........................Second Corporal
Smith, Dewey...........................Third Corporal

PRIVATES.

Allen, Thos., Sr.	Driggers, Joel	Grooms, Wesley
Allen, Thos., Jr.	Driggers, Elisha	Haggard, John
Adams, Abner	Driggers, Robinson	Huff, Thomas
Altherson, James	Davis, A.	Hyatt, Thomas
Barber, Frederick	Dangerfield, Starling	Harrison, Benj.
Barber, Benjamin	Davis, Jenkins	Howard, Abram
Barber, Edward	Davis, Hamilton	Howard, James
Barber, Joseph	Driggers, Andrew	Howard, Wade
Barber, William	Driggers, Daniel	Howard, Gabriel
Baxter, Delly	Driggers, Henry	Mears, John
Bunch, Henry	Driggers, Mack	Miers, Thomas
Bunch, Wm. M.	Donnelly, John	Monroe, George
Bunch, Wm.	Devenport, David	Nettles, Richard
Brothers, John	Edminson, Charles	Nettles, Rhett
Baxter, Daniel	Fryer, Edward	Powell, Thomas
Bexley, John	Fryer, James	Parker, John
Burbage, James	Fryer, Robert	Perry, William
Brothers, James	Fryer, Wesley	Paramore, Allen
Connerley, Charles	Fryer, William	Peyler, John
Donnelly, Benj.	Grooms, James	Stevenson, Benj.

Stoutamier, David	Wiggins, Lewis	Winningham, Daniel
Stanby, James	Wannamaker, Abner	Winningham, Edward
Tumblestow, Henry	Weatherford, Robert	Winn, Thomas
Turner, David	Weatherford, Lemuel	Winn, Frank
Thomerson, J. G.	Winter, Robert	Way, Pink

COMPANY D, 11TH REGIMENT.

Harrison, Jno. J. .... Captain
Gooding, John J. .... Captain
Hucks, Henry K. .... Captain
Gooding, McD. .... First Lieutenant
Gooding, Wm. J. .... Second Lieutenant
Bowers, J. W. .... Second Lieutenant
Thomas, Phillip. .... Second Lieutenant
Sauls, Osborne J. .... Second Lieutenant
Jenkins, Thomas. .... Second Lieutenant
Mole, John A. .... First Sergeant
Hodge, Lewis. .... First Sergeant
Corbin, Chas. .... Second Sergeant
Cook, Constantine. .... Third Sergeant
Cook, Washington. .... Fourth Sergeant
Owens, Jno. A. .... Corporal
Thomas, James. .... Corporal
Rivers, Joseph T. .... Corporal
Shipes, Wm. D. .... Corporal
Mixon, Wm. T. .... Corporal

PRIVATES.

Altman, Abram B.	Gooding, Jas. W.	Rivers, Jacob M.
Altman, Owen	Gooding, Richard	Rivers, Robert H.
Altman, Edward	Gray, Jacob W.	Rivers, Geo. M.
Bulger, Henry P.	Hall, Edward	Roberts, Jno. B.
Brunson, Thos. D.	Hall, Alexander	Rentz, Charles
Brunson, Phil. J.	Hodges, Jas. P.	Sinclair, Peter D.
Barnes, Wm. B.	Hull, Wm. H.	Stanley, Jno. J.
Barnes, Sylvester	Joyner, Frederick G.	Stanley, George E.
Bennett, Jas. W.	Kearse, Blake W.	Stanley, Alexander
Crews, Wm. L.	Kearse, John F.	Stanley, Thomas
Crews, Jerry B.	Lewis, Wm. H.	Stanley, Benjamin
Crews, Chas. E.	Lewis, John	Shipes, John
Crews, Isham	Lucas, Shadrack	Shipes, Jas. P.
Crews, Jno. E.	Lightsey, Jno. F.	Strickling, Jno. C.
Crews, John	Mason, David A.	Thomas, Vincent J.
Cook, Kinsey	Mason, Wm. W.	Terry, John M.
Corbin, Edward	Matthews, Robert N.	Thames, Frank
Fennell, Wm. A.	Owens, Thomas	Tyson, Jno. A.
Fennell, Geo. M.	Page, Robert L.	Warren, Thos. R.
Gooding, Eldred B.	Rivers, Frank D.	Williams, Sam'l W.

COMPANY E, 11TH REGIMENT.

Mickler, Jno. H. . . . . Captain
Smith, Wilson. . . . . First Lieutenant
Tuten, Thos. S. . . . . Second Lieutenant
Hamilton, Thomas. . . . . Second Lieutenant
Smith, Jesse W. . . . . First Sergeant
Fitts, Jno. A. . . . . Second Sergeant
Mew, Alex. C. . . . . Third Sergeant
Woods, David. . . . . Fourth Sergeant
Crosby, Alex. W. . . . . Fifth Sergeant
Mew, Sam'l K. . . . . First Corporal
Fitts, Chas. R. . . . . Second Corporal
Smith, Jno. W. . . . . Third Corporal
Morgan, A. Greene. . . . . Fourth Corporal

PRIVATES.

Airs, William	Fields, Richard	Mulligan, George
Aul, Greene	Finley, R. Augustus	McFail, John
Allen, John	Farris, Joe	McLane, Henry
Aughley, Jos. J.	Farris, James	Nix, Henry E.
Bennett, William	Ghelston, Richard F.	Nix, Joseph R.
Bennett, R. D.	Ginn, Andrew C.	Nix, William
Bennett, J. L.	Ginn, Wm. R.	Preacher, John
Brooker, John	Geohagan, David B.	Parnell, J. R.
Brooker, Edward	Garvin, Hamilton	Reynolds, Robert
Brown, Edward	Godley, Wm. B.	Rouse, William
Cook, Abram	Harley, Jos. N.	Rivers, F. Tyler
Cook, Jackson	Horton, R. Frank	Rivers, Jno. D.
Crapes, Jonas	Horton, Geo. W.	Rushing, Albert
Crapes, Jefferson	Horton, Henry E.	Rushing, Hausford
Crapes, Henry T.	Hull, Enoch	Ruth, John
Cone, J. Cooper	Hull, Samuel	Shuman, W. Samuel
Cooler, Frank	Horton, Solomon	Smith, Andrew H.
Cooler, P.	Hammond, Wm. R.	Smith, Ben F.
Daly, Patrick	Hall, Ben	Smith, Charles
Daring, J. Tom	Hall, Edward	Smith, W. Jasper
Dean, Andrew	Hall, Alexander	Smith, Jas. W.
Dean, Robert	Jarrell, James L.	Smith, Jas. G.
DeLoach, Frank	Jarrell, Richard	Smith, Thomas H.
Dobson, Charles	Jarrell, Robert	Smith, Jno. L.
Dobson, Jacob	Jeffords, Thos. J.	Smith, G. Washington
Dobson, Jno. S.	Jones, James P.	Steed, W.
Dobson, Wiley	Law, Abner	Wells, W. Barton
Dobson, W. Ferdinand	Law, Robert	Wiggins, Ben W.
Ferguson, Geo.	Lawton, Ben T.	Winn, Barney B.
Ferguson, Willis	Langballe, Fred	Winn, Richard C.
Fitts, Thomas H.	Mulligan, Wm. H.	Winningham, Geo. W.
Furse, William	Mulligan, Bernard	Zehe, John
Freeman, Albert	Mulligan, A. Gideon	

30—H

COMPANY F, 11TH REGIMENT.

Elliott, W. W...Captain
Wyman, B. F...Captain
Jenkins, Richard M.....................................First Lieutenant
Morrison, Jno. T.......................................First Lieutenant
Fuller, William.......................................Second Lieutenant
Mixon, Jesse N..Second Lieutenant
Wyman, Wm. H..Third Lieutenant
Wyman, E. H...Third Lieutenant
Jenkins, M..Sergeant
Moore, G. W...Sergeant
Smith, Bryce...Sergeant
Gooding, Thomas...Sergeant
Mixon, James...Sergeant
Mixon, W. B..Sergeant
Miley, Martin..Sergeant
Terry, Wm. M...Sergeant
Griner, Jesse..Sergeant
Cleland, D. B..Corporal
Smith, Chas. C...Corporal
Crosby, D. W...Corporal
Blocker, A. W..Corporal
Parnell, Frank...Corporal

PRIVATES.

Anderson, Robert	Davis, James	Heape, Benjamin
Blocker, Thos.	Davis, Charles	Heape, D. B.
Brown, Charles	DeLoach, James	Horton, Benjamin
Boldt, Richard	Edwards, F. P.	Horton, Moses
Condon, Jerome F.	Ervin, Samuel	Horton, Job
Cook, Barney	Fitzgerald, Ed.	Hutson, C.
Cook, John	Fennell, Arthur	Hutson, B.
Cook, Steven	Fennell, William	Hutson, W.
Cook, Berry	Fitts, Edward	Howard, A.
Cook, F.	Freeman, Benj.	Hay, E. G.
Cook, Middleton	Gantt, Eldred	Jenkins, Benj.
Creech, H.	Garvin, Hausford	Johnson, John J.
Crews, Edward	Garvin, Wilson	Lightsey, Henry
Crews, James	Gooding, Perry	Lubkin, F.
Crosby, Emanuel	Griner, Ralph	McFeer, Henry
Crosby, Steven	Hall, Ben	Mears, James
Crosby, David	Hall, Alex.	Mills, Benjamin
Crosby, George	Hall, Ed.	Mixon, Jno. A.
Cuthbert, F.	Hamilton, Charles	Mulligan, F. J.
Cuthbert, W. H.	Howard, Charles	Nix, J. D.
Davis, C. F.	Heape, Audley	Nix, Joseph

Padgett, J. R.	Smith, Benjamin	Walls, S.
Peeples, Abram	Skillings, Edward	Wyman, H. Hastings
Peeples, John	Simmons, A. J.	Wyman, Hay
Phillips, John	Trusals, William	Youmans, J. R.
Rosier, R. A.	Thomas, James	Youmans, R.
Roberts, Wilson	Tuten, A. J.	Youmans, Jerry
Rivers, John	Ulmer, Thomas	Youmans, Washington
Smith, Samuel		

COMPANY G, 11TH REGIMENT.

Maguire, John J...Captain
McMillan, W. D...Captain
Wolf, W. M..First Lieutenant
Brownlee, Jno. H.......................................Second Lieutenant
Clayton, H. W..Second Lieutenant
Brownlee, S. H...Second Lieutenant
Riggs, J. S...Sergeant
DeCosta, B. A..Sergeant
Isaacs, Zachary..Sergeant
Smith, E. A..Sergeant
Lynes, Jacob...Corporal
Lemacks, M...Corporal
Stutts, Thomas...Corporal
Way, T. R..Corporal

PRIVATES.

Ahrens, John	Hastings, Mike	Muckenfuss, Isaac
Bedon, John	Hiatt, J. H.	Muckenfuss, G. P.
Benton, S. J.	Hutson, Robert	O'Connor, Baltz
Bowen, H. H.	Hutson, W.	Pendarvis, J. B.
Bradley, Mike	Isaacs, E. R.	Pendarvis, W. P.
Brownlee, W. P.	Larissy, O. B.	Riggs, E. R.
Brownlee, J. W.	Larissy, T. L.	Salisbury, John
Brownlee, F. L.	Leman, L. B.	Scott, John
Brownlee, J. P.	Lemacks, T. H.	Smith, John
Brownlee, E. A.	Lee, William	Smith, Elijah
Brownlee, T. W.	Lord, Richard	Stokes, Thaddeus
Cantwell, J. M.	Lyons, Benjamin	Stokes, E. A.
Canton, Richard	Malloy, Mike	Stokes, Henry
Carr, Terrance	Martin, W.	Stutts, G. H.
Clayton, M. H.	Martin, J. H.	Stutts, Jno. R.
Colter, Wm.	McMahon, Terrence	Thornely, John
Cummings, Benj. W.	Mims, Joseph	Tuttle, D. M.
DeWitt, William	Mims, David	Tuttle, D. T.
Grinaway, John	Mims, Pinckney	Tuttle, O.
Gosley, Henry	Muckenfuss, G. L.	Viawd, Peter

Wade, R.	Way, William	Dunn, John
Way, B. R.	Weathers, William	Smith, Samure
Way, M. D.	White, J. H.	Brown, W. P.
Way, T. H.	Whitsel, John	**Traxler, D. H.**
Way, Thomas	Willis, Alfred	

COMPANY H, 11TH REGIMENT.

Weathers, Jacob..Captain
Cannady, D. S...Captain
Raysor, Thos. E...Captain
Howell, J. S. A......................................First Lieutenant
Wilson, W. G..First Lieutenant
Minus, J. P.......................................Second Lieutenant
Appleby, F. B......................................Third Lieutenant
Millard, L. C......................................Third Lieutenant
Howell, F. E...Sergeant
Appleby, A. W...Sergeant
Ackman, S. W..Sergeant
Utsey, D. W...Sergeant
Appleby, A. R...Sergeant
Easterling, Emory...Sergeant
Shuler, P. W..Sergeant
Murray, J. E..Sergeant
West, John D..Corporal
Weeks, Zack...Corporal
Shuler, Y. B..Corporal
Bryant, M. C..Corporal
Murray, W. B..Corporal
Westbury, L. D..Corporal

PRIVATES.

Ackerman, Rogers	Cannady, Chas.	Heaton, Peter
Appleby, P. S.	Creel, John	Hussey, W. J.
Beaglin, Wm.	Currie, S. M.	Hill, David
Bradwell, O. P.	Crook, W. T.	Infinger, W. A.
Brothers, C. P.	Clark, M.	Infinger, G. N.
Bowman, D. R.	Durr, Peter E.	Judy, J. A.
Byrd, T. D.	Durr, John	Judy, J. W.
Bull, John	Ferris, W.	Judy, Jacob
Bunch, Wade	George, W. K.	Jackson, Durant
Bunch, W. J.	Godfrey, James	Jackson, Porter
Cannady, H. C.	Harley, T. W.	Kizer, J.
Cannady, W. T.	Harley, T. D.	Lochlier, John
Cannady, J. P.	Harbeson, A. T.	Lochlier, W. N.
Cannady, L. D.	Heaton, Phillip	Lowe, Zack
Cannady, J. A.	Heaton, C. T.	Lowe, L. W.

Lofton, Stephen	Pendarvis, Enoch	Stokes, T. M.
Mallard, Isaac	Pendarvis, J. D.	Stokes, J.
Mallard, John	Pendarvis, H. L.	Thomas, H. L.
Mallard, C. H.	Pendarvis, J. O.	Traxler, J. D.
Mallard, A. H.	Pendarvis, J. B.	Utsey, D. D.
Murray, Henry	Patrick, George	Utsey, C. J. D.
Mizzles, G. W.	Patrick, W. S.	Utsey, J. C.
Mizzles, T. R.	Pierce, George	Utsey, J. T.
McAlbaney, Wm.	Reeves, C. D.	Wimberly, John
Metts, Adams	Richardson, T. D.	Wimberly, J. S.
Metts, Thomas	Raysor, B. S.	Wimberly, George
Metts, John	Sheider, J. W.	Westbury, David
Metts, David	Sheider, Mack	Westbury, T. H.
Murray, W.	Syphrett, J. W.	Walters, W. J.
Murray, A. D.	Seigler, James	West, T. D.
Murray, F. M.	Seigler, Urel	West, J. D.
Mims, J. T.	Summer, Geo. T.	Weeks, L. E.
Proctor, S. J.	Stokes, T. R.	Weeks, T. M.
Proctor, L. W.		

COMPANY I, 11TH REGIMENT.

Campbell, W. L..Captain
Loyless, Edward B.....................................Lieutenant
Dandridge, Rich'd J...................................Lieutenant
Campbell, Robert......................................Lieutenant
Reilly, Jno. C..Lieutenant
Spell, Eldred...Sergeant
Langdale, Jas. S. H...................................Sergeant
Smoke, Andrew J.......................................Sergeant
Sanders, Joseph.......................................Sergeant
Beach, Henry T..Sergeant
Linder, Thomas R......................................Sergeant
Grant, Joseph...Sergeant
Pelham, Jas. E..Corporal
Sanders, Griffin G....................................Corporal
Breland, Chas. J......................................Corporal
Tant, Spartan G.......................................Corporal
Williams, Jas. E......................................Corporal
Schmidt, Martin.......................................Corporal

PRIVATES.

Avant, Jno. W.	Bailey, Jas. B.	Beach, L. B.
Avant, Lewis B.	Benton, Joshua	Beach, Lones
Anderson, Chas.	Bazzle, John	Beach, Richard B.
Adams, James	Bazzle, Steven	Beach, Clem
Adams, Henry B.	Bazzle, William	Bishop, Henry
Buchanan, Jas. B.	Beach, Joseph	Campbell, Daniel P.

Craven, John	Hiott, Malachi M.	Simmons, Jno. M.
Craven, Alex. J.	Hiott, Edward	Simmons, William
Craven, Thomas	Hutson, Joseph H.	Smoke, Henry
Craven, James E.	Harris, William	Sauls, John •
Craven, Martin	Hughes, Nathan	Sauls, James
Craven, George	Herndon, Henry G.	Sauls, Charles
Carter, Joseph	Herndon, Clem	Sauls, George
Carter, Henry A.	Higgins, William	Sauls, Peter
Carter, Richard	Higgins, T. H.	Strickland, Henry H.
Carter, Reuben	Higgins, Morbis D.	Sullivan, Daniel
Carter, Isham	Hickman, W. Rhett	Sullivan, George
Crosby, Steven	Johnson, Julius	Sullivan, Wm.
Crosby, Jno. D.	Kinard, Isaac	Sullivan, Huggins
Crosby, Henry	Lemacks, Silas	Tant, Olin
Crosby, John	Larisey, Richard	Valentine, Henry
Crosby, Gooding	Lane, Edward	Valentine, Joseph
Crosby, Abram	Lane, Albert	Walker, Richard D.
Compton, Thadeus	McMillan, Jas. N.	Willis, John
Davis, Charles C.	Murray, Andrew	Way, George
Dawdy, James C.	Miller, Henry	Wiggins, William
Dewitt, James A.	Martin, William	Wiggins, Simeon
Felder, David A.	Martin, Stephen	Witsell, Emanuel
Gassett, James A.	Martin, Solomon	Warner, Henry
Griffin, James S.	Martin, Hausford A.	Warren, Daniel
Hiott, Lawrence P.	Martin, Henry	Warren, Perry
Hiott, Daniel	Mitchum, Jesse	Warren, Joseph
Hiott, Nathaniel	Morris, Thomas	Warren, Malachi
Hiott, Thomas	Noble, James	Wasson, George
Hiott, Peter	Noble, William	Warren, Richard
Hiott, Wilson	O'Brien, Wm.	Yewley, James
Hiott, Lucius	Sanders, James	Osborne, Geo. E.
Hiott, Jno. M.	Sanders, Lawrence	Pelham, Oswald G.
Hiott, John	Sanders, William	Parker, James
Hiott, Joseph	Smith, Charles	Robertson, Jno. C.
Hiott, Benj.	Smith, John	Robertson, Lewis
Hiott, Samuel	Spell, William	Ritter, Richard

COMPANY K, 11TH REGIMENT.

Hay, Richard G................................Captain
Boatwright, John..............................Captain
Gantt, Frederick H.......................First Lieutenant
Murdaugh, J. H...........................First Lieutenant
Murdaugh, L. B...........................First Lieutenant
Johns, William...........................First Lieutenant
Cassidy, Frank...........................First Lieutenant
Stephens, J. W...................Brevet Second Lieutenant
Gantt, Eldred L...............................Sergeant

Cummings, John.. .. ..Sergeant
Gantt, Richard P.. .. ..Sergeant
Hickman, G. B.. .. ..First Corporal
Jones, Joseph R.. .. ..Second Corporal
Godley, Wm. S.. .. ..Third Corporal
Cummings, Frank W.. .. ..Fourth Corporal

PRIVATES.

Adams, L. B.	Godley, J. B.	O'Quin, Edward
Boatright, Thos. W.	Griffin, William	Padgett, Daniel, Sr.
Branch, J. E.	Green, H. B.	Padgett, Daniel
Buchannan, J. S.	George, Aleck	Padgett, James
Benton, James	Heape, John J.	Padgett, Stephen
Brant, R. H.	Hickman, J. Medicus	Padgett, Henry W.
Branch, Giles	Hickman, W. Albert	Padgett, Joel
Buchannan, J. D.	Hiers, Jasper T.	Padgett, L. B.
Bishop, William	Hiers, W. J.	Padgett, Josiah
Benton, Babe	Hiers, Jacob	Padgett, Jacob
Beverly, Jack	Hiers, A. J.	Padgett, Frank
Broxton, John	Hiers, G. McDuffie	Padgett, Martin
Carter, W. O.	Hiers, John	Padgett, Abram
Carter, William	Johns, A. P.	Pelham, J. B.
Carter, J. R.	Johns, John	Peters, J. Albert
Carter, W. J.	Johns, George	Polk, Thomas
Carter, Isham	Jones, L. B.	Polk, Wilson O.
Connerly, D. C.	Jones, Zack	Polk, Isaac
Corbett, James	Jones, Joseph, Jr.	Polk, Frank M.
Cummings, Wm.	Jones, Newton	Polk, Jacob T.
Crosby, Daniel	Lane, A. J.	Polk, Madison
Copeland, W. A.	Mears, H. W.	Pelham, George
Copeland, J. R.	Mears, J. F.	Richardson, Jacob
Copeland, Elzy	Mears, John S.	Richardson, James
Dopson, J. W.	Mears, James	Rizer, Thomas P.
Dopson, Nathaniel E. H.	Mills, Benjamin A.	Rizer, John
Fender, Ransom	Mills, John	Rentz, George W.
Fender, G. C.	McMillan, Rich'd F.	Rentz, Aaron
Fields, J. D.	McMillan, J. H.	Rentz, Jacob, Sr.
Folk, J. C.	Morris, Thomas	Rentz, Jacob, Jr.
Folk, Adam L.	Mills, James	Rhodes, Thomas H.
Folk, J. J.	Murdaugh, Josiah, Jr.	Sauls, Benjamin
Folk, Perry	Nettles, William	Shaw, Jno. M., Sr.
Folk, W. C.	Nettles, W. D.	Shaw, Jno. M., Jr.
Fralix, A. E.	Nettles, Cuthbert	Smith, Martin H.
Fralix, D. S.	O'Quin, W. R.	Smoke, A. E.
Fralix, T. J.	O'Quin, J. H.	Smoke, Joshua
Fralix, R. M.	Owens, Charles J.	Stephens, R. R.
Fralix, Gabriel	Owens, O. B.	Stone, Matthew R.

Stone, Allen B.	Trowell, Jonathan	Walker, Albert M.
Smith, Dick	Varn, Gabriel	Walker, L. B.
Thomas, James E.	Varn, Aaron	Walker, Henry
Thomas, Martin	Walling, John D.	Walker, A. E.
Thomas, Ransom	Warren, B. A.	White, Duncan
Thompson, Washington	Walker, John E.	Wiggins, John

BROOKS' BATTALION OF REGULARS.

Brooks, J. Hampden.. .. ..Lieutenant-Colonel
Goodwyn, Chas. T.. .. ..Assistant Adjutant, Lieutenant
Martin, Vincent F.. .. ..Captain
Brooks, U. R.. .. ..First Lieutenant
Teuten.. .. ..Second Lieutenant
Minott, Jno. C.. .. ..Captain Co. C
Simkins, Eldred.. .. ..Acting Captain
Wardlaw, David Lewis.. .. ..Captain Co. D
Pinckney, B. G.. .. ..Captain Co. E
Goodwyn, Chas. T.. .. ..Lieutenant, Acting Adjutant

ORIGIN OF BROOKS' BATTALION.

In 1864, when the Northern armies had the world from which to recruit their ranks, and even our slaves had been armed against us,—while the Southern armies were being rapidly depleted, and, perhaps, four-sixths of those who were fighting had been wounded—the authorities in Richmond conceived the idea of enlisting in our ranks foreigners among the Federal prisoners, hoping that, like the redoubtable Dougal Dalgetty, they would care very little on which side they fought. To command such an organization no ordinary officer was needed. Courage was a *sine qua non*, and he should have military knowledge. experience and judgment. Covered with wounds and with honor, Capt. J. Hampden Brooks, who, in his own person, had illustrated the courage of the Brookses and Butlers on many a bloody battlefield, was selected to command them. A serious mistake was made in allowing a large number of Northern men to enlist, many pretending to be Englishmen. Among those selected were Irishmen, Germans, Spaniards and one Italian who could scarcely speak English.—Extract from history of Brooks' Battalion by Vincent F. Martin.

These men soon decided to kill all the officers and return to the Northern army, but were betrayed by one of their own men whose name was Sinner; he was an orderly sergeant and a vile sinner, too, in their estimation. The other orderly sergeants were courtmartialed and shot—the men sent to Florence, S. C., and locked up in prison, and the officers were soon with their respective commands again.

U. R. BROOKS,
Editor.

CHARGE OF HAGOOD'S BRIGADE*

(By Joseph Blyth Allston.)

Scarce seven hundred men they stand
　　In tattered, rude array,
A remnant of that gallant band
Who erstwhile held the sea-girt strand
Of Morris' Isle with iron hand
　　'Gainst Yankees' hated sway.

Secessionville their banner claims,
And Sumter, held 'mid smoke and flames,
And the dark battle on the streams
　　Of Pocotaligo:
And Walthall's Junction's hard-earned fight,
And Drewry's Bluff's embattled height,
When, at the gray dawn of the light,
　　They rushed upon the foe.

Tattered and torn those banners now,
But not less proud each lofty brow,
　　Untaught as yet to yield:
With mien unblenched, unfaltering eye,
Forward, where bombshells shrieking fly,
Flecking with smoke the azure sky
　　On Weldon's fated field.

Sweeps from the woods the bold array,
Not theirs to falter in the fray,
No men more sternly trained than they
　　To meet their deadly doom;
While, from a hundred throats agape,
A hundred sulphurous flames escape,
Round shot, and canister, and grape,
　　The thundering cannon's boom!

---

*Written in the summer of 1864, immediately after the charge referred to,
which was always considered by the brigade as their most desperate encounter.

Swift, on their flank, with fearful crash
Shrapnel and ball commingling clash,
And bursting shells, with lurid flash,
    Their dazzled sight confound:
Trembles the earth beneath their feet,
Along their front a rattling sheet
Of leaden hail concentric meet,
    And numbers strew the ground.

On, o'er the dying and the dead,
O'er mangled limb and gory head,
With martial look, with martial tread,
March Hagood's men to bloody bed,
    Honor their sole reward;
Himself doth lead their battle line,
    Himself those banners guard.

They win the height, those gallant few,
A fiercer struggle to renew,
Resolved as gallant men to do
    Or sink in glory's shroud;
But scarcely gain its stubborn crest,
Ere, from the ensign's murdered breast,
An impious foe has dared to wrest
    That banner proud.

Upon him, Hagood, in thy might!
Flash on thy soul the immortal light
Of those brave deeds that blazon bright
    Our Southern Cross.
He dies. Unfurl its folds again,
Let it wave proudly o'er the plain;
The dying shall forget their pain,
    Count not their loss.

Then, rallying to your chieftain's call,
Ploughed through by cannon-shot and ball,
Hemmed in, as by a living wall,
    Cleave back your way.

Those bannered deeds their souls inspire,
Borne, amid sheets of forked fire,
By the Two Hundred who retire
    Of that array.

Ah, Carolina! well the tear
May dew thy cheek; thy clasped hands rear
In passion, o'er their tombless bier,
    Thy fallen chivalry!
Malony, mirror of the brave,
And Sellers lie in glorious grave;
No prouder fate than theirs, who gave
    Their lives for Liberty.

MONUMENT TO HAGOOD'S BRIGADE NEAR PETERSBURG, VA., SHOWING FRONT VIEW—ERECTED BY WM. V. IZLAR.

MONUMENT TO HAGOOD'S BRIGADE

Here
A Brigade
Composed of the
7th Battalion
The 11th, 21st, 25th and 27th
Regiments,
South Carolina Volunteers
Commanded by
Brig. Gen. Johnson Hagood
Charged
Warren's Federal Army
Corps
On the 21st Day of August,
1864
Taking Into the Fight 740
Men
Returning With 273

No Prouder Fate Than Theirs,
Who Gave Their Lives
To Liberty.

On the opposite or west side of the die is a 15-inch bronze shield of the State of South Carolina.

On the four sides of the base of the monument are inscriptions; that on the east or side fronting Halifax road being as follows:

HAGOOD'S BRIGADE.

On the north side are the letters,
C. S. A.

On the south side are the letters,
A. N. V.

On the rear or west side of the base is the following inscription telling the history of the monument:

Placed Here by Wm. V. Izlar,
A Survivor of the Charge
Aided by Other
South Carolinians.

MONUMENT TO HAGOOD'S BRIGADE NEAR PETERSBURG, VA., SHOWING REAR VIEW—ERECTED BY WM. V. IZLAR.

LIST OF ILLUSTRATIONS OF VOL. I.

LIST OF ILLUSTRATIONS OF VOL. II.